THE TAMILS

A PORTRAIT OF A COMMUNITY

NIRMALA LAKSHMAN

ALEPH BOOK COMPANY
An independent publishing firm
promoted by *Rupa Publications India*

First published in India in 2025
by Aleph Book Company
7/16 Ansari Road, Daryaganj
New Delhi 110 002

Copyright © Nirmala Lakshman 2025
The image credits on pp. 391–92 constitute an extension of the copyright page.

Jasmine illustration: Apoorva Lalit 2025

Endpaper illustration: Shutterstock/Bhuvanesh S.

All rights reserved.

The author has asserted her moral rights.

The views and opinions expressed in this book are the author's own and the facts are as reported by her, which have been verified to the extent possible, and the publishers are not in any way liable for the same.

The publisher has used its best endeavours to ensure that URLs for external websites referred to in this book are correct and active at the time of going to press. However, the publisher has no responsibility for the websites and can make no guarantee that a site will remain live or that the content is or will remain appropriate.

No part of this publication may be reproduced, transmitted, or stored in a retrieval system, in any form or by any means, without permission in writing from Aleph Book Company.

ISBN: 978-81-1963-507-8

1 3 5 7 9 10 8 6 4 2

Printed in India

This book is sold subject to the condition that it shall not, by way of trade or otherwise, be lent, resold, hired out, or otherwise circulated without the publisher's prior consent in any form of binding or cover other than that in which it is published.

Also by Nirmala Lakshman

Degree Coffee by the Yard: A Short Biography of Madras
Writing a Nation: An Anthology of Indian Journalism (edited)

THE
TAMILS

BOOK III
THE AGE OF TRANSITION

19. Turmoil and Tumult: The Madurai Sultans and the Vijayanagar Kings	215
20. The Nayaks in Tamil Country	227
21. The Grand Marathas of Thanjavur	234
22. Tamil by Birth, Muslim by Faith	240

BOOK IV
THE AGE OF THE EUROPEANS

23. The Merchants of Colonization	255
24. Christendom in Tamilakam	267
25. From Company to Empire	280

BOOK V
THE AGE OF FREEDOM

26. Revolt, Rebellion, and the Road to Freedom	289
27. A Society in Flux	301
28. Chennai That Was Madras	310
29. Awakenings and Transformations: The Freedom Struggle and the Dravidian Movement	322
30. An Unprecedented Freedom	334
31. A Progressive and Paradoxical State	353
Epilogue: The Tamil in Us	371
Acknowledgements	384
Image Credits	391
Notes	393
Bibliography	419
Index	427

Contents

Introduction: This Jasmine Country	ix
1. Emergence	1

BOOK I
THE AGE OF POETRY

2. Literature as History	13
3. Of Heroes and Kings	23
4. Life of the Times	31

BOOK II
THE AGE OF EMPIRE

The Pallavas	40
5. Lions of the Earth	41
6. Kanchipuram: A Confluence of Cultures	53
7. Divine Origins and Earthly Arrangements	68
8. The Citadels of Faith	77
The Pandyas	86
9. Madurai and the Acme of Pandya Culture	87
10. No Faintness in Their Hearts	107
11. Enterprise and Opulence: Aspects of Pandya Society	121
12. Abnegation, Devotion, and Faith	128
The Cholas	144
13. The Tiger Crest: The Great Chola Monarchy	145
14. The Facets and Functions of Chola Society	161
15. Reaching the Sky: An Imperial Vision	171
16. Pinnacles of Artistic Vision	181
17. The Spires of Faith	194
18. The Cheras: The Emporium of India	201

*To my mother,
Menaka Parthasarathy,
who gave me all things Tamil and whose
light and love inspires me every day.
And in loving memory of my father,
Srinivasan Parthasarathy.*

Introduction

This Jasmine Country

A fertile heartland, overlooked by rugged mountain ranges on one side and silhouetted by a long sandy coast and a vast sea on the other, cradles an ancient yet enduring civilization. This civilization has persevered for more than 2,500 years. It finds celebration in the literature of the Tamil Sangam—a confluence of poets and scholars that emerged as early as 400 years before Christianity. The terrain bears a remarkable continuity of language, culture, ideas, and beliefs. These elements have been shaped not only by their roots in antiquity but also by the natural openness of the Tamil people—an openness that embraced the march of kings and soldiers from the north of the land, traders from West Asia, as well as seafarers and explorers who arrived from distant shores to mingle with the local people and make this region their home.

The ancient Tamils classified the topography of Tamilakam, their land, into five distinct categories. Each category was symbolized by a flower indigenous to that region: the kurinchi, a rare mountain bloom; mullai, the fragrant jasmine flourishing in the forests; the blue water lily of neytal, representative of the seashore; the desert flower of palai, emblematic of the arid lands; and marudam, also known as the queen's flower, of the lowlands. Beyond representing physical attributes, these descriptions encapsulated themes of life and death, as well as the continual flow of generations. This landscape, etched into collective memory and interwoven with life, is luminously reflected in Sangam poetry—compositions that are over 2,500 years old, yet hold relevance today.

At the core of this evocative poetic imagery lies a keen understanding of the human condition based on metaphors stemming from nature. According to the Tamils, the whorls imprinted on white conch shells underfoot in neytal lands echo the patterns of the universe. Bamboo and long grass blanched by the summer heat along the desert pathways of dry palai surfaces symbolize life's challenging journey. Secret waterfalls concealed within hidden hillsides and the scent of red earth mingled with pouring rain can transform into an unexpected union of young lovers. In the ancient Tamil worldview, the solitude of a warrior king facing a hero's death, a mother's anguish at the loss of a child, or the betrayal of a lover can merge with the fabric of nature itself. The custodians of this civilization's values were the dreamers—poets, bards, and storytellers. Reflect then upon the collective refinement that defines Tamil culture.

Sangam refers to a coming together, a meeting, or a congress, primarily comprising poets, scholars, and kings—a form of assembly that reportedly began several centuries before Christianity and occurred periodically over time. Poems and writings from these academies, many of which were secular, were surprisingly only rediscovered by scholars in the nineteenth century, although some had been commented on in earlier centuries. The renowned poet, translator, and scholar A. K. Ramanujan recounts a meeting between the famous Tamil scholar U. Ve. Swaminatha Aiyar, who had just moved to Kumbakonam, and a liberal-minded civil judge, a munsif, who questioned Aiyar about his wealth of knowledge. When Aiyar recounted his knowledge of the Sangam texts in detail, the judge was disappointed and unimpressed, asking him why he had not studied the 'old texts'. This left the erudite Tamil scholar, later known as the Father of Tamil, puzzled and aghast that he knew nothing of these old texts. Ramanujan writes that Aiyar then 'devoted the rest of his long life to roaming the villages, rummaging in private attics and the storerooms of monasteries, to unearthing, editing, and printing classical Tamil texts'. Most of these were palm leaf manuscripts, delicate and crumbling, although some had been copied onto paper or parchment after the advent of printing.

Much of what we know about early Tamil culture and ways of being can be inferred from these poems. Ramanujan points out that 'they embody values but do not speculate or philosophize about them'. The physical landscapes reflect various states of mind; there are interior or Aham poems and Puram or poems of the exterior. Therefore, whether it is about quarrels, war, honour, pride, lust, ethics, lovers' meetings, or simply nature and its elements, they provide us with an astonishing glimpse into a civilization seeded many thousand years ago, rich in its marriage of sustained sophistication with simplicity.

The fixed geography of the land did provide the Tamils with some unique advantages. Whether these people were the original inhabitants of India or wanderers who came from the Indus Valley is not a settled question—historians, epigraphists, and archaeologists continue to debate the issue—but the land they occupied and thrived in was the southernmost region of India. Delineated in the present day as Tamil Nadu, the region stretches from the southern point of the peninsula called Kanyakumari, where the blue green waters of the Bay of Bengal meet the Indian Ocean, up to the border with Andhra Pradesh, 750 kilometres to the north. In the west lies Kerala and to the northwest lies the state of Karnataka. The mountains of the Western Ghats in the west cradle miles of green fields and flat lands watered by the river Kaveri and its tributaries. Further south flows the Thamirabarani or Porunai watering the partly arid lands of southern Tamil Nadu. At the very tip, in Kanyakumari, the Arabian Sea meets the Bay of Bengal in the Indian Ocean. The jewelled Coromandel coast lapped by the Bay of Bengal runs down the eastern shoreline to Kanyakumari's shores. The sea here provides a vast fishing population with an active livelihood, although one punctuated by poverty and tragedy. The lives of the fishing community also embody an aspect of Tamil culture that is distinct and unbroken across the centuries. The poet Sarojini Naidu, whom Mahatma Gandhi called India's nightingale, gave voice to the Coromandel fishers:

> Rise, brothers, rise, the wakening skies pray to the morning light,
> The wind lies asleep in the arms of the dawn like a child that has cried all night.
> Come, let us gather our nets from the shore and set our catamarans free,
> To capture the leaping wealth of the tide, for
> we are the sons of the sea!

On the other side, many hundreds of miles away, the Western Ghats, or the Sahyadri, the Benevolent Mountains, loop down, forming a perceptible backbone for the peninsula, straddling several southern states. The mountains are rich with green deciduous forests, somewhat denuded in places today, but still providing varied vegetation that thickens the air with the heady scent of eucalyptus along with the aroma of the tea gardens near the beautiful hill stations of Coonoor and Ooty. Here they are known as the Nilgiris, Blue Mountains, standing tall at the very edge of the Ghats and spreading a diffused blue light over that part of the Tamil country. The gaur, the mountain bison, roams freely in this region, and occasionally the night traveller will encounter the gleam of a panther's eyes in the undergrowth. Parts of the Mudumalai wildlife sanctuary, a protected area and home to the ancient Indian elephant and several endangered species, including the magnificent Bengal tiger and an innumerable variety of birds, also border Tamil Nadu.

Between the mountain ranges and the sea lie tracts of dry red earth, green paddy fields, and pebbled riverbeds. The river Kaveri, originating in the Kodagu hills of Karnataka, and revered in legend and song, flows through Tamil country, as do the rivers Palar, Pennar, and Thamirabarani and their tributaries. In the hot summer months, the dust from the plains through which these rivers run rises like a fine gossamer garment, veiling and unveiling centuries, stories, and secrets that define and depict a people. In the sweep of rain in the monsoon, the Tamil region gleams with its own heartbreakingly beautiful tapestry, splintering identities, and dissolving certainties of who people are and what their histories really say. Under the amorphousness, however, is a sense of surety. Being Tamil encompasses many things, including the myriad journeys of a people, it is a distinct heritage, although it may have evolved and mutated over centuries and geographies. It has also been impacted by the contemporary and by the everyday yet retains an essentially Tamil kernel.

These days, the highways of the twenty-first century criss-cross the Tamil countryside, yet leading off them are ancient tracks and remote villages that encapsulate traditional ways of living. However, the intrusion of the contemporary world is never far, and today's Tamilian negotiates it with great ease. In small sleepy towns that dot the gleaming, asphalted freeways, the crackle of remote signals from the atmosphere triggers numerous WhatsApp interactions between small farmers and wholesale buyers in nearby cities. The blare of a film song from a mobile phone contends with a modern version of an old Tamil hymn played from a flower stall near an ancient temple, the two strains signifying that the Tamil people are as comfortable with the modern as they are with the old ways and their traditional moorings.

The cities and towns of Tamil Nadu have their own histories and stories to tell. Chennai, once Madras, a sliver of sandy terrain cut out from a blue bay and bought by an impecunious English agent, Francis Day, trying to make his way in the world, is now India's fourth-largest city. Madurai, the city of temples, of jasmines, the seat of the Sangam congregation, written up by Megasthenes, the Greek ambassador to the Mauryan Empire, and flourishing under the ancient Pandyas and Nayaks, is as energetic and bustling as it was two millennia ago. Thanjavur, where Rajaraja ('king of kings') built a magnificent temple to Brihadeeswara (the Immense God) more than a thousand years ago, and once the capital of the glorious Cholas where history's shadows fall on stones, speaks to a culture of high art, music, and dance. Cities like Coimbatore, now the second-largest city in Tamil Nadu, and a centre of innovation, signal a proud industrial modernity; the city is famed as much for poultry breeding as for 'wet grinders' (a peculiar appellation for a particular kind of blender that is oriented to Indian cuisine) that it exports to other parts of the country and the world beyond. In between are smaller towns, scattered along the alluvial plains, in the Kaveri basin, the rice bowl of the Tamil country: Tiruchirappalli (Trichy), Chidambaram, Srirangam, Pichavaram, Poompuhar, Velankanni (the town of Our Lady of Good Health), Kumbakonam, standing from the Sangam age and often called the 'Cambridge of South India' because of the disproportionate number of geniuses that emerged from there, and Nagore of the healing dargah. There are other small towns with traditional lifestyles, trying to preserve the old and yet scrambling to embrace the contemporary. Karaikudi in Chettinad, with the breathtaking heritage homes of the Chettiar community; Pondicherry, the last bastion of the French in South India, with its ghostly remnants of French life reflected in street names and crumbling architectural facades; and Kanchipuram (Kanchi), the ancient town of the Pallavas, the town of a thousand temples and home of resplendent silk saris, cling proudly to their unique legacies. Even fleeting visits to these places offer up menus of legend and story, mutated, exaggerated, and often distorted, but capturing something of what it means to live and die there.

The Tamils are inheritors of a disaggregated culture and history, stemming from the diverse historical experiences of caste and community. But they unite broadly in the emotional bandwidth of language and particular sentiments. These sentiments, while being honed to a pan-Indian identity also importantly express a separate Dravidian cultural self within a larger structure. The consciousness of this Dravidian selfhood, particularly in the context of political and cultural expression, is integral to the Tamil identity.

Archaeological finds from mankind's dawn demonstrate the presence of human beings in the region as far back as the Palaeolithic Age. Burial sites in Adichanallur, and urns and potsherds with inscriptions in the antediluvian Tamil Brahmi script, going as far back as 1000 BCE, have been discovered. However, these pale in comparison to other astonishing finds: the famous stone hand axe, for instance, found in Attirampakkam, some 80 kilometres north of the city of Chennai, testifying to an advanced people, who, like several similar communities of wandering *Homo sapiens* in other parts of the world, pioneered this marvellous all-purpose tool 1 to 1.7 million years ago. At an exhibition called India and the World, curated by the Chhatrapati Shivaji Maharaj Vastu Sangrahalaya in Mumbai in collaboration with the British Museum, one of these hand axes was exhibited. Looking at this beautiful object, a stunning teardrop, chiselled to fineness and dazzling like a jewel, I reason that although early man vanished like the dinosaurs after a certain time, his inventiveness and perseverance live on in the DNA of the Tamil people of today.

Much later, before the wanderers who arrived to fill the northern regions of the subcontinent, the proud moorings of a Dravidian civilization added weight to the notion of a distinctive identity. In addition to caste and community, the identities of the Tamils rest often on the notion of ooru or place of origin. E. Valentine Daniel, the anthropologist, observes that the notion of ooru is very intrinsic to the Tamil person, especially in rural areas and is derived from a strong spatial notion, which in turn is intimately connected to the person's own experience. For the Tamil villager, ooru is likely to have more resonance, coming as it does from a person-centric and highly individualized relationship experience rather than the larger constructs of state and nation. The notion of ooru carries with it a rich emotional content that includes not only the physicality of the ancestral place of origin, where perhaps centuries of family connections exist, but also ties in with a deeply felt bond or religious affinity with a family god, the kula deivam, which many Tamil Hindu families hold as sacred and even critical to the family's well-being and continuance.

Language and Culture—the Unbroken Line

The shifts of history, deep and impactful, emerging from the mists of centuries, carry with them a continuity of tradition that remains alive. This is perhaps one of the major strengths of Tamil culture; for instance, Sangam-age poetry, mentioned earlier, still flourishes and is frequently recited. Aham and Puram, the internal and external, find easy place in modern parlance, and early philosophies find expression through the tracts of modern poetry. Children in rural classrooms continue to shout in unison: 'karka kasadara karpavai katrapin nirka adharku thaga', translated loosely as 'learn flawlessly, without blemishes, and stand true to what you have learned'. These were early insights instilling the value of knowledge and character from the *Tirukkural*, a remarkable and morally intuitive secular text of 1,330 couplets by the poet Tiruvalluvar. Considering that it is dated anywhere from 300 BCE to possibly around 500 CE, its place in the Tamil stratosphere remains undiminished. As a child, I was made aware of this by a constantly exasperated Tamil tutor who came by to school me in the language and would throw out couplets from the *Kural*. 'Agara mudhala ezhuthellam, aadhi bhagavan mudhatre ulagu' he would pronounce at the beginning of each lesson, underlining that the first letter of the language is the letter 'A', without which one cannot speak or write, much in the same way that the sun, the first deity, is the beginning of all things, even as God is, and crucial to the survival of humankind. In harking back to an ancient reflection, the poor man probably hoped that his truant ward would begin to delve into and absorb the beauties of the language, and in time appreciate the philosophical nuances of an eternally relevant text.

This constant and concurrent presence of the old with the new is inherent to Tamil culture. Apart from literature, contemporary Tamil music, theatre, dance, art, and film are replete with references to classical literature, and to reinvented stories depicting a continuity that spans epochs. Several scholars have suggested that the conscious reinforcement of this idea of continuity in language and culture is what powered a strong revival of Dravidian culture and political consciousness in the early twentieth century in Tamil country.

Both linguists and historians attest to the hoariness of Tamil and other Dravidian-origin languages, although controversies continue to rage over whether the Indus Valley civilization was of the early Dravidian people, and whether the script and engravings on the Indus Valley seals were of a prototype Dravidian language or not. However, the indisputably classical nature of Tamil (recognized by the Government of India as one of the country's classical languages only in 2004) has come from the acknowledgement that Tamil did originate from this prototype Dravidian language and developed singularly over the millennia. Its amazing continuity from earlier than 500 years BCE to the present time gives it a unique and noteworthy status in the history of humanity. The notion of the language as 'mother', transmuted with some level of passion into an anthropomorphic mother goddess (Tamizh Thai), was fuelled by linguistic pride, particularly at the time of Tamil revivalism in the nineteenth century, and later during the political movement of the early twentieth century. As Sumathi Ramaswamy in her scholarly study *Language Devotion in Tamil India* points out, 'For her devotees, Tamilttay (Thamizh Thai) is a singular figure with her own unique biography, a repertoire of deeds that cannot be reproduced, and a range of powers unfathomable. There is literally no one like her. Yet it is clear that she joins a pantheon of comparable female icons of the nation such as Bharata Mata, "Mother India", Britannia of England, Marianne of France, Guadalupe of Mexico and the like.'

And, yes, Tamil is distinct and has evolved separately from the Sanskritic language groups, it has assimilated certain aspects of that linguistic tradition. David Shulman, professor of Humanistic Studies at the Hebrew University in Jerusalem, offers a superb cultural history of the language in his book simply titled *Tamil*. He emphasizes, '…one cannot get along in Tamil without Sanskrit words. They were there at the beginning, and they are there now…'. Shulman's work stands as a lyrical paean to Tamil, unveiling the story and trajectory of the language like a musical composition. It provides fascinating insights into the intricate evolution of the language and its expression. 'To know Tamil' can also mean 'to be a civilized being', he says. 'Tamil means something like knowing how to love.' Shulman says that purists of Dravidian ideology may not agree, but 'Tamil is astonishingly rich in Sanskrit loan words...' although these Sanskrit words 'tend to be Tamilized'. The movement towards a robust non-Sanskritic expression of Tamil, and indeed the avoidance or substitution of Sanskrit-origin words, gained momentum with the Dravidian movement. This movement was fuelled by a fervent passion for the language and culture. However, it could be perceived as somewhat neglecting the inclusive and open-minded nature of the Tamils, as it proscribed influences from centuries of diverse cultures, words, and ideas brought by people who genuinely loved and lived Tamil in the first place.

Though the figures are approximate and likely an understatement, as of this writing, an estimated 80–90 million people around the world identify as Tamil. As of May 2024, 89.6 million people worldwide speak Tamil, with 80 million native speakers in India. The predominant presence of a majority in India's southern peninsula doesn't diminish the potent sense of Tamil identity among those residing in various corners of the world or even within the broader Indian subcontinent. The poet Cheran, residing in Canada, aptly captures this sentiment, stating, 'The sea has drained away / Tamil has no territory / Kinships have no name'. No matter where Tamils are settled, the celebration of 'Tamilness' is interwoven with daily life. My sisters and I were raised in a liberal, cosmopolitan household, deeply steeped in Western education, yet rooted in the heart of Madras for two generations, with origins in Kumbakonam, the renowned temple town nestled in the heart of the Kaveri delta. The Tamil identity within us flowed seamlessly, like the famed 'degree' coffee of Kumbakonam. Thus, a harmonious coexistence between a pan-Indian, urban, Anglicized identity and our Tamil heritage existed, much like it did for many of our contemporaries.

We had some exposure to snippets of poetry by Subramania Bharati, the illustrious Tamil poet, and we were equally familiar with the compositions of Thyagaraja, the eighteenth-century poet-saint whose Telugu and Sanskrit verses resonated in our home. While we studied Kabir ke dohe in school, Tamil tales were shared with us over leisurely meals of rasam sadam. My mother narrated the story of Paari Vallal, the generous Tamil ruler who left his chariot behind for a creeper. This, my mother explained, exemplified how boundless generosity should be practised. The narrative unfolded thus: Toward the end of the Sangam age, Paari, a powerful king of Parambu Nadu, paused his golden chariot to quench his thirst at a stream. Upon his return, he discovered a delicate jasmine creeper had wound itself around the chariot wheel. The magnanimous king, renowned for his benevolence as much as his courage and prowess, left his chariot behind for the creeper to ascend. The ancient Sangam text *Purananuru* extolled him in a couplet, stating that while the earth was nurtured by rain-bearing clouds, they had their own Paari! Benevolence was a highly esteemed virtue for Tamils; so much so that this king's courageous acts and his patronage of the arts and literature were overshadowed by his generosity. He became known as the king who offered his chariot to a creeper—mullaiku ther kodutha mannan.

Certainly, we were also acquainted with the Ramayana, stories from the Bhagavatam, and we were taught Sanskrit slokas to dispel our childhood fears and perhaps kindle early spiritual inclinations. Among the slokas, my mother firmly included The Lord's Prayer (her own brand of enlightened spirituality) to the list, thus introducing the universality of the divine early on. Christmas was part of our upbringing as well—unfortunately not the Tamilized version of our neighbours, but rather a version imported from England. The Nativity scene was reenacted with dramatic flair with white-skinned, rosy-cheeked dolls, a twinkling Christmas tree adorning the space, and carols warbled with a distinctive English accent.

The wave of westernization permeated numerous aspects of our lives. However, this influence did not diminish the deeply embedded, yet distinctly visible Tamil essence that coloured our everyday existence. From the intricate kolam patterns drawn with rice flour at our doorstep each morning to invite auspiciousness and nourish the ants, to our daily fare of dosai and idli, rice and rasam, to the uniquely Tamil festivals like Pongal, to the melodies of the nadaswaram accompanying the processions of deities, the rootedness in Tamil customs, culture, and ways of life was instinctive, much as it remains across various communities throughout the Tamil region.

Ideas of Identity

Tamil culture and Tamil identity evoke a distinctive sense of pride. The more benevolent aspects of this overarching pride are encapsulated in the simple sentiments of the poet Bharati, who asserts, 'senthamizh nadenum podhinile inba then vandhu payudhu kadhinile, engal thanthayar nadenum pechinile oru shakti pirakudhu moochinile'—'when Tamil is mentioned, honey pours into one's ears, and when we speak of the land of our ancestors, strength flows into our breath'.

However, there exist troubling elements within the seemingly benign Tamil cosmos. Tamils possess another facet, with caste and kinship strongly influencing their sense of identity. Senior journalist B. Kolappan explains that what the Tamils greatly value is a sense of honour (often misguided), rooted in caste pride regardless of one's caste affiliation. The extreme form of caste pride can manifest as violence often leading to death, perpetuated by prejudiced and narrow-minded ideas that contradict the more generous and open-minded nature of the Tamil community.

The origins of the caste system in ancient Tamil societies are documented in Sangam literature, particularly in works like the *Tolkappiyam*, the earliest grammatical work in Tamil by Tolkappiyar. Interestingly, as with literature (as mentioned earlier in this chapter), initial social organization mirrored geography and topography. People belonging to the kurinchi, or hilly regions, had specific occupations, while those in mullai or pastoral areas engaged in different work. People residing in neytal, the coastal regions, were involved in maritime activities, while those in marudam worked in agricultural tracts, cultivating grains and food. Those living in palai, the sandy areas, pursued other forms of employment. The migration of people between these regions implies that castes might not have been as rigidly stratified in early history.

The emergence of concepts like 'untouchability' appears to have taken root during the Pallava period and persisted into the eleventh and twelfth centuries CE, continuing into the twentieth century until it was legally banned. Unfortunately, the echoes of this practice continue to persist under the radar and often even openly today. With the advent of Buddhism, Jainism, Islam, and Christianity, social migration to these religions meant an escape from the rigours of caste hierarchies for those who were amongst the most underprivileged. However, over time, both Christianity and Islam, while abandoning formal caste structures, still retained traces of them in practice. Additionally, it is noteworthy that the introduction of Christianity and Islam to Tamil shores witnessed a remarkable fusion of the new religions with the old. Often, the new faiths did not abandon their original Tamil cultural and social foundations.

The dark side of caste is painfully evident even today in many forms, for instance, as honour killings incited by caste groups, particularly when marriages occur between Dalits and caste Hindus. This is an area where the principles of the Dravidian movement appear to have had very little influence. At one end, the Tamils can be reformist and egalitarian, and at the other extreme they will not hesitate to wield a machete and hack to death anyone assaulting their perceived sense of honour, especially when young people belonging to different caste groups elope and marry. Heart-wrenching stories recount tales of youthful love crushed by merciless familial opposition. However, there are faint indications of change in recent times. Some young people, often the direct victims of such tragedies, are now approaching the courts, securing convictions, and defying oppressive familial and caste regulations.

Caste-based discrimination and prejudice continue to exist, deeply entrenched in parts of Tamil Nadu. Although laws against discrimination are in place, they are violated with impunity, especially in the context of temple rituals and processions. In these settings, the Dalit presence is still unwelcome, as powerful local caste interests continue to hold sway. The reprehensible practice of providing two types of glasses at tea shops—one for Dalits and the other for non-Dalits—although prohibited by law, stubbornly persists in certain rural areas of Tamil Nadu.

Even in a traditional Tamil sport like jallikattu or bull baiting, casteism can prevail. In places like Singampunari in Sivagangai district when Dalit youth tried to participate in the sport they were attacked on account of their caste. However, in the recent large-scale yet mostly peaceful agitation in 2017 over the Supreme Court of India's ban on jallikattu, there seemed to be a collective resurgence of Tamil identity. Several thousand individuals, primarily comprising young IT professionals, students, and lawyers, came together to protest on Chennai's Marina Beach. Although the ban was temporarily lifted with the local government passing an ordinance, this bull-taming sport, mostly practiced in specific parts of the state, abruptly transformed into a symbol of Tamil culture. The ban was perceived as an assault on 'Tamilness'. While the sport indeed traces its origins to ancient Tamil culture, the exaggeration of its role as a repository of Tamil culture was fuelled by impassioned social media comments. Some analysts have suggested that these protests might also have been instigated by Tamil films. Matinee idol Rajnikanth starred in a famous film involving bull-taming called *Murattu Kaalai* (1980), and Kamal Haasan's film *Virumandi* (2004) prominently featured bullfighting. However, the practice of rubbing chilli powder on bulls, injuring their vertebrae, and forcing alcohol down their throats to confuse them before they enter the bull ring to be harmed and dominated is in no way a representation of

Tamil culture. In a newspaper commentary during the protests, writer and historian Ramachandra Guha expressed that the way the jallikattu protests were conducted and portrayed did a disservice to the Tamil people. He likened the attempt to reduce Tamil identity to jallikattu to the farcical and tragic endeavour to reduce the Indian identity to flag worship. In this book we will be examining multiple aspects of what makes Tamil culture, the mosaic of experience and expressions marked in stone and metal, in literature and art that makes it what it is.

∽

This book is a personal journey of discovery: what it signifies to be part of this distinct group of people, dissimilar in many ways from their fellow Indians, yet bound by numerous similarities. Many Tamils themselves are acutely aware of this prevailing sense of 'Indianness'. '*Mannum Imaya malai engal malaiye* (The peaks of the Himalayas are ours),' sang Bharati, expressing the strong pan-Indian connection that many Tamils feel. This sentiment persists, despite the firmly held belief that the presence and spirit of Tamil people often go unnoticed and misunderstood by many beyond the Vindhyas, frequently tainted by prejudice.

This is an account of the great Tamils—their histories and stories that have enriched the granary of Tamil life, contributing to its often esoteric existence, and building layers of richness for those who will partake in the future. This book is about the Tamils who created these stories, who went to war, wrote songs, made music, painted, and danced, wove silk and cotton, worked with stone and metal, built churches, mosques, and temples, created marvellous structures that have outlasted generations, and generously shared their crafts with others because they believed in the value of preserving and passing down their precious knowledge. As much as it encompasses grand and magnificent edifices, this book also embraces humble shrines, village deities, and the numerous guardian gods of rural life that still dot the Tamil landscape, being worshipped and revered as much as the more prominent deities. It is a personal narrative that reflects multiple voices and stories I heard and places that I visited over four years of researching this book. And as Walt Whitman said, 'Do I contradict myself? / Very well then, I contradict myself, / (I am large, I contain multitudes).'

This book also describes the contributions of writers, philosophers, and geniuses who have left an indelible impact on Tamil culture, as well as on Indian and universal thought. It delves into opposites—the refinement and heights of Tamil culture, but also, the violence stemming from centuries of prejudice, a narrowness and closed-mindedness bred from fear and ignorance that at times led the Tamils down a path of bigotry and intolerance.

From the annals of history to the present day, there are tillers of the land who have cultivated rice, the region's staple food, that has sustained the Tamils for millennia. There are communities of artisan weavers who spend hours at their looms, weaving and narrating a distinct Tamil story through silk, sungudi, and kalamkari weaves, crafting zari and muthangi—pearl-studded garments—for the gods. There are potters working their wheels to create vividly painted mud pots, known as mann paanai, and blacksmiths labouring in their forges to cast copper plates and coins. Painters employ colours and canvases to craft intricate Tanjore paintings. All these stories must be recounted, their efforts, achievements, and tragedies recorded, and their rightful place in the Tamil universe recognized.

This book takes the form of an anecdotal and personal journey, marshalling facts and weaving together the long tale of a civilization, its history, and its culture spanning centuries, progressing steadily through millennia. It delves into reflections on identity—some enduring and authentic, others illusory—all of which depict characteristics and ways of being that stem from the Tamils' finely honed and unique imagination. Tracing the chronology of Tamil life across centuries, this book also attempts to delve into the lives of ordinary people, visible through the structure of societies across the ages. Inevitably, there are narratives of rulers, glimpsed through literature, legends, records, and inscriptions.

During numerous road trips over the past few years, I had the privilege of being accompanied by experts well-versed in the history of the land, they knew well the shrines and caves, as well as the towns, cities, mountains, and woodlands of this land of jasmine. They generously shared their insights and time, enriching my understanding. Conversations with historians, archaeologists, and Tamil experts shed profound light on the multiple Tamil narratives that coexisted.

Listening to these experts, I journeyed with them while observing the landscape from which life flourished—from the paddy fields, jasmine groves, mango orchards, and sugarcane fields. Here, where rivers of stories and legends flowed, one can trace the path of centuries, ancient kingdoms, rulers, the arts of war and peace, and the diverse philosophies of humanity, all resonating under a Tamil sky. This narration includes multiple Tamil communities and their histories, at times in their own voices, presenting Tamil heroes, their creativity, achievements, aspirations, and how they perceive their Tamil identity. This book is largely subjective; it is a portrait rather than an academic study. It strives to provide an accessible account of the Tamils and their history for those interested in the subject but not necessarily familiar with it.

Chapter 1
Emergence

Questions about origins of things are easy to ask, but difficult to answer. Still, it is perfectly natural for the human mind to persist in its curiosity about how it all began.

K. A. Nilakanta Sastri, historian

TAMILAKAM OR THE ABODE OF THE TAMILS OF THE PRE-COMMON centuries demonstrates the existence of a sophisticated and ancient civilization. If we travel further back, through millennia and prehistory, and examine the evidence from excavation projects, remarkable discoveries from the peninsular region of South India stand revealed.

The incontrovertible evidence of early humans walking this region as far back as about a million to 350,000 years ago comes from some significant discoveries; from superbly carved pear-shaped multipurpose hand axes, many jewel-like in their aspect, which have been found in certain places in Tamil Nadu, and mainly in Attirampakkam in Tiruvallur district, about 60 kilometres from Chennai. Similar hand axes have been found in parts of Europe and in Africa, testifying to an amazing gamut of common skills across populations in different parts of the world during the Palaeolithic Age. Did these itinerant groups of people make vast journeys across the world, or did they split from each other, carrying their knowledge and skills and go on to create new communities on whom they stamped their evolutionary genius? We may never have an answer to this.

The first hand axe was discovered in Pallavaram, a suburb of Chennai, and a cleaver was found in 1863 in Attirampakkam again near Chennai, by Robert Bruce Foote, a multifaceted Englishman whose passions included geology, archaeology, anthropology, museology, and painting. Along with geologist William King, he later found several hand axes, cleavers, and scrapers in Attirampakkam. Foote has been fondly called the 'father' of Indian prehistory, as his discoveries set the calendar further back on human presence in the south Indian peninsula. In recent years, researchers from the Sharma Centre for Heritage Education, led by Dr Shanti Pappu and Dr Kumar Akhilesh, have published in journals like *Science* and *Nature* about the subsequent discovery of numerous Acheulian tools discovered at this site. These have been scientifically dated to much earlier than hitherto assumed of tool usage among prehistoric humans—earlier than in Europe and calling into question the theories of migration of the first humans from Africa. In 2011, Dr Pappu and her team reported the discovery of stone artefacts buried in the lowest sediments of excavations suggesting a middle Palaeolithic culture in the region. She affirms that the research 'represents a paradigm shift in thinking...suggesting a far greater antiquity and a more complex story than we thought. At Attirampakkam, we have a wonderful sequence contained in a single stratigraphic continuum and showing a long process of evolution'. The shift to the middle Palaeolithic phase from an earlier period of hunter-gatherer hominids is a deeply crucial and complex point in human evolution, and it is an amazing fact that the Tamil region was one of the places on earth where this transition happened.

Fast forward over an undocumented period to archaeological finds 500 to 1,000 years before the start of the Common Era. It is from this period that a somewhat linear progression of the lives of the Tamils can be established. Information about this period comes from specific excavations in places like Adichanallur near Tirunelveli, which reveal burial urns. Conventionally, the Sangam age, a loose nomenclature, has been used to define a period of roughly six centuries, between 300 BCE and 300 CE. Recent discoveries such as the excavations at Kodumanal near Erode and Porunthal near Palani and those at the Keezhadi site near Madurai among others take this era further back by a couple of centuries. The most recent theories suggest that the Sangam age began as early as 500 BCE. Also, the evidence for this period was largely thought to be only from the literature of the age, but these excavations have brought to light corroborative material that adds fascinating insights into the lives of the early Tamils.

The burial urns found in Adichanallur contained pieces of jewellery such as stone beads, terracotta beads, a gold diadem, bronze figurines, iron spears, arrowheads, and copper bangles. A great amount of baked earthenware has been found as well. Other small vessels include those with lids decorated with floral designs, of which close to a thousand are still intact. A few burial urns held skeletal remains, one of a mother and child. They had markings and symbols on them thought to represent tribal afflictions. There were iron implements and weapons, suggesting a vibrant and active community and settlement. Another unique find has been that of a palm-sized bronze figurine presumed to be of a mother goddess, possibly a fertility figure, with wide hips and a gold diadem around her head. In the late nineteenth and early twentieth centuries, Alexander Rea, an English archaeologist who was among the early excavators in the area, was the one who first found a few gold ornaments which indicates an active trading community as gold is not innate to the area. Many of these discoveries are now housed in the Government Museum at Egmore in Chennai, along with numerous other artefacts from the excavations at the site. As the Adichanallur site has been the focal point of interest for numerous archaeologists and scholars from around the world from the nineteenth century onwards, many artefacts have found their way to a couple of museums in Europe.

A recent visit to Adichanallur with Dr Yathees Kumar, the chief archaeologist of the site, was revelatory. Thirteen trenches are currently being worked upon closest to the riverbed; further afield are the rest of the 125 acres that are being excavated. As has been cited, the original site of a possible ancient settlement was indicated by Rea, more than 120 years ago. With advanced technology such as remote sensing, Yathees Kumar says much more accurate excavations are possible. Seventy-five urn burials have been found around the current excavation, out of which two are pit burials. These are likely to be from before the Iron Age, and carbon dating indicates the date of the urns as 980 or 1000 BCE. Husks of millets and paddy in stoneware have been found and these are dated to 1500 BCE. In ceramic assemblages and in broken bits of pottery, mounds of ancient rice have been found. As mentioned earlier, skeletal remains of humans of the same period have also been found at this site. There is evidence of a continuity of burial practices from the fourth century BCE back to 1500 BCE, contrary to the earlier notions that there were gaps in the continuity of human existence in the area. In the same locality, there are indications of a temporary human settlement from 400 to 200 BCE.

Redware urns have been found in these pits, says Yathees Kumar, with beautiful lids in place, as well as the later period black stoneware. We see a near perfect black polished bowl with a beautiful lid. It was here that the gold diadem, and bronze objects including a decorated lid along with a dagger, a spear, and a sword were found. These are all secondary burials, as the primary burial would have occurred in another place and the bones preserved in these urns. This site must have been that of an important personage, notes Kumar, with simpler objects buried with people who were lower down in the social hierarchy.

What these digs testify to is the existence of a distinctly sophisticated style of civilization. Former superintendent archaeologist of the Archaeological Survey of India (ASI), T. Sathyamurthy, who was involved in two seasons of excavation, suggests that only about 10 per cent of the area has been dug up as of now. Unfortunately, work on the vast, unexplored portions of the site has been abandoned over the last decade, and it is only recently that public interest petitions have led the Madras High Court to question why the ASI has not pursued these excavations for such a long time. Political interference, squabbles between the ASI and the state government, as well as frequent transfers of key personnel involved in these excavations has led to a sorry situation where priceless treasures remain locked below the surface. The ASI has now set up a site museum at Adichanallur.

The historians and archaeologists I encountered in Tiruchirapalli and Madurai suggest that whatever has been unearthed in recent times turns on its head hitherto held notions of Tamil civilization's antiquity. Carbon dating and other scientific ways of verifying and confirming dates are being systematically done by sending the excavated material to specialist institutions abroad. While there is wide agreement now on pushing back the timeframe of what has come to be known as the Sangam age stemming from recent archaeological discoveries, experts seem to differ somewhat in terms of their theories and conjectures about the early history of Tamilakam.

In Pudukkottai district is another recent discovery preceding even the Sangam age, of a prehistoric settlement in the area. Rock paintings, Iron Age weapons and implements, sophisticated pottery with markings, and beads from a variety of stones, many with small, precise holes in them, have been excavated here. Specifically, in Kodumbalur, black- and redware dating as far back as 2,500 years have been found. Dr J. Raja Mohamad, archaeological expert and historian, says several megalithic burials of the Iron Age have been found in the Tiruchi–Pudukkottai region.

Dr Mohamad, scholar, researcher, former assistant director of museums, Chennai, is the retired curator of the government museum in Pudukkottai town. An authority on Tamil Muslims, especially on the maritime history of the Muslims of the Coromandel coast, Dr Mohamad's sense of history is qualified by an exemplary need to demonstrate authenticity. He speaks with great passion. 'I was fortunate to be part of the extensive field work that was done, and the report was completed in 2015,' he says. Raja Mohamad suggests that these cave paintings are probably closer to 3,000 years old, and date back to well before the Sangam age. The unearthing of iron implements in the area as well as a few megalithic burial sites indicate that parts of the region seem to have had continuity of habitation from prehistoric times. A cave temple of the ninth century and inscriptions from the third century BCE have also been found in the Kudumiyanmalai area. Raja Mohamad stresses that advanced centres of civilization existed before the Sangam period and in the centuries leading up to that time. 'A civilization cannot sprout all of a sudden, there is evidence of a strong line of continuity from earlier periods up to the Sangam age and beyond,' he says emphatically. We talk about the confusions of historical perspectives, about the need for a more nuanced and fact-based reading of history and politics.

Another excavation in the Tamil region, Kodumanal village near the town of Erode, has yielded rich material that corresponds roughly with the Sangam centuries. Kodumanal is referred to in two places (as Kodumanam) in the Sangam work *Patthitrupattu*. An important trade centre, it connected ancient Muziris on the Malabar coast with Kaveripoompattinam or Poompuhar on the Coromandel coast. Excavations have revealed numerous silver Roman coins, carved beads, broken bangles, quartz, amethyst, and topaz, fine gold wires, beads with holes, stones of all kinds—carnelian, agate, beryl, cat's eye, and lapis lazuli, utensils and bowls among various other artefacts. The renowned expert of early south Indian epigraphy, archaeology, and history, Dr Y. Subbarayalu, head of Indology at the Institut Français in Pondicherry and editor of the *Historical Atlas of Tamil Nadu*, a path-breaking work, Professor K. Rajan of Pondicherry University, and Professor Raju of Thanjavur among others were actively involved in the Kodumanal excavations, with Rajan and his team repeatedly visiting the site to discover evidence of more than a hundred potsherds or pottery fragments with inscriptions in Tamil Brahmi. Writing in *Frontline* in 2012 after that season's excavation, journalist T. S. Subramanian reports, 'In the period between the fourth and third centuries BCE, to the first century BCE, Kodumanal was an important industrial and trade centre with links to northern parts of India, as is evident from recent excavations.... People who lived there extracted iron from its ore and forged steel; spun cotton using spindle whorls and made textiles; manufactured thousands of beads from semi-precious stones such as quartz, carnelian, sapphire, beryl...cut exquisite bangles from conch shells; used bronze to make artefacts.' The archaeological teams discovered very specific structures that proved the existence of kilns and furnaces, all verified by scientific dating. One prized artefact was a potsherd with the names 'Samban' and 'Sumanan' written in Tamil Brahmi, suggesting that parts of the industrial complex or indeed the whole complex may perhaps have been owned by this family.

In 2013, Rajan reported that a major excavation revealed,

a complete gemstone industry. The four trenches laid in the central part of the habitation mound yielded the industry in different stages of manufacture…this site survived as one of the important trade cum industrial centres between the 5th century CE and 1st century BCE…. The bustling industrial activities brought traders, artisans and skilled labourers from different parts of India. The occurrence of a large number of Tamil Brahmi inscribed potsherds with names of North Indian origin and Prakrit affiliation supports this view….

The habitation part of the site yielded a number of graffiti bearing potsherds…the most common graffiti marks are the sun, swastika, star, ladder…fish, bow and arrow, wheel, cart, etc…. Though the exact connotation of these symbols, individually or in compound form cannot be easily guessed at…. More than 500 potsherds using Brahmi letters were recovered at the site….

Most of them were proper names like Atintai, Makintai, Masa, Kuviran, Sumanan, Campan, Santhai Veli, Pannan, Pakan, Atan, etc.

In the Sivagangai district outside Madurai city is the Keezhadi site that has been the subject of much controversy in recent years owing to the sudden transfer of a young superintending archaeologist, K. Amarnath Ramakrishna, midway through the explorations in 2017. Ramakrishna and his team had brought to light the fact that the yield of thousands of artefacts at the site confirmed the existence of a highly urban civilization that synchronized with the Sangam period affirming an evolved south Indian culture. Other than the sites at Arikamedu and Kaveripoompattinam, Keezhadi is the only other extensive habitation site, as the others are largely burial places. Ramakrishna and his team identified 293 possible locations along a 200 kilometre stretch for excavation and then zeroed in on an area of 100 or so acres, mostly coconut groves and largely privately owned. In 2015, the located site yielded 7,000 indicators of antiquity, including structures like brick walls, ring wells, and drainage systems. Over 5,500 artefacts were also unearthed revealing incontrovertible evidence of a civilization (carbon dated to certify the period) coinciding with the Sangam age. This has allegedly proved irksome to some political interests who have been reluctant to accept the emergence of a distinct secular (no religious relics have been unearthed yet) habitation at this time and place. Notwithstanding the dubious reasons for the transfer of the enterprising young archaeologist from the Keezhadi site, the work there had been mired until recently, in various stand-offs and funding issues between various agencies. And with the courts having to frequently intervene, the progress of the excavations suffered, but work has been resumed recently. While the ASI did the first three seasons of excavations, the Tamil Nadu State Department of Archaeology has done the next six seasons of excavations.

On a hot May morning, I drive out of Madurai city to the Keezhadi site. The dilapidated chaos of contemporary urban India is evident everywhere. Cinema posters on half-broken walls, unruly goats foraging in trash cans, and the blare of horns from disorderly vehicles, all too familiar sights and sounds in Tamil Nadu, confront me. I pass by the famous Vandiyur Mariamman temple's teppakulam or sacred pond where the idols of Meenakshi and Sundareswar are set afloat in a colourful ritual on the night of Thai Poosam (first full moon of the month of Thai) each year. There is no water in the tank now, only an overgrown morass of green weed. The tar road narrows and crossing the railway tracks we bump and bounce down trajectories of mud and red earth with the dust rising behind us.

Indologist David Shulman in a recent lecture in Chennai spoke about dust in the south Indian universe. In its motley forms it is soil, it is specks of gold, the reddish stuff of passion, it is eroticism, it is death and regeneration, it is the essence of life itself, he had said on what he called a bottom-up view of the south Indian firmament. As I drew closer to the site, I recalled that Shulman mentioned how frequently classical Tamil literature touched on the topic of dust, right from the Sangam age to the *Kamba Ramayanam* and more. It seemed only apt that my visit to this ancient Tamil site should be through this fine pink cloud, irksome somewhat to our modern-day allergic sensitivities, but nevertheless the same essence that was stirred up millennia ago, physically as well as in the minds of writers and poets. As we leave the dust tract behind, we reach a coconut grove in which there are makeshift tarpaulin tents and beyond that a group of women squatting on geometric beds of earth, chipping away at bits of stone that they hold in their hands almost as if they were carving something. The sun begins to beat down on the workers and yet they are absorbed in their work and barely look up at the strangers who have arrived. We meet Sakthivel, the onsite archaeologist. He is a wiry, energetic man whose initial reluctance to give away too much information soon changes.

Sakthivel speaks with passion about the discoveries at Keezhadi. 'The name is Kondhahai actually,' he explains. 'Keezhadi is the name of the revenue area.' It certainly sounded more like old Tamil. Sakthivel tells us that the project has been so dogged with various kinds of controversies between the state government, the ASI, and the Tamil Nadu Archaeology department, that it has severely affected the progress of the work. Pon Vasanth, the young journalist who has accompanied me to the sites, points out that public interest litigations have also brought the courts into the picture. Issues of compensation to the private owners of the coconut groves have not been properly resolved yet either. Despite all the hurdles, in Sakthivel's view, the findings here have been nothing short of remarkable. He speaks of unearthing stone beads the size of mustard seeds with holes drilled in them and a hoard of glass beads as well as painted potsherds with markings. 'Bits of ivory, possibly earrings, ivory dice and conical gold beads' have also been found, he says with obvious pride.

'It was a local schoolteacher, V. Balasubramaniam, who first discovered a mound and found bits of terracotta,' says Sakthivel. 'Keezhadi's finds now surpass most other sites, it is clearly a habitation site, whereas many others are burial sites although they had plenty of artefacts as well,' he says. A little further away are the original excavations where the archaeologists found troughs, a double-walled furnace, and several brick chambers with brick floors, ring wells, and drainage systems. 'It is possible that textiles were dyed here,' says Sakthivel. 'The combination of an industrial site and a habitation place is what makes this place extraordinary, this was a highly urban civilization,' he says.

Sakthivel also reminds us that about 150 kilometres away is another important site, in Alagankulam village, further down in Ramanathapuram district, on the banks of the Vaigai River where a stockpile of Roman coins, more potsherds, and beads were unearthed, roughly from the same time period. Positioned on an estuary, it was likely to have been a port town. 'It is also a Sangam age settlement. We know all this for sure as the material is sent abroad for carbon dating.' For about a century, the existence of an ancient Tamil civilization had been deduced from the Sangam texts. More recently, this has been confirmed by these archaeological findings.

Another source that has contributed to proving the existence and supremacy of the ancient Tamils are very old inscriptions that have been carefully studied and documented by various scholars and expert epigraphists and historians like Iravatham Mahadevan, whose contributions to the field are immense. Mahadevan's work on Tamil Brahmi writing, the precursor to classical old Tamil, has been pivotal to the understanding of Tamil history, beginning from 300 to 400 BCE. Mahadevan has recorded incredible finds in caves, rock faces, on burial mounds and stones, on coins, and on vast amounts of broken pottery. In an article, Mahadevan says, 'The most important historical inscriptions include those of Nedunchezhiyan at Mankulam near Madurai, the Cheral Irumporai dynasty at Pukalur and Atiyan Netuman Anji at Jambai…all assigned to the period from the period of the 2nd century BCE… coinciding with the Sangam age described in the earliest Tamil anthologies.' Mahadevan describes other important discoveries, such as the copper coins of Peruvazhudi, a Sangam age king, and the silver coins of Chera kings inscribed both in Prakrit and Tamil Brahmi.

There are a large number of inscriptions, dated to possibly around 400 to 300 BCE, in places like Porunthal and Kodumanal, at sites which were likely to have originally been the caves of Jain and Buddhist monks. Shulman writes about the 'sensational' discoveries of Tamil Brahmi inscriptions that were found at Jambai in South Arcot district and in Pukalur near Tiruchirappalli as mentioned earlier. 'The Jambai inscription marks a donation by *satyia puto atiyan netuman anci*…the chieftain whom we know of from several references in Sangam heroic poetry,' writes Shulman.

A scholarly paper titled 'Archaeology and the Cankam literature with special reference to pots and hero stones' was presented and later published in a special volume by Professor Y. Subbarayalu at the World Classical Tamil Conference held in June 2010 in Coimbatore. The paper underlines that the archaeological evidence that has surfaced in recent years with regard to the dating of Sangam literature include '1) potsherds with Tamil Brahmi inscriptions excavated from Arikamedu, Alagankulam, Kodumanal and other ancient sites in Tamil Nadu and those from a couple of sites in Egypt; 2) Roman coins and other antiquities; and 3) the recently discovered four memorial stones with Brahmi inscriptions.' In a perceptive analysis of the archaeological evidence, Subbarayalu states that the pottery with Tamil Brahmi from the sites mentioned above can be dated from 200 BCE to 100 CE. He points out that nearly one-fifth of the names on the pottery are recognizably Prakrit names, and do not use non-Tamil letters. Some are Tamilized, such as Kuviran which is derived from Kubira or Kubera. Another name Camuta is a Tamilized version of the Prakrit Samuda. Other names based on Prakrit influences include 'star names such as Asatan, Asalay(a), Mulan, Visakan….' A few women's names of Prakrit origin are also found on the potsherds, such as Tevvai, Tattai, and Kutaly. In the cave inscriptions (in the caves used by Jain monks) he observes an equal proportion of Prakrit origin names and Tamilized names.

What is very significant about Subbarayalu's findings is that though there is a conspicuous presence and influence of Prakrit, it was not widespread in terms of impacting literacy in these places. What it really accounts for is the presence of immigrant Prakrit-speaking people at these sites. Subbarayalu says, '[L]iteracy was confined to only the elite sections of society, particularly the merchants, their craftsmen associates, the ruling people, besides the monks.' The movement of merchants and the trade in places like Kodumanal and Alagankulam meant that these places were busy centres of exchange. With regard to the identity of the people whose names were inscribed on the pots, they are possibly 'the Prakrit-speaking merchants...(who were) instrumental in the beginning in introducing the Brahmi script into the Tamil country. This must have happened soon after the Brahmi script in its full form was available in the Magadha region during the Maurya rule early in the third century BCE,' Subbarayalu says. 'The spread of the knowledge of writing through the traders is an important consequence of this development', implying that the traders and craftsmen from these areas played a crucial role in the growth of writing. There is more Prakrit in the pottery, and a more Tamilized language in the caves of the Jain monks, which included other elite members of society such as the kings who were the patrons of these monks and their disciples.

While the three great monarchies of Tamilakam that came a few centuries after this age have left a great deal of material evidence of their glory, for a long time, this period of early Tamilakam was lost in the realms of literature, myth, and travellers' accounts. Now, with plenty of excavated evidence in hand, we have incontrovertible evidence about the origin of the long and glorious civilization that is Tamil.

BOOK I
The Age of Poetry

Chapter 2

Literature as History

It looks like a skilled man's work of art, this jasmine country.

Ahananuru 134

THE DEVELOPMENT OF A RICH CLASSICAL TAMIL IDIOM FROM THE hoary Tamil Brahmi language came to a 'superb finish' in the Sangam poems, according to Nilakanta Sastri. Let us then look at Tamilakam 2,500 years ago through the lens of literature. Imagine a land effulgent and green, yet also dotted with teeming towns and cobbled streets, where merchants traded wares brought from distant shores, women adorned with sapphire ornaments yearned for their secret lovers, and poets wrote of the valour of kings. Imagine millets and other grains sown and tended in fields, yielding harvests of plenty in some seasons, and dry despair during times when a merciless sun scorched an earth with no respite from rain. Imagine the clatter of horses and chariots, the sway of tall elephants, blooming cassia peeping from behind small hamlets, and the tramp of herdsmen as they moved their cattle through the forests. Imagine scholars bending over their work in dim rooms, and the rolling drums and funereal cries rending the air announcing a hero's death.

This was the kind of civilization that flourished in the southern peninsula of India, and whose story was largely brought to light and sourced from poetry written on palm leaf manuscripts, lost for many centuries but rediscovered in the nineteenth century. Passionate scholars like U. Ve. Swaminatha Aiyar's almost serendipitous discovery, and the joint efforts of other academics like C. W. Thamotharampillai who worked to compile, catalogue, and revitalize the manuscripts reveal the extraordinary genius that was Tamil culture in 300–500 BCE and up until 300 years or so in the Common Era. In addition to this, with epigraphical, numismatic, and archaeological evidence surfacing since the late nineteenth through the twentieth and twenty-first centuries, and up until recent decades, the sophistication of the age has only been further validated.

This period of history in Tamilakam has come to be known as the Sangam age, because much of the information about that age comes from the literature of the time, from a confluence or sangam of poets that occurred roughly between 300 BCE to about 300 CE. Although some scholars do not feel comfortable with the nomenclature defining the age, this gathering was supposedly the Third Sangam. The first two assemblies are thought to have happened several thousands of years before this, although there is no actual historical record of the earlier convergences. Legend has it that three academies lasted about 9,990 years and had 8,598 poets participating. Although quite problematic in terms of historical accuracy, this has been mentioned in the *Tolkappiyam*, the earliest extant work on Tamil grammar. Such referenced dates and years notwithstanding, the central myths surrounding the poems and tracts persist despite the fantastical dating described in the ancient texts of the period. Interestingly, in an article in *The Hindu* published in 1960, a time before the major archaeological finds, Sastri cautions against overenthusiasm and exaggeration. 'All of us have a natural propensity to claim the highest possible antiquity for our own civilisation and culture and we are apt to prefer data which favour such a view and overlook...the rest of the evidence,' he says somewhat wryly.

The legends of the sage Agastya, which appear in the lore of both North and South India, describe him as the head of the first Sangam. The legend goes that he had deities like Shiva, Muruga, and Kubera accompany him in that assembly of poets, a story that the historian and Tamil scholar David Shulman retells with an unaffected indulgence. The emergence of the first Tamil grammar compiled by Agastya, called the *Agattiyam*, along with some works of early Tamil literature, is thought to have emanated from this time. While there is no actual physical record of Agastya's work on grammar, it has been quoted and referred to in other classical literature, such as in the work of the poet Nakkirar. The first recorded work of Tamil grammar, however, is among the earliest of Sangam texts, the *Tolkappiyam* by Tolkappiyar, who is said to have been a disciple of Agastya and who quotes the latter's work extensively in his own compendium of grammar. The exact date of the *Tolkappiyam* is not known but conjectured as being either in the sixth century BCE, just before the Sangam era or contemporaneously along with the Sangam poems, and indeed even a bit after, that is, anywhere between the fifth and sixth centuries CE. There is another school of thought that suggests that the work was layered and produced over several centuries. We must remember that works like these might have been written on palm leaves but also were part of a hoary oral tradition and communicated over centuries. In another rather engaging legend connected to Agastya, it is said that before he set off for the South, the sage asked Shiva to give him the blessing of knowing good Tamil, a sentiment that maybe many modern day Tamilians could probably identify with.

> They say the Tamil land where I am headed
> Is full of poetry.
> Everyone there has studied Tamil and has achieved
> Sweet Tamil wisdom…
> So kindly heal my ignorance and give me
> The book of natural correct Tamil…
>
> —*Thiruvilayadal Puranam*

For many of us who grew up with stories of gods and sages, Agastya's name pops up in diverse contexts. Known as a major contributor to several hymns of the Rig Veda and to other Vedic texts, he is mentioned in various scriptures and in epics like the Ramayana and the Mahabharata. The story goes that the reason he was sent down south beyond the Vindhya mountains was to balance the weight of the subcontinent, and he subsequently instructed the Vindhyas not to grow until he came back north. Of course, they waited, and he never returned, ensuring perhaps a permanent ease of movement between the north and the south! However, the legends of Agastya have also been viewed as reflecting vested interests in the Aryanization of Tamil culture. But as Shulman and many other modern-day linguists and historians point out, notwithstanding the more blatant incursions from the North, most of the permeation and the commingling of cultures and language traditions occurred much more subtly and over the ages, beginning even centuries before the Sangam age, despite the physical hurdles of crossing the Vindhyas.

It must also be mentioned that given the Tamil predilection for setting things into a firm proto-Dravidian context, many conjectures and theories have arisen about these early settlers and their dissimilarities from the Aryan wanderers who came into the Indo-Gangetic plain from Central Asia. The question as to whether these people were the original occupants of the Indus Valley is still unresolved. Notwithstanding racial theories and evolutionary features, it is abundantly clear that in many regions of Tamilakam, these forebears of the Sangam period were apparently already an urbane group of people. What came after, in the era that has come to be known as the Sangam age, was a further flowering, confirmed by new archaeological discoveries, detailed in epigraphs, on coins, and in the accounts of outsiders who travelled to this southern peninsula, where, as the literature of the age says,

> The traveller is safe on the highway.
>   Sellers of grain shelter their kin…
>
>   ….

Hunger has fled.
And taken disease with her.

—*Pattitrupattu 13*

As a primary source of information about the time, the 2,381 poems composed by 473 poets (around 102 poems of the poems having unknown authorship) deal with love, death, war, nature, philanthropy, heroism, courage, and relationships, in short, the whole range of human experience. They were composed not just by poet-scholars but also by women, priests, chieftains, peasants, merchants, and warriors, and even by those who laboured as potters and blacksmiths.

Spanning several hundreds of years, these poems dealt with Aham, the interior world, and Puram, the exterior world, and their creators linked the landscape of their time with their everyday living, and with their most meaningful life experiences. 'The ancient poets composed in Tamil for their Tamil corner of the world of antiquity; but as nothing human is alien, they have reached ages unborn…' says Ramanujan, the translator of these poems of the Sangam. He also points out, 'these poems are *classical*, i.e., early, ancient; they are also "classics", i.e., works that have stood the test of time, the founding works of a whole tradition. Not to know them is not to know a unique and major poetic achievement of Indian civilization.' Apart from the *Tolkappiyam*, the most well-known of these poetic anthologies are the *Ettuthokai* and *Pattupattu*, with numerous poems within these anthologies, such as *Ahananuru, Purananuru, Kuruntokai*, and several other works.

Tolkappiyam is the grammatical treatise that classified poetry into Aham and Puram. The well-known literary critic and scholar K. Kailasapathy notes that while these poetic conventions were set up in the grammar, 'both categories of poetry had, notwithstanding this division, a fundamental unity.' For convenience, the grammar of early Tamil poetry classified 'love' and related states as the inner, and the 'heroic' as the outer. 'Those treating wars, exploits of kings and chieftains, the splendour of courts, and the liberty and munificence of heroes may be called heroic poems; those in which the love theme is predominant may be called love songs. It is in this general sense that one can accept the categorization of poetry into *Aham* and *Puram*,' says Kailasapathy. Kailasapathy writes that the *Tolkappiyam* prescribes that the names of lovers should remain anonymous, but heroes can be named in poems. He adds, 'We do not know enough of the motives and other factors that helped shape these grammatical rules.' The fact of a highly evolved set of rules in the treatment of attributes like love, munificence, heroism, and valour in this ancient grammar reflects a literature that was extraordinarily advanced and refined. The *Tolkappiyam* has three books dealing with units of literary practice, from letters and words to content. This text provides indispensable insights into the ancient world of Tamils.

With the physical environment intricately connected to ways of life, the land was demarcated into five distinct landscapes or tinai: kurinchi, mullai, marudam, neytal, and palai. And the word tinai, according to Martha Ann Selby (who teaches South Asian Studies at the University of Texas at Austin) also stands for context, and 'this (context) is sweeping, and includes geographical space, time and everything that grows, develops, and lives within that space and time, including emotion.' Everything in the immediate surrounding was interconnected: the earth, soil, trees, clouds, leaves, flowers, sadness, anger, despair, courage, and joy were almost codified symbols, and layered into all these elements were human relationships and emotions, gods, and lovers. We can see how much these landscapes provided for particular stories and histories, how these specific settings set the early pace for the rise and fall of kingdoms and led to the establishment and progress of Tamilakam through the centuries.

The kurinchi landscape, which stands for the mountainous regions of Tamilakam, includes parts of the Western Ghats and smaller mountains like the Palani Hills, the Aanamalai and Yercaud hills near Salem, and is described in the Sangam poems as being the space of wildlife, lush forests, thick with teak and bamboo, with copious waterfalls, red rock, and pouring rain. The rare kurinchi flower that blooms once in twelve years is the region's symbol. Horses, bulls, tigers, and elephants roam the slopes, and the hill tribes gather honey in the deep forests. These people, called kuravar, vetar, and kanavar, besides being honey-gatherers, are also hunters and cultivate bamboo rice. The deity that they worship is Murugan, known later as Skanda or Karthikeya, and the associated mother goddess is Kotravai.

The cool climes of the verdant hillsides represent various human moods and emotions, such as lovers meeting in secret, with their quarrels and reconciliations; all these are revealed in the exquisite poetry written at the time. The context moves from the intensely personal to the larger landscape—to exemplify, here is a poem in the *Kuruntokai* text that reflects this tinai:

'What She Said'
Bigger than earth, certainly,
higher than the sky,

> more unfathomable than the waters
> is this love for this man
> > of the mountain slopes
> > where bees make rich honey
> > from the flowers of the kurinchi
> > that has such black stalks.
>
> —Tevakulattar, *Kuruntokai*

The magnificence of the surrounding dissolves into the overwhelming love the girl feels for her lover, and yet the context is the anchor of her feelings. And in 'What She Said to Her Girl Friend' is a more intimate depiction of this world:

> In his country
> summer west wind blows
> flute music
> through bright beetle-holes in the waving bamboos.

The kurinchi tinai is home to the velir, or hill chieftains, who married into royal houses and often took their brides from the ventar or crowned kings, some of whom belonged to the existing ruling dynasties.

If we look at the marudam and mullai landscapes as other critical sites of early Tamil history, it is easy to see how these well-considered divisions or contexts set the stage for later civilizational development. For instance, the fertile river banks of the marudam tinai saw the growth of agriculture; irrigation and the plough brought prosperity to these regions, and the more privileged ventar, or kings, established themselves in these areas, setting up hierarchies and elite groups. The Kaveri riverbank was the backdrop against which the mighty Chola empire later grew. In this Sangam period some minor kings of the early Chera, Chola, and Pandya dynasties ruled, mostly in contention with each other, and at other times in situations of uneasy peace. Among the Cheras, the more reputed ones were Udiyanjeral and Senguttavan, an almost mythic hero king whose legendary exploits were written up in *Purananuru* by Paranar, an important poet of the time. Senguttavan's maritime successes were also recorded in some of the Sangam writing.

The Chola kingdom's most famous early king was Karikal, and the Pandya kingdom's early rulers like Nedunchezhiyan have also been listed in the Sangam poems. Among the velir or chieftains, seven of them known as Kadaiyelu Vallalgal—Paari, Ori, Malayan, Elini, Peygan, Aay, and Nalli—were each known for their outstanding attributes and peerless valour. They were also generous patrons of many Sangam poets like Kapilar, Avvaiyar (the legendary woman poet), Nallathanar, and Perunchithiranar. Some of these poets also functioned as diplomats and advisers to these chieftains and their families. For instance, the poet Kapilar supposedly took charge of Paari's young daughters after his death, and much of this is referenced in the poetry. Similarly, Avvaiyar advised her patron Adhiyaman, underlining also (at least in legend) an important role for women in public spaces.

A great deal of information about the velir and ventar comes from texts like the *Purananuru* which praises many of these chieftains and kings through heroic poetry. The sway of kings, that is the ventar, was usually over land that was classically marudam, that is fertile land where the early settlements first took root, as mentioned earlier, and probably partially mullai; indeed, in many cases the kingdoms bordered or extended into kurinchi tinai as well. These would roughly correspond to the river basins of the Kaveri, the Tamarabarani, the areas around Uraiyur (near modern-day Tiruchi) and Kaveripattinam, where the Cholas and several velir chieftains ruled. Madurai, which thrived for centuries beginning with the early Pandyas, is also of marudam tinai. Fertile rice fields, abundant crop lands, prosperous farmers ploughing the soil while paying tithes to their overlords, fruit orchards, and vegetable patches, with town centres and cities of great affluence teeming with craftsmen and markets and goods signalling a growing prosperity for the people of the region marked the marudam landscape. Just beyond these small semi-urban dwellings surrounded by extensive pasture lands and green flowering forests was mullai tinai. In the twenty-first century, this area comprises the base of the Western and Eastern Ghats, including the contiguous areas around Salem touching the Yercaud Hills and the grasslands connecting modern Coimbatore with the Nilgiris.

Sangam poetry describes marudam's flower as the queen's flower of the lowlands and mullai's flower as the jasmine. The emotions associated with marudam tinai is the joyful meeting and union of lovers, and the imagery and symbols this landscape encapsulates are ponds and lakes with dancing freshwater fish, lazy buffaloes soaking up the sun, mango groves and harvests of plenty, with Indra being the main deity. Mullai tinai is associated with forests and the heroine's grief at separation from her lover as well as the patient wait for love's return. The smell of red soil churned by pouring rain, clouds scudding across grey skies, pastimes like bull taming, the carefree spirit of cowherds and shepherds with their sheep grazing in the pasture lands, are evocative of this landscape and its deity Mayon, an early form of Krishna or Vishnu.

And the beauty of mullai lands is evoked thus:

> Rains in season,
> forests grow beautiful
> Black pregnant clouds
> bring the monsoons and stay...
> ...and fallen jasmines.
> cover the ground...
> ...Friend, drive softly here.
>
> —*Ahananuru*

Next, if we look at the description of neytal, or the seashore, Sangam poetry offers stunning imagery, often laced with humour such as in the poem below:

> O man of the seashore
>   where old women
>   dry their wet streaming hair
>   and look like a flock
>   of herons in the bay...
>
> —Ammuvanar, *Ainkurunuru*

Neytal's representative flower is the water lily, and the deity Varuna, not surprisingly the god of rain. Neytal stands for sunset, for the early days of summer, for fisherfolk, for small wooden boats, conches, pearls, and seashells; for where the fishermen who brave dangerous sharks on the high seas and the sandy beaches where lovers have clandestine meetings. The 'bustling city of Korkai' or Colchi is mentioned in the neytal Sangam poems as well as in the *Periplus*, where merchants from far away, the Yavanas, possibly Arab seafarers, as well as Roman and Greek sailors, traded in the pearl fisheries and were engaged in lucrative commerce in the bustling port cities. Sangam poems like 'Pattinapalai', part of the *Pattitrupattu* anthology, written in praise of the Chola king Karikal, speak of the glory of Kaveripattinam or Puhar, the port where the Yavanas conducted brisk trade, and the colourful portraits of these merchants as well as the local traders or vanikars is vividly depicted. Interestingly, trade between pon vanikan and uppu vanikan is mentioned in some Sangam texts, suggesting perhaps that there was a system of barter between traders, who exchanged paddy or pon for uppu or salt. Consequently, borders between marudam and neytal grew blurred as people moved between the regions.

Neytal lands were the concourses of the inland regions to the sea. Apart from trading, the impact of an extended fishing community stretching along the coastline spawned its own unique culture, contributing greatly to the local economy. The *Ahananuru* describes these communities in some detail and the poet Nakkirar is said to have belonged to the fishing community; they were known variously as minavar, parathavar, valayar, karayar, and other titles. Both Ptolemy and Pliny reference the fishing communities all along the coast of modern-day Kerala, which was then part of Tamilakam.

The palai or desert land is often described as scattered across Tamilakam and usually at the junction of kurinchi and marudam or even mullai. The *Tolkappiyam* does not recognize palai as a proper tinai, although other Sangam poems speak of parched, dry lands, high noon, blazing sun, and desert areas with wild animals like the tiger and the wolf searching for water in the wilderness. Cactus is predominant in the region. The goddess worshipped by those living on such lands is Kotravai. The desert area is known for its dangerous journeys, usually undertaken by desperate lovers, desertion, and a sense of loss; travellers and bandits are therefore the principal subjects of the poetry of palai.

In his *History of South India,* Nilakanta Sastri provides a detailed description of Tamilakam: 'The land was fertile, and there was plenty of grain, meat, and fish; the Chera country was noted for its buffaloes, jackfruit, pepper, and turmeric. In the Chola country, watered by the Kaveri, it was said that the space in which an elephant could lie down produced enough to feed seven, and a *veli* of land yielded around a thousand *kalams* of paddy...'. He goes on to comment on the sense of social solidarity that prevailed; apparently, diversity of social levels was of little consequence to the Sangam poets, who wrote with equal fervour about the mighty as well as the humble.

We know too that while Vedic gods were also worshipped in this period, heroes slain in battle were routinely worshipped as well. In addition, there were local gods and goddesses which in later centuries fused into other deities. Murugan, Shiva, Mayon (a version of Vishnu or Krishna), Varuna, Indra, and Kali were among those worshipped. Caste structures did not appear to be rigid and while there is some mention of Brahmins and merchant castes in the poems, strikingly the varna or caste structure does not seem to have operated with any degree of rigidity in the Sangam age, although the Brahmanas or Brahmins were sometimes called upon to advise monarchs. Jainism and Buddhism had also made inroads into Tamilakam although they established themselves more strongly a few centuries later. However, two epics that were composed at the end of the Sangam age, *Shilappadikaram* by Ilango Adigal and later, *Manimekalai* by Sattanar, make many references to the Sangam period. These later texts provide useful insights into the advent of Jainism and Buddhism in Tamilakam although Buddhism had made incursions into Tamilakam even during the reign of Chandragupta Maurya.

The five tinai with their Aham and Puram poems energetically demonstrate the evolution of communities in Tamilakam. It is not very difficult, when we look at the later growth and evolution of Tamilakam from these geographies, to see where and why particular cultures, kingdoms, people, cities and all their stories took root and unfolded. What remains at the core of these earliest days of the region's history is an unquenchable sense of exuberance, what Sastri calls the 'joyous faith in good living'. This is evident in the Sangam poems in rich detail, documenting as they do with great insight not just human nature and emotions but provide an astonishing record of life as it was lived over 2,000 years ago, with all the values that the period reflects; good, bad, heroic, cowardly, brave, treacherous, loving, and grieving are often recorded without judgement.

Chapter 3

Of Heroes and Kings

Forbearance of kinsmen's wrongs,
a good man's shame over other men's poverty,
honour without blemish in acts of war
courtesy in the courts of kings

Purananuru 157

TAMIL CHILDREN ARE OFTEN RAISED ON STORIES OF AVVAIYAR, THE woman poet who, among other things, was the supposed author of *Athichudi*, the alphabetic aphorisms that pithily teach good values. While this particular Avvaiyar is said to have lived roughly in the tenth century, during the heyday of the Chola monarchy, there was an earlier Avvaiyar who lived during the Sangam age, equally famous in legend and song whose stories are also part of Tamil folklore. This Avvaiyar's poetry finds a place in the *Purananuru* collection. There is also a third Avvaiyar who had similar attributes and the merged and received wisdom from these three women poets is such that even now, each year on a particular day, an 'Avvai' festival is conducted in the Viswanathaswamy temple in Vedaranyam in Nagapattinam district, where the poet is supposed to have had a fabled encounter with Lord Muruga. But that is another story for another time; at this point the first Avvaiyar's great influence on a couple of Sangam age rulers as recorded in the literature shows that apart from writing poetry, she seems to have had some sort of advisory role in the circle of the chieftain-king Adhiyaman and the ruler Paari mentioned earlier. Of the many references to the achievements of the rulers of this time, the standout one is the recognition of wisdom above valour and other accomplishments. The story goes that Adhiyaman was given a special gooseberry or 'nelli' which had the power to bestow eternal life to anyone who ate it. Rather than eat it himself he hands it over to Avvaiyar, saying that it is more befitting for her to eat it as it would allow her to always be available to offer sage advice and good counsel to the Tamil people. Tamil will flourish and Tamil culture and heritage will be safeguarded if she lives, was the king's thought. An oft-retold story, it depicts a valiant king who esteemed wisdom above his own life—it was perceived as illustrative of the kingly virtues of the age.

While the stories and accounts of kings and chieftains who held sway during this time come largely from Sangam age poetry, in recent decades, inscriptions and notations on coins and on rock faces and stone walls have been deciphered, and the discovery of several copper plates with information about specific kings and chieftains have added a vast amount of knowledge to the material about Tamil polity and the social functioning of the people of the Sangam age. Scholars like Kesavan Veluthat of Delhi University point out that the period of nearly thousand years cannot be viewed as 'a single unchanging entity'. He writes that because of the now varying categories of sources of information about that society 'it has been more profitably considered as representing the various stages in the biography of social formation—its emergence, maturing and dissolution'. Although Veluthat accepts that the dominant view is that this world is best represented through these early anthologies of Tamil literature, he asserts that the texts are now recognized as being composed over a vast period and belonging to different strata.

Sastri says that to begin with, the Tamils firmly believed in the 'immemorial' antiquity of the three great dynasties, the Chera, Chola, and Pandya. Notwithstanding the fabled rule of these kings as perceived in popular lore, their glory days came much after, in the centuries post the Common Era. However, they began to establish their territories even during the Sangam period. The pillars of the Emperor Ashoka, inscribed between 270 and 230 BCE, names these three dynasties, and the inference is that they were not in any way under Ashoka but on good terms with him. Often, the three dynasties warred with each other over boundaries; many petty chieftains owed their allegiance to one or the other of these kingdoms and aided them to flourish or founder until the Pallavas firmly captured power around the seventh century CE.

Marudam tinai extending to mullai and parts of the kurinchi are largely the spaces where kings and chieftains sought to establish their rule. Fertile rice-growing areas were considered the biggest prize and adding these areas to a king's territory meant more wealth and more power to the ruler. At the top of the heap were the muventar, or the three crowned kings of the Chera, Chola, and Pandya dynasties. Feudatory chieftains under these kings, the velir who owed fidelity to these monarchs, had to pay them tithe regularly as well as all manner of produce from their territory and although subject to the greater political control of the overlords, they functioned independently and also switched loyalties from time to time.

In his seminal work *Tamil Heroic Poetry*, Kailasapathy discusses the bardic traditions of early Tamil poetry. As noted, most of the actual information about heroes, chieftains, and warriors comes from the poetic anthologies of the Sangam age such as the *Purananuru*, which with *Patthitrupattu*, is Kailasapathy says, 'historically the most valuable'. The couple of hundred or so poems in these anthologies deal as much with chieftains, including those ruling in tribal areas, the kurinchi tinai, as they do with the exploits of the more powerful kings including the early Pandya, Chera, and Chola rulers.

While a great deal of the information (including those from inscriptions written in Tamil Brahmi) deals with names that are obscure, Sastri managed to put together a chronology of a few generations up to the third century CE. From an early Cheral (Chera) name, Uthiyan Cheral (c. 130 CE) to Yanaikatchey Mandaran Cheral Irumporai (c. 230 CE), and Ilanjetchenni (c. 165 CE), and Karikal (c. 190 CE) of the Chola dynasty and Pandya kings like Nedunchezhiyan (c. 210 CE) details are sketchily available in the poems, but much of the information about them is also handed down via oral traditions in stories about their deeds and valorous acts. For instance, Uthiyan Cheral, probably the first Chera ruler, and Karikal Chola who were contemporaries were said to be frequently at war against each other seeking to expand their suzerainty. The story goes that Uthiyan Cheral's back was injured in the Battle of Venni (130 CE) against Karikal, and unable to bear the shame, he starved to death and his companions did the same as they could not bear to part from him. An injury on the back could indicate that the king was in the process of retreating, hence his great shame. This is also beautifully described in a poem: 'Like the heroes who, wishing to go to the unattainable world, gave up their lives along with Cheralathan, on hearing with mixed feelings (the news of) his intended voluntary death (by starvation) in the devastated field of Vennil, where to his utter abashment he was wounded on his back when he fought with Karikala of (the) glittering weapons'. Known as Vanavaramban, meaning one whose kingdom reaches the sky, he extended his territory eastwards and northwards. The port town of Muziris is said to have flourished with brisk foreign trade during his time. Information about several Chera kings is available in *Pattitrupattu*, the Sangam work.

Karikal Chola is perhaps the most fabled king among the early Cholas and works like *Pattinapalai* speak about his heroic life and his numerous exploits, including the great victory at Venni where he defeated many foes. The origin of his name too is encased in various legends. One interpretation is that as a child he was burnt and hence the name, which means black-legged. Another story suggests that his mother had marked the soles of his feet with charcoal which mysteriously reduced his weight so as to enable the royal elephant to lift him easily and bring him to his coronation in Uraiyur. Another reading of the name says kala meaning death and kari meaning the elephants of the enemy amounts to 'one who brings death to the enemy's elephants'. As a young man, it is said Karikal's enemies conspired and stripped him of his birthright and cast him in prison from where he escaped in a heroic manner. Scholars quote this passage often: 'Like the tiger's cub of curved stripes and sharp claws that grows imprisoned in a cage, the prince grows proud and hard in the guarded house of his foes. Like a long-trunked elephant which falls into a pit when trapped, but breaks with its tusks the steep sides, fills the pit with earth, steps over and makes its way to its mate, so calculating his plans minutely the prince scaled the thick walls, unsheathed his blade, put to death the many guardsmen and regained his rightful inheritance...'

Pattinapalai says of Karikal, 'He could uproot mountains; fill up the sea; pull down the sky and make the moving air stand still'. Like Karikal, the power of other kings was exalted as well. The poems and, in particular, inscriptions of the period also commend their munificence and their concern for their people. There are descriptions that suggest the existence of an impartial justice system, and although an autocracy, the accessibility of rulers was a noteworthy feature of ancient Tamilakam. For instance, as mentioned before, women poets like Avvaiyar who were not necessarily nobly born served as ambassadors and advisers to several kings. The poet Kapilar was also an adviser and later became a very close friend of Paari the chieftain about whom stories have been told and retold over generations.

Apart from Paari, Tondaiman, Adhiyaman, Ay, Evvi, and Irungo were among the more prominent chieftains. Of the Adhiyaman clan, Netuman Anci was perhaps most well-known, and his name and title of 'Satyaputo' is recorded in the Tamil Brahmi inscriptions found in Jambai in Tirukoyilur in Villupuram district. The *Purananuru* and *Ahananuru* celebrate this king whose power was on par with the Chera and Chola kings at a certain point in time. Paari was a great patron of literature with numerous bards stationed in his court. The villages and land under his overlordship have been described in the poetry as being extremely prosperous, the envy of the monarchs who laid siege to Parampunadu and tried unsuccessfully for years to seize it until they finally did. Paari died in battle, leaving his poet friend Kapilar to look after his young daughters. The haunting beauty of the lands that Paari owned are a recurrent theme in Kapilar's poetry. Tondaiman Irandiriyan, the chieftain whose prowess finds mention in the *Purananuru*, is another ruler who was quite possibly an ancestor of the Pallava kings who came later. A later branch of the Tondaiman dynasty also ruled alongside the Pallavas. These kings had their capital in Kanchipuram. There is a lovely and oft-told story of how Avvaiyar who served as Adhiyaman's ambassador made the long journey to Kanchipuram to the court of Tondaiman who was preparing for war with her patron Adhiyaman. Under the pretext of admiring Tondaiman's armoury, she complimented him on their sheen and newness (implying the lack of usage) and remarked that her ruler's weapons were lying in the blacksmith's foundry, broken and in need of repair as they were in constant use. Tondaiman got the message that his opponent was battle ready and changed his plans. The poet had successfully averted a war.

While there was no organization that remotely resembled a 'state', kings like Karikal frequently sought to expand their territories through battle, bringing under their control areas that could be cultivated and bring prosperity to its inhabitants. Karikal famously tried to control the floods from the Kaveri by raising its banks, promoted irrigation tanks, and reclaimed forest lands for agriculture. Interestingly, while the cycle of stories about the prowess and achievements of Karikal are described in the Sangam poems, the epic *Shilappadikaram* also speaks of Karikal as the conqueror of many regions of North India even up to the Himalayas and of him receiving tributes from the counties of Magadha, and Avanti, present-day Patna and Gaya districts in Bihar and part of Madhya Pradesh respectively. The glorification and exaggeration of the might of kings, tales of their valour, and honourable deaths were the subjects of not only the poets and bards of these courts but also of the other anonymous writers whose work is part of the Sangam corpus. Whether the monarchs of Tamilakam conquered parts of North India or not is a moot point, but as Kombai S. Anwar, historian and documentary film-maker, says, the description of fauna and flora that could have only existed in North India mentioned in Sangam poetry leaves one to wonder whether people from Tamilakam did make journeys beyond their immediate habitation to distant lands.

Although much of the insight into the lives of the Tamils comes from Sangam literature, as well as from inscriptions and excavations, a great deal of fascinating evidence also comes from the accounts of outsiders who had connections with Tamilakam and further cements our knowledge about this remarkable period. Kautilya, or Chanakya, as he was called, philosopher and politician of fabled cunning who served as adviser in the court of Chandragupta Maurya, wrote of trade routes to the South and buying pearls from Madurai, the city of the Pandya kings. The Greek historian Megasthenes, who was sent as ambassador to Chandragupta's court, has written accounts of his journey to India and his work *Indica* has been quoted in the accounts of later historians. He has mentioned a 'Pande' kingdom and speaks of a portion of land in the South that extends towards the sea. This was around 300 BCE, when the early Pandyas were ruling in Madurai, the main base of the Sangam age. The edicts of Emperor Ashoka, the grandson of Chandragupta Maurya, mention the Tamil kingdoms of the Cholas, Pandyas, and Cheras in the second century BCE. The Roman historian Strabo in the first century CE writes of the presence of Pandya emissaries at the court of Emperor Augustus. He has referred to ambassadors from 'Dramira' (an appellation given to Tamil country), and there are details of trade between the Tamil lands and Rome. Strabo drew his material from the accounts of others and did not actually travel to India. Pliny the Elder, in the years just before the first century of the Common Era, writes about Tamil ports in his records. Numerous Roman coins found at various archaeological sites in Tamil Nadu also testify to the vigorous trade relations between the two regions. Many gold medallions which were found were not used as currency, according to Karashima, who says they were 'hoarded as treasure'. Pliny the Younger (first century CE) in a letter to the Roman people was said to have bemoaned the fact that Roman gold was being depleted for the exchange of pepper from the Western Ghats, which Pliny did not find very appealing in terms of taste. Pepper from Tamilakam also went to China and continued to be the main commodity exported from the region.

Another interesting confirmation of the prosperity and affluence of Tamilakam during that time comes from a document scripted by an unknown merchant, whose account, *The Periplus of the Erythraean Sea,* is dated possibly around the first century BCE. It is said to be the first direct historical record of the voyages to Asia by traders from the West. 'Periplus' in Latin means circumnavigation, and while there are a few other periplus-documenting journeys to Africa and Asia, this is the one complete but short text. This 'shows every sign of being the work of a man who had himself been to most of the places he mentions…' according to G. W. B. Huntingford of the Hakluyt Society. The Erythraean Sea is the Red Sea, and we are told that most of these early voyages were undertaken by either Greek merchants or traders from Egypt. The unknown author of this periplus catalogues some marvellous journeys through Arab lands, Asia, and then India, listing local marts of trade. He speaks of Kalliena (Kalyana in Bombay harbour) in the Hakluyt edition, of Limurike, a corrupt version of Damirike, the Tamil country, of 'Dakhinabades', the Dakshinapada or the South where 'there are two very celebrated marts…from them is brought down to Barugaza in wagons, from Paithana a great deal of onyx stone, and from Tagara much common cloth…all sorts of muslins and some other goods….' He documents journeys to the Travancore coast of the kingdom of Kerala, and numerous other ports and places of trade including Muziris and Nelkunda in what is described as the 'kingdom of Pandion'. Imports to these places are listed in the account—'large quantities of coinage, chrysolith, damasks, antimony, and coral, copper, tin, lead and also wine'. The exports from this region are large quantities of pepper, pearls of 'excellent quality' and also 'ivory, Chinese cloth, Gangetic spikenard, Malabathron, from the interior…precious stones of all kinds, diamonds, sapphires, tortoise shell….' The cotton from the region was said to be like gossamer, beryl from Coimbatore and soft silks were also exported. Rivers alluded to in the text are the Periyar and the Tamarabarani, and there are also references to Uraiyur, near Tiruchirappalli, which was the seat of the early Cholas.

The port of Puhar is celebrated in works like *Pattinapalai* as the place where big ships docked and emptied their merchandise on the beaches. Paraphrasing a passage from this text, Sastri writes: 'Under the guardianship of the gods of enduring glory, horses with a noble gait had come by the sea; bagfuls of black pepper had been brought in carts; gems and gold born of the northern mountain, the sandal and agil from the western mountain, the coral of the western sea, the products of the Ganges (valley), the yield of the Kaveri, foodstuffs from Ceylon, and goods from Kalagam…all these materials, precious and bulky alike were heaped together in the broad streets overflowing with their riches.' The original author seems to have mixed up exports and imports as pepper was only exported, but the exchange of goods from other parts of India and from Sri Lanka and possibly horses from Arabia indicate that as much as things, people must have also moved around a great deal.

Kombai Anwar, whose well-researched documentary film *Yaadhum* (2013) and other work on the Tamils challenges stereotypical notions of the early presence of Islam in the Tamil country, points out that Sangam literature frequently mentions trading with 'Yavanas', possibly a reference to foreign traders, most likely Arabs, for pepper, which was known as 'black gold' and perhaps horses as mentioned above. Anwar says that while the larger focus studies of early Tamil history primarily emphasize trade with the Romans, there were also actual, regular visits to Tamil regions by the Arabs as well. The Arab merchants sailed in with vast quantities of gold to ports like Muziris in return for pepper and other goods from the sea.

Srinath Perur, travel writer and translator, says that Muziris in South India was one of early India's most important trading ports, and was part of Sangam terrain under the rule of both Pandya and Chera kings. He quotes the *Ahananuru* collection of Sangam poetry which describes Muziris as 'the city where the beautiful vessels, the masterpieces of the Yavanas stir white foam on the Periyar…arriving with gold and departing with pepper'. Another Sangam poem speaks of the port as the city 'where liquor abounds', which 'bestows wealth to its visitors indiscriminately'. The connections between the Arabs, the people of the Mediterranean, and South India is beyond dispute; but additionally, there are details in old Chinese records indicating contacts with Southeast Asia and China. Karashima says that old Chinese records mention a country called Fu-nan in the lower Mekong valley where an Indian Brahmin called Kio-chen-ru (thought to be Kaundinya) was chosen as a ruler—and he is supposed to have changed the local laws to conform to that of India. The discovery of Tamil Brahmi inscriptions and some artefacts from South India in places like Cambodia and Vietnam all point to brisk and vigorous connections between distant lands and the Tamil country.

Chapter 4

Life of the Times

…The general impression left on the mind by this early literature is one of social harmony, general contentment arising from a widespread zest in life and opportunities for enjoying its good things.

K. A. Nilakanta Sastri, historian

Diverse accounts and descriptions emanating from poetry and literature as well as from copper plates and stone inscriptions in Tamil Brahmi make it easier to visualize the actual functioning of Tamilakam in these early centuries and examine the life it gave to its communities. The boundaries of Tamilakam of the Sangam age extended from the Bay of Bengal in the east down to Kanyakumari in the south; it included most of modern-day Kerala and extended up to the Andhra regions with the Krishna and Tungabhadra rivers bordering the north. Tamilakam was divided into three kingdoms—Chola, Pandya, and Chera, with smaller feudatories within areas under their control. These kingdoms were marked by fluid borders, internecine warfare, and frequent power struggles. Also, they vied with one another in terms of arts and achievements. Uraiyur, and later, Puhar was the capital of the Cholas, Madurai was the main city of the Pandyas, and the Cheras ruled from Karur or Vanji as it was called. As a symbol of their equal status the kings were referred to as 'Muvar' or the 'crowned three'. While as mentioned earlier there was no real sense of 'state', with no large system of taxation, except the tithe that was collected from feudatories, and a defined hierarchy among different levels of overlordship, what was unquestionable was the authority vested in the king as the supreme ruler.

Agriculture was extensively practised, and rice cultivated in marudam was a much sought-after commodity; some of the urns found in Adichanallur and in a few other sites had husks and millets in them. In fact, a lot of the pottery found in recent excavations have remnants of burnt rice and husks in them. As agriculture was the mainstay, water and rain were highly valued. Irrigation was also a valued practice, and in times of peace kings paid attention to this but were often distracted by their adversaries and battles. In a scholarly paper in the *Indian Journal of History of Science* published in 2016 titled, 'The Agricultural Practices as Gleaned from the Tamil Literature of the Sangam Age', T. M. Srinivasan says that the Pandya ruler Nedunchezhiyan was exhorted by the poet Kudapulaviyunar in *Purananuru* to carry out irrigation works to benefit his subjects.

> That which men call food comes from water
> mingled with earth.
> Those who bring together earth and water in unison
> create
> The means for bodies to exist in this world, for life
> to be!
> Those who construct dams so that the water collects
> On low ground in the fields are assured, in this
> world, of glory!
> Those who build none will have no renown
> enduring in this world.

The writer gives another example. The poet Avvaiyar also advises thus in *Kondraivendan*, a collection of one-line quotations: 'Niragam porundiya uragattiru', meaning, 'reside in a place where there is plenty of water'. The anxieties over water and its conservation as well as a veneration of it is deeply etched in Tamil literature and life. In fact, in the *Tirukkural*, thought to be composed at the close of the Sangam period, Tiruvallur devotes a whole section to water and rain called Van Sirappu—In Praise of Rain.

We have also looked at how the five ecosystems of marudam, neytal, palai, kurinchi, and mullai were represented by particular flora in the poetry. Interestingly, while regional varieties of rice were consumed in the different tinai such as mountain or wild rice in the kurinchi areas, other grains were also cultivated. Honey, avarai beans, tubers, white paddy, and bamboo were the staples in the kurinchi terrain, while in mullai lands kollu or horse gram, varagu, or millet and spotted avarai were grown. In marudam, with an abundance of water, white and red rice was cultivated, and all manner of fruits and grains and vegetables were grown. In neytal, there was a preponderance of fish and salt and palai was left with scrubs and thorns resulting in either barter or stealing of crops by people who lived in such desert conditions.

It is clear, therefore, that prosperity abounded in the lands of the marudam more than in any other region and both the early Cholas of the Sangam age and the later Cholas benefitted greatly from the geography of their kingdom and especially from the Kaveri. Srinivasan says, 'The fertility of the soil in the Chola country was not only enhanced by the waters of the Kaveri but also the alluvial deposits left by the river.'

The Pandyas too benefitted from the great rivers of Vaigai and Thamirabarani, and the prosperity of human settlements in these regions as well as the subsequent development of sophisticated urban centres in Tamilakam all grew organically over the centuries. While those who lived in riparian areas were usually farmers or ulavar, peasants known as velan-kudi, tillers, and their headmen going up to the velir and ventar in hierarchy, the social grouping in neytal lands usually consisted of fisher folk, minavar, and oarsmen as well as those involved in salt panning. In mullai tinai there were shepherds or idaiyar and cowherds or ayar who subsisted on animal husbandry, shifting agriculture, and raising specific crops. The people of the mountains, in the kurinchi areas were usually small farmers called kalamar, hill people called kanavar, and hunters known as vetar and kuravar.

This leads us to the question of caste or jati in this period. There have been diverse opinions among scholars on the origin and stratification of caste groups in South India. It is now largely accepted that caste did exist in the Sangam period—it has even been mentioned by Tolkappiyar who wrote about the four-fold divisions in society. However, it was not stratified, and neither was casteism much in evidence. There are practically no accounts of any practice of untouchability in that time. To give an example of the fluidity of caste, it was perfectly acceptable for a Kshatriya to marry a woman of a higher caste; a Brahmin could become a king, or as in the case of Nakkirar, be a carver of conch shells. Similarly, Vaishyas could engage in war and handle weapons. Social organization did not appear to be based on birth but rather on occupation and although by the time of the Sangam, the Aryan influence was very much present, it could be argued on the basis of the historical evidence we have at present that the social construct that prevailed in Tamilakam of that period was still largely defined by the tinai concept where residents of certain regions chose to find particular occupations suitable to that terrain. This meant that a shepherd could move from say mullai to marudam and become a farmer; or a hunter from kurinchi could also move to the plains and become a cultivator. Caste groupings tended to follow this loose structure based on occupation, it was only much later in the mediaeval period that they become more rigid.

Sastri wrote several elaborate articles on the social structures of Tamilakam in the Sangam age. From the poetry, he captures the life of the times:

The unlettered hunters…spent the day in hunting for food and were aided by low caste pulaiyar who beat their drums so hard that their strong arms turned red. The shepherd with his curved lips wore a garland of green leaves and dust laden clothing as he tended to his small-headed flock of sheep…they used beds of straw and leather, and their womenfolk engaged themselves in churning the curd early in the morning and in the sale of buttermilk and ghee for grain in the course of the day. The houses of the Brahmins were marked by a small shed in front where a calf was tied to one of the posts, and the threshold was smeared with cow dung; they had idols for worship inside and were not approached by dogs or cocks…the women of the house cooked fine food for offering to the gods and guests…. Learned Brahmins were fond of public disputations and challenged their rivals by hoisting a flag indicating their purpose. The fisherman of Puhar (Kaveripattinam) had their huts on the foreshore, worshipped the fish bone as their deity, and enjoyed many pastimes in their free time. Numbers of wandering minstrels (*panars*) and their womenfolk (*viralis*) who accompanied their songs with appropriate dances moved from one royal court to another getting presents in return for the entertainment they offered…

As stated earlier, kings and chieftains were at the top of the social hierarchy. Many of them held daily durbars, called nalavai, and justice was meted out in the royal courts. Obviously, differences in functioning and temperament existed in various rulers over the ages, including the constant goal of territorial expansion, but by and large it was an autocracy tempered by the idea of benevolence and the need to do good for one's citizens. The courts were filled with advisers, ambassadors, and a few of them famously included women poets like Avvaiyar. Whether kings took heed of the advice of these counsellors or not, they were accorded a great deal of respect in the royal courts. Many of them were poets who contributed to the body of literature and the epilogues of several anthologies indicate either the munificence of the ruler or their niggardliness.

A description of the court of Karikal quoted by Sastri gives a glimpse of courtly life. A poet who was warmly received by the great Chola king says, 'In his palace beautiful women wearing fine jewels and sweet smiles often poured out and filled the ever-ready goblet of gold with intoxicating liquor, unstinting like the rain; thus, drinking my fill and chasing out my fatigue and my great distress. I felt a new elation. In good time he plied me with soft-boiled legs of sheep fed on sweet grass, and hot meat cooked at the point of spits, in large slices...when I said I would have no more of these, he kept me on and gave me sweets to eat made in various shapes and of excellent taste.' This poet stayed so long at the court that, '...by eating flesh by day and night the edges of my teeth became blunt like the ploughshare after ploughing the land'. He soon begged permission to leave.

Outside of the royal establishments, ordinary people followed the ways of their occupations. The literature speaks of shepherds, farmers, hunters, fishermen, blacksmiths, merchants, weavers, and carpenters. Their contributions to the local economy as well as to trade outside the region added to the wealth of Tamilakam. Of course, it was not the perfect society often espoused in the poetry; women, for instance, were mostly well regarded but the lot of widows was grim and they were relegated to the edges of society. Women from the upper strata were known to have committed sati which was highly regarded. However, one must also remember that a substantial amount of Sangam age poetry was written by women, although many were anonymous. Interestingly, in the two early Tamil epics, *Shilappadikaram* and *Manimekalai,* the strongest characters were women. *Kalithokai,* a Sangam work, describes how women played by the seashore, participated in temple festivals, and often freely chose lovers. However, they were socially subject to the authority of the men in their lives and did not own property nor did they enjoy any legal rights.

Many of the Aham poems have women as protagonists. Even if they are prostitutes or those who have taken another's man, there is a strong and not necessarily censorious articulation of their situation. The voices of women are clear, and as Ramanujan says, women are central in the world of Aham poetry. For instance, in *Kuruntokai,* several hundred poems are assigned to the woman's voice, to her girlfriend, or to her mother. Much of the imagery is physical, referring to her eyes, her shoulders, her skin, her breasts, the texture of her hair, and also the glittering ornaments she wears. Her state of mind, her rage and despair, as well as the deep sense of betrayal by lovers who cheat, is captured in the poetry, obviously reflecting the ethos of that world. However, despite the sense of freedom that emanates from the poems in terms of the women's position in society, the slow stratifications that begin to appear in the external world also impact the position of women. The power of chastity in a woman is emphasized through many stories in the literature with the chaste and righteous woman's devotion to her husband being potent enough to bring him back from the dead. This is a favourite and oft-recurring theme in many of the poems.

Looking at music and dance in the Sangam age, the *Tolkappiyam* suggests that each of the five tinai had their own music as well as a particular musical instrument associated with them. Flutes, drums, and different types of yazh, a string instrument, were in popular use. The poems themselves describe how scores of these instruments were made. *Nattrinai, Paripatal,* and *Kalithokai* were anthologies said to have been cast in a musical mode. According to some scholars, the origins of early Carnatic music occurred in these centuries. Viraliyar and koothiyar are different kinds of women dancers mentioned in the *Tolkappiyam* which lists numerous dance forms like the koothu or more formalized styles that were precursors of Bharatanatyam, although that came later. The recent discovery of astonishing rock paintings in caves near Tirumayam Fort, which depict dancing figures, are evidence of dance forms that existed during that period. *Pancha Marabu* and *Kootha Nool* which appear to have emanated around the same period as *Tolkappiyam* are texts that defined dance forms of the time. It must be noted however, that like the poets at these princely courts, dancers and musicians too depended on the patronage of kings for survival.

Music and dance were integral parts of Sangam culture. Poetic compositions were often set to music and sung in the courts and in temples and public spaces. A great deal of religious fervour found expression through music and dance forms of this period. The *Tolkappiyam, Ettuthokai,* and *Pattupattu* anthologies shed light on Tamilakam's religious beliefs in the Sangam era despite much of the work being of a secular nature. The variety of spiritual practices range from hero stone or ancestor worship to animistic beliefs, living as these people did, very attuned to nature in this early period. Initially, the inhabitants of the five tinai largely worshipped particular gods based on aspects of nature most crucial to their existence. Murugan was the deity of kurinchi.

Mayon was the god of mullai, Indra was worshipped in marudam areas, Varuna in neytal, and the goddess Kotravai in mullai and palai lands. She was also the goddess of war and victory. Scholars argue about whether these local deities evolved from the native inhabitants and were later absorbed and transformed into a larger Vedic structure or whether their origins were indeed from a Vedic prototype. Mayon of the shepherds later came to be worshipped as Krishna or Vishnu and the mother goddess of many attributes, Kotravai, metamorphosed into Durga and later the more benign version, Parvati.

Though indigenous beliefs and practices such as funerary rituals like urn burial originated in ancient Tamilakam, there was a parallel body of Vedic beliefs demonstrably practised by the people as well. For instance,

Sangam age kings were said to have performed Vedic yagnas as part of their kingly duties. Apart from Murugan, Siva, Krishna, and Balarama, who were worshipped, other deities were added to the pantheon such as Brahma, Indra, and Varuna thought to be linked to regions of the north. A fluidity of religious practice seems to have prevailed, and with the peaceful coexistence of Jainism and Buddhism which had entered Tamilakam perhaps even around the time of Emperor Ashoka, there was a robust expression of tolerance and accommodation in religious practice.

It has been suggested that Jainism came to South India as early as 600 BCE. Caves around Madurai, Tiruchirappalli, and Thanjavur have been found with Jain inscriptions that are thought to be from the fourth century BCE. The critical Tamil Brahmi Jain inscriptions in Jambai belonged to the second century BCE. Further, many rulers of the Sangam age were thought to have been practising Jains until some of them became Hindus. A theory suggests that both the *Tolkappiyam* and *Tirukkural* were written by writers who held Jain beliefs. Buddhism was also prevalent at this time and certainly the travels and sojourn of Arab traders and merchants brought prosperity as well as Islam to places like Korkai, an important trading post in Pandya country. The entry of Islam into South India was quiet and almost unobtrusive. The peaceful coexistence of people of different faiths was a cornerstone of Sangam society.

BOOK II
The Age of Empire

The Pallavas

The first major dynasty of Tamilakam, the Pallavas ruled for over 400 years. It was an age of great flowering in art, culture, religion, and society. The era of the Pallavas set the foundation for the great empires that came after.

Chapter 5

Lions of the Earth

*The concept of a sacred lineage of kings starting from
Vishnu became significant for sovereignty.*

Noboru Karashima, historian

THE BOY ON THE PROW OF THE ROYAL SHIP WATCHED THE disappearing shores of a land that had been home to him and his family for several generations. The shoreline, blurred by the growing distance and by his tears, was the final image of a carefree life. He trembled with fear and anticipation, shaken by the forces that had impelled him to volunteer to take up the crown of a distant land when his older brothers had balked and fearfully refused the unexpected offer. The reason he had agreed to take on the challenge was because he wanted to please his beloved father whose affection he constantly craved. Father would perhaps finally recognize his worthiness, thought young Pallavamalla. The year was 731 CE, and the royal prince was twelve or thirteen years old.

Pallavamalla knew from his childhood that a different destiny awaited him. He was somewhat of a loner, his head filled with dreams of crossing the seas, of conquest, and building great edifices. His father, Hiranyavarman, who ruled a south Asian kingdom far from his native land in southern India, was first offered the crown as a direct descendant of Simhavarman (c. 535–580 CE), one of the first Pallava rulers, but he did not want to rule the kingdom in Tamilakam. Hiranyavarman's great-great-grandfather Bhimavarman was the brother of Simhavishnu (c. 555–590 CE) and they were both sons of Simhavarman. Bhimavarman had left the Pallava kingdom in South India and established his own kingdom in a region thought to be a part of modern-day Cambodia. The young child, Pallavamalla, who had grown up on stories of the mettle of his ancestors, the great Pallava kings of Tamilakam, was asked to accept the throne his father did not want. The 'purity' of the line had to be preserved, according to a courtly delegation that arrived from Tondaimandalam in Tamilakam, and the malla (meaning 'wrestler' or 'warrior') sons of Hiranyavarman were considered 'pure'. So, they appealed to Hiranyavarman who was torn between letting his young son go and keeping him within the safe confines of his own kingdom.

Hiranyavarman was then told by an ascetic that this young prince, above all others, had the mark of Vishnu on him. This was Dharanikondakoshan, a great scholar and seer, who prophesied that the young prince would become the emperor of vast lands one day but would never return to his family or see his father and adopted land again.

The Pallava dynasty came into prominence with Simhavishnu driving out the Kalabhras with the help of the Pandya ruler Kadungon in the mid-sixth century. The origins of the Pallava rulers are mired in a variety of theories, some of which we touch upon below. However, Simhavishnu was the first great Pallava ruler who established a firm Pallava line of kings. Pallavamalla (described above) was a descendant from another branch of the family; he was Simhavishnu's brother Bhima's descendant and ascended the throne some two hundred years later. The dynasty was the first large consolidated south Indian empire and ruled for about 400 plus years. The story of bringing and installing the rightful heir to the great Pallava throne after two hundred years of a flourishing dynasty is important as it was imperative to secure a powerful ruler to hold the growing empire together. This tale of bringing the rightful heir, the boy prince from across the ocean, is told in the magnificent but semi-faded carvings on the walls of the Vaikunta Perumal temple in Kanchipuram built by this very same Pallavamalla, who came to be known later as Nandivarman, and was one of the greatest kings of the Pallava dynasty.

The story goes that these kings who came to rule Tondaimandalam or North Tamilakam after the Kalabhra period were keen on strengthening their line and so propounded a theory of divine origin and every successor had to be of the same bloodline to ascend the throne. Even among them there was a distinction between the Bhagavata kings (worshippers of Bhagavan the Great God, or Vishnu) and the Maheshwaras (those who belonged to the sect of Shiva the Great Ruler). The young Pallavamalla belonged to the Bhagavata side which was considered superior. When Parameswaravarman II died without an heir in 731 CE, there was chaos and civil strife, and a faction of the royal family led by a prince called Skanda opposed young Pallavamalla. The prince landed on the sandy shores of Tondaimandalam against the backdrop of violent conflict in Kanchipuram, the Pallava capital, but he ultimately prevailed and became one of the greatest rulers of the Pallava dynasty. Despite the vicissitudes of life, Nandivarman Pallavamalla as he came to be known, ruled for a long period of sixty-five years, fought wars, expanded his kingdom, and built the most beautiful temple to his beloved God Vishnu just as he had been determined to do as a young boy.

The scholar and historian Dennis Hudson elaborates in intricate descriptive detail the coronation of Nandivarman, carved across several panels in the Vaikunta Perumal temple. The boy king, 'sits upright and gazes forward. His pendent legs are spread apart, his feet rest on a footstool probably placed on a tiger skin, and his hands rest on his thighs. A cord appears to descend from each side of his head along each shoulder…to cross the centre of his bare chest and pass under the opposite arm…these garments probably represent the uterus from which he is born a *kshatriya*, one who possesses the might and power known as *kshatra*….' Bowls of sanctified concoctions are poured over the head to anoint the king—despite the damage to some of the images in that panel, the might and solemnity of the occasion is obvious. Hordes of figures in worshipful postures are carved on the lower registers, the royal umbrella displaying the king's insignia almost looks like it is fluttering in a breeze, there are ministers, priests, angels, and goddesses, and interestingly, Nandivarman's queen (whom he must have married later) can also be identified standing next to him.

The Pallava period of what is known as the Simhavishnu line that Pallavamalla belongs to is considered the most formative period of south Indian culture. However, it is necessary to understand, before we plunge into the glories of the Pallava kings with the capital city Kanchipuram as their fulcrum, that in the period prior to the advent of the Pallava rule, there was no clear dominant dynasty that controlled the region. The dominions of the early Tamil rulers—the Chola, Pandya, and Chera kings and those of smaller chieftains or the velir were splintered by frequent internecine wars and then a group called the Kalabhras or Kalappalar disrupted the rule of many of these smaller kings and took over most of Tamilakam. This was a dynasty that held sway in Tamil lands for about three hundred years post the Sangam age. There are no historical details available at all about this period in Tamil history, either in literature, in lithic or metal inscriptions, except the Pulankurichi inscription of a king called Chendan Kurran ascribed to 270 CE. Because of this, a fallacious perspective that labels this period as a dark age has been put forward. The Pulankurichi inscription written in classical Tamil speaks of land grants, of administrative units, and Vedic sacrifices.

The first copper plate of the Pallavas was that of Simhavarman. The copper plates and stone inscriptions do not often give direct details of rulers, but much can be inferred from them as they are dated by scientific methods that clarify dates and periods. This first copper plate recorded a grant made by Simhavarman to the Jain community. It does not give any details about the ruler but mentions his son Simhavishnu the prince, the yuvaraja, and his achievements. Hero-stones of Simhavarman and Simhavishnu have also been discovered recently, and Simhavishnu is considered the actual founder of the dynasty, the king who established Pallava power in this period. A copper inscription of the time states that Simhavishnu not only suppressed the Kalabhras but went on to conquer the whole region up to the Kaveri. It also adds that he came into conflict with the Pandya king and the ruler of Ceylon. As his name indicates, he was a worshipper of Vishnu and had the title of Avanisimha, Lion of the Earth. While the territory up to the Kaveri was brought under the Pallavas, Simhavishnu also successfully cleared much of northern Tamilakam of the remaining Kalabhras, and extended Pallava rule to all of northern Tamil Nadu and across much of southern Andhra Pradesh of the present day. The grandiosity of the Avanisimha title reflected the growing might of this dynasty which consolidated power across northern Tamilakam, going down to Tiruchirappalli right up to the Kaveri. Through the might of successive rulers who followed Simhavishnu, the Pallava dynasty grew strong; the Pandyas who ruled further south, from Madurai, were always wary and watchful of their powerful neighbour and often engaged in battles with them. But their main rivalry seems to have been reserved for the Chalukya kings who ruled in Karnataka. The two fought fiercely and regularly over two centuries. The cause and origin of this near perpetual war with the Chalukyas was never really known, but the gaining and losing of territory between the two was a feature of Pallava rule.

There is much debate around the origin of the Pallava kings, including far-fetched ones that suggest they came from Persia as their name is akin to the Pahlava rulers of that region. Of course, that is dismissed by most historians. However, several expert scholars such as Sastri and the remarkable C. Minakshi say that these kings were possibly feudatories of Andhra rulers, the Satavahanas, and later grew in power and extended their rule across the northern Tamil region. The fact that the early administrative practices and systems of the Pallavas resembled the Satavahanas further corroborates the theory that they took over large parts of Tamilakam after the Andhra dynasty lost control of that area. The Pallava use of Prakrit and Sanskrit also underlines the likelihood of their close association with the Satavahanas, as the Andhra dynasty used both languages. The Cholas, who came after them both in terms of royal suzerainty as well as sustained power, were merely small chieftains at the time of the Pallava ascendancy.

Another popular theory suggests that a Chola king called Ilantiriyan was a Pallava ancestor, emphasizing the Pallavas' Tamil origin, as there are references to Kanchipuram in the lore associated with that king. The theory also offered the Cholas a sense of connection and a line to the Pallava monarchy. An additional legend underlining this Tamil connection comes from Naccinarkkiniyar, the writer who annotated Tamil classics around the fourteenth century and the same story is told in the epic *Manimekalai*. The theory is that a Naga princess called Pillivalai had a liaison with a Chola prince, Killivalavan; he subsequently left her saying that if she floated any child of their union on the sea with a tondai (creeper) around its neck and if it survived, he would recognize it as his heir and give it a kingdom (possibly Tondaimandalam came from that). A baby was born to her and sure enough the child called Ilantiriyan was set afloat, survived the voyage, and is said to have become the first Pallava ruler. A further story of the Pallava origin, inscribed in the Kasakudi copper plates, and carved on the walls of Vaikunta Perumal, refers to a baby born on a bed of sprouts to a celestial maiden and the legendary warrior Ashwatthama, the son of Drona, the preceptor of the Kauravas and Pandavas in the Mahabharata.

One of the earliest inscriptions of this dynasty, aside from the copper plate of Simhavarman mentioned above, written in Prakrit, was also dated to the reign of Simhavarman. It was found on a stone pillar in Manchikallu in Guntur district in Andhra and was related to land grants that were made in the king's name. Interestingly, although much of recorded history only speaks of the dynasty from the time of Simhavishnu, there are twelve copper plate characters in Sanskrit giving a continuous genealogy of the Pallava kings for about eight or nine generations from 350 to 550 CE. Most of the charters, both in Prakrit and Sanskrit, relate to gifts to Brahmins and a couple of them are about gifts to temples.

There is also a reference recorded in the Allahabad Pillar of Samudragupta, the great Gupta emperor, in relation to the name of Vishnugopa of Kanchi. Scholars think that if Samudragupta, in the course of his conquests, inscribed the name of Vishnugopa as one of the kings he vanquished, it must certainly be that he was an important enough early king of the Pallavas; they were somewhat well established by then, possibly even for a couple of generations, as the inscription has been dated to the first half of the fourth century. The Kalabhras probably took over from these early Pallava rulers.

More than thirty copper plate inscriptions, covering the period from the fourth century CE to the early part of the ninth century CE have been found across the region. These plates and inscriptions give direct proof of the rulers, their donations, and throw some light on aspects of governance. The ones found in Maidavolu, Hirahadagalli, and in Gunapadeya in modern-day Andhra Pradesh are in the Prakrit language written in Brahmi script. The Maidavolu plates record a land grant of two villages made in 305 CE to an official and was issued from Kanchipuram, from the prince, Yuva Maharaja Sivaskandavarman, of Bharadwaja gotra, of the Pallava royal family. These plates are now in the Madras Museum. The Hirahadagalli plates discovered in Bellary in Andhra can be dated to 338 CE and are again a grant made by the same prince who was now the king—he was named Siva Skandavarman, or Skandavarman. He performed the Vedic sacrificial rituals of Ashvamedha, Vajapeya, and Agnishtoma. The Gunapadeya copper plate records an order from a queen, Charudevi, the wife of Yuva Maharaja Vijaya Buddha Varman. There are several other early Pallava copper plates such as those found in Omgodu, Udayendiram, Nedungaray, Sakrepatna, Chendalur, and in other places in modern-day Karnataka, Andhra Pradesh, and Tamil Nadu. This gives an idea of the size of the Pallava realm. Many inscriptions largely specify grants of villages called Brahmadeyas to Brahmins who were favoured by the rulers.

One of the early significant rulers of the dynasty, Skandavarman, belonged to the Bharadwaja gotra and was also called the Supreme King of Kings devoted to dharma. Sastri draws a genealogy chart which suggests that this king's father could have been called Simhavarman whose dates are roughly fixed between 275 and 300 BCE. The next mention of a Pallava king is the Vishnugopa reference in Samudragupta's Allahabad Pillar which we touched upon earlier.

The Allahabad Pillar inscription, originally inscribed with Ashoka's edicts (one of a few remaining ones), also had additional inscriptions written almost six centuries later during the rule of the Gupta emperor Samudragupta. The second set of inscriptions were essentially a prasasti or poem of praise about the king by his minister Harisena, listing his achievements. There are lines inscribed on the pillar which describe Samudragupta's southern campaign and mentions the name of Vishnugopa of Kanchi, one of the many kings of the southern regions whom he defeated. Samudragupta returned these kingdoms to the respective rulers, possibly out of expediency, but apparently Vishnugopa did not take the defeat well. The corroboration of Vishnugopa's defeat at the hands of Samudragupta in the fourth century can now be seen in a blank panel among the richly carved ones in the Vaikunta Perumal temple with a solitary figure in a corner, the significance of which is the topic of much discussion among scholars. Writing about the panels relating to the Pallavas on the Samudragupta pillar in Allahabad, C. Minakshi states: 'The only incident which could have shaken badly the Pallava rule in its early stage was the invasion of Samudragupta. The defeat of Vishnugopa of Kanchi…and the terror inflicted in the hearts of the Southerners must have caused some obstruction to the continuity of Pallava rule…and the sculptors of Pallavamalla who sought to portray the whole of Pallava history…did not fail to mark this critical point… The single figure in this panel is probably the defeated Vishnugopa with a *mukuta* or crown on his head and represented in a very downcast mood.' The connection with Samudragupta is also remarkable in another sense; it speaks to the active interaction between the Gupta kings and the rulers of the South. Other Pallava rulers of note were Buddhavarman and Kumaravishnu I, whose names are mentioned in both Prakrit and in Sanskrit charters such as in the Velurpalaiyam plates. There is, however, a lack of historical detail about these Pallava kings, and there are no further references to them after this time for a period of close to 200 years when the Kalabhras controlled these lands until they were finally subdued by Simhavishnu.

Let us then take a leap forward in time and take a quick look at what we know about some of the prominent rulers of the later Pallava dynasty descended from Simhavishnu. These rulers have been referred to as the Great Pallavas. Mahendravarman I, Simhavishnu's son (who ruled between 590 and 630 CE), was the king who is thought to have commissioned the renowned structure of Mamallapuram, also known as Mahabalipuram, a UNESCO World Heritage site that continues to draw tourists even to this day. Of the monuments in Mamallapuram is a group of monolithic pyramidal structures called the Five Chariots or Pancha Rathas of the legendary heroes, the Pandava brothers of the Mahabharata, and forty other monuments and temples including the beautiful Shore Temple, a celebrated tourist spot of which more remains were found post the tsunami of 2004. Mahendravarman I was the ruler who began the celebrated tradition of rock-cut temples and moved later to constructing structural temples built of stone. There is much in legend, inscription, and in recorded history about him. Tamil lore is replete with details of his genius: he was an intellectual, known as Vichitrachitta, or curious minded, a poet, a painter, who had the title of Chitrapuli, meaning a tiger of art. He was also an architect, a musician, dramatist, polymath, and warrior. In an almost childlike way, he apparently loved titles or birudas, and some of them were in an early version of Telugu, to appeal to the people of that region. One can imagine the richness of the temple structures that Mahendravarman built: the cool, distinctly rock-cut temples, introducing new elements and styles of sculpting; the sudden drama of rising gopurams along the sandy shores and blue waters of the Bay of Bengal. Mahendravarman is said to have constructed a lighthouse in Mamallapuram to guide ships and sailors to safe harbour. The Mandagapattu inscription in the oldest temple of the region (in Villupuram district), hewn from rock, proudly proclaims that Vichitrachitta (Mahendravarman), built an eternal structure for Brahma, Shiva, and Vishnu without using brick, timber, mortar, and metal. The inscription is in Sanskrit written in Grantha script.

Mahendravarman consolidated the lands of his kingdom although there were constant battles with his contemporary, the Chalukya king Pulakesi II, to whom he lost some of his northern territory. There is mention in the Kasakudi copper plate of some details of his victory in a battle in Pulalur in Chengalpattu district. Obviously the Chalukya king came very close to Kanchipuram at that time. The inscriptions of Mahendravarman in Pallava Grantha can also be seen on the Rock Fort in Tiruchirappalli which establishes that the Pallavas held this Chola territory all the way up to the south bank of the Kaveri river. While the Pandya empire will be explored in another chapter, we must keep in mind that many early Pandya rulers coexisted with the Pallavas and indeed it is likely that the Pandya king Kadungon who ruled from 575 CE to 600 CE joined hands with Simhavishnu Pallava to defeat the Kalabhras.

Mahendravarman was initially a follower of Jainism which was widely prevalent across Tamilakam during his father's rule. The king reconverted to Saivism at the instigation of Tirunavukkarasar or Appar, the Shaivite saint. There are contradictory stories surrounding the conversion and corresponding legends supporting the various theories that were propounded, but there was certainly an excess of Shaivite religious zeal emanating from the king and court that prompted great temple building activity. Apart from Mamallapuram, Mahendravarman built rock-cut temples in several places across his kingdom such as in Mahendravadi, Pallavaram, Mandagapattu, Mangadu, Dalavanur, all celebrating the legends and power of Shiva and the philosophy of Saivism. An inscription in a Pallava temple in Tiruchirappalli mentions Mahendravarman's reconversion to his original faith. With renewed royal patronage Saivism flourished throughout the kingdom. Mahendravarman also wrote a satirical play in Sanskrit called *Mattavilasa Prahasana* which made fun of Jain priests as well as Buddhists and Shaivites, focusing on inebriated priests and their paramours and mocking certain aspects of organized religion. The Bhakti movement which saw a reinvigoration of Saivism and Vaishnavism took firm root during his time.

Mahendravarman's son Narasimhavarman I ruled from 630–668 CE and shared his father's passion for art and for building temples. He was also known as Mamalla, and likely added to and completed some of the structures in Mamallapuram. In military might, this Pallava ruler waged a mighty war with the Chalukyas, defeating their persistent enemy the Chalukya king Pulakesi II in a fierce battle, and captured Vatapi or Badami, the Chalukya capital. Narasimhavarman was called Vatapikondan (one who won Vatapi) after this victory. Obviously, he restored the lost glory of his family by capturing Vatapi. He also avenged his father Mahendravarman's defeat earlier—Pulakesi had defeated the Pallava ruler at the Battle of Pulalur. Narasimhavarman's general Paranjothi, a great warrior, is said to have aided his victory. Paranjothi later became an ascetic called Siruthontar, one of the Nayanmars, or Shaivite saints and was thought to be a physician as well. Thirugnanasambandar and Appar were two other Shaivite saints who lived during this time. Narasimhavarman is credited with the expansion and consolidation of the Pallava empire, sending a naval expedition to Sri Lanka and keeping the Chola and Chera kings under his suzerainty. It was in his reign that Hiuen Tsang, the Chinese explorer and Buddhist scholar, visited Kanchipuram and described the prosperity and contentment of its people in his writings.

Kalki Krishnamurthy, the novelist and magazine editor, wrote two popular serialized novels—*Parthiban Kanavu* and *Sivagamiyin Sabadam*—set during the time of these Pallava kings depicting fictionalized versions of a dramatic tale of love and loss and betrayal involving Mahendravarman, Narasimhavarman, Paranjothi, the Chalukya Pulakesi, and of course the novel's heroine, Sivagami, a poor sculptor's daughter who stole the king's heart. My mother recalled how these newly published romance novels were widespread favourites in the 1950s among many young women of her generation and their serialization in magazines would have many young readers eagerly looking forward to each instalment. Later, Kalki would write another hugely popular novel based loosely on a Chola king called *Ponniyin Selvan.*

After the rule of Narasimhavarman, his son Mahendravarman II ruled for two years before he was succeeded by his son Parameswaravarman I, who was considered an efficient ruler and able administrator and continued in the family tradition of engaging (fighting) with the Chalukyas. Unfortunately, he lost the capital Kanchi to the Chalukya king several times before regaining it more permanently. He was also a poet and undertook temple-building like his ancestors. Then came Narasimhavarman II or Rajasimha (690–728 CE) of Kailasanatha and Shore Temple fame.

This Rajasimha, another flamboyant Pallava ruler, was an unusual king. As the descendent of the original Mahendravarman who built the Mamalla edifices, this king is said to have also added to those structures and went on to build other numerous temples, including the stunning Kailasanatha temple in Kanchipuram. From all accounts, Rajasimha was a charismatic personality much like his ancestors Mahendravarman and Mamalla. Sastri says that his rule was marked by great literary activity as well, and the scholar and rhetorician Dandin spent time at his court. Like some of his predecessors, Rajasimha was proud of his naval force and there was great maritime activity during his time; he is also said to have sent ambassadors to China. The inscriptions in the Kailasanatha temple state that he created a utopian kingdom for his subjects which was likened by poets of the time to the Krita Yuga, or the Golden Age described in Hindu lore

One of the peculiar predilections of this king was to give himself numerous titles in the vein of his ancestor Mahendravarman I. He gave himself devotional titles such as Ishana Sharana (he who has surrendered to Shiva), Shiva Chudamani (the crest jewel of Shiva), and philosophical ones including Tattva Vedi, Itihasa Priya (the lover of history), and Doordarshi (one who is far sighted), among several hundred other such similar titles. In all, he assumed nearly 350 titles. These are inscribed all around the Kailasanatha temple. They fall into distinct categories such as the grouping mentioned above, but perhaps the one that sums it all up is Atyanta Kama Pallava—the Pallava whose desires are without boundaries—a name that he gave himself. This could well be interpreted as the king being interminably engaged in the welfare of his people or as one who had endless desires for the public good and indeed for himself as well. This title is inscribed in other places too, such as in the Ganesha Ratha in the Shore temple. Many of Rajasimha's titles were imperial, such as Chakravarti (emperor), Raja Raja (king of kings), Kshatriya Simha (lion of warriors). There were titles of valour—as in Maha Malla, like his famed ancestor, Rana Jaya (victorious in battle), Aparajita (the unconquerable), Unnatha Rama (equal to Rama in battle), and then there are the titles that proclaim him the connoisseur, Kala Samudra (the ocean of the arts), Kavi Prabodha (the patron of poets), a musician par excellence, Veena Narada (equivalent to Narada on the veena) among others. Another inscription mentions that the king is a master in the philosophy of Shaiva Siddhanta and is the first epigraphical reference to this body of thought anywhere in Tamil Nadu. And ironically, the king also called himself Guna Vineeta—one who is extremely modest.

There is a reference to the king's accomplishment in dance as being the equivalent of the sage Bharata, who first encoded this dance form into the *Natya Shastra,* the primary text of the traditional performing arts. Dr Nagaswamy, archaeologist and epigraphist par excellence, says that this is the earliest reference to Bharata in any inscription in India. The entire ethos of the *Natya Shastra* is etched on the walls of this temple in the sculptural depictions.

Kingship was regarded as divine and firmly hereditary. As we saw, when Parameswaravarman II died without an heir in 731 CE, Nandivarman from the collateral line (but descended from Simhavishnu), took over the crown. Nandivarman II was also known as Pallavamalla and was a descendant of Simhavishnu's brother Bhimavarman. Whether the collateral descendants of Simhavishnu actually ruled in a region of Cambodia or not is not proven according to some historians, but the fact remains that the Pallava rulers had consistent and long-term trade and cultural relations with Southeast Asia.

There are twenty-five inscriptions of Nandivarman II in stone and metal in the Vaikunta Perumal temple alone. The many war scenes depicted in the panels if corroborated with the copper plates such as the Udayendiram grant show the various defeats and victories of the Pallava kings. Minakshi's close examination reveals that Nandivarman's defeat at the hands of the Chalukyas is clearly represented. Similarly, his victory in various battles such as in Mannaikudi against the Pandyas is likely depicted with the great Pallava general Udayachandra, in battle scenes with foot soldiers, standard bearers, horses, and caparisoned elephants and drummers. Interestingly, in one of the panels one can clearly see a Chinese figure carved as part of a coronation panorama, a remarkable attestation to the phenomenon of travellers from China and parts of Southeast Asia to South India. We know, of course, that the Chinese traveller Hiuen Tsang visited Kanchipuram. It is fascinating to think that beyond the early trade exchanges, there was an exchange of culture and learning that was significant enough for these ancient sculptors to include it in their depiction of art; surely an indication of the value of the presence of these travellers and monks who sought these shores to learn these new philosophies. The interactions of culture and scholarship brought about a mutual cultural enrichment.

Before he established himself on the throne, Pallavamalla had to subjugate the Chalukyas. Nandivarman challenged them with the might of the Rashtrakutas behind him, having married a Rashtrakuta princess called Reva. Nandivarman's son and successor Dantivarman ruled for fifty-one years after him. However, he was not a capable ruler and lost much territory to the Pandyas. His son Nandivarman III ruled from 846 to 869 CE and seemed to have made up for his lacklustre father by managing to retrieve some lost territory and forcing the Pandyas to retreat. He was also a patron of art and literature, taking after his glorious ancestors, and maintained a powerful fleet.

Then there occurs a seminal point in Tamilakam's history which ultimately led to a massive upsurge in the fortunes of the Cholas (hitherto obscure chieftains whose overlords were the Pallava rulers). This occurred at the battle of Sripurambiyam near Kumbakonam, which took place around 880 or 885 CE. It was a battle between the Pandyas and the Pallavas. The Pallavas won, but the benefit of the victory went to the Cholas who sided with the Pallavas in the battle. The sons of Nandivarman III, born of different mothers, went to war with each other to decide who would rule after the death of their father. Eventually, Nripatunga, the son by the king's first wife, was anointed king and was quite successful battling enemies with the help of his ally, the Pandya king Varaguna. But fratricidal war soon broke out between Nripatunga and his half-brother Aparajita. The Pandyas and Cholas supported opposite factions. In the end, the Chola-backed prince Aparajita won and ascended the throne. Ironically, his vassal Aditya Chola who was given lands and wealth in gratitude by Aparajita attacked Tondaimandalam and went to war against the Pallava ruler and killed him. That signalled the end of Pallava rule and the rise of another mighty dynasty, the Cholas, to whom we shall turn in a while.

Chapter 6
Kanchipuram: A Confluence of Cultures

...the golden temple of the tall Power of the King,
whose moat surrounds the flower that never closes—when you think of him in all
four places standing, sitting, reclining, and striding, your sorrows vanish.

Poykai Azhwar, eighth century CE

A GARISH AREA OFF A TEEMING HIGHWAY THAT LEADS OUT OF CHENNAI announces the entrance to the ancient temple town of Kanchipuram (or Kanchi). The road stretches like a wide moat leading to an old citadel, except that instead of revealing any specific architectural grandeur, what comes into view is a stack of small residences, shops, and roadside eateries, all leaning into one another in familiar disorganization, signalling the haphazard twenty-first century urban arrangements of small-town India. Billboards and posters peeling off dilapidated walls, with goats grazing in nearby dustbins, belie the earlier majesty of this old temple town.

And yet, from about the fourth century CE, for a period of over five hundred years, this was the beating heart of Tamilakam, ruled by the Pallava kings and one of the country's greatest cities. A verse attributed to the Sanskrit poet Kalidasa says, 'pushpeshu jati, purusheshu Vishnu narishu Rambha, nagareshu Kanchi', which roughly translates to, 'as the jasmine among flowers, as Vishnu among Gods and Rambha among women, so too Kanchi among cities'. My friend, the historian Chithra Madhavan, who is travelling with me, points to the low-lying areas below the moat-like road. 'This used to be a huge lake filled with lotuses,' she says. 'A wide-open space leading to the grandeur that was the old city of Kanchipuram.' And now, unregulated construction even on this once historic lake surface attests to a skewed urbanization that disrupts a celebrated landscape famed for over a hundred temples, monasteries, and mathas that stood for a specific philosophical order, as well as its renowned weaves and silks.

Although it is a quiet town in the context of modern Tamil Nadu, Kanchipuram is a treasury of not just Pallava history but tells the story of a crucial phase in the development of art, culture, administration, and architecture in the Tamil ethos. As a citadel of Jain, Buddhist, Vaishnava, and Shaiva learning and worship, in many ways the town itself exemplified the generally syncretic cultural moorings of the Tamil people.

Culturally, this Pallava capital was a microcosm of India's secular fabric at the time. Set between the Palar River and its tributary Vegavati, the various 'sectors' of the city, Buddha Kanchi, Jaina Kanchi, Shaiva Kanchi, and Vishnu Kanchi, as they were called, co-existed side by side, largely peacefully, at least initially. Parallel faiths, parallel worship that was distinct and different, and yet pulled humanity's threads together in a common reel appeared to be this city's ethos. An ancient poem of the pre-Christian era calls this place a city of festivals that was admired across the world. Scholars like Hudson suggest that the city was built in the shape of a mandala, a circle at the centre from which it expanded outwards to a 'squared realm whose east-west axis crosses its north-south axis to form a sacred centre'. The mandala is a symbol that is in both Buddhist and Hindu philosophies, representing the cosmos, with the universe and indeed the human self at its meditative centre. Hudson sees this construct in the layout of ancient Kanchi, a blueprint which governed the way humans and gods dwelled together. Other architectural texts suggest that both Kanchi and Madurai were laid out in the form of a lotus, the padmakara or lotus plan.

Interestingly, the concept of a mandala has made its way into western thought. Carl Jung, the influential Swiss psychologist and psychoanalyst, famously acknowledged that he gradually discovered what the mandala really is, '...the Self, the wholeness of the personality, which if all goes well is harmonious'. So, the ancient Tamils obviously intended to order and structure their lives around a significant concept that tied in with a perception of universal harmony with the individual at its core. Kanchipuram laid out thus was for many a pivotal point from which they could contextualize themselves through geography, structures, texts, and indeed the multiple manifestations of the philosophical streams of Jainism, Buddhism, Saivism, and Vaishnavism—all flowing down the centuries from the girdle of the Goddess (Kanchi means waist girdle as well as a local tree of the same name). The spiritual nature of the city is remarked upon by Hiuen Tsang, who reached the Pallava territory in the seventh century: 'This country is about 6000 li in circuit; the capital of the country is called Kanchipura...There are some hundreds of *sangharamas* and 10,000 priests...They all study the teachings of the Sthavira...school belonging to the Great Vehicle....' The text goes on to say, most interestingly, that the Buddha, or Tathagata, 'in the olden days, when living in the world, frequented this country much; he preached the law here and converted men and therefore Asoka-raja built stupas over all the sacred spots where these traces exist.'

While there is no actual evidence of the Buddha's visit, Kanchipuram was considered a sacred space by the Buddhists. Bodhidharma, the founder of Dhyana Marga, who lived in the sixth century, was thought to be a prince of Kanchipuram. A volume compiled by scholars that commemorates the 2,500th anniversary of Buddha Jayanti at the Madras Museum in 1956 references this 'Chan' or 'way' (as it came to be known in China) and mentions how it was later transported to Japan where it grew into Zen. Dinnanga, a great Buddhist scholar and philosopher, was born in Simhavaktra, a suburb of Kanchipuram. The renowned teacher Dhammapala, who later became the head of Nalanda University, was also born in Kanchipuram and studied under Dinnanga in the city. There were many such Buddhist and Jain scholars and monks who travelled throughout the Tamil country including to the south, where the Pandyas ruled, and benefitted from royal patronage until Saivism became the dominant belief.

In the previous chapter, we spoke about the prevalence of Jainism in much of Pallava country and its spilling further west and south across Tamilakam. Indications that Pallava rule extended up to the Kaveri is evident from vatteluthu (alphasyllabic script) inscriptions of the fifth and sixth century CE on the rock face of the Rockfort Temple of Tiruchirappalli. As Jain beds have been found on the hillside, it is a definite indication of habitation by Jain monks. The strong and pervasive presence of Jainism, especially during the early Pallava periods, was because of firm royal patronage fanning out from Kanchipuram.

The Pallankoyil copper inscription, the earliest bilingual inscription found in the area, records King Simhavishnu's grant of land in the sixth century, on which the Tiruparittikunram Jain temple complex was built. There are two temples on the granted land; the smaller one, the Chandraprabha temple, belongs to the Simhavishnu era, and the later Trilokyanatha could have come from another period, given that there are Chola and Vijayanagar elements in the temple.

Before we move on to other important cultural aspects of the nearly 600 years of Pallava presence and suzerainty in Tamilakam, let us look at two important Pallava temples in Kanchipuram that highlight many of the ways in which religion permeated into various aspects of society, culture, and language. One is the unique Kailasanatha temple, which was built around the same time as many of the Mamalla temples, around 700 CE, and as mentioned earlier, by the Pallava king Narasimhavarman II, who was also known as Rajasimha. The second is the Vaikunta Perumal temple, built a bit later, but also reflecting Pallava history and one of the earliest examples of what became traditional Dravidian temple architecture.

Despite frequent war, especially with the Chalukyas, we know now that this was a period of relative calm with Pallava rule firmly established. There was time enough for these rulers to create structures which reflected their power, and which firmly erased any ideas of them being outsiders not native to the region. Temples became important institutions for managing local resources, providing employment to a whole host of craftsmen, and gradually became the fulcrum of economic activity; in addition, they were a means of social control by the rulers and their representatives.

The Kailasanatha temple, built entirely of sandstone (with minimal use of granite for support) was originally called Rajasimheshwara Pallava Griham, an obvious reference to its builder-king. Rajasimha called his beloved temple Kanchi Mahamanihi, the jewel of Kanchi, and the temple is said to be the inspiration for many others that were built later in South India. These include the Chalukya king Vikramaditya's Virupaksha temple in Pattadakal in northern Karnataka, and the Brihadeeswara temple built by Rajaraja Chola in Thanjavur (there is an inscription in Kailasanatha recording Rajaraja's visit where he calls it 'a great structure').

The Chalukya king Vikramaditya II, who captured Kanchi several decades after Rajasimha's time, was apparently so astounded by the beauty of this temple that he did not confiscate its treasures, nor did he destroy it. To avenge a century-old attack on the beautiful Chalukya capital of Badami, Vikramaditya is said to have marched into Kanchi after defeating the Pallavas. The Pallava king at that time was a thirteen-year-old boy who had fled Kanchipuram; but the conqueror who was conquered by the beauty of the Kailasanatha temple turned honourable victor and assured the citizens of Kanchipuram their safety, returning all the treasures of the temples including that of Kailasanatha. His benevolence is recorded in a Kannada inscription on a pillar in the mantap at the temple.

Visitors to the temple cannot help but be amazed by the opulent array of carvings on its walls and niches, the yalis (mythological creatures with the head and body of a lion, and trunk and tusks of an elephant), the bhuta ganas (divine servitors) expressing merriment, and other carved tiers four storeys tall speaking of the splendour of Shiva in every possible form—Shiva the cosmic dancer, Shiva in battle, Shiva the sublime, Shiva as the bearer of the Ganga, and Shiva as Kala Samharamurthy, the destroyer of Time and Death. One of the most beautiful sculptures is that of Shiva as Dakshinamurthy—each image is different and distinctive but has that same inscrutable smile, celebrated by a king who also wanted to publicly proclaim his devotion.

The robustness of the carvings never compromises the intricacy of aesthetic detail; the synchrony of line and form combine with striking creativity to reveal a softness as well as an energy and movement in the stone. An inscription in the temple says, 'Kailasa leelam apaharati' meaning that this Rajasimheshwaram even robs Mount Kailash of its beauty. The images of Somaskanda (the family grouping of Shiva, Parvati, and their son Skanda), a favourite Pallava icon and deeply entrenched in the Pallava psyche, are always carved on the back wall of every Pallava Shiva temple. Behind the family of Shiva, Parvati, and Skanda, stand Vishnu and Brahma, attesting to their own devotion to the trio. An important but small shrine with its own gopuram dedicated to Shiva within this magnificent structure has an inscription describing it as Mahendra Varameshwari Griham, a shrine for Ishwara, built by Mahendravarman, who was Rajasimha's son but unfortunately pre-deceased him.

A series of smaller shrines line up in front, built by Rangapataka, a queen of Rajasimha's, as evident from two inscriptions. In one she has been described as being 'a beautiful banner among women, as dear to Rajasimha as Parvati to Shiva, and surpassing Lakshmi in having the grace and favour of Vishnu'. She was obviously not just beautiful but wielded considerable power and has praised her husband in the shrines she built. Among the inscriptions in the temple is one that roughly translates to say that 'this Emperor, who has vowed to protect the whole realm, this conqueror of the world, who like Narasimha Vishnu is known for his valour only needs a glance from her to do her bidding'—such was her power over him. There is a deep sense of the personal that permeates the temple but does not diminish its grandeur.

Despite the plastering over of much of the carvings (which was a practice to preserve them right from the Pallava days to the present) by the ASI in attempts at preservation, their singular beauty is striking. However, much of the original plaster seems to have fallen off in many places and has been replaced in the nineteenth and early twentieth centuries.

The temple reflects the move towards the Trimurti cult—that is the worship of Brahma, Vishnu, and Shiva. This fixation with the Trimurti grouping is a special Pallava concept. Shiva as a dominant image with Vishnu and Brahma as tertiary figures can be observed wherever the Trimurti is depicted in Kailasanatha. It appears that the Shiva image is always depicted with four hands and in some niches, where there is a male image with two hands, it is likely to be that of the king Rajasimha.

All the way around, carved on the granite slabs that support the sandstone structure, is a lengthy twelve-stanza Sanskrit inscription that runs along the entire base of the edifice. Composed by Rajasimha himself, it is the dedication verse of the temple. One phrase in the inscription 'Harasya Hara Haasa Roopam Athi Maanam Athi Adbudam'—'the mysterious soft smile of Shiva that enchants you and smites the heart in a measureless spire that is greatly wondrous' is a metaphor for the temple itself, according to many experts.

The temple was also the tallest structure of the times, and the king himself in another inscription refers to its towers as 'touching the sky' and the row of deva kulikas (or little shrines) all around as 'crusted jewels, enclosing the beautiful main shrine of Rajasimha'. The entire complex is a perfect rectangle with squares within, and although some architectural and sculptural additions were made in the fourteenth century, the integrity of the original eighth century structures has been maintained, including the pyramidal structures above the sanctum sanctorum and the boundary walls as well as all the other smaller shrines.

Built to mathematical precision, two squares, the inner one of 64 square feet and the outer of 81 square feet, are worked into the architectural plan with the outer square invoking the planets and stars and the inner square representing the twelve months of the year. There are no walls or sculptures on these squares, and they are used to mathematically plot the basic design. The walls of the main shrine are built within a third square, and right in the centre is the sanctum sanctorum with the lingam. The plethora of carved images that enclose the main shrine depict the many manifestations of Shiva and Parvati. Directional deities, that is the guardians of the eight directions, the Ashta Dikpala, who according to tradition guard these spaces, are also represented. There are also pada devatas, deities of each of the little mathematical squares, standing lions, and gods with their consorts. In between, on the plain walls, are thirty-two manifestations of Parvati as matanga kanya, kadamba vanavasini, veena gana vinodini, and more. This is the only temple in India where such manifestations are sculpturally depicted, according to the epigraphist and historian Dr Nagaswamy. Another point of interest to the visitor is the beautiful calligraphy used in the inscription listing Rajasimha's titles. The script is striking and elegant. There are swans, snakes, flowers, and creepers twirling in intricate beauty on the stone surfaces. Nagaswamy says the two lines above the calligraphy are in archaic Grantha and ordinary

Grantha, and the topmost line is in the Devanagari script.

Just as magnificent as the Kailasanatha temple is the Vaikunta Perumal temple, one of the fourteen Divya Desams in Kanchipuram extolled in the poetry of the Azhwars. Its original name is Parameswara Vishnugraham or Paramecchuara Vinnagaram, with the former mentioned in inscriptions and the latter cited in the pasuram of Tirumangai Azhwar, the poet saint who lived in the ninth century CE. Parameswara is normally an appellation of Shiva, but as it only means the greatest God, for the worshippers of Vishnu too it made sense.

Each visit to the Vaikunta Perumal temple shines a new light on the history carved on its panels, on the fervour of religiosity and philosophy as well on more material and mundane matters that reflect the life of the times and the continuities that exist up until today. This was the first temple in Tamilakam that had three vertically aligned sanctums, with Lord Vishnu seated on his throne on the ground floor, Vishnu as Sayana Perumal (Lord that is Reclining), and the top vimana meant to house the standing Vishnu left empty as no one knows where the idol is. A couple of other temples such as the Koodal Azhagar temple of the Pandya period, and the Sundaravadana Perumal temple in Uttaramerur in Kanchipuram district (late Pallava construction), have followed this model. This temple, however, with its unfinished front gopuram and stunning prakara (the enclosure wall that surrounds the sanctum sanctorum) has marvellous sculptures of sandstone, with the handsome standing Pallava lions facing inwards towards the main shrine. According to Hudson, these lions could well have embodied the conquering power of Goddess Durga as the lion is her mount. We know that the lions are a leitmotif in Pallava architecture, and this Vishnu temple is no exception. The outside walls too have these leaping lions, embodying Pallava magnificence.

As one approaches the temple, one can see a complete complex within a rectangular enclosure. This enclosing wall is stretched into a colonnade that runs all the way around the main shrine. There is a depth between this outer prakara and the main shrine. Within the main shrine is a narrow prakara that can be used for circumambulation. Two stairways lead to the next floor, one for climbing up and the other for coming down, but quite hidden from view by narrow doors. As historian George Michell says, 'the vimana tower as viewed from outside the complex appears to rise seamlessly above the enclosure walls, disposing the triangular mass of the superstructure over a broader area, thereby achieving an imposing composition'. At the entrance, the gopuram base alone stands unfinished, and it is likely that this structure was built later, during the Vijayanagar days. Some scholars say that this temple is possibly the most mature expression of Pallava architectural style. It is easy to agree with this. It does not have the opulence and the overload of visual impact of the Kailasanatha temple, but there is a remarkable cohesion in the various structural elements which provide for an integrity and unity of design. Inside, the simplicity of sandstone is used with intricacy and genius on the carved panels that run almost all the way around the structure. Inscriptions on the panels praise Vishnu and his manifestations or relate the story of the Pallavas, their fabled accomplishments, and their rich genealogy.

The seated Vishnu on the ground floor is magnificent in his kingly splendour. The shanka (conch) and chakra (discus) are held in his back pair of hands and of the front pair, one is in the abhaya mudra, fingers facing up in a gesture of protection, and the other in a gesture of giving, the varada mudra. The priest who showed the arati, the flame that lights up the idol, on one of my visits points out that although the splendour of the image is awe inspiring, there is a benignity, a flowing benevolence, and he is seated in lalitasana, the posture of royal ease. Tirumangai Azhwar addresses him as Krishna in his poetry. 'The vast Sky forever black / The Lights of Sun and Moon / The Earth and her Mountains / All continue at the navel / Of Kannan with the Lotus Eyes, / Whose place is splendid Kanchi / With her tall surrounding walls….' The Sayana Perumal or Vishnu lying on Adisesha the divine serpent is on the first floor.

Tirumangai Azhwar says more in his poem on the temple. 'In a time long ago / He lay down on a soft sturdy bed, / An immense shape in the Ocean / The colour of the black gem / Who gives boons here in Kanchi / With its necklace of villas… / The cosmos and its eight directions, / Earth with her billowing waters / Along with sky, fire, wind and such. / My father ate. / The Lord whose place is Kacchi (Kanchi) / Brilliant from the glowing light / On each mansion floor….' Clearly the representation of Vishnu was carefully conceived, and it was Tirumangai's devotion that saw Vishnu as Krishna on all three floors. A standing Vishnu, likely of the same black stone, must have been in the topmost chamber, but now that chamber is empty. Although its disappearance has been noted in the annals of south Indian temple history, the mystery surrounding its absence remains unsolved.

Let us now turn to perhaps the most striking aspect of the temple—the bas-relief sculptures on panels running contiguously on the colonnaded prakara around the main sanctum. In the late nineteenth century, the British archaeologist Alexander Rea, one of the first appointees to the ASI (he excavated a sarcophagus near Pallavaram), published some enlightening tracts on Pallava architecture and sculptures, including of many temples like the Kailasanatha, but failed to properly identify the subject matter of these panels. He felt that they depicted the Puranas in all probability. Later, in the early twentieth century, the French archaeologist and Indologist Gabriel Jouveau-Dubreuil, described as a pioneer in Pallava studies by many present-day archaeologists and experts, and who brought to light several new antiquities of the Pallava era scattered across several areas of Tamil Nadu such as Melacheri, Panamalai, Singaperumal Kovil, Mahendravadi, etc., also seemed to feel that the sculptures were of a 'general signification' and did not particularly reference Nandivarman Pallavamalla who built the temple. However, Minakshi's *Historical Sculptures of the Vaikunthaperumal Temple* offers a detailed interpretation, largely agreed by later scholars, which suggests that the panels depict the genealogy of the Pallavas as well as incidents from Nandivarman Pallavamalla's life.

Many of the panels have already suffered the ravages of time and, despite current efforts at preservation, the soft crumble of sandstone mars some of the sculpture. The original sculptures have been much plastered over. The upper row appears to be distinct from the lower one, and there is not always an obvious connection between the two. The detailed carvings include the facial expression of the figures, the curved fingers of the chamara bearers, poised with the decorative hand fan over the king, the crowd at a coronation of a beloved monarch standing in worship and admiration, battle scenes, and the depictions of gods and goddesses.

In another panel is the depiction of the most popular tale of Pallava origin—that of a baby born of a celestial maiden Menaka to Ashwatthama on a bed of sprouts—the word Pallava meaning sprouts. This same story, according to Minakshi, is referred to in the Kasakudi plates. However, in the Rayakota copper plate grant, she says the celestial nymph is not mentioned, instead a Nagi is described as the mother. So, an entire series tracing the Pallava royal lineage carved in rich detail finds space on a wall, the emphasis being on the divine origin of the dynasty descending from Vishnu.

Pallava temples were by no means confined to the historic city of Kanchipuram. About 50 kilometres down the coast from Chennai is Mamallapuram. It is here that one finds the magnificent Shore Temple (partly submerged yet clearly visible) and other rock-cut edifices with the style of architecture and sculpture similar to the Vaikunta Perumal temple, the Kailasanatha temple, and several others in Kanchipuram. It is now a part of the UNESCO protected group of monuments and a World Heritage site. The pride of many Tamils and marked as a favourite tourist spot, Mamallapuram draws more than a million visitors each year. The town was the commercial capital of the Pallava kings (Roman and Chinese coins have been found here) as well as their port and trading centre for sustained maritime activity from different countries.

Mamalla was the title of the Pallava king Narasimhavarman I, after whom the place was likely named. Interestingly, Hindu temple architecture of the now familiar Tamil or Dravida style, does not really predate the Pallava period, that is, not before about mid 600 CE. Although the body of beliefs, the philosophical traditions and even rituals have a hoarier past, as we already know, this specific way of constructing temples, carving them out of rocks, began in the Pallava period. As mentioned earlier, the Sangam age temple-building style was quite different—the structure was mainly constructed in brick. Michell writes, 'However, the Dravida style may not have been a Pallava invention. Buildings in a rudimentary version of this idiom were erected at a slightly earlier period by the Chalukya rulers of the Deccan region, as at Aihole and Badami in northern Karnataka.'

There is also a theory that the name Mallai (or Mamallai) was used earlier by Vaishnava saints. Another name for the location was Kadalmallai, referenced by Tirumangai Azhwar. Tirumangai Azhwar sang at the temple here and, in his work, there are descriptions of the port city of Mamalla with anchored ships laden with treasures of all kinds. Legend also has it that one of the first Azhwars, Pey Azhwar, was born on a bed of red lilies in Mamallai, adding to the town's cache of Vaishnava lore.

When I visited Mamallapuram with T. S. Subramanian, journalist and editor, along with Dr G. Thirumoorthy, a veteran of the ASI and former professor of Ancient History and Archaeology at the University of Madras, I heard about some puzzling aspects of the place. Perhaps one of the most significant ones was that unlike the temples of their capital Kanchipuram, these monuments were left unfinished, and the work appears to have been abruptly halted. Supposedly first built or initiated by Simhavishnu in the sixth century, and as mentioned earlier, enhanced by Mahendravarman, and Narasimhavarman I, further additions were made by the latter's great-grandson Rajasimha. He is said to have added to these edifices significantly, and possibly been its main constructor. Despite so many generations of rulers continuing the work, it is a matter of mystery as to why much of it remains unfinished.

One of the earliest articles by the British on the place was published by

William Chambers in 1788. Chambers thought the monuments appeared to be 'the remains of a great city that has been ruined many centuries ago; they are situated close to the sea between Covelong and Sadras, somewhat remote from the high road that leads to the different European settlements. And when we visited them in 1776, there was still a native village adjoining to them, which retained the ancient name, and in which several Brahmins resided, that seemed perfectly well-acquainted with the subjects of most of the sculptures to be seen there.' James Fergusson, called 'the first historian of Indian art', says in 1876, that this was probably the most visited place near Madras. And centuries before, Ptolemy referred to this place as Malange.

The day we visited, the area was overrun with tourists and tour guides; ubiquitous but nondescript waste was piled up curbside and the site was replete with unruly traffic, and a plethora of eating stalls and a phalanx of souvenir vendors. There was also the pervasive presence of loudspeakers making frequent announcements, signage with tall historic claims, and a host of other boisterous if not disorderly sights that are familiar in small town India, especially those that harbour 'tourist' attractions. When I asked why the ASI did not have more control over the many small historic structures that we saw, I was told that control by local politicians and small businessmen with political affiliations made it almost impossible to keep to any semblance of order or have the area cleaned up.

Mamallapuram is a stunning collection of unfinished Pallava structures and located on the shores of the Bay of Bengal. Mamallapuram, an ancient Pallava port, has been erroneously connected to Mahabali. There are over forty ancient structures mostly of the seventh and eighth centuries in this port town, but the main monuments are the Pancha Rathas, the five chariots celebrating the heroes of the Mahabharata, monolithic structures hewn from rock, Arjuna's Penance, the largest free standing bas-relief open air structure in the world, the beautiful Shore temple and the rock-cut cave temples known as the mandapa vihara—the Adi Varaha cave temple, the Tiger Cave are among these.

Although an extensive discussion on the many architectural marvels to be found in Mamallapuram is beyond the scope of this book, it's worth mentioning some of the more distinctive sculptures and features of the complex. To start with, the famous bas relief, Arjuna's Penance, close to the Five Ratha set of monuments, may not be about Arjuna after all, as some experts suggest that it is an image of Bhagiratha instead. It is, nevertheless, the biggest open-air bas-relief in the world with ninety distinct sculptures.

Carved on two huge boulders, it is a magnificent sight. Arjuna stands on one leg, all skin and bone, praying for Shiva to grant him the Pasupathi weapon to defeat his enemies the Kauravas. Shiva is pleased with his strenuous efforts and appears in a majestic form with his hand extended in varada mudra or boon-giving gesture. All the celestial bodies, such as Surya and Chandra, the Gandharvas, fantastical birds, animals, including an army of elephants followed by children, and prancing deer, all in a very lifelike fashion, gather to witness the marvellous spectacle. (Apparently, Indira Gandhi, when she visited, became so enamoured of the image of the deer that she organized for it to be used in the rupee note.) In another row are forest people, and between the boulders, the sea and carved waves with many creatures swimming in it, all rushing to see Arjuna and the munificence of Shiva. Male and female nagas or snakes fold their hands in adoration. An image of Vishnu is also carved below the Arjuna carving with sages and deer around him.

Thirumoorthy conjectures that as there are no idols in the sanctum of the Pancha Rathas, except in the Pidari Ratha which has a statue of Durga, it could well have been just a model of a temple to show foreign explorers of ancient times that this place was a hub of international tourism and a trade centre in the sixth century. It also reveals to visitors an exemplary way of temple-building, showing different styles of architectural construction from rocks, suggest experts. Straight ahead of us in the ratha or chariot complex, in a hollowed-out sandy surface, is the first chariot, the Dharmaraja Ratha. Next to it stands the Bhima Ratha and in alignment with the other Rathas—the Arjuna Ratha, the Nakula-Sahadeva Ratha, and the Draupadi or Pidari Ratha with an image of Durga. The Pidari Ratha was the only place where worship was apparently conducted. Thirumoorthy points out the differing shapes of the bases, pillars with the sitting lion, the standing lion, and the squatting lion. Interestingly, the work of these sculptors started on the top, in the uppermost tier, and many of the lower levels remain unfinished. The bhuta ganas carved below the Dharmaraja Ratha are sculpted to appear as if they support the entire structure. There is a beautiful carving of Garuda with Vishnu almost in motion in prayoga mudra as if he were about to unleash his divine chakra. The distinct elongated face, thicker lips, and the aquiline nose exemplify the typical Pallava style differing from that of Chola or Pandya sculpture. The earliest Nataraja sculpture in Tamil Nadu is to be found on the front tier c. 630 CE, small yet startling in its beauty, a leg raised, ready to stamp out mankind's ignorance. The subtle smile on Shiva's face as he performs his cosmic dance is both dazzling and moving. The next panel shows

Shiva as Rishabanthaka, leaning gracefully with his fingers resting lightly on a rishaba (a Nandi or bull). Even in miniature it seems as if the hand and fingers pulse with life. The facial expression is one of transcendental bliss, and to see so much vitality and expression in a small frieze atop a vimana in a 1,500-year-old temple is astounding.

Magnificent sculptures of Shiva and Vishnu, ganas with musical instruments, dancing girls, Krishna as Kaliya mardhana, a beautifully carved Ardhanariswara with each side depicting specific aspects of gender (such as one arm being feminine and the other a stronger male arm), and numerous animal images, especially the Pallava lion, all find play and space on the sculpted walls of the rathas. There are also carvings of Indra on Airavatham, his elephant, on the wall of one of the rathas, and one remembers that like Surya, Indra was a god favoured by the Pallava kings.

Obviously, these sculptors were dedicated to carrying out the instruction of the Pallava monarch and worked with sustained efforts to produce these beautiful carvings. We see examples here of unusual craftsmanship, for instance, an entire stupa-like structure in the Buddhist tradition, hewn from a single rock base, which would have had wide popular appeal. To corroborate the theory that all the five Ratha structures were sculpted as 'models' of Pallava artistry for the benefit of traders and foreign visitors and not for worship, is the fact that none of the carved stupas or kumbhas have a kalasam, or metal top, usually installed in a place of worship, says Dr Thirumoorthy.

So, who then were the sculptor or sculptors of Mamallapuram? While traditionally across Tamilakam there are general terms found in inscriptions that describe the nature of the work that people do and their skills, such as tacchan, acariyan, tattan, rathakaran, that is, carpenter, master labourer, metalworker, chariot maker, specific names of craftsmen were hardly ever mentioned. There are no names on any of the actual structures in Mamallapuram, although images of the Pallava kings in some of the caves and in the rathas have been identified as being those of Simhavishnu, Mahendravarman I, Narasimhavarman I, and Parameswaravarman.

However, and quite unusually, a few names of artisans are carved on low rocks in Pooncheri near Mamallapuram and are believed by scholars like Dr R. Nagaswamy to be those belonging to the Mamallapuram artisans. Inscribed in Pallava Grantha…the characters read 1) Kevattapperuncattan, 2) Gunamallan, 3) Payyamillipan, 4) Catamukkiyan, 5) Kaliyani, 6) Namah Tiruvorriyur Abhajar, and 7) Kollan Semagan. Experts have suggested that we can easily identify the profession of two people. One is Kevattapperuncattan, and then other is Kollan Semagan. The first person was possibly a stone mason and that too perun-taccan which means chief mason or carpenter. The second person was perhaps a blacksmith who may have been the supplier of chisels, hammers, and other implements required by the sculptor.

Other experts are also convinced that there is an image of the sculptor on the rock face of Arjuna's Penance. The rock was unfinished below the level of the standing Shiva, and this is exactly where we see the sculptor—sthapathi or stone mason working on a sculpture. He is chiselling the lower portion of a bhuta gana, sitting to the right of Shiva's chest.

Whether a link can be made, first, between the name on the rock near Mamallapuram, Kevattapperuncattan, as one of the sculptors, and further if the image on the rock mentioned above refers to him or not is a moot point, but it says much about the relative anonymity of the creator or creators of such marvels, with both the master craftsmen and the humbler skilled workers ascribing almost everything to the monarch. Whether these were acts of modesty or whether anonymity was imposed on these master craftsmen by the sheer weight of feudal, political, and social structures is a matter of conjecture. However, notwithstanding the anonymity from the point of view of posterity, these people must have been highly regarded by the local people and amply rewarded as well. Dr K. V. Raman, the veteran archaeologist, has pointed out that 'these artisans were patronised by kings as well as by the village assemblies who granted tax-free lands to them. They were referred to in the inscriptions as *bhumi dana* (land donation), and *irai ili nilam* (tax free land)...some special privileges were granted to them. An inscription states that artisans of some villages were permitted to blow the double conch on auspicious and bad occasions, beat drums and wear chappals wherever they went and plaster their houses.'

The small elements of stylistic unity in the depiction of various aspects and features show that these structures could be from a group of similarly trained craftsmen by one master and indeed can be dated to one specific period. An important point is that apart from a few of the cave temples, in general, the Mamallapuram structures were not places of worship, and successive dynasties and rulers did not overlay, embellish, or add in any way to these rock-cut edifices. The names of the Five Rathas were also given to them much later for popular appeal, and were not named originally, although the Shore temple was called the Atirachandeswara temple after the idol there.

There is another Pallava site near Mamallapuram which reveals an astonishing and recently unearthed piece of archaeological evidence. That evidence demonstrates that this area's history and offerings originated well before the Pallava construction and offers substantiation of the existence of a Sangam age habitation.

In 2005, Thirumoorthy and his team found the only remaining Sangam age temple of the region which they have dated to 300 BCE. They first thought it was a Chola construction but changed their theory about the temple's provenance after they found Pallava remnants and also evidence of a Sangam age structure evidenced by the roof tiles. Obviously, there were three phases of temple-building here with Pallava and Chola superstructures on top of the Sangam age remnants. This has been described in an earlier chapter.

A few hundred yards away another small but intact cave-like Pallava structure can be seen. This is famously (but wrongly) called Tiger Cave, as the carved images are of half-lions or yazhi, a Pallava favourite. Beautiful bas-relief sculptures of Somaskanda (the word is a combination of Shiva, Uma, and Skanda), the favourite sculptural grouping of the Pallava king Rajasimha, are carved inside the mantap-like structure. The repeated depictions of leaping lions could be further proof that it was Rajasimha's construction, as obviously it was another favourite motif of the king, given that it reflected his name.

The inscriptions here are in exquisite Pallava Grantha. The dynamic carving of a stylish Parvati with her parasol, with her ganas and weapons, Vishnu and Brahma positioned above, the dwarapalakas (the guardians of the temple) are all elegantly carved with prime positioning for Shiva and his family. Thirumoorthy says that the historian K. R. Srinivasan thought that this space could have been a durbar hall for the king and not a temple for worship. He points out the peculiar acoustics of the place, where a quietness is palpable, despite the sea being only a few yards away.

Chapter 7

Divine Origins and Earthly Arrangements

The city seems to have been continuously enlarged to accommodate the growing needs of a capital and mercantile centre...

P. Shanmugam, historian

SO, WHAT DID THE LONG RULE OF THE PALLAVAS THAT LASTED OVER SIX centuries establish and achieve? We can glean a great deal from the arduous research of C. Minakshi who was the first woman to obtain a doctorate from the University of Madras in 1936. A student of the renowned historian Nilakanta Sastri, she was a trailblazer in the study of Pallava history. Her research was entirely based on a direct study of inscriptions and literature from which she gathered a great many details about administration and social life under the Pallava rule. It looked at subjects like revenue, taxation, irrigation, famine, and some other topics not much dwelt upon earlier. However, it must be noted that many of these subjects were dealt with in isolation and not integrated into a larger argument. The larger contextual discourses in relation to the period came much later with historians like Y. Subbarayalu, Noboru Karashima, Rajan Gurukkal, Kesavan Veluthat, R. Champakalakshmi, and others who analysed socio-economic processes, politics, and power relations in these empires of Tamilakam and gave us deeper insights into the mediaeval world order of these early kingdoms.

From Minakshi's work, we get descriptions of the marvellously intricate world of the Pallavas, their elaborate systems of local governance, educational institutions in Kanchi that focussed on knowledge as well as training called ghatikas, intricate systems of agriculture, urban growth, taxation, trade, social life including caste and political hierarchies. They were all set in place which ensured the development of literature, the arts, and military might and naval strength which carried Pallava culture across the seas to Southeast Asia and Sri Lanka.

The Hirahadagalli copper plates mention the names of administrators and the larger political units that the Pallavas created. Visaya is one such name and Rastra or Rastrika is also mentioned as a smaller unit mentioned in various Pallava grants. Kottam, nadu, and ur are other names of geographical units.

By the time of the Great Pallavas (third to ninth centuries CE) the caste system was somewhat in place. We saw earlier that the Vaikunta Perumal temple depicted the descent of the Pallavas from Brahma and the rishis, the implication being that there was a Brahmin origin for this royal dynasty which was also Kshatriya in effect. They described themselves as Brahmakshatriyas, according to K. K. Pillay. David Shulman calls this 'polities formed around Brahmin royal dynasties and infused by Brahmin and Sanskrit ideologies… germane to the Pallava state model'. Therefore, not only was value accorded to Brahmins by the kings with gifts of lands and villages, but because of the positioning at the top of the social structure, the gradual element of superiority of the caste began creeping in. The Kurram plates of Mahendravarman I indicate that he maintained and supported caste divisions. The Pallavas exalted the Brahmins. Minakshi says that there are plenty of references to Brahmins and Kshatriyas in epigraphy but less so of the other castes. Pillay speculates in his book *The Caste System in Tamil Nadu* that it is unclear whether some nomenclature refers only to professions during this period—these later evolved into caste identities. For instance, he feels that those who worked as drummers, the tattalikottuvar, are described in inscriptions as musicians attached to the temple and it initially referred to those that beat the metallic drum during the time of temple offering regardless of the caste they belonged to. Minakshi suggests that Brahmins also undertook this task, and it was only later that these groups formed castes. Obviously, a level of fluidity existed in terms of identity groupings until it became stratified in the centuries that followed. Another caste name that has been found in inscriptions is that of Kadavar. This could well be the same as Kaduvetti, a name that was used to refer to the Pallavas as people who cleared forests and made them suitable for human habitation. It could also be a reference to those who lived in forests. This later became a specific caste name. Later Pallava inscriptions described other groupings such as uvaiccan, agambadiyar (an agricultural caste), idaiyar, ilavar, and other profession-based names which in time solidified into caste identities.

There isn't a great deal of information about women in Pallava inscriptions, except for a few names mentioned as pious women making grants to temples. These were obviously women of some means. Also, we know that there were many Jain monks who were women and in service of the public. The Shaivite saint Tirunavukkarasar's sister Tilakavathiyar has been written up in Sekkizhar's *Periyapuranam* as a near saint herself and being instrumental in the saint's spiritual development. Of course, there is an indication of Pallava queens as in the Kailasanatha temple where Rangapataka, Rajasimha's favourite queen, is described in superlative terms. Another anonymous queen is referred to in a separate Kailasanatha inscription; she is described as 'full of loveliness, sharpness, grace and cleanliness who seemed to be the masterpiece of the Creator'. There is mention in other inscriptions of the virtues of Reva, a Rashtrakuta princess who was the wife of Nandivarman Pallavamalla and her munificence in making grants to temples. Most of these queens, especially the wives of the later Pallava monarchs such as Dantivarman, have been described as 'crest jewels' of the family, skilled in the arts and of beauty and learning.

A council of ministers supported the king with his duties; there is a specific reference to such a council in one of the panels of the Vaikunta Perumal temple. The Hirahadagalli plates mention amatya, that Minakshi interprets as 'councillor' whereas she says that the word mantrin is also found which means 'diplomat'. Mahatras is another name for them as evident in an inscription of Pallavamalla in a Vaikunta Perumal panel. The term mahamatra is also inscribed and it is said that Paranjothi who served Narasimhavarman I was from a mahamatra family. Minakshi alludes to a lovely description of Nandivarman's prime minister in the Kasakudi copper plates. 'Brahma Sri Raja who was a friend of the world; who was filled with all virtues as the ocean with a heap of gems; who was famous, modest, handsome, and long lived; whose speech was never rough; who was distinguished among men; who just like Brihaspati, the chief minister of the Lord of the Heavens, was the chief minister of the Pallava king Nandivarman, the Lord of the earth and the delighter of the peoples' eyes and hearts, who was refined by nature and education....' The lines go on to praise the Pallava king and his semi divine attributes but is evidence, however exaggerated, of the status and power accorded to an important minister at this court.

More details from the Vaikunta Perumal temple panels indicate that these ministers of the king assisted in carrying out the king's orders about matters like grants and endowments both to temples and to their chosen subjects. Apparently, they also gave advice on military matters and indeed Nandivarman was exhorted by his ministers to take on the Chalukyas. Sometimes the prime minister, as in the case of Brahma Sri Rajas, was also the chief purohit or priest of the king and took care of all the pujas of the king and his court. Many ministerial berths were hereditary in nature.

In the royal courts, Sanskrit and Prakrit were the languages largely used. However, what is known as Pallava Grantha (evolving from Tamil Brahmi) has been extensively used in many of the inscriptions. The encouragement for reading, writing, and scholarship came from the patronage bestowed by the rulers on educational institutions that were called ghatikas. The various copper plates refer to the ghatika of Kanchi, an institution of higher learning largely peopled by the Brahmins who studied sacred lore and grammar. Most of these survived on royal patronage, but often this was not sustained and continuous owing to quarrels and issues that sprang up between the patrons and the scholars of these institutions. The Buddhist monasteries were also great seats of learning, as we know from the Chinese monk-travellers Fa Hien and Hiuen Tsang's accounts of the many monasteries they encountered during their travels to the country. Fa Hien belonged to the late fourth and early fifth century, and most of his travel was to Buddhist viharas in Central and North India, but he has mentioned, according to Minakshi, the Nagarajikonda Hill, which was a Buddhist stronghold in pre and early Pallava times. Hiuen Tsang's visit to the South is recorded in inscription and in his own accounts.

From a variety of inscriptions, it is clear that the treasury of the Pallavas must have been vast. With wealth pouring in from conquests, from the spoils of war and taxes, the rulers spent generously on grants and endowments including to Brahmins, temples, royal servants. There was also a lot of investment in the military given that there was almost incessant war with the Chalukyas.

Regarding justice and the courts, one of the greatest Pallava rulers, Mahendravarman I, whose play *Mattavilasa Prahasana* has been mentioned earlier, himself made fun of judicial corruption in his play. A tongue-in-cheek reference to the adhikarana, or apex court in Kanchipuram, speaks of how a quarrel cannot be resolved impartially in this court and the subject says, 'Why, this man has heaps of riches drawn from the revenues of many monasteries; and with it he can stuff the mouths of the court officials at pleasure. But I am the maid of a poor Kapalin whose only wealth is snake's skin and sacred ash and what riches have I here that I should go into the court?' Corruption was apparently no stranger to public processes. All the villages had assemblies and courts that were under royal supervision and control. Pallava inscriptions indicate that a judicial body called Dharmasena also existed to continuously dispense justice, often through committees that operated regularly.

Other notable aspects of Pallava rule include development of irrigation and water storage. There were many tanks in existence, often named after kings or local chiefs. There are plates (now in the British Museum) that mention the Pallava queen Charudevi making a grant of land to the Rajatataka or King's Tank, the recipient of which was the God Narayana at a place called Kadaka, which has not been identified. Tanks were built in places like Mahendravadi just outside present-day Chennai which still has a large half-ruined tank likely built by Mahendravarman. The Mamandur tank which has water to this day and is thought to be the largest and prettiest tank in the district has some Chola inscriptions, but it was constructed during the Pallava period. There were many other tanks such as the one in Kaveripakkam, the Marudadu Eri in the Wandiwash area, and the Kanakavalli Tataka and other tanks all of which are recorded in temple inscriptions as well as in the inscriptions of the kings in copper plates. Most of these were rain fed. The Palar has been mentioned as the source of water for a few tanks. Wells were also dug in various places with royal permission and managed by village assemblies. Pallava charters of the seventh and eighth centuries CE, relating to Brahmadeya and Devadana grants, indicate that among the privileges awarded to many such villages was the right to dig wells, both small and large. Water supply from all these sources was also made available for irrigation of fields by canals which were constructed across the realm. The present Uyyakondan Vaykkal which takes off from the Kaveri and supplies the town of Tiruchirappalli is the original Vairamegha Vaykkal of the Pallavas.

We learn too that there were many famines over the years. The land was often starved of rain. Even though villages were all well-served with deep wells and canals, and self-sufficient when it came to the cultivation of fields, severe famines often occurred. Frequent warfare with the Chalukyas coupled with the drought that was caused by the lack of rainfall often led to starvation among much of the population—this was alluded to in the stories of the Nayanmars, in works like the *Periyapuranam*. The seventh and eighth century poet and grammarian Dandin, who was a powerful presence in the court of Rajasimha, has described in his work the *Avantisundari Katha* the terrible state of the Pallava capital of Kanchi which was ravaged by both war and famine. An account by a Buddhist monk and teacher Vajrabodhi who came to Kanchi in 689 CE says: 'The king of Kanchi had been suffering for three years from a terrible disaster; the king Narasimhapotavarman implored the help of the pious minded Vajrabodhi, who, by means of prayers brought on rain.' The fact of this severe famine is also borne out by the Velurpalaiyam plates of Rajasimha which indicate that he had to reorganize the ghatikas or religious schools in the city owing to the distress. Notably Sastri has also mentioned the existence of a pancha (famine) vara committee which was possibly set up at the village level to provide against famine. The Velurpalaiyam plates also contain a reference to this committee.

The Brahmadeya came to be firmly established in mediaeval India, beginning in the settled kingdoms of the fourth century, as a practice of rewarding Brahmin advisers and preceptors of kings and princes with villages and large tracts of tax-free land. These were rich, cultivable lands, and they were given these in return for services rendered to the kings. Many early inscriptions attest to this. For instance, land gifts to the Brahmins were described in the Kuram plates of Parameswaravarman. A member of the royal family, a relative of the king Vidyavinita Pallava, is said to have donated land as well as built a temple. The earliest Pallava grant of land mentioned in the Maidavolu plates registers the gift of a village to two Brahmins. There are other similar grants by later kings, and these were entirely tax free, and no levies were paid to the king's treasury. Karashima suggests that there was a mutual dependency of relationship between the king and the Brahmins. 'A king needed the authority of the Brahmanas for the legitimation of his sovereignty and the Brahmanas had to depend on the king's support for their living'. He also says that Nandivarman Pallavamalla was said to have invited several hundreds of Vedic scholars from North India when he ascended the throne in 731 CE. It must be noted that while the owners of these Brahmadeya lands enjoyed a variety of rights including the collection of taxes from the tenants, they could not gift or sell the property. Other communities also inhabited these villages or leased these lands from the Brahmin owner who derived the maximum economic and social benefit out of this. Obviously, the owners of these lands offered great support to their princes and feudal lords, which included the fealty and service of the communities and labour that lived therein. The Brahmadeya phenomenon will be discussed later, but it's important to note that the system was initiated by these early rulers of Tamilakam.

Speaking of villages, many had a ruling body or committee. These were called variyam and gana and shared the work of the people or perumakkal and it is likely that the ruling committee took charge of specific tasks. While there is much more information about the functioning of these committees and sabhas in the Chola periods, there are a few inscriptions that mention variyam in the late Pallava period. An inscription dated in the ninth year of Dantivarman records a private endowment for dredging the Vairamegha tank every month—the variyam is instructed to use the money only for this purpose; from inscriptions such as these one can infer that such committees had a lot of other work that they were responsible for in the villages. In addition, the sabhas which oversaw different kinds of work such as irrigation, looking after agricultural lands, administering local justice, etc. were also formed in as many as twenty villages in the later Pallava period according to the Ulalur inscriptions in Minakshi's account. A brief look at taxes during the Pallava period reveals some interesting details. The Hirahadagalli plates mention that both sugar and salt were manufactured by the administration and there was a royal monopoly on these. This meant there was no private manufacture of sugar or salt. There was a tax on agricultural produce that went straight to the king although there is no indication as to the amount of irai or tax that the king had to be paid from agriculture. Tax was levied on those belonging to many professions—on toddy tappers, cattle breeders, washermen, drummers, goldsmiths, the producers of ghee (possibly because it was a luxury product), and a fee had to be paid to the vaiyvan or village headman which was a hereditary post. A small kanikkai [offering made to a ruler or deity] had to be given to the king when there was a wedding in a family. This custom of Rajasambavanai persisted for a long time. There were other taxes too such as amounts collected from quarries; people paid taxes to the village headman who in turn paid a portion to the king. It appears that the Brahmadeya lands had special exemptions unlike other villages that had to pay tax as well as give a portion of agricultural produce either to the village headman or the king. Areca nuts, oil seeds, paddy, medicinal plants, coconut palms, and cotton were among the produce grown.

The art of the Pallavas, as exhibited in the temples, set a new standard in terms of both architecture and sculptural and mural expression. Equally in music, in the 600 odd years of dynastic rule, royal patronage as well as the infusion of spiritual poetry emanating from texts such as *Thevaram* and the *Nalayira Divya Prabandam* gave rise to singing in temples, a practice that remains to this day, although the ways in which these compositions are sung today are very different from the original expression.

Tondaimandalam's prosperity and indeed its sovereignty declined around the late ninth and early tenth century. The constant battles with the Rashtrakutas, Chalukyas, and Pandyas had weakened the borders, and the military might that the Pallava kings were so proud of. Fratricidal wars, which we spoke about earlier, opened the advantage to the Cholas who were up until that time feudatories of the Pallavas and in alliance with them. After the famed Sripurambiyam or Tirupurambiyam battle in 880 CE, Aparajita, the Pallava ruler, defeated the Pandya ruler, Varaguna Pandya. This signalled the decline of the Pandyas; the Pallava ruler who was victorious in this battle found that, in time, his overlordship was challenged by Aditya Chola who was his vassal. Finally, the Chola chieftain went to war with the Pallava king who was ultimately felled. It seems symbolic that a ruler of once vast lands should be killed in battle, and atop a royal elephant, all the panoply of success unable to stave off mortality. And indeed, like kings and men, the kingdom too crumbled, torn down by internecine strife and attacked by outsiders, and yet their glory remains to this day, etched in inscriptions on stone and copper plates, glimpsed in the literature of kings and scholars, and resplendent still in the temples they left behind.

As much as the Pallavas attained great salience for their vast contributions to art, to temple building, to fashioning social and political order, to building institutions of governance, to creating ports and towns that were the marvel of that world, we know that the writing and literature of the age also revealed dexterity and depth of scholarship and philosophical vision. Generations of various communities of the age lived by their beliefs and the wisdom accumulated through times of strife and peace, appeared to be shared by all. Nowhere did I find this more telling and indeed poignant as when I read the inscription embedded in the walls of a well, constructed during the Pallava period.

Twenty kilometres outside Tiruchirappalli, in a quiet village called Tiruvellarai, is a temple for Vishnu called the Pundarikaksha temple. In lieu of the usual temple tank, this temple has a swastika-shaped well situated close by. Maintained by the State Archaeology Department, it is an arresting construction, although sadly public conveniences have been thoughtlessly built adjacent to it by this government body, in an 'act of vandalism disregarding the rule of no construction within 100 metres of a protected monument,' says T. S. Subramanian, journalist and editor, who along with Dr Vedachalam, the expert epigraphist and archaeologist, accompanied me on a visit.

The well at Tiruvellarai is unusual: it has four entrances with four deities guarding it and its large and elegant design was obviously meant to give easy access to the public. To see water inside this beautiful stepwell, and the people negotiating the steps to procure it, makes one wonder if a sight like this would not have also been seen a millennium and more ago.

The swastika symbol originally signalled auspiciousness, spirituality, and well-being in Buddhist, Jain, and Hindu contexts. The word itself in Sanskrit means 'conducive to well-being'. However, with the Nazi adaptation of this symbol with a right-facing tilt, it has created a negative reaction to the design itself although even ancient European religions have referenced it as a positive symbol of luck and prosperity. In the context of the well in Tiruvellarai, which was built more than a thousand years ago, in 800 CE, it was obviously deliberately designed to signal auspiciousness and well-being as normally wells in Tamilakam were circular in shape. The import of this well is much more than its shape. Vedachalam tells me that the well reveals two interesting facts. One, a clear inscription which mentions that it was built in the time of Dantivarman, the Pallava ruler. The inscription states that in the time of Dantivarman this well was dug on the south side of the village of Tiruvellarai. It declares that the well was built by Alampakkam Kamban Araiyan, the younger brother of Vijaya Nalluzhan of Alampakkam. He was probably an official of Nandivarman the second, and therefore highly regarded in his village. The name of the well is Maarpidugu Perung Kinaru, marapidagu means thunderbolt, and likely a title of the king, and perung kinaru means 'big well'.

Having established the date of the well's construction, Vedachalam points to another inscription, which is a short philosophical poem. Just consider the wisdom in this: Sri kandaar kaanal ulagathil kadhal saidhu nillaadhe / pande paraman padaitha naal paarthu ninru naiyadhe / thandar moopu vandhu unnai thalara siedhu nillamun / undel undu mikkadhu ulagam ariya veidhinay. This roughly translates to: Do not fall in love with this impermanent world, neither wait in fear for the day that God has marked for your death. Do not wait till old age to do dharma, use whatever you need for yourself and whatever you have left, leave it for the world to see.

More than 1,200 years ago, in this water-starved, drought-ridden region, someone followed the principle which has been inscribed on the walls and built this well for the benefit of the people of the locality, so much so that it has lasted to this day. Beyond the construction, the inscription too stands as a code to live life by, underlining a discernment and wisdom that prevailed in the era of the Pallavas.

Chapter 8

The Citadels of Faith

Though the kings of the earlier period followed Brahmanical political practice, Sramanic religions like Jainism and Buddhism were also quite influential.

Noboru Karashima, historian

A CITY OF MULTIPLE FAITHS, A CITY OF FESTIVALS, AND A FULCRUM FOR wandering monks, Kanchipuram was one of the cradles of Jain, Buddhist, Shaivite, and Vaishnavite thought and expression in South India. From about 500 years after the advent of the Common Era, in northern Tamilakam, over which the Pallava kings established their suzerainty, several religious philosophies prevailed and were patronized and supported by the Pallava rulers of Kanchi. A general spirit of harmony existed, especially in the early years of the establishment of Pallava rule after 550 CE, when Jainism and Buddhism were the dominant faiths, entrenched as they were in the royal courts. However, with the advent of the Bhakti movement, a reformist drive, which went on for several centuries across Tamilakam, there was a gradual shift in royal support that saw the slow decline of Jainism and Buddhism not only in Kanchipuram and the Pallava kingdom, but elsewhere in the Tamil country. Even within the Brahmanical sects, by which one means the followers of the Vedic and Puranic philosophies, and not the Brahmin caste (broadly, adherents of Hindu philosophy although that word had not been coined then), there were fierce differences. One sect's faith was sometimes considered heresy by the other or considered paramount. For instance, Bhagavata worship is the worship of Bhagavan Vishnu or Lord Vishnu. In this form of worship, the focus of spirituality is Bhagavan, or the Lord, with the particular form or deity subsuming other traditions including Saivism within it.

The ideology of Bhakti can be traced back to the Sangam age, to the glimpses of early devotional poetry discussed in an earlier section. As a concept, it was reformist as well as poetic in nature and offered an alternative to the rooted and often severe philosophies of Jainism and Buddhism. These religions had earlier offered a strong pull to those who had struggled with social oppression and the ritualistic rigours of the early Vedic religion, but from the seventh century onwards, groups of reformers and poet-saints, the Shaiva

Nayanmars and Vaishnavite Azhwars, offered ordinary people a new way of worship that was emotional, personal, temple-centred, and yet integrating all the crucial tenets of the Brahmanical or Vedic religion, that is basic Hindu tenets. In time, a fierce opposition to Jain beliefs and tenets grew, especially after these poet-saints obtained royal patronage from the Pallava rulers.

Let us go back a little to establish the context. Roughly in the first few centuries of the new millennium, the Tamil lands were overrun by the Kalabhras. As previously noted, there is very little by way of information either from inscriptions or literary sources about the Kalabhras although Sastri suggests that a few Buddhist texts speak of a Kalabhras king, Accutavikanta, during whose reign Buddhism received much patronage in the Tamil country. There is, however, one inscription, the Pulankurichi inscription, which also refers to the Kalabhras. Roughly for a period of 300 years, from about the third to the sixth century CE, these unknown rulers held sway over most of Tamilakam. Sastri says, 'When the curtain rises again towards the close of the sixth century A.D., we find that a mysterious and ubiquitous enemy of civilization, the evil rulers called Kalabhras (Kalappalar) have come and upset the established political order which was restored only by their defeat at the hands of the Pandyas and Pallava as well as the Chalukyas of Badami....' Current thinking does not posit the characterization of the Kalabhras as being 'evil', but suggests that due to the paucity of information about that period, orthodox history tends to view this time as a 'dark' period.

Scholars theorize that they were Jains from the north or possibly what is present-day Karnataka. The institution of a community of monks called the Dravida Sangha in 470 BCE indicates that this period marks the ascendancy of Jainism—the role of a monk called Pujyapada and his disciple Vajranandi in the dissemination of Jain doctrines was apparently significant. Pujyapada was said to be the first acharya of the Dravida Sangha which he established in 470 CE in Madurai, according to Devasena, the author of a Jain religious work called *Darsana Sara* in the ninth century. The Jain sanghas were also apparently formed around that time and probably were centres of proselytising and the teaching of Jain philosophy. Further historical evidence of the dominance of Jain practice exists as there is a reference to Vajranandi in the Pallankoyil copper plate of a grant of Simhavarman, the father of Simhavishnu, of the Pallava dynasty about the grant of a village called Sramanasrama and 'other gifts' to the Jain temple of Vardhamana at Jaina Kanchi in the third quarter of the sixth century.

It is important therefore to note that Tamilakam witnessed the firm establishment of Jainism, which came a bit after Buddhism but prevailed dominantly up until the seventh century. Again, after some marginalization of Jainism in the face of Vaishnavite and Shaivite revival (the Bhakti movement), it picked up and flourished strongly up until the sixteenth century. We can see here the hold of various religious tenets and how Tamil culture, history, spirituality, and art were impacted by various creeds across the span of centuries.

Although during the time of the Pallavas, there is no evidence of a functioning Buddhist vihara in either Kanchipuram or Mamallapuram, however, at Nagapattinam, there is a ruined Buddhist vihara which was popularly known as the Chinese Pagoda and called the Tower of Malla (by Marco Polo). The Kalyani inscription found in Burma (present-day Myanmar) refers to this very same Chinese pagoda, with travellers like Marco Polo also mentioning this. The Kalyani inscription clearly says that travellers visited Nagapattinam and went on foot to worship the image of the Buddha in a cave constructed by the king Narasimhavarman II. Royal patronage for Buddhism obviously existed, although this was less in evidence compared to the support for Jainism and later for temple building and the Brahmanical faith.

While the numbers of practising Jains and Buddhists slowly saw a decline during the later years of Pallava rule, Buddhist and Jain ghatikas flourished until the last days of the Pallavas. We hear about these schools that taught Buddhist and Jain doctrines from travellers like Hiuen Tsang. He speaks about the more than hundred monasteries in Kanchi and 10,000 monks. He mentions a particular vihara and a stupa 'about a 100 feet high which was built by Asoka-raja' as the most important place for a large gathering or a Sangrama where reputed thinkers would meet. Hiuen Tsang says that the monastery connected to the stupa functioned as the intellectual centre for the elite. Dennis Hudson says that this monastery may have been the royal monastery that the Pallava king Mahendravarman mentions in his play *Mattavilasa Prahasana*. It is conjectured that many of these were built by the earlier more tolerant Pallava kings. As far as Jain institutions are concerned, there were several patronized by kings like Mahendravarman before his conversion from Jainism. Pataliputra in South Arcot district was one such monastery where, according to the *Periyapuranam*, Appar resided before his reconversion to the Vedic faith. Jain scholars from these monasteries scattered across Tamilakam established a strong connection with the local population, roaming the countryside and debating their theological perspectives with their opponents.

Jain history and contributions remain an important facet of the history and shaping of Tamil culture, and indeed of the Tamils themselves. Jain monks, scholars, and monasteries were widely supported across Tamil society by rulers, merchants, and lay people who provided them with space for living and teaching across Tamilakam. We must remember too that some of the greatest Tamil literary works which had a strong Jaina undertone were ascribed to this period. These include the great *Tirukkural* by Tiruvalluvar, written sometime between the second century BCE and the fifth century CE. It is considered to belong to the group of didactic poetry called *Kilkanakku* or Eighteen Minor Works. Scholars have pointed out that the poetry is distinctly in a post Sangam mode and composed in the venpa metre. Details of Tiruvalluvar and his work are better positioned in the chapter on the Pandya kingdom and will be elaborated there as it has been suggested that while he could have been born in or around present-day Chennai, more specifically in Mylapore, he supposedly lived most of his life in Madurai. The poet himself gives no clue about his time or whereabouts.

To go back to the Jainism-Brahmanical conflict, a well-known tale of persecution and torture sourced from Brahmanical accounts is the legend of Tirunavukkarasar, popularly known as Appar, a Velalla from Tiruvamur, considered a contemporary of the Pallava ruler Mahendravarman I. Although born into a pious Shaivite family, he and his sister Tilakavathiyar (who also became an ascetic and whose life was written up by the poet Sekkizhar in *Periyapuranam*), were orphaned at an early age, with Tilakavathiyar also losing her betrothed. The young boy, then called Marulnikki, shocked by the family tragedies, took to Jainism, much to his sister's dismay (she was a devout Shaivite). He even joined a Jain monastery to gain mastery in Jain thought and practices. However, the story goes that his sister prayed to Shiva to turn him back to Saivism. In Jain lore it is acknowledged that he gained mastery over the philosophy and was known as Dharmasena. Tilakavathiyar fervently prayed for her brother to return to the fold. Afflicted by sudden and severe colic pain that would not abate, Marulnikki or Dharmasena turned to his sister for help. She advised him to beg Shiva for forgiveness and rubbed holy ash on him but to no avail. It was only when he sang verses of devotion and forgiveness spontaneously in front of the lingam that his pain abated. Legend has it that a voice from above then named him vagisa or Tirunavukkarasar meaning 'king of the holy tongue'. The Pallava king Mahendravarman, who was Jain, was angered by the poet's conversion to Saivism and demanded that he recant his new-found faith. The story (not corroborated by any historical evidence) retold in oral form in the *Thevaram* is that the poet-saint resisted the king and said he was only answerable to God and to no king. The king ordered that he be burnt in a kiln and his ashes brought to him. But Appar, as he came to be called, was found seated unharmed in the kiln. The poet-saint then burst into the now famed *Thevaram*, 'Masil veenaiyum...' which speaks of finding shelter at Shiva's feet which is akin to the divine music of the veena. The stories recount the various methods of torture that were employed, from administering poison to him, to having him kicked by the royal elephant. Appar sang a song invoking the elephant-headed Ganesha, and the royal elephant then went around him three times and bowed to him, leaving him unharmed. He was also thrown into the sea with a stone tied to him, but he surfaced, singing that his faith would save him. The persecution by the Jain establishment evoked a response from him that was expressed in his hymns. Some frequently quoted lines are: 'We are slaves to no man / Nor do we fear death. / Hell holds no torment for us / We know no deceit / We rejoice... / We bow to none.' In the end, Mahendravarman himself became a Shaivite. The many *Thevaram* poems of Appar challenge head-on some of the tenets of the Jainas. He regrets his association with the Jains and calls them wily and wicked without an awareness of the truth that is Shiva.

Building up the Bhakti movement, Tamil lore houses accounts of many miracles performed by these saints and speaks of the coming together of several of the Nayanmars, most prominently Appar with the much younger Sambandar who sang his first *Thevaram* or poem in praise of Shiva at the age of three. Sambandar who was born in Sirkali had also mastered the Vedas at the age of three and gathered many disciples around him, making visits to Shaivite shrines and temples, singing and composing hymns. When he met Tirunavukkarasar, the little boy saint embraced him as a father, hence he came to be known as Appar. Perhaps the most vociferous opponent of the Jains was Sambandar, who took them on in his hymns and poems, continuously deploring everything about them from their names to their doctrine. Sundarar, another Nayanmar, initially a householder with two wives, is said to make up this prominent trio of saints who wandered around Tamilakam and beyond, composing and singing hymns in over two hundred temples across the region. For instance, Appar is said to have walked from Kanchipuram to Tirukazhikundram, Tiruvanmiyur, Mylapore, Tiruvottriyur, and Kalahasti among other places. This trio is also said to have performed various miracles, together and alone, bringing both a resurgence of faith and reflection among the laity for many of whom the Vedic texts and philosophies in Sanskrit were not accessible. The essence that people gleaned, enjoyed, and absorbed was complete devotion to Shiva the godhead, whose grace they believed would remove their negative karma. In that sense, Brahmanical philosophy or Vedanta was eschewed in favour of simple devotion. Manikkavachakar, another Shaivite saint, came some years later but is also considered among one of the prominent preacher-poets of the Bhakti movement.

It was not just the use of Tamil in the hymns and poems that drew the public to this movement, but also the fact that these saints belonged to a variety of castes—Brahmins, cobblers, farmers, merchants, princes, and even robbers. The historian Champakalakshmi points out that it is important to differentiate between those who propagated the Bhakti cult and those who were canonized—whose compositions became a part of temple ritual and worship. Although there were sixty-three Shaivite poet-saints, the most prominent were the four mentioned above whose work was included in ritual singing and recorded in inscriptions.

Now to the Azhwars or Vaishnava saints. Between the fifth and ninth centuries, the Azhwars were responsible for the spread of Vaishnavism or specific worship of Vishnu-Narayana as the supreme godhead. Their poetry, compiled later into one body of work by a Vaishnavite theologian called Nathamuni around the tenth century, was called the *Nalayira Divya Prabandam*—that is 4,000 verses. The shrines they sang about in their verse came to be known as the 108 Divya Desam. The earliest Azhwars came before many of the Shaivite saints and were twelve in number with a few of the later Vaishnavite saints being contemporary with the Nayanmars.

Ramanujan in his *Hymns for the Drowning* says the term Azhwar means 'one who is immersed in God'. Other interpretations suggest that Azhwar also indicates 'one who rules' borne out also by the fact that the woman poet Goda who was one among this constellation of poet-saints was more famously known as Andal or, 'she who rules'. The first three or Mudal Azhwars, called Poygai Azhwar, Pey Azhwar, and Budhat Azhwar, were supposed to have lived around the fifth or sixth century CE or a little after, and are clearly located in the Pallava era. They lived in and around Kanchipuram, Tirupati, and the Mamallapuram area. Champakalakshmi says that the early Azhwar Bhakti has been characterized as derived from the Bhagavad Gita, and is a relatively quiet expression of adoration, service, and loyalty, with a personal connection to God. While the temple is the centre of their religion in a generic sense, according to Champakalakshmi, they refer to Venkatam, Mallai (i.e. Mamallapuram), and Tirukoyilur as three important locations of Vishnu worship. Their geographical environment is thus clearly confined to the northern part of Tamilakam, says Champakalakshmi.

According to myths, these saints are considered by devotees to be the incarnation of Vishnu's divine weapons. Legends speak of the divine births of the three. Poygai Azhwar, the one who composed the first pasuram or stanza called Mudal Tiruvanthadhi in praise of Vishnu, was thought to be a manifestation of his conch called Panchajanya, symbolizing that which could bestow enlightenment or gnana. According to stories, he was born in a lotus leaf in Kanchipuram. Budhat Azhwar was the kaumodhaki, Vishnu's gada or mace, born in a kurunkathi flower in Mamallapuram, and Pey Azhwar was said to be a manifestation of Vishnu's sword, his nandaki, born in Mylapore among the red lilies.

There is a lovely apocryphal story of the three of them variously reiterated which I frequently heard, whenever I spoke about the Azhwars. Many Vaishnava households seem to have a repository of such tales passed on down the generations, each version as fantastical, philosophical, or as matter-of-fact as the storyteller was inclined to make it. The story goes that once the three of them travelled separately to Tirukoyilur to worship Perumal, or Lord Vishnu. On the way, each arrived at Rishi Mrikandu's dwelling and sought shelter as the rain was hammering down and it was a terribly stormy night. They found shelter in the thinnai (front porch) of the house. As all three had sought shelter, they found they had to stand close to each other and huddle in that narrow space, where 'only one could lie down, two could sit and three could stand' as oft detailed in many narratives. They were so delighted by this chance encounter that they paid no heed to the inclement weather or the lack of physical space as they huddled together and grew absorbed in discussing their like-minded devotion and passion for the Lord. The three of them then suddenly felt that a fourth person had arrived in that small space, pressing up against them. They were baffled but could not see anything as it was pitch dark. In between the flashing lightning, they sensed a radiance. The story goes that it was Vishnu himself who appeared amongst them, eager to listen to their discussion and witness their devotion to the divine. One of Vishnu's appellations is Dehalisa, or Lord of the Porch.

According to the narrative, each Azhwar lights the lamp of knowledge with their words to dispel the surrounding darkness. 'Vaiyam thahaliyaka,' says Poygai Azhwar: the world is the lamp base, the sea is the ghee, the sun is the wick, and a garland of verse is strung together for the feet of the lord who wields the flaming discus, so that he may free us from the ocean of misery. This is a paraphrasing of that first verse of the first pasuram or andhadhi, the verse form in which the last word of one line forms the first word of the next line. The collection of the works of the three is the beginning of the *Prabandam* compilation of what would become 4,000 verses later. 'Anbe thahaliyai arvame neyyaga inguruku sindai idu thiriyaka,' says Budhat Azhwar in the next andhadhi: 'My love is the lamp of intent, my thought is the inspiration and my knowledge the wick with which I light up my service to the Lord.' Pey Azhwar, the story goes, was so inspired by the verses of the first two which illuminated the radiant presence of Vishnu that he followed up with an ecstatic verse, singing 'Tiru kanden tirumeni kanden', meaning, I saw the lord, and I saw his holy form. Each Azhwar supposedly then sang one hundred verses which formed the beginning of the *Divya Prabandam*.

In the Pallava era particularly, Tirumangai Azhwar's story deserves mention. A man who robbed travellers to pay off his debts, he turned into a devout bhakta of Vishnu. In his early years, Tirumangai was said to have won his spurs as a military commander but later fell on bad times. He fell in love with Kumudavalli, the beautiful daughter of a healer, who declared that she would marry him only if he turned to Vaishnavism and constructed a thousand temples to Lord Narayana. The story goes that he resorted to highway robbery to fund his temple-building and thereby gain his girl. One day, when he attacked a bridegroom on the road and tried to remove his jewelled toe ring it would not come off. The bridegroom revealed himself to be the Lord and Tirumangai was stunned and later learned the sacred philosophy from Lord Narayana himself. The first ten verses of Tirumangai's work *Periya Tirumozhi* speaks of this. He was a vassal of Nandivarman Pallavamalla and was given a small principality to rule. He also sang several verses in praise of the king who built the Vaikunta Perumal temple

Combining the formal ritualistic worship of earlier times with such personal identification with God (as above) and using the philosophy of individual surrender to a divine being had great popular appeal. Another important aspect of these poet-saints was that they belonged to diverse social strata; from Brahmin to Paraiya, although those whose devotions were expressed with lyricism tended to come from the Velalla (cultivators) and the ruling class or Kshatriyas. Tamil was also accorded primacy, with hymns being composed in the local vernacular, while still following Vedic and Puranic doctrine and philosophies. The cavilling and eschewing of the Jain and Buddhist way of life by many of the Shaivite and Vaishnavite poet-saints as being essentially alien to the Tamil ethos slowly caught hold of the public's interest. Many wanted freedom from the more rigorous lifestyle imposed by Jain philosophy and found all of that in the newly emerging notions of bhakti, the total surrender to a personalized deity. The poetry of the Bhakti saints whether of the Vaishnavite or Shaivite canon imagined the divine in all possible forms, as lover, as parent, as friend, and as child. The notion of pilgrimage also took root with communities of bhaktas following in the footsteps of these poet-saints and visiting the places where they sang and celebrated the divine. The temple, deriving inspiration from the cosmos, reflected an accessible divinity to everyone in the community.

The revivalists also carefully incorporated the earlier deities of the Sangam age into the Brahmanic world view synthesizing the multiple ways of worship of the Tamil people. Even the temple was related to the innermost sacred Self and God. For instance, regarding the structure of the Vaikunta Perumal temple, Hudson says that 'the tall enclosing prakara wall defines this mandala of five concentric circles, each symbolising a level or layer (kosha) of God's body whether visible or invisible to us'. The human correlation of the divine koshas, or sheaths of the body, are perceived in such a way that the outermost prakara wall is equivalent to the skin of the body and the innermost sanctum hidden inside is analogous to the hidden life, the jiva or soul that owns our body. This extrapolation does find a parallel in the Vedantic idea of the body being composed of five sheaths which can be peeled away like an onion (an oft-repeated phrase)—to go from the gross to the innermost subtle core. The Taittiriya Upanishad describes these as being the panchakosha, beginning with the annamaya kosha, the gross body nourished by food, then the pranamaya or the vital breath that pervades the entire body, next the manonmaya which is the mind and the sense organs which are reactive to human experience. The vijnanamaya kosha is the fourth sheath, the discerning intellect, and, finally, the anandamaya kosha is the subtlest sheath that reflects the soul or atman and is the seat of bliss which evolves from an awareness of the Self. The subtle weaving of the more profound concepts of Hindu philosophy with the material world of temple and ritual grew more appealing as the Bhakti movement gained ground.

The Pandyas

A dynasty that lasted several hundreds of years and gave cultural and historic continuity to extensive regions of the South, the Pandyas, celebrated even in the early Sangam literature of the pre-Christian era, were rulers under whom art, literature, and architecture flourished. They exhibited tolerance of other faiths, and their achievements took Tamil culture to a great pinnacle.

Chapter 9

Madurai and the Acme of Pandya Culture

He saw the Pantiyan's great city of Maturai and rejoiced in his heart.

Shilappadikaram

KANNAGI WALKED THE LONG AND DUSTY ROAD ALONGSIDE HER husband Kovalan. There was little relief at that time of year when the southwesterly wind blew hot and muggy and the broad trees that lined both sides of the road stood stately and still, offering no respite to the tired travellers. The journey had been a long one. Kannagi looked at her husband, lost in thought, and she frowned, remembering the bitter battle to win him back. Kovalan on his part was musing about his own great betrayal of his beloved wife, wondering what had led him to Madhavi, the dancer, and the few years when he had let down Kannagi by abandoning her. The worst thing, Kovalan knew, was that Madhavi was as blameless as Kannagi; he was the one who had erred, he was the one who had crossed lines, betraying two women, and as he walked with his wife towards the city, he heard 'like distant thunder the sound of the morning drums'. It sounded ominous to Kovalan. The great city of Madurai loomed before the weary travellers and the banners on its ramparts 'appeared to stop them'…warning, 'don't enter'. However, his karma seemed to be beckoning him, thought Kovalan. Perhaps this was the road to the end. But Kannagi, for her part, felt suddenly optimistic, and resolved that this new place, this glorious city, would bring them luck and a new life. The story's tragic denouement is well known.

Shilappadikaram, or *The Tale of the Anklet*, is one of the more popular tales that has riveted the imagination of the Tamils, a tale of love and betrayal, of jealousy and justice, where a wronged wife rails against a king whose miscarriage of justice leads to the death of her faithless husband. Her rage burns the city of Madurai, which the author of *Shilappadikaram* calls the immortal city. In this epic poem, supposedly composed by the monk-prince Illango Adigal in the fifth century, he speaks of the city of Madurai as 'the yawning treasure chest of thousand-eyed Indra', a city of tall mansions, and crowded streets with a profusion of riches. In its marketplaces, the poem says, ornamented chariots, coats of mail, jewelled goads, potent medicines, white yak tail fans, boar-faced shields, leather shields, and gloves are in plenty; things of gold, copper, bronze, ivory and sandalwood, incense and scents, wreaths of flowers and garlands and shops with precious gemstones—faultless diamonds, rubies, sapphires, and sardonyx—all the envy of kings are seen here in abundance. The poem describes cloth merchants piling high their bales of silk and cotton, and traders wandering everywhere with their bushels and measures to weigh copious amounts of grains and spices like black pepper. Even the folk who live outside the city feel its fragrance in the wind as they tell Kovalan: 'The south wind from Maturai blows here. Feel it. / It is redolent of the divinely fragrant, thin, soft mix / Of eaglewood paste, the aroma of the saffron / The civet, the goodness of sandalwood paste, /and musk blended together. On its way it hovers / Wreaths of pollen laden, red water lilies, / And the newly opened petals of the champak…/ It caresses the smoke from kitchen fires, / The smoke from the broad streets lined, / With shops where appam and cakes are fried / The fumes of incense swirling from terraces / where men and women have fun together….' The *Shilappadikaram* is, of course, a work of the imagination; in the poem, the city is reduced to ashes by the wronged wife. The description of Madurai here is a testament to its culture and prosperity in the first half of the first millennium of the Common Era, although its story goes even further back than the context of the poem and has been described in legends and in fragmented accounts and literary texts. Beginning with its origins, Madurai's cultural wealth, shored up by the long rule of the Pandya dynasty, has had a deep impact on Tamil culture, serving as pivotal point from which one can understand the contributions of the Pandyas.

However, though the city of Madurai has been in existence for about 2,500 years or so, due to a multiplicity of factors, structures and relics that are older than 1,500 years are not easily found within the city itself because of successive invasions over the centuries and chaotic urbanization in modern times. The Madurai of today is a typically contemporary city of pollution and disorder and, barring a handful of places, much of a sense of historicity is absent within the precincts of the city. Nevertheless, the small hillocks that surround the city carry definitive evidence that this was a place of ancient habitation and bustling activity at least 200 to 300 years before the Common Era.

The excavations at Keezhadi described in an earlier chapter date the Madurai region to the Sangam age: the discovery of artefacts point to a time between the third century BCE and second century CE. Burial urns and rock art in Kizhavalalu from a much earlier time, to about 500 BCE, takes the region's civilization even further back. The earliest Tamil Brahmi inscriptions have been found in Mankulam, about 20 kilometres outside of Madurai, and more have been found in other places too like in the Arittapatti rock-cut caves which were inhabited by Jain monks who made this area the epicentre of Jainism.

The *Thiruvilayadal*, a sixteenth-century literary text by poet-saint Paranjothi, places Madurai in the realm of legend, myth, and spirituality, and recounts that sacred games and wonders were performed by Lord Shiva in and around Madurai, referring frequently to the city's divine origin. There are many stories of Shiva in this epic poem, but one tells of a beautiful kadamba forest where, in a pond filled with golden lilies, a marvellous Shivalinga glows with mystical properties. Kulasekhara Pandya, the king of nearby Manavur, comes to worship this lingam and that night Shiva appears to him in a dream and tells him to clear the forest and build a city. He does so according to religious and other prescribed rules and Shiva himself appears over the new city on the day of its consecration. Drops of nectar from his locks fall on the city, purifying it, and so it gets the name of Madurai—Mathuram is a Tamil word for sweetness, madhura in Sanskrit means the same. Another story speaks of Indra, the king of the gods and his elephant, Iravatham, who were both cursed by the sage Durvasa, finally finding redemption by Shiva's grace in the same kadamba forest at the swayambhu (self-manifested) lingam. He builds a magnificent temple around the lingam which later became the famous Meenakshi Sundareswarar temple. The temple itself is an integral part of the Madurai story and we will go into more detail about it a little later.

There are other names for the city. Kutal is one, referring to the fact that a congregation or kutal of poets, the famed Sangam, was held there. More fully, it was called naan-mata-kutal, traditionally interpreted as the 'junction of four terraces', according to the epigraphist Iravatham Mahadevan. A second century BCE inscription in Tamil Brahmi found in a cave refers to the city as 'matiray' meaning 'walled-city' according to Mahadevan. Malligai Maanagar or city of jasmine is another of the city's names, and the *Thevaram*, the poetic compositions of the Shaiva saints, call the city Thirualavai. Additional names include Kannipuri and Sivalokam and there is a suggestion that the marudam trees that once flourished in the area could have been so named because of the marudam tinai or landscape which has a rich biodiversity and gave the city its name.

The other early references to Madurai are recorded in several Sangam works supposedly belonging to the second and third centuries BCE. While the relationship between recorded historical fact (as in epigraphy), and literary references and allusions can be deemed to be tenuous, the wealth of literary material about Madurai cannot be overlooked as we examine this pivotal centre which was the political, cultural, and religious focal point of a bustling empire.

Madurai was considered the seat of Tamil poetry and grammar and the assembly of poets which was later called Sangam took place in the city. The Pandya kings were also among the participants. Legends have it that the first Sangam was held over 4,000 years ago and the next one, 1,000 years later, although there is no historical evidence for any of this. These assemblies were said to have lasted for several centuries with the sage Agastya presiding over the legendary first Sangam supposedly held in the Madurai that became submerged by the sea. The third Sangam, whose date is again fuzzy, is nevertheless mentioned in many poems referring specifically to Madurai, such as in the *Kalithokai*. 'When I bade him goodbye from my heart, did he not promise to return in this season when those from Koodal with tall mansions, wise people who are praised by those living in all the countries, enjoy reciting new verses?' The anonymous poet takes cognizance of the poets' congregation as well as of Kutal, which, as mentioned earlier, is another name for the city. Madurai is also referred to very specifically by name in the *Paripatal* poems that were probably composed in the Sangam era. A translation of some of the *Paripatal* poems, *The River Speaks: The Vaiyai Poems from the Paripatal* translated by V. N. Muthukumar and Elizabeth Rani Segran, specifically on the Vaiyai (Vaigai) River, lyrically expresses the river's flow on whose banks a people and a civilization build their lives. In the *Paripatal* the city is celebrated as a place that drew its life from the river. 'In the town of Kutal / which receives the waters / that take away the sorrows of the land, / bards and dancers / sing in praise of the Vaiyai,' says the poet. In *Madurai Through the Ages*, D. Devakunjari also quotes from the *Paripatal* and says that at the landing stages near the river, boats with fantastically carved prows were moored, and behind them rose a moat that guarded the city. Beyond that there was a rampart protecting the city's towers. Other Sangam age poems like Patirruppattu, Nedunal Vadai, and Tirumurugattru Padai also celebrated Madurai and its cultural riches.

There are a few indirect references in some datable records such as in the Ashoka edicts which also refer to the many south Indian kingdoms that were outside the Mauryan empire. Madurai, as the Pandya capital, is mentioned in the second and thirteenth edicts, which also include the names of the Chola, Satiyaputa, and Keralaputa kings and territories.

The Vaigai river's presence was intrinsic to the city's early growth and development, although in recent decades, as in other parts of India, the same sad tale of environmental degradation is apparent here with the river running dry in the seasons when rain is scarce. There are smaller and equally historic tributaries of the river which are mentioned in texts like the *Paripatal* and *Shilappadikaram* which include the Silambar (later known as Nupura Gangai), Peraruvi, Sitharuvi, Sathiyar, Majamalaiyar, and several others like the Krithamal, a river considered to be as old and sacred as the Vaigai itself. The Gundar and Varattar, other larger rivers originating in the nearby hills and feeding into the Vaigai, are said to have been sites of habitation in the Palaeolithic or Neolithic ages with excavations yielding stone-age implements in these river basins. These tributaries also created verdant forests—places like Alagarmalai, Sirumalai, and Palanimalai are even today storehouses of various medicinal herbs and have added to the diversity of the region's biosphere. However, currently, these rivers and streams have also been reduced to narrow channels with scarcely any water, all reflective of a new ecosystem of pollution, haphazard construction, and destruction which has turned modern-day Madurai into a city of frequent water shortages.

To go back to the pre-Christian and early post-Christian centuries, the sights and sounds of Madurai are depicted in great detail in *Maduraikanchi*, an oft-quoted text which is embedded in the *Pathupaatu* body of poems of the Sangam age and written by Mangudi Maruthanar, a poet in the court of the Pandya king Nedunchellyan. A translation by Vaidehi Herbert conveys the bustle and commotion of this urbanized agglomeration: 'In the huge city where drums roar constantly / festivals are celebrated on the wide streets / thunangai dances are performed…/ there are communities with fragrances / and there are many citizens with abundant wealth, / in the middle of that fine country praised by poets….'

This poem also describes a city of enormous wealth with day and night markets, with sellers and buyers jostling for wares: 'things in the market of Koodal do not get decreased by selling / or get increased by the new things that are brought in….' There are merchants who buy gold and gems, and sell exotic imported things and yet are righteous, says the poet, while rich women stroll down the streets, their gold anklets jingling with their stride, and fragrances spread as they walk wearing their bright earrings. They live in mansions that 'rise up to the sky, with many doors and windows through which a little wind blows with music'. This is a sophisticated picture of an elegant and advanced environment. Among other things, it describes 'older women of fine beauty / with long braids of white hair / like white conches in the huge ocean', revealing a mature perception of beauty that is not confined to a stereotype; the poet also speaks of soldiers spent from war, pious pilgrims worshipping at the citadels of diverse faiths, the Jains, the Brahmins, and the Buddhists. While a poetic imagination tends to colour reality, it is striking that the poet reveals a fine eye for detail of the city's pursuit of inclusiveness. Similar heightened images of the city appear in various texts of the Shaiva saints, in the works of the Nayanmars in the ninth century for instance, who touch upon the glories of Madurai in their poetry. Norman Cutler in a scholarly essay points out that in the poem *Thirukkovaiyar*, composed by the poet saint Manikkavachakar, which is in praise of Shiva, there are insights into Tamil geographies such as Tillai, Chidambaram, and Madurai. The poet-saint writes: 'Did you go to study sweet Tamil verses / at the academy of Kutal, / high walled city of the lord / who dwells in my mind and in my heart /...or did you go to study music where they play the seven tones?' Shiva is the lord who dwells there in his local manifestation as Somasundara and as the poet says he lives in his mind and heart too. It seems as if Madurai and the Lord are synonymous for the poet. Madurai is perceived as the temporal abode of Shiva and an anchor of Saivism as well as the established space of literature and music.

This then, even in the pre-Christian, and in the first centuries of the first millennium, was a land of poetry and piety as well as that of natural and mineral riches, flourishing for centuries under the Pandya dynasty of kings with Madurai as the capital city. Even as early as the third century BCE, this was a city that was known across India, points out award-winning senior archaeologist, scholar, and pioneer epigraphist V. Vedachalam, who accompanied me on multiple visits across Tamil Nadu, elaborating that from literature like the *Shilappadikaram*, we know that Madurai was the hub for north–south travel, and the most important nerve centre along the Dakshinapada (the Southern Way), gradually adding commerce and trade to the spiritual appeal of the city. The identity and origins of the traders who came to the city would be known from the flags that they flew over their places of trade. The local Tamil people were accommodating to these outsiders says Vedachalam, inclusiveness was always a hallmark of Tamil culture, he adds.

The long rule of the Pandya kings in much of southern Tamilakam contributed to many significant developments in the south of India. As epigraphist R. Nagaswamy points out, the Pandyas were the only dynasty in India that had a continuing presence and indeed rule in some form or the other for more than 2,000 years, with their first mention being in the inscriptions of the Emperor Ashoka in the third century BCE and as a dwindling yet active power until the seventeenth century CE. Because of the long reign of the Pandyas, Madurai has continued to be an important city for over eighteen centuries.

Today the gopurams of the Meenakshi temple stencil Madurai's skyline, and the narrow streets leading up to it bustle with frenetic activity. It seems as if the temple's vast interior vistas house an entirely separate universe; the fragrance of Madurai malli, the GI-tagged jasmine, competes with sandal paste and frankincense; mounds of turmeric and kumkum, and coloured glass bangles are stacked enticingly, and artefacts of stone and wood as well as brass and copperware household items jostle alongside small images of gods and deities in an appealing display. They beckon the locals as well as visitors to these shops and sustain a unique economic zone within the temple's precincts. While the temple with its strategic location has come to symbolize the city itself in the popular imagination, an array of historically significant structures that have emerged over different centuries—such as the Koodal Azhagar temple dedicated to Vishnu; Ladan Kovil, sacred to Murugan and hewn out of rock; the remarkable caves of the ascetic Jains that fringe the hillocks around Madurai the Yanaimalai; and in later centuries the Kazimar Periya Pallivasal or the Big Mosque; and the graceful St. Mary's Cathedral dating back to the 1800s—stand testament to the syncretic development of the city despite periods of internecine strife that left their impact.

Initially, natural caves and rock-cut temples set the stage for centuries of piety and sacred explorations, while the Sangam period originally gave the city an emblazoned, richly literary identity, and a specifically Tamil culture. Epigraphy, as the renowned historian and epigraphist K. V. Raman pointed out, is what has given us the most material about the cultural and social histories of the Pandya kingdom.

Travelling from Madurai further south, beyond Ramanathapuram and Tuticorin, and down to Tenkasi and Tirunelveli, where the Thamirabarani River flows, one encounters several fascinating aspects of Pandya heritage lands. Beginning on the fringes of Madurai, beyond the crouching hillock called Yanaimalai (so called because it looks like a sleeping elephant) that borders the city, down highways, across riverbanks, and green paddy fields, through mud roads and small towns, one encounters some extraordinary relics—temples, sculptures, cave paintings, and inscriptions that offer a treasury of insight about the Pandyas, illuminating the life of the times.

Some unusual structures and temples that still stand are a testament to the Pandya vision of piety, history, and aesthetics. 'Even looking at a place like Yanaimalai one can understand the distinct history of the region,' says Vedachalam. The earliest inscriptions in Tamil Brahmi belonging to the first century CE are found in these hills. There are also bas-relief structures carved by Jain monks, of the ninth and tenth centuries CE (although Jain settlements in Tamilakam began as early as 300 BCE). On the other face of the Yanaimalai hill there is a Narasinga Perumal cave temple (also called Yoga Narasimha temple) built in 770 CE, belonging to the early Pandya period, and there is yet another cave temple to Subrahmanya in these hills.

According to Vedachalam, the Guptas in the fourth century seem to have begun this tradition of creating cave temples in places like Udayagiri near Sanchi, where the earliest such temples have been found. In the sixth century CE, in Karnataka, the Chalukyas constructed such temples in Badami and Aihole, and then the Pallavas, who were contemporaries of the Pandyas, followed suit. More than thirty such cave temples of the early Pandya period have been excavated, according to Vedachalam, such as those in Tirumayam, Pillayarpatti, Arittapatti, Yanaimalai, Kunnathur, Tiruparankunram, and in other parts of south Tamil Nadu. In the foothills of Yanaimalai is the Ladan temple of Subrahmanya.

The Ladan temple, a simple structure, is a fine example of early Pandya art of the eighth century CE. The temple itself stands at the foot of the hill and is scooped neatly out of the hillside. An inscription in vatteluthu in this temple states that a wandering monk called Vatta Somayaji Parivirajakar created this temple. The unusual posture of a sitting Subrahmanya, wearing a belt across his chest, with Devayani, his consort, by his side is in an inner sanctum, while on the outside wall, the crusted granite shows the pillars of a mandapam. The two pilasters have carved bhuta ganas on the side, and Subramanya's symbols of a cock and peacock are also carved on the pillars, thus establishing the identity of the deity. Instead of the usual dwarapalakas or gatekeepers, two images of mendicants or Brahmins are carved, each holding a lotus flower in his hand.

A certain creative freedom seems to have existed in the conceptualization and execution in this early Pandya temple unlike the more established style of contemporary Pallava sculptures. There is no worship here currently, and the slightly forlorn monument is tucked away among small dwellings with goats and chickens wandering about, a little startled by our presence as they clearly feel that we are intruders in their home.

The Yoga Narasimha temple, in the Yanaimalai foothills, was built in 770 CE by Maduraikavi or Marankaari who was a minister at the court of the Pandya king Parantaka Nedunchezhiyan. An inscription in vatteluthu states that the temple was finished by the minister's brother Maran Eiynan. There are no details about why the temple was not finished by the original constructor. It is another example of the early Pandya cave temple, and an impressive sculpture of Narasimha is carved from the rock. There are several early Pandya inscriptions here including an unfinished one from Sundara Pandya's rule (around 1216), mentioning his victories against the Chola king. Multiple tales abound about the temple and its origins including one in the *Thiruvilayadal Puranam* which says that a Chola king who could not win the battle against the Pandya ruler sought the help of Jains who with their mystic powers created a giant elephant to kill the Pandya ruler and destroy his capital. But the Pandya king fervently prayed for help to Shiva, who sent his Narasinga Asthram, a powerful weapon which turned the elephant into a hill and hence, the legend says, the name Yanaimalai came about. Stereotypical references to Jain defeat and the triumph of Brahminical religion over the Samanar or the Jain view was a frequent and recurrent theme in many of these mediaeval texts and legends.

There are innumerable Jain monuments in this region, and indeed they are a very remarkable on-ground testament that assert a strong practice of the faith across southern Tamilakam especially around Madurai. Archaeologists affirm that there are more than a hundred such sites in the Pandya-ruled region. There are tales of the first journeys of Jain monks from the north, some walking down with the great Jaina seer Bhadrabahu about 300 years before Christ and spreading the word of Mahavira and his teachings. Professor Kanaka Ajithadoss, a gentle Jain scholar, contends that it is not factual that the Jain faith appeared at a particular instant in time. Tamilakam was conducive for Jain asceticism for many centuries before it was firmly established, he says, as acceptance of the faith as a way of life among common people is almost a prerequisite for enabling the practice of the more austere aspects of the faith.

One of the most spectacular demonstrations that captures the pristine and almost incandescent beauty of Jain art can be found in the caves of Sittanavasal in Pudukkottai district. As the name Sittanavasal suggests, this is a gateway and abode (vasal) of the siddhas or monks. The town of Pudukkottai itself still bears the relics and stamp of antiquity, with ancient burial mounds and significant cave art from pre-historic times, including the recent discovery of 3,000-year-old symbols etched on a cave in a nearby village called Malaiadipatti. The area is replete with vestiges of ancient societies and communities, each leaving its own imprint, from dolmens, stone circles, and cists to luminous cave paintings almost inconspicuous at times, and at other times quite dramatically noticeable.

On a balmy pre-monsoon morning, when the sun's rays were gentler than usual in this heat-trapping terrain, we drive to Pudukkottai. A garland of small hillocks leads us to a natural cavern on one hillock with seventeen Jain beds carved on the rock floor dating back to at least 200 BCE. Several of these rock beds even have pillow arrangements carved in stone, and many have Tamil Brahmi inscriptions ascribed to the second century BCE. One reads: 'eruminatu kumulur piranta kavuti itenku cirupavil ilayar ceyta atit-anam'. This means, 'bed made by Ilayar (the younger) of Cirupavil for Kavuti born in Kumulur in Eruminatu'. Scholars suggest that Jain monks like Kavuti probably used this place to perform their severe vow of slow starvation to death called sallekhana. Incidentally, sallekhana is an avowed Jain practice described in texts like *Ratnakarandaka Shravakachara*, a Jain householder's code of conduct which says, 'When overtaken by portentous calamity, by famine, by old age or incurable disease, the Aryans obtain for the sake of merit, liberation of the body by Sallekhana'. The text advises that a person 'having purified the mind by the renunciation of friendship, hatred, ties and acquisitions; having forgiven his relations…sought forgiveness from them…viewing with a strong mind but aloofness all that he does…so shall a man enter on the performance of this great vow not to be completed save by his death'. In other words, there were specific conditions for ritual suicide; although the Rajasthan High Court deemed this as unlawful in 2015, in the same year the Supreme Court allowed this as part of Jain philosophical and religious practice. The word attitanam or adhistanam in the context specifically means a place where such crucial vows are fulfilled, and resolutions undertaken.

Many inscriptions in Tamil and vatteluthu in these caves indicate that they were used from the second century BCE through the fifth and sixth centuries CE as well and right up to the thirteenth century CE. This particular bed also has other inscriptions from later periods all the way up to the thirteenth century and today they stand as a testament to a living tradition of Jain practice that existed for several centuries with monks of succeeding generations using them. This suggests that there was a conscious and cultivated intent to imbibe and practice the strictest of Jain tenets by the Jain monks who sheltered here.

On the western side of the hillock, the superb wall and roof paintings of the Sittanavasal caves highlight an unexpected luminosity of Jain art, which contrasts with the generally more severe practices and expressions of Jain thought. As we walk up the small hillock towards the cave, there is a mandapam in front, and behind that an inner cave.

Vedachalam and archaeologists like T. N. Ramachandran say that this site is clearly of the early Pandya period. Likely, these caves were painted at the time of the Pandya king Srimara Srivallabha whose name appears in inscriptions and in legends as a multifaceted ruler, a Bhagavata (worshipper of Vishnu), as well as a patron of Jain monks who apparently found his rule hospitable enough to calmly pursue their meditations and teachings. It must be remembered that with Jain presence in Tamilakam even as early as the second century BCE, these natural caves were favoured shelters for them to live out their ascetic existence. The paintings, although faint now and subject to moderate levels of defacement and graffiti in the years before the site came under the purview of the ASI, appear to be evocative of a more refined era where art, literature, philosophy, and the temporal came together and offered a wider vision of human existence.

Faded paintings of apsaras reminiscent of the Ajanta cave paintings are depicted on the two front pillars at the entrance of the cave. Though the faces are somewhat indistinct and faint and almost fully obliterated, the shape of the torso tilted to the left indicates a posture that while being sensual also expresses a distinct dance position, the talasampohita karana. The elongated earlobes are decorated with patra kundalas, which are long earrings, and her wrists are covered with delicate bracelets and bangles, while her neck is adorned with a close-fitting choker and other necklets flow from her neck to cover her breasts. There is a gorgeously designed ring on her finger, and it seems as if no detail is too small for the artist to record the beauty of this apsara. The adjacent pillar shows another apsara in a pose called ardheracita karana, the contours of her frame fitting neatly into the pillar. The subtle movement in the postures of both apsaras captures the grace of the artist's vision and expression. We observe a royal couple clearly defined on another wall. This is likely the Pandya king Srimaran Srivallabha and his queen who supposedly visited the temple in a show of their patronage. Even though it was a time of Brahmanical (Hindu) revivalism with the Bhakti movement in full flow, as mentioned earlier, the tolerance of this king is clearly on display in his support of this Jain temple.

Scholars have pointed out that there are two layers of paintings here, one superimposed on the other. The later layers were of the Pandya period and despite the peeling plaster and fading lines, the intrinsic power of the paintings leap out at the visitor. The layered work is attested to with the glimpse of an inner surface of colours, which is superimposed by the art that came later when the temple was renovated by Srimaran Srivallabha, the Pandya king who ruled from 815 to 862 CE.

Beyond the immediate splendour of the pillars in the cave there is an austere image of Parsvanatha, the twenty-third renunciant teacher, a Tirthankara who supposedly lived and taught in seventh century BCE. Two other Tirthankaras, ascetic in their form, are carved into niches on the walls. And almost in contrast is a magnificent ceiling painted with a Michelangelo-like diligence. An amazing blue lake limpid in a forgotten sunlight washes over the unsuspecting visitor. Here, lotuses bloom, pink and white, fish abound, some of them leaping joyously to the sky, elephants bathe twirling lotus blossoms in their trunks, some of them spraying streams of water; buffaloes graze at the water's edge tilting their heads in curiosity and exotic birds fly in and out of the lush vegetation that surrounds the lake. There is nothing that is immobile on that surface. Dancers welcome the traveller from green banks, monks dip into the lake's blue waters and offer prayers.

The playfulness of the scene contrasts almost startlingly with the general austerity and asceticism of Jain philosophy. While there have been (and still are) multiple interpretations of the significance of the blooming lotuses related to Mahavira's life and Jain philosophy, scholars are in general agreement that this lake is Khatikabhumi, the heavenly tank where the faithful greet the monks who are moving on their journeys of self-discovery towards enlightenment.

It is also a place for a democratic congregation, the samavasarana—which is often found in Jain art—a space where the Tirthankara sits on a dais and preaches to all beings, man, animal, and bird, who gather there to understand the essence of Jain philosophy. The emphasis is on equality among all living things. There is a distinct joyfulness in the depictions on the ceiling; despite the fading surfaces and the progress of time, the monks who created these wondrous surfaces knew about life's richness while on the path of monastic rigour. S. Paramasivan, an archaeological chemist who in the 1940s worked on the Sittanavasal site, says, 'The art of painting in the cave temple at Sittanavasal, in the Kailasanatha temple at Kanchipuram, and the Brihadeeswara temple at Tanjore is almost as great as at Ajanta. But the craftsmanship is very much superior to the northern craftsmanship. It represents a long period of artistic training and apprenticeship reaching the highest watermark in the Chola paintings at Tanjore.'

Both Jain monuments and Hindu cave temples flourished equally under royal patronage until the Bhakti movement gained momentum from the tenth century onwards. For instance, when we visited Kazhugumalai, that most magnificent Jain edifice carved on a rock, we saw that only a few hundred yards away, the Shaivas had also created an astonishing (but unfinished) temple called Vettuvankovil, hidden initially from sight on the side of a hillock. Climbing up the patchy hillside, one would expect to see a slope and a view from the top of the hill; instead, rising up without warning is a structure of extraordinary beauty. This is an early Pandya temple, possibly belonging to the eighth century. Its splendour is simply breathtaking. 'This is a remarkable treasure that rises, cut out from under a seemingly buried surface,' says Vedachalam. The temple's structure is a magnificent construction carved out of a huge rock of granite as if emerging from a crater blasted out of the surrounding rock, with its gopuram cut first from the top. We look down a few storeys at the layers of carved walls, tier upon tier sculpted with intricacy and great artistic intelligence. Every single symbol of divinity carved in this stone reveals a rich range of expression and emotion. No image here is too small to not reflect humanness. The interplay of these deities and the positioning of numerous sculpted animals and birds with musicians, dancing girls, with bhuta ganas, the guardians and servitors of the gods, also show a cohesion and an understanding of a composite universe. Notwithstanding the movement of time and the passage of centuries, it underlines that the essential nature of life in all its playfulness and mystery remains the same. Vedachalam describes the vimana of the temple as 'the jewel of the Pandyas'.

This tradition of cutting down from the top of the rock and chiselling down the layers and building and carving this temple is most unusual, especially in Tamil Nadu, according to Vedachalam. 'In this same period, this style of temple building is evident in Ellora. The early Pandyas have built this in the eighth century. There are no inscriptions here, but it is possible to date this temple and architecture. So, at one end are the marvellous Jain sculptures and at the other end this. The designs on each stone reflect a great artistry. To indicate that this is a Shiva temple, you can see the four nandis on four sides. There is a rare carving of Dakshinamurthy on the southern side, playing a mridangam or drum, something that is not seen elsewhere in Tamil Nadu. There is a smile on the face of Dakshinamurthy, as if he is enjoying his own music,' Vedachalam says. He also points out the sculptures of Vishnu as Narasimha and Brahma, emphasizing that both deities are featured although the temple is primarily for Shiva. In the lower tier, monkey-faced bhuta ganas seem to be looking at each other, playing a variety of musical instruments, their expressions reflecting an absorbing interaction. Female figures comb and dry their tresses, stone musicians come alive with their different instruments, rose-tinged parakeets take flight, elephants leap with joy, and Parvati gazes lovingly at Shiva, a small smile on her face. The sun and moon intrude as well, balancing life and nature; indeed, the whole of the cosmos is reflected in these sculptural expressions. The distinct style of Pandya sculpture and art with its singular features clearly sets it apart from the Pallava and later the Chola style.

The art historian C. Sivaramamurti has described this as the most beautiful free-standing monolith of the Pandya period which recalls the famed Shiva temple at Ellora. This beautifully hewn rock temple was likely built during the reign of the Pandya king Parantaka Nedunjadayan. T. S. Subramanian says, 'From above the temple looks like a rising lotus…the sight gives one an ethereal feeling and drives home the sheer magnitude of the work that went into its making.' Subramaniam adds that 'no one knows why this was left unfinished and what was the nature of the exact calamity that overtook the sculptors'.

There are two slightly divergent interpretations about the origin of the name of the temple. One story is that a master sculptor was at work carving one portion of the temple. Unknown to him, his long-lost son who had run away from home in his childhood had also been engaged as a sculptor to work on another part of the temple. One day the master sculptor who was passionate, possessive, and proud of his work heard the echo of a hammer in another part of the temple. Up until then the younger sculptor's work had perfectly synchronized with the older man's, but on that fateful day, there was a discordant sound of a hammer, and the master sculptor realized that someone else was working on his beloved temple. In a fit of rage, he swung his hammer in the direction of the sound and the hammer went flying through the air and hit the young sculptor who died instantly. When the older man ran to see what kind of damage his hammer had done, he saw his own son dead on the ground. The father was so filled with grief and remorse at the accidental killing of his son that the temple construction was abandoned, leaving the temple unfinished. Another version suggests that the rivalry between the father and son (as both were sculptors) was so intense that when the son mocked his father saying that he would never be able to complete the work, the father swung his hammer at him, and the young man was struck dead. Shocked by his own deed, the father gave up the work and so the temple remained unfinished; the son's words were prophetic in a tragic way.

Many such stunning edifices that lie scattered from North Tamilakam all the way down to the tip of the peninsula below the flowing Thamirabarani date from the early Pandya period, and although many of them were renovated by the Cholas and later the Vijayanagar rulers and the Nayaks, the firm stamp of the Pandya builders cannot be missed. Of the numerous Pandya temples scattered around the region, many structures were commissioned and initially constructed during various periods of Pandya rule with characteristically Pandya-style architecture. This included a towering vimana or the roof above the deities, and huge entrance gopura or gateways as well as pillared halls called mandapas where gatherings would occur and music and dance performances as well. The later Pandya rulers post the Chola resurgence adopted many Chola-style elements. The grandest Vaishnavite shrine, called Bhooloka Vaikuntam or Heaven on Earth, is the Ranganathaswamy temple in Srirangam, a small green island on the Kaveri a few kilometres from Tiruchirapalli, which was Pandya in origin, but has distinct Nayak and Vijayanagar inputs with each dynasty contributing to its architectural magnificence. The foremost of the 108 Divya Desam, the holiest of Vaishnavite shrines, the approach to this splendorous temple is deceptively simple. One would think that the meandering village road would lead to sleepy hamlets secured on the Kaveri's banks but instead one drives into a giant complex of gateways and gopurams, twenty-one in all, each enclosed by giant fort-like walls. Benoy K. Behl says, 'the concentric arrangement of walls around the sacred centre is a *mandala* which expresses the essential structure of the world. From the innermost point where the Divine is seen as all pervasive... All that there is in one's life and in the world is seen as emanating from the still centre of the cosmos....' The stupendous sculpture of Ranganathaswamy reclining on Adisesha, the divine serpent, moves devotees who constantly throng the sanctum sanctorum. The goddess Ranganayaki, his consort, is housed in another beautiful shrine within the complex. A charming legend speaks of a Muslim princess who came across an image of Ranganathaswamy and became so enamoured of the Lord that she travelled to Srirangam from far away and died on the steps of the temple. She came to be known as Thuluka Nachiyar, and her image is painted on one of the walls of the temple complex.

Similarly, the beautiful Vatapathrasayi temple at Srivilliputhur, another temple that is part of the 108 sacred Vaishnavite shrines, whose sacredness is glorified in the Vaishnavite canon *Nalayira Divya Prabandham* is of Pandya origin. Here is where the poet-saint Andal lived and worshipped her lord Vishnu, and ultimately married him, or as the legend goes, merged with him in Srirangam. Here too, the distinct Dravidian style of architecture showcases stunning murals and paintings, as well as artistic elements from later periods after the Pandyas. There are Pandya, Chola, Nayak, and Vijayanagar inscriptions found in this temple. The Nelliappar temple in Tirunelveli district is another unique example of the amalgam of diverse styles of Dravidian art and architecture. Founded by the Pandya rulers with its unique musical pillars, this temple was further built up by later dynasties.

No writing on the marvellous temples, caves, and structures in and around Madurai can be complete without mention of the magnificent Meenakshi Sundareswarar temple. This is not only a symbol of the Madurai of today, but it has stood for centuries from its legendary origins to its popular present-day appeal, through the vicissitudes of time, withstanding the ravages of war and occupation, rebuilt many times and yet standing tall with its towering gopurams right from the Pandya period through the Nayak era (when a lot of restoration and rebuilding took place), all the way down to the nineteenth century. In the context of this temple a story must be told: the British collector of Madurai, Rous Peter, was the temple's administrator between 1812 and 1828. Although a Christian, he had great respect for the Goddess. He was also very popular and well liked in the city and the nobility of his character earned him the name of Peter Pandian. Every day as he crossed the temple on the way to his office, he would get down from his horse, remove his hat and shoes, and would go past the temple barefoot, bowing his head in obeisance to the deity. One night, there was a very heavy downpour, and the Vaigai was in spate. The collector who was asleep in his bungalow was awakened by the sound of anklets and found that a small girl, dressed in silk and gold jewels, was urgently but smilingly beckoning to him. 'Follow me, Peter, come this way,' she said. Bewildered, he followed her, running outside into the pouring rain. When he turned back to look, his entire house had collapsed and was washed away, and the little barefoot girl had vanished. He believed that it was the Goddess Meenakshi who saved him. He donated a beautiful pair of padukas (footwear) to the Goddess, encrusted with rubies and diamonds for the barefoot girl who had rescued him. He settled in Madurai after retirement as he never wished to be far from his deity. As per his request, he was buried in the churchyard that faced the temple so that he would always be able to worship her. To this day, during the temple's Chitra festival, Rous Peter's padukas known as Peter Padukam are placed in front of the Goddess as part of worship.

As Meenakshi's prominence grew, especially from the Vijayanagar and Nayak times, the main deity, Chokkanathar or Shiva the mendicant, transformed into Kalyana Sundareswarar, Meenakshi's handsome bridegroom, and came down to marry her. Her magnificence soon became Madurai's magnet, and as the empress goddess, offerings and rituals are to her first and only then to Shiva.

Every visit to this complex structure, which is a mini universe of commerce, religiosity, and cultural expression, yields new discoveries. From the Pudu (new) Mandapam built by Thirumalai Nayak in the seventeenth century, and the thousand-pillared mandapam built by Ariyanatha Mudali (a great draw for tourists and worshippers) to accounts of several vanished murals that were grossly painted over, there are many stories to be told. Beginning with its legendary origins, and the tale of a self-manifested or swayambhu lingam in the kadamba forests, the temple has grown steadily over the centuries; its present-day manifestation has been built under the patronage of several dynasties, from the Pandyas and the Cholas down to the Vijayanagar and Nayak kings. The temple area sprawls over 17 acres of land today and is enclosed by a wall that is 847 feet in length and 797 feet in breadth. As mentioned earlier, this temple, dedicated to Shiva, was called Thirualavai, Alavai being another old name for Madurai. The Shaivite saint Thirugnanasambandar composed and sang a hymn about Shiva residing in the Alavai temple after his triumphant refutation of Jain beliefs.

Here, in this chapter, only the early establishment of the temple undertaken by the Pandyas is looked at, as much of the temple's grandeur came from later structures and edifices, with each dynasty that succeeded the Pandyas building additional shrines as well as prakara (the outer pathways enclosing the inner sanctums) and adding to the friezes and edifices. The details of the building of many of these are carved on inscriptions within the temple complex. About 70 per cent of the structures within the temple are of the Vijayanagar and Nayak periods. During the early Pandya rule, there were multiple edifices, carvings, inscriptions, and bronzes across Tamil Nadu, but there is not a single Early Pandya inscription within the current precincts of the Meenakshi temple. The bronzes currently in the temple are of a much later period, of the fourteenth century, suggests Vedachalam. However, there are three sculptures that are discernibly of the early Pandya period.

As far as the temple itself is concerned, the assumption is that in the early years the temple is likely to have conformed to the basic Vastu and Agamic strictures and would have probably had the garbhagriha, the ardha mandapam, the kitchens, the yaga salai, and the tank. An indirect literary reference in *Maduraikanchi* indicates that processional deities went around the temple streets even in these early times, which suggests that multiple rituals of worship were going on inside the temple. One aspect that seems persistent in Madurai, right up to the present day, is the communal fervour and public participation in these street festivals, particularly in areas around the temple. Community involvement added layers to ritual worship and bolstered the importance of the temple which always was a hub of socio-economic activity and artistic creation, offering sustenance to the many hundreds of people involved in its ecosystem. K. V. Raman mentions an inscription in the Meenakshi temple which states that a land grant was given to a musician as life pension or jivita. He was given the title of Pandya Vaadyamaaryar according to the inscription. Raman points out that another inscription gives details of eleven musicians who were experts in playing different instruments and they too were honoured by the temple administration.

There is a story that Thirugnanasambandar, the early proponent of the Bhakti movement, who came to Madurai to cure the Pandya king of an illness and convert him to Saivism from Jainism at the secret behest of his queen Mangayarkarasi, met the queen at the temple and guaranteed her that he would heal the king and bring him back to the fold. It was as if the backdrop of the temple provided the much-needed reassurance that the queen was looking for. It had also by then become a bustling and popular place of worship.

Dr Porchelvi Jeyaprakash, a scholar of Tamil literature, said that Thevaram poems of Thirugnanasambandar which mention the temple, when it was probably only a brick structure in the seventh century, reiterate that Shiva lives there. Dr C. Santhalingam, archaeologist and epigraphist, who is the secretary of the Pandya Nadu Centre for Historical Research in Chennai, corroborates this and says it would have certainly been only a brick structure built with lime and mortar when Sambandar sang 'this Alavayil is the place where Annal (Shiva) resides with Angayarkanni'. The rough extended translation of the Thevaram *padhigam*, refers to Shiva as Kabali who lives in 'naan maada koodal', the junction or pavilion of four roads (which is Madurai), in a temple that has long and tall compound walls. And this is the place, the poem goes, that houses he who is an ascetic and prefers to live in a cremation ground. It appears that the main deity at this time, Shiva, was known as Chokkar, or Chokkanathar, and Angayarkanni was the name of the Devi, his spouse.

However, despite the firm establishment and patronage of Tamil by the Pandya kings during the centuries of Pandya rule, in the Nayak period, the Telugu-speaking rulers who had an affinity to Sanskrit changed the Tamil appellations of these deities to Meenakshi and Sundareswar; and of course, these are the names that are now more popular. And with Meenakshi's sway overriding that of her husband's, the temple itself came to be known as Madurai Meenakshi Kovil.

We must not forget that Madurai is a city of festivals and with cultural traditions dating back centuries, many of them had their roots in the Pandya era and continue in some form or the other even in the present day. The famed Jallikattu or bull-taming festival in January, for instance, is an event that is rooted in tradition and is controversial but continues to be prevalent. In popular lore it is suggested that the sport is more than 2,000 years old, a fact that is sometimes disputed. The sheer strength of native bulls such the Kangeyam Pulikulam, Malai Madu, are displayed to the pride of their breeders and owners, and the bulls are pitted against human opponents who hold on to the animal's hump and try to tame it. Brutal injuries are often inflicted on the bulls and have given rise to vehement opposition and calls to ban the sport for its barbarism and cruelty from animal rights activists and others. However, it is emblematic of a display of prowess, of human control over animal, and many Tamils see it as a matter of local cultural pride. The Chithirai festival in April is a semi-religious festival which also attracts people from the villages outside the city.

The Madurai Nayak kings were instrumental in establishing the Chithirai festival, after the time of the Madurai Sultanate. The festival is one of the Madurai temple's biggest annual events. In the early years it was the reiteration of royal power sanctified by divinity, almost a reclaiming of identity after Muslim rule. Public participation is exuberant with the narrow streets milling with devotees, and processions and pageantry all celebrating the wedding of the Goddess to her beloved Shiva (called Somasundara). Meenakshi's brother Vishnu as Azhagar also arrives with pomp and splendour to participate in the wedding.

Just as these festivals are unique to the city, there are objects that reflect an 'only in Madurai' flavour. There are specialities like the *Jigar Thanda*, a popular cooling drink widely available in the bustling shopping areas, made of almond resin, khoya, and sarsaparilla or nannari as it is called. Its origins are unknown except that there is a possibility that with the Madurai region being a major seafaring and trading route, the drink could have come from the coastal regions where there were a lot of traders from other places, as the Jigar Thanda are not Tamil words. Then there is malli poo idli (soft as jasmine idli), bun parotta, textiles such as the specially dyed kattuchayam and sungudi saris, brought in by the Saurashtrian communities that migrated to Madurai under the patronage of Thirumalai Nayak in the seventeenth century. These are some of the things that are exclusive to Madurai. Known as thoonga nagaram, the city that never sleeps, its vibrancy is reflected in the effervescence of its people as much as it is in the fact that many of the activities—social, commercial, religious, and the festive happen without pause, rolling from day into night. This distinct identity has been nurtured and cherished by local people who feel the weight of their city's unique heritage and relay it to outsiders with obvious pride.

To understand this region's Tamils, it is necessary to situate the area's history in the generations of Pandya rule—from the banks of the Vaigai to the fertile lands of the Thamirabarani river deep in the south—and to comprehend its impact on the Tamil people of this terrain.

Chapter 10

No Faintness in their Hearts

They fear evils that other men fear, but never sleep over them
Give their lives for honour, will not touch a gift of whole worlds
If tainted

Ilam Peruvaluti, *Purananuru 182*

DURING THE CENTURIES OF SUSTAINED RULE OF THE PANDYAS, TAMIL language, art, architecture, literature, and music saw a budding followed by a great flowering. Right from the pre-Christian centuries of the Sangam age, and all the way down to the mediaeval era and beyond—a span of 1,500 plus years—these people left a strong mark on the civilizational standards of the Tamils. The early chieftains, and later, the kings of the Pandya dynasty were warriors and rulers who were often individually named and heralded in fable, in literature, in inscriptions, and in art, but what is remarkable is that there is great evidence of an originality of approach and a pioneering way of thinking sustained over several generations and this can only be wrought by a collective of people—albeit at the behest of a king or kings—who had the imagination and spirit to build small towns, new capitals, ports, create systems of taxation and land grants, organize water supply, bring about agricultural transformation and, among other things, generate a substantial legacy of temple building, patronizing and encouraging multiple cultural activities, and early on, installing a strong structure of administration as well as intricate arrangements for the dispensation of justice.

If we look at the origins and early stories of the fabled Pandya rulers, their descent from the moon is touted in panegyrical literature as Nilakanta Sastri says in his detailed account of the dynasty. C. Sivaramamurti, the renowned art historian, epigraphist, and museology expert writing on Kazhugumalai, the Pandya rock-cut shrine, says there is a mention even in Kalidasa's *Raghuvamsa* of a Pandya prince who is one of the suitors of Indhumathi, a celestial maiden who later marries into the clan of the emperor Raghu of the dynasty of Rama. This prince is described as of a 'dark complexion, wearing a bright and long pearl necklace and with his body smeared with red fragrant sandal paste looking like a dark red mountain covered with red laterite and with a sparkling stream running down its slopes....' In the same text, the Pandya ruler's might is described as such that even the mighty Ravana is said to have sought peace with him rather than face him as an enemy. The more realistic (and possibly earliest reference) is still the mention in the Ashoka edicts although, as Sastri says, there is no evidence of the Mauryan kingdoms expanding into Pandya territory. Y. Subbarayalu says that the antiquity of the first Tamil kings can be traced back to several hundreds of years before the Common Era with Greek and Latin accounts referring to the rulers of Lymyrike or Damirike, and a reference is also made in the *Periplus of the Erythrean Sea* to the Chera kings of Kerala and the Pandya king in Madurai.

Apart from such stories and legends of Madurai's origins, some of the earliest historical detail that can be found are references in the *Periplus* which speaks of the many seaports of South Asia including the ones in Tamilakam. The riches of the Pandya kingdom, of which Madurai was the capital, are described in the *Periplus*: an abundance of spices, diamonds, precious stones, and silks, much like the description in the *Shilappadikaram*. Fragments from *Indica*, the work of Megasthenes (350–290 BCE), the Greek ambassador of Selecus Nikator who visited the court of Chandragupta Maurya, the great Gupta ruler, mention the Pandya kingdom. Megasthenes is referenced in the works of later writers like Arrian, who was also Greek, and wrote largely about the expeditions of Alexander the Great into Asia. Arrian finds the work of Megasthenes quite reliable although historians like Strabo and Pliny the Elder in the first century CE dispute some of his more fantastical accounts. Some twentieth century scholars like E. A. Schwanbeck and J. W. McCrindle have also found his work largely credible and have worked on translations of the fragments. While Megasthenes has written of Pataliputra, the capital of Chandragupta Maurya, of the Punjab region, and the plains of the Ganges and Yamuna rivers, he has also specifically mentioned the Pandyan kingdom ruled by a 'daughter of Herakles'. Whether the name Herakles is generic, or linked to the Greek Hercules, these ancient travellers seem to have nevertheless found this a convenient appellation. Megasthenes's fragments as made available by McCrindle states:

> The Pandean nation is governed by females and their first queen is said to be the daughter of Herakles... Herakles begat a daughter in India whom he called Pandaia. To her he assigned that portion of India which lies to southward and extends to the sea, while he distributed, the people subjected to the rule into 365 villages, giving orders that one village

should each day bring to the treasury, the royal tribute, so that the queen may always have the assistance of those men…

Apparently this Pandaia was a much-favoured daughter. The account further states that 'the sovereignty (of the land) Herakles entrusted her, was called after her name (sic), and she received from the hands of her father 500 elephants, a force of cavalry 4000 strong. And another of infantry consisting of about 130,000 men'. The account by Megasthenes speaks of sea pearls and other gems that Herakles obtained for his daughter in these lands and from these seas.

Indirect references in datable records such as in the Ashoka edicts also refer to the many south Indian kingdoms which were obviously outside of the Mauryan empire. Madurai as the Pandya capital is mentioned in the second and thirteenth edicts, which also includes the names of the Chola, Satiyaputa, and Keralaputa kings and territories.

As mentioned in the earlier chapter, the references to these early Pandya rulers are largely in the Sangam poems. The Chera rulers are mentioned frequently, and there are many references to the muventar, the three rulers of the monarchies of the south, and as Sastri puts it, there were also 'a number of minor principalities ruled over by petty warrior chieftains, vying with one another in the arts of war and peace'. These chieftains feature in many of the poems and many of them are precursors to the later Pandyas. It must be kept in mind that the production of Sangam literature extended over several generations and, according to Sastri, 'we may assign a length of say, 150 to 200 years for the period represented in these works.' He also points out that the kind of references made in Sangam texts like *Maduraikanchi* to ports, ships, and merchandise of various kinds like pepper, wine, silk, and pearls are also mentioned by the mariners, the geographers, and voyagers from distant climes in various records testifying to the veracity of these accounts.

Poetry may swerve from fact, and indeed, most of us are conditioned to look for factual proof of historicity, but these poems, touching as they do on untiring heroes, warrior kings, strong women, and secret lovers, do draw from a cache of community memories, and even if the poems do not always represent a specific ruler, they represent not just ideal attributes but possibly expectations and likely some realistic qualities evident in these rulers albeit exaggerated by a poetic imagination. Consider this:

Great king
You shield your men from ruin,

...And your kingdom
Is an unfailing harvest
Of victorious wars

—From *Pattitrupattu*

There is a valorization of might and magnanimity, and notions of honour and kingly courage are clearly described in these poems. Apart from such literary references whose verisimilitude can be questionable, more concrete (if confusing) material is available in copper plates and inscriptions, but it is still all only slivers of information. As K. V. Raman points out, in spite of a very long record of unbroken rule, historical detail of the Pandya rulers is paradoxically among the briefest that is available today. However, the significant contributions made by Iravatham Mahadevan in the reading of the Brahmi inscriptions which are all around the Pandya country have enabled us to discover and comprehend names of several villages, towns, kings, chieftains, merchant classes, and dynasties, adding to the knowledge of the period.

The earliest mention of a Pandya king in an inscription is that of Nedunchezhiyan in Tamil Brahmi. This is of the second century BCE in Mankulam and is inscribed in the caves used by Jain monks as elaborated in earlier chapters. His name is clearly spelled out and, apparently, he generously donated these rock shelters to the Jain monks. There are two inscriptions in Mankulam that mention him. One of the inscriptions, as described earlier, mentions Katalan Valuttiyan, an officer who donated this cave on the king's behalf, and Raman points out that the suffix 'valutti' is a 'characteristic appellation of the Pandyas'. What this means is that there was a clear affiliation between this king and Jainism as he excavated beds in the caves for the use of Jain monks. There is a debate among scholars if this same Nedunchezhiyan was also a Sangam age Pandya king known as Thalaialanganathu Seruvenra Nedunchezhiyan as he won a legendary battle—Seruvenra—meaning one who defeated his enemies, who overcame hostility—at Thalaialanganam. V. Vedachalam in his book *Parakrama Pandyapuram*, jointly authored with M. Chandiramurthy, suggests that the reference in Mankulam is to this same king. Another king of this early period is Palyagasalai Mudukudumi Peruvazhudi. The Sangam text *Maduraikanchi* mentions a Palsalay Mudukudumi Peruvazhudi, a slightly altered version of the name but is nevertheless thought to be the same person, and he is reputed to have performed several thousand yagnas or Vedic sacrifices and hence was known as pala yaga salai, that is, 'he of many sacrificial spaces'. Sivaramamurti has described Mudukudumi Peruvazhudi as 'a great conqueror and a liberal patron of literature'. Sangam literature says that these kings wore neem flowers as garlands and this flower was decreed the royal flower, while the royal emblem of the Pandya kings was a pair of fish. Apart from specific information on Mudukudumi, several early Pandya rulers names are available to us such as Palyanai Selkuzhu Kuttuvan, Pazhaiyan Maran, Pandyan Arivudai Nambi and others with fascinating appellations such as Pandyan Chitra Madathu Thunjiya Nanmaran—'the king who slept in the pavilion with beautifully painted murals' and Pandyan Velli Ambalathu Thunjiya Per Vazhuthi, 'the king who slept in a shrine of silver'.

More important epigraphical information has surfaced in the Velvikkudi grant, which is a series of copper plates probably of the eighth century CE (currently housed in the British Museum in London) recording the grants of land and other details of kings and their deeds mentioned in general terms. The grant itself was made during the rule of Parantaka Nedunjadayan who ruled for fifty years from 768 CE to 815 CE. They were in all probability issued during the year 770 CE. These multiple copper plates are held together by a thin copper ring. They are inscribed in Sanskrit and Tamil. The Sanskrit portions are written in Grantha script and the Tamil in vatteluthu and are a distinct source of information on a great many of the early Pandya kings, battles won, and grants made. Another set of copper plates, the small and large Chinnamanur plates belonging to a slightly later age, also refer to names of rulers. The Velvikkudi grant mentions Palyagasalai Mudukudumi as the original donor of the lands of Velvikkudi village. The gift of land, according to the copper plate, was to be enjoyed 'by the donee and his descendants for long, *nidu bhukti*, before the Kalabhra interregnum at the end of which came the Pandya restoration under Kadungon,' according to Sastri.

The copper plate with Palyagasalai's name suggests that he was an ancestor of Parantaka Nedunjadayan. There is an interesting story that was narrated by Subramanian that he heard from Dr Poongundran, senior epigraphist and scholar of Tamil history, who said Palyagasalai Mudukudumi had donated huge tracts of land, and a village called Velvikkudi (its present-day location has not been identified) close to Cholavandan near Madurai to Korkai Kizhan Narkottran. When the Kalabhra rulers took over southern Tamilakam, all the land grants were annulled, including that of Narkottran, and lands were seized from all those who possessed them. This is also mentioned in the Velvikkudi plate and the Kalabhras are referred to as 'kali arasar', a pejorative term meaning 'degenerate rulers'. After the extended Kalabhra rule in Tamilakam which lasted roughly between 300 CE and 550 CE, a Pandya ruler Kadungon overthrew them and re-established the Pandya dynasty in Tamil Nadu. According to Poongundran, one of the descendants of Korkai Kizhan Narkottran called Narsingan alias Kamakaani approached the king Nedunjadayan Parantaka and petitioned for the return of Velvikkudi village to him and his kin. The king was probably sceptical about the claim and insisted that Kamakaani show him proof and to produce the record that Kamakaani's ancestor had indeed been given the grant of Velvikkudi from Palyagasalai Mudukudumi, the king's ancestor. The village chief or nattar found mention of this in one of the plates and the king ordered the return of the land and a new copper plate was issued to Kamakaani with the details of the boundaries of the village and beyond. The story goes that this Kamakaani generously distributed the newly regained land to many of his relatives.

In his book *Pandya Nattu Varalatru Murai Samuga Nilaviyal*, Vedachalam says, 'The early Pandya dynasty, from the days of the king Kadungon, became powerful in stages and metamorphosed into a puissant kingdom by the end of the 9th century CE. The boundaries of the Pandya kingdom widened spectacularly. The conquests of the Chera, the Chola, the Pallava and the Kongu Nadu territories led to economic prosperity. The boom in agriculture and commerce, and burgeoning religious activities stamped the Pandya rulers with authority. Material prosperity, a strong army and the fine tuning of the administration resulted in large agrarian *nadus* being brought under the control of the rulers.'

Before we look at the record and details of specific rulers, it must be borne in mind that historians describe the Pandya dynasties as divided between various time periods. The first or early phase is roughly between 575 CE and 985 CE. This was the period when the dynasty firmly established itself and before the Chola dynasty started asserting themselves. However, one early Chola king, Parantaka Chola (r. 907–955 CE), defeated the then early Pandya ruler Rajasimha II (r. 900–920 CE). The second phase, which was from 985 CE to 1070 CE, was the period when the Pandya territory came under Chola rule, and their lands were reduced vastly to a mandalam or territory of the Chola empire. The middle Pandyas, 1070 CE to 1190 CE, continued under the yoke of the Chola rulers. In the fourth phase, the Pandya rulers re-asserted themselves and freed themselves from the Chola yoke and this period is roughly between 1190 CE and 1271 CE. In the final phase, for about a hundred years from 1271 CE to 1368 CE, there were periods when the dynasty was strong and then came the final decline.

The Velvikkudi copper plates speak of Kadungon, one of the early Pandya kings who, as previously noted, along with the Pallava king Simhavishnu, is credited with having driven out the Kalabhras from the Tamil country.

Kadungon was said to have defeated many petty chieftains and destroyed 'the bright cities of unbending foes'. The Velvikkudi inscription describes him as 'a resplendent sun (emerging) from the dark clouds of the Kalabhras'. Sastri says that a statement in the Tamil part of the inscription clearly indicates that he had an active role in putting an end to the Kalabhras interregnum and 'bringing about the restoration of his own dynasty, as he is said to have abolished by his strength the claim of others to the earth and established his own claim on a firm basis. Subbarayalu reminds us that before Kadungon, some details of the king Cendan Kutran and his son Cendan who were probably Kalabhras are available in the Pulankurichi inscription, including the fact that they had their political centre at Madirai or Madurai before Kadungon took over. Another source of information about the Kalabhras is from the Pulankurichi inscriptions, one of which talks about two kings called Cendan Kutran and Cendan. It is in a transitional script and is dated to 500 CE. Subbarayalu says that it 'is clear that Cendan Kutran and his son were fairly big kings ruling over an extensive territory and some sort of official establishment. His political centre was at Madirai or Madurai where the Pandyas of the Kadungon line start ruling from the early seventh century. So, it is likely that Cendan Kutran and his family members who preceded Kadungon belonged to the Kalabhra family who were later overpowered and replaced by Kadungon.'

Sastri's account of the Pandya kingdom although complex and even turgid in places mixes evidence from inscriptions with corroborating literary references and is quite possibly the most expansive source of information on this dynasty. Drawing from his work, it is possible to build a chronology of these kings, which, unlike the Chola kings, is still somewhat meagre in detail. Kadungon was succeeded by his son Maravarman Avani Choolamani who ruled from 600 CE to 625 CE. This king continued the work of his father and maintained the kingdom as he inherited it although he did not add much to it. Again, there is some information on this king which only comes from the Velvikkudi plates which indicate that he had enormous wealth including 'an elephant brigade which defeated all kinds of enemies'. From his time onwards, Pandya kings tended to use the coronation titles of Maravarman and Chadayavarman.

There is a little more detail about his successor Chezhiyan Senthan or Jayantavarman, who ruled from around 625 CE to 640 or 650 CE. Sastri says his rule may have extended even beyond these years. He has been described as a brave warrior whose other name was Vanavan, indicating perhaps a victory over the neighbouring Cheras. He is also known to have established a just and temperate rule. The Velvikkudi grant praises him as 'the king of kings', 'a king who ruled the earth without blemish', and 'the Chezhiyan who wielded the bow and arrow and decimated the murderous elephant brigade of the enemies'. A stone inscription of Chezhiyan Senthan can be seen in a rock-cut Siva temple in a village called Malaiadikurichi, near Sankarankovil in Tirunelveli district.

Maravarman Arikesari was the next king—a powerful monarch who ruled for fifty years until 700 CE or so—and went by many names: Pandyan Ninraseer Nedumaran, Koon (hunchback) Pandyan, and others. That the period of his rule extended to fifty years is borne out by the discovery of two lithic inscriptions in vatteluthu which clearly attest to his regnal years. Nedumaran also had many birudas or honorific titles and was the ruler who expanded Pandya territory, coming frequently into conflict with the rising Pallava dynasty, and more specifically with Mahendravarman. He also fought the Cheras and the Cholas and is said to have won twenty-five battles. Information about him not only comes from the Velvikkudi plates, but also from other copper plates such as the Sinnamanur plates. Vedachalam, in his recent Tamil book, *Pandyan Ninraseer Nedumaran*, co-authored with A. Kalavathy, on Nedumaran, talks about the Kooram and Sinnamanur copper plates which also mention Nedumaran's disputes with the Pallava king Narasimhavarman. This battle took place in a village called Sankai Mangai. Vedachalam suggests that in the several battles that took place between the Pandyas and Pallavas, Nedumaran must have won only at Sankai Mangai. The Pallavas must have become victorious later and stopped the advance of Nedumaran. Nedumaran's rule extended from Madurai and Pudukkottai to Ramanathapuram, Tirunelveli, and right up to Kanyakumari.

It is a commonly held view that Nedumaran alias Koon Pandyan converted to Jainism and then became a Shaivite again under the influence of Thirugnanasambandar, the Shaivite saint and poet who was said to have cured him of his hunch (after which he came to be known as Sundara Pandyan or Beautiful Pandyan). Sambandar is also said to have healed the king of a chronic stomach ailment. He had been invited to Madurai to cure the king at the behest of his queen Mangayarkarasi (a Chola princess who was the daughter of Manimudi Chola) and a minister called Kulachiraiyar. Vedachalam and Kalavathy however say that there is no reference in Sambandar's poems to suggest that he had cured the king of his hunch or even of the fact that the king was a Jaina first. However, many accounts refer to the constant dialectical duels held between the two faiths across the kingdom at this time, and the frequent outbreak of clashes between the two communities. Some scholars, however, doubt that there were extreme points of violence between the two faiths such as the notion of texts being burned, practitioners being tortured and put to death, etc., but agree that Jainism significantly declined from around this period.

Nedumaran's son, Kocchadayan, also known as Ranadhiran, succeeded his father and waged bitter wars against his neighbours. He had titles like Vanavan, Sembiyan, and Solan suggesting that he gained victories over the Chera and Chola kings of that time. He subdued and attacked the Marathas in the city of Mangalapuram which is likely to be modern-day Mangalore. This king's successor was called Maravarman Rajasimha, and his name is mentioned in the larger Chinnamanur plates and in the Velvikkudi plates. The Madras Museum plates call him Pallavabhanjana, and the Sanskrit portion of the Velvikkudi grant mentions that he defeated Pallavamalla who is said to have fled from battle. In a highly ornate Tamil portion of the grant, it has been mentioned that he won a series of battles and defeated Pallavamalla who was deprived of numerous elephants and horses during these pitched battles. So, there is little doubt that he was a contemporary and opponent of Pallavamalla. Also, territorial expansion was steadily happening with references in these plates of this Pandya king 'renewing Kudal, Vanji and Koli'. This is a reference to the capitals of the Pandyas, Cholas, and Cheras, so the power of Rajasimha was very great indeed. The king is said to have crossed the Kaveri and brought about the subjugation of Malakongam which is in the modern Trichy-Thanjavur region. The Malava king who was reduced to subjugation gave his daughter in marriage to the Pandya king. From the Malava country Rajasimha proceeded to Pandikodumudi where he 'worshipped the lotus feet of Pasupati and gave away with great pleasure heaps of gold and lustrous gems'. This perhaps means that the conquests of the Pandya king extended up to Kodumudi. We also learn that he contracted a relationship with the Ganga king. The details of this transaction are given later in the Velvikkudi plates. The various copper plates that have been mentioned have a wealth of detail and are credibly dated, so the authenticity of the information is acceptable. This king is said to have performed many yagas—Gosahasras, Hiranyagarbhas, and Tulabharas, and to have donated generously to the Brahmin priests who conducted all these rituals, much of it to offer them succour from financial woes.

There is a great deal of discussion about the historicity of the names and titles, the battles fought and a fair amount of detail on the administration of these early Pandya rulers in Sastri's book *The Pandya Kingdom*, wherein he draws from a lot from other experts—historians and epigraphists like the pioneer Venkayya, who wrote prolifically on south Indian history and studied hundreds of inscriptions in Tamil Nadu. While the focus of Sastri's account is on epigraphy, he draws amply from literary sources as well. The discovery of multiple lithic inscriptions after Sastri's time and the valuable contributions of later epigraphists like Mahadevan and Nagaswamy have added much richness to the existing material, adding to a greater and more layered understanding of this dynasty.

We find that kingship was passed on through sons and grandsons during these early Pandya periods with the direct bloodline predominating for several generations. For instance, the king that succeeded Rajasimha was his son Parantaka Nedunjadayan, by the Malava queen, and he was the donor of the Velvikkudi plates and issued the Chinnamanur and Seevaramangalam copper plate grants as well as the Madras Museum plates. He was a powerful king in the mould of his ancestor Nedumaran. This king's numerous names on inscriptions in Trichy, Kazhugumalai, and Yanaimalai refer to him as Jatila, Parantaka Nedunjadayan, and Varaguna Maharaja among other names. There is a lot more material available on Nedunjadayan unlike the earlier rulers, as his inscriptions are available from his third regnal year, the Velvikkudi one, to the forty-third year of his rule at Eravadi, and he probably reigned for nearly fifty years, between 766 and 815 CE. It was Parantaka Nedunjadayan Varaguna who excavated the Yoga Narasimha temple at Yanaimalai in 770 CE and the Tiruparankunram temple near Madurai, both of which stand as fine examples of early Pandya architectural styles. Of course, there were battles fought and victories won, but in addition, many of these rulers, particularly Nedumaran and Nedunjadayan, also fostered the growth of agriculture, established administrative structures, built numerous temples and in general were attuned to the welfare of their citizens. Nedunjadayan who was learned also had the title of Panditha Vatsalan.

However, battles and territorial acquisitions seem to have dominated the king's agenda and many inscriptions reflect this. For instance, even the smaller victories over local uprisings have been recorded such as the win over a local chief Ay Vel by Nedunjadayan in one of the Velvikkudi plates. Other interesting details that emerge from these inscriptions include the names of ministers who apparently had substantial powers in bestowing grants. For example, one of the inscriptions names someone called Marangari, who was also called Madurakavi and is often confused with the Vaishnavite saint Madurakavi as they are of the same period, and this minister (likely the uttaramantri or chief minister), built a stone temple for Vishnu and on its consecration made the gift of rich lands to the Brahmins near this temple. Again, it must be emphasized that this Madurakavi is not likely to be the Vaishnavite Azhwar of the same name and period and most historians are agreed about that. Nedunjadayan's patronage saw the excavation of several well-known rock-cut temples such as the Ladan temple and the Yoga Narasimha temple of Yanaimalai which are of this period.

When Madurakavi died around 770 CE, his brother Maran Eyinan became the uttaramantri and made additions to the Vishnu temple that his brother had built. Curiously, a host of other members of the same family seem to have been given prominent positions in Nedunjadayan's courts reminding us that a predilection to nepotism in the corridors of power is not a new phenomenon.

Sastri suggests that the military exercises and expansion programmes of the king brought a lot more permanent territory to the Pandyas. The Madras Museum Plates speak of unnamed enemies as well as famed warriors with titles like Adigan of the Bright Lance who was aided by the Pallavas and the Kerala forces in his battle to contain the growing aggression of this king. Sivaramamurti says that an inscription in Kazhugumalai mentions Nedunjadayan's 'conquest of Malainadu, and his destruction of Ariviyurkottai and Karunanadan, a member of the Ay family of chieftains who were friendly with the kings of Venad.' Venad is south Travancore and apparently this king also captured Vilijnam which was great trade emporium. Nedunjadayan's territory extended well into Thanjavur, Coimbatore, and Salem districts.

The son of Nedunjadayan, Srimaran Srivallabha, who ascended the Pandya throne around 815 CE, and likely ruled till 862 CE, extended Pandya territory further, even up to Ceylon and had titles like Ekavira and Prachakrakolahala. The Sinnamanur plates mention his success over the Keralas, Simhalas, Pallava, and the Vallabha. The famed Sittanavasal cave paintings in Pudukkottai district near Madurai which are a testament to the genius of piety of the Jain monks may have been executed around this time. While Pallava and Pandya architectural forms are evident in these caves, an inscription states that under the patronage of the Pandya king Srimaran Srivallabha (c. 815–862 CE) Ilan Gautamanenum Madurai Asiriyan supervised the renovations and added a mukhamandapa. That is, a teacher or master craftsman from Madurai, thus explicitly declaring the provenance of the place. We shall discuss this later as we continue to explore the multifaceted genius of the Pandyas.

In 862 CE, Srimaran was succeeded by his son Varagunavarman II who faced a crushing defeat at the hands of the Pallava king Aparajita (mentioned in an earlier chapter) at the battle of Thirupurambiyam near Kumbakonam. The Pandya king, confident of a victory, wanted to take advantage of the declining Pallava power, and its ruler Aparajita. But Varagunavarman had obviously not bargained for an alliance of his enemies. The Pallava forces brought together a father and son who were Chola feudatories—Vijayalaya Chola and his son Aditya Chola—and the king of western Ganga called Prithvipati also joined them. The Udayendiram plates mention the tragic fall of this Ganga prince in battle, but his allies won, and legend has it that, shocked by such a resounding defeat, Varagunavarman became a monk. The decline of the Pandya dynasty began after this watershed battle. Varagunavarman also died childless, and the kingdom then went to his younger brother Sri Parantaka also known as Viranarayana Sadayan. The Sinnamanur plates, according to Sastri, have Sanskrit verses that carry some specific information about this king; that he captured a 'haughty' king called Ugra near Kharagiri together with his elephants 'whose tusks were reeking of the blood of opposing forces killed in battle', that this king endowed many agraharams and devasthanams and his queen Sri Vanavan Mahadevi resembled Lakshmi and Indrani, the consorts of Vishnu and Indra.

In 1958, in Dalavaipuram, another find of a copper plate provided more valuable information about many of these early Pandya kings. Apparently, the donor of this plate was Parantaka Viranarayana Sadayan, the younger brother of Varagunavarman and Srimaran's son, as mentioned above. It speaks about Kadungon and Jatila Parantaka and the many battles they won; it details in glorified terms that Srimaran Srivallabha won victories against the combined force of his enemies including the Cheras, the Cholas, the Kupakas, the Gangas, and the Kalingas. We learn that Varagunavarman continued to be king even during the time when these copper plates were issued by his brother Viranarayana. It is surmised that they jointly held the throne for some years. Interestingly, the copper plates mention Varagunavarman's devotion to Shiva and this zeal of the king was eulogized by the Shaivite saint Manikkavachakar, thereby possibly establishing the date for Manikkavachakar.

The last of the mediaeval Pandyas was the son of Parantaka Viranarayana, Rajasimha II, who ruled from 907 CE to around 931 CE. He was the donor of the larger Sinnamanur plates. He was defeated by Parantaka Chola who captured Madurai and unseated the Pandyas, putting a temporary end to five hundred odd years of continuous dynastic rule. Sivaramamurti says Parantaka Chola who defeated the combined forces of the Pandyas, and their allies, and conquered Madurai and parts of Si Lanka got the title of Maduraiyum—Ilamum. Rajasimha fled to Sri Lanka and then sought refuge in the Chera country. Significantly, and perhaps poignantly, he left behind his royal insignia in Sri Lanka.

Cholan Thalaikonda Veera Pandyan, meaning The One Who Had the Cholan's Head, ruled between 946 CE and 966 CE and as can be inferred from his title, he defeated the Cholas temporarily, but with the advent of Rajaraja Chola the Pandya kingdom was converted into a mere mandalam of the Chola kingdom.

Fast forward some years. With Kulottunga Chola, the king who ruled the Chola and Pandya regions between 1070 CE and 1120 CE, the Pandyas obtained a level of autonomy albeit under the gaze of the Chola king. After this time there was some restoration of lost Pandya glory with a line of kings and rulers, the Pandyas of the Second Empire, as Sastri calls them, whose fabled wars brought them wealth and glory with a decisive change in the power relationships between the Chola overlords and the Pandya feudatories. After Jatavarman Kulasekhara Pandyan ascended the throne in 1190 CE, 'from this time on till almost the end of the thirteenth century the power of the Pandyas attained a great strength and expanded as far north as Nellore and Cuddapah; a succession of able and truly distinguished rulers in the main line made this Second Empire a real power in the politics of South India in their age.' There are numerous inscriptions often carrying a profusion of names and cognomen, frequently of a contradictory and confusing nature (say several historians) which nevertheless offer strong evidence of the literary and artistic achievements of these Pandya kings. It is during Jatavarman's rule that a kind of renaissance of the Pandya rule occurred, and they shook off the yoke of Chola rule. Aspects of his son Maravarman Sundara Pandya's rule, which began around 1216 CE, are recorded in numerous inscriptions such as those found in Tirunelveli district which refer to his victorious campaigns against the Chola king during which he is said to have set fire to Thanjavur and Uraiyur and laid waste the surrounding countryside. There is a fascinating story about this king, victorious from battle, worshipping at the shrine of Nataraja of Chidambaram. Apparently, during this sojourn, he became overcome with emotion and vowed to return to his enemy the crown and kingdom he had lost. The vanquished Chola king and his son were brought before the victor.

They prostrated before him, and true to his word, he restored the kingdom to them as a religious donation. This event is recorded in one of his inscriptions and whether it was an act motivated by political compunctions or one of pure generosity, he 'raised himself and his country in the estimation of his contemporaries'. That the Chola king in later years again took up arms against Sundara Pandya is another story; the Chola ruler was again vanquished and left defenceless, losing everything, including his chief queen.

In addition to Jatavarman Sundara Pandyan, other Pandya rulers of note from this period include Maravarman Kulasekhara Pandya and Jatavarman Veera Pandyan (possibly his son). Interestingly, Marco Polo, the great Italian traveller who visited the Pandya kingdom during this time, speaks of 'five royal brothers' and 'five crowned kings'. Chinese sources who seem to have had diplomatic connections with 'Ma'bar' in 1280 also mention 'the five brothers who were Sultans' during this period. However, the main monarch seems to have been Maravarman Kulasekhara. After his death his two sons, Jatavarman Veera Pandyan and Jatavarman Sundara Pandyan, fought for the throne, signalling the tragic end of the Pandya dynasty. The two brothers had different mothers and apparently their rivalries not only weakened their control of the kingdom but embittered the last years of Kulasekhara Pandya and finally led to his murder. Malik Kafur, representing the Delhi ruler Alauddin Khilji, invaded Madurai in April 1311. Ostensibly he had come to assist Sundara Pandya in the fratricidal war that was raging. Wassaf, the Persian writer, and Amir Khusrau of Alauddin Khilji's court have accounts about the invasion from the north—by 1323, the Madurai Sultanate was established.

The Pandya kingdom's story sees a progressive decline from then onwards, and although these later rulers clung to some vestiges of power through the control of some meagre territory, they were all under the suzerainty of the sultanate and later the Vijayanagar kings. Driven further south by other expanding empires and controlling only some territory, the last of this dynasty's rulers continued till about the seventeenth century, after which they went into obscurity. The long centuries of steady rule were finally marred and wracked by internecine war and saw the dissolution of a power that had set the standard of civilization from the Sangam age onwards.

Chapter 11

Enterprise and Opulence: Aspects of Pandya Society

Since my eyes rejoiced to see the glory and the great doings
of the Pantiya kingdom I stopped here blessing the king.

Shilappadikaram

ALTHOUGH A REMARKABLE WORK OF THE IMAGINATION, THE *Shilappadikaram* is also valuable for its detailed and accurate descriptions of several aspects of the Madurai of early Pandya times. Prosperity clothed the city, creating a society that was affluent but hierarchical, caste-oriented, militaristic, and yet filled with opportunities. There were streets dedicated to the four castes, as well as a grain merchants' street, cloth merchants' street with bales piled high indicating a brisk trade, gold merchants' street with four kinds of gold, and tall mansions reaching the sky, streets of the rich, streets that had dwellings of courtesans and dancers, a street for musicians, for the makers of wheeled carriages and markets whose air was filled with the scent of spices. The poem's descriptions give us a glimpse of a layered social order and an economy that relied on a feudal structure of governance with the king as the sovereign lord and head of the social structure.

Other than the *Shilappadikaram,* texts like *Maduraikanchi,* another lengthy Sangam work of the third or fourth century CE ascribed to the poet Mankuti Marudan, also describe in detail the activities of the people in the streets, in the dwellings and in the courts. Through this one can glean that in the early Pandya days, a high level of enterprise, opulence, as well as a well-oiled social machinery supported the free functioning of an active commercial society with trade and agriculture as the mainstay. Creative expression was reflected in achievements in music, poetry, the performance arts, temple building, and in other arts that had a distinct Pandya signature. A description of the king's court in *Maduraikanchi* reflects the pomp and splendour of the early Pandya court.

In the audience hall rested the handsome Pandya. He wears only a single piece of clean starched cloth on his waist. Over it is clasped a jewelled belt. On his bare arms above the elbow, are armlets of pure gold beautifully wrought. On his broad shoulder, fragrant with sandal paste, is a priceless necklace of brilliant pearls besides a wreath of flowers. Around him stand a group of sturdy warriors, his trusted captain, heroes who have captured many a fortress, or slaughtered fierce elephants in battle, veteran chiefs whose coats of mail have been battered and bruised in many a fight. Actors and minstrels and the lute players display their skill in the presence of the monarch and receive chariots and elephants as presents.

The king had a group of people around him called kulus and ayams, all part of the king's entourage consisting of priests, physicians, astrologers, ministers, spies, and messengers. There are references to royal perfumers, dressers, heads of the elephant corps, and others. One Puram poem offers cautionary advice to the ruler saying that the effect of moderate taxes to replenish the royal treasury was far better than the ruler inflicting heavy taxation which would render him deeply unpopular.

The nearly 2,000 years of Pandya rule left behind some exceptional systems of administration and social order, details of which emerge largely from stray references in inscriptions and copper plates and, as mentioned above, from literary sources as well. In the Sangam poems which tend to valorize some early Pandya rulers, the anonymous poet of a Puram poem offers advice to the ruler.

> Although a monarch's power may seem to depend on his ferocious battle elephants, fleet of war horses, tall, bannered chariots, and fearless soldiers, it has its real foundation on justice. Therefore, be not partial to thy subjects, nor deal unjustly with strangers. Be valiant as the fierce sun, benevolent as the mild moon and generous as the clouds which shower rain so that there may be no poverty in thy land…therefore give alms freely to those who seek thy charity. Spend thy days joyfully drinking daily of cool and fragrant wine brought by Yavanas in their good ship…

This indicates, again, a society of high sophistication where although the ruler was the most powerful, poets and bards who often served as advisers could offer guidance to the ruler.

The king ruled with the assistance of his ministers and the main minister was called uttaramantri, prime minister. Another minister was known as mahasamantas, particularly in the reign of the king Jatila Parantaka. Matangajadhyaksa was the name of an officer in charge of elephants, and this is referenced in the Madras Museum plates. Other titles included Parantaka Virar and Tirumalai Virar—these were possibly references to those in charge of a cohort of soldiers or regiment. Marangari was the name of an officer who was skilled in battle, a poet and orator and served as a minister as well. 'The Five Great Assemblies' of the king included people's representatives, physicians, priests, ministers, and astrologers. The rulers also frequently recognized the courage and contributions of ordinary soldiers, and they were routinely honoured by the king for their bravery. Many fighters received endowments from the royal treasury in their name as is evident from the inscriptions on copper plates. These early Pandya rulers were generous patrons of the arts and encouraged both Sanskrit and Tamil.

The brisk trade with the West during the early Pandya centuries has been recorded by Greek and Roman writers. This trade was sustained and stable over a long period of time and contributed to the economic prosperity of both regions. Roman coins found in India date as far back as the first few decades of the Common Era from the time of the Roman emperors Augustus and Tiberius. From the Malabar coast in the west to the east coast, an abundance of Roman coins have been found belonging to the first and second century CE. Copper coins have also been discovered in Madurai in riverbeds and it has been suggested that a great number of them could have been used for trade among the Romans themselves. Strabo has said that a Pandya king sent an embassy to Rome. Pliny spoke of a 'King Pandion' and 'Madoura'. It is quite conceivable that Roman sailors and merchants spent months in the Pandya region, spending gold and silver while purchasing pearls and trinkets for the ladies of Rome. Madurai and Uraiyur were the chief markets from where pearls were exported, and the fisheries were located at places like Korkai. Pliny even complains in 70 CE that India drained Roman gold to the value of a million pounds 'giving back her own wares which are sold among us at fully a hundred times their cost'. Black gold, that is pepper, was greatly popular with these western nations and was a major source of revenue to Tamilakam. One of the names for pepper was yavanapriya, that is, beloved by the foreigners. Legend has it that when Rome was attacked by enemies, many of them would demand thousands of pounds of pepper as part of ransom arrangements.

Internal trade flourished in early Pandya times. *Maduraikanchi* refers to the trade in salt as a big business which was carried out by humble people living in small huts. Maduvellilai was an important salt-producing centre. Ships and carts loaded with salt, tamarind, and dried fish were carried across the region on wooden carts as well as on the backs of donkeys. Rice and cotton cloth were transported and sold to other regions. Streets of towns tended to be called by the names of the trades as mentioned above; for instance, vanikar theru, merchant street, had groceries, clothes, ornaments, and goods of all kinds. Kalamar and ulavar who were cultivators of wet and dry lands also had houses in the towns.

While many of the towns that were described in early literature like Madurai, Karur, and Poompuhar were fortified and prospered from trade including with that of the ancient Roman world, we must bear in mind that outside of these places there were numerous tribal and rural communities who were exposed to attacks from neighbouring rulers and chieftains as well as from marauding vagrant groups, so many of the poor in these towns suffered great hardship. Cattle thievery, crop burning, random killings, and destruction of village dwellings was not uncommon. A curious mix of extreme wealth and dire poverty seems to have been the order of the day during the first few hundred years of Pandya rule.

The kingdom as a whole was divided into the following major divisions—valanadu (fertile region), kurram (collection of villages), and grama (village). Mangalam, kudi, and ur were descriptors affixed to villages or grama. Gifts of land and indeed of whole villages to temples began in the early Pandya period and continued during the Chola period. Although the concept of Brahmadeya, the process or the granting of villages and large tracts of land to Brahmins, was a major feature of the Chola administration, this practice began in the Pandya period. Land not donated as dana or charitable contribution to temples was often given as Brahmadeya by the rulers. Obviously, the existing owners or tillers were either removed as owners or came under the jurisdiction of the new landlords. Rajan Gurukkal points out that earlier historians like Sastri, even when they recognized the possibility of a less than peaceful transfer of land from agriculturists to the new Brahmin landlords, rarely referred to any process of resistance. The new owners, not being agriculturists themselves, had to develop novel relationships with the original cultivators, and this is unlikely to have always been a harmonious exercise. Gurukkal says that the Dalavaipuram copper plates describe an incident of encroachment at Comacikurricchi village where the original Shudra landholders reclaimed a portion of the land that was given as Brahmadeya. This move was spearheaded by the kilavan or the headman of the clan. In this case, according to the inscription, the appropriated portion was renamed Maturataranallur. When there was conflict and resistance, the Brahmins often sought the help of the king to restore the land to them. Such an event where the king used force to quell the resistance has been mentioned in the prasasti (introductory verse) of certain copper plates, praising this as a meritorious act of the king. In time, the general boost that the Brahmins received socially from royal patronage diminished the resistance and gave the Brahmin landholders an inbuilt advantage that served them multigenerationally in the accumulation of wealth and resources. The Cholas further consolidated the Brahmadeya system.

In terms of local governance, administration at the village level appears to have vested in village assemblies. A 1,200-year-old inscription of the Pandya king Maran Sadaiyan Varaguna at Manur village in Tirunelveli district gives details of elections to such assemblies. This king ruled roughly between 767 CE and 815 CE and the inscription is dated to 805 CE. There is a difference of opinion among epigraphists and historians as to whether the inscription details the qualifications needed to become members of the village assembly or if the inscription refers to the constitution of the village court. Be that as it may, this inscription dates back 100 years before the famed Uthiramerur inscription of the Cholas which details in a clear manner the constitution of the village assembly, the village courts, the number of votes that the public is entitled to, and other matters. The Manur inscription of the Pandya king is at the Ambalavana Swamy temple in Manur where elections were held. Manur was established as a brahmadeyam well before the time of this particular Pandya king, underlining the fact that the establishment of the village assembly and local courts probably occurred earlier than the eighth century. The assembly, according to the inscription, was summoned by the beating of a drum, the perungurri sarri, and the makkal sabhai or people's assembly, gathered at the stated hour to discuss local matters. Attendance and membership were restricted to property holders, small farm cultivators, and learned people. Some people who attended were not given a full vote and only half a vote and a code of conduct was prescribed. Importantly, no royal officers or representatives of the king attended these gatherings. Thiruninravur, another small temple town near Chennai, had a written constitution, and other temples in places like Manimangalam and Pazhaya Seevaram in Chengalpattu district, Dadsamudram near Kanchipuram, Sithamalli and Thalaignayiru near Thanjavur, Jambai in Villupuram district, and Ponnamaravathy near Pudukkottai, all have temple inscriptions that mention local elections and assemblies. Obviously, even from the days of early Pandya rule, participation by local people in these assemblies, even if not entirely democratic in nature, existed across many parts of Tamilakam, which points to the dynamic role of many of these local agencies in the dispensing of justice and in wielding power and authority over local matters. Caste and land ownership also played a role in the composition of these assemblies.

Although some scholars suggest that caste divisions were not rigid in the early mediaeval Pandya period, some caste distinctions especially among the Brahmins, the Vellalas (the non-Brahmin landowners) and those in lower-ranked professions such as fishermen and scavengers did exist. Shepherds and huntsmen called Aiyar and Vedduvar respectively were ranked below the cultivators or Ulavar. The artisans—goldsmiths, carpenters, potters, blacksmiths, and others—were ranked below them. Although there was no slavery per se, the prevalent social order dictated that lower ranked people had to make way for the higher castes when passing in the streets. Several Sangam poems offer a glimpse into the clothing of people. Lower-ranked people did not wear an upper cloth, whereas soldiers, the king's officers, and nobles wore full dresses. It appears that women barely covered their chests although the wealthy ones covered their upper bodies with multiple ornaments made of gold and precious gems while lower classes of women used cheaper beads, conch shell bracelets, and adorned themselves with flowers.

In terms of social customs, mediaeval literary accounts indicate free interactions between men and women, especially among the vendors and hawkers, village workers, as well as those working in wealthy households. Women of the upper strata tended to be less visible except in the palaces and royal courts, although they were no less open to free dealings with the opposite sex. Stories of illicit love affairs, extramarital relationships, elopements etc., were not uncommon, as we have noted in texts like the *Shilappadikaram*. Concubinage was socially accepted. Notions like honour and courage were highly regarded, especially among the warrior class, and an exhibition of cowardice was tantamount to death.

We know that the Pandya dynasty lost out first to the Pallavas and then to the Cholas after their first period of strong rule and while they continued to wield power over small areas, they were largely eclipsed by the Chola might that took over the whole of Tamilakam. The Pandyas raised their heads again from the twelfth century onwards with kings like Jatavarman Sundara Pandya who ruled between 1251 CE and 1293 CE. His period was a time of great territorial expansion for the Pandya dynasty. By this time, a great many Arab traders had settled in the Malabar area and many local citizens had converted to Islam.

Marco Polo who came to the Malabar region during the reign of Jatavarman Sundara Pandya or possibly a little later, during the reign of his son Maravarman Kulasekhara Pandya, has provided an account of the Pandya kingdom which gives us several interesting insights.

> The province is the finest and noblest in the world. The name of the king ruler is Sundar Bandi Devar. In his kingdom you find very fine and great pearls… You must know that in all this province…there is never a tailor to cut a coat or stitch it, seeing that everybody goes with unstitched pieces of cloth. It is a fact that the king goes as bare as the rest; only around his loins he has a piece of fine cloth, and around his neck he has a necklace entirely of precious stones—rubies, sapphires, emeralds, and the like…

We hear in Marco Polo's account that a great part of the Pandya kingdom's wealth is lost in their newfound fascination with horses: 'Here are no horses bred; and thus, a great part of the wealth of the country is wasted in purchasing horses…indeed this king wants to buy more than 2000 horses every year and so do his four brothers. The reason why they want so many horses every year is that by the end of the year there shall not be one hundred of them remaining, for they all die off.' Wassaf, the Persian writer and historian (who some historians say never visited the Pandya kingdom), says in his account of the rule of Maravarman Kulasekhara Pandya: 'They bind the horses for 40 days in a stable with ropes and pegs in order they may get fat; and afterwards without taking measures for training, and without stirrups and other appurtenances of riding, the Pandya soldiers ride upon them like demons.' Marco Polo also points out that the people are idolaters and worship the 'ox' because they find them to be excellent creatures.

Marco Polo describes other facets of Pandya society that he finds fascinating including the fact that many people bathed twice a day and looked down on those who did not do so. He also notes that they smeared their bodies with sesame oil and cleaned their houses with cow dung. He finds that there is great interest in astrology and magic and is amused by the fact that mighty duels can occur if anyone spits on anyone else, leading often to the death of one of the contestants. They are strict at dispensing justice, he says, but lechery is not counted as a sin.

Chapter 12

Abnegation, Devotion, and Faith

In theology...philosophy and at the liturgical level, they carried out innovations with a more liberal attitude towards the lower orders of society...

R. Champakalakshmi, historian

THE GREAT SOUTHERN WAY OR DAKSHINAPADA, OF WHICH MADURAI was the centre point, is an ancient route that has been described by many writers and travellers. There's an interesting encounter in the *Shilappadikaram* where a traveller meets Kannagi and Kovalan and describes at great length the two paths leading to Madurai. The traveller, a Brahmin from Mankatu in the Kutaku Hills, says that his own journey took him 'to see the splendour of Vishnu praised and adored / by many as he lies with Lakshmi reposing on his chest /...in the islet caressed by the rolling / waves of the mighty Kaveri.' This is a clear reference to Srirangam, about 140 miles away from Madurai. This is obviously a well-travelled man who not only made a long and arduous journey but was wise in his knowledge of local geography. 'Since my eyes rejoiced / To see the glory and great doings / Of the Pantiya kingdom / I stopped here blessing the king', he says. The traveller elaborates on the many paths to Madurai. On one path, 'you will see the cadamba with its branches spread out / the dried toothbrush tree, / the sirissa with its scorched stem / the bamboo with its withered leaves....' This is obviously an arid pathway, with the poet describing thirsty deer crying for water. Once the 'Pantiyan's Little Mountain' is crossed, fertile lands and verdant forests lead to the great city of Madurai. Other magical pathways are described; a cavern that wipes out 'all illusions', ponds that sparkle, troublesome deities and nymphs that could accost travellers who are advised to prevail over distractions—the direct path to Madurai then opens to them. Once the road is clear, the profusion of wealth that the city presents is described—rich merchandise, ornate dwellings, and a prosperous citizenry. The city's reputation as a commodious hub of many things had reached far and wide across India even from around 500 BCE.

With the impact of the Bhakti movement, from about the ninth century onwards, the temples around Madurai, especially the Meenakshi temple, had acquired a spiritual heft that created an expanding universe of rituals, ceremonials, festivals, and traditions, such as the annual Tirukalyanam or the wedding of Parvati to Shiva, which even today is celebrated as a community event in the streets of Madurai. There are also festivals specific to communities and their temples which have been in place for centuries. And, despite the growth and firm establishment of the Vedic or Brahmanical religion, especially after the ninth century, local traditions and ways of worship continued to have a hold on many of Madurai's citizens and were sometimes placed above the worship of the Brahmanical deities. Such local deities and practices of worship that go back several centuries, as in the popular Kochadai Ayyanar temple near Madurai, in which the guardian deity of the village is worshipped, are common across the region. Local folk heroes like Madurai Veeran (probably the most popular among them) hold a strong place in the hearts of the city's residents. This warrior's story is one of the defiance of caste hierarchy in pursuit of love, which led to his death. Madurai Veeran fell in love with a royal princess who was under the protection of Tirumalai Nayak. Although he was favoured by the Nayak king for his valour and made a general, the fact that he belonged to a low caste and dared to fall in love with a woman of a higher caste and elope with her enraged the king who had him mutilated and put to death. His lover committed suicide as did his first wife, Bommi. As a warrior who was already a local hero, he was accorded semi-god status after Tirumalai Nayak himself constructed a shrine for him. His image is enshrined at the east gate of the Meenakshi temple, and his legend lives on in street plays and songs. The deification of many defiant local heroes and heroines camouflages the caste and honour crimes often committed against them.

Interestingly, Madurai also has a host of secular festivals with a hoary history such as Meen Pudi Thiruvizha, where fishing competitions are held in villages close to Madurai, the most famous being the festival at Tiruvadavur, near Melur, where entire families participate in catching fish. This tradition supposedly goes back more than 400 years. These prize catches would be taken home as offerings to their local deities. Another much established fishing competition takes place at Kallanthiri village near Azhagar Kovil where five nearby temples join to celebrate, and close to 5,000 people congregate every year to catch fish in an atmosphere of revelry and merriment.

Traversing the dusty country roads that circle the villages near Madurai, I noticed the unusual spectacle of hundreds of painted terracotta horses massed together near a hamlet. The sight was startling in its unexpectedness; quiet green fields, sleepy hamlets with little human movement and then, suddenly, a burst of colour and a crowd of strident presences, much like the army of terracotta warriors in Xi'an in China. The horses looked lively and although the paint had worn off, they appeared real; symmetrically arranged, animated and energetic, they had obviously been fashioned with great devotion to detail. Some of them were crafted standing on their hind legs as if raring to go and others were decoratively posed—bejewelled warrior horses painted with coloured necklaces and garish bridles, teeth bared, sometimes grotesquely so. This phenomenon is obviously not at all an uncommon sight across several districts such as Pudukkottai and Sivagangai, where local people worship their guardian deity called Ayyanar by the votive offerings of these horses. The festival is called Puravi Eduppu, which is an offering of the horses to Ayyanar, a fierce watchman of the village who in his nightly rounds protects the community from harm. The origins of Ayyanar worship can be traced back to the 2,000-year-old tradition of worshipping hero stones, that is the honouring of village heroes who in time become elevated to village gods. Local potters are commissioned to make the terracotta horses by farmers who offer these horses to these gods in gratitude for rain or for a plentiful harvest. In the summer months they are taken in procession with song and dance to be dedicated to the temple where they are positioned till they disintegrate. Village and folk traditions of faith and worship passed on from generation to generation hold a central place in rural communities.

Travelling to Madurai and further south, beyond Ramanathapuram and Tuticorin and down to Tenkasi and Tirunelveli where the Thamirabarani flows, it is possible to encounter fascinating aspects of the Tamil heritage that originated in Pandya times, a heritage which is often obscured by the Pallava rule in north Tamil Nadu and by the grandiosity of the Chola empire that followed it. However, as we have seen, much of the origins of recorded Tamil culture, including the language itself, was nurtured and fostered in the nearly 2,000 years of Pandya presence in these places in the far south.

Speaking of living traditions, I have touched upon the role that Jainism played in shaping Tamil culture, especially its literature. Some of Tamil's literary works had a strong Jain undertone, notably those composed in the early pre- and post-Christian years. These include the *Tirukkural* by Tiruvalluvar, written sometime between the second century BCE and the fifth century CE. The exact date of its composition is not known, although most scholars date it to the third century CE, nor is much known about its creator but literary references indicate that Valluvar spent time in Pandya country, although the poet also is said to have lived in Mylapore, which would have been part of Pallava terrain. As previously noted, the text is considered to belong to the group of didactic poetry works called *Kilkanakku* or Eighteen Minor Works.

These 1,330 verses of the *Tirukkural* embody primary life principles in three books, aram, porul, inbam—that is, of virtue or goodness, of wealth or practical wisdom, of love. In pithy, crisp language, complex moral and philosophical ideas are conveyed. Each verse has only seven words in the venpa metre, a classical metre used in Tamil poetry. The *Kural* is totally secular in nature and packs a punch in its delivery of practical wisdom. David Shulman has suggested that this may not have been a unitary work unlike the traditional view that it all flowed from the pen of a remarkable poet who was sometimes even ascribed mystic powers. So great is the impact of what he wrote, that to this day the Tamils' veneration of him knows no bounds. His couplets adorn public spaces in Tamil Nadu and many places are named for Tiruvalluvar. The verses have also found a way into regular Tamil lexicography. One of the most interesting points about this work is that the author's religious affiliation is never overtly mentioned.

The work is a secular masterpiece. Its distinction comes because of its timeless relevance to multiple aspects of the human condition. Among the concepts and subjects it takes into survey are courtesy, goodness, nobility, valour, and the temptations of love. Gopalkrishna Gandhi states that it 'uses the pathways of analysis and contemplation to advance a state of balance in private living and public duty....' The translation into Latin of the *Kural* by an Italian Jesuit serving in the Madurai mission, Constanzo Beschi, brought Valluvar's work to the outside world, but he did not translate the third book dealing with the subject of love, perhaps in keeping with his priestly avocation. Apart from a couple of other translations into French and German, the first English translation of the entire work was done in 1886 by the Christian missionary G. U. Pope whose remarkable work in the world of Tamil literature and culture will be looked at later. Pope conveyed to English readers, as Gandhi states, 'Valluvar's vision of the totality of life'.

Legends suggest that Tiruvalluvar was born to a Brahmin father and a Dalit mother in Madurai and raised by a weaver (valluvan). This seems to satisfy the cosmos of Tamil values, underlining his appeal across communities. His wife, Vasuki, however, who was portrayed as an exemplary woman partnering this ideal husband has been viewed as being submissive and under the husband's domination, to the discomfiture of admirers like Periyar E. V. Ramaswami. Gandhi, in his excellent translation of the *Kural*, dwells on some of these issues in his introduction. He writes, '… gender equality is not a concept that detains

Valluvar. Indeed, the parity and equality between man and woman is outside his imagining except in what Periyar E. V. Ramaswami calls the "state of love and desire".' The first two books of the *Kural* firmly denounce courtesans and offer a negative view of such women while the third book is all about love. That he was a Jain is generally accepted although it was never proclaimed in the text as Gandhi points out, but the theme of 'compassion for all life' is strongly prevalent. Gandhi, however, says that 'what comes as a surprise in this sage-like author with his Jainism-evoking ardour for vegetarianism and non-killing is his expertise in war. Valluvar's understanding of the mechanisms of war, warfare, battles, battlements, and of combat…is serious. His almost inborn sense of the use of animal power in battle is astounding….'

Other masterpieces of this time include the *Shilappadikaram*, mentioned earlier, *Nannul, Manimekalai,* and other works classified under The Eighteen Minor Works as well as *Civakacintamani*. Their authors were votaries of Buddhism and Jainism. In *Shilappadikaram,* after the wronged Kovalan is avenged by the wrathful Kannagi, she ascends to heaven with his body. Shulman has pointed out a version of this story is played out in the Teyyam rituals of North Malabar—tales of injustice, violent death, and an evolving divinity. The core narrative is linked to Kerala as well as Madurai. The sequel to this story, *Manimekalai,* is the tale of Kovalan and Kannagi's daughter who becomes a Buddhist nun and is another tale of unrequited love and tragedy. Written by a grain merchant who was called Cattanar, it also reflects a permeability of philosophy and language in much of the literature of the times often authored by people of the Jain and Buddhist faith.

Jain contributions of that time went beyond literature. Iravatham Mahadevan, the foremost epigraphist and leading scholar of the Tamil Brahmi and Harappan scripts, has underlined their importance: 'No survey of Jainism in the Tamil country can be complete without mentioning the enormous contributions made by the Jainas from the earliest times up to the 16th century…mention must be made of at least of such outstanding works by Jaina authors like *Tolkappiyam* and *Nannul* among the grammatical works, *Shilappadikaram, Civakacintamani* and *Perunkatai* among the epics, the immortal *Kural* and *Nalatiyar* among the ethical works and *Tivakaram, Pinkalantai* and *Cutamani* among the lexicons.' Mahadevan adds, 'To this already formidable record may be added what is the most basic and fundamental contribution made by the Jainas to Tamil, namely the development of a script for the language leading to literacy and the…efflorescence of Cankam literature in the early centuries C.E'. The script of Tamil Brahmi called the Grantha is in plenty of evidence in the inscriptions of the Jains found scattered across the Tamil country offering us incontrovertible evidence of a rich, heterogeneous culture.

We move then from the literary into a more evidence-based recording of historical detail, particularly about administration, donations, and religious affiliations with the discovery of numerous inscriptions belonging to the early centuries of the millennium. According to Mahadevan, recent discoveries assign many of these to the second century BCE. Subramanian, however, says that trade existed between the north and south even earlier—by the fourth century BCE. This is attested to by the fact that northern black polished ware was found in Korkai and Azhagankulam in the Pandya country and Kodumanal in the Chera country. A hoard of Mauryan silver punch-marked coins was found in Bodinaickanur in the Pandya country.

The earliest Tamil Brahmi inscription is in an area called Mankulam, close to Meenakshipuram near Madurai. In the hills around Madurai, close to thirty Tamil Brahmi inscriptions have been discovered. The Mankulam inscription, the earliest, belongs to the second century BCE, and refers to a king called Neduncheliyan. Varichiyur, Kongarpuliyankulam, Kizhavalalu, Arittapatti, Anaimalai, and Tiruparankunram atop a steep hill are some of the other places where such inscriptions have been discovered. Tamil Brahmi inscriptions datable even to the first century have also been found at Azhagarmalai specifically mentioning how a goldsmith, pon kolvan, a trader in ploughshares, kozhu vanikan, a textile merchant, aruvai vanikan, and a salt merchant, uppu vanikan, had all donated rock-cut beds for the Jaina monks who resided there. Most inscriptions are largely Jain and indicate a dominant presence of the community in the area which was essentially Pandya nadu. It is thought that Jain monks moved into Tamilakam from the north and west. The spread of Jainism in the south gained momentum after the migration of the Jain saint Bhadrabahu with his 12,000 followers to Shravanabelagola now in Karnataka sometime in the third century BCE and these disciples fanned out further south across Tamilakam. Therefore, one reason for the spread of Jainism in South India was the work done by Jain monks from the north, another important reason was the existence of trade routes by land and sea, and the resultant commerce between the Jain traders in the north and their counterparts in the south.

The Jain monks brought with them the Ashoka Brahmi script which gradually became Tamil Brahmi, as ancient Tamil did not have a script at that time. By about the third or fourth century CE, this developed into what is known as vatteluthu. And some of the Madurai inscriptions are in vatteluthu. The Jain monks lived in rock caverns of hillsides near natural springs, surrounded by verdant greenery. It is thought that the local chieftains, traders, and merchants who sought their wisdom sculpted beds for them in these caves. The monks carved out a brow-like structure at the entrance to the cave so that the rain would fall like a curtain in front and would not enter the cave. Jain monks were also vaidyas or physicians and made grooves in the rocks to prepare their medicines, and such are still present in these areas near the caves.

Vedachalam, one of the archaeologists who discovered this site, wryly points out that the Jain monks were clever with their choice of habitation. 'The city of Madurai saw a great traffic of people pour through its precincts as it was an important city in those times. There were traders, travellers, merchants, people of diverse communities, and these Jain monks would propagate and preach to the locals and the visitors then retire to these caves.'

These places would have served as a monastic abode, as a medical facility, and as a palli or teaching place. Vedachalam also says that these monks would go down to the village and ask for food only from the houses of certain people. 'They never sat down and ate,' he says, 'and neither did they collect food in a container. They stretched out their palms and took only as much food as their palms could hold and ate standing.' So, it was a disciplined and controlled relationship with food.

We visit Arittapatti, another important Jain cave. On the eastern side of the hill in Arittapatti is a natural cave with two Tamil Brahmi inscriptions. Next to that, of a later period possibly during the tenth century, carved on the rock side are Tirthankara images, with vatteluthu script nearby. In the inscriptions, this hill is referred to as Tirupunayan malai. The word punayan means 'float', Vedachalam explains. 'The one who becomes the float that helps you cross the ocean of samsara'. The inscription reads, 'In the name of Purkottu Karanathar, Acchanandi Munivar (who) worshipped this "divine body" (thirumeni)'. The second Tamil Brahmi inscription mentions that Silivan Adinan Oliyan gave this mulahai or cave for the monks.

It is clear from these caves that a large segment of society followed the Jain and Buddhist faiths. Professor Kanaka Ajithadoss, a specialist on Jainism in Tamil Nadu says, 'Jainism was a popular religion of the masses...with Tamil people adopting its philosophy, thought and practice for more than two thousand years...'. As mentioned earlier, a marked decline of the visibility of Jainism (not so much the philosophy), slowly occurred in Tamilakam from around the late sixth century and in the early seventh century owing in large measure to a distinct and strong revival of the Shaivite and Vaishnavite traditions. There was a quiet continuation, however, albeit in a form that absorbed local traditions and rituals and were made more palatable to the public after the eighth century. The rather challenging philosophy of anti-theism, anti-rituals that the earlier Jains practised that were countered by the Bhakti movement, were now transformed into a more theistic expression with the original caves slowly being adorned with sculptures depicting the Tirthankaras in places and began to look more akin to Pallava- and Pandya-style temples.

The acme of early Pandya Jain sculptural and artistic manifestation must indeed lie in Kazhugumalai. When we climb up the hillock on the northern side, a gentle shower sends us scurrying for cover beneath a rock. It is the perfect time for Vedachalam to tell us the story of this unusual place. The place, he says, is called Tirumalai and is also known as Araimalai. Towering carvings and the bas-relief sculptures of rows of Tirthankaras on the rocky hillside are to the right of our climb. This was once an eminent place of Jain learning and living, a famed monastery, a progressive spiritual centre and a Jain college that thrived for 400 years from around the eighth to the twelfth century. From across Tamilakam and indeed from Kerala as well, ascetics have stayed here, studied here. Interestingly, women ascetics were also welcomed here and accorded an equal status with the male monks. They taught male students, were scholars themselves, and the inscriptions indicate that more than fifteen Jain nuns worked and taught here. The ascetics were called kuravar, adigal, and the women were called kurathi and referred to in most respectful terms. Although one would expect the male and female ascetics to stay separately, it appears that they stayed together, very unusual for those times but nevertheless accommodated with the monks practising abstinence. Vedachalam shows us an inscription which describes a donation in the memory of a female teacher by a male student.

A dazzling array of carved Tirthankaras, each under their three-headed umbrellas, close to a hundred in number, stretch across the side of the rock. One superbly sculpted Tirthankara is on a lion pedestal with a triple umbrella over his head. Celestial maidens lead him in a procession playing musical instruments and there is an atmosphere of joyfulness as the monk is obviously on the road to enlightenment. There is another standout carving of a Tirthankara with his guardians; a yaksha who looks frightening with his wife the yakshi, Ambika, under a kalpakavriksha. There is also a carving of a lion, two children, and a female figure that appears to be the maid servant of the yakshi. There is a tragic story behind this depiction. Ambika, a simple young woman, is accosted by an ascetic who begs her for food. Forgetting that she must first complete a death anniversary ritual with her husband, she feeds the starving mendicant. The family arrives to find that the food meant for the ancestors has been given away and are angry with Ambika and tell her to confess her mistake to her husband. He becomes enraged, beats her, and drives her away along with the children. When Ambika goes to the ascetic for advice, he tells her that she must return to her husband and she hesitates, sitting by the hillside praying for help for her hungry children. Lord Indra (apparently a part of the Jain pantheon) sends her the kalpakavriksha, the bountiful wish-granting tree and she is then able to feed her young ones. Hearing of this marvel and realizing that she is an advanced soul, the husband decides to take her back and walks towards her. Seeing her husband coming towards her, Ambika, fearing for her life, jumps to her death. Upon her death she is transformed into a being of gold, a yakshi, by the Tirthankara Neminatha as she showed compassion and care for the mendicant seeking food. In her heavenly abode, her thoughts turn to her children on earth and Indra bestows her with a boon that she can return to her earthly life at times and at other times, she may stay and serve the Tirthankaras. Ambika then serves as a yakshi as well as a wife and mother until one day, her ever suspicious husband, who cannot quite believe his wife's ethereal nature, demands proof and to see her golden body. When she shows herself to him, he is so dazzled that he covers his eyes. Vedachalam points to a frieze. 'See that carving of the man covering his eyes, that is the husband. He of course becomes so ashamed of his suspicions that he dies by suicide. He too becomes a yaksha, a simha or lion which finally becomes a vehicle that constantly bears Ambika.'

The final frieze of this story shows a beautiful Ambika standing in a half-bent posture of grace akin to the goddess Parvati as Vedachalam points out, the dangling kamandala in her ears, her hand resting lightly on the head of her servant maid and the lion and her now frightened husband and children at her feet. The writer Uma Maheshwari, in her book on Tamil Jains, points out that one of the most distinguishing features of Tamil Jainism is the worship of the yakshi…'within the structural edifice of the Jaina temple complex. Among the most popular yakshi…are Padmavati the *yakshi* of Parsvanatha, and Ambika…the *yakshi* of Neminatha'. She believes that yakshi worship is like the worship of Amman or the goddess, stemming from perhaps the earlier versions of the mother goddess or the village deities 'from whom it is easier to seek boons, while the *tirthankaras*, who are beyond wordly attachments... do not grant boons to laity'.

Let us look now at the revival of the Brahmanical religion and the new postulates of faith that blossomed in the heart of Tamilakam. Champakalakshmi suggests that Bhakti as a concept had its roots as far back as the Sangam age, for example in the *Paripatal*, a Sangam classic, speaks for the first time of the temple as a milieu of worship and also the idea of a godhead whether it was Mayon, Mal (Vishnu), or Murugan. The writer Archana Venkatesan, drawing from Kamil Zvelebil, the great expert on Tamil literature, says that the *Paripatal* is 'probably the earliest literary testimony of the Bhakti movement in South India, if not in India as a whole'. She adds that 'in the *Paripatal* poems, the panegyric, a staple of *puram* poetry becomes the favoured mode to produce poetry.' Later, Bhakti as a base for the expression of a deeply personal connection with a favoured deity was elaborated by the Azhwars and the Nayanmars, each group passionately turning to personal devotion through compositions of devotional poems and song. It was spread over a time span of about three centuries and more beginning around the sixth century, and up to the ninth century and beyond. The proponents espoused a personal and passionate connection with Vedic or Puranic religious philosophies through devotion to a supreme deity whether it was Shiva, or Vishnu and his incarnations. This had an impact across the Pallava, Pandya, and the Chola periods with the flame of spirituality becoming a fire of religiosity. Here we will look at the Bhakti saints who largely lived in Pandya country.

A Shaivite domination of the polity began to take root with the shift of power to the Pandya rulers who fervently embraced the faith and undoubtedly pressed it on those within their spheres of influence. Setting fire to sacred texts, torturing monks, and mocking the Jaina faith was a common occurrence. Champakalakshmi says that Sambandar was 'a crusader and his denunciation of the Jains and Buddhists was instrumental in bringing about their decline at the royal court of the Pandyas.' He constantly refers to the 'false doctrines of the heretic Jain and Buddhist monks'. She also says that Sambandar claimed that the fire that the Jains aimed at him was redirected as a disease to afflict the Pandya king, and by curing the king he proved the superiority of Saivism. 'The enemy was not the Brahmanical or the Puranic religion, but Buddhism and Jainism which were alien to Tamil culture. Hence it is represented in their hymns that kings who had been seduced by the false doctrines of the Jains and Buddhists were being rescued and brought back to the true religion'. We must keep in mind too that the Jain community slowly repositioned itself by absorbing features of the majority community, for instance, their yakshi were slowly made into female Hindu goddesses and other aspects of worship changed in order to blend with the larger community.

The crusades mounted against Jainism and Buddhism by some proponents of Bhakti such as Sambandar emphasize again that their mission was less about reforming aspects of the Brahmanical or Puranic religion and more about ensuring the dominance of their beliefs. Indeed, both Appar and Sambandar underlined the sanctity of the Vedas.

However, before we move into looking at the revival of the Brahmanical religion through the Bhakti movement, it is important to note some underlying facts about the so called 'decline' of Jainism or the 'revival' of the other. Uma Maheshwari makes an important point which should be kept in mind when the chronology of community histories is examined. She questions the idea among some scholars of placing a 'living' community within set periods of time and to speak of 'dominance' and 'decline' as these by and large reflected only political and state patronage. The notion of 'decline' may be only from a particular viewpoint she asserts, such as during the time of the Bhakti poets and even here 'the Tamil Jaina communities narratives reflect a situation where you find them constantly trying to assert their identity. Conflict is seen as the constant or the sub text. One sees a minority community consistently negotiating and working out ways of survival: moving from marginal to mainstream, and marginal time and time again.'

Uma Maheshwari also notes that in the context of the question of persecution during the Bhakti era, while there may be a recounting of myths and tales, the socio-political paradigm which is at the root of it all is often ignored by mainstream scholarship. She gives examples of 'the Shaivite exaggerated myth making within the Brahmanical temple-land owning paradigm'. One example from the *Periyapuranam* says that the small Tantiatikal Shaiva temple tank near Tiruvarur was surrounded by Jain lands and pallis on four banks. The Shaivas wanted to make it bigger by removing the Jain settlements. The Jains protested. The poet Sekkizhar mentions that Shiva appeared in the dream of the king to command destruction of the Jain settlements at this place. She adds that 'these stories signify the efforts at land appropriation and seeking control over the sources of cultivation'. The infusion of these kind of aspects into the Bhakti paradigm makes it a complex issue well beyond a spontaneous regeneration of pure devotion.

Looking at the phenomenon of Bhakti, the Azhwars, and a little later the Nayanmars, brewed an emotional and devotional lexicon based on the Puranic myths and temple iconography that found resonance with both lettered as well as unlettered people. The songs and hymns and poems of praise were all in Tamil. Scholars have been careful to point out, however, that there was a continuing if complex relationship between the two, that is temple iconography and Bhakti poetry. In fact, historians like Keshavan Veluthat and Romila Thapar have argued that beyond the personal and individual foray into devotion, much of the legitimization of Bhakti literature came through support from temples which, in turn, were used by the state, i.e., the kings and ruling elite, to secure political hegemony.

The spiritual honing of the verses came from Vedic (that is Sanskrit) sources although the emotional surrender via forms of Bhakti were all anchored in the vernacular.

The Azhwars, twelve in number, lived across two to three centuries, and included the famed Andal, the only woman in this group of poet-saints whose story has been retold and re-enacted in music and dance over the centuries, with versions ranging from celebrating her as a saint and goddess to feminist interpretations that acclaim her courage and determination. Her two literary works include the *Tirupavai*, a collection of thirty verses, and *Nachiyar Tirumozhi*, a collection of 143 somewhat more erotic verses, many of which exhibit an intense longing for communion with her beloved Vishnu. The latter were not very popular with the more orthodox Vaishnavites because of their eroticism.

The other Azhwars were Tirumazhisai Azhwar, Kulasekhara Azhwar, Andal's father Periyazhwar, Tirumangai Azhwar, Nammazhwar, Thondaradippodi Azhwar, Madurakavi Azhwar, and Tiruppan Azhwar, all drawn from diverse castes and backgrounds. Four of them, Nammazhwar, Maduraikavi, Periyazhwar, and Andal, were all from the Pandya country. The *Tiruvaymozhi*, *Tiruviruttam, Tiruvasiriyam*, and *Periya Tiruvanthadhi* composed by Satagopan Nammazhwar, added a thousand plus verses to the *Divya Prabandam*. He is perhaps the most prolific contributor to this body of work. Nammazhwar's writing is highly philosophical. In works like the *Tiruvaymozhi* he distils the essence of Vedic thought. The *Tiruviruttam* is a hundred-verse poem that is in the same tradition. Archana Venkatesan, who has done a marvellous translation of Nammazhwar's work, sees it 'as both heir and progenitor in a long and illustrious lineage of Tamil poetry'. To reiterate the Vedic connection in terms of religious philosophy, she points out that Vishnu is praised as the (source of) Vedas…and the presence of epithets…serve to capture the indivisible relationship between Vishnu and Vedic philosophy. However, as verse 64 of the work says: The masters of the earth cleave / to the weighty words of the Rg Veda / to praise faultlessly / the feet that spanned the worlds. / I depressed subdued by fate / simply recite sacred names I've learned / like one who can't eat ripe fruit / and make do with raw ones. The implication here is that scholars who have mastered the Vedas can comprehend more, but for the subject, the recitation of the sacred name is all that can be mastered. Clearly, this means, that a subtle primacy is granted to those who know the Vedas, but space is also given to the simpler ways of connecting with the divine—the recitation of sacred names. The final stanza in the poem also confirms this and emphasizes the notion of surrender, a cardinal principle in Vaishnavism. Maran who wears as a garland / the foot of those who recite Tirumal's divine names / that lord of Kurukur where good people praise him / sang a plea of one hundred verses / those who master them / won't ever be trapped in the quicksand / of delusory birth its wicked fate / the misery of this false world.

Venkatesan, however, goes on to point out 'though the impulse of Bhakti was radical in a number of ways—advocating community, enfolding women and lower castes as part of the group, asserting the efficacy of devotion as an equalizer before god—it also stressed the value of Sanskritic Brahmanical temple-based ritual and liturgical tradition.'

Scholars have pointed out that women in the corpus of Bhakti hymns were seen largely as devotees, and while poets often assumed a feminine voice when they expressed their passionate longing for god, they also reaffirmed family relationships and social structures. For instance, although ultimately she was held up and worshipped as a goddess, Andal was forbidden to express her love and longing for Vishnu (her erotic poetry clearly underlines her intense desire, and leads to her ultimate merging with the deity, an aspect that was considered outside the pale of society). Karaikal Ammaiyar, considered one of the Nayanmars, had to shed her femininity. These two examples of women who were in apparent public view but outside the normative familial structure indicate that those who crossed the bounds of patriarchy could not literally and metaphorically continue to live. One merged with the deity and the other gave up her beauty and ultimately even her human form. We know too that inscriptions in the many temples in the Thanjavur, Madurai, and Tiruchirappalli regions reveal that many women who made contributions by way of grants to temples are by and large referred to as daughters, wives, and mothers of important men of the region. Karaikal Ammaiyar's story is told by Sekkizhar in *Periyapuranam,* which is a work of literature composed around the twelfth century. It is full of stories of the miracles of these Nayanmars and is considered an important hagiographical source. Many Thevaram hymns were also added to this and came to be known as *Tirumurai*. According to legend, Karaikal Ammaiyar's original name was Punitavati, and the story goes that her husband Paramadatta, a merchant prince, once gave her two mangoes, one of which she gave away to a mendicant who came to her door and whom she perceived as Shiva himself. Her husband ate one mango when he returned and liked it so much that he asked for the second one. As she had given it away, she prayed to Shiva that she should not have to disappoint her beloved husband. Lo and behold, she found a mango appearing miraculously between her folded hands. When he asked her why the second mango was much more delicious than the first, she told him the truth of its origin and he asked her to procure another one. Again, another mango appeared, but before he could eat it, it disappeared. Realizing her greatness, he left her, saying he could not live with her anymore and that she was a goddess and not his wife anymore. Her divinity was too much for him to bear and Punitavati herself then shunned her human form and prayed that she may shed her femininity. This is a clear instance that she had gone beyond the pale of normative functioning, so she became a skeleton or a ghoul and is said to have walked on her head to Mount Kailash, much to the astonishment of Parvati and Shiva who then called her his mother (thereby removing connotations of sexuality) and granted her boon, which was to not have any more births. Having granted her wish, he asked her to witness his cosmic dance in Thiruvalankadu where she composed and sang the beautiful Thevaram 'Arpuda Tiru Andhadhi'.

Apart from stories of the Muvar, that is Appar, Sambandar, and Sundarar, the stories of miracles around many of the Nayanmars are popular to this day in Tamilakam, with versions told and embellished and retold across generations. One of them is the story of Nandanar, a cobbler born in a poor Dalit family in Adanur, who as a maker of drums and other musical instruments worked in leather. He was a great devotee of Shiva and went to the Shiva temple in nearby Thirupunkur to see his beloved deity. Being a Dalit, he could not go into the temple and could only see his god from outside. However, a stone Nandi blocked his vision, and he prayed fervently to see his lord, a wish which was granted by the Nandi moving out of his way. He then prayed ardently and thanked Shiva, cleaned the temple precincts, and dug a pond which became the temple's tank and is still there today. He next yearned to go to see Nataraja in Chidambaram. When he finally made it to Chidambaram, he was overjoyed but again he could not enter the temple and wept outside the temple walls. Shiva appeared in a vision to the temple priests and asked them to prepare a pyre and to let Nandanar in. He walked into the temple and walked through the pyre unharmed. The story goes that he moved towards the sanctum sanctorum and disappeared under the foot of the dancing Nataraja, merging with the deity.

Another popular tale is of the miracle of Thinnan or Kannappa Nayanar, a hunter from Kalahasti. He was devoted to his Lord Shiva and would bring him offerings of the meat he hunted every day. One day he noticed that one of the eyes of the lingam was bleeding. Without a thought, he plucked out his own eye and placed it on the lingam. The next day he noticed that the other eye was bleeding and was about to pluck out his second eye when Shiva appeared and saved his beloved devotee. Tales like these were a mix of local Tamil tradition and infused Brahmanical notions such as the purification element of walking through fire. At the same time, there are aspects such as the offering of blood and game by Kannapan to the deity, underlining a peculiar Tamil tradition of faith that had to be demonstrated through pain.

In many temples even today, as I travelled across Tamil Nadu listening to priests narrate the sthala puranam or history of the place, there is always a curious if almost unconscious mix of local lore infused with Puranic traditions. Many of the most beautiful sculptural elements in these temples were depictions of legends and stories of Shiva or Vishnu, with the rich detail involving not only aesthetics of a high standard but evoking beyond beauty a sense of story depicted with humour and skill in many instances. A sense of community was strong with the local temple as the focus of many activities. Festivals always involved and invoked folk elements. The singing of Tamil hymns was distinctly rooted in a southern musical tradition.

The intent of the Thevaram saints was to propagate the highly personal connection with the temple deity in addition to establishing their links to the Vedic works and philosophy. Champakalakshmi, however, suggests that the Vaishnavites were more successful than the Tamil Shaivas 'in relating the Sanskrit Vedic tradition to Tamil Vaishnava doctrine. (The Tamil Shaivites) could not directly relate their tradition to the Vedic *Sruti* or revealed literature. However, it has been shown that the Shaiva *patikams* exhibit a close similarity to the Sanskrit *stotra* or poems of praise, and their affinities with early Sanskrit litanies have been stressed.'

To perceive the Bhakti movement simplistically as bringing about social reform and progress is to ignore some of its deeper socio-political implications. As mentioned earlier, the zeal with which some kings like Pallava

Mahendravarman and the Pandya king Nedumaran eschewed Jainism and took to the Brahmanical religion or reconverted to it at the persuasion of people like Appar and Sambandar resulted in the decreased royal patronage of Jainism, which in turn affected many Jain establishments. Their philosophical hegemony over the laity declined, although Jainism continued to have a strong presence in the area that is now Karnataka.

The Bhakti movement contributed to a significant breaking down of caste barriers as many of the poet-saints belonged to non-Brahmin communities. The broad democratization of religion is evident in a lot of temple-building activities across Tamilakam which stemmed from the need to canonize and deify the works of the Nayanmars. The temple served the Bhakti movement well by incorporating a range of worship and ritual from the tribal and folk traditions to the more elaborate Sanskritic traditions. They were also becoming citadels of local power and instruments of control for rulers as it was the hub of a great deal of economic activity. The temples where the poets sang the glories of Shiva came to be called padal petra sthalam, or places where the Shaiva saints had sung and thus ennobled them, and the temples sanctified by the Vaishnavite Azhwars were called Divya Desam and scattered across Tamilakam in Pallava, Chola, and Pandya territory.

The deeply personal element is at the crux of Bhakti poetry. It is the universality of the human experience, coupled with a longing for the divine, expressed in the most profound way—mystical, musical, spiritual verses that served and nurtured the Tamil psyche well; whether it was in thousand-pillared temple mandapams, in the recesses of cave temples, or in celebration of processional deities that were carried around the streets. I recall that on a visit to the Brihadeeswara temple in Thanjavur, Jaykumar Bharadwaj, the young man who accompanied us—a modern day entrepreneur and cultural expert—spontaneously burst into an elevated and profoundly moving rendering of a Thevaram hymn and this I thought was an exemplar of the Tamil mind, which regardless of the passage of time and centuries is capable of pulling up the words and verses that are continually relevant to the human experience.

The Imperial Cholas

With the Chola dynasty, Tamil civilization attained its high-water mark, especially from the tenth to the thirteenth centuries when the Imperial Cholas transformed Tamilakam into a rich repository of culture, literature, and the arts. The multiple dimensions of this extraordinary empire constitute a proud legacy of the Tamil people.

Chapter 13

The Tiger Crest: The Great Chola Monarchy

Let me speak out to this rich country's king! Be easy of access at fitting times, as though the lord of justice sat to hear, and right decree. Such kings have rain on their dominions at their will!

Puram 36

THANJAVUR, THE CAPITAL OF THE CHOLAS, WHOSE FORTUNES WERE tied up with the whims and fortunes of the Chola monarchy, is today a quiet jewel in the heart of Kaveri country, known as the rice bowl of Tamil Nadu. The river's ebb and flow also perfectly reflect Thanjavur's journey in history. Its early beginnings were as the capital of the rising Chola monarch, Vijayalaya Chola, displacing the smaller town of Uraiyur as the capital of an empire in the making. Unlike Madurai or Kanchipuram, Thanjavur then had a plethora of rulers of different dynasties who held sway after the Cholas, such as the Nayaks and the Marathas, followed by British rule, all of whom gave this city an edge and a character quite unlike any other major Tamil city, barring Chennai.

As in many parts of India, much of the impact of various historical periods can be felt, even intangibly at times, in many of the cities with roots in mediaeval empires. All these cities have a shared history of faith, culture, literature, and the arts, which although distinct in expression, have many common threads that run through them. Notwithstanding the ravages of war, as the kings constantly fought one another, the cities themselves stood as symbols of the achievements of not just the ruler, but of communities and people who were tillers, artisans, sculptors, painters, teachers, weavers, and builders, all of whom made these cities what they were and what they are today.

In the Sangam age, the Chola dynasty already existed, and there are plenty of legendary, literary, and poetic references to them. They were mostly chieftains and petty kings. After the Kalabhras were defeated by the Pallavas and the Pandyas around the sixth century, the Cholas held some small territories under the aegis of these bigger monarchs. Thanjavur, their great capital city, however, does not find reference in the Sangam period, although there is a seventh-century reference in literature, in the *Divyaprabandham*, where the Vaishnava saint Tirumangai Azhwar refers to a Vishnu temple in the area as Tanjaimamanikovil. But the town itself came into prominence only during the time of Vijayalaya Chola from whose line the Imperial Cholas descended. Uraiyur, just outside modern-day Tiruchirapalli, was the original Chola capital and has been mentioned in Sangam literature. Architectural excavations have revealed Sangam age artefacts in the region. Uraiyur was also called Kozhiyur locally as it was named after a hen (kozhi) that supposedly defeated an elephant in battle. Mention must also be made of Poompuhar (or Kaveripoompattinam), which was the port city of the early Cholas and was their headquarters until Vijayalaya Chola captured Thanjavur from the Muttarayar clan and made it the capital of the Chola kingdom. The move to Thanjavur was a smart decision, as the city was watered by the Kaveri and its tributaries—the Vennaru, the Vadavaru, and the Grand Anicut canal. The surrounding fields and riverbanks had rich alluvial soil which made it highly suitable for paddy production, although Thanjavur city itself is in the drier belt, the New Delta region as it was called in the colonial period, and came under good irrigation only in recent centuries. References to the Muttarayars, whom Vijayalaya Chola defeated, can be found in the Sendalai inscriptions of the eighth century that mention Tanjaik-kon, or Lord of Tanjai, and Tanjai narpukalalan—he of the good name of Tanjai—epithets that are references to the Muttarayar king Suvaran Maran. In addition, one inscription says that poets and bards 'remain singing on the state of Tanjai, appearing amid fields ever filled with water. (They sing)...to cause destruction to the Pandya, and (bring) success to the Pallava Mara (who) advanced that day to battle'. Obviously the Muttarayars later switched their loyalties to the Pandyas, supporting Varagunapandian, the Pandya ruler, which underlined the fact that they did not and indeed could not function independently. In the ninth century, Vijayalaya, the Chola king, seized complete control of the city of Thanjavur, defeating Ilango, the Muttarayar chief, thus setting the stage for the rise of one of the greatest dynasties that ever ruled from the south of India.

A few hundred years later, the Thiruvalangadu copper plate of Vijayalaya's descendant Rajendra Chola I in the eleventh century makes a direct reference to Vijayalaya's conquest of Thanjavur. 'He (Vijayalaya) of the solar race took possession of the town of Tanchapuri which was picturesque to the sight, was as beautiful as Alaka, the chief town of Kubera...had reached the sky by its high turrets and the whitewash of mansions.... Having next consecrated there the image of Nisumbasudani whose lotus feet are worshipped by gods and demons.... He, by the grace of that Goddess, bore just as easily a garland the weight of the whole earth resplendent with her garment of the four oceans....' Thanjavur town was obviously viewed as an attractive place even in these early years and soon became the setting for centuries of Chola rule.

Thanjavur-based historian Kudavayil Balasubramaniam, an authority on the Cholas and their various temples, says that Vijayalaya consciously built Thanjavur up to a great level of grandeur, and this was sustained all the way through Rajaraja's time when the magnificent Brihadeeswara temple was built. Several stone inscriptions in the temple speak of the city's magnificence, including details of its well-laid streets. But in 1024 CE, ten years after his ascension to the throne, Rajendra, the son and heir of Rajaraja, shifted the capital to Gangaikondacholapuram and it was as if the whole of Thanjavur was moved there. Merchants, traders, shopkeepers, soldiers, and common people all moved from Thanjavur and even the Periya Kovil was deserted. That was Thanjavur's first fall. When the later Pandyas recaptured Chola lands after the decline of the dynasty, they felt the need to re-establish semi-ruined Thanjavur again. The Pandya king Maravarman Sundara Pandya I had destroyed the Thanjavur palace earlier and the Sangam-age Chola palace in Uraiyur, the old capital, was also demolished. All this was revenge for the years of subjugation that the Pandyas experienced under Chola rule. The Pandyas then needed a place from which to administer the Thanjavur area and therefore set up in Nandi Puram, which was an old Pallava palace built by the Pallava king Nandi Varman II on the outskirts of Thanjavur. This palace had also been used by the Chola kings. and originally it was known as 'a place of a thousand lingams'.

Subsequently, a Pandya general called Samantha Narayanan Tondaiman was assigned the task of further reviving Thanjavur and, therefore, set up in his own name within the precincts of the original Thanjavur town, a small temple called Samantha Narayana Vinnagaram with the Yoga Narasimha of the Pandya style as the main deity. He also built a tank for the temple, now called Samantha Kulam, which remains to this day. Land between the temple and the tank was given to 108 Brahmins, who built their houses there, and the place was renamed Samanthanarayana Chaturvedi Mangalam. An inscription detailing the grant in the Periya Kovil on the eastern gateway near the steps between the main temple and the ardha mandapam can be seen even today. So, a new town quietly came up within old Thanjavur and land grants were given not just to this Narasimha temple but also to all the 108 Brahmins of the Chaturvedi Mangalam.

Post the twelfth century, after Chola power declined, Thanjavur suffered further vicissitudes from time to time. The end of Pandya rule saw the arrival of Malik Kafur and his lieutenants, who took over most of South India. Then followed Vijayanagar and Nayak rule, after which the Marathas arrived, and their stamp on Thanjavur included new arts and cultural interventions, which added layers to the rich fabric of Tamilakam's culture. As a separate principality, the British Raj then swallowed up the city while retaining the last Maratha ruler as a puppet.

The city's prominence and grandeur peaked during Chola rule. Established as the capital of the Chola kingdom in the mid-ninth century, the stage was set for a long dynastic rule which took Tamilakam to great heights in various ways. With their temple building, their art, their religion, their literature, and their forms of administration, the rule of the Cholas eclipsed earlier periods of Tamil history in terms of magnificence, power, and glory. For over 400 years, the Chola dynasty held sway across South India including modern-day Kerala, Karnataka, and parts of Andhra Pradesh. At the height of Chola power, Rajendra I sailed the seas and raided and captured with his powerful navy parts of Sri Lanka, Java, Sumatra, parts of Burma, Kedah in Malaysia, the Lakshadweep islands, and the Maldives. He marched his armies across the Gangetic plain to Kalinga and Bengal, bringing back with him the spoils of war—precious statues, sculptures, gemstones, and even water from the Ganga, a perfect and symbolic affirmation of Chola achievement and territorial expansion. All the territories on his long march all the way up the east coast from Tamilakam to Bengal were subdued by him.

In an earlier chapter, we have already briefly looked at the Sangam-age Chola kings with whom the dynasty originated. Regarding their origin, like many royal dynasties of ancient India, the Chola kings claimed descent from the sun (although at some point a lunar genesis is also mentioned). The epigraphical records of the Chola kings are mostly inscribed in the Leiden copper plates, the Thiruvalangadu copper plates of Rajendra Chola (discovered in 1905), the Anbil plates of Sundara Chola, and the Kanyakumari inscription of Virarajendra Chola. Other sources of information on these kings are from references in literature.

The two stand-out names of the Sangam age are Karikal and Kocchenganan (others like Killi Valavan, Koperuncholan, and Nallan Killi also appear in the Sangam poems). Karikal's achievements have already been mentioned. The Shaivite poet-saint Thirugnanasambandar as well as the Vaishnavite poet-saint Tirumangai Azhwar have referenced Kocchenganan in their hymns, praising the king's piety. In addition, there are fables to be found about some other noteworthy Chola kings; tales that are part of Tamil lore and retold in many Tamil households such as the one about Manu Needhi Cholan. This king was so seized by the notion of justice that he had his own son killed by running a chariot over him, as the son had killed a calf in the same manner. The cow in its great grief had rung the bell of justice in front of the king's palace and the king who had installed the bell to ensure that every citizen could ask for justice was now faced with this terrible situation, but he delivered justice all the same.

The other well-known story is that of Sibi Chakravarthi, the emperor who saved a dove from a vulture by giving the predator flesh from his own thigh to eat in place of its intended prey. The king supposedly used a scale with the dove in one pan and his own flesh in the other, but the pan with the dove in it remained heavier than the one with the king's flesh until the king put his entire weight in the balance. While these apocryphal stories may testify to the strength and personal ethics of the Chola rulers, there are other stories, according to historians, that portray them as brutal, vengeful, and driven by greed and ambition.

We know that during the time of the Kalabhras, roughly for about 300 years, the three kingdoms of the Pallava, Pandya, and Chola went into obscurity, until the Pallavas and Pandyas (separately or together) defeated the Kalabhras in the late fifth century. After this, the Pallavas ruled North Tamilakam while the Pandyas re-established themselves in the south. The Cholas at this time were feudatories of the Pallavas.

When Vijayalaya Chola captured Thanjavur from the local Muttarayar chief, he was still a vassal of the Pallava ruler, and technically it was terrain that was under the Pallava king. Vijayalaya then built up the Chola territory that extended from Thiruttani in the north up to the banks of the Vellaru, near Pudukkottai, in the south. There is not much additional detail about him except that the Pandya king Varaguna again tried to capture some Chola country. He reached the banks of the Kaveri and camped there; apparently that operation failed. After Vijayalaya, his son Aditya Chola, who is credited with further Chola expansion, was crowned as king in Thanjavurpatnam in 871 CE. An invasion of Kongunadu early in his reign has been recorded as well as the fact that he took the town of Talakadu. The Anbil copper plates say that he also built temples along the Kaveri belt, from the Sahyadri mountains to the sea, signalling a steady expansion of Chola territory.

Next, as previously noted, a fratricidal war broke out in the neighbouring

Pallava country, between the two royal Pallava half-brothers, the sons of Nandivarman III, Nripatunga, and Aparajita, with each wanting to rule after their father's death in 869 CE. Vijayalaya Chola's son, Aditya I, whose reign began in 871 CE, took the side of Aparajita. The Ganga king Prithvipati I also supported Aparajita, while Nripatunga had the Pandya king Varaguna on his side. A great battle ensued between these kings at Thirupurambiyam near Kumbakonam. Aparajita and his allies, Aditya and Prithvipati, won the battle although Prithvipati tragically lost his life.

Today the area is green and lush with paddy fields and birds flying low over standing water. It is hard to imagine a field of bloodied bodies and gory outcomes in this verdant and peaceful part of the Kumbakonam region, but it was at this precise time in history that the tide seemed to have distinctly turned for the Chola kings. Aditya was well rewarded for his part by his Pallava overlord Aparajita, who gave him more territory around Kumbakonam. Obviously, he was not only a remarkable warrior and clever diplomat but a king who made full use of all his opportunities.

After they lost in Thirupurambiyam, the Pandya king Varaguna was preoccupied with his domestic affairs and died soon after. He was succeeded by his son Parantaka Viranarayana. Meanwhile, Aditya Chola went to battle with his erstwhile ally, Aparajita the Pallava, overthrew him and deprived him of his territory. The ruthlessness and cunning of Aditya set the Cholas on a trajectory of acquisition and war. The Thiruvalangadu plates, which list the complete genealogy of the Chola kings, say Aditya overthrew 'the strong Pallava ruler'. The Kanyakumari inscription calls him Kodandarama or the one who slew the Pallava king who was seated on an elephant. It was a great victory, after which Aditya gained Tondaimandalam, and annexed it to Chola territory. Aditya then embarked on several other military campaigns to expand his kingdom—eventually expanding it up to the borders of Rashtrakuta. He married a Rashtrakuta princess, a daughter of Krishna II, whose name was Ilankon Pichchi. She became his senior queen. In the twenty-third year of his reign, he is said to have also married a Pallava princess.

All the information on Aditya is from plates and inscriptions—the Anbil plates, the Thillaisthanam inscription, and some others describing territories and gifts made to loyalists as well as to temples. For instance, Aditya was a close friend of the Chera king of the time, Sthanu-Ravi, and the Thillaisthanam inscription records a gift made by a Kadamba-Madevi, the wife of a general Vikki-Annan, whom both Aditya and the Chera king favoured. These two monarchs jointly gave Vikki-Annan a 'throne, a palanquin, drums, a palace, bugles an elephant corps and the hereditary title of *Sembian Tamila-vel'*. Obviously, the generosity implies that a lot of confidence and trust was reposed in this individual, who must have been of great support to both Kings.

Aditya died in Tondainad, near Kalahasti in Chittoor district, in 907 CE. His son and successor, Parantaka Chola, built a sepulchral temple in his memory called Kodandarameswara or Adityarameswara. Parantaka apparently neatly managed to usurp the crown from his older half-brother, Adittan Kannaradevan, who was the son of the senior Rashtrakuta queen and by all accounts the rightful heir; the circumstances surrounding the takeover are not clear. There could have well been a war of succession with Krishna II, the Rashtrakuta king interceding on his grandson's behalf, but obviously it was to no avail. Parantaka thus acquired a vast stretch of land from Kalahasti to Pudukkottai, in addition to what his father had conquered—Tondaimandalam and Kongunadu. Parantaka's reputation is that of a fierce warrior. He ruled from 907 CE to 955 CE. During his rule, he expanded the Chola kingdom to a considerable extent. First, he began by invading the Pandya country, which was under a king called Rajasimha II, and although his incursions into Pandya territory began as early as in the third year of his reign, it was only around 918 CE that he subjugated Madurai in a battle at Vellur, earning him the title Madurantaka. The Udayendiram copper plates of 921 CE refer to this victory: 'His army having crushed at the head of a battle the Pandya king together with an army of elephants, horses and soldiers, seized a herd of elephants together with Madhura…he bears in the world the title of Sangrama Raghava (Rama in battle) which is full of meaning.' The inscription goes on to say that even the Sri Lankan king, who was an ally of the Pandya ruler, was afraid of what Parantaka would do to Sri Lanka.

The Sri Lankan king's fears came true, for in a 923 CE record we find that Parantaka has a new title: Maduraiyum Illamum Konda Parakesarivarman—alluding to the defeat of both the Sri Lankan and Pandya rulers by Parantaka. The *Mahavamsa*, a Sri Lankan work on the history of that island, compiled by Sinhalese monks in the fifth century CE, mentions this attempt by Parantaka to conquer Sri Lanka. Parantaka was diverted from this, however, by frequent military incursions into his kingdom, notably by the Rashtrakutas on his northern border.

Parantaka also extended power in other directions; the Udayendiram copper plates say that he uprooted two Bana kings who were supporters of the Rashtrakuta king and annexed their territory which is in the present-day Andhra region; he also conquered the Vaidumbas and subjugated them. It is clear then that Parantaka, who was called Samarakesari, that is one who wins battles, and Veera (fearless) Cholan, fought numerous wars to extend his territory. Some were at great cost to himself—for example in the Battle of Takkolam, fought in 949 CE, against the Rashtrakuta king, Krishna III, he tragically lost his son Rajaditya. The prince was sitting on an elephant and was struck by an arrow shot by Butuga II, a Western Ganga feudatory of Krishna the Rashtrakuta king. As Rajaditya had died on his elephant, he was given the heroic title Aanaimel Thunjiya Thevar, or one who attained martyrdom on the back of an elephant. The Leiden plates of Rajaraja in 1006 CE say:

> ...the historic Rajaditya having agitated in battle the imperturbable Krishnaraja along with his army, with his sharp arrows falling in all directions while on the back of an excellent elephant had his heart split by the thrust of sharp arrows and mounting a celestial car went to the world of heroes.

Heartbroken by the death of his son, Parantaka died in 955 CE; earlier, his second son, Gandaraditya, had taken over the reins of the kingdom around 950 CE. During Parantaka's rule, in its heyday, the Chola kingdom extended from Nellore in the north to Kanyakumari in the south. The Cholas lost some of the northern territory at the end of Parantaka's reign, with the king a broken man, beset by personal as well as political tragedies.

Parantaka had other sides to him. He was a great administrator, and a devout Shaivite who built some beautiful temples in Chola country. Pullamangai near Thanjavur is a little jewel of a temple which we will look at in detail in the next chapter. Parantaka's temples had clean lines and were generally small in scale; inscriptions point to a spirit of religious tolerance that seems to have prevailed during the period of Parantaka I. The Thiruvalangadu plates describe Parantaka as 'the bee at the lotus feet of Siva' and say that he covered with gold the temple of Siva at Chidambaram. Parantaka's record in governance was praiseworthy. For example, the Karandai plates speak of his contributions to agricultural growth as he dug many canals and provided waterways across Chola country.

Parantaka's second son, Gandaraditya, ruled a meagre eight or so years. Gandaraditya was a pious man prone to spiritual activities. He voluntarily gave up the kingship and became a renunciate, his throne passing to his younger brother, Arinjaya. Gandaraditya's spiritual accomplishments include a hymn with eleven verses on the temple at Chidambaram, contributions to a Vishnu temple and a Jain temple. A sculptural frieze in the Umamaheshwara temple at

Konerirajapuram built around 973 CE shows the king and his queen, Sembian Mahadevi, carved in a worshipful stance to the main deity.

Sembian Mahadevi was an unusual woman. She built and repaired more than a dozen temples in South Arcot, Thanjavur district, Kumbakonam district, and Chengalpattu district. Her sense of history in an age when the focus was likely to be only on the immediate glories of the period was remarkable. So also her attitude of fairness. For instance, while repairing a Pandya temple built by Varaguna Pandya, who was a mortal enemy of the Cholas, she carefully preserved the Pandyan king's inscription while the temple was being renovated and placed it back after the repairs were done, adding an additional inscription that placed her own renovation as well as his in an accurate historical context. Sembian Mahadevi was the daughter of Malavarayan, a nobleman who was in the court of Parantaka and Gandaraditya. A woman of substance, her contribution to Chola creativity as a princess and later queen were considerable. She conducted herself with great wisdom and dignity through the years of reign of her husband, her brother-in-law, Arinjaya (956–57 CE), his son, Sundara Chola Parantaka II (957–70 CE), his son, Aditya Karikala (957–69 CE), and that of her own son, Uttama Chola Karikala (970–85 CE). She also lived well into the reign of her grandnephew, the great Rajaraja, and acquired a reputation as a wise, pious, and stable matriarch in a family that was plagued by intrigue and early deaths.

Besides her interests in building and repairing temples, she set up a tradition of metal casting that gave Chola bronzes much of their beauty and grandeur. A lot of the early Chola bronzes available with us today, including the beautiful ones at Konerirajapuram and Thiruvengadu, are from her time. Systems of mass production of these bronzes for temples were apparently encouraged by her direct involvement in the processes. She not only managed to remain outside the fray of royal intrigue and politics but was a trusted and much sought-after figure, whom the Chola kings turned to for advice and counsel. The other notable fact is that unlike a few other Chola queens within the family who committed sati on the demise of their husbands, Sembian Mahadevi did not choose to, and in her later years, focused more on the development and patronage of art and culture.

Soon after Arinjaya Chola, Parantaka's youngest son, ascended the throne, he lost his life in battle against the Rashtrakutas, in a place called Arrur. The Rashtrakutas kept biting off tracts of territory from Chola lands, and until Rajaraja's time they continued to lose control over vast areas they had brought under their suzerainty. Arinjaya was succeeded by his son Sundara

Chola. Sundara Chola was also known as Parantaka II and ruled from about 957 CE to 970 CE; he recovered some of the lost territory of the Cholas from the Rashtrakutas. His success in securing the northern borders of the Chola kingdom made the kingdom more prosperous and secure. Sundara Chola died in a palace in Kanchipuram and was known after that as ponmaligai-tunjina deva or the lord who died in a golden palace. He was a man of many parts; he encouraged both Sanskrit and Tamil literature. Moreover, he had a tolerant attitude to other faiths, especially Buddhism.

A murder mystery unsolved to this day emerged during the last years of Sundara Chola's reign with the murder of his son, Aditya Karikala II. An inscription from Udayagiri states that the local sabha of Sri Veeranarayana Chaturvedi Mangalam had confiscated the properties on the king's orders from three Brahmins as they were liable for treason, having killed Aditya Karikala, Sundara Chola's heir apparent. Aditya Karikala, after a victory over the Pandyas in 964 CE, had cut off the Pandya king Veera Pandyan's head, brought it back triumphantly to Thanjavur, and displayed it in front of his palace. To avenge the death of the Pandya king, three top officials in his administration allegedly killed Aditya. However, several historians like Sastri say that it was Uttama Chola, the son of Gandaraditya, who conspired to have Aditya Karikala killed, as he saw him as a threat to his own possible accession to the throne. Uttama was not satisfied with the subordinate role assigned to princes of the blood in the administration of the kingdom; and he perhaps convinced himself that the throne was his by right, and that his cousin and children were usurpers.

The Thiruvalangadu plates, while glossing over the story, make some enigmatic statements. 'Aditya disappeared owing to his desire to see heaven…', a euphemistic reference to his death. A rough translation of these plates suggests that after the shock of the murder, 'with a view to dispel the blinding darkness caused by the powerful Kali (Sin) entreated Arulmolivarman (later Rajaraja I) versed in the *dharma* of *ksattra,* (but) did not desire the kingdom for himself even inwardly as long as his paternal uncle coveted the country'. Clearly in the indication of covetousness, there is the hint of conspiracy. The third view, quite absurdly, was that Arulmozhi Varman wanted the throne for himself; but this has no credence at all, given that after his brother's death he insisted that his uncle, Uttama Chola, rule before him. By all accounts, the Chola royal family were quite united, and Arulmozhi Varman displayed great maturity in not claiming the throne until it came to him in the ripeness of time. This prince believed that during his time as crown prince during

Uttama Chola's kingship, he could quietly learn politics, warfare, kingship, and the arts, before the beginning of his own great reign.

Successive Chola rulers displayed a remarkable sense of political craft, military expansion, and efficient administration. They fostered the arts with their magnificent temples, murals, and structures, and decentralized to some extent their control over local governance. On the other hand, they were ruthless in their wars and conquests. Decapitation, severing the heads of enemies and betrayers, having elephants trample enemies to death and other kinds of cruelty were not at all uncommon in the courts of the Chola kings.

Uttama Chola, known as Madurantaka Uttama Chola (because he firmly brought Madurai under the Chola overlordship), ruled for fifteen years from 969 CE to 985 CE and named Arulmozhi Varman his crown prince. Several stone inscriptions of Uttama Chola's period have been found mentioning the names of his queens and his ministers. Curiously, the earliest Chola gold coin mentioning his reign was once in the possession of an Englishman, Sir Walter Elliot. He reproduced it in a drawing since the actual coin was lost; it showed a seated tiger (the Chola emblem) and a fish to the right, with a legend of Uttama Chola in Grantha. The tiger crest was the emblem of the royal Cholas.

In 985 CE, on the death of Uttama Chola, his nephew, the crown prince Arulmozhi Varman, born to Sundara Chola and his queen Vanavan Mahadevi, came to the throne; his coronation name was Rajaraja I. Arulmozhi Varman has since been the subject of myths and stories including in the novels of Kalki Krishnamurthy and now a successful two-part film by popular film-maker Mani Ratnam. Notwithstanding the exaggerations of creative retelling, this prince occupies a special place in the hearts of the Tamils for his courage, his administrative capabilities, his mastery over several subjects, and his piousness which never came in the way of clear-headed action. He ruled till 1014 CE.

The historian S. R. Balasubrahmanyam, who has brilliantly and in exacting detail studied all the Chola temples from the earliest days to the end of the dynasty's rule, says that the Cholas were perhaps the most gifted of the dynasties that ever ruled India. He says that Rajaraja I can 'legitimately claim to have laid the real foundations for the glory and longevity of the Chola empire. He was a great soldier and general like Alexander of Macedon, Julius Caesar, and Hannibal. The Cholas had the great good fortune of his being followed by a line of successors equally adept in the arts of war and administration.'

Rajaraja's first important act was to conquer the Cheras, destroying their fleet at Kandalur Salai and capturing Vizhinjam. He next 'destroyed the splendour of the Pandyas' by regaining lost territory from them. Plagued as the Cholas often were by the Rashtrakutas, Rajaraja brought back under Chola control all the land lost to them during the battle of Takkolam. The princes of the Eastern Chalukyas were pacified and made into allies—he married his daughter, Kundavai, off to Vimaladitya, the younger Chalukya prince. Next, he annexed large areas of Karnataka, Andhra, and even Kollam and Kudamalainadu (modern-day Coorg). He also subjugated the Western Chalukyas who had taken much of the Rashtrakuta land. Then he overran the kingdom of Kalinga, present-day Odisha, following which he invaded Sri Lanka. According to the Thiruvalangadu plates, Rajaraja I 'excelled Sri Rama by crossing the sea, not with the aid of a causeway built by monkeys but by using ships and conquering Lanka.' Rajaraja had built up formidable naval fleets that ultimately controlled all the islands off the Arabian Sea. At the height of his power, his kingdom extended from Sri Lanka in the south to the Tungabhadra basin in the north and the Mahendra mountains in the Northeast.

Besides his renown and ability as a warrior and military strategist, Rajaraja excelled at governance, innovating and executing several pioneering concepts. For instance, he organized a land survey quite unlike anything ever done before by any ruler in India. The survey was extremely detailed, including the measurement of small bits of land, details of systems of irrigation, boundaries, and tax revenues. It was carried out by a large cadre of revenue officers, accountants, ledger keepers, and executors of royal decrees. Additionally, it was established at all levels, from villages to the more central units (Balasubrahmanyam points out that some decades later, William the Conqueror performed an elaborate survey just like Rajaraja's in England). Rajaraja also implemented his own sophisticated system of governance, which had both accountability and a large degree of autonomy. The Cholas' systems of administration were to an extent adopted from the Pandyas' systems, then restructured and refined continually over the course of Chola rule.

Rajaraja also showed a great deal of religious tolerance. Apart from his ardent devotion to Shiva and therefore to temple-building, he also aided other creeds; the Leiden copper plates speak of his contributions to Buddhist viharas. Of course, his greatest contribution was to the world's architectural heritage: the building of the marvellous Rajarajesvaram or Brihadeeswara temple in Thanjavur, dedicated to his beloved deity, Shiva. He began building the temple probably in the nineteenth year of his reign, and it took over seven years for the building to be completed. The stones for the temple were brought from quarries that were not close by, and it has also been suggested that he used slaves from Sri Lanka to transport and install them. We will look at this architectural masterpiece in a subsequent chapter.

While it seemed like Rajaraja would be a difficult act to follow, Madurantakan, who came to the throne in 1012 CE (and was called Parakesarivarman Rajendra Chola Deva), set himself up to mirror his father's achievements. His father installed him on the throne, and he came to be called Rajendra I. Rajaraja died in 1014 at the age of sixty-seven of natural causes. Rajendra inherited an extensive kingdom from his father, all of Tamilakam, most of Andhra, Karnataka, and Sri Lanka. The empire was already trading with the East Indies and China, and Rajendra carefully maintained the strength of his navy to ensure continuance of this commerce. Having inherited a stable administrative set-up with a bureaucracy in place, Rajendra turned his attention to military activities. He clearly wanted to not just safeguard the land he inherited, but also to expand his borders, as if by vying with his father he could prove himself his father's equal. The equation between the father and son is interesting; Rajendra's attitude to his father ranged from utmost respect, admiration, and filial piety to an unexpressed rivalry and perhaps a need to outdo his father, which manifested itself in Rajendra's many splendid projects like Gangaikondacholapuram which reflected both facets of the relationship.

Rajendra set out first to extend his empire. At the age of twenty he had conquered the Western Chalukyas, after which he was known as the 'ornament' of the Chola race. He captured the lands between the Krishna River in the north and the Tungabhadra in the south and firmly ensured that the Chalukya capital was in his hands. Then he moved on to the Chera and Pandya rulers and ensured their subservience to him in a victorious campaign. The Thiruvalangadu plates detail some of this. 'Rajaraja's son, the Master of Policy took possession of the bright spotless pearls, the seeds of the spotless fame of the Pandya kings.' And the line that follows says, 'after establishing there his own son Sri Chola Pandya for the protection of the Pandya country. The light of the solar race then proceeded to the conquest of the West.'

The copper plates mention Rajendra's takeover of Kerala. 'The fearless Madurantaka crossed the Sahya Mountain and forthwith set upon...Kerala in great force and there ensued a fierce battle which brought ruin upon kings... after having conquered the Kerala kings and harrowed the land guarded by the austerities of the lord of the Bhrigus, the prince returned to his capital, the abode of prosperity.' Rajendra then went on to place the responsibility of governing Kerala and the Pandya country on his son, whom he crowned as viceroy in Madurai and gave the title of Jatavarman Sundara Chola Pandya, a name that tied the prince to the Pandya country. Rajendra next invaded Sri Lanka and recovered the Pandya crown that had been deposited there. The Karandai plates say that he conquered the island, and his expedition was 'thorough and complete' and that 'the king of Ceylon out of fear, came and sought the two feet of Rajendra as shelter'. Rajendra then went on to capture Kadaram, or Kedah in Malaysia—and the king of that country simply ran away. The Cholas were now a cardinal part of the chain of maritime trade from west to east and stretching all the way up to China. Fragments of inscriptions in Tamil found in places like Sumatra were evidence of a long history of trade relations, and the naval expeditions and suzerainty over Kadaram and even parts of Cambodia added lustre to Rajendra's list of military achievements.

Apart from Rajendra's military successes (especially in the Gangetic plain), he was an able and successful ruler like his father before him. He encouraged the arts and had great literary interests, setting up schools and colleges which brought him the title of Pandita Chola. He also built twenty-five temples, some in Pandya country, and brought back numerous beautiful bronzes as spoils of war to his kingdom. However, his most remarkable achievement was the construction of his new capital at Gangaikondacholapuram. The king, having been seized of the idea of celebrating his success in conquering areas beyond the Gangetic plain, built this new capital in a village not far from Thanjavur. Like his ancestor Vijayalaya before him, who moved his capital from Uraiyur to Thanjavur, Rajendra moved his capital from Thanjavur to Gangaikondacholapuram. The entire structure and machinery of government was shifted, and Thanjavur was left quite derelict for many years. The new city was also known as Gangaikondacholisvaram and remained the Chola capital for approximately 250 years from about 1025 CE till 1279 CE, when the Chola empire collapsed.

Gangaikondacholapuram was an extensive and well-planned city by all accounts, with architectural principles derived from ancient classical texts on the subject. It was strongly fortified with two walls, entirely built of burnt bricks, and had its own artificial lake. The streets and gateways were named Rajaraja Peruvali and Rajendra Peruvali after the king and his father, and most of the kings who succeeded Rajendra were crowned there. Although only the Rajarajesvaram temple remains now (this temple was also called Rajarajesvaram), the site of the palace and details of the surroundings such as the tanks and canals that were dug are detailed in several epigraphs and inscriptions. There is an apocryphal story about the lake, saying that water from the Ganga was transported manually to fill it, involving thousands of people carrying pots of water on a long, arduous trek from the Ganga in the north to Gangaikondacholapuram in the south. It is interesting, though, that although the temple at Gangaikondacholapuram was built in the likeness of the Rajarajesvaram temple in Thanjavur, legend has it that Rajendra was careful not to have it rival the Thanjavur temple in scale and ensured that the vimana was at a lower height than that of the Thanjavur temple. Rajendra too died of natural causes in 1044 CE at age eighty, although some accounts hold that he was around seventy-three or seventy-five when he died. His chief queen, Vanavan Mahadevi, is said to have committed sati after his death.

Rajendra was succeeded by his three sons, Rajadhiraja I, Rajendra II, and Vira Rajendra (aka Vira Chola), who ruled one after the other. Although talented and militaristic, they did not measure up to the successes of their father and grandfather. They were often caught up in the task of preserving the boundaries of the mighty empire and rebuffing the small rebellions that occurred regularly. Their sister, Ammanga Devi, was married off (in what proved to be a fortuitous political move) to the Eastern Chalukya ruler, Rajaraja Narendra. The offspring of that marriage, their son Rajendra, who was also called Kulottunga I, inherited the great Chola throne in 1070 CE after the death of his Chola uncles and their heirs, all of whom died young. The Chola kingdom again saw a great level of stability until 1120 CE. A strong ruler, Kulottunga I abolished certain taxes and ensured the welfare of his subjects, at the same time guarding and strengthening the borders of his kingdom. He too was a temple builder, supported Buddhist monasteries, and was credited with having sent an embassy of seventy-two people from his court to China. As Sastri says, 'by introducing a fresh, and possibly more vigorous yet closely related stock of kings to rule the empire, and by amalgamating at a critical time the resources of the Eastern Chalukya kingdom with the Chola, it ensured a continuous and active life for the empire of Rajaraja....'

Several capable Chola rulers followed Kulottunga. His son, Vikrama Chola, ruled after him till 1135 CE and was followed by Kulottunga II. The latter ruled till 1150 CE and was a very devout Shaivite, apparently to the point of bigotry. Well-known poets like Sekkizhar, Kambar, and Pugazhendi lived during his reign. His son, Rajaraja II, ruled after him from 1150 CE to 1173 CE, during which he built the beautiful Airavatesvara temple in Darasuram. In addition, Rajaraja apparently cleared several blockages in the Kaveri River for the benefit of his citizens.

Several rulers followed this king, and Kulottunga III of this line was another great Chola ruler. The last Chola ruler was Kulottunga III's grandson, Rajendra III, who ruled from 1246 to 1279 CE, after which, in 1286, the Pandya king Jatavarman Sundara Pandya conquered the Chola kingdom.

The 450 years of Chola rule brought great richness to the story of Tamilakam. There was an immense flowering of architecture, painting, sculpture, and literature. The several hundred temples that these kings built showcased the architectural and artistic genius that they encouraged. Militaristic expansion was followed by the establishment of far-sighted methods and structures of administration and governance. The qualities of these rulers were recognized in numerous copper plates. As the larger Leiden plate says, with not a little exaggeration:

> As long as the moon crested deity (Siva) sports with his consort on the Kailasa mountain, as long as Hari (Vishnu) performs his meditative sleep (Yoga Nidra) on the serpent couch on the ocean of milk, as long as the light of all the world dispels the dense darkness…so long may the Chola family protect from danger the circle of the whole earth.

Chapter 14

The Facets and Functions of Chola Society

The Chola kingdom grew...into an extensive and well-knit empire, efficiently organized and administered, rich in resources...

Nilakanta Sastri, historian

THE IDEA THAT THE CHOLA STATE WAS A CENTRALIZED ONE WITH THE king in control at the head, an efficient bureaucracy, and a well-developed revenue system has been established by historians like Nilakanta Sastri while scholars like Kesavan Veluthat argue that the 'concept of a highly centralised state cannot be reconciled with the presentation of the autonomous and vital local groups'. Veluthat suggests that the king was more like an overlord, a suzerain over many local chiefs and magnates. He also says that these landed magnates were used by the king and his agents for the collection of tax revenue rather than using the established and highly functional bureaucracy which Sastri says existed. Scholars such as Burton Stein have questioned the conventional framework of historiography of historians like Sastri and others, although some of Stein's observations, while very valid, do not always take other complexities into account. Be that as it may, it is not within the scope of this study to get into elaborate academic discussions about these social constructs, but it is important and necessary to highlight that there are radical reinterpretations of the mediaeval set-up under the Chola kings that came after Sastri's work. Y. Subbarayalu's *South India Under the Cholas* is a case in point. While Sastri's *The Colas* continues to be the most authoritative work on Chola dynastic history, Subbarayalu's analysis and interpretation puts together the accumulated knowledge of later years. According to Veluthat, Subbarayalu's contribution 'to the understanding of the history of this region, particularly the economic, social, and political processes and structures under the Cholas has been immense'. Subbarayalu's studies clearly set out the constituents of the Chola state, the king, the political and social organization, and the slow stratification of caste groupings.

As we will recall, the more than 400-year-old Chola rule passing through the hands of twenty or more kings saw the establishment of certain types of administration. We must remember that in the early years of Chola rule, just before their expansion in the tenth century from Chola-nadu (mostly under Rajaraja I, and after the Pallava decline) there were many smaller chiefs who had a subordinate relationship with the Chola kings and ruled their own nadus, which were about 100 square metres of territory. Many of these chieftains married their daughters off to the Chola rulers from time to time. They maintained their small courts, donated to temples, often in the name of their Chola overlords, and gave military help to their kings in times of war. These chiefs were padikaval or watchmen to the kings and guarded their localities; they, in turn, took sizable revenues from local artisans and others by way of tax. The nadus or territories of these kings were slowly incorporated with consummate skill by Rajaraja into his kingdom under a category called valanadu. The chiefs who were thus absorbed into the larger Chola territory were rewarded by being recruited into the Chola bureaucracy. They served as important ministers in the imperial court.

The Chola rulers vigorously encouraged Brahmin settlements, the Brahmadeyas, particularly all along the fertile Kaveri basin. This practice of donating huge tracts of lands to Brahmins began in the days of the Pandya kings, as we've seen. The setting up of such social hierarchies and privileges which became problematic later with unequal access to wealth and resources was set in motion during these centuries. Veluthat says, 'Most *brahmadeyams* revolved around a temple and that institution was the nerve centre of many social activities. A whole new ideology was disseminated from the temple through the exposition of the *puranas* and *itihasas*.... All these helped in legitimising the principle of social stratification.... Accordingly, the *brahman* priest and the...ruler occupied the highest position in society. This helped in strengthening and validating newly formed monarchies. Thus, the state, which was the creation of the upper class in the stratified society, received its legitimacy in the hands of these new idealogues.' Generally, many village lands in the central parts of the Chola kingdom were communal holdings while Brahmadeyas were owned by individuals. By the twelfth and thirteenth centuries, these holdings became bigger and bigger, with individuals owning entire villages. The early centuries of Chola rule saw the establishment of sabhas in many Brahmadeyas, which were assemblies or corporations that conducted village business. Inscriptions have yielded a lot of information about them. Sometimes the Brahmins were brought in from elsewhere and settled in these lands, and they were called Brahmadeya kilavar. They had rights of cultivation and overlordship. In Velanvagai or non-Brahmin villages, where ownership rested with the Vellala or cultivators, including the non-Brahmin landed gentry, many were asked to forfeit their lands to Brahmins as mentioned.

In time, particularly from the tenth century onwards, the status of kings became elevated until it reached its acme in the eleventh century. Their titles reflected this. From peruman or great person, they took on titles like tribhuvana chakravarti—emperor of the three worlds. Udaiyar was another title as was ko. A king's titles sometimes were the same as those used for deities, and the king was also considered a comrade of the deity in some cases and called tolan. Queens and princes were mentioned in the inscriptions with honorific titles like pillaiyar up to the eleventh century after which they were indirectly referred to in eulogies. In the earlier years of Chola rule the king had several officers—adhikari, srikariyam, and nadu-vagai. There were about 100 adhikaris by the time Rajendra I came to the throne and some of them had the king's titles prefixed to their names, to show that they represented royal authority and were loyal to the king. Some records mention a group of officers called naduvirukkai, who worked with the adhikaris and tended to be Brahmins. There was a revenue office called puravuvari and tinai to look after tax collection. These were all officers of the king and appointed by him. Tirumantira-olai or olai was the king's scribe and had to write down and record royal orders on the spot.

The kings ruled through groups of such officers and representatives, who were sent across their territories. The basic unit of the Chola territory was the nadu and used to denote larger territories as well as distinct agricultural divisions. Apart from the central territory which was the Chola-nadu, there were other territories which came under Chola rule such as Pandya-nadu, Tondai-nadu and Malai-nadu. Some of these territories had other suffixes like kurram, kulakkil, erikil, nilai. The valanadu is a term for a larger administrative unit than the nadu. Nadus were usually from 20 to about 200 square kilometres in extent.

There was, however, a fluidity in administrative arrangements over decades and years. The basic settlement was a habitation site; it, along with surrounding agricultural land, was called ur. Those that were not Brahmadeyas were called velanvagai villages. In the early years of the Brahmadeya, the nattars were the main landholders of these velanvagai villages. In some villages, agricultural labourers called paraiya lived in separate settlements called cheris. Artisans had separate quarters as did coconut tree climbers and toddy tappers, who were called ilava. As inscriptions show, in some villages, washermen and water distributors also had separate quarters. The Brahmadeya was partially exempted from taxes unlike the Velanvagai villages. The Brahmadeya villages were often named for the king or queen or donor and had mangalam or chaturvedimangalam added to the name such as Kundavai Chaturvedimangalam. The Karandai plates say that over 1,080 Brahmin families were settled in Brahmadeyas in the early eleventh century. The devadana, which are temple lands or temple villages, usually had the term nallur added to the name. The creation of multiple Brahmadeyas meant that more irrigation systems such as canals and ponds were created. Separate lands called vettaperu were set up for this purpose. Subbarayalu says that some Brahmadeyas came to be called taniyurs, or independent villages, and some were grouped together to form new nadus. The cultivators who were tenants of these places were called ulukudi. There were caste-based corporate bodies that functioned at the village and at the supra village level. The urar was the corporate body of the Vellala landowners, the sabha was for the Brahmins, and the nagarattar was the body for the nagaram or merchant and trading villages.

We have observed in an earlier chapter how Rajaraja I created land records that measured almost every square inch of his kingdom as early as in 1000 CE. Rajaraja came to be called Ulagalandha Cholan, or the Chola who measured the world. There were accurate registers of land in every village, and temple inscriptions that provide fascinating details of Chola life also give an insight into administrative aspects. Even the kinds of measures and measuring rods that were used to measure land, the length of roads and canals, and the weights for weighing produce and commodities have been meticulously named and documented. Bamboo measuring poles called tiru ulagalandhakol and iluvaipaddikol were used to measure and classify agricultural lands. Padaikkol and manaikkol were names of other measures that were used. The full length of a measuring rod has also been specified in a carving at the Varadaraja Swamy temple in Kanchipuram.

The Chola government apparently did not interfere in the functioning of the local bodies although records of the tenth and early eleventh centuries suggested that an official could have sat in at some of the meetings. Government representation was mainly for tax collection. The local accountant, called ur-kanakku, was mainly involved only in local bodies like the urar, the sabha, or the nagaram. This local accountant was supposed to be an unbiased neutral person and was also called madhyasthai; he was a link with the government for tax collection.

Two inscriptions detail the penalty that befell the accountants who failed to discharge their duties. One is an inscription from Pullamangai in Thanjavur district dated to 973 CE, which says that the madhyastha of the Brahmadeya land had to forfeit his service tenure land since he failed to submit proper accounts of the paddy dues, and the money collected from the Vellalas and the Brahmins of the village. In another instance, recorded in an inscription 1001 CE from Thiruvidaimarudur, a subordinate accountant absconded without producing proper accounts, so his landed property was seized and confiscated by a senapati, the king's official.

Let us look briefly at the Uttiramerur inscriptions of the later Pallava and the Chola rulers which describe the self-governance system of Uttiramerur even from around the seventh century, and from Parantaka Chola's time in the early tenth century up to the reign of Kulottunga in the eleventh century. The village records indicate that some of the Pallava rulers took a great interest in the temples in this area. Nandivarman II founded and named the village Uttarameru Chaturvedimangalam. Not only did this Pallava ruler donate land for this village in the eighth century, but also set up the first sabha mandapam, the village assembly hall, and this is made clear in the inscriptions in the Vaikunta Perumal temple in nearby Kanchipuram.

After the Cholas captured Tondaimandalam, and with the tenth century witnessing agricultural expansion under the Chola rulers, more inscriptions were created regarding the administration of the time. Beginning with Parantaka Chola, who brought in a system of village assembly with elected officials, all the way up to the time of Aditya Karikala and his brother Rajaraja I, there were copious donations and grants made to the temples in the region, and the active functioning of the village assembly was boosted and supported by the royal courts. Experts who have deciphered the inscriptions and records here indicate that they cover a variety of subjects from the appointment of teachers, the construction of mandapams, elections to the village assembly, endowments for cure of snake bites, endowments for worship such as ritual offerings from food to flowers, punishments for accidental murder, testing for gold purity, and many other curious subjects.

The Uttiramerur inscription of 920 CE is 'a veritable classical written constitution of the village assembly that functioned 1000 years ago. It gives astonishing details about the constitution of wars, the qualifications of candidates standing for election, the disqualifications, the mode of election, the constitution of committees with elected members, the functions of the committees, and the power to remove the wrong doer, etc. (sic).' The expert epigraphist V. Venkayya who has translated the inscription verbatim, provides details:

King: Parakesarivarman who conquered Madurai.

Date: On the sixteenth day of the fourteenth year.

Royal Order: Whereas a royal letter of His Majesty, our lord, the glorious Viranarayana, the illustrious Parantakadeva, the prosperous Parakesarivarman was received and shown to us.

The Village: We, the members of the assembly of Uttaramerur-Caturvedimangalam, in its own sub-division of Kaliyurkottam

Settlement: Sitting with us and convening the committee in accordance with the royal command, made a settlement as follows according to the terms of the royal letter for choosing once every year this year forward members for the Annual Committee, Garden Committee and Tank Committee.

The inscription goes on to say that there will be thirty wards and those that live in these wards shall assemble and choose kuda olai (tokens drawn from a pot to select officials), that everyone must own more than a quarter veli of tax-paying land, live in a house built on his own site, and his age must be below seventy and above thirty-five. It also says that the person must know the mantra-brahmana and must be capable of explaining it to others. The disqualifications are many in number for anyone who has been on these committees and not submitted accounts or who has accepted a bribe. It clarifies which relatives of this person shall be forbidden from entering their names in the pot for office including aunts, uncles, cousins, in-laws, and others. Also, a foolhardy person, one who has committed incest, one who has 'taken forbidden food', and one who has performed ritual expiation for sins committed were among those excluded from participation in the pot ticket that enabled them to get on to committees.

The inscription further describes the mode of election whereby the names from the thirty wards are put in a pot, and a great assembly of the entire village is summoned. A young boy is asked to choose some tickets, transfer them to another pot in front of the assembly, from which one is drawn for each of the thirty wards and given to the madhyastha, the arbitrator who must receive it with all his fingers open and palm exposed. Members are thus chosen for the Garden Committee, the Tank Committee, and the Annual Committee. 'The great men of these three committees thus chosen for them shall hold office for full three hundred and sixty days and then retire', reads the inscription.

While this inscription provides a detailed description of democratic functioning at the grassroots, it must also be seen in the broader context of applicability in a Brahmadeya (we must remember that Uttiramerur is a Brahmin settlement) where there were already landowners who could qualify for these committees. There were plenty of people who were outside the pale of these qualifications and were not permitted to participate in these so-called 'democratic' functions and exercises. Nevertheless, the inscriptions of the area do give remarkable insights into the lives of the people even as they tangled with the structures around which their lives were built.

One aspect that must be highlighted at this juncture is that jati or caste became stratified. Inscriptional evidence attests to the existence of castes with hierarchies among them. We are all aware of the occupational origins of the caste structure, but it grew more structured in these times; from the tenth century onwards, even tribal groups who were outside the pale of society began to be incorporated into caste divisions. The inscriptions of the eleventh century mention donors to temples with their caste identities. The Brahmins occupied the highest rank in the caste hierarchy followed by the landholding Vellala, and the merchant caste which was considered almost equal to the Vellalas. The Paraiya were considered lower in the hierarchy and were agricultural labour. Leather workers, artisans, and herders were considered as service groups. Their respective assemblies were also caste oriented and that too increasingly in the centuries that followed. Another new aspect that emerged from this period is that with the expansion of the Chola empire, many tribal communities were roped in to defend the empire as part of the military and were also part beneficiaries of the conquered wealth of other territories which would have trickled down to them. A Chola inscription of the twelfth century mentions the palli people as the holders of kani (hereditary land rights) in the northern areas. This community is clearly described as martial, according to Subbarayalu. Once they became settled, the term nattar was added to their names. Other communities like this were the surutiman, nattaman, malaiman who also settled into agricultural life and were called nattars.

A further feature of social groupism that grew more pronounced during Chola rule was the left hand (idangai) and right hand (valangai) divisions among the castes. These distinctions also existed in Pandya times but emerged more strongly in the Chola period. It impacted the Vellala community the most and surfaced among traders and those in the military. Originally these were groupings of Chola Army regiments and initially there were no implications of one group being superior to the other. Many people belonging to hill tribes came down to the plains in the twelfth century and joined these groupings. Caste affiliations within these groupings, however, prevailed. The Brahmins seem to have been excluded from these groups. However, the two divisions were not fixed social groupings but were potential formations that were polarizing at times. Burton Stein drew up a chart of left-hand and right-hand affiliations and suggests that only ten out of the sixty-eight castes that he names are of the left-hand division. For instance, merchants and artisans were often bracketed with the right-hand group, and some weavers with the left-hand group. This classification also occurs among military personnel, who, after service, became peasants and cultivators. It is quite possible that these two divisions may have originally even started in the military and later became general nomenclature. In tenth century inscriptions of Rajaraja, right-hand divisions in the army have been named. Information about the left-hand divisions appeared for the first time in the inscriptions of Kulottunga Chola in the eleventh century. By implication, right hand meant a more influential, higher level group and the left hand denoted a lower level group of people.

An inscription which has a diktat about water usage is found in the entrance gopuram of the Koneriswarar temple at Ponnamaravathy in Sivagangai district. The inscription dates to the Pandya king Sundara Pandyan in the thirteenth century, and orders that his army battalions should not drink water from the uruni or water tank at Ponnamaravathy which was called idangai (left hand) meekaman. This was done at the behest of the donors who had made gifts to the temple. Obviously social pressures at times fostered such attitudes. These divisions or at least a perception of them strengthened during the Vijayanagar period and persisted till the time of the British.

With inscriptions as the main source of information on this period, historians have sought to study them in the context of a changing socio-political order during the centuries of Chola rule. Subbarayalu says the history of the Tamil country could not have been written without the help of inscriptions whether on stone or copper plate. They also largely relate to religious donations from royal dynasties and wealthy donors which often included the merchant class. Other than donations, there are many that refer to land sale and land lease including details of new settlements. As they are not subject to revisions, they are the most reliable source of the information regarding the society of the time. As a caveat, one must remember that the inscriptions largely reflect the upper strata of society. The status, lives, and livelihood of those outside the pale of this social strata, such as the poor and the landless, are by and large not subjects of such records and rarely feature in them.

Chola society starting from Parantaka I's time in the tenth century, while hierarchical with the Brahmins held in high regard, also integrated other groups ranging from dancing girls, the devaradiyar, to merchants and shepherds (sankarapaddiyar, idaiyar, manradi, etc.) all of whom contributed to the units of economy in which they were positioned. Inscriptions in temples indicate that the shepherd community was quite closely involved in the functioning and rituals of the temple. The more affluent among them donated cattle, perpetual lamps, and other ritual items. In fact, an inscription of Rajendra Chola's time indicates that if someone promises to donate ghee to the community, and for some reason fails to keep his commitment, his community would step in and honour the promise. Some women of the shepherd community were also philanthropic and made donations to local temples. As temple dancers played an important role in temple rituals, they were well regarded and, in this time, accorded respect. The deterioration of their status seems to be a later phenomenon.

Polygamy appears to have been common especially among the nobility and kings. The inscriptions do not say much about women but the literature of the times, which was largely religious in nature, includes impassioned poetry from women poet-saints like the Shaivite Karaikal Ammaiyar and Andal who worshipped Vishnu. These women were radical in the sense that whether the reality of their lives mirrored their poetry or not, they liberated themselves from stereotypical roles at least in the imagination as revealed in their poetry. Andal, for instance, dared to see the Lord as her lover, and Karaikal Ammaiyar shed her youth and physicality to be in service to Shiva. The fervour and faith of these poet-saints, both men and women, of the Shaiva, Vaishnava, Jain, and Buddhist traditions are dealt with elsewhere, but it is important to note that some exceptional, perhaps even imagined, situations existed for women in a society that was slowly changing its idiom. We must not forget Sembian Mahadevi's role as materfamilias for the Chola rulers was a highly visible one, and an inscription of her period also mentions the name of one of her ladies—Nandi Peru Kadatti. A few other women are mentioned as being present at these early Chola royal courts. One is specifically named as a singer, Nakkan Pattalagi. There are no other details about the general status of women, but a few village records indicate the practice of sridhana, an amount gifted to a woman at the time of marriage, which also included property, and it appears that she had some level of control over it.

In its heyday, as many of the inscriptions bear out, Chola society with the temple as the major fulcrum, fanned into complex networks of trade, tillage, and activities with transactional constituents that kept the wheels of the local economies going and fed into the working of the larger political structure of the kingdom. As David Shulman says, there were '…networks around each of the great temples, drawing into this inherently political arena the peasant villages with their assemblies, pastoralists living off their herds, soldiers, courtiers, brahmins, ritualists, artisans, accountants, washermen, dancing girls, tailors, watchmen and other service workers—all of whom contributed to the temple economy and lived to no small degree off its fruits.'

Chapter 15

Reaching the Sky: An Imperial Vision

...The Hindu temple functions as a place of transcendence, a place where man may progress from the world of illusion to knowledge and truth

George Michell, historian

THE STATELY STONE VIMANA OF THANJAVUR'S BRIHADEESWARA, THE temple of the Great Lord, towering against the expanse of sky had always drawn the young scholar S. K. Govindaswami. Studying at Annamalai University in Chidambaram, some 100 kilometres from Thanjavur, he would make frequent journeys over dusty roads by bus and train, spending his meagre savings travelling to this old historic town and wandering in the temple precincts. He would run his palm over the roughly hewn stones of the temple walls etched with carvings in old Tamil and spend hours deciphering the scripts carved into stone a thousand years ago. He was fascinated by the temple's great façade, its exceptional architecture, and the stories that its stones revealed. The country was waking up to a sense of its own history as the struggle for freedom from the British yoke slowly gained momentum, and Govindaswami like many other young men of that time felt a strong connection to Tamil history, and in this case, to the story of the great Cholas. He felt intuitively that there were more secrets that the great temple would reveal.

In 1930, the twenty-eight-year-old Govindaswami and his friend T. V. Umamaheswaran Pillai made their usual trek to the Periya Kovil (Big Temple) as is popularly known. As they wandered inside, a sleepy sentry cautioned them about dark passages and uneven floors. Govindaswami felt a sudden and inexplicable frisson of excitement as both men climbed up the narrow winding stairs into the circumambulatory passage above the sanctum sanctorum. The passage walls, 7 feet wide, were crusty with falling plaster. At first Govindaswami saw what he described as 'paintings of late and degenerate age whose linear contortions and chromatic extravagances' were a disappointment as he had hoped to find fine murals of an even earlier time. Govindaswami did not give up, as he 'felt' in the 'dim religious light of a small oil lamp' the possible existence of more paintings in the narrow circumambulatory passage around the sanctum sanctorum. He went back a year later in April 1931 and under the bright light of a baby petromax lamp, his efforts paid off to reveal a landmark discovery. On further exploration and inspection of the western wall under the cracked plastering, exactly as he had dreamed, he found beautiful frescoes of a much earlier time. Govindaswami gave *The Hindu* a scoop on 11 April 1931. Describing the moment of discovery, he writes: 'A gentle touch and the whole mass crumbled down, exposing underneath a fine series of frescoes palpitating with the life of older days.' He was delighted by his discovery of figures of men and women, birds and flowers, horses and elephants, yakshis, apsaras, and majestic figures, including one seated on a tiger skin. He was aware that his discovery would mean that Chola mural art would now be comparable to the Pallava paintings found in the Kailasanatha temple in Kanchipuram. He writes, with a disarming degree of unselfconsciousness, 'the discovery of these paintings is of great importance to the history of South Indian art.... The Cholas may now be believed to divide the honours equally with the Pallavas not only in South Indian architecture and sculpture, but in South Indian painting.'

In a follow-up article on 7 June 1931, Govindaswami, now writing with more authority and clarity, points out that after Buddhist Ajanta and Jain Sittanavasal, and the few fragments of mural art found in Kailasanatha temple, the mural art of the Brihadeeswara temple has 'extended the frontiers of Indian painting'. Here, he says, one does not find a layer of clay, cow dung, and powdered rock as in the case of Ajanta; instead, a thin coating of white lime plaster is applied directly to the wall. It is a combination of tempera with fresco, and the forms are drawn delicately but 'strengthened with forcible (sic) blacks and reddish browns, always firm and of uniform thickness.' Shiva is portrayed here in different manifestations, and the story of Sundaramurti Nayanar (Sundarar) is pictured in three panels, as is the great hall of Chidambaram, says Govindaswami. He states that the repetitive representation of the strong figure of a king on occasion alone and sometimes with his queens is of Rajaraja, always in a prayerful mode. Govindaswami firmly believed that these paintings were contemporaneous with the building of the temple in the eleventh century.

This remarkable finding excited the interest of historians of the time like Nilakanta Sastri. There were other developments, too. Although the temple had been declared a historic monument in 1891, it was only after the discovery of the paintings that serious efforts were made to protect the temple. Sadly, Govindaswami died in 1941, around the age of thirty-eight, and did not live long enough to revel in his fame or pursue his interests. The accurate identifications that Govindaswami made about the stories on the walls, the techniques of painting used for the murals, and the naming of the figures of saints, gods, and the king on the narrow walls was a great contribution to the history of art in South India. The feat of profusely documenting this hitherto unknown art was left to later archeologists and conservation experts like Dr Sathyamurthy, Dr P. Sriraman, and photographer R. Thyagarajan. The murals were 15 feet tall and 10 feet wide and would not fit in single frames and had to be photographed in 40 to 50 frames and then digitally assembled. The dark, ill-lit passage posed further challenges to documentation with the space between the two walls being less than 7 feet. Using the technique of montage, Thyagarajan, who was also an artist, captured the paintings without sacrificing the artistic elegance of the paintings or their aesthetic value. This documentation was then compiled in a book by Sriraman titled *Chola Murals: Documentation and Study of the Chola Murals of Brihadiswara Temple*, which interpreted the stories of the panels. The work of documentation and preservation began in 2004 when the digital camera first came to India.

On a visit with Sriraman to the temple, he explains the history of the murals. First, he shows us the sixteenth-century paintings commissioned by the Nayak rulers (with the intent to display their own brand of creativity) which overlaid the Chola murals. The Nayak paintings, he points out, are drab in colour, using largely black and red with poor technique; in theme too, they are limited, with repeated representations of Shiva as Tripurantaka, says Sriraman. Govindaswami's discovery of the Chola murals added a great dimension to Indian painting whose reputation had hitherto rested only on the Ajanta cave paintings.

Notwithstanding the fact that Rajaraja was personally involved in the construction of the temple including the murals, it must have been a daunting task for the master painter, given the narrow and poorly lit circumambulatory passage. The themes of the paintings were misinterpreted in the early years of their discovery, says Sriraman, but have now been properly identified. What makes them stand out is the level of detail in each segment and the incomparable artistry in perception and execution. There are many painted scenes; most of them outstanding in their depiction of chosen subjects, such as one of the king and his wives listening to the wisdom of the guru in a cavern on a verdant hillock. But it is not a static scene; on one side of this canvas under a magnificent banyan tree, its sacredness depicted with the symbols of Shiva, a cobra is seen trying to attack a group of monkeys, and the birds and animals nearby scatter in agitation. The genius of the artist captures the movement of these frightened creatures in this frame with great cinematic skill; each of the monkeys displays a posture of fear and flight from the cobra. There are other dazzling scenes. The painted hillocks in some panels are a quiet riposte to active movement, there are sages quietly engaged in philosophical discourse, and the wild animals do no harm here. There is obviously deep spiritual intent in all the stories and representations; Shiva and Parvati float celestially in one panel high above the clouds and there are portrayals of Shiva as Dakshinamurthy and Bhairava. As ardent Shaivites who patronized many of the Nayanmars, the poet saints who lived through the Chola period, the temple's murals include stories of these saints and in particular that of Sundaramurthi Nayanmar and Cheraman Perumal, who were contemporaries.

The vivid telling of the Sundaramurthi story best captures the genius of this unknown master artist. As Sriraman says in his book, the murals in Brihadeeswara are the result of the persona of the patron (Rajaraja) and that of the painter. 'While Rajaraja's memory was inerasably etched in the annals of history, the Chola painter, like most brethren of his fraternity of this ancient land, has completely vanished into oblivion without any record mentioning him.'

It is apt at this point to talk about Brihadeeswara as a whole, as it is the most extant and visible symbol of Chola power and might. Turning off the highway towards Thanjavur, no matter how many times one visits and drives over the bridge towards the city, the vision of the towering vimana against a sky which could be a cloudless blue or a soft twilight pink is completely breathtaking. The structure with its unpolished stone finish is soaring and audacious—an engineering marvel of the Chola period and an architectural innovation that defied existing parameters of construction. One of its many marvels is that the sacred chants of the priests echo all the way up to the top of the vimana and bounce back below. Rajaraja may have begun construction in 1003 CE, and the temple was probably finished in 1010 CE.

The magnificent vimana of Brihadeeswara rose on the skyline of Thanjavur in the year 1000 CE. Rajaraja ascended the throne in 985 CE and ruled till about 1012 CE or 1014 CE. By this time, Thanjavur had established itself as a great cultural centre, and the remarkable focal point of a highly organized kingdom. Royal patronage flowed in support of temple building and all kinds of arts; the king's passion and vision in building this great temple reflected his keenness to mirror the great exploits and successes of the royal Chola line, and to diligently record the establishment of such a great venture. It was also about showcasing his ardent devotion to Shiva. Although the family's passion for temple-building was in ample evidence generations before Rajaraja's time and there are beautiful Chola temples in the Kumbakonam-Thanjavur belt reflecting this, Rajaraja took this to great heights (literally), especially with this temple, which he called Rajarajesvaram, with the 216-foot vimana.

The execution of this architectural masterpiece involved not just meticulous planning and vision but a different way of thinking which ensured that it functioned and survived as an independent institution that supported many people—artisans, artists, craftspeople, officials, and a great many others in long-term arrangements. The temple was a world unto itself; and innumerable endowments made it a focal point that sustained a myriad art forms, like music, devotional dances, and painting.

Before we get to the internal features, let us look at the external structure of the temple and its precincts. The outer walls of the temple have a moat-like construction around it. The overall area is a rectangle of some 240 metres by 122 metres. It consists of four structures; the actual garbhagriha or the sanctum sanctorum, which contains the vimana, the ardhamandapam, the mahamandapam, and the shrine that houses the Nandi. The Nandi presently installed there is of a much later period, possibly of the fifteenth or sixteenth century, and there is no clear idea of the location of the original Nandi, although a smaller one inside the temple could have been the original one. On the outer prakara, there are shrines for Subrahmanya and Amman.

If you pause at the entrance of the temple complex from the east, there is the Keralanthakan Tiruvasal, a gopuram, the citadel on top of a gateway, constructed to commemorate Rajaraja's victory in Kerala. Historian Jayakumar Bharadwaj says there is a prasasti (lines of praise) in an inscription that refers to the king's victory in Kandalur Salai after which he goes on to capture the rest of Kerala. A hundred metres inside is the Rajarajan Tiruvasal, named for the monarch and leading to the central complex which houses the main shrine. The temple was built according the makutagama, which is a set of rules for temple-building, and this agama is unique in that it allows you to place the deity in the sanctum sanctorum before building around it, which was the way this temple was constructed.

Two mighty dwarapalakas or guardian deities, eighteen feet tall, are on either side of the entrance. They must have both been carved from the same boulder that was probably dragged there by elephants trained for the work. One of the sculptures shows an elephant being swallowed by a snake. The snake is the size of the dwarapalaka's toe and the dwarapalaka is holding a mudra called vismaya hasta, a gesture of wonder, which indicates that God is so large that he can hold everything. It is a depiction that is likely inspired by a Thevaram of Thirugnanasambandar, the *Tirukailai Padigam,* where he mentions this concept. The traditional sculptor obviously was someone who had to master 'forty fields of knowledge', had to be knowledgeable about the puranas, be a scholar, an engineer, a geologist who knew about stones, and an expert in the Natyashastra apart from having musical expertise. He had to be a person of passion and vision who could depict the philosophical aspect of the legends through a carefully conceived image or series of images before he could become a sthapathi or master sculptor.

The plethora of carvings on this outside wall depicting legends related to Shiva in his various forms opens into a vast internal courtyard. Some stucco images were repaired in later years, but all the granite sculptures are of the Chola period and some of them are depicted in unusual forms. There is, for instance, a stunning Vallabha Ganapathi seated next to the figure of Devi, and on the other side is a Subrahmanya riding on an elephant, which was originally his vehicle. Arunagirinathar, the poet-saint of the fifteenth century, sings about this Subrahmanya: 'Thanjai gopurathai amarntha perumane'—the lord who sits on the gopuram of Thanjai.

The temple itself is constructed of granite. Significantly, it is not a local stone and there is no granite available nearby, so it is likely that it was obtained from places as far away as Pudukkottai and Tiruchirappalli. The quantum of granite that was transported and used for building was enormous. The total weight of the masonry used was about 1.5 million tons. They would have obviously required at least double the amount of masonry than that which was finally used. The sheer logistics of transporting these stones, dressing them, bringing additional sand and other material required for construction was an incredible achievement. S. R. Balasubrahmanyam, one of the foremost experts on Chola temples, monuments, and art, says that the stones were raised by an artificial inclined plane to the required height. Some experts have said that this inclined plane itself had to start several kilometres away from the town to ensure that the final point would rest at the height of the vimana. 'It is a rare feat, considering the limited technology of the age. With great engineering skill the downward thrust of the heavy stone superstructure has been well distributed. The *Linga* is huge, and it is housed in a double-storied *garbhagriha* supporting the upper part of the *srivimana,*' he writes, adding 'the steep upward sweep of the *srivimana,* resembling Meru, with needle-like stupi at the top seems to point the devotee the path to the lap of the Lord of the Universe'.

Like the Chidambaram temple, the concept of empty space symbolizing the divine, and as being formless, was also applied here with the priests tossing flower offerings into the air rather than on the lingam directly. The king's unwavering devotion to the lord of the dances, Adavallan, standing for omnipresence, manifested in various ways in the temple; from actual images of Nataraja and other forms of Shiva cast in metal to naming measures and weights Adavallan, so that everyone had to use the word while transacting. The words Adavallan and Dakshinameruvitankar, which was another type of measure, was repeated in all the temple records hundreds of times, enabling devotees to constantly utilize the terms. The inscriptions in the temple indicate that there were more than sixty-six images cast in metal for the temple, including images of the king, his queen, and his guru.

The vimana, probably the most stunning feature of the temple's architecture, rises to a height of 63.4 metres from the floor of the inner courtyard. The first tier of the sanctum sanctorum is filled with sculptures of Shiva in various forms, such as Bikshantakar, Virabhadra, Lingodhbhava, Dakshinamurthy, and other manifestations. Interestingly, in the same tier there are sculptures of Ganesha, Vishnu and his consorts, Gajalakshmi and Saraswathi, in addition to Mahishasuramardini and Bhairava. Another marvellous set of stone carvings, depicting in detail eighty-one karanas or postures of Bharatanatyam, expressed by Shiva himself, sits on the second tier. Above these floors, about thirteen stories high, atop the vimana sits a single block of granite, weighing eighty tons, above which rises the final stupi (the moulding at the end of the vimana) which was originally covered in gold.

Rajaraja spent a great deal of time on this temple, almost up to the end of his life. Despite all the wars he waged, and the time taken with administering his vast kingdom, this temple project was the closest to his heart, which is why he went about recording everything on its walls. All endowments, gifts, gold, vessels, ornaments, sculptures, even the vast sums of cash that were donated, were meticulously recorded. The names of the donors including the king, his queens, his sister Kundavai, his ministers and officials are all to be found here. According to R. Nagaswamy, this is the only temple 'wherein the builder himself has left behind a large number of instructions on the temple's construction, its various parts, the daily rituals to be performed for the Linga, the details of the offerings such as jewellery, flowers and textiles, the special worship to be performed, the particular days' and so on. To find suitable planetary positions for temple celebrations an astronomer called Perunkani was appointed, and his name has also been recorded in the inscriptions. A portion of the taxes collected for the royal treasury from villages was allocated to the temple. The inscriptions describe in profuse detail the exact measurements of tax-paying villages, the lands exempted from tax such as tanks, temple lands, artisans' residential areas, some agricultural lands, etc. Another listing includes details of salaries paid to those in service of the temple. These were broadly categorized as those involved in rituals such as priests and others, those who were administrative staff—accountants, treasurers, etc. and those involved in temple service such as sweepers, tailors, watchmen, jewel makers.

Sriraman says, 'In addition to donating wealth, Rajaraja made many administrative and religious arrangements for the temple. Singing and dancing were two inseparable ways of worship during the Chola period. Accordingly, to recite the Tirupatiyam, the collection of hymns of the servitors, he appointed forty-eight *pidarars* and musicians to accompany them. The longevity of the arrangement…(was) guaranteed by the clause that provides for deputing a suitable person from either their family or anyone as a substitute.' A large endowment was also made to maintain 400 dancers and their staff. As the Lord of the Dance was very important to the king, dance was always celebrated in the temple. To assist the dancers during their practice and performance, dance masters and musicians with various musical instruments were also appointed. 'In addition, the farsightedness of Rajaraja is clearly reflected in the appointment of a chief accountant, sub-accountant, astrologers…holders of the sacred parasol, water sprinklers, a person to maintain lamps, potters to supply ceramics, washermen to wash clothes, barbers, tailors…' and other menial staff, all for the upkeep of the temple. Also, the inscriptions attest to the appointment of 143 guards for the temple—these were drawn from different regions of the kingdom to ensure safety as well as a wider representation. The names of villages from where these guards were drawn figure in an inscription on the Rajarajan gateway.

Kudavayil Balasubramaniam, the Chola expert, talks about the principles behind Rajaraja's operations in the temple. All the performers of the temple were considered as being owned by the deity, so they were not exploited in any way and their talents were never diverted to the palaces, he says. The salaries of the 1,000 odd people employed at the temple were paid from the king's treasury and not from the temple's treasury, which only maintained the management staff. The king firmly believed that all were equal in the temple; as an example, the chief architect of the temple, Kunjaramallan, was given the name Rajaraja Perunthacchan, and the barber was called Rajaraja Perunavisan in the records. Whether this was grandiosity or generosity is perhaps less of an issue than the fact that Rajaraja had his own vision of how this world should be.

Another insightful point is made by Kudavayil Balasubramaniam that illustrates the nature of these endowments and how they were self-sustaining. It is commonplace even today to donate ghee lamps to temples in fulfillment of a wish or for family welfare, and those who want to keep this going make repeat offerings of ghee to the temple. In Rajaraja's temple, to keep the perpetual lamp going for one's family welfare, one had to deposit 96 female goats or 36 cows or 16 bulls. The goats had to be of a fertile age, and they would usually litter a hundred plus baby goats. Among the goats that were donated, a few male goats had to be given as well. This would be taken on record at the temple. Then impoverished interior villages would be identified and the goats or the cows and bulls, whichever was donated, would be given to these poor villagers. The villagers would have to enter into an agreement with the temple authorities to give adequate ghee every day from the animals for the donor's perpetual lamp. When the agreement was made initially it was written down as '96 sa va, moo va, per aadu, or 36 sa va moova perumpasu'. This means goats or cows that never died; and a constant number of breeding animals had to be maintained. The records specify that this arrangement is for as long as the sun and moon shine, implying that it is in perpetuity and will support generations. If extra milk or ghee or offspring accrued to the village families, they could do what they liked with it, provided they kept to the original agreement. This system supported poor rural families financially. The Chola societal sensibility was thus an expansive one. It also underlines the fact that apart from piety and worship, the temple served as the base that held a lot of strands of the community together and supported it economically.

Like Thanjavur, nearby Kumbakonam also featured prominently during the 450–500 years of Chola rule. While not much is known of its early history, the two prominent Shaiva poet-saints Tirunavukkarasu and Thirugnanasambandar both visited this town, close to the banks of the Kaveri, and sang at its most sacred temples. In the *Ahananuru*, there is a reference to the Cholas having a strongly guarded treasury at Kumbakonam. This must be in the period of the early Cholas, but along with Uraiyur and later Thanjavur, it remained an important bastion of the Cholas.

The great battle of Tirupurambiyam was fought between the Pallava and Pandya rulers near Kumbakonam in the ninth century. Later the territory of

Kumbakonam was ceded to the Chola king Aditya Chola, Vijayalaya Chola's son, who had assisted the Pallava ruler against the Pandya king. There was also a Chola palace at Pazhayarai in Kumbakonam and with the Chola kings giving the town importance and building beautiful temples in the region, it also grew commercially, became more prosperous and came into greater prominence in the centuries that followed.

Chapter 16

Pinnacles of Artistic Vision

Innumerable endowments helped the temple in becoming an active locus for art forms like music, continuous recitation of hymns, devotional dances, and paintings.

P. S. Sriraman, historian

SCATTERED OVER THE VERDANT LANDSCAPE OF THE KAVERI DELTA, IT IS often a serendipitous encounter to find tiny temples tucked away amid green rice fields and sleepy villages, reflecting in their quiet and serene beauty the greatness of the Chola builders. A short distance away from Thanjavur is the hamlet of Pasupathikovil in Papanasam taluk. The roads are narrow but smooth, and wind through small villages. Nestling between palm trees and emerging into sight suddenly is an exquisite temple, the Alanthurainathar temple at Pullamangai in Pasupathikovil. Shiva here is also known as Brahmapurishvarar. Coming from the grandiosity of the Rajarajesvaram temple in Thanjavur, or beautiful Darasuram, or indeed from some of the other magnificent temples built by the Chola kings in this area, this little gem is astonishing in the specific aspects it presents. In many ways, its beautifully presented facets portend some of the rich details of later Chola temples, but its uniqueness lies in the fact that the relative quiet of the location and the smaller scale of structure does not in any way diminish the strength and beauty of early Chola artistic vision. Built in the time of Parantaka Chola, worship here in the current period appears to be quite laid-back. During several visits to this temple, we noticed that the usual flurry of visitors was not much in evidence. Instead, a few stray chickens were running around, unperturbed by visitors; occasionally, a few local people would peer in at the deity inside and appeared quite nonchalant about the stunning sculptural legacy of this small temple.

Tirupullamangai was the old name of the village where this Chola temple stands, and now it just goes by Pullamangai. The Shaivite poet-saint Thirugnanasambandar sang here, and the temple is glorified in the sacred hymns of the *Thevaram* as one among the 275 padal petra sthalam or shrines sung at by Shaivite poet-saints. It was possibly a brick structure in the seventh century, and later rebuilt as a stone temple by Parantaka I in the late ninth or early tenth century. Like Tirunageswaram in Kumbakonam, Moovarkovil in Pudukkottai district, and the Koranaganatha temple in Tiruchi district, this is one among the very few intact early Chola temples, and the architecture reflects some Pallava features. The transition towards a new architecture is evident in the style of the ardhamandapam, or the entrance porch, which is a Chola feature. The yellowish sandstone of the temple walls, streaked with roseate veins, catches the sun's rays, illuminating the exquisite carvings on the walls and niches. A large area of wall is covered with inscriptions in the Tamil of the tenth and eleventh centuries recording gifts of land, sheep, and other goods to the temple. There is also a record of a village quarrel and a meeting of the village assembly which was held in front of the temple when it was called Tiru Alandurai. The earliest inscription in the temple belongs to the eleventh year of Parantaka Chola's reign, roughly 918 CE. It refers to the king as Parakesari, an epithet that these kings of the Vijayalaya line used. Though the epithet of Parakesari is not tagged with a name, it is clearly about Parantaka I, according to Vedachalam. Details of a village assembly that met at the temple, details of a gift of land by a Ganga feudatory Sembiyan Mahabali Vanavarayar, and other inscriptions of land donations are mentioned here.

The most striking intact carvings reveal the superb aesthetics of the early Chola style of sculpture. The plethora of tiny sculptures narrating stories and legends from the Bhagavatam, the Ramayana, and fables of Shiva makes this a veritable museum, a treasury of Chola art. A magnificent Ganesha sits with his attendants. There are floating deities flying above him, fierce bhuta ganas, the demon-like demi-gods who attend on these, their higher lords. Below him there are symbols of prosperity—fruits and flowers.

The cornices and base mouldings are carved with angels and fairy creatures. Then there are dramatic scenes of the death of Vali, killed by Rama, being mourned by his peers, their small faces contorted with grief. A mighty Gajasamharamurthy, a fierce aspect of Shiva slaying the mad elephant (in other words, the human ego) is in one of the smaller niches—his demeanour is so ferocious that an image of Parvati standing nearby shows the baby on her hip slipping down as she steps back in fear. All this is captured in exquisite and miniature detail. 'The noblest artistic expression of Parantaka I's time is found in the *devakoshta* sculptures of the Brahmapurisvarar temple at Pullamangai,' avers Balasubrahmanyam. Devakoshta are the niches for subordinate deities, and the niches here are filled with unusual figures—a medley of tiny musicians, dancers and demons, alligators and crocodiles, the makara, with torana or flower garlands spilling from their mouths, all in a merry congress of devotion to these supreme deities. Then there is Shiva as Lingodhbhava, Brahma with his hand in a gesture of reassurance, and a serene Vishnu, slender yet powerful, cast in the new Chola style.

The Tirunageswaram temple or Nageswaraswamy Kovil in Kumbakonam town is probably of Aditya Chola's time, that is of the tenth century, and although many additions were made during the Nayak period in the sixteenth and seventeenth centuries, this is also an example of the new vigour in architecture that came with Chola rule. This temple has lifelike representations of the figures of Brahma, Durga, and other forms like the Ardhanariswara, as well as a beautiful panel depicting the Ramayana. The Ramayana sculptures indicate the popularity of these stories across several centuries of Pallava, Pandya, and Chola rule and across regions. More importantly, there was apparently little sectarianism, with a Shiva temple often housing the legends of Vishnu. The divisions came later. While these sculptures are less embellished than later Chola sculptures, the sculptors' talents are just as honed here, and the innate beauty of the human form is captured with great felicity. The Surya shrine is important and is visited as a boon-bestowing deity.

There are more than a hundred such early Chola temples, and some outstanding sculptures are visible across small and big temples throughout the Kaveri belt and even further south in erstwhile Pandya country (which gradually became Chola territory). For example, Vijayalaya Chola built the Nisumbasudani temple to celebrate his capture of Thanjavur, and this is a striking early Chola construction. A clear transition from the Pallava to Chola art form is evident in the sculptures of the Vijayalaya Choliswaram temple on Narthamalai hill near Pudukkottai; some of these sculptures can be seen in the Pudukkottai government museum.

The Moovarkovil at Kodumbalur is a few kilometres from Pudukkottai and is another graceful example of early Chola architecture. It is a complex of three temples, two of which stand, and one of which is in ruins, with only the base remaining. Although small in scale and structure when compared to other Chola period edifices, there is a quiet grace about the lines of the carvings; the sculptures are sensitively executed with an almost fluid moulding and the expressions on the faces of Shiva and Parvati and a host of other figures like Tripurantaka are filled with lifelike emotions. Built by Bhuti Vikramakesari Irukkuvelir at the end of the ninth or early tenth century, the Irukkuvelir clan were supporters of the Chola rulers. This ruler was a subordinate of Sundara Chola and there are inscriptions here in Sanskrit and in the Grantha script about this clan's chief and his two queens. The genealogy of nine generations of Irukkuvelir chieftains, who also endowed a monastery nearby, is mentioned in the inscriptions. The sculptures here stand in quiet isolation within the niches of the ancient walls as these are not places of regular worship; and in the expanse of a flat green landscape where the fields meet sky, their beauty stands out more.

The entire region is green and water-fed with spreading acres of paddy and small villages huddled in-between. Near Kumbakonam is the ancient city Pazhayarai, described sometimes as Kumbakonam's twin city. The region around was also called Aiyaratalli, or land of a thousand temples; many temples that are still standing here are mentioned in the *Thevaram* and have recorded visits by the Shaivite poet saint Sambandar. As we drive by it is easy to see how habitation quickly grew in these areas, temples large and small springing up from Pallava and Chola times right up to the Vijayanagar period. Pattisvaram, Darasuram, Mettrali, Keithali, Vadathali, Tirunandipura Vinnagaram, and several other villages with important temples dot the region. Both Azhwars and Nayanmars sanctified these temples with their visits, and the area grew in religious as well as political importance. There was significant migration from Kannada and Telugu-speaking regions, especially in the Vijayanagar and Nayak periods and many pilgrimage spots emerged here, such as the Mahamaham tank in Kumbakonam, which is a confluence of the tributaries of Kaveri and is a place that has acquired spiritual significance.

At Srinivasanallur is another Chola jewel, the Koranganatha temple, which was probably built in the Aditya Chola period in the ninth century. In this small early Chola shrine, just as in Pullamangai, the sculptures seem to come alive. There is a sense of movement in these panels where ancient stories are told, and in the other spaces where the sculptures stand alone, an indescribable beauty emanates from the chiseled faces such as from a serene Dakshinamurthy (Shiva). Rishis listen in rapt attention to his words, a lion and a deer sit submissively, a Mahishasuramardini (Durga who conquered the demon Mahisha) is beautifully carved above, a yali emerges from the mouth of a crocodile, and in the soft light of the morning sun, the minutiae of expression and emotion on these carved faces as well as the costume and jewellery on all these figures appear real.

The Cholas stamped their own style subtly on the erstwhile Pandya places of worship with the mark of their artistry, although in the early years they were careful enough to retain many Pandya features in these structures. In the tenth and eleventh centuries when the Pandya territory came fully under Rajaraja I and Rajendra I, their heirs were given the titles of Chola-Pandya, and Rajendra's sons administered Pandya territory, stationing their battalions there to prevent any Pandya uprising. In the Tirunelveli region, the Cheranmadevi temple, Mannarkoil, Tiruvalisvaram, and Brahmadesam are examples of Pandya region Chola temples. The Thamirabarani river, also called Porunai now, retaking its ancient Tamil name, originates in the Podhigai hills and flowing through this verdant region of Ambasamudram, joins the sea at Punnai Kayal, a journey of 100 kilometres or so. The road that one drives on is almost like a riverbank in some places with water right next to the tarred road. An avenue of Marudham trees, the *Terminalia arjuna,* an ancient tree species which a Sangam landscape is named after, lines this highway.

These places clubbed together were called Rajaraja Chaturvedimangalam, a vast area made up of all these villages and small towns that had been converted by Rajaraja to a vast and fertile Brahmadeya. The splendours of these temples, their towering structures, sculptures, and beautiful images of deities remain to this day a strong testament to the consistency that was the Chola aesthetic, although some of them were renovated in later centuries. Many original vatteluthu as well as classical Tamil inscriptions of the early Pandya, Chola, and Vijayanagar periods can be found in these temples.

Cheranmadevi is named for the wife of an early Pandya king Cheravan Mahadevi, says Vedachalam; when Rajaraja took over these lands it was renamed Niharili Chola Chaturvedimangalam (niharili means that which one cannot come near). This is a town with many temples, the more important ones being the Shiva temple and the Ramaswamy temple built in Rajaraja's time which has an ashtanga vimana (a vimana with eight aspects). This architectural style is also found in other temples in south Tamil Nadu such as in Tirukoshtiyur, Koodal Azhagar Perumal temple, and Mannarkoil. Three beautiful, tiered shrines stand here housing a standing Vishnu, a reclining Vishnu, and a seated Vishnu. Among the many inscriptions, an eleventh century one talks about the Vaikanasa, or Vishnu worshippers pledging to light a perpetual lamp and recording that they would proffer twice the amount of the required ghee should they ever fail in their task. Another eleventh-century inscription notes the gifting of land to the temple to provide employment to a watchman to guard the temple.

In Mannarkoil near Ambasamudram, one notices again the eight-sided vimana. This is another outstanding structure. Built by Cheramannar Rajasimhanar, a Chera king in the eleventh century (Rajendra Chola's time), there is a foundation inscription at the temple to this effect. Again, the Vishnu here is in three forms—reclining, seated, and standing on three tiers. The temple is said to be the place where the Chera king-turned-saint Kulasekhara Azhwar spent the last thirty-odd years of his life, so there is a shrine in his honour which was built by Cheramannar Rajasimhanar. In the nearby village, which is called Brahmadesam, there are more striking sculptural masterpieces on view. From Pandya through Chola and then the Vijayanagar kings, this temple underwent several restorations. There is a beautiful yali mandapam here, and among the sculptures is an outstanding Bikshadana, the mendicant form of Shiva who seemingly comes from the forest, and as he walks by the rishi patnis (the spouses of the sages), a panorama unfolds. It appears that the women were stopped in their tracks by his beauty—the sculptures are of a woman combing her hair, her comb slipping as she is transfixed by him; a woman who is dressing stopping midway, and a woman who is cooking poised with a ladle raised above her head. There is a host of other figures as well, with rishis and gods sculpted in detail and almost lifelike in expression and aspect. The anonymous sculptor or sculptors' artistic liberty (perhaps mischief) heightens the irony of human reactions in the face of utmost devotion.

By the time of the Imperial Cholas, temples, particularly the larger ones, became centres of economic and administrative activity, cultural productivity, and were the fulcrum of the local universe. Rajaraja set in place a complete system of donations and payments, ritual practices, records of the people in employment, and cultural activities in the temple.

One of the most important temples of Chola times, besides the ones already mentioned, is the Nataraja temple at Chidambaram, also known as Tillai. It was probably built to its present form in the ninth or early tenth century. The name Chidambaram emanating from chitr-ambalam means the state of consciousness or enlightenment; it was the family temple of the Cholas and briefly served as a Chola capital. Nataraja, the cosmic dancer, is the main deity here and various Chola kings embellished the temple, adding to its grandeur; many renovations were undertaken by successive rulers even up to the seventeenth century.

It was Parantaka I, a staunch devotee of Nataraja, who made the Chidambaram temple the Chola family temple and its deity Nataraja, also known as Adavallan, their kula nayaka or family deity. The Tiruvalangadu copper plates describe the king as 'a bee at the lotus feet of Parantaka'. Balasubrahmanyam says that the plates add that Parantaka built a silver mountain (Kailash) and a golden house called Dabhra Sabha. The house became known as Hema Sabha or Ponnambalam and Parantaka acquired the title of pon veinda Perumal or the lord who covered the roof with gold. References to the temple constantly appear in the Shaivite hymns of many of the Nayanmars, most specially in the work of Appar and Sambandar of the seventh century, and in the hymns of Sundarar in the eighth century. Another Tamil poet-saint Tirumular of the seventh/eighth centuries also devotes an entire chapter to Chidambaram in his work *Tirumantiram*. To this day it continues (as in the case of many other prominent temples in Tamil Nadu) to be one of the most popular and spiritually significant shrines of the region. Nagaswamy says, '…the sanctity attached to the temple of Chidambaram reached new heights in the 12th and 13th centuries…the four gopuras had come into being…and the great veneration (given) to the Shaivite saints gave a new orientation to the several projects of temple building by the rulers.' Nagaswamy also says with the main temple vimana, and, subsequently, the gopuras (which were considered to be the holy mountain Meru and thereby vested with spiritual significance), the emphasis of worship shifts from the sanctum sanctorum to the gopuras so much so that even the sight of these towering spires from a distance was supposed to confer spiritual benefits.

The temple itself is a vast complex and houses the much-acclaimed 1,000-pillared mantap; there are other multiple structures as well with murals and superb sculptures of dancers and deities, on the gopuras, on the base walls, and on pillars. There is the magnificent shrine to the consort of Shiva, Parvati, who is in the form of Sivakami. We know that Rajaraja, like his ancestors, was devoted to this temple, and the frieze in the Brihadeeswara temple depicting him and his three queens worshipping at Chidambaram underlines this. There is an apocryphal story that says the Thevaram hymns of the Shaivite poet-saints, which were scattered across many palm leaf manuscripts, were stored away inside the Chidambaram temple, and when the king wanted to examine them, the priests refused, saying that unless Appar, Sambandar, and Sundarar (who had all died a few centuries before), appeared before them, they would not allow the king to see the manuscripts. The king and his cohorts cleverly took idols of the three Nayanmars with them, and the story goes that the gates opened magically and access to the manuscripts was obtained. Thereafter, Rajaraja was said to have encouraged the revival of Thevaram recital in Shaivite temples across Tamilakam.

Among the later Chola kings, Kulottunga I donated to the temple a beautiful gemstone given to him by the king of Khamboja (Cambodia), although the whereabouts of this is not known now. The king's sisters, Kundavai and Madurantakai, donated golden bowls to offer water to the deity and set up endowments to maintain flower gardens and provide food for the devotees who came to the temple. Vikrama Chola, Kulottunga's son, gave expensive gifts to the temple including the spoils of war, covering the temple's assets with gold and silver and pearls. A single individual called Naraloka Vira, who played an important role in the victories of the wars waged by the Chola kings, contributed immensely to renovations of the temple including to the mantaps and the sanctum sanctorum. Other contributions included the provision of various services such as installing streetlights, planting gardens for flowers, creating areca palm groves as well as relaying streets fanning out from the temple for the deity's processional route. He also built a bathing ghat and water tanks for the temple and became more famous for his munificence than for his military exploits.

Two other significant Chola temples are the Choliswaram (also called Rajeswaram and Brihadeeswara) temple at Gangaikondacholapuram and the Darasuram temple, whose facets reflected a high point of the Chola art of temple building. We know that the city of Gangaikondacholapuram was built to commemorate Gangaikondan, the one who brought the Ganga, that is Rajendra I, and replaced Thanjavur as the Chola capital. The spoils of his wars in Odisha, in Karnataka, and in other places were brought to the Gangaikondacholapuram temple, such as the sculpture of Surya the sun god in his chariot, a Mahishasuramardini sculpture, a Bhairavi sculpture, and a few more. It is important to point out that bringing back trophies of war, including images of deities, was common practice and this was not confined to particular kings or communities.

It is obvious that although Rajendra admired his father Rajaraja greatly, he wanted to bring distinct and new creative features to the Gangaikondacholapuram temple. For instance, the temple vimana's base is square at one level, called nagaram, then octagonal, or dravidam, where the corners are cut off, and then circular or vesaram, when the ends are further shaved, whereas in the Brihadeeswara temple the base is square and tapers off at higher levels. This was a major sculptural change that Rajendra made at Gangaikondacholapuram. While this temple has an undeniable elegance, it is much smaller and slimmer in overall stature than the Brihadeeswara temple with its grand edifices. The beauty of the complex of structures hits the eye and their square plan has a pleasing visual impact. The courtyard, the ardha mandapam, and the sanctum sanctorum are reminiscent of the Brihadeeswara temple, but its scale is smaller, and it's shorter when compared to the Brihadeeswara—historians believe that this is deliberate and a mark of respect from Rajendra to his father.

The soil here being looser, the temple's base structure is wider than that of the Thanjavur temple. The display of sculptures is more visible than in the Brihadeeswara temple and there are stunning details in the carving. The tall images of deities have exquisite panels around them that tell the legends of Gods and saints; the panel details are important to note in that they express secular images of people and the activities of the times although against a backdrop of religious lore. There is a beautiful image of Chandikesvara, the servitor of Shiva, with a shrine of his own, and the other niches have sculptures of Saraswathi, Nataraja, Durga, and Vishnu.

The Airavatesvara temple at Darasuram in the Kumbakonam district, now a protected UNESCO heritage site, was built in the twelfth century by Rajendra II and is another fine example of the special artistic energy that the Cholas seemed to possess, resulting in an exuberance of creativity. The visual impact of the carved pillars never ceases to amaze even if one visits several times. The master sculptors of this time had obviously developed very fine tools for carving; the minute details, whether it is of gods or people or elements of nature, reveal a genius of hand and eye that is incomparable. This is the only place where the entire *Skanda Purana* (verses in commemoration of the stories of Shiva), an eighth century text, is carved in exquisite detail on small panels on four stone pillars. What immediately catches the visitor's eye is the temple's ardha mandapam in the shape of a chariot that is being pulled by elephants and horses. There are griffins and yalis that also seemingly pull the chariot. This mandapam is called Rajagambhira Tirumandapam and is perhaps the most beautiful part of the temple. The ceiling has a captivating carving of Shiva and Parvati sitting on a lotus and there are other beautiful carvings including that of Saraswathi, an unusual six-headed Subrahmanya, Lingodhbhava, and a unique Ardhanariswara. The set of fading murals on some of the walls is again a testament to the painting skills of the Chola artists.

It appears as if Rajendra II, a highly accomplished and successful ruler, wanted to set out an all-encompassing view of the world as he experienced it. There are panels of dancers executing perfect poses and stories of saints and poets retold on pillars, all carved in intricate detail including their clothes, thong-like footwear, even toenails and ribs. The celestial wedding of Shiva and Parvati, Ganesha with a veena, Ravana lifting Mount Kailash, and a host of other mythological incidents are also carved on these walls. The master sculptor and his team must have been given liberal artistic licence by the king, as there is a great deal of humour apparent in these micro carvings. In the tiny two- or three-inch panels many ordinary events of life are carved, with the miniature human figures having a host of expressions on their faces reflecting joy, sorrow, and fear; the scenes range from showing a woman in childbirth, to frolicking mermaids and women gymnasts. It seemed as if the king wanted to showcase an entire radius of human activity and emotion. Darasuram thus represents an imperial might that is always cognizant of its limitedness—spiritual devotion was at the forefront for the Chola kings but intertwined with it was a practical awareness of earthly passages as well.

Chola Bronzes

No writing on the Cholas and their history can be complete without touching on the sacred bronzes that often reflect the high point of Chola artistry. We must bear in mind that even as we acknowledge the rulers for their military exploits, their patronage of the arts, and their administrative capabilities, the execution of their vision was done by hundreds if not thousands of craftsmen. These people often laboured under difficult circumstances but despite this they created masterpieces that are collectively the rich legacy of the Tamils. Unknown and unsung, these were the people who were largely responsible for the priceless works of art that have come to define the heritage of the Tamils. The bronzes of the Chola period were made by hereditary sculptors whose experience and knowledge were steeped in the art form for several generations; and from the proliferation of bronzes in Tamilakam, apparently, there was steady employment for sthapathis. Job Thomas, Professor Emeritus of Art History at Davidson College, and an expert on Chola art, says that it is 'puzzling however that in the innumerable inscriptions of donations to the temple, there is no reference, individually, or collectively to them.' The Cholas were not averse to identifying ordinary people in their inscriptions as is evident from the numerous names of dancers, scribes, carpenters, and others in the Thanjavur temple, but the perplexing omission of any sthapathi names is intriguing. The overall notion of monarchical benevolence and the king taking care of the well-being of his praja, or people, was a widely held mediaeval notion, but how much of this was selective and how much was applied is another matter. To this day, however, the bronzes are a superb symbol of the artistic vision and expression of the Cholas and are universally admired.

The great French sculptor Auguste Rodin, on being shown early photographs of some Chola bronzes, wrote lyrically about a Shiva Nataraja bronze from Velankanni in 1913. It is believed that Rodin saw the photos taken by a wealthy Russian aristocrat Victor Goloubew, a collector, who founded a journal called

Ars Asiatica, dedicated to the arts and architecture of the Far East. Two of the Shiva bronzes, the Tiruvalangadu Natraj and the Velankanni Shiva, were published as six images in the magazine, and Rodin wrote about it in acute detail from different perspectives. Looking at Shiva from the front he says,

> ...the pose is familiar, but it has nothing banal about it, because in every pose nature intervenes so much! Above all, there are things that other people do not see, unknown depths, the wellsprings of life. There is grace in elegance; above grace there is modelling, everything is exaggerated; we call it soft but it is most powerfully soft! Words fail me then...

There were several images that were made for temples. Legends also impute 'self-manifestation' regarding some images, especially those of lingams. The main deity in the sanctum sanctorum is often made of black granite but in many temples the deities in the adjacent shrines and all processional deities are of bronze. Sthapathis followed specific texts, the *Shilpa Sastras* or the rules of sculpture, which described how images needed to be cast—with all the attributes of divinity including postural details. To determine proportions, two types of iconographic rules were followed, called talamana and angulamana, which specify details such as the length of the palm to equal the length of the face, the length of the image to be nine times that of the face, and other proportions of the image. Similarly, the postural minutiae of images in the standing, sitting, and reclining positions are also prescribed and the sthapathis followed them, additionally taking inspiration at times from literary texts and adding to the images of deities. These Chola bronzes were made by a method called the 'lost wax process' (identical to the modern 'investment casting')—this involved making a reference statue with beeswax, building a mould around it, heating the mould to melt the reference statue, then pouring molten metal into the mould. There is a lot more to the process, but it is noteworthy that the sthapathi had to cast the entire image as a single piece.

The finished bronze images were consecrated and stationed in temples, and purity not just in the making and casting, but also in the installation was of great importance. As the Bhakti movement popularized image worship with both Vaishnavite and Shaivite poet-saints singing at these temples, public participation in temple worship increased enormously during these periods. The bronzes were largely processional deities who were paraded around the streets of the temple in small rural villages as well as in other habitations. The intimacy of the relationship with the deity was fostered by the more personal expression of devotion. For instance, as Vidya Dehejia points out, Appar's poem to Nataraja at the Chidambaram temple states Shiva's beauty is so great that it would be worth forgoing the ultimate goal of severing the cycle of rebirth on earth to have another chance to gaze at his beauty. Similarly, the beautifully cast images of Vishnu evoked a passionate response; for example, the twelfth century poet-saint Vedanta Desikar was mesmerized by the beauty of Ranganatha at Srirangam and sings: 'Oh lord of Ranga / I see the exquisite curves of your calves / the lustre of anklets bathes them in colours / swift runners between armies in times of war / … to catch the liquid light of your beauty / …my soul stops running the paths of rebirth.'

Images of Vishnu cast during this period are seen in different temples to this day. By and large most Vishnu bronzes depict a timeless transcendence first expressed during the days of Kulottunga I. This expression of bronze art sees a bejewelled deity with two rear arms bearing the conch and the discus and one front hand either on the thigh or with palm facing forward from a downward pointing arm to surrender at his feet; the other arm is raised in benediction. This is the most defining aspect of Vishnu images, the most grounded in terms of stability, evoking an emotional response from the bhakta or worshipper. Other details of this classical image of Vishnu usually include a tapered crown or mukuta, a veshti with tapered folds, and jewellery caved around the neck. The grace and beauty of an imagined Vishnu is sought to be portrayed in this kind of bronze depiction; many of the hymns of the Azhwars also try to reflect compelling majesty of Vishnu. For example, Kulasekhara Azhwar in the ninth century longed to be a step in the shrine of Venkateswara (Vishnu) so that he may gaze at him constantly even while providing a surface for the pious to tread on as they visit the Lord's shrine. 'O Lord, O Venkata / Would that I were a step / at the entrance to your shrine, / trodden upon by devotees, by gods and apsaras / who crowd to worship you / Ceaselessly I need to see / your lips of coral hue. / May I lie as a step upon your threshold?'

At the Thanjavur Museum several fine examples of Chola bronzes can be seen, such as the Nataraja of Tiruvalangadu, the Somaskanda (Shiva, Parvati, and Skanda grouped together), belonging to the eighth century or the early Chola period, and the bronzes of the Brihadeeswara temple. Subramanian reminds us that the Thiruvalangadu Nataraja is one of the finest of this period and portrays Nataraja performing the Ananda Tandava. 'The image was cast on the lines of the *dhyanasloka* in Thevaram and its poetic description where the poet-saint Appar sings of Shiva as having "arched eyebrows, lips as red as a kovai fruit, a beatific smile and a raised golden foot".' Sivaramamurti says, 'it is a classical example and the best known of its kind anywhere in the world...the physical proportions and the flowing contours are blended into a pose so amazing that Rodin...considered this to be the most perfect representation of rhythmic movement in the world'.

The Tiruvengadu bronzes in the museum like the Kannappa Nayanar, the Ardhanariswara, and the Bikshadana exemplify a high point in bronze-making. There are other outstanding examples of Chola-era bronzes on display—Tirthankara statues from Tindivanam, Buddha statues from Nagapatnam, and the Murugan bronze from Gangaikondacholapuram from the time of Rajendra Chola. There are also images of the Shaivite saints including Karaikal Ammaiyar.

However, many superb bronzes of this era have been stolen, lost (even from the Brihadeeswara temple, for instance), or exported and installed in museums abroad. Of the sixty-six images described in the inscriptions of Rajaraja at the Thanjavur temple, only two remain. John Guy, senior curator of South and Southeast Asian art at the Victoria and Albert Museum in London, has said that when several invasions occurred in Tamil Nadu in the fourteenth century, many bronzes were secretly buried, often in temple premises or sent elsewhere for safekeeping for fear of them being requisitioned by the victors. A lot of the jewellery and gold donated to temples was also lost, and much of the accounts of the pillage of the remaining wealth are recorded by the occupiers. Madurai was a prize as was Srirangam and Chidambaram. In fact, in 1976, Nagaswamy was instrumental in discovering some bronze idols in a 'dark' room in the Chidambaram temple which were subsequently valued at several crores of rupees and secured. Nagaswamy said, 'A good number of metal images in the Nataraja temple belong to the age of (the) Chola king Kulottunga I. Naraloka Vira, who was the commander in chief under the Chola emperors...has contributed immensely to many temples particularly in Chidambaram'. The high numbers of beautiful ancient bronzes in proliferation in Tamilakam, especially from the Chola era, stand testimony to the great aesthetic and production value of these deities and their central role in the lives of the people.

Chapter 17

The Spires of Faith

South India is studded with gigantic temples fascinating in their beauty and imposing in their appearance...

C. Sivaramamurti, art historian

JEWEL-LIKE TEMPLES SCATTERED ACROSS CHOLA LANDS PROVE THE draw of faith in much of the Chola epoch. Intense temple-building activity went on throughout the Chola centuries, and temple rituals and festivals were the essence of everyday life. Faith flowed into community activity, fostered by the Bhakti movement, where poet-saints as mentioned in earlier chapters composed and sang paeans of worship to Vishnu and Shiva. The temples of wood and brick made way for stone structures beautified by stunning sculptures and tall spires all combining to create a new idiom of Dravidian architecture. We saw what the Pallava contribution has been in this regard, and as described in earlier chapters, the Cholas added to the wealth of space for worship in the temple or kovil. Ko means the residence of God and also the place where a king lives, thus bestowing a god-like transcendent position to the king. Let us look at a few unique aspects of some of these temples which reflected the grandeur of their vision and the beautiful execution of their art across Tamilakam among the local people drawing both king and God into the local communities.

Beginning with the Sangam age, the early Chola rulers (who, as we know, were small chieftains) were given to worshipping the deities who were popular during the Sangam age such as Murugan, Kottravai, and Mayon. In parallel, Buddhism and Jainism coexisted with Hinduism, especially in the early Chola period. There were also other philosophies like the Ajivika, an ascetic way of being, which believed in determinism without the notion of free will—this prevailed across parts of Tamil Nadu in the early post-Common Era. As noted, although ardent Shaivites, the Chola rulers were by and large tolerant and supported both Buddhist and Jain schools of learning and monasteries. The Jinalaya or Jain spiritual centre comprising temples, small rock-cut shrines, a cave with faded Chola paintings (and later with Vijayanagar paintings) in Tirumalai, 40 kilometres from Tiruvannamalai, is a case in point. Kundavai, the sister of Rajaraja I, built this place of worship for the Jina, a Jain name for an enlightened being. The numerous inscriptions found here are from the ninth century right up to the fifteenth century CE, in Tamil and Grantha scripts from the Chola through to the Vijayanagar periods and indicate that numerous gifts and donations were made, including tax-free land grants to support this complex just as in the case of Hindu temples. Buddhist viharas were also supported by royal patronage, although Buddhism was not as active a faith as Jainism during the mediaeval period in Tamilakam.

The tolerance of other faiths by Hindu rulers and influential members of society was not always steady or consistent and varied during phases of mediaeval history. We must not forget the animosity of certain Shaivite Bhakti poet-saints like Sambandar towards Jainism. Stories of persecution were not just a part of Jain lore but even evident in later hagiographical works about these Shaiva and Vaishnava saints such as in Sekkizhar's *Periyapuranam*. Historians such as Champakalakshmi suggest that in the context of a wide popular base of support for both the Vedic religion as well as the Shramanic ones, conflict grew around the need to acquire royal support and patronage, especially around centres of economic and political power.

By the ninth and tenth centuries, Hinduism or the Vedic religion had become the most powerful religion in the region and the full-blown impact of the music and poetry of the Bhakti saints was felt across Tamilakam. The songs and spontaneous outpouring of these poets were compiled by later scholars like Nambi Andar Nambi and Nathamuni who, a century or so later, made many of these compositions and philosophies widely available to the public. Faith was further fortified as these compositions were in Tamil. And when the Shaivite saints' hymns, the *Thevaram*, was chanted at temples by the odhuvars who were expert reciters (but not priests), the entire community was drawn into worship. Similarly, the *Nalayira Divya Prabandam* of the Vaishnavite canon again brought the intimacy of language, the Tamil that people knew, into the fold of faith with great emotional and religious fervour.

In the Kaveri belt, as we know, with the Chola kings sponsoring temple-building activity, especially after the ninth century, they slowly became centres of power and focus for village communities. There was much more too that emanated from these temples apart from economic support for local activities. People felt the emotional tug of a more personalized relationship with local divinities; for instance, to witness processional deities—beautifully bejewelled and garlanded Gods—accompanied by music from the tavil, nadaswaram, and mridangam carried on the shoulders of the faithful, moving through small streets, stopping at doorways where awestruck villagers made their offerings was a magnet for the faithful. Elaborate temple rituals that were magnificent spectacles often involved local people and showed the power of not just the deity but also that of the king who ultimately controlled the temples, including much of its finances. This further shored up community faith in these times. Beginning with the early and middle Chola periods, the power, the wealth, and the artistic vision of the Imperial Cholas was sustained for over two hundred years.

The utsavamurti or processional deities in these temples were treated with as much reverence as the main deity. The main deity was consecrated with great religious fervour and kings like Rajaraja created endowments for the perpetual cooking of meals for the deities. Each day special food was made in the temple, silk and cotton fabrics were wrapped around the deities, and they were decorated with ornaments and fresh flowers. Incense was offered and learned priests chanted and sang the praise of God. With festivals or utsavam being an intrinsic part of village and small town life in Chola times, the entire community would turn up to participate and religious fervour grew, moving beyond the orthodoxies of caste. With the temple as the hub of the local economy these festivals also provided a spur to a more secular economic growth across local society.

Many of the prominent poets of this time were of the Pandya country, but some lived in Chola territory. The great Vaishnavite reformer Ramanuja who came a century after the advent of the Bhakti poets was born in Sriperumbudur in the eleventh century (near modern Chennai) when the area was under the Chola ruler Kulottunga I. He also later lived in Srirangam, Tirupati, and Melkote. Kulottunga was a fierce Shaivite who belonged to the eastern Ganga line of the Chola dynasty. He supposedly set himself up in strong opposition to Ramanuja, who was a Vaishnavite philosopher, but legend has it that Kulottunga later turned into a follower. Ramanuja's philosophy of non-dualism advocated total surrender to Vishnu as the Supreme Deity. Unlike the Advaita Vedanta philosophy of Adi Shankaracharya, who is believed to have lived in the eighth century, and who proposed a deeply impactful liberating notion of the human soul and the true nature of reality (which was perceived as a unified whole), the Vishishtadvaita set of beliefs propounded by seers like Ramanuja which while strongly theistic, also promoted a broader concept of Vaishnavism. This was reformist in nature and included the accommodation of non-Brahmin elements in temple rituals. Many mantras could only be recited by Brahmins and were kept secret. There is the famous legend of how Ramanuja, despite strict orders from his guru to keep the sacred Vaishnava mantra secret, climbed the vimana of Tirukoshtiyur temple and loudly declaimed the mantra for everyone to hear. The streets around the temple then reverberated with the sound that energized and moved the ordinary people who had gathered there, breaking the barriers of caste and presumed sacredness with his compassion. As for Shankara's Advaita Vedanta philosophy, it stressed the unity or oneness of the universal consciousness of the Brahman. Self-realization or enlightenment, known as moksha, meant freedom from the cycle of birth and death emerging from meditation, study, and a sense of discrimination. His treatises on the Upanishads and other texts in Sanskrit went far beyond the simpler profession of Bhakti or faith and devotion and rank among the finest expressions and explorations of Hindu spiritual thought.

Shankara is said to have travelled the length and breadth of India establishing mathas or schools; his philosophy still made space for a godhead whether Shiva or Vishnu. The inscriptions of Shankara are available only from a later date, from the time of the Vijayanagar rulers, but this had a deep impact on Hindu philosophy. Another school of thought, the Shaiva Siddhanta, which became very popular in Tamilakam after the twelfth century, drew from the Shaiva saints of the ninth century. This philosophy and other offshoots of the Shaivite tradition not only positioned themselves against the Shramanic religions but also the orthodoxies of Brahmanical Saivism.

Shaiva Siddhantha surged in popularity due to the dissemination of the *Thevaram* which the Nayanmars had composed, and which was sung at more than 285 Shaiva temples built by the Chola rulers. A few of them like the Airavatesvara temple at Darasuram built by Rajaraja II in the twelfth century has exquisite miniature sculptures depicting events in the lives of the sixty-three Nayanmars; the story goes that the king consulted Sekkizhar in the building of this temple. The incidents of the lives of these saints including tales which reveal the essential simplicity of many of these lives albeit laced with miraculous events touched a chord with the local people, so whether it was a tale of a Nayanmar who was a soldier turned saint, or women saints sitting in front of Shiva, or even the story of the Chola king Ninraseer Nedumaran who was converted from Jainism to Saivism, there are multiple stories carved all around the temple in small rectangular panels in beautiful detail.

The Devalaya Chakravarti or the 'emperor among temples' as the Brihadeeswara temple was called has been discussed in some of the earlier chapters, but more details of the builder's intent and some of its special facets need to be highlighted. Its architectural marvels, its murals, and the significance of the sculptures all draw as much from a spiritual base as from Rajaraja's desire to build such a grand monument. His ambition was well expressed and to this day the spires of the Brihadeeswara are as inspiring as they were in the Chola period. We must remember that Rajaraja was a king whose spiritual inclinations matched his vaulting ambition. For example, he was fascinated with the idea of Meru, an imaginary mountain peak beyond the peak of Kailash, the abode of Shiva, symbolizing infinity. The arch inside the vimana of this temple supposedly stands for Kailash and beyond is Dakshina Meru (the Meru of the south), a term Rajaraja used and specifically mentioned in an inscription in the temple. He also created in this Dakshina Meru what he imagined in the mythical—Parvati on a golden mountain peak with Ganesha and Subrahmanya. This entire set cast in bronze was taken out on the streets during festivals and was part of the processional entourage. The people of Thanjavur not only marvelled at such splendour and beauty but were struck by their emperor's devotion. Similarly, in the sculptures of Tripurantaka, a version of Shiva that destroyed a demon, carved in many places in the temple, Rajaraja seems to have fancied himself as Shiva, and this is another leitmotif that runs across the temple.

The great frescoes and murals of the temple have also been discussed in earlier chapters, but it is important to note that at the heart of the stunning artistic expression is a strong element of faith that was part of the king's character. We know that as a devotee of Shiva, the king felt a deep kinship to the eighth-century Bhakti poet-saint Sundarar who described himself as Shiva's close servitor. Rajaraja wanted to be a devotee like that and called himself Shivapathasekharan or 'one who carries the Lord on his head'. The king's piety is apparent in his humble clothes depicted in many of the murals. His fascination and reverence for the story of Sundarar is set out in marvellous detail in the murals. As an enlightened soul in Mount Kailash, Sundarar is in the service of Shiva the Supreme Being and yet, overcome by desire for two apsaras or heavenly damsels, he is sent back to earth by Shiva to satiate his material desires. Sundarar is upset at this demotion to earth but is assured by Shiva that he would be redeemed at the appropriate time. He is then born into a devout Brahmin family in Navalur and is named Nambi Aruran. When he reaches a suitable age, his marriage is arranged, and a wondrous scene showing the marriage preparation and festivities is painted on the walls. Cooking for the wedding feast, a collective activity, is beautifully presented—vessels with food in them appear to be ready to eat, there are people cutting vegetables and stirring pots—it is almost as if the aromas of the feast are wafting in the air.

Both stone and metalware are shown and were obviously common at that time. There is an incredible level of animation in these scenes; people are scurrying about; guests are watching the arrival of the bridegroom, and the shamiana-like textile above the dais is realistically drawn with repeated motifs of geese in the same posture and facing the same direction—suggesting that the block printing method was available to the painter. There are numerous other depictions, from minute patterns to the grand figures of sages and queens and the king himself worshipping the various forms of Shiva in many of the panels in the passage. It was almost as if the grand details of the wedding had to be fully illustrated to contrast later with the saint's renunciation and devotion to Shiva.

Among the assembled guests in the marriage frieze is a tall old man, his slightly bent figure indicating his advancing years, holding a palm leaf deed with the signature of Nambi's ancestor. Shiva declares that Nambi is his eternal slave and cannot enter a marriage, and the expressions of shock and disbelief among the gathered guests have been marvellously conveyed by the painter. The deed has the signature of Nambi's ancestor who has promised him to Shiva, and the outraged Nambi, who calls the old man pitta or the mad one, travels along with some elders to the temple at Tiruvennainallur, where the old man proves that there is an original document preserved at the temple indicating the same. The old man reveals himself as Shiva and claims his bondsman for life before disappearing. The once reluctant Nambi, now enlightened, seizes the ascetic life with joy. Shiva asks him to compose his first hymn using the word 'mad' that was used on him earlier, saying that he did not mind the negative epithets and Sundarar's first composition begins with the words 'Pitta piraichudi', meaning, 'oh mad man with the crescent moon, how can I not be yours?' There is more to the story, which is told in detail in the twelfth-century poet Sekkizhar's *Periyapuranam*, but Rajaraja's deep interest in the life of this saint is evident in the elaborate depiction on these temple walls. There are also remarkable depictions of Sundarar with another poet-saint Cheraman Perumal, his contemporary, who traverses the spiritual path along with him. Another panel is a magnificent portrayal of Shiva as Nataraja, the family deity of Rajaraja, and the king is seen offering worship at Chidambaram. This image has a great impact on the viewer, and the panel must have been a special commission of the king whose devotion to Nataraja and to Chidambaram is also evident.

The great secret of the temple, the Chidambara Rahasya, in essence is also summed up in the underlying philosophical concept which went beyond the theistic expression 'Andamum Pindamum Onru', meaning that the human body and the cosmos are one and the same—a much cherished belief that emanated from these early times. The indivisibility of all things is the secret; so, when the curtain of maya or illusion is opened by the priest during puja, it reveals empty space. The sky is the akasha lingam, meaning there is no main deity, and the presence of the divine is everywhere and not restricted to any one space.

We must not forget as we acknowledge the spires of faith that cocooned Chola society that, regardless of frequent antagonism expressed at various periods towards Jainism, many Chola kings including Rajaraja I were supporters of Buddhist viharas and Jainalayas. Sivaramamurti says, 'That other religions were actively encouraged can be seen in Raja Raja Chola's splendid gifts to Buddhist monasteries.' The Kundavai Jainalaya, the serene Jain temple constructed and donated by Rajaraja's sister Kundavai, standing on a green hillock is another example of royal patronage to other faiths. Built along the tiered hillside of rocks and boulders, this stunning edifice is in Tirumalai village which is located between Polur and Arni. A free-standing 17-foot image of a Jain Tirthankara Parsvanatha, the twenty-third Tirthankara, attracts pilgrims from across Tamil Nadu. At the ground level is a beautiful shrine dedicated to Mahavira, the twenty-fourth and last Tirthankara. The image is made of stucco and behind are faded wall murals of the Chola and Vijayanagar times and several inscriptions of the ninth and fifteenth centuries can also be seen on the walls of the temple complex. 'They belong to the periods of Parantaka I, Sundara Chola, Raja Raja, his son Rajendra I, the latter's son Rajendra II and Raja Raja III,' says Subramanian. According to Ajithadoss, 'The simple architecture of the pillars indicate Chola origin. The maha mantapa was a later addition in the thirteenth and fourteenth centuries.' There is evidence here among the faded murals, the paintings of the Jain gathering, the samavasarana, the carvings of soaring angels with lotuses and inscriptions indicating donations and support to the temple, of a once active place of worship although there is no worship here at present.

Faith in the Chola era was therefore multilayered and complex. At one end were fiercely held religious beliefs that decried and were even hostile to other religions like Jainism, and at the other end was an expansive philosophical view of the oneness of all things, that is, non-dualism. Chola belief systems, as we saw, also included a deeply held faith in salvation through a personal devotion and intense connection to God and the Cholas used their creative instincts, their art and architecture, and their splendid imagination to bring many strands of faith together.

Chapter 18

The Cheras

The Emporium of India

The fine ships of the Yavanas come with gold and leave with pepper...

Ahananuru 149

SET IN A LUSH GREEN COAST EXTENDING FROM THE ROLLING mountains of the Western Ghats all the way down to the tip of the continent, enclosing backwaters where the glistening sea formed inlets and small islands dotted the waters was a gateway to a great and wondrous land. Here, the air was filled with the aroma of exotic spices, and though the broad walkways that hugged the shore were rough and uneven they were conducive to the loading and unloading of goods from distant shores. A sailor turned merchant from Phoenicia, who unusually for that time and circumstance, was not unlettered and had a smattering of both Greek and Latin was filled with the excitement of the voyage as his ship neared the glimmering port. He had travelled from a faraway terrain to this marvellous coastline and decided to capture his expeditions in a log. He assiduously chronicled important details of the long days of voyaging where for miles on end only the horizon was visible, and the sea alternated between terrible roughness and days of calm. The ship had wended its way down the African coast. He wrote:

> Directly below this place is the adjoining country of Arabia, in its length bordering a great distance on the Erythraean Sea. Different tribes inhabit the country, differing in their speech, some partially, and some altogether. The land next the sea is similarly dotted here and there with caves of the Fish-Eaters, but the country inland is peopled by rascally men speaking two languages, who live in villages and nomadic camps, by whom those sailing off the middle course are plundered, and those surviving shipwrecks are taken for slaves... Navigation is dangerous along this whole coast of Arabia, which is without harbours, with bad anchorages, foul, inaccessible because of breakers and rocks, and terrible in every way...

It seems to have been a different experience in India. As the ship casts anchor after it enters Indian waters, our merchant sailor notes a remarkable exchange; of goods from western shores in return for much desired treasures from these parts—almost a calm contrast after their rough voyages. The ship with its merchant sailors docked on Tamil shores after a sojourn further north and discovered Muziris, an old port city on the banks of the Periyar River. This is the first time these travellers became aware of the great wealth of port cities like these, built by the kings of the region, the early Cheras who ruled the western coast of the subcontinent. The *Periplus* was the log maintained by the anonymous merchant sailor and he speaks of voyaging down the river to the south of the country:

> Then come Naura (Kannur) and Tyndis, the first markets of Damirica or Limyrike, and then Muziris and Nelcynda, which are now of leading importance. Tyndis is of the Kingdom of Cerobothra; it is a village in plain sight by the sea. Muziris, of the same kingdom, abounds in ships sent there with cargoes from Arabia, and by the Greeks; it is located on a river (River Periyar), distant from Tyndis by river and sea five hundred stadia, and up the river from the shore twenty stadia. Nelcynda is distant from Muziris by river and sea about five hundred stadia, and is of another Kingdom, the Pandian. This place also is situated on a river, about one hundred and twenty stadia from the sea....

Damirica or Limyrike is Tamilakam, the Tamil country. The journal goes on to say:

> Besides this there are exported great quantities of fine pearls, ivory, silk cloth, spikenard from the Ganges, malabathrum from the places in the interior, transparent stones of all kinds, diamonds and sapphires, and tortoise-shell; that from Chryse Island, and that taken among the islands along the coast of Damirica (Limyrike). They make the voyage to this place in a favourable season who set out from Egypt about the month of July, that is Epiphi.

The Malabar coast was a welcoming place for traders from Rome, Egypt, Arabia, and other parts of West Asia like Mesopotamia and Persia who, well before the advent of Islam, were engaged in exporting pearls, pepper, and other gems to the Arab world and beyond. Tamilakam derived great prosperity during the early Chera rule from the trading of spices, ivory, timber, pearls, and gems. Around the same era or a little after (between the first and third century CE) Muziris has also been mentioned in the Sangam poem, *Ahananuru*. Muziris is clearly referred to in relation to Koodal, that is Madurai:

> …west of Koodal city where flags sway, belonging to the victorious Pandiyan king with many tall, fine elephants, who surrounded with uproar the wealthy Musiri town of Cheran, where, causing the huge beautiful Periyaru river's white foam to become muddied, the fine ships of the Yavanas come with gold and leave with pepper…

Another poem in this collection refers to the city as a place which bestows wealth on its visitors and as a place where liquor abounds. A further reference to Muziris also was made by the Roman historian Pliny, again of the first century, and the dates dovetail to the Sangam-era poems. He called Muziris 'the first emporium of India'. In a fifth-century map of the world as seen from Rome, Tabula Peutingeriana, the town of Muziris is shown prominently as well, all this underlining the fact of a strong connection between the Roman world and the Chera-ruled region.

The numerous references to gold, gemstones, and jewellery as gifts to those who pleased these early rulers is an indication of the availability of ample valuable resources in the Chera kingdom. During these early Christian centuries, the links that connected the west to the east came from the voyages of western explorers who quickly found amazing wealth particularly in the western coastal region and drew benefit from trading. Pliny records that 'Muziris was the first emporium of India' adding that 'the station for ships is at a distance from the shore and cargoes have to be landed and shipped by means of little boats…There reigned there, when I wrote this, the Coelobothros.' The *Periplus* says 'Musiri, a city at the height of prosperity was two miles from the mouth of the river on which it is situated and was the seat of the Government of the kingdom under the sway of Kaprobothras.' While pepper was the main export, there were other local products such as ivory, pearls, spices, and silk. The writer Srinath Perur quotes Federico De Romanis of the University of Rome Tor Vergata: '…this was a centre of paramount importance for Roman trade…what made this absolutely unique was the considerable amounts of black pepper exported from Muziris. We are taking about thousands of tons.' Recent excavations in the village of Patnam near Kodungallur have yielded artefacts, Roman amphorae, tools of iron and lead, gold ornaments and semi-precious stones, possibly intended for export. Many historians feel that this could possibly be the location of the famed and legendary Muziris.

Beyond the Muziris reference, the Girnar inscriptions of Ashoka specifically refer to Keralaputra, Keralaputo, and Satiyaputo. In early Tamil literature the Cheras are referred to as Cherala and Cheraman. The word Kerala does not appear in the Sangam works and is Prakrit in tradition. The term puto was assumed by some dynasties in the south (like the Satavahanas), and a silver coin has been found that bears the term putasa or puto, and on the obverse is the Tamil word makan ('man' in Tamil). The historian and epigraphist R. Nagaswamy says the Cherala Puta of the Ashoka records stands for Cheraman; the Chola and Pandya rulers did not use the Cheraman epithet. In addition, Nagaswamy explains that terms like Atiyaman and Cheraman were popular in Ashoka's court, suggesting that the Tamil regions were actively connected with Ashoka's Pataliputra. The reverse was also true, and Ashoka sent his emissaries to the southern kingdoms. Beyond all these references it is well-known that caches of Roman gold coins have been found in many parts of Tamil Nadu, particularly along the earlier mentioned trade routes. Ptolemy has also mentioned Ay, a chieftain of the southern Kerala region, and in the early Sangam poems such as the *Purananuru*, in the *Patthitrupattu* compilation, there is a chronological reference to some of these early Chera rulers.

The early history of the Chera rulers is hazy as the references are only in literature. An apocryphal story in the *Purananuru* says that a Chera king, Perum Chorru Udiyan Cheral Athan, fed the two opposing armies of the Pandavas and the Kauravas during the Mahabharata war. Perum Chorru is an obvious reference to a lavish filling of the stomach of huge armies of soldiers, and while this speaks to the king's generosity, highlighted in the *Purananuru*, it also indicates a familiarity in the deep south with the stories and legends of the north such as the Mahabharata. Even though there is obvious confusion about dates and the era, the poem nevertheless implies that agriculture must have flourished with bountiful harvests that were able to feed vast armies, revealing a prosperous southern region ruled by the Chera dynasty.

In the term Muventar, or the Three Crowned Kings, referring to the Chera, Chola, Pandya kings, the triumvirate of rulers who ruled Tamilakam from the Sangam age to the thirteenth century, the Chera ruler is firmly ensconced. The term Muventar finds mention in the edicts of Ashoka and in the accounts of Megasthenes, the Greek historian and traveller. The Vanpukazh Muvar or the Three Celestially Famed Kings, are mentioned in *Tolkappiyam*, the first Tamil grammar text. We know the history of the Pandya and Chola rulers who dominated Tamilakam across centuries beginning in the post Sangam era, validated by inscriptions, copper plates, and literature. Like them, the Chera kings were clearly of Tamil origin and held sway across western Tamilakam all the way up to Coimbatore and across the Palakkad Gap, providing a clear passage for the movement of goods and for trade between the inland and the Malabar coast. From the Sangam poems only a skimpy genealogy of the Chera rulers is available; epigraphical evidence regarding the Chera rulers comes from a rare inscription found in Pugalur.

According to Sastri, the *Patthitrupattu* is the primary source of information on the Chera kings. The Udiyan Cheral who fed armies could have well been an ancestor of the Sangam age Chera king of the same name. This Udiyan Cheral's period can be roughly attributed to 130 CE. However, many historians are clear that he was not the founder of the dynasty and there were Chera kings before him as the Ashoka inscriptions indicate. His son and successor was Neduncheral Adan who had the title of Imayavaramban or 'he who conquered the Himalayas'. This claim was reflected in the Chera emblem of a bow against the backdrop of a mountain. He was also called adhiraja or primary king, as he supposedly vanquished many crowned kings, won naval victories, and took into custody some Yavana traders. (The Yavana traders who were active at that juncture meant only Greeks, Romans, and some Arabian merchants; in time, this term was also extended to describe the Arab traders.) After a somewhat turbulent rule marked by military conquests, Neduncheral Adan and his Chola counterpart fought a battle where they both died, and their queens committed sati.

Before we get to the other known Chera rulers, an idea about the geography and spread of this kingdom would be pertinent. The Sangam-age Chera capital was Karur, also called Vanchi. Present-day northern Kerala, the Kongu area of Tamil Nadu, extending up to Salem and Coimbatore, was part of their empire. Although the Cheras were probably the oldest among the three crowned kings of Tamilakam, the borders of their territory were fluid and they frequently lost land to other rulers, particularly the Pandyas. Like Muziris, Tondi was another ancient port city of the early Cheras—the extent of the Chera kingdom then was from Alappuzha in the south to Kasargod in the north. But in the eighth and ninth centuries the Cheras of middle Kerala and the Kongu Cheras detached to form a separate kingdom. By the thirteenth and fourteenth centuries, with the development of Malayalam, these regions evolved into Kerala, with the local Zamorins who were Hindu kings, and other chieftains taking over, and they were thereafter separated from Tamilakam.

With this, the later Chera rule and the rule of subsequent smaller chieftains and kings were more a part of Kerala's history than that of Tamilakam.

Nevertheless, the early intertwining with Tamil history and the fact that they were an integral part of early Tamil polity makes them relevant to this study. Kodungallur was the capital of one branch of the original Sangam Cheras, who carried the name kuttuvan in their lineage, such as Chenguttuvan. Nearby Muziris was their port. As mentioned, another breakaway group of Cheras called themselves Kongu Cheras and established Karur as their capital. Thousands of Sangam age Greek and Roman coins have been unearthed in the Karur region on the banks of the Amaravati River, the biggest discovery of ancient coins in Tamilakam. In addition, Tamil Brahmi inscriptions and brick structures have been found in recent archaeological excavations. Recent excavations have yielded potsherds inscribed in Tamil Brahmi, Roman amphora pieces, and rouletted ware. Kaolin, a type of clay ware, and russet-coated ware have also been found, attesting to a continuing and intensely close contact with Rome. Karur was an important trading and political centre at that time. In nearby Pugalur, Chera inscriptions have been found with the addition of the 'porai' name. This is important epigraphical evidence about the Cheras. The use of epithets like Irumporai and Ko Adan are clearly references to the Chera dynasty. Three kings have been specifically named, says Vedachalam: Ko Adan Sel Irumporai, his son Perum Kadungon, and the latter's son Ilan Kadungon. Only a crowned king could take the title of Adan, and Perum Kadungo means senior ruler, Ko is another title reflecting royal status.

When Ilan Kadungon was still a prince, he made an interesting donation to a Jain monk called Moodha Amanan Athur Sengayvan. The donation was an entire abode created by Ilan Kadungon for this monk and his fellow monks, including carved stone beds and other structures intrinsic to a Jain shelter. Two of the coins that were discovered had names of kings engraved on them. One bears the name Kol Irumporai, and the other, Kolli Porai. Another coin has the name Ma Kottai inscribed on it and yet another has Kuttuvan Kottai inscribed on it. The Porai coins are clearly dated to the first century CE, and the Ma Kottai coin is from the second century while the third coin, the Kuttuvan Kottai, has been dated to the third century CE. This firmly places the kings, the literature, and the archaeological evidence between the first and third centuries—the dates of the Sangam era.

To go back to the *Patthitrupattu*, the Sangam age anthology, it talks about the ten decades of ten Chera kings; each king's name is mentioned, and ten songs are dedicated to every ruler, so there are a hundred poems in this work. The first and last set of ten poems are unavailable. Remarkably, the names in the later poems are said to be the very same names that were discovered at

Pugalur in the inscription as mentioned above, thus corroborating the evidence in literature. All the poems in this anthology are hagiographical in nature; the first few of the 'tens' refer to the earlier dynasty of Cheras, the Imayavaramban dynasty, and the later poems are about the Irumporai rulers. All the poems have a poetic epilogue at the end called patikam and were originally found in palm leaf manuscripts. According to U. Ve. Swaminatha Iyer, who discovered the Sangam manuscripts, commentaries on this anthology came only after the thirteenth century. There is mention of several deities like Shiva, Murugan, and Korravai in the poems and the subject matter is largely in the nature of puram, or exterior themes, such as war, violence, and the deeds and exploits of the Chera kings. There are references in the poems also to the just nature of the Chera rulers, their generosity and large heartedness. A Tamil writer Nallamur Periyannan, delving deeper into *Patthitrupattu*, says the poems also speak about the Chera system of administration, about harbours, villages, and the beautiful countryside, its woodlands, rivers, and sandy shores.

Patthitrupattu is remarkably detailed about the number of years each king ruled; Imayavaramban Neduncheral Adan, for instance, ruled for fifty-eight years, Palyanai Selkelu Kuttuvan ruled for twenty-five years, his successor, Kalangaikanni Narmudi Cheral, was king for another twenty-five years. The text thus talks about the entire Chera Sangam lineage with Kadal Pirukottiya Senguttuvan, who was the son of Imayavaramban, ruling for an astonishing fifty-five years, almost as long as his father. The poems are ascribed to different poets. Kumattur Kannanar has sung about the heroic king Imayavaramban. Palai Gauthamanar, another poet, sang about a king called Palyanai; Kakkai Padiniyar wrote on Aadukotpadu Cheralanathan; and two well-known Sangam poets Kapilar and Paranar composed poems about kings such as Selva Kadungo Vaazhiyathan and Kadal Pirakkotiya Chenguttuvan. Although *Patthitrupattu* is the main source of material on these ancient Chera rulers, the *Purananuru* has some information on the Chera kings. Another later literary work, *Kalavazhi Naarpadhu*, talks about the Chera king Cheraman Kanaikaal Irumporai who was imprisoned by a Chola ruler. The story goes that when the Chera king requested his prison guard to give him water to quench his thirst, the guard delayed bringing water to him, deliberately disrespecting him. The king was so humiliated and anguished by this, that he refused to drink any more water and died shortly thereafter. This legend highlights the sense of honour and pride that many mediaeval kings defined themselves by.

Other kings were Chelva Kadungo Azhi Athan, Thakadur Erintha Perum Cheral Irumporai, and the eighth king, Kudako Ilam Cheral Irumporai. With the unavailability of the first and tenth compilations of *Patthitrupattu*, the names of the remaining kings of the dynasty are lost to history.

To go back to the earliest recorded king of the Chera dynasty whose name we know, Udiyan Cheral Adan, who, apart from the mythical feeding of the armies (which was probably done by an ancestor of the same name as mentioned earlier), ruled the land well and the kingdom was very prosperous under him, having become wealthy by foreign trade especially by sea. His royal kitchen is said to have been set up at Kulumur, now identified with Kulukur in North Travancore. Udiyan Cheral patronized poets and carried the title Vanavaramban. His kingdom was vast, and he is said to have ruled from the west coast to the east coast of the entire southern peninsula at one time, and purportedly (as written in the poems) had a powerful elephant corps and cavalry which he efficiently deployed during war.

Udiyan's son, the famed Imayavaramban, is credited with many important conquests including the capture of a gold-producing region, Konganam, which gave him access to enormous amounts of gold. He made rich donations of gold and jewellery to temples; he also gifted 500 villages in Umbarkadu to the local communities. As mentioned earlier, the Chera emblem of the bow against the backdrop of a mountain was credited to him, and he supposedly carved a bow on a rock face in the Himalayas, which gave him the title 'conqueror of the Himalayas'. Another narrative about him says that he captured and imprisoned many Yavanas (a common name used for Greek, Roman, and Arab traders) and poured ghee over their heads, but this seems uncharacteristic, as most Chera rulers encouraged trade from overseas as it contributed to their economic prosperity.

Imayavaramban was succeeded by his brother Palyanai Selkezhukuttuvan, who was a very pious ruler following the Brahmanical religion and performing many yagnas. He was also called the leader of the Malavas, a group of people who lived in the Kolli and Paccur areas. Like the rulers before him, he controlled the entire area between the east and west coasts of Kerala. The next to rule was Imayavaramban's son Narmudi Cheral, who apparently was a great Vaishnavite and worshipped at the Tiruanantapuram temple. This king won decisive victories over local chieftains, Anji of Tagadur and Nannan of Pulinadu. The poet Kapiyanar, whom he patronized, was given 40 lakh gold coins, according to literary sources.

Chenguttuvan, another son of Imayavaramban, whose mother was the Chola princess Manikilli, ruled next. When her brother Killi, a Chola chieftain and king, was attacked by nine other Chola princes, Chenguttuvan defeated them all. Chenguttuvan is considered by many as the greatest among the early Chera rulers. He won against the Kongars, travelled on military expeditions to the north in aid of a Satkarni ruler, then defeated and captured the Yavanas (and obtained the title of Kadal Pirukottiya, or the conqueror of the seas) and built up the wealth of Muziris, the Chera port city of great wealth and prosperity, which for many centuries during mediaeval times was fabled for its affluence. Chenguttuvan was a man of letters, and like many other Chera kings, was an active patron of poets and literature. He also built a temple for Kannagi, the heroine of the *Shilappadikaram*. Sastri says that establishment of the Pattini cult, that is the worship of Kannagi as the ideal wife, occurred in the time of Cheran Senguttuvan. The stone to make the first image of Pattini or the divine chaste wife was brought from the Himalayas and specially bathed in the Ganges before it was brought to Chera country.

Another king, Chelva Kadungo Azhi Athan, was panegyrised by the famed poet Kapilar as a great king who promoted and supported the arts and was adored by the literary community. He gave a gift of 100,000 gold coins to Kapilar, and apparently bestowed an entire hill on the poet and 'all the land that one could see'. One can recall that Kapilar was first at the court of Pari, the heroic local chieftain mentioned in an earlier chapter; he moved to the Chera court after Pari's death and was obviously well regarded and accommodated. Another fabled act of generosity emanated from this king's son, Perum Cheral Irumporai, who supposedly gifted his entire palace, throne and 900,000 kanam (a land measure) to a poet called Arisil Kilar, who immediately returned all the gifts but remained as minister in the king's service. Ilam Cheral Irumporai, the next king who was the seventh Chera king, expanded Chera rule considerably; he was the overlord of Tondi, Kongar Nadu, Kuttuvar Nadu, and Puli Nadu. Perum Kadungo ruled from Vanchi and was an eminent poet himself—these last three kings were the ones whose names are in the Pugalur inscription.

Two eminent Chera rulers of the eighth century CE must be mentioned. One is the Vaishnavite poet-saint Kulasekhara who came to be known as Kulasekhara Azhwar and wrote the celebrated *Perumal Tirumozhi* in Tamil and *Mukundamala* in Sanskrit. *Perumal Tirumozhi* has been recited at the Srirangam temple ever since the eleventh century. A revised second version of this, *Tetrarum Tiral*, was also recited there, and this has been recorded in a Chola inscription of Kulottunga Chola in the same century. Kulasekhara was born in Vanchi, and his father abdicated the throne in his favour, confident of his son's capabilities. In his own work, he refers to himself as Kongar

Koman, the ruler of Kongu, with his capital at Kollingar, which has been identified as a village at the foot of the Kolli hills. Some historians suggest that this Kulasekhara was the first king of the newly revived Chera dynasty; he mentions in his own poems that he is the lord of Kolli, Kudal, and Kongu. Kodungallur was also an important city and region that he ruled over, and he built a temple called Trikkulasekharapuram in Kodungallur. In his later years he travelled to Mannarkoil in Ambasamudram, and stayed there after discharging his kingly duties, spending his days in devotion to his favourite deity, Rama. There is an inscription to this effect belonging to a later century describing his presence at Mannarkoil. Considered the seventh of the twelve Azhwars, his religious compositions are a part of the Vaishnavite canon of *Nalayira Divya Prabandam*, and his philosophical concepts have had an impact on Vaishnava tenets and practice. However, before he opted for the spiritual life, he is said to have secured his kingdom after several military exploits. In general the Chera region at that time was prosperous and trouble free.

Another much celebrated Chera ruler called Cheraman Perumal was someone whose life is mired in lore. Most of the information on him comes from legends and apocryphal stories. What is most interesting is that many faiths of the time claim him as their own and this perhaps attests to the syncretism and openness in communities at that time with Jain, Buddhist, Hindu, and Islamic stories involving the same king. He is believed to have lived towards the end of the eighth century and possibly in the early ninth century with his capital at Tiruvanjikalam. His deep sense of piety and spirituality probably endeared him to diverse communities. Cheraman Perumal was described as an ardent Shaivite by the poet Sekkizhar in *Periyapuranam*. He was the contemporary and dear friend of Sundaramurthi Nayanmar (Sundarar), the poet-saint who contributed more than a hundred hymns to the *Thevaram*. Sundaramurthi's concept of Shiva was that of a close friend, and he was known as tambiran tolan or friend of God. Cheraman, like his friend Sundaramurthi, was the author of highly devotional works of a literary nature such as the *Tiruvarur-mummanikkovai*. As they were close friends, the story goes that at the end of their lifetime, the two travelled to Kailash together on their last journey, with the king having opted for an ascetic life after renouncing his wealth and power. Sundaramurthi rode a white elephant and Cheraman a white horse as they reached the heavenly abode of Shiva.

The story of the king framed in Islamic terms says that Cheraman had a dream one night that the moon had split into two. When he asked his courtiers about the significance of this, no one could give him a satisfactory explanation. One wise person, however, said that this had to do with the revelation to Prophet Muhammad. Intrigued, the king and some of his associates from court crossed the Arabian Sea to meet the Prophet. He achieved his objective, converted to Islam, and directed his subjects to build a mosque in Kodungallur. On his long journey back, he fell ill in Salah, a city to the south of Oman, and passed away there. The mosque was however built, and today the Cheraman Mosque is reputedly the oldest continuously operating mosque in the country, worship there commencing in the seventh century.

Cheraman's story fades into obscurity around 825 CE. Sastri credits this king with wisdom, tolerance, and piety but casts doubt on his conversion to Islam. Scholars like S. Divan of Palayamkottai say that this Cheraman Perumal was an entirely different Cheraman around whom the Shaivite stories are woven. 'There were many Cheraman Perumals,' says Divan. Nevertheless, the existence of such legends does indicate that there was communal harmony in Chera country, possibly because of their long history of tolerance and success in integrating into their communities the strangers who landed on their shores.

Beside the fabled city of Muziris, there were also ports like Bandar, famous for its pearls, and Kodumanam, renowned for its rare jewels. The hills of the Chera country had mines from which precious stones were extracted, and there were skilled artisans who worked in all manner of arts from jewellery-making to refitting ships, according to the literary texts. Although agriculture flourished in the Chera country, the economy grew largely on account of trade. While there was frequent war between the territories ruled by the Chera, Chola, and Pandya kings, land borders were always fluid. However, for long periods of time the Chera kings indeed had suzerainty over vast areas and ruled from Karur or Vanji in Trichy district up to Muziris on the western coast. Southern Karnataka and the Konkan region also came under Chera rule.

To organize trade to their treasury's advantage, Chera kings issued coins in the region. Sastri mentions the unearthing of a Roman 'factory' or 'settlement' in Arikamedu near Karur, where a hoard of Roman punch-marked coins has been found. Nagaswamy places them in three categories; punch-marked Roman coins, punch-marked Tamil coins, and local currency. The fact that Roman coins were used locally indicates a possible small Roman settlement as early as in 25 CE. Although not all historians concur on the idea of an actual settlement, the fact of brisk trade is undeniable. Literary references speak of coins with names like ka, pon, kanam, and kasu. Parameshwara Lal Gupta, a numismatist, says that of the hoards found, 184 of the silver punch-marked coins were from Kottayam district and another silver hoard with 34 silver punch-marked coins were from Iyyal village in Cochin district. Among these are 12 Roman gold coins and 71 Roman denarius, he says. Although most locally issued coins have been described as Pandya coins, given the length and extent of Chera rule, this idea needs to be re-examined. These local copper coins have emblems on them that reflect Chera rule such as elephants with or without riders, sometimes square in shape, with an auspicious symbol above the elephant such as the Chakra, Srivatsa, and Chaitya, which apart from being Chera emblems are Buddhist symbols as well. The frequent use of elephants and their might as symbols of power was also common in Chera royal life. Even later Chera coins of the mediaeval period which are indisputably of Chera origin carry the emblem of the bow, the palmyra tree, and the elephant.

After the Sangam age, like with the other royal dynasties of the south, the Cheras seem to disappear. It is most likely that given the rule of the Kalabhras over the entire south, a time of which there is no record or inscription, the Cheras went into obscurity. Around the eighth century they resurfaced and established themselves in Tiruvanjikalam, making it their capital, says Vedachalam. However, by this time, the Cheras were not as powerful as they once were. Caught up in several wars between the Pallava and Pandya kings, they never really reclaimed their once powerful status. Up until the eleventh and twelfth century the Chera kings were on the landscape of Tamilakam after which, with the development of Malayalam and their own unique identity, they edged away from Tamil polity and developed a separate history.

BOOK III
The Age of Transition

Chapter 19

Turmoil and Tumult

The Madurai Sultans and the Vijayanagar Kings

The pupil of the eye has never seen a place like it, and the ear of intelligence has never been informed that there existed anything to equal it in the world...

Abdur Razzaq, Persian ambassador and writer

THE GREAT EMPIRES OF THE MEDIAEVAL AGE DECLINED AND VANISHED due to frequent internecine wars, weak leadership, and administrative dysfunction. The Chola empire with boundaries that stretched across the seas, began to crumble in the twelfth century after a long reign, and met its end in the early thirteenth century. The once unassailable territory, which extended from the shining seas of the Indian Ocean to lands beyond, and in the north, as far as the Ganga, met a significant defeat at the hands of the Pandya king in 1215 CE, spelling the dynasty's doom. The ultimate defeat of Rajendra Chola III by the Pandya ruler Maravarman Kulasekhara Pandya in 1279 CE, following years of constant strife between them, was the final nail in the coffin. The Pandyas did not last long after dethroning the Cholas. Kulasekhara Pandya died in 1308 CE during a succession war. One of his sons sought the aid of the Delhi sultanate and that opened the door to the Delhi sultans venturing southward.

According to Sastri, the first forays of the northern rulers were more about 'pursuing a policy of plunder and loot' rather than territorial expansion. The notion of subjugating territories in the south came later, with expeditions to regions like Warangal in the Telugu lands led by Malik Kafur, a general who initially served as a slave to Alauddin Khilji and later developed a close personal relationship with him. Malik Kafur's excursions resembled raids more than attempts to capture territory.

By this time, both Telugu and Malayalam had evolved as distinct languages. In the decades that followed, Telugu, Kannada, and Marathi speakers journeyed to Tamilakam, ruling in some parts and coexisting with the local population in others. Some of these regions slipped outside the borders of Tamilakam and fell under the rule of various dynasties and rulers. Despite the many negative aspects of invasion and plunder, the inroads made into places like Telugu Warangal, Devagiri of the Yadava kingdom, and large portions of the Deccan sowed the seeds of a syncretic culture.

Malik Kafur and subsequent rulers like Muhammad Bin Tughlaq established capital cities in conquered southern regions before retreating to Delhi, giving rise to a new Deccani culture. Within this cultural synthesis, a fusion of Hindu and Muslim traditions occurred, influencing the Urdu and Telugu languages, as well as festivals, foods, and customs that are still observed today in the Nizami culture of Hyderabad. The arts of sculpture, painting, and architecture were impacted by the confluence of these cultures. Naturally, these traditions permeated various segments of society, resulting in local adaptations, and becoming the culture of specific communities. The enduring beauty of these traditions continues to foster unity and togetherness among Hindus and Muslims.

Meanwhile, Malik Kafur's army overran numerous minor kingdoms in central, eastern, and western India. He laid siege to their fortifications, stormed their bastions, and carried back vast treasures from these places to Delhi.

The initial foray of Malik Kafur into South India is highly controversial, with opposing perspectives regarding his march into the Pandya kingdom and the nature of his actions. In 1311, he embarked on his journey southward, leaving destruction in his wake. As has been noted, it is surmised that one of the warring Pandya brothers invited him to the region. Upon his arrival in South India with his army, several accounts attest to his attack on the Meenakshi temple in Madurai, devastating the sanctum sanctorum. Apparently, he also looted treasures from the Chidambaram temple, reportedly damaged the Srirangam temple, and committed severe cruelties against the local population. Numerous Shaiva and Vaishnava temples also suffered destruction.

However, historian and scholar Raja Mohamad has argued that considering Malik Kafur spent only around twenty-seven days on his southern sojourn, it is unlikely that he could have conducted all the attacks attributed to him. He suggests that his plundering and looting were on a par with that of several other mediaeval Indian kings. Hindu kings also had a history of attacking other Hindu kings and seizing trophies of war, including statues and sacred symbols from enemy holy spaces. Raja Mohamad cites the example of the Chola kings, who conquered and destroyed temples in places like Sri Lanka.

On the other hand, several scholars emphasize that some Muslim rulers and their lieutenants, like Malik Kafur, engaged in significantly more plundering and destruction. Vedachalam points out that whether it was Rajaraja or Rajendra, plundering seemed to be the norm, citing the example of war trophies collected by Rajendra from Pandya temples in the south and from faraway places like Bengal. Malik Kafur, as a non-Hindu, was likely more aggressive in his campaign and in collecting treasures from kings and temples. Accounts from those who travelled with him, and contemporary writers, support this perspective. Temple accounts, including a few inscriptions, also record the closure of many temples, such as Chidambaram, and the hiding of temple treasures out of fear of further destruction.

Malik Kafur's expeditions paved the way for the establishment of the Madurai sultanate. During this period, many Hindu temples were dismantled, and idols and temple treasures were concealed. According to historian Andre Wink, the mutilation and destruction of Hindu idols and temples constituted an attack on Hindu religious practice, with the Muslim destruction of religious architecture aimed at eradicating vestiges of Hindu religious symbols. Scholars like Richard Eaton have pointed out that a ruler's power and identity is closely tied in with the central temple of his kingdom, and in inter-regional conflicts, capturing the temple symbolizes the subjugation of the defeated ruler. 'The temple was normally looted, redefined or destroyed, any of which would have had the effect of detaching a defeated raja from the most prominent manifestation of his former legitimacy'. Eaton gives the example of the Pallava king Narasimhavarman I looting the Ganesha image from Vatapi, the Chalukya capital. The Pandya king Srimaran Srivallabha brought back a golden Buddha from Sri Lanka and the Chola king Rajendra I brought back many idols from his conquests. This demonstrates that temple destruction was not only done by Muslim rulers in the places that they conquered but by Hindu rulers as well. A strong contrary view is held by several other experts such as B. Narasimhaiah who says, 'The Mohammedan invaders were particular in looting temples which were repositories not only of wealth but also of knowledge and culture.' Our primary focus here, however, is on the ongoing history of the Tamil region, which at this juncture, experienced significant political instability. The constant rivalry between the brothers Sundara Pandyan and Veera Pandyan, which led to the ultimate collapse of the Pandya kingdom, was preceded by various political intrigues involving a range of actors. These actors included Ravivarman Kulasekhara, the Chera king who ruled Travancore, as well as Malik Kafur and Khusrau Khan (both lieutenants of Alauddin Khilji), Muppidi Nayaka of Nellore, Prataparudra, the Kakatiya ruler, and several others whose power struggles resulted in the fragmentation of once stable kingdoms.

There were three invasions of the south in the fourteenth century, primarily targeting Madurai, Tiruchirappalli, and the South Arcot district. These invasions were led by the Delhi sultans. Malik Kafur initiated these invasions by sacking the city of Madurai in 1311. Subsequently, Khusrau Khan launched an attack on the city, and a third assault was carried out by Ulugh Khan, later known as Muhammad Bin Tughlaq. By this time, nearly all of South India, most of the region south of the Deccan, had come under the control of the Delhi sultanate.

The Madurai sultanate, also known as the Ma'bar sultanate, eventually broke away from Delhi. In 1335, Jalaluddin Ahsan Khan declared independence and began issuing gold and silver coins in his own name from Madurai. The Madurai rulers held power for about forty years, with eight sultans ruling during that period. Notably, the Moroccan historian Ibn Battuta, who travelled through Asia and Africa and provided an account of the sultanate, was the son-in-law of Jalaluddin Khan.

For about a hundred years from the thirteenth century onwards, Tamil polity experienced disruptive and fragmented rule. Five politically divided states—namely, the Madurai sultanate, Hoysalas, Kakatiyas, Suenas of Devagiri, and the much-diminished Pandya kings in the far south—kept fighting each other. This continued until the establishment of the Vijayanagar kingdom in 1336 CE, which unified the region to the south of the Tungabhadra River under one large empire, a Karnataka empire, with Vijayanagar as its capital.

Before this unification, the Suenas of Devagiri and the Kakatiyas of Warangal had been gradually declining. The Hoysala king Ballala III, who 'bent before the aggressor (the Delhi sultan) but did neither prostrate nor succumb', grew old and alone, attempting to wage war against the northern invader with little success. He ultimately died fighting the Madurai sultan in the south near Trichy in 1342.

The troubling impact of Muslim rule, which introduced a host of unpopular policies, gave rise to opposing forces, including a new brand of Shaivism, that grew into a fierce opposition against Islamic rule. Many Hindu kings attempted to unite to overthrow the yoke of Muslim rule. Two brothers, Harihara and Bukka, the sons of Sangama, the chief courtier at the Hoysala court, rebelled against the Delhi sultanate and founded the state of Vijayanagar in 1336 CE. Their avowed intent was expansionism, and the conquest of the territory controlled by the sultans. They also confronted the Madurai sultanate and established their kingdom, which encompassed vast lands south of the Deccan, rich in agriculture, minerals, and natural wealth. To underscore their imperial stature, an ambassador from their court was dispatched to China to the Ming dynasty's court. Throughout these endeavours, the brothers were aided by Madhava, a minister of Sangama's court, who later became known as Vidyaranya, serving as their secular adviser and spiritual mentor. He later became the head of the Sringeri Sharada Peetam, an important religious institution.

Legend has it that the site of the kingdom's origins was Kishkinda, the place of the monkey gods, the Vanaras of the Ramayana. Hampi, the capital, was supposedly another name for Kishkinda, and from this fabled city extended the Vijayanagar kingdom. The Tungabhadra River flowed through the region, and the temple of Virupaksha stood there, esteemed by the local population and revered as Pampa Kshetra, the holy land of Parvati, who did penance and subsequently celebrated her marriage to Shiva in this place. The temperate climate, cool forests, hills, and the waters of the Tungabhadra made this an ideal location for the foundation of an empire. According to B. Narasimhaiah, retired Superintending Archaeologist with the ASI, Hampi, Hosapattana, and the town of Vijayanagar are possibly the same. The name of the city has also been found in an inscription from 1356 CE. Notably, early Vijayanagar architecture, including that of temples, followed the late Chola and Pandya styles.

The city of Vijayanagar, with its central citadel, splendid buildings, and lush gardens filled with fruit trees, flowering trees, and rare herb gardens, was well-documented by foreign travellers of the time. The Persian ambassador Abdur Razzaq, who was in the city in 1443, wrote: 'The pupil of the eye has never seen a place like it, and the ear of intelligence has never been informed that there existed anything equal to it in the world....'

Towards the late fourteenth century, the Vijayanagar empire extended its rule over the Tamil regions. The condition of Tamilakam at this time was dismal, to say the least. The plight of the poor was severe, as class differences had become amplified, and they suffered under the oppression of landlord cultivators. One of the sons of Bukka, Kumara Kampana, captured territory in Tamilakam, which included the Madurai, Trichy, and Kanchipuram regions. Based on his exploits in Tamilakam, his wife, Gangadevi, who was a poet, wrote *Madura Vijayam*, celebrating the Vijayanagar victory and the routing of the local rulers. Kumara Kampana also brought Rameswaram under Vijayanagar rule. The Madurai sultan had been overthrown, and Vijayanagar rule was established over most of Tamil Nadu. However, the situation of tenant farmers and landless labour did not see much improvement in the immediate aftermath of the Vijayanagar takeover, leading to riots by the left-hand groups against landlords in the Trichy and Thanjavur districts, continuing off and on well into the fifteenth century.

In terms of stabilizing the empire, the Vijayanagar rulers had rivals and neighbours in the Bahmani sultanate, which had established itself in the Deccan north of their territory. These two kingdoms, sharing a border, were often at war with each other. The Bahmani kingdom had already established itself as a progressive state that welcomed talented immigrants from the Muslim world and had strong connections with its Islamic counterparts in West Asia. The Vijayanagar king at that time, Devaraya, also began to welcome some of these immigrants to Vijayanagar, realizing that beyond being a Hindu bastion, he had to have a broader vision for his empire. During his long and prosperous reign, he introduced new ideas in administration, the military, and among the polity. Abdur Razzaq commented that Devaraya had a diverse court with scholars of many faiths, writers, and scientists present. He also enlisted Muslims in his army. The city's architecture incorporated some facets of the Islamic style in its buildings. Some of these mediaeval rulers showed an acute perception of the value of communal harmony. The glory of the Vijayanagar kingdom would last for over two hundred years, despite violent court intrigues, attempted murder, conspiracies of succession, and even the slaying of some rulers from time to time.

In time, the dynasty changed hands, and the third family that ruled over the empire was called the Tuluva dynasty. The greatest ruler of Vijayanagar was Krishnadevaraya, who belonged to this family. His father was a general in the army of the Saluva king, Narasimha Devaraya. Tuluva Narasa Nayaka, Krishnadevaraya's father, acted as the regent for the young sons of the earlier ruler who was murdered. After the so-called rule of the last two princes of the Saluva dynasty, who ruled under the regency of Narasa Nayaka, his older son by his first wife, Vira Narasimha, ascended the throne. After Vira Narasimha's death, his half-brother Krishnadevaraya, whose mother was Nagala Devi, the second wife of Narasa Nayaka, came to the throne. He ruled from 1509 to 1529. The impact of his rule was far-reaching and impressive. The earliest inscription of him is from 1509, and his coronation was celebrated on the date of Krishna Jayanthi. Paeans of praise were composed, suggesting that he had some of the same divine qualities as Krishna, according to his worshipful subjects. Domingo Paes and Duarte Barbosa, Portuguese travellers who visited the kingdom, have commented on the brilliance of Krishnadevaraya, his great capabilities, and the general prosperity of the kingdom. Robert Sewell in his book, *A Forgotten Empire*, paraphrases the accounts of Paes who met the king in 1520. Paes says that he was a real ruler, physically strong, a fine rider, blessed with a noble presence. He commanded his armies in person, was able, brave, and statesmanlike and was a man of much gentleness and generosity of character. Paes writes that 'he was gallant and perfect in all things'. The only 'blot on his escutcheon, is that after a great success with (a) Mohamedan king he grew to be haughty and insolent…no monarch such as Adil Shah could brook for a moment such a humiliation as was implied by a peace the condition of which was that he should kiss his triumphant enemy's foot'.

Apart from successful military campaigns in which Krishnadevaraya expanded Vijayanagar's territory, repelling the Bahmani forces in the north, and bringing Odisha, Telangana, and large parts of the south under his sway, he also strengthened a somewhat weakened kingdom. Recognizing the value of consolidation for long-term stability, he implemented good governance norms throughout his realm. During his military campaigns, in addition to leading his troops in battle, his humanitarianism was evident as he reportedly personally tended to the wounded. Beyond being a capable administrator, he was a great patron of the arts and attracted poets and scholars to his court. He was a scholar himself and authored the epic poem *Amuktamalyada* in Telugu; he also wrote poetry in Sanskrit. His inscriptions, found across South India, were in Sanskrit, Tamil, Kannada, and Telugu.

Sastri, extolling Krishnadevaraya's virtues, cites a Telugu poet from his court, Allasani Peddana, who said that 'he (the king) was in no way less famous for his religious zeal and catholicity. He respected all sects of Hindu religion alike, although his personal leanings were in favour of Vaishnavism. Krishna Raya's kindness to the fallen enemy, his acts of mercy and charity towards the residents of captured cities…his great military prowess…the royal reception and kindness he bestowed upon foreign embassies…his imposing personal appearance, his genial outlook…his love for literature and religion and his solicitude for the welfare of his people…mark him out as one of the greatest of…monarchs.'

In Tamil Nadu, he undertook the restoration of many important temples that had fallen to the onslaught of invaders. His Dig Vijaya, a victory tour of his kingdom, took him as far south as Rameswaram. He also added structures to the Ananthapadmanabhaswamy temple in Thiruvananthapuram. He visited the Meenakshi temple in Madurai and celebrated his birthday with a grand puja, distributing 500 gold coins to the gathered crowd. He offered prayers at the Azhagar temple in Madurai and even stayed there overnight.

Nearby is the Rakkayi Amman temple, where he built the Krishnadevaraya mandapam.

Among the significant temples he renovated was the Varadaraja Perumal temple in Kanchipuram, where he rebuilt the partially demolished sanctum sanctorum and constructed a large 100-pillared mandapam in the temple premises. T. S. Subramanian highlighted the restoration of the beautiful lime-washed sculptures of the kalyana mandapam. T. Satyamurthy, a former Superintending Archaeologist of the ASI, called the sculptures in this temple 'the jewels of Vijayanagar architecture'. Krishnadevaraya, around 1525 CE, covered the vimana of the temple with gold sheets.

Achyuthadevaraya, Krishnadevaraya's brother and successor, built the mandapam in the Varadaraja Perumal temple in 1530. In true Vijayanagar style of aesthetic excess, the pillars of the mandapam showcase an array of fantastic sculptures, from mythical creatures to dancers, musicians, and deities. An intriguing sculpture of a horse rider depicts a man with a beard and moustache on only one side of his face, wearing pleated trousers. The sculptor may have been influenced by the appearance of Portuguese traders on the shores of the Vijayanagar kingdom, whimsically capturing this on the temple walls. A small metal sculpture of Krishnadevaraya with one of his wives is installed in a niche at the temple. This sculpture, a few inches tall, is found near the Perundevi shrine at the temple. The king is seen standing with folded hands, with a sword tucked behind his left hand and carrying a dagger. He wears a tall conical crown studded with gemstones and a diminutive queen stands next to him. A much larger dwarapalaka is seen standing near the pair. The inscriptions in the temple, in Telugu and Tamil, provide details about the restoration activities undertaken by Krishnadevaraya.

In the Ekambareshwar temple in Kanchipuram, Krishnadevaraya built an outstanding structure, a raja gopuram. An inscription in Tamil and Telugu at the temple attests to this. In the Tiruvannamalai temple, he constructed four entrance gopurams and a mandapam. The raja gopuram, usually positioned in the east, was the most prominent and came to be termed as raya gopuram in honour of the raja or king, associated with the majesty of these structures. Another magnificent gopuram built by him stands in the Srirangam Ranganatha temple. Beautiful metal statues of the king with his two wives can be found in Tirupati. Krishnadevaraya lavished gifts on the Tirumala temple, demonstrating his devotion to the deity.

The Vijayanagar rulers seemed to have a fascination with mandapams. They constructed numerous mandapams or pillared halls of different dimensions and for different purposes. The older Dravidian temples mostly only had an ardha mandapam and a maha mandapam, but these kings built numerous halls such as the vasanta mandapam, kalyana mandapam, neeradum mandapam, unjal mandapam and nritta mandapam, providing space for a variety of social and religious functions which drew the local community to these temples.

The arrival of these new rulers was a welcome relief, especially in places like Madurai, as the people were allowed the freedom to congregate in temples. In addition to these recreational mandapams, the Vijayanagar kings, especially Krishnadevaraya and Achyuthadevaraya, built numerous teppakulam or temple tanks, encouraging community involvement. Hindu revivalism was helped by this strong royal patronage. From a new kind of temple architecture to influencing changes in lifestyle and food habits, the rule of these kings of the Vijayanagar clan and later the Nayaks impacted the Tamil population. For instance, the Tamil staples, dosai and idli, came from that period, according to S. Kannan, a Madurai-based historian and scholar. Temple offerings in Tamilakam used to be simple milagu amudhu (pepper rice enriched with ghee), thayir amudhu (curd rice) and in places like Karaikudi, pasiparuppu kummayam (now renamed as Ashoka halwa). In the Vijayanagar-Nayak periods, more food was added, and the reference to these prasadams or offerings included a description saidu ittavi, meaning 'made and cooked', so ittavi soon became idli and similarly dosai came to be a Tamil food. The acculturation that occurred in Tamil society at this time took it to a new trajectory that was quite different from the earlier linear flow of Tamil history, particularly up to the ninth century.

Vedachalam notes that during the Vijayanagar and Nayak periods, many mandapams were built in the precincts of both Vishnu and Shiva temples. He mentions the pudu mandapam in the Meenakshi temple, formerly known as vasanta mandapam. The sight of beautiful floating deities under dark night skies drew the hushed devotion of the throng of people who would gather to witness these festivals. The mandapam's construction was overseen by Tirumalai Nayak, featuring sculptural portraits of many Nayak kings on the pillars and walls, including Viswanatha Nayak, an earlier ruler, depicted in postures of welcome and worship of the deities as they float by. The plethora of sculptural offerings, including those of Tirumalai Nayak and his wives, though not as finely honed as Chola sculptures, offer a more human and less perfect representation, as seen during multiple visits to these places. The revivalist imagination is exuberant, as evident in the numerous additions to the Meenakshi temple. Even the famed Golden Lotus tank, one of the earliest structures of the temple, was renovated in the sixteenth century. There is a Nandi with a mridangam, Shiva ganas in different postures of worship, and a host of other sculptural offerings, including a Vishnu with an udukku, an ancient percussion instrument.

The Vijayanagar-Nayak additions to the Meenakshi temple are numerous, although the deity herself is depicted in the old Pandya style, with two arms instead of four as is customary in the Amman temples of northern Tamilakam. Her allure and magic are evident from the constant throngs at her shrine. The fish-eyed Goddess wears a karanda makuta or tiered crown typically depicted on sculptures of south Indian goddesses, holding a lily in her right hand and the left in lola (or dola) hasta mudra, a posture where the hand hangs down gracefully from the sloping shoulder and relaxed arm, conveying both relaxed stability and grounding.

Another mandapam built in the seventeenth century, adjacent to the gorgeous Azhagar temple in Madurai, has jewel-like paintings on the ceiling. The mandapam is plain and has been used as a primary school, a storeroom, and perhaps even as a sleeping place for itinerant travellers. During the time of the Vijayanagar–Nayak rulers, like in the pudu mandapam of the Meenakshi temple, this was a place for gatherings and spectacles and for festivals like the rites of spring for the people of the surrounding communities. In those days, the Azhagar temple was quite outside Madurai city, and each geography had its own celebrations, thus widening the base of devotion and spirituality among ordinary folk who were largely unlettered. The deity, Vishnu, from within the temple would be brought and placed at the centre of the mandapam. Vedachalam points to a mirror image painted on the ceiling. This is where the story begins, he says, the early part of the Ramayana, painted exquisitely and in mini panels across the entire ceiling in consecutive manner beginning with King Dasharatha's longing for a child and going on to depict the yagna the king did, and subsequent birth of the four royal princes to his wives. What sets these series of paintings apart is the minutiae that reveal several insights into the customs of the era. For instance, when Dasharatha's queens go into labour, one of them is seen delivering the baby standing up while she is supported by two women of the court. There are other scenes; the details of the royal children being bathed, being put to sleep and, in one panel, where the king distributes his largesse to a gathered crowd to celebrate his sons' births, the diverse depiction of people in these paintings in terms of looks and demeanour suggests that the influx of migrants into Tamilakam was not uncommon.

It was not just the influx of migrants, but the general cosmopolitan courts of the Vijayanagar kings which fostered a more 'Persianate' or 'Islamicate' environment. Whether it was architecture, art, dress, etiquette, trade, or even warfare and diplomacy, the permeation of a variety of influences even though not too strong in the Tamil regions brought changes to the way people lived. The historian Lennart Bes points out an interesting aspect in a kalamkari painting of the time where a Nayak ruler, probably of Madurai or Thanjavur, wears a kabayi (a Muslim style garment) in a military procession but wears a dhoti in other parts of the painting where he is engaged in domestic activity. Apparently, many Islamic appellations were also adopted by these Hindu kings and nobility. The Vijayanagar court set a tone of cosmopolitism which may not have entirely percolated to the southern regions but had an impact nevertheless especially later when the Marathas came to Thanjavur.

Other aspects of the kingdom of Vijayanagar include the emergence of the Nayak administrative structures evolving from the Vijayanagar king's main court, from where support was needed to rule an expansive kingdom. The land was divided into large administrative units called rajyas. The Nayaks, who ruled different rajyas, were military leaders under the kings and had to remit taxes to the rulers while fulfilling various duties. Inscriptions in Tamil Nadu, dating back to the Vijayanagar period, provide extensive details about these Nayaks. Fernão Nunes, the Portuguese horse merchant who stayed in Vijayanagar city during this period, also commented on the growing power of the Nayaks.

After Krishnadevaraya, his brother Achyuthadevaraya, although a capable leader, found that in the later years of his reign, he was losing his grip over the vast provinces he ruled. In Tamilakam, Nayak governors were appointed in Madurai, Gingee, and Thanjavur. These governors gradually freed themselves from the overlordship of the Vijayanagar rulers but, in some cases, continued to owe fealty to them. The reason why the Vijayanagar kings initially appointed these chiefs in territories seized from Muslim and Pandya rulers was that the regions were becoming difficult to manage directly. Besides, they wanted to reward old loyalists who had served them, and princely or royal relatives were placed in these new political structures.

It's important to note that the Portuguese had established themselves on the western shores of India by this time, with small trading outposts in Goa under the control of a governor. We'll take a closer look at the European traders who turned rulers in a later chapter. In the fifteenth century, during the rule of a later Vijayanagar ruler, Venkata, who had already lost much of the territorial gains made by earlier Vijayanagar kings, the Dutch and the English began to establish themselves on the east coast. Rebellion in Tamilakam, as well as in other regions like Kolar and parts of the Telugu country, was sporadic. Lingama Nayak in Vellore led a revolt against the Vijayanagar ruler, but he was eventually quelled. The attention that the rulers devoted to the distant provinces was significantly less than what they allocated to the Telugu and Kannada regions. While the old Chola administrative setup and structures persisted in some parts of Tamilakam, tax and tithes were forcibly collected by central administrative officers representing the king, causing their rule to become increasingly unpopular among ordinary people. Consequently, maintaining the unity of the kingdom gradually shifted towards emphasizing policing and militaristic operations in these provinces, rather than focusing on civil matters and administration.

Despite the 'Persianate' influences in society and the slow seeping in of multiple cultures in Vijayanagar, the political situation was different. The Portuguese had territorial ambitions in the kingdom even as Krishnadevaraya came to the throne in 1509 and the additional and constant threat from the 'Muhammadan activities on the northern frontier', was a challenge to the stability of Vijayanagar. The South, that is Tamilakam, was somewhat protected from these external forces, but internal dissensions broke out as Vijayanagar rule slowly crumbled and the Nayaks, the viceroyalty of various regions of the South, took control and became the new royalty.

Chapter 20

The Nayaks in Tamil Country

The history of the Nayaks…comprises the history practically of the fifteenth, sixteenth, seventeenth, and the first third of the eighteenth centuries, and carries the history of South India from the best days of the empire of Vijayanagar to the eve of the British occupation of the Carnatic.

S. Krishnaswami Aiyangar, historian

AN HONEST SCULPTURAL RENDERING OF TIRUMALAI NAYAK, ONE OF the greatest Nayak rulers, in the pudu mandapam of the Meenakshi temple in Madurai, is an almost audacious proclamation of the might and confidence of the Telugu Nayak rulers who came to control Tamilakam for about two centuries after the decline of Vijayanagar. The king stands palms together in a gesture of prayer and supplication, his rotund stomach jutting out slightly above a decorative veshti. The joined palms and bejewelled hands are by no means a gesture of solicitation; the posture of the king is overbearing despite depicting a less than perfect figure, and behind him in timid decorum stand three of his queens, shy and humble in demeanour, heads downcast, with the third and last queen almost turned away from the group. The lifelike rendition of these figures marks not just realism but hints at excess. These stucco statues summing up the grandeur and garishness of some of the Nayak art and architecture seem to reflect a kind of peaking of artistic expression during this period. Everything was ornate and grand—from pillared mandapams to gopurams, vimanas, and murals on temple walls.

We recall that while the great Krishnadevaraya and later Achyuthadevaraya had much of the Tamil regions under their suzerainty, the slow disintegration of a once magnificent Vijayanagar empire led to a scramble for control in Tamilakam by their erstwhile subordinates, the Nayak regents of their territories. Until they established themselves as local powers, these Nayaks were administrators and tax collectors under the Vijayanagar overlordship. The most prominent in Tamilakam were the Nayaks of Gingee, Thanjavur, and Madurai, with Madurai becoming the most prominent among them.

Karashima notes that the number of Nayaks mentioned in Vijayanagar inscriptions in Tamilakam totals about 500, both big and small. Robert Sewell's

A Forgotten Empire published in 1900 provides much detail on the Vijayanagar and Nayak kings. These Nayak stewards maintained soldiers for the king and forwarded the taxes they collected to the royal treasury. Karashima quotes the Portuguese horse merchant Fernão Nunes who was in Vijayanagar at the time of Achyuthadevaraya and inferred from local inscriptions that the Nayaks had to remit a certain amount of the money from their collection to the royal Vijayanagar treasury and also maintain a small army for the king as well as carry out general administration in the territories through other agents. Apparently, in the early years of the Nayak stewardship, the Vijayanagar rulers would move them around often to prevent them from becoming locally entrenched and with their own power centres.

However, the system wasn't always smooth and well-coordinated: maladministration and landlord oppression are recorded in some inscriptions in Tamil Nadu such as in the Tevur inscription. A valangai/idangai rebellion against the Nayaks and their overlords occurred in 1429 when oppressed peasants rose against them. This appears to have been a significant event, noteworthy enough to merit mention in a permanent record. In the Vellar and Kaveri/Kollidam valleys, a series of inscriptions from Aduthurai, Tiruvaigvur, and Elavanasur in Korukkai detail the agitation. It wasn't just directed at the Vijayanagar rulers but also at the Nayaks, the military, and the holders of official tenure such as the Vellalas and the Brahmins. 'We, the people belonging to *Idangai 98* and *Valangai 98* assembled here in full strength and let the following be engraved on the wall of the temple....' Then they proceed to name a host of officials, warning that if they 'try to oppress us in collusion with the government officials, we shall never submit to such oppression... If there appears any single person among us who helps the intruders, betrays us...we shall assemble as of today and we shall degrade him in the caste hierarchy.' The threat of lowering one's caste seemed to be viewed as a severe punishment. In any case, as Karashima points out, it appears that in the Tamil country, especially among the lower strata of society, people suffered greatly under the arbitrary and oppressive administration of the Vijayanagar army and officials. The collusion between wealthy landlords and the government seems to have further exacerbated their misery.

Despite the hardships faced by the dispossessed, whose situation became increasingly vulnerable, especially in rural areas affected by rain and drought, the social and administrative machinery continued to operate as established in the more orderly days of Kumara Kampana. An early Vijayanagar representative or viceroy to the Tamil region, he was a prince of royal blood who managed to establish more stable administrative structures in these far-flung regions. He also managed to secure more resources from the centre for these regions in the fourteenth century. However, by the beginning of the seventeenth century, with the gradual disintegration of Vijayanagar rule in many regions of South India, Nayak rule emerged. Initially semi-independent, these Nayak rulers eventually broke away entirely from their overlords in Vijayanagar, who were dealing with a declining empire. According to Sathyanatha Aiyar, who wrote a detailed account of the Nayaks in 1924, their rule in Tamilakam from the late fifteenth century through the eighteenth century 'carries the history of South India from the best days of the empire of Vijayanagar to the British occupation of the Carnatic.'

A pioneering but somewhat unreliable source for the history of Nayak rule, particularly in Madurai, comes from the writings of J. H. Nelson of the Madras Civil Service in 1868. Nelson apparently relied too heavily on information from the Jesuits stationed there, and on Tamil and Telugu chronicles of the region, which later historians considered undependable. According to Aiyar, William Taylor's *History of the Carnataka Governors* from 1835 provides some brief but more reliable information. There are other works in Sanskrit and Telugu that shed light on the rule of the Nayaks in Madurai and Thanjavur. Of interest are also letters from Jesuit missionaries in South India to their European headquarters. Aiyar draws from epigraphical information in Sewell's *List of Antiquities*, which contains epigraphical information about this period. Importantly, temple paintings, sculptures, and inscriptions offer diverse information about this period of Tamil history, particularly from the Madurai, Thanjavur, Ramanathapuram, Tirunelveli, and Tiruchirappalli areas.

The greatest of the Nayak rulers, Tirumala Nayak, ruled from 1623 CE to 1659 CE. After the downfall of the rulers of the Vijayanagar dynasty, the most powerful independent Nayak rulers who emerged in the seventeenth century were the Nayaks of Madurai, Thanjavur, Gingee, and Vellore. Even earlier, after the Battle of Talikota (1565), the Vijayanagar rulers faced a steady decline, and the Nayaks, whom they had set in place, ruled for about 200 years, until about 1736. Pockets of Tamilakam were held by the descendants of the earlier Muslim rulers but, by and large, until the Marathas came to Thanjavur, the rule of the Nayaks prevailed. The earliest Nayak of Madurai was Nagama Nayak, who was initially a trusted lieutenant of Krishnadevaraya and had been sent to control the Pandyas. Later, he declared himself free of Vijayanagar control. In a strange turn of events, his own son, Viswanatha, was sent by Krishnadevaraya to subdue him, which he did—he took his father back to Krishnadevaraya as a prisoner. Viswanatha then brought Madurai back into the imperial Vijayanagar fold. The king later pardoned Nagama.

Viswanatha assumed his father's position in Madurai after Krishnadevaraya's death and took control of Tiruchirapalli. He cleared forests, cleaned up the Kaveri, and paid attention to the restoration of temples, such as the Ranganatha temple in Srirangam. The Koyiloluhu records indicate that Viswanatha spent about three lakhs of pon or gold on this temple. He also utilized his general, Ariyanatha, to bring various rebel elements in the south of Tamilakam in line. Viswanatha and his general were credited with bringing stability and growth to the region by enhancing agricultural production and installing irrigation systems through the construction of tanks and waterways. After establishing a level of peace and order, local powers were deputed under a system called palayam to local chieftains called palayakaran or polygars. Territorial divisions were handed over to them, and they had to defend these places and assist in the defence of forts like those in Madurai and other locations. They also took care of law and order and administered local justice. They collected taxes from the local people and handed over a portion to the Nayak ruler. They maintained troops and protected people in their areas and repulsed dacoits and robbers from their territories. Much later, they fought the imposition and advancement of British rule, and their heroism and patriotism became legendary.

Initially, the Nayaks wanted to settle many of the local chieftains under their suzerainty, especially those who had been devoted to them, to reward them in a way and allow them to maintain a mini government under them. The more important palayams were Sivagangai, Wodayarpalayam, Ariyalur, and Panchalamkurichi, the territory of the legendary Veerapandiya Kattabomman. There was a constant tussle between the peasant farmers or tillers of the land in polygar territory, and a high degree of oppression of the cultivators at times. The kaval or watch was another set up like the polygar system—these officials were responsible for the well being of the villages and they in turn enlisted groups like kallans and maravas to help catch thieves. The historian K. Rajayyan, says that the idea here was, 'set a thief to catch a thief'. At some point the polygars and kavalkaras merged, as the Nayak rulers could not pay two separate establishments and had to focus on dealing with the Mughals whose intrusions into Nayak terrain had slowly intensified. Many rural areas and villages were affected by the interminable conflicts between warring groups, so the polygars became very powerful as protectors under the Nayak rulers particularly between 1650 and 1760. Rajayyan points out that the tax burdens under the name of deshakaval became intense, particularly for poor villagers.

Along with the polygars, the Nayak rulers, who were Reddy and Naidu communities, dominated large swathes of Tamilakam. It must be kept in mind too that the Nayaks were Telugu-speaking like the Vijayanagar rulers before them and with many people from Telugu lands in north Tamilakam pouring into the more southern Tamil regions, the Nayaks reduced the Tamils to a more subordinate status. Those who ruled and held power had either wrested it from local lords or belonged to princely families of the Telugu fold. We have noted the general impoverishment of the region and the simmering discontent of ordinary people, but it appears that these rulers lived well. The Nayak rulers led lives of pomp and splendour. They gave charity to Brahmins and maintained harems. One Nayak ruler of Madurai, according to a traveller, had as many as 700 wives.

Viswanatha Nayak was followed by many rulers including sons, nephews, and generals who assumed positions of regional power. As mentioned earlier, Tirumalai Nayak, whose brother Muttu Virappa Nayak was described in Jesuit records as 'the powerful prince of this country', was a ruler who had to contend with the fallout of civil wars stemming from Vijayangara. It was during his reign in the early seventeenth century that Roberto de Nobili, an Italian ecclesiastical, established the Madura Mission with the avowed aim of not only spreading Christianity but also Indianizing it. Aiyar describes De Nobili as a man of 'towering intellect' and a 'penetrating personality'. De Nobili arrived in Madurai in 1606. His brand of proselytizing involved adapting Hindu customs and an Indian/Tamil way of life, which ultimately proved to be successful.

Tirumalai Nayak was, without question, the most remarkable ruler from this dynasty. Most of Tamilakam came under his rule and his territory extended from Kanyakumari to the Kaveri, including Salem and Coimbatore. He ruled from Madurai. The Jesuit records say that he had 200 wives. He waged successful wars, primarily with the goal of making Madurai a strong independent kingdom, separate from the overlordship of Vijayanagar. He formed alliances with the neighbouring Nayaks of Thanjavur and Gingee. He was determined to elevate the region from a province to a kingdom, and he appeared to achieve that with the assistance of his polygars. He gained control of Mysore, invaded Travancore, and subjugated Kilavan Sethupathi, the local chieftain, to take control of Ramnad. He sought the assistance of the Portuguese in this endeavour. Aiyar quotes an interesting and illuminating extract from F. C. Danvers, who states:

The Naique of Madurai sent his ambassador, Ramapa, to the Viceroy on the 13th August 1639, to give an assurance on his account to the King of Portugal that in consideration of the assistance sent to him...he undertook to give the King of Portugal a fortress in Pampa...or wherever he might desire one, with a Portuguese captain, 50 Portuguese soldiers, 100 lascars, 3000 pardaos for the maintenance of the same...

The Naique also gave permission to all those who might desire it to become Christians, and promised to furnish gratuitously to the King of Portugal all the assistance he might require.

The assumption was, of course, that Tirumalai Nayak would pay for the Portuguese. He further offered to build eight churches for them.

Aiyar comments that these conversions were 'held to imply ipso facto, a change of political loyalty from the Indian ruler to the Portuguese king'. It must be mentioned, though, that Tirumalai Nayak was said to have loved Christianity and protected the religion based on his own personal principle of freedom of conscience.

One other noteworthy Nayak ruler was Rani Mangammal, who became regent upon the death of her son, Ranga Krishna Muttu Virappa, in 1689. Vijayaranga Chokkanatha was crowned king when he was only three months old and was raised by his grandmother, the regent Rani Mangammal, as his own mother had died by suicide. She proved to be a capable and strong steward of her grandson's realm. In a world marked by male intrigue, conspiracy, and brutality within the court and across her territory, she demonstrated extraordinary strength and capability. While she did engage in warfare, her preference was diplomacy and peace. She cleverly accepted the supremacy of the growing Mughal empire in exchange for the freedom to govern her kingdom's affairs.

Rani Mangammal personally led several military campaigns, some marked by shrewdness and others by great courage. Aiyar notes, 'her vigor and diplomacy gave the Nayak kingdom a longer tenure of life than it otherwise would have had.... Her prudent administration in an age of storm and stress marks her out as a ruler of high repute.' She exhibited remarkable tolerance toward both Christianity and Islam, providing grants for the maintenance of mosques and supporting Christian missions. Additionally, she was an extremely devout Hindu and made generous grants and donations to temples. In more secular aspects, her legacy extended to building roads, inns, shelters for pilgrims and travellers, and giving great attention to irrigation schemes. Her inscriptions on the banks of the Uyyakondan Channel in 1687 and 1704 bear witness to her contributions.

Tragically, Mangammal met a grim end after a productive regency of eighteen years. She was reportedly involved in a relationship with one of her ministers, Achaiya, and grew increasingly unpopular as she was unwilling to relinquish control when her grandson turned eighteen. Consequently, she was arrested, imprisoned, and ultimately starved to death, according to many accounts.

When Nayak rule came to an end a couple of centuries years after its inception as a distinct entity from the Vijayanagar empire, it was largely due to ineffectual rulers who followed Mangammal. Apart from some of the rulers mentioned here, the rest of them proved to be weak administrators and failed to adapt to the changing economic and political landscape. While some smaller chieftains and rulers under them, like the polygars, fared better, these later Nayak rulers lacked the ability to maintain their military strength and keep their subjects content. Their incompetence weakened the kingdom and gradually paved the way for foreign rule.

Chapter 21

The Grand Marathas of Thanjavur

The condition of the members of this royal house while wearing the purple of power and now divested of it, is remarkably striking and impresses the traveller with sadness at the departed greatness.

William Hickey, memoirist

'SHE IS LIKE A VIOLET, EXISTING IN SECLUSION AND SORROWING IN secrecy.' So wrote the memoirist William Hickey, an English lawyer who worked as a Pleader in the days of the Raj. He was speaking of Thanjavur which at that time (1856–1857) had just fallen into the hands of the British under the infamous Doctrine of Lapse law as the last ruler did not have a male heir. Much of British annexation of Indian territory from the maharajas occurred by this proclamation by the British Governor General Lord Dalhousie that when a ruler had no heir to follow him, the territory would 'lapse' to the British. Hickey writes '…the independence of the Tanjore Mahratta dynasty was forced to terminate in A.D. 1857, by the ruthless hand of Annexation'. Before its crumbling though, Thanjavur was no shrinking violet, and neither was it in the doldrums. When the dynasty of Maratha rulers established their rule in the ancient Chola capital of Thanjavur, an unusual amalgam of culture occurred. Religious and literary work, music and dance, language and science, all saw a flowering and a synthesis of multiple cultures that prevailed in the region. Much like the Deccani culture further north, Tamilakam, while cradling its own civilizational values opened itself up to the winds of cultural change that came from a variety of sources.

Known as a 'successor state', following the dissolution of Nayak rule across much of Tamilakam, in the sixteenth and seventeenth centuries, the chaos that prevailed in the region led to the capture of Thanjavur by the Bhonsles who were related to the Maratha emperor Shivaji. Another story from Hickey recounts the origins of these famed Maratha kings who at one point built up large territories across India and put up a fierce resistance to the Mughals. According to Hickey, a small time silladar, or cavalry owner of a modest and irregular regiment, called Mallojee Bhonsle who was successful in the discharging of his duties had a patron called Jadow Rao. During the

A near perfect jar with a beautifully crafted lid—black and redware found at the Iron Age burial cum habitation site at Adichanallur.

Urn burial site excavated at Adichanallur near Tirunelveli by the ASI in 2021 and 2022. The age of the site is between 1384 BCE and 665 BCE.

A well laid-out Sangam age site, about 2,000 years old, which could have been an industrial site. This is probably a dyeing vat in a vast brick structure excavated by the ASI at Keezhadi near Madurai.

A multi-tiered terracotta ring well discovered by the ASI at Keezhadi. Ring wells are a sign of advanced water conservation systems.

Top: One of the earliest Tamil Brahmi inscriptions of the third century BCE found at Mankulam or Meenakshipuram near Madurai.

Bottom: On a hillock near Arittapatti village, close to Madurai, are the caves of Jain monks with stone beds and an early Tamil Brahmi inscription dating to the second century BCE.

The empty sanctum sanctorum, which must have had a sculpture of Murugan, was excavated by the ASI at the Salavan Kuppam Murugan temple near Mamallapuram in 2005. The boulder behind has two inscriptions indicating that a Sangam age Murugan temple existed there.

The five unfinished great stone monolithic rathas of the Pallavas at Mamallapuram, seventh to eighth century CE.

Top: A surfeit of sculptures including that of Shiva and Parvati at the Kailasanatha temple, Kanchipuram.
Bottom: A series of pillars supported by lions and a long running panel of sculptures portraying the history of the Pallava dynasty at the Vaikunta Perumal temple at Kanchipuram, eighth century CE.

Top: Bas-relief of Jain Tirthankaras seated on lotus pedestals in three rows, beautifully sculpted on a hillside in Kazhugumalai, an important Jain centre, seventh to eighth century CE.

Bottom: The yakshi Ambika and her children with a lion and a kalpavriksh tree. This stunning bas relief shows her children and her husband, his face totally blurred by the dazzle of her golden appearance. Carved on the hillside in Kazhugumalai.

Top Left: Standing Brahma at the Pasupathi Kovil, also called Brahmapurisvara at Pullamangai, Thanjavur district, a classic early Chola stone sculpture of the tenth century.

Top Right: Early tenth century Chola sculptures of Ganesha and his servitors at the Brahmapurisvara temple in Pullamangai, Thanjavur district.

Bottom: A beautiful painting showing a lotus pond with a swan, fish, and sanyasi on the ceiling of the Jain rock-cut shrine at Sittanavasal.

Top: An overview of the Airavatesvara temple with the vimana in the background and chariot-shaped mandapa at Darasuram, Kumbakonam.

Bottom: The tank, the northern gopuram, and the thousand-pillar mandapa inside the Nataraja temple at Chidambaram.

Top: The Keralantaka Tiruvayil (entrance) at extreme right, the Raja Rajeswaram entrance, and the Nandi mandapa at the Brihadeeswara temple at Thanjavur.

Bottom: Inscriptions in Tamil running to a length of more than 100 metres on the northern outer wall of the Brihadeeswara temple at Thanjavur.

Top: The hollow vimana, which is an architectural marvel of the Brihadeeswara temple, Thanjavur.
Bottom: Gangaikondacholapuram temple built by Rajendra Chola I around the eleventh century CE.

Top: The majestic vimana of the Brihadeeswara temple at Gangaikondacholapuram.

Middle: Vijayanagara paintings depicting episodes from the Ramayana and with label inscriptions in Tamil, at the Vasantha Mandapa at Tirumal Iruncholai temple near Madurai.

Bottom: The Golden Lotus Tank and one of the soaring gopuras of the Meenakshi temple at Madurai.

Top Left: This Nataraja bronze of ethereal beauty is from Kulasekara Nallur near Tiruvidaimarudhur in Thanjavur District. It belongs to the Kulottunga Chola II period.

Top Right: A rare group bronze of early Chola period portrays Krishna with Satyabhama and Rukmani.

Middle: A panel sculpture of Shiva marrying Parvati at the Meenakshi temple.

Bottom: Series of sculptures of the Nayaka rulers who patronized the Madurai Meenakshi temple, at the Pudhu Mandapam.

Top Left: The Chola seal in the Tiruvalangadu copper plates.
Top Right: The Tiruvalangadu copper plate charter displayed at the Government Museum, Chennai.
Bottom Left: The Lakshminarasimha bronze, fourteenth century, Kulithalai, Tiruchirappalli District.
Bottom Right: A painting of Portuguese traders arriving in a ship with their horses to be sold to Vijayanagara rulers at Tiruppudaimarudur.

Top: The top panel of painting of women and the panel below shows the debate between the Shaivite saint Sambandar and Jain monks and the burning of Jain manuscripts at the Tiruppudaimarudur temple, near Tirunelveli.

Bottom: Luz Church in Madras, built in 1516 by the Portuguese.

Top: A view of the North Street of Fort St. George
Bottom: A view of St. Thomas Mount, near Madras.

Top: Marina Beach, Chennai.
Bottom: Chennai's Central Railway Station.

festival of Holi one year, Mallojee took his five-year-old son Shahji to the residence of his patron where the young boy started to play joyfully with Jadow Rao's young daughter, Jeejee, and the children threw Holi colours at one another as is the custom. Watching the children play, Jadow Rao carelessly and perhaps with some measure of delight turned to the gathered company and said, 'they are a fine pair' and turned to his little daughter and asked '…well girl, wilt thou take this boy as thy husband?' Hickey says, '…the circumstance occasioned a great deal of laughter, but the mirth was disturbed by Mallojee Bhonsle rising up and saying, "take notice friends, Jadow has this day become a contracting party with me in marriage"… Jadow seemed astonished and was mute'. The story goes that Jadow tried to make light of the matter, but it appeared that Mallojee determinedly built a fortune with palaces and more horses to bring himself on par with Jadow Rao. With his newly acquired wealth, Mallojee even raised a command of 5,000 cavalry which also elevated him socially—he now became Mallojee Rajah Bhonsle. So assiduous were his efforts that in the end, Jadow Rao had no excuse but to agree to marry off his young daughter to the Bhonsle heir.

This set in place the famed Maratha dynasty, for Jeejee and her husband Shahaji were the parents of the warrior Shivaji who went on to conquer and rule over a large swathe of territory in the north and west, and later in the south as well. Shahaji had another son by another wife; this half-brother to Shivaji and Sambhaji was called Venkoji or Ekoji. After the death of Shahaji, his kingdoms on the Western coast, of Satara and Kolapore, went to Shivaji, and the southern territory of Thanjavur went to Venkoji or Ekoji who became the founder of the Tanjore Maratha dynasty. The Marathas, who were initially small jagirdars or land administrators, soon became a force to reckon with for the Mughals, the sultans of Bijapur, the Golkonda sultanate and for the advancing European colonial powers. Shivaji's forces expanded the bounds of the Maratha empire—he started by taking over declining neighbouring kingdoms such as Bijapur. He was crowned chatrapathi or emperor in 1674 in Raigad Fort.

Maratha rule in the Tamil south had more to do with Venkoji than Shivaji. The ascension of Venkoji to the Thanjavur throne was not achieved without a battle. The rule of the Thanjavur Nayaks came under fire from the Madurai Nayak ruler of that time, Chokkanatha. This Thanjavur Nayak, Vijayaraghava, was killed, and his brother Alagiri was placed on the throne in 1673 by the Madurai Nayak. Vijayaraghava's son sought the help of the sultan of Bijapur who sent his commander, the Maratha Venkoji, with his forces to help with the situation. Venkoji seized the Thanjavur throne and later when the many sultanates came under the control of Shivaji, the Thanjavur portions were left to Venkoji by his brother. Venkoji was crowned king in 1676 and the Nayak rule in Thanjavur ended once and for all with the entry of the Marathas. Shivaji, meanwhile, also conquered Gingee, and Vellore and left another brother, Santaji, in charge of these areas. Later, after Shivaji's death, Venkoji defeated Santaji so that Gingee and Thanjavur came under Venkoji's rule. The Maratha rule in the Telugu-speaking Tamil regions resulted in an amalgam of culture much like that of the Deccani culture, fostering a new blended ethos of art, music, and literature, which had a deep impact on Tamilakam. Venkoji's three sons inherited the throne one after another. First, there was Shahji who ruled from 1684 to 1712, followed by Serfoji I who ruled from 1712 to 1728, and Tulaji or Tukkoji ruled from 1728 to 1736. None of these reigns were trouble free, with the Sethupathis of Ramnad and the Mughals gnawing away at Maratha territory. After Tulaji, Pratapsimha or Pratap Singh ascended the throne; by now the Thanjavur Marathas were quite weakened with the British constantly making treaties with them for the purpose of gaining territories from them. Tulaji was already paying taxes to the nawab of the Carnatic and to the East India Company. Within a few years, the Maratha successor Serfoji II, who had been adopted by Tulaji from a collateral branch, had to pay so much to the British administration that he soon found that he had very little of Thanjavur left to him. Serfoji was the last Maratha ruler to have power. He had to cede his lands to the British for protection from his enemies and ended up having sovereignty only in Thanjavur and surrounding areas. He was also paid one fifth of the state's land revenue and a pension of '100,000 star pagodas'. However, Serfoji's patronage of the arts during this embattled period saw a flowering that was quite unusual despite the chaos of political administration.

The historian and documentary film-maker Kombai Anwar points out that many cultural traits of the Mughals were shared by the Marathas, 'including a love for music and dance. The Thanjavur Marathas who inherited the court of the Telugu-speaking Nayaks enriched the *durbar* with Marathi traditions and the courtly traits of the North', he says. Anwar writes about a telling portrait in one of the halls of the Brihadeeswara temple which depicts the Maratha rulers and the various important people of the courts, during the time of Shivaji II, a son of Serfoji and the last ruler of Thanjavur. Two dancing girls and a couple of soldiers are seen and one of the dancers is clearly Hindustani and the other is south Indian. 'The painting of the *tawaif* or courtesan is a reminder of the time when the sounds of tabla, harmonium, *sitar,* and *sarangi* competed with the tinkle of the *ghungroos* (ankle bells) of the dancing girls in royal *durbars* across Tamil Nadu.' Apparently, another portrait of the Maratha court currently in the Victoria and Albert Museum showing three Hindustani dancers in action shows that their costume is of north Indian origin; this is further evidence of the confluence of cultures and relationships nurtured in the arts across cultures. The Thanjavur Quartet, the maestros of dance, brothers Chinniah, Ponniah, Vadivelu, and Sivanandam flourished at that time and set in place the flowering of Bharatanatyam, the Sadir which came just before that was performed to a high degree of refinement by the devadasis or temple dancers who also danced at the courts of kings. The exploitation of the devadasis will be discussed in another chapter, but these dancers developed Sadir into a complex performance by adding features like alarippu, jatiswara, varnam, padam, and other such forms in the performance. The development of the arts, music, and dance saw its pinnacle during the period of Serfoji. The Thanjavur veena, also known as Saraswathi veena, was perfected in the Thanjavur court. Serfoji also developed a great interest in Western music, possibly because of the early influence and encouragement of his Danish teacher, Reverend Christian Friedrich Schwartz, a missionary under whose care Serfoji's uncle Tulaji had entrusted him. Reverend Schwartz also sent Serfoji to study at the Lutheran Mission in Madras for a period. A vibrant synthesis of the arts occurred during the time of both Serfoji and his son. Many portraits like the ones mentioned above give ample proof of the commingling of cultures, especially that of Deccani and Hindustani with the Marathi and Tamil. Another difference between paintings of this period and earlier periods is that there was a distinct shift to portraiture in addition to painting murals of deities and depicting stories from religious literature in temples. What is striking about painting at this time is that rulers like Serfoji developed a great fascination with European culture. Consequently, much of the art of this time included a more European way of dressing and comportment; this was something Thanjavur artists tried to capture in their portraits. Mention must also be made of the more traditional Thanjavur style paintings where deities were captured in a more classical manner and a distinct style developed where the pigments on the canvas were also encrusted with precious and semi-precious stones and gold leaf was also used.

From ophthalmology to cooking, to art, music, and literature, it was Serfoji's deep interest and enthusiasm that created a distinct court culture whose influence pervaded across Tamilakam. Maharaja Serfoji loved cooking and compiled a book of all the court cuisine. Soon this developed into fine fusion food, and these dishes were enjoyed across the region. There is another story that suggests that due to the unavailability of kokum, during the visit of the Maratha emperor Sambhaji to Thanjavur, the palace in Thanjavur resorted to using tamarind and this turned out to be a tasty success. Hence, the name sambar for a staple favourite of the Tamils today.

Serfoji was said to be something of an ophthalmologist himself and carried a surgical kit around with him. The Saraswathi Mahal Library has records in English of the cataract surgeries he conducted. His interest in medicine, especially in indigenous herbs and local types of medicinal practice, led him to set up Dhanvantri Mahal for research in medicine. Serfoji's remarkable education made him a polyglot; he was proficient in Tamil, Telugu, Urdu, Sanskrit, German, French, Dutch, and Latin. The Saraswathi Mahal Library, built by a Nayak ruler, was vastly enriched by Serfoji, who was a great bibliophile as well. He added maps, coins, rare manuscripts, and about 4,000 books from across the world, some of them marked up with his comments in his own hand. In addition to this, the library had 46,000 manuscripts in print and palm leaf manuscripts as old as 400 years. There are classics as well as rare works of Jain, Vaishnava, and Shaiva origin including commentaries on Sangam works. There is literature of the Maratha court in Modi, the script that was used as a royal language. Serfoji has been credited with setting up the first printing press in Devanagari in Thanjavur. The other contributions of Serfoji included the setting up of rest houses or chathrams across the region and establishing several schools and colleges with a distinct orientation to English education. Along with Vedas and Shastras, he advocated the learning of mathematics, science, and languages in these schools. Tamil along with Marathi was the language of the court and these rulers even before Serfoji knew that accepting the local language would help them with their administration especially in terms of accounting (they used local accountants who were called karanams) and for revenue collection.

As far as the economic situation was concerned, throughout the rule of the Maratha kings, the bureaucracy, largely made up of Telugu and Maratha immigrants, reduced the role of Tamil labour, pushing them into poverty. The bureaucracy lived off large tracts of land awarded to them by the Maratha rulers. The local labour was given 'service' land called maniams, where many of the tillers and peasant farmers were forced to work, eking out a miserable living while their earnings dwindled to a pittance. Meanwhile, some artisans and crafts people prospered, as the royalty and nobility had a great appetite for the arts. The buildings in the Thanjavur Palace complex were built during the rule of the Nayaks and then added to by Serfoji and his son Shivaji II. The Maratha kings also spent a great deal on bolstering temple activities by supporting festivals and rituals by way of material goods as well as by adding structures such as gopurams, the towering gateways, and large prakara that underlined their grandeur.

Under Maratha rule and patronage another area of the arts saw a flowering. A renaissance of sorts in Carnatic music occurred; this was Carnatic music's first revival post the Vijayanagar empire. Hindustani music, which had already been refined by Persian music, had a lot of impact on the evolution of Carnatic music. The musical genius, the poet-saint Purandaradasa, who composed his lyrics in Kannada during the days of the Vijayanagar kings was the predecessor to the masterminds of Carnatic music, and his music impacted them immensely. The great composer Thyagaraja, who was born in Tiruvarur in 1767, and moved to Tiruvaiyaru where he lived the rest of his life, composed his 2,400 plus kirtis there. His music had a profound impact on ordinary people as it was akin to the poetry of the Bhakti saints several centuries earlier. The emphasis on inspired spiritual content with much of it especially anchored to Lord Rama, combined with a profundity of emotions that ranged from simple devotion to more complex notions of surrender and enlightenment, ensured a great legacy that set in place much of what is now Carnatic music. Similarly, Muthuswami Dikshitar (1776–1835) and Syama Sastri (1762–1827) were other great musical geniuses of that time. The three of them are known as the Musical Trinity and have had a powerful impact on the development and stability of Carnatic music. A more popular evolution was the development of the nottuswara, where Carnatic compositions were infused with marching melodies and western musical instruments were also used. Serfoji instituted a 'Tanjore band'.

The Maratha support of the arts, music, and literature were all institutionalized by the creation of centres of learning and teaching patronized by rulers like Serfoji. With the winds of change blowing because of the advancing foreign presence in Tamilakam, especially of the British, adaptations of cultural traits of the diverse constituents of the local populations including in lifestyle and in social mores produced a new dimension to the Tamils of that region. Tolerance, curiosity, and a happy commingling and fusion in arts and culture did not however mask the slow ceding of political rights to the foreigners, who ultimately took over the region.

Chapter 22

Tamil by Birth, Muslim by Faith

I feel I have to be the best version of a person belonging to my religion. I am an ambassador of my own faith.

Rana Safvi, writer

EVEN BEFORE THE DAWN OF THE CHRISTIAN CENTURIES, PENINSULAR India, particularly the eastern and western coasts—the Malabar and the Coromandel—saw the arrival and departure of trading ships that found the wealth of this region astonishing in many respects. There was a bounty of goods ranging from spices and precious metals to silk, cotton, pearls, corals, and cardamom in addition to several other commodities. Black pepper was in high demand in the West—it was bought for gold by the traders. Apart from buying and selling, the traders, who were largely Arab, found the Malabar coast and the Coromandel a convenient halting ground for further travel up the Indian Ocean towards China and other Southeast Asian countries. And the land itself was welcoming; the people of the coastal regions from Gujarat to the Konkan and the Malabar were friendly and inviting, and the climate was salubrious for many traders to soon turn into settlers.

When the Arabs became Muslims, possibly in the late seventh century, they brought their new religion to South India. Raja Mohamad, an expert in the maritime history of Tamil Muslims, speaks at length about the history of Tamil Muslims. Raja Mohamad has set up a research centre for Islamic Tamil Culture under the aegis of the Jamal Mohamed College in Trichy and points out that within approximately thirty years of the inception of the new religion, Muslim Arab traders brought it to the southern shores of India.

Trade between the Arab countries and South India, both by way of the Malabar coast and the Coromandel coast, had been going on even during the Sangam age, as early as 200 CE, as recorded in Sangam literature. Anwar points out that today, when the UAE and India speak of linking the dirham and rupee for trade, it harks back to a 2,000-year-old connection, when the gold dirham coins of the Arabs poured into the region and were used as local currency. An inscription in Thanjavur's Periya Kovil refers to gold dirhams. There are copper plates which talk about active trade guilds, the Anjuvannam, or body of traders, that were functioning as early as the seventh century CE and oversaw transactions. One such is the Tarisapalli or Quilon Syrian copper plate, which is attributed to the year 849 CE. The guilds, made up of West Asian traders, were active all along the Malabar coast and subsequently on the Coromandel coast as well. Gold dirhams are recorded in property transactions and disputes were settled upon providing the proof of such dealings.

Raja Mohamad says that many Arab merchants settled down in Tamilakam and married local women; thus, a distinct community of Tamil Muslims was born. He further notes that many downtrodden communities in the region took to Islam because it offered them an escape from their often difficult social conditions, including poverty and caste oppression. Contrary to popular notions, there was no forced conversion, he says. The principles of Islam were disseminated by the traders and many local people embraced the religion. During the later mediaeval period, although trade weakened and the traders who came from western shores declined in number, the Tamil Muslim community grew in numbers from mingling with the local population but retained their separate identity right from the eighth century onwards. There are copper plate inscriptions and stone inscriptions that corroborate this. Raja Mohamad however ruefully points out that a great lacuna exists even in scholarly studies of south Indian history that give little or no space to Tamil Muslim history, and even to the presence of such a community in India. There is a small, little-known mosque in Tiruchirapalli, which has an authentic inscription from 736 CE that indicates the age of Muslim presence in the area. The Pallavas were ruling there at that point in time, and there was obviously a small population of Muslims in the Trichy area that necessitated the construction of a mosque. Raja Mohamad and his research teams are currently tracing the growth of many of these Tamil Muslim communities, examining literature, inscriptions, and even folklore to build a record. Apparently, there was a complete synthesis with the local people, and several south Indian Islamic historians concur that, barring their practice of religion, they followed local customs and lifestyles and were culturally Tamil in identity.

When the Malabar coast was under the rule of the Chera kings, and other small-time chiefs, it was still Tamil country, and many Muslims of that region (present-day Kerala), belonged to a community called Mappila, whose origins were from the Arab trading community as mentioned earlier. They were also known as Moplahs, and historically known as Chonaka Mappila or Moors Mopulars, indicating a descent from Arabs or Persians from West Asia. Mappila originally means 'great child' and was also a term for son-in-law, either an honorific bestowed by the local Hindus whose daughters they married or implied 'honoured guest' and was often used to refer to foreigners. Chonaka Mappila and Yavanaka Mappila were terms that were also used to distinguish them from the Nasrani Mappila (the St. Thomas Christians) and the Juda Mappila (the Jews of Cochin).

Until the Europeans took over the spice trade, this community of Muslims was very prosperous and contributed to the affluence of the region. During the rule of all the early Tamil kings, the Chera, Chola, and Pandya, regardless of the changes of territorial administration, the Tamil Muslim traders were highly regarded by the ruling kings as they brought in foreign exchange, meaning gold, and most importantly functioned ethically in business because of their strict adherence to the moral code of Islam, says Anwar. They also brought in new technology and systems of administration for which they were rewarded by being given places of worship and land. The community was highly respected in the mediaeval period and by and large the Tamil Muslims continued as a peaceful community, quietly taking in those from other communities who felt disadvantaged or who experienced deprivation in their own communities.

We can also briefly consider the perspectives of Marco Polo, the Italian merchant and explorer, whom Sastri refers to as that 'prince among medieval travellers', who visited the Coromandel coast in 1292 after a two-year voyage to China and Asia, landing in Pandya country. The region frequented by the travellers and merchants from Arabia was known as Ma'bar which means 'ferry' or 'passage' in Arabic. The extent of the land 'is from Kulam (Quilon) to Nilawar', according to another contemporary Muslim chronicler. Marco Polo says of Kayal, the chief emporium of the Pandya kingdom, that the ruler to whom it belongs 'possesses vast treasures and wears upon his person a great store of rich jewels. He maintains great state and administers his kingdom with great equity and extends great favours to merchants and foreigners so that they are very glad to visit his city. It is at this city that all ships touch, that come from the west, as from Homos and from Kis and from all Arabia, laden with horses and other things for sale. And this brings a great concourse of people from the country round about, and there is great business done in this city of Cail....'

He also confirms the observations of some Muslim chroniclers who say that owing to the unfavourable weather conditions of Tamilakam and an ignorance of dealing with horses, fresh and frequent imports of horses became necessary.

Islam spread further across the Malabar coast between the thirteenth and fifteenth centuries and the Hindu rulers, the Zamorins of Calicut, strengthened trade ties with the Arabs with the increased sale of pepper, cardamom, and textiles, because of which all the western coastal regions became very prosperous. As we know, this trade had been brisk even earlier, and there is a Muslim inscription of 752 CE in Patalayini Kollam in North Malabar which attests to this. The Tarisapalli copper plates also speak of the grants given by local rulers, one of which is in Arabic, and mentions the name of eleven Muslim traders as witnesses to the grant. The traveller Ibn Battuta, who visited Calicut between 1342 and 1347, writes of the city's prosperity in his records. The Persian ambassador to the court of the zamorin, Abdur Razzaq, who visited Calicut in 1442, described the city:

> Security and justice are so firmly established in this city that the wealthiest merchants bring towards that place from maritime countries, considerable cargoes which they unload and unhesitatingly send into the markets and bazaars without thinking…of the necessity of checking account or keeping watch over the goods. The officers of the customhouse take upon themselves the charge of looking after the merchandise, over which they keep watch night and day when a sale is effected, they levy a duty on the goods of one-fortieth part; if they are not sold, they make no charge whatsoever…

After the twelfth and thirteenth centuries, with these regions drifting away from Tamilakam's purview (although the Pandyas gained whatever was left of the Chera kingdom at that time), the focus shifts entirely to Muslims in the lands that constitute present-day Tamil Nadu and how they integrated into society. In *Yaadhum*, Anwar brings this aspect to vivid life. The stunningly beautiful opening scene of the film shows the processional deity of Ranganatha from the local temple paraded through the streets of Kombai in Theni district, the hometown of the filmmaker, and passing the mosque with people of both faiths either watching or participating in the procession. The next scene is of the worship at the mosque and after that we see Kombai's madrasa, where young Muslim boys and girls learn the Quran with their diligent young teacher. In a town with a majority Hindu population and much smaller Muslim population and a few Christian families, it is moving to see the quiet practices that determine communities against a larger backdrop of harmonious living; the simple taken-for-granted friendships and camaraderie between people of demonstrably different faiths who live in an unquestionable state of harmony. Anwar recalls in his narrative that the processional sight was something that had always been a part of his childhood. During this festival, Muslims are honoured, as they look after the temple's account, says Anwar. The temple's idol has an interesting history. It was said to have been gifted by Tipu Sultan of Mysore to Kombai's temple in the eighteenth century. When Tipu was camping in Dindigul he visited the zamindar of Kombai who had a breed of dogs with him known for their fearlessness and loyalty. Tipu included them in his army and in return presented a beautiful idol of Ranganatha to the temple at Kombai. This was one example of how in small towns and villages across Tamilakam a sense of amity often existed between communities.

Anwar decides to explore his Tamil Muslim identity, and the film traces the journey and history of the Tamil Muslim as expressed through architecture, music, and other cultural aspects including food and spices. Anwar's journey takes him to Vaishnavite places of worship such as Alwarthirunagari; he travels to Pulicat, Kayalpatnam, and other historic towns, taking in mosques and temples and excavations. He notes the bas relief sculptures of the Thirukkurungudi temple, which shows Arab traders arriving in boats to Tamilakam's shores; he speaks of the Dravidian architecture in Muslim mosques in Tamil Nadu, Kerala-style timber mosques in Kerala, and of how a Muslim family has been maintaining the fence of a yaga kundam, or ritual fire pit, in Madurai for generations in a Shaivite sacred space. There are other examples that Anwar shows where Islam lends itself to local culture, while holding firm to the practice of the faith. In an interview with *Frontline*, he says, 'When I undertook the journey of tracing my roots, I came across many surprises. It was a recollection of many good things. All the religious functions and festivals I captured in *Yaadhum* at different places in Tamilnadu and Kerala point to only one thing to me: peaceful co-existence.' Apart from this, the reclaiming of a specific identity of Tamil Muslims is at the core of this thought-provoking film. 'I am a Tamil by birth and a Muslim by faith,' says Anwar.

This kind of synthesis is very common in the small towns of Tamil Nadu, says Raja Mohamad, and needs to be highlighted. The misconception of Islam being an Arab import, and that the Muslims of the south are essentially foreigners, needs to be dispelled. Another point to be noted is that although many Tamil Muslims started in trade big and small, they moved to agriculture in places like Cuddalore, Tiruchirapalli district, and Chidambaram. In South Arcot district, agriculturists from Muslim communities specialized in betel nut cultivation, especially in places like Kulithalai, says Raja Mohamad. In Thanjavur district, Muslim agriculturists were large landowners as well as small farmers and like their non-Muslim counterparts they engaged in the cultivation of a variety of crops, especially paddy. With the stereotyping of the community as being mainly traders, their engagement with agriculture and other occupations was largely overlooked.

To go back to the early periods, Raja Mohamad says that even in Rajaraja's court a Muslim was appointed as a senior minister. Rajendra Chola also appointed a Muslim, Tirumandira Olai Nayagam, who functioned as a prime minister. The Thanjavur inscriptions mention a Sonegan Samur (a variation of the name Jaffar) who was given lands and the title of Paranjothi by the Chola kings. It is very clear that the inscription uses the term 'Sonegan', but there has been opposition to this reading, and the word 'Cholagan' was sought to be introduced to obscure the fact, as Sonegan simply means Muslim, says Raja Mohamad. The experts finally concurred, and the distortion was corrected. The early epigraphists like K. V. Subramaniam and Hultz had also read the inscription as 'Sonegan' and recorded it, he adds. Anwar points to another fascinating inscription in the Thanjavur temple which says that this same Sonegan Samur was one of two people who were administering payments to the temple dancers. He was also an extraordinary musician, says Anwar, and was given the title of Rajendra Kala Vidyadharan. Another gift, an ornament given to the deity in the Periya Kovil called Sonegan Shidukku, was recorded in an inscription in the temple.

Islam obtained firmer footing in Tamilakam in the ensuing centuries with the transformation of the traders into settlers. It must be mentioned that there were early settlers from the Arab countries on the Gujarat coast as well, and many of the earliest mosques in India can be found in Gujarat. But much of the earlier Islamic history of the country is buried because of the dominance of the Delhi sultanate and Mughal narratives. Muslim settlements continued to grow all along the coasts of Tamil Nadu and subsequently fanned inwards to Pulicat, Kanyakumari district, Nagapatnam, Kilakkarai, Kayalpatnam, and later, Thanjavur, Ramanathapuram, and Tirunelveli districts. Many Arab traders who continued to travel back and forth, contracted temporary marriages with local women for a stipulated period, and provided for them in return for room and board. The children were left in the care of their mother. There were others who settled in South India permanently and branched into occupations other than trade.

As mentioned earlier, there were inscriptions in the early mosques right from the eighth century in Trichy and Kayalpatnam that underscore the endowments and grants given by the later Pandya rulers as well as the spread of Islam, including Sufism, in these regions. There is a story that the Zamorin of Calicut, who was a Hindu, even gave the traders permission to convert his subjects to Islam, particularly from the fishing community. One or more children of a family was converted to Islam to ensure more manpower for their ships. The idea was to build a naval presence in the region with the help of the Arab traders and local fishermen would create support for Arab merchants by converting to Islam. The Arabs also introduced horses to the south. The development of Arabic Tamil was another outcome of the Tamil settlements on the Coromandel coast. To enhance communication between the locals and the Arab traders, a link language soon developed, especially for writing, where Tamil words were written in Arabic script, and this was called Arabu-Tamil or Arwi. This was in use even in the eighth century and used by the Muslims in Sri Lanka.

About social customs and rituals, Raja Mohamad observes that many Tamil customs have been retained in Tamil Muslim communities even after they converted to the new religion. For example, in some Muslim families, wedding rituals such as tying black beads on a bride, planting the muhurta (auspicious) pole at the wedding venue, doing the ritual of arati, etc. are practised, and these are entirely Tamil customs which are not used in Islamic marriage ceremonies in other parts of the world. They are not considered un-Islamic by and large, he explains, although some religious teachers may question this. Naming ceremonies, nose and ear piercing and other aspects like casting horoscopes (although they are never used for ascertaining compatibility of prospective brides and grooms) are commonly practised among Tamil Muslim families. It appears that this is more about Tamil cultural moorings than religion.

Social divisions are not caste hierarchies in the Tamil Muslim community. They are loose community-based structures and like in early Hindu society, based originally on professions. These divisions are flexible and based on the original occupation of the communities and not rigid or hierarchical. Marriages between these groups is not uncommon. As for group names, Sonegan is the term for those of Arab descent; Thulukkar means one who rides a horse—in Tamil Nadu it is sometimes used to describe Muslims in a generic sense. There is a coastal Muslim community known as Sha'afi, Anwar says, whose prayer methods and interpretation of Islamic personal law are slightly different from others. Interestingly, in places like Kilakkarai and Kayalpatnam there are Sha'afis who follow the matrilocal system even today, says Anwar. The bridegroom goes to the bride's house after marriage and becomes part of that family. Houses are settled on the girls. From Pulicat to Sri Lanka and in parts of Kerala, such a system is still followed.

The Marakkayars are descendants of the Arab traders; they were originally boat and ship makers and ship owners. Many Muslims of the coastal regions and in places like Kilakkarai, Kayalpatnam, and Nagore are Marakkayars. Muslim maritime towns in the south were dominated by elite Sunni Muslim trading families who were Marakkayars and who continued to maintain ties with the Arab and West Asian nations for trade and pilgrimage. Pearl, chank shell, and ruby trading as well as shipbuilding and shipping continue to be dominant businesses of Marakkayars. As this community continues its close association with Muslim nations outside of India, it also belongs to a particular school of Quranic law and maintains a separate social identity among the Muslims. In many ways, the Marakkayars' wealth and social influence gave scope for them to turn their coastal towns into centres of Islamic piety and influence by building mosques, madrassas, dargahs, and other religious institutions right from the fifteenth and sixteenth centuries. The Periyapalli, or mosque, in Kayalpatnam was one such grand edifice built in 1331. Kilakkarai and other towns also have imposing and elegant mosques, most built in the Dravidian Tamil style that were the fulcrum of Islamic worship and practice. In time, the Marakkayars also built elaborate houses in these towns which were called mohullas and were grouped together in family-based neighbourhoods. This is a distinguishing feature of wealthy Marakkayar towns.

It must be noted, however, that after the Portuguese arrived on these shores, the shipping business of the Tamil Muslims was affected. The establishment of cartazes, a Portuguese licensing system that was created in the sixteenth century to aid Portuguese trade and commerce in the Indian Ocean and to control their monopoly over a wider area, became a hindrance to local traders. It was mainly Muslim and Malay trading ships that were affected by this, and their trade, especially the spice trade, suffered hugely on account of the cartazes. Following this, the East India Company set up its operations, which also impacted the shipping industry that the Muslims were involved in. The first ones to be affected by colonialism were the Muslims, says Anwar, 'you can say that they were the outer shields for the Indian economy'.

Labbai is the name of another group of Muslims. Originally of Arab descent too, these were people who came into Tamilakam as helpers. Apparently, these helpers or assistants would respond to the call of their masters with the term 'labbaik', which translates roughly to 'here I am'. The children of these settlers were called Labbai, and this appellation was also used for Hindu converts to Islam. Besides trading, they took up tanning, weaving, mat-making, and agriculture. Some of this community speaks Urdu in addition to Tamil. The 1881 Census describes them as 'thrifty, enterprising, and industrious' and calls them the Coromandel Moplahs. They are, however, considered distinct from the Marakkayars. Those who speak Tamil among the Labbai are another distinct community called the Rowther, who relate to the horse trade and are cavalry men and horse trainers. They were also called Guthirai Chettigal. A small but powerful group of Tamil Muslims speak a language called Dakhni and describe themselves as descendants of the Muslim kings of the Deccan (who at one point controlled many southern regions). There are other smaller Muslim communities in Tamilakam such as the weaver community (there is epigraphical evidence of their origins in the sixteenth century) called Panchu kotti and Achchu katti, who live in specific textile-producing regions. However, it must be mentioned that there is hardly any awareness of community affiliations among Tamil Muslims of the present day.

Just as local Tamil customs, cultural practices, music, and language were a part of the Tamil Muslim community, it is important to note that the architecture of the mosques of Tamilakam, particularly in the early centuries, followed the Dravidian idiom and adopted many facets of the Dravidian style of construction. In his book *Islamic Architecture in Tamil Nadu*, Raja Mohamad shows this took place in numerous mosques across Tamilnadu. He suggests that as the early Arab merchants and settlers did not have any architectural schemes for mosque building, and since the early Muslims only required a public space for daily prayers, they constructed prayer spaces in the Hindu temple style using local materials and local builders. It must be mentioned that the Indo-Islamic style of architecture refers to the distinct style of mosque construction in North India which is different from the architectural idiom of the south.

Palli, a word meaning 'place of worship', was constructed in Muslim settlements. Jain temples were also known as palli, and Raja Mohamad explains that the early mosque or palli was in the form of a small mandapam, like the ones found in temples made in the local style of architecture; however, care was taken to avoid any sculptural representation. It was also called kallupalli, or stone temple, and closed on three sides with the eastern side left open. There were no minarets or minars, and the walls were of stone supporting a stone ceiling. Many such early mosques were built along the coastline and later in the hinterland; Anwar says that many local non-Muslim rulers also gave land and supported such construction in the early years of the settlements.

The kallupalli in Trichy, Makkah Masjid, was built in 734 CE and was subject to multiple renovations and rebuilding. The mosque looks like a small mandapam and is supported by six pillars. These pillars are in typical Dravidian style with square bases, and a rectangular roof slab made of granite is positioned above the mihrab, the niche in the wall of a mosque that indicates the direction of Mecca, that one needs to face while praying. An Arabic inscription in the rectangular slab above the mihrab says that this mosque was built by Mohamed Ibn Hameed Ibn Abdullah in the Islamic year Hijri 116, that is 734 CE. Further the names of the four Khalifas, the Islamic religious and political leaders, are mentioned in the inscription.

In Tirunelveli district, as we have already noted, Kayalpatnam, one of the earliest Muslim settlements in the southern peninsula, was a prosperous port city and some of the important early mosques of the mediaeval period were constructed there. A couple of these mosques were partly demolished, for example the tenth century Karuppudaiyar Palli. This mosque near the seashore has been destroyed up to the plinth level and a modern construction sits on top of it now. According to inscriptions found at this site, Veera Pandyan, the Pandya king, had endowed devadanas for the maintenance of this mosque and for the conduct of five daily prayers. Another ancient mosque at Kayalpatnam that Raja Mohamad mentions is the Kadarkarai Palli, which has completely disappeared either due to sea erosion or from Portuguese razing. There are details in the inscription about the endowments made by Jatavarman Kulasekhara Pandyan to this mosque. One of the king's titles was poovinkizhathi and this title is also referenced in this inscription. The mosque is likely to have been constructed in the early thirteenth century.

Raja Mohamad says that a typical Dravidian style construction can be seen in the Irrataikulam Palli in Kayalpatnam with pillars supporting a stone mandapam. The pillars are in typical Pandya style with highly decorative motifs, but most of them are now plastered over, and the square shape of the mihrab was subsequently restructured to be semicircular with an arch added to it. While a lot of the ornamentation has been removed, the beauty of the unrenovated portions remains, showing its antiquity. During the first few centuries of Islam's presence in Tamilakam, this was the favoured style of construction. Adopting the local idiom for mosque construction was not extraordinary in any way—for example, mosques in other parts of the world such as China and Mali used local architectural styles.

There are a few other ancient mosques in Kayalpatnam where there is a clear indication of support from the ruling Hindu king of that time. Raja Mohamad points to the Kodimarathu Siru Nainar Palli, a Dravidian-style mosque which has been subject to a lot of renovation, which was liberally endowed by Arikesari Parakrama Pandyan in the fifteenth century. In the inscription, the mosque has been called Thurukka Nainar Palli and Sonakappalli. A great point of interest in this mosque is a thirteenth-century inscription which says that the dowry rate for girls to marry is very high, because of which many girls in the area remain unmarried. The inscription details a maximum amount for dowry and the sridhanam or gifts for the bride.

The Juma Masjid in Kayalpatnam, a fourteenth-century structure which was renovated in later centuries, has a remarkable connection with temple architecture. The walls are made with pilasters in typical Dravidian style, and there is a hexagonal mandapam in front, very similar to the ones found in temples. There is a central adhistanam, or shrine, and there are ornamental pillars in the mosque which are alternately square and hexagonal following Dravidian design. Other mosques like the Juma Masjid at Periyapattinam, the Juma Masjid at Pulicat (where early Arabs also traded in textiles), and old mosques in towns like Vedalai and Kulasekharapatnam all continued this tradition of following the Dravidian idiom in mosque construction up to the fourteenth century.

In the film *Yaadhum* (2013), as Anwar moves forward in his journey searching for lost roots, he finds a victory stone on the outskirts of Kayalpatnam, erected by the king of Wayanad, Udhaya Marthanda Varma. The fourteenth-century inscription of this Hindu king records the renovation and renaming of a mosque in this location as the Udhaya Marthanda Perum Palli. The granting of certain special concessions to this mosque is evidence of the integration of Islam with a Hindu milieu, says Anwar. He then discovers a temple inscription of the thirteenth century at the Jagannatha Swamy temple at Tirupullani temple further up the coast near Ramanathapuram. The inscription is of Maravarman Sundara Pandya II, who ruled in the thirteenth century, and this inscription records the grant of land to a Muslim Sonegar at Pouthramanickapattinam which is not identifiable today.

In nearby Kilakkarai, which is a major Tamil Muslim settlement and an old Tamil port, one can see one of the finest examples of Dravidian-style mosques. Vallal Seethakathi Sahib, a philanthropist, is said to have built the mosque here in the seventeenth century; he was said to be a close confidant of Kilavan Sethupathi, the ruler of Ramnad. The film shows the mosque's stunning interior, with strong decorative stone pillars, a high roof, elements that one would find in a south Indian temple. The nearby nineteenth-century mosque built by Habib Arasar also follows this tradition.

Raja Mohamad speaks of an important stage in the development of Islamic architecture in Tamil Nadu after Madurai was annexed by the commander of Alauddin Khilji, Malik Kafur. There was much chaos during the forty-year administration of the Madurai sultanate, and it did not result in any greater impact in the direction of Islamic art or in the spread of Islam, says Raja Mohamad. However, in the style of the architecture of the sultans of Delhi, the dome first appeared as a feature of south Indian mosques during this period, and a new Dravida-Islamic style developed, particularly in the mausoleums and dargahs that were built for kings and saints. Although minarets and domes were introduced in this epoch, some elements of the Dravidian style remained; it is important to note that observations from travellers like Ibn Battuta confirm that the newcomers from the north conformed to the customs and traditions of the south except in matters of religion.

At times even these religious lines are happily blurred, especially in Tamil Nadu. In one of our exploratory visits to the Tirunelveli region, we passed a small town where the crowded market street was full of traders and bustling with activity of all kinds. A small temple almost jutting onto the main road arrested our attention. We noticed a Muslim man and woman pausing at the entrance and bowing their head reverentially at the two gigantic colourfully painted deities that dominated the small mandapam. We observed that the man applied a small amount of vibhuti to his forehead while the young woman clasped her hands together in a gesture of reverence. When we asked them why they prayed here, prompt came the reply: 'Ella deivamum onru thane?' —aren't all gods the same? Mian Jan was a small farmer from Nagapatnam and was visiting his newly married daughter, the young woman Sannah Bibi, who was with him. The other locals, who quickly gathered there, said that the deity was called Vandi Marriccha Swamy, and was a potent remover of obstacles and a favourite deity in this small town. The male and female deities were the guardians of the town, they told us. They did not seem surprised by the prayerful presence of the Muslim visitors. Similarly, the sight of Hindus praying at dargahs and mosques is not at all unusual in the Tamil country.

There are numerous examples of such amity between members of religious communities in the villages and small towns dotted across Tamilakam. In Thanjavur, where my mother grew up in the progressive post-Independence household of my grandfather, she relates how she and her siblings were always fascinated by the Bawasa kadai, or the Bawa Sahib store, on a main road in Thanjavur. They would sit there for hours, watching the Muslim owner making attar: he would allow them to smell the different scents while they escaped the rigours of homework. The road was called Iyyan Theru, the lord's street, with a temple at the end as well as a flourishing Muslim shop, which was the mainstay and meeting point of the residents of that road. My uncle's wife, who was a new bride in the family and given to learning new languages, wanted to learn Urdu, which was duly arranged.

This demonstrable good will and harmony among neighbours is a hallmark of Tamil culture and persists at the core of the Tamil sensibility.

BOOK IV
The Age of the Europeans

Chapter 23

The Merchants of Colonization

*The Europeans needed spices, cloves, pepper, indigo, pearls, silk, calico....
However, they found obstacles to their commerce in the simplicity
and frugality that marked the life of the Tamils.*

K. Rajayyan, historian

THE HEROES OF EXPLORATION WAS A BOOK THAT I WAS FASCINATED BY AS a young child. Full of colourful drawings, maps of the ancient world, and portraits of swash-buckling heroes who sailed the seas in voyages of important discovery, it was almost as if the world had to wait for these adventurous men to reveal what existed across dangerous waters. We heard of Prince Henry the Navigator from Portugal, who was one of the earliest European princes to send ships to the waters of West Africa, although he personally never undertook any of these exploratory voyages himself. We were regaled with tales of heroes like Magellan (whose patron was Henry) and others like him who brought glory and wealth to their countries spreading prosperity all round. We learned about William Hawkins and Sir Francis Drake and his ship the *Golden Hind* on which he set out to circumnavigate the globe. The real story is, of course, much darker and more sinister; for instance, while opening up the west coast of Africa, the Portuguese, beginning with Prince Henry, set in place the system of transatlantic slavery. So, the quest for trade and wealth, as we now know, was also about slavery, the greed of corporations, and the subsequent impoverishment of many societies. In Tamilakam and in India the Europeans came to trade and became colonizers.

Well before the time of the famed Portuguese explorer Vasco da Gama who sailed to India in 1498, Europe had experienced many a tantalizing taste of the riches of the East. From the time of the early Arab traders, even before the advent of Christianity, merchants and traders had come to western India's shores, from the Malabar coast up to Gujarat and a brisk exchange of goods between India, North Africa, and West Asia already existed. Trade with the ancient Greeks, Romans, and Arabs was mostly by the Mediterranean route up to West Asia, and overland it was never direct but handled by Arab merchants. This changed over the centuries and in the mediaeval and modern eras, links began to develop between European society and Tamilakam. The Renaissance and the Reformation in Europe beginning in the fifteenth century, changed the shape of that continent. Great progress in science and explorations across the globe as well as the growth of trade, ship building, and the arms business, meant that power structures, economies, as well as commerce underwent structural changes. In 1453, Constantinople, the capital of the Byzantine empire, was captured by the Ottomans, and this meant that goods that travelled from India via Constantinople were blocked by the Turks. The goods used to be sent via the Red Sea to Berenike and Argada and then to Alexandria and thereafter by land to the West. In the face of the new European upheavals and hostilities, the need to continue to maintain brisk trading with India and the rest of Southeast Asia and China became a pressing matter and this was a strong motivation to look for new routes and indeed stable and safe routes.

The eastern part of the trade routes to India had hitherto been controlled by the Arabs and further up by the Italians (the Romans) and the Greeks. The need to discover new sea routes was also necessary to break the Arab and Italian monopoly of trade with India. The Portuguese were determined to find a way and decided to travel all the way down the African coast, avoiding the Red Sea altogether. This meant crossing the much feared Cape of Good Hope with its history of stormy weather and terrible shipwrecks. Meanwhile, Christopher Columbus also set out to find India from Spain and ended up travelling westwards and reached America in 1492. The Portuguese explorer Vasco da Gama, the son of a provincial nobleman, but well connected in court, was asked to lead an expedition to find a route to India by the Portuguese king, Manuel I. The Portuguese felt that following the expeditions of Bartholomew Diaz, who actually rounded the Cape of Good Hope prior to Vasco da Gama, signalled possibilities that would allow them to shrug off any trade dependence on the Italians or Muslim traders. Da Gama's voyage began in 1497 from Lisbon with four ships weighing about 120 tons each. They carried with them a couple of stone pillars to commemorate what they felt would be a triumphal outcome. In 1498, Vasco da Gama landed near Calicut and although welcomed by the Hindu Zamorin, the local leader, and allowed to trade in spices, there was hostility from the local merchants who were largely Muslim, and the Arab traders as well. Nevertheless, he returned to Portugal with spices as well as five or six Hindu kings in tow to announce his success and to introduce the king to the customs and beliefs of the Hindus. He sold the spices and other commodities for a huge profit, at sixty times the price. The Portuguese were even more convinced now of the need to build trade with India. Meanwhile King Manuel styled himself Lord of the Conquest, the Navigation and the Commerce in Ethiopia, Arabia, Persia, and India.

Vasco da Gama made two more voyages to India and the king made him a 'Dom' and amply rewarded him. He finally died in Cochin in 1524 but not before playing politics in that region, in Goa and Cannanore, among its leaders. There are several accounts that speak of the cruelties inflicted by da Gama on his return visits to the Malabar coast and by his successors. Large-scale violence and massacres were perpetrated especially in Malabar. One account says how in 1525, the Portuguese caught one of the richest merchants in Cannanore, Mamalli Marakkar, and cut his hands off and hung him on a public wall as a warning to other locals. By 1510, the Portuguese had acquired Goa from the sultan of Bijapur whose territory it was and made it its headquarters in South India.

On the heels of Vasco da Gama, another Portuguese explorer Pedro Cabral landed in India and got permission from the Zamorin to set up trading stations in Calicut, Cannanore, and Cochin. The Portuguese then asked the Zamorin to expel the Arab traders from the west coast. Battles broke out between the two groups of traders and many lives were lost in these conflicts, especially because the Portuguese had superior arms at their disposal. The trading centres became settlements and on orders from the royal court in Lisbon, governors were appointed to safeguard the trading centres and the settlements around them. The first governor who was appointed to protect Portuguese interests was Francisco de Almeida. S. Kannan says that he pursued a 'blue water' policy to ensure Portuguese domination in the Indian ocean. A forced blockade of non-Portuguese ships, including Indian ones, and a system of paying cartez or a heavy fee for plying on the waters deprived many local people of their livelihood at sea. The next governor was Afonso de Albuquerque who, although he was in control only from 1509 to 1515, was the person who captured Goa. It is important to note that a policy of expansion was pursued by this governor, even beyond the Indian coast, and the Portuguese captured Malacca and parts of Sri Lanka as well. Albuquerque encouraged the Portuguese to marry Indian women and forced conversions to Christianity right from the time of da Gama. All the west coast settlements were crown sponsored, whereas the expansion in the east coast was mercantile, by private merchants. They set up trade centres in Punnakayal in Tuticorin district, Vedalai in Ramanathapuram district up to Nagapatnam, Devanampattinam in Cuddalore district, and in

Mylapore, San Thome, and Pulicat. Luz Church at Mylapore, a version of which still stands today, was built by the Portuguese in 1516 and the San Thome Church was built in 1522.

It must be mentioned at this point that there was a great interest in India from the Roman Catholic Church via the court in Lisbon, ever since the time of the first voyages to promote Christianity in the Malabar region. Under the padrado real or royal patronage, the papacy granted the Portuguese monarch the right to make ecclesiastical appointments at all their missions overseas, and missionary operations increased at a great pace. Although the initial focus was on trade, as soon as the settlements expanded there was a steady and often heavy-handed effort at conversion of both Hindu and Muslim communities.

Although Goa fell away from Tamilakam, much of the conquered territory at the time of early European adventurism included large parts of present-day Andhra, Kerala, and Karnataka—at the time, they were all part of Tamil country.

The arrival of early Jesuit missionaries like Roberto de Nobili from Italy to the Portuguese settlement in Goa, brought with it a gentler approach to the conversion of local people to Christianity. Nobili's approach was unusual and heralded a new aspect to the arrival of Christianity in South India. We will discuss this, but it is important to note that his approach to conversion and the spread of Christianity was opposed by the earlier Portuguese missionaries. At this time printing became prevalent, and manuscripts were sent from the western coast to Portugal to be printed. Henrique Henriques, a Portuguese merchant, introduced printing in Tamil.

The Portuguese, meanwhile, continued their acts of piracy on the high seas. The imperial Mughals, who always had their eye on southern territories, bitterly opposed them. The Portuguese had an ally in the Paravar community. The Paravars were a maritime community in coastal Tamil Nadu, dealing with trade and pearl fishery since the time of the Pandyas, and were loyal to the Vijayanagar rulers. The Portuguese took over this community promising them protection; many of them were converted to Christianity including a mass conversion in which 50,000 people in Tuticorin converted. Already in charge of many of these southern coastal towns of Tamilakam, it became easy for the Portuguese to expand their control over the territory.

The arrival of other merchants of colonization, the Dutch, the Danish, the French, and the British soon sparked bitter rivalry among these groups. Soon enough, the influence of the Portuguese began to wane, especially after assaults by the Vijayanagar and Nayak forces. In rapid decline in Tamil Nadu, they continued to hold Goa, and, in fact, were the last colonial power to leave India. The Portuguese also began to focus on the other side of the earth—in the sixteenth century, an interest was sparked in exploring and conquering Brazil with all its mineral and natural wealth and their attention shifted there, even as their power declined in India. However, they left behind many military innovations in India. They were the first to use body armour, matchlocks and other new kinds of guns and pistols, and the first shipbuilders of multi-storey ships. Goa was also famed for producing intricate gold and silver work, another craft that came from Portuguese settlers. The beautiful churches of Goa are a legacy of the Portuguese presence. Tamil absorbed many words from the Portuguese such as alamari, which comes from armario, jannal from janela; chave is saavi, mesa is mejai. The word veranda is also from the Portuguese. Other words include annasi or pineapple, and peepa or jug.

The Dutch came hot on the heels of the Portuguese into India. The Dutch East India Company was established in 1602, although its main intent was to trade with the Indonesian islands and Malaysia rather than India. The Dutch came to Tamilakam in 1605 and established trade centres in Masulipatnam, Pulicat, Nagapatnam, and Karaikal. There were other places in India, in the north, where they established trade settlements. Kottar near Kanyakumari, then Tuticorin, and to the north, Karaikal, Port Nova (Parangipettai), Tenganapatnam, which was just north of Port Nova, and Sadras or Sadurangapatnam, in Pulicat, which the Dutch acquired from the local Nayak ruler; this was their local capital or stronghold. They constructed a fort called Geldria in Pulicat in 1613, from which they traded slaves. These were people from Bengal, Tenganapatnam, Karaikal, and Pulicat where often famine and hunger and food shortage led to such exploitation. The Danes who also landed on the southern coasts and created a settlement in Tarangambadi (Tranquebar) engaged in the same kind of slave trading. Kannan says that there was a brisk slave trade from many parts of India, in addition to Asia, Africa, and of course further east. Many of the slaves ended up in royal or noble houses scattered across Europe. They were all colloquially referred to as Moorish. The Danes and the Dutch were both bitter rivals of the Portuguese whom they detested. The Danish territorial activity and active trading in India did not last beyond three decades, but they founded the Danish Lutheran Mission which challenged the Jesuits. All the earlier missionaries were Catholic. Heinrich Plutschau and Bartholomeus Ziegenbaulg were the first Protestant missionaries to come to India, sent by Frederick IV, the Danish king. Apart from their proselytising work they also translated religious work into Tamil.

Ziegenbaulg is credited with the first translation of the New Testament into Tamil. He also published other books in Tamil: *Needhi Venba, Kondrai Vendhan, Ulaga Needhi*. A fellow missionary John Bishop Febrius translated the Old Testament into Tamil.

The Dutch were far more interested in acquiring wealth through trade and were certainly not interested in empire building in India. But they fought the British fiercely for territory. In the Battle of Hooghly, in 1759, they were defeated by the British. Finally, in 1824, the Anglo-Dutch Treaty was signed whereby the Dutch relinquished all their possessions in India in favour of the British. One of the best-known legacies of the Dutch is the fort in Pulicat. It was not just a fort then but also served as a residence and a warehouse. The Pulicat cemetery is an example of a new type of architecture. The Dutch traded largely in cotton and spices and the cotton trade was soon picked up by the British. But the Dutch like the Portuguese did not have a great and lasting impact on Tamil Nadu.

Let us now turn our attention to the arrival of the British in India. Tantalizing tales of exotic and mysterious India with its vast fortunes to be had for the taking had long haunted the European imagination. In 1600, a motley group of bankers, aldermen, merchant sailors, and modest clerks met in the City of London to discuss the possibility of expanding trade with India and the Indies. The most prominent among the people assembled was the mayor of London himself, Stephen Soame. Now these Englishmen had already heard of the great wealth that the Dutch had acquired from the Indies, particularly by way of their spice trade. There was a sense of urgency at the meeting; several British expeditions, including those to America, had not quite succeeded. An older company called the Levant founded by Thomas Smythe would also become part of the new initiatives being planned and added several people to this diverse group of men. These men founded the East India Company with the intent to trade in textiles with India—cotton, indigo, chintz, and silks as well as in salt, pepper, spices, and tea. The Dutch far outdid them at that stage, but of course this was the beginning of the founding of the British empire in India. The original charter of the East India Company, which was a joint stock company with many more investors, clearly stated that this was the Governor and Company of Merchants of London trading to the East Indies. The group of 200 and more received their royal charter from Queen Elizabeth I, which gave them a monopoly of trade for fifteen years with countries east of the Cape of Good Hope and west of the Straits of Magellan. The charter also specified that any trader who did business without license from the Company would forfeit his ships and cargo, would have to pay a heavy fine, half of which would go to the Crown and half to the Company and could also suffer imprisonment at 'royal pleasure'. William Dalrymple, the historian, says the charter granted them 'semi-sovereign privileges to rule territories and raise armies.' He adds, 'the wording was sufficiently ambiguous to allow future generations of East India Company officials to use it to claim jurisdiction over all English subjects in Asia, mint money, raise fortifications, make laws, wage wars, conduct an independent foreign policy, hold courts, issue punishment, imprison English subjects and plant English settlements.'

The first ship of the East India Company to land in India was the *Hector* steered by Captain William Hawkins in 1609. Hawkins was entrusted with the duty of procuring a licence from the Mughal emperor Jahangir to start a factory in Surat where he had landed. Upon arrival he was apparently kidnapped by the Portuguese who extorted money from him and demanded that he buy a licence to do business as well as seek permission of the Portuguese king. After some tribulations at the hands of the Portuguese, he managed to extricate himself from them and made his way to Agra where the emperor held court. Hawkins was entertained by the Mughal king who was curious about these foreigners and let him linger in the Mughal court but permission for factory building was not given. Jahangir instead organized an Armenian wife for Hawkins who waited long in the Mughal court, but nothing came of his efforts. Jahangir probably found Hawkins amusing and a great curiosity and called him English Khan. After many years Hawkins was asked to depart from the Mughal court due to pressure from the Portuguese and died on his way back home.

The next Englishman to descend on Jahangir's court was Sir Thomas Roe. Roe came to Surat in 1615 and made his way to Agra to present his credentials as the English ambassador of King James I. He hoped for a better outcome than his predecessors. There are several portraits of Roe and Jahangir—one of them shows Jahangir surrounded by his courtiers and Sir Thomas with doffed hat trying to present his papers. The imperiousness of Jahangir is obvious; he was not impressed by the paltry gifts that were presented to him and ended up having the ambassador frustrated by the slow progress of the request for a firman, the permission to open a factory at Surat. Sir Thomas was finally able to get this done after a few years of hanging about the Mughal court. He meticulously wrote a journal, which is kept at the British Library today, and which reveals his contempt for the Mughals while still working at establishing a connection with them. N. S. Ramaswami, historian, says, 'Roe was well aware of the dignity of his country and of his own importance. He was not a man like Hawkins before him who would complacently accept an Armenian bride Jehangir condescendingly chose for him...he was sagacious.' While he did not get the exact permission he wanted, by the time he left India, he managed to set up factories in Surat as well as in other places like Masulipatnam, Agra, and Ahmedabad. This was the beginning of Britain's long relationship with India. Roe is important because through him the East India Company finally got its foot in the door. However, at this point, the English still had to contend with Portuguese intrigue and hostility from the Dutch as well.

The old spice trade while still relevant was overtaken by the new European interest in textiles. The Dutch were already exporting cotton and the British soon followed suit. They found that Masulipatnam (later known as Machilipatnam) on the Coromandel coast was an important centre for trade in textiles. Ptolemy mentions the town of Maisolos from where fine muslin cloth was traded in Greek and Roman towns. Centuries later, in mediaeval times, nearby Golconda also became the centre of the famed diamond trade, but the muslin trade continued into the sixteenth and seventeenth centuries, with a new form of artistry emerging in textiles with local weavers and painters, the chitrakars, using their talents and creating stunning designs called kalamkari. The Europeans called this 'painted cloth' and these were exported in vast amounts from the Masulipatnam area, and particularly from small towns close to Masulipatnam such as Petapoli and Palacole. The beauty of these was that it was all done with vegetable dye using locally grown roots like madder and other plants for colour; even after the passage of time, these 'paints' remained fresh and beautiful on the cloth. The British were intrigued by the families that worked together from grandfather to grandson in the business, using these natural dyes; the trade in these textiles became extremely profitable and popular. The Masulipatnam textiles, including muslin, cotton, and chintzes, were soon hung in Mughal courts as well as in London and in fashion-conscious country estates in England. Ramaswami writes, 'Masulipatnam chintz was becoming popular in England by 1620. A fashionable home noticed in 1641 contained a suite of hangings consisting of "four pieces of Indian pintadoes and curtaines of the same suite with a valence thereto and four little Indian carpets."' Eight years earlier, Samuel Pepys bought for his wife 'a chint, that is a painted East Indian callicoe for to line her new study'.

As the British expanded their presence, their European rivals were pushed back. The Dutch found that after seven decades of rivalry they were slowly losing their possessions and territories to the British. But the British didn't have it their own way everywhere as the Dutch and the Portuguese were very powerful. Sometimes, the only way forward was through tactical alliances. Bombay, for example, was gifted as part of the dowry to Charles II by the Portuguese king on the marriage of Catherine of Braganza, his daughter, to Charles. At that time only Surat was important on the west coast, but a foothold in Bombay meant that Britain could start developing trade in the west—they shifted their base or capital to Bombay from Surat. In 1632, the sultan of Golconda gave permission to start factories in coastal Andhra. The English were savvy enough to realize that they would be better off if they looked for trade opportunities down the Coromandel coast rather than focus on the already crowded western coast and regions; they felt that there was more promise in the southern territories and sent their agents to explore and set up trading posts. In 1639, Francis Day founded the city of Madras on a strip of land that was given to him by the Vijayanagar king of Chandragiri-Vellore, Venkataraya III. He built Fort St. George on the sandy terrain which appeared to be a good anchorage for trading ships. Soon Madras became the headquarters of the British on the Coromandel coast.

In 1652, Madras became an administrative unit that was called a presidency. In 1685, it was given the status of a formal presidency. In 1688 Madras had a municipal government with a mayor. In 1690, the English established a factory at Calcutta, and later built a fort there called Fort William which became the capital of British India. So, Bombay, Madras, and Calcutta became the three presidency towns of the English settlements in India. By way of clarity and context, let us look at the phases of English presence and imperialist expansion in India. Phase one therefore occurred from 1612 to 1757 when the Battle of Plassey took place. During this phase, the English were just traders who made huge profits; in phase two, from 1758 to 1857, they turned producers and owners, buying land, taking over territories, and gradually and insidiously destroying Indian industries. In phase three, which commenced after the first war of Indian Independence took place in 1857, India became a subject nation of the British empire (after the British government took over from the East India Company in 1858). From 1857 to 1947 the exploitation of India and Indians by the British was rapacious.

If we look at British ascendancy in the Carnatic region, one must be aware of the three Carnatic wars that occurred which gave the English a very solid and strong base in the region. These wars were because of Anglo-French rivalries. The French East India Company had been set up in 1664 and was authorized by King Louis XIV to set up trade, conquer territories, and was encouraged to add to the glories of France much in the same way as the other European powers. Pondicherry was their capital and they also held possession of other places like Karaikal. In 1746, the French seized Madras.

The French had replaced the Dutch as rivals of the British East India Company which was slowly gaining in presence and power in the south. Initially, like several other European powers, the French entered Surat and set up a factory there in 1668. The French East India Company had been created under the aegis of Cardinal Richelieu in 1642. After Surat, another factory was established by the French in Masulipatnam, and in 1674 the French acquired Pondicherry from the sultan of Bijapur and set up an administration. Joseph François Dupleix was the first governor of the French territories in Tamil Nadu. He had great ambitions to expand French territory in South India. Soon Karaikal, Yanam, and Mahe were brought under French control.

Keeping pace with the French were the British. India's share of the global economy was around 27 per cent in the 1700s. The growing interest in acquiring land, becoming producers, and furthering their own commercial interests were critical to the global expansionist plans of the British and the French. A great surge in demand for textiles as well as raw cotton and the continuing interest in pepper and other spices kept Indian artisans and producers busy. Moreover, allied industries like shipbuilding and metalwork also flourished but soon the producers grew impoverished owing to skewed and unequal taxation rules, unfair trade practices, sustained exploitation, and other damaging aspects that were central to the functioning of the East India Company.

Before we look at the Anglo-French Carnatic wars, after which the British established their supremacy over the region, it would be instructive to look at how Indian rulers and rebels were faring as the British kept trying to advance their cause. Large parts of India were under Mughal rule in the north, but the power of the Mughals was declining. In the south, particularly in Tamilakam, the British were slowly taking over territories that were once under the Vijayanagar kings and later under the Nayaks and the Marathas. The Poligars put up stiff resistance. Famously, Veerapandiya Kattabomman fought against the stiff imposition of taxes by the British in the eighteenth century. He and his small force of fighters took on British troops and even killed an important commandant. Kattabomman's story became the stuff of legend. One of the Tamil actor Sivaji Ganesan's most well-known roles was that of Kattabomman who challenged Jackson durai about the taxes he had to pay to the white man's regime, asking: 'Why should I pay you taxes? The skies pour and the earth receives; did you come with us to the fields to plant seedlings, to pluck branches...did you grind turmeric for our happy girls?' This dramatized declaration by Kattabomman in the film was echoed for decades after as not only a tribute to Sivaji's ability to move Tamil audiences but also as a rallying cry to bolster the self-worth of Indians enslaved for generations by colonial rule.

This particular palayakaran was initially a peace-loving administrator of Panchalamkurichi who turned to rebellion. Panchalamkurichi which came under the domain of the nawab of Arcot had been surrendered to the British under the Carnatic Treaty of 1792. An accumulation of arrears in taxes led the British Collector Colin Jackson to harass Kattabomman despite the latter having cleared most of the arrears. Jackson would deliberately insult Kattabomman in multiple ways including by summoning him to meetings, making him wait, and then demanding that he travel hundreds of miles to meet him in another place where he would keep him standing for up to three hours before humiliatingly interrogating him. Kattabomman was continuously attacked and provoked by the British until he could take it no longer and retaliated. Although he was captured, tried, and hanged, his story continues to resonate with Tamils.

British ascendancy in the Tamil areas emerged after the defeat of the French in the Carnatic region. The First Carnatic War was fought between 1740 and 1748, and this arose mainly from rivalry between the British and the French. It was strange that South India should be a proxy stage for a war in Europe between the two countries—the War of Austrian Succession, which was going on in Europe, but it proved to be an opportunity for both countries to display and exercise their might in South India. The British destroyed French ships off the Coromandel coast, in retaliation, the French under Dupleix captured Madras and Fort St. George in 1746. A young Robert Clive was one of the soldiers who was asked to take an oath to not take up arms against the French—he and a handful of others who refused were imprisoned. The story goes that they disguised themselves as Indians and escaped to Fort David near Cuddalore which was then a British possession. The Carnatic nawabs also got involved in this. Anwaruddin, the nawab of Arcot who ruled between 1744 and 1749, supported the British and the French, meanwhile, sought the help of Chanda Sahib, who was later the nawab of the Carnatic. Both forces fought at the Battle of Adyar in 1746. The war ended with a treaty, the Treaty of Aix la Chapelle, which was signed in France in 1748. Neither side had any decisive victories during this period, although the French extended their power and influence across the region and in other parts of India during this time, and their superiority over the British was established.

However, in the immediate aftermath, war broke out again. The Second Carnatic War was fought between 1749 to 1754. This time, local dynastic disputes were the reason for the war. Nazir Jung of Hyderabad, Anwaruddin of Arcot, and the British were ranged on one side. Muzaffar Jung of Hyderabad, Nazir Jung's nephew, Chanda Sahib, and the French were on the other. Nazir Jung wanted to become the nizam of Hyderabad, and Anwaruddin joined the fray in the hope of strengthening his own position against his perpetual enemy Chanda Sahib. The initial victory went to the French. This was at the Battle of Ambur in 1749. Muzaffar Jung and Chanda Sahib, with the help of the French, managed to capture Arcot and Muzaffar Jung did end up becoming the nizam as he had wanted. In 1751, Clive, who had risen in prominence, successfully led the British to capture Arcot and win the war, ending up with the Treaty of Pondicherry in 1754. The British then placed Muhammad Ali Khan Wallajah on the throne as the nawab of the Carnatic. The Third Carnatic War broke out in 1757; a year prior to this, renewed conflict between the British and the French, known as the Seven Years' War, took place in Europe between 1756 and 1763. In 1758, the French, under Comte de Lally, captured British forts at Cuddalore and Vilijnam (in Kerala). Following this, in retaliation, the English attacked the French fleet at Masulipatnam which had grown into a significant trading port for many Europeans. In 1760, another decisive battle was fought at Wandiwash where the British led by Sir Eyre Coote were victorious. The British also captured Pondicherry in 1761 and almost fully destroyed the French city. The Seven Years' War meanwhile came to an end with the signing of the Treaty of Paris which ended the Carnatic War in India. The British confined the French to certain places by way of this treaty. In time, by 1801, the British took complete control, appointed a governor, and created the Madras Presidency. Having suppressed and routed all other foreign forces, the British became the sole masters of India.

Chapter 24

Christendom in Tamilakam

> *…Evangelical missions had developed within colonial culture. It is therefore not surprising that at the same time that European merchants were viewing India as a place to gain wealth in moveable property, European missionaries were viewing it as a place to gain wealth in souls.*
>
> D. Dennis Hudson, scholar

MADURAI, NOVEMBER 1606. THE MONSOON RAIN LASHED THE CITY, AND the streets were flooded. A strange white figure in a dhoti and a priest's tuft waded unsteadily on wooden sandals through the city's narrow lanes. He seemed unaffected by the wind and rain; striding purposefully, he was a man on a mission. People cowering from the rain stared at this odd figure, not quite knowing what to make of this strange white man, the likes of whom they had never seen before. He seemed like one of the priests in the temple and yet his colouring was so pale that they wondered if he were stricken with some sort of illness. Roberto de Nobili smiled to himself, quite aware of the consternation of those around him. When he reached his destination, a small, low-roofed house that looked modest though welcoming, he was greeted with joy by the men and women who came out to receive him. The curious ones who lingered outside decided that they would stay and find out more about this unusual person.

Missionary, scholar, and nobleman, Roberto de Nobili was an Italian who could count two popes among his kinsmen; his father was a nobleman in the Italian court and brought up the young Roberto with every privilege. However, the young boy turned to religion and became a Jesuit priest and scholar, opting to travel to far-flung lands to spread the word of Christ. This Jesuit priest's entirely radical way of bringing people into the fold is a remarkable chapter in the development of Christianity in Tamilakam.

Commanding as they did the seas and much of the west coast and even regions further to the interior, the primary goal of the early Europeans in India, especially the Portuguese, was trade. They were fiercely anti-Islam due to the constant clashes with the Moors in continental Europe which reflected in their dealings with Muslims in India. This further motivated them to convert many locals to Christianity although their methods often left much to be desired. The Portuguese had scant regard for local faiths and customs, destroyed numerous temples and were ruthless in their treatment of the locals, especially those who resisted conversion.

De Nobili brought with him an entirely different approach to conversions. He realized that an intellectual and emotional approach was needed to get local people into the Christian fold. He first arrived in Goa and went to Cochin. After a brief stay there, he moved to Madurai where he adopted the garb of an Indian sanyasi. He wore a small tuft and three threads, not unlike the Brahminical sacred thread; but he claimed that these represented the Holy Trinity. He learned Sanskrit, Telugu, and Tamil and followed Hindu or Indian customs; in the process of acculturation with the local population he found a way forward to teach the Christian doctrine. He used the vernacular for words like the Bible, calling it Vedam. Poojai was used for Mass, prasadam for grace, etc. He consciously engaged with upper-class literate Hindus and persuaded them to accept the Christian doctrine. He was called the 'white brahmin'; Max Mueller has called him the first European Sanskrit scholar.

He worked assiduously to translate several catechisms and texts into Tamil, and although the Portuguese did not quite appreciate his approach, he continued to draw people to him. While there was scepticism in the Catholic Church about his methods and the Portuguese bishop in Goa opposed his ways, the Pope approved, and the humaneness of his approach was understood, including all the accoutrements such as the sandal paste, the sacred threads, and the tuft.

There are, however, criticisms of de Nobili especially by some present-day commentators, who suggest that positioning himself as a kshatriya, or soldier, descended from Roman royalty, amounted to deceiving simple, credulous people. He declared: 'I was not born in the land of the *Parangis* (foreigners) nor was I ever connected with their race...I came from Rome where my family hold the same rank as respectable *rajas* hold in this country.' He called himself Tattvabodhar, the one who teaches reality.

De Nobili died in Mylapore, Chennai, in 1656, having contributed much to Tamil Christian literature and philosophy, including learned treatises on the Christian texts in Tamil. In the centuries that followed, others like de Nobili who adopted a novel approach to communicating the word of Christ include C. J. Beschi, Robert Caldwell, G. U. Pope, and Andre Dubois. They were all scholar-missionaries, ethnographers, linguists, and historians, lovingly adopted into the Tamil fold and, as Susan Bayly says, 'their writings are still an important source of first-hand observations and analysis'. The work of these foreign missionaries shaped a course for the spread of the Christian doctrine in Tamil Nadu.

To go back even further to the actual origins of Christianity in India and in Tamilakam, many centuries before the advent of the Jesuit missionaries, and in the immediate aftermath of the crucifixion of Jesus Christ, 'Doubting Thomas', one of his twelve disciples, landed on the Malabar Coast in Muziris in 52 CE. Apostle Thomas was the first messenger of Christ in India. Given that the date of Jesus's crucifixion is 33 CE, and that two decades later St. Thomas sailed to India, the Christian community here is likely among the oldest in the world. St. Thomas is said to have travelled all across the western Malabar coast (modern-day Kerala) to spread Christianity and establish churches there. There are currently many communities of Thomas Christians in Kerala who revere him as their founder. They are also known as Syrian Christians as the group's ancestors used Syriac in liturgy. The earliest community in the Tamil area as it then was, were these Thomas Christians.

Susan Bayly says 'the legends of St. Thomas predate the arrival of the Portuguese in south India, and for centuries the Syrians' foundation accounts have maintained that the group is descended from local men of high standing—usually described as the members of the elite Keralan Nambudiri Brahman caste group—who were converted by St. Thomas during his stay in Malabar'. Of course, this ultimately was an important aspect of the history of Kerala. In the early years, these Syrian Christians were part of the trading groups in Malabar and soon became a powerful and wealthy local community actively engaged in the pepper and spice trades.

During his time on the Malabar coast, St. Thomas set up at least seven churches including ones at Palayur, Paravur, Quilon, Niranom, and at the Cranganur-Malankara site. He is said to have performed many miracles which brought a great many people into the Christian fold including some of the royalty of the area. Later, he went eastwards to Mayilapur with the intention to build a church. Some scholars such as Arthur Coke Burnell, W. R. Phillips, and James Hough have strongly disagreed with the extent of his travels in the region and disputed his stay in the area, but others have pointed out that *The Acts of Thomas*, a work from around the second century, talks about his martyrdom taking place 'outside the city' on 'a mountain'. A few centuries later, as K. V. Raman points out, Marco Polo (in the thirteenth century), without mentioning Mayilapur by name, says that 'the body of Messer Saint

Thomas the Apostle lies in this town having no great population... Both Christians and Saracens frequent it on pilgrimage'.

St. Thomas is said to have lived in Little Mount and walked down the shore to Mayilapur to preach every day. His discourses attracted a lot of people including the local ruler. One fateful day he was attacked and killed, some say accidentally, by a fowler who was aiming for the peacocks who frequented the area; others say that he was deliberately killed by enemies and buried in Mayilapur. A church was built over his mortal remains, but the relics were dispatched to Edessa in Mesopotamia, then taken to Italy for safekeeping as the Moors had taken over Mesopotamia at that time. Some relics remain to this day in Madras. Historian V. Sriram says, '...the Portuguese had no doubts about St. Thomas having once been buried in Mylapore, and by the early sixteenth century, were attracted to the place and built San Thome.' St. Francis Xavier, during his mission in South India, is also said to have visited the said tomb of St. Thomas. Portuguese interest in this area was further underlined by another legend: sailors who were confronted by a severe storm were guided to the shore and safety by a bright white light, in gratitude for which they built a church there in the sixteenth century; it was dedicated to Mary and called Luz Church, luz meaning light.

The Portuguese presence in San Thome and the surrounding areas steadily augmented the spread of Christianity especially Roman Catholicism. From the sixteenth to the eighteenth century, the Portuguese worked closely with the Holy See to shore up their presence in the region. The Portuguese royal patronage of the church was called padroado and their close relationship with their citizens in South India helped a deeper percolation of Christianity. However, as mentioned earlier, the Portuguese methods of conversion were brutal. The king of Portugal in 1546 sent a memo to the Portuguese rulers in India that they should discover and reduce to fragments all forms of idols. Then the Goan Inquisition in 1561 persecuted thousands of Hindus and Muslims, many of them recent converts to Christianity, in the belief that they were not really immersed in the faith.

A. X. Alexander, retired Director General of Police, Tamil Nadu, an expert on the history and growth of South India's Christians, explains that the east coast Christians and those in southern India are distinct from the Kerala Christians, that is the Thomas Christians. This was largely because of St. Francis Xavier, a Jesuit who was later canonized, who moved from Goa to southern Tamil Nadu—to places like Tuticorin where a community of pearl fishers called the Paravas (many of whom had already been converted) received him. Pearl fishing is an important avocation for the southeastern fishermen, says Alexander, 'Our pearls even went to the court of Cleopatra and to the Roman emperor Augustus, so much so that the Roman Senate chastised the emperor for denuding Rome's gold reserves in favour of the pearls from South India'.

At that time, the hostilities between Muslims and the Europeans which were constantly on the boil (from the eleventh to the fourteenth century) impacted the relationship between the Portuguese and the Muslim traders in South India. Edgar Thurston, the botanist and anthropologist who was the British superintendent of the Madras Museum from 1885 to 1908, compiled a seven-volume study called *Castes and Tribes of Southern India* along with his colleague K. Rangachari. He quotes J. Hornell who says the Paravas had control of the pearl fisheries from time immemorial and were the most powerful community in the country around Korkai. Thurston says,

> ...the *Maduraikanchi* text of the Sangam period describes Korkai as the chief town in the country of the Parathavar and the seat of the pearl fishery, with a population consisting chiefly of pearl divers and chank cutters. When the Pandya kingdom was powerful, the Paravas had grants of certain rights from the monarchy, paying tribute from the produce of the fisheries, and receiving protection and immunity from taxation in return'. ...they were exempt from tribute or subjugation to the Rajahs, having a chief of their own election who drew revenue from the whole people, which in process of time had spread itself from Quilon to Bengal.

Importantly, the word Parava itself means the 'sea', and a Paravan is one who can command the seas—which meant he could be a boat maker, a merchant prince of the seas, a steerer, and any other person who was occupied with seafaring.

In time, 'the Moors', as Thurston calls them, or Muslims, had also spread themselves across these southern regions and were in competition with the pearl fishery operations, seeing that it brought considerable wealth to the Paravas. Also, the Paravas were not paying any tithe to local leaders, therefore there were ongoing disputes between the Muslims of Kayalpatnam and Keezhakarai with the Paravas, many of whom were Hindus at that time and some who had been converted earlier. The Paravas were soon assisted in their fights against the Muslims by John Da Cruz, a Chetty (not Chettiar) from Kerala. Earlier, Da Cruz, a man of some substance, had been sent by the Zamorin of Calicut as the ambassador to Portugal. The young Portuguese king was impressed by John Da Cruz and gave him the right to import horses into India; he was greatly favoured at the Portuguese court and had gained much influence. Over time, Da Cruz fell out with the Zamorin who sided with the Muslim traders against the Paravas; he wrote several letters to the Portuguese king asking for assistance for the Paravas to fight against the Muslims. In return he offered to convert all the Paravas to Christianity and make them loyal subjects of the Portuguese crown and citizens of Portugal. Forty thousand Paravas were converted to Christianity at one stretch. Many families even today can trace a family connection back to this time, much like the Goans.

Another local community called the Maravas was also converted by the Jesuits, and it was clearly a marriage of convenience says Alexander. It suited the purpose of both groups as both the Portuguese and the Paravas wanted relief from the Muslims. Starting from the villages around Rameswaram and Kanyakumari and right up to Cochin and Kollam, thousands were baptised in the Goan Church and given individual Christian names, and European ones at that, such as Fernandes, Rodrigues, etc. There was a single bishop in Goa whose jurisdiction was up to Indonesia during that period, and all ecclesiastical matters came under him. One can understand, of course, that with so much at hand and so many converts, all the bishop could do was to pronounce them all Christians, give them new names but not teach them Christian doctrines or values.

Francis Xavier, the Spanish missionary mentioned earlier, was of aristocratic lineage, and along with a Portuguese fellow student Francis Ignatius of Loyola set up the Society of Jesus (the Jesuits) in Portugal to spread the word of Christ across the seas. These two brilliant young students who along with a few others steeped in Christian doctrine got permission from Pope Paul III in 1540 to set up this new religious order. They were asked by King John of Portugal to go to India and beyond where he held a lot of territory, to re-instil Christian values among the Portuguese, many of whom they felt, had gone astray, and also to spiritually uplift the new converts. When Francis Xavier arrived in Goa in 1542, he also felt that the newly converted, especially in the southern and eastern coasts of India, needed a spiritual lift and more instruction in the faith; after spending time in Goa he moved to the pearl fishery coast to preach to the converted Christians. He would ring a bell as he walked the village streets and hundreds of people including young children would gather to listen to his catechism. He built as many as forty churches along the coast and was said to have performed several miracles that drew more people to the faith. He also visited the tomb of St. Thomas at Mayilapur.

The other invaluable contribution of St. Francis Xavier, according to Alexander, was his translation of Latin prayers into Tamil, having committed them to memory in the Tamil himself. Within about three months of his arrival, he had translated the Lord's Prayer, the Creed, and the Ten Commandments into Tamil. He appointed kanakupillai or accountants to keep track of how many Christians existed in the region and how many became Christians. These accountants would be summoned periodically before Francis Xavier, with the converts brought there and if the prayers or catechisms were not properly recited, the stipend of the kanakupillai would be reduced, he adds. Alexander says the stipend was sanctioned by Queen Isabella of Portugal from the money that was allocated to her for her shoes.

Francis Xavier moved on from South India after living in the pearl fishery coast for two years to Indonesia, Japan, China, and Sri Lanka. Deified in the places where he worked, St. Francis, although he did not speak Tamil like some of the other Jesuit figures, was very highly regarded across the region; particularly in Tuticorin, he was the central figure in the devotion of the Paravas and in other local Christian communities. It was as exhausting as it was exhilarating for him. In his letters he writes with honesty about his daily rounds. '…it often happens to me to be hardly able to use my hands from the fatigue of baptising; often in a single day I have baptised whole villages. Sometimes I have lost my voice and strength altogether with repeating again and again the Credo and other forms.' Susan Bayly says that it was Francis's personality and 'charismatic authority' that endowed mechanically learned rites with a level of coherence.

So, with faithful adherents to St. Francis across the region, the main Parava town of Tuticorin has a church called the Church of Our Lady of Snows, the name coming from a Roman basilica of the fifth century where it snowed in midsummer. It has a beautiful statue of the Virgin Mary which the Portuguese brought from Manila, a gift from the nuns of Manila to Francis Xavier, initially housed in Punnakayal, then moved to Tuticorin. In Tuticorin, the church and the festivities surrounding it soon acquired a special status. Alexander says its annual festival 'transcends religion', and crowds of people, Hindus, Muslims, and Christians throng the town. There is a strong Tamil cultural anchoring here, with festivals and rituals conducted somewhat in the manner of Hindu temple festivals. This Madha is considered the guardian of the fishermen, says Alexander, adding that it is called 'Ezhu kadal thurai yega adaikala madha' 'the Mother and Keeper of Seven Villages'. She is even referred to as Parameshwari, an appellation of the Hindu goddess Parvati.

The head of the fishermen, the jati talaivan, or head of the caste, presides over the church festivals emphasizing the hierarchy as well as caste traditions of the Paravas despite their conversion to Christianity. The elite and wealthy among the Paravas such as the jati talaivan make generous contributions to both the church and its attendant festivals. Like several other Christian communities across the south, the Paravas follow many of their original Hindu customs for family events like weddings and other occasions. The intonation of the scriptures in this church is a strange and sonorous mixture of Latin and Tamil. Alexander says a lot of the Latin has even been done away in favour of Tamil hymns. 'The accent is on local customs these days' he says. 'As in Hindu temples they cook Pongal as an offering and Christmas celebrations are also like a Hindu festival,' he adds.

Earlier, rites in the Hindu style were also followed at the church's car festival, the Pon Ter Vizha. Tamil was the language in use and, unlike the Goan Christians who were heavily under the influence of the Portuguese, the Paravas held on to their Tamil moorings. Susan Bayly points out that flags and banners with emblems of Vishnu, Shiva, and Murugan are on display, and the Golden Car stops at the houses of the patrons, much like the Hindu car festivals which also honours donors and patrons.

The fact that the position of a jati talaivan exists is an implicit recognition of a strong community and caste identity, carried over from times when many such communities were Hindus for centuries before they became Christian. The problematic issue of caste as it has existed in Hindu society, its oppressive, pervasive presence expressed through discriminatory practices and often with violence, had driven many communities to convert, especially among the Dalit population. Unfortunately, certain levels of caste discrimination also permeated into many Christian communities in Tamil Nadu. Thol Thirumavalavan, Member of Parliament and leader of the Viduthalai Chiruthaikal Katchi, has pointed out that Christianity in India has become 'flexible' to the caste system. While it is not within the scope of this work to engage with the complex and significant issue of caste in Tamilakam, it must be mentioned that those who turned to Christianity did not always enjoy the same privileges of upper-caste Christians such as the Reddiars and Nadars, and discrimination has not always been successfully staved off.

Journalist D. Suresh Kumar, who has studied this phenomenon, says that voices against such discrimination are growing both within the church and outside. He points out that even several decades ago a book like writer Bama's *Karukku* (1992), was 'a searing indictment of caste-based oppression in the Church and its institutions (that) exposed the hypocrisy of the Church which had come to be dominated by the upper castes.' Likewise, Father Mark Stephen's novel *Suvargal* depicted the need to bring down walls in cemeteries that divided the tombs of Dalits and upper-caste Christians. His other work *Yathirai* highlighted the fact that Dalits were consistently denied the right to participate in church organizations and festivals. Suresh Kumar points out that the Hindus who converted to Christianity 'refused to shed their caste identity, so today there are Christian Nadars, Christian Reddiars, Christian Mudaliars and Christian Yadavas, and this privilege of the dominant caste over the Dalits within the church establishment has led to tension'. An example of this was when the Arokia Matha Church in Thachur village in Kanchipuram, which had been built over 175 years ago, had to be closed for ten years in the late 1990s following a dispute between the Reddiars and the Dalits over the burial of two Dalits in the church cemetery which the Reddiars objected to. Clashes broke out and a heavy deployment of the police was called in. However, there is a constant and continuing effort to reform and eradicate caste-oriented practice through public hearings and other interventions from within the Christian community.

Robert Hardgrave's seminal book, *The Nadars of Tamil Nadu* (2006), highlights in detail the position of the Christian Nadar community in the south Indian hinterland, the caste discrimination that drove them to embrace Christianity, and their quick upward mobility as landowners and traders. The name Nadar also stood for 'those who ruled the land' and as they were also called Shanar earlier, that name was dropped in favour of Nadar. Overcoming visual caste recognition by abandoning the societal rule that Nadar women among other castes could not cover their breasts, a practice that existed in the Travancore area, the women braved riots and opposition from other Shudra communities and were aided by a proclamation from Queen Victoria who supported the right of groups to opt for their own lifestyle. The community consciousness of this group grew and while religious affiliations were different, both Hindu and Christian Nadars continued to view each other as brethren and followed similar social customs.

Other groups such as the Vellalas, Pillais, Mudaliars, Maravas, and Kallars and some Brahmin communities also steadily took to Christianity from the seventeenth century onwards. A Brahmin-Catholic family we encountered in a street in Trichy spoke in antiquated Brahmin Tamil and explained that they follow Hindu customs while adhering to the Catholic Christian faith. The small street, tucked away behind one of Trichy's main roads, was colloquially known as Agraharam street and had always been home to the generations of Brahmin Christian families who live here.

Another missionary whose impact was profound like that of St. Francis Xavier was John de Britto, a Portuguese Jesuit who came to South India to the Madurai mission in 1673. He called himself Arul Anandar and performed mass conversions among the Maravar community. As he venerated St. Francis Xavier, the method of teaching that he followed was modelled on the approach of St. Francis. Susan Bayly says that de Britto 'presided over dramatic mass baptism ceremonies…including men of rank and power in the Marava chiefdoms. There were conversions within the household of the Sethupathi ruler of Ramnad; the commander of the Ramnad army became a Christian, and in 1692 the Sethupathi's kinsman Tadiya Tevar, Polygar of the Siruvalli domain, also declared himself a convert.' De Britto tried to Indianize the Madurai Mission and free it from Portuguese domination, and much like his predecessor de Nobili, he too adopted saffron or yellow robes and turned vegan. He taught Christian doctrine in a gentle and persuasive way. When de Britto exhorted the Maravar prince Tadiya Tevar to send away his multiple wives, one of them complained to the Sethupathi king of Ramnad. The king, already tired of the catechists, began to persecute the Christians. De Britto was sentenced to execution. The missionary is said to have willingly offered his neck to the executioner. The sand dune at Orur, where the execution took place, is said to have turned red with his blood; a shrine was constructed there which has become a hallowed pilgrimage point and a place of prayer and miracles for millions of the faithful.

A little after John de Britto, we have the appearance of Constanzo Beschi, a remarkable Christian polyglot, missionary, and visionary whose intellectual capabilities were immense. Beschi was an Italian who came via the Portuguese court to the Madurai Mission in 1711. Like de Nobili before him, Beschi adopted the garb of a Hindu sanyasi, and totally Tamilized himself and his approach to teaching Christianity. He learnt Tamil, Telugu, and Sanskrit and compiled the first Tamil lexicon, a Tamil-Latin dictionary; he also translated important Hindu devotional works including the *Thevaram, Tirukkural, Nannul,* and *Thirupughazh.* Beschi was responsible for introducing the dot in Tamil consonants.

His extraordinary composition the *Thembavani* has 3,615 stanzas and an unusual subject—the life and work of St. Joseph of Nazareth. Beschi was fearless and up to all the challenges thrown at him by the ruling dispensation of many rajas of the region. Known as Viramamunivar and Dhairyanathar, the courageous one, he stood up for his convictions despite frequent persecution. And until the end of his days, he held on to his cultural beliefs and a Tamil identity.

Two other missionaries belonging to the Anglican Church, G. U. Pope (who came to be known as Tamil Thatha or grandfather of Tamil) and Robert Caldwell (a Scot who came to work in India for the London Missionary society in the early nineteenth century) furthered the cementing of Christianity and Tamil. The Reverend Pope was ordained in the Church of England and started learning Tamil even as a teenager, joining the Anglican mission at the age of fourteen. His translation of the *Tirukkural* was called the *Sacred Kural*. It is Pope's translation that apparently drew Mahatma Gandhi to the *Kural*. Reverend Pope's translation of the *Tiruvacakam* was also highly acclaimed. After over forty years in Sawyerpuram, Tuticorin district, and later in Thanjavur, Pope left his beloved Tamil Nadu to teach at Balliol College in Oxford. Much revered by Tamils to this day, Pope's statue, like those of some other Tamil stalwarts, stands on Chennai's Marina Beach. One of his last requests was for his tomb to be inscribed with 'A Student of Tamil'. In a copy of his last sermon which he delivered at Balliol, he wrote a simple foreword in his own hand. 'In the heart of this my last sermon lie truths which harmonize with all that is best in *Tiruvacakam* and Siva gnanam. I am very old. May the Father bless you and yours.'

Like others before him, Robert Caldwell, who joined the Madras mission in 1838, saw the importance of learning Tamil in his proselytising efforts. He soon acquired great proficiency in the language and his in-depth study resulted in his voluminous work *A Comparative Grammar of the Dravidian or the South Indian Languages* (1856), where he set up a clear divide between the Aryanized language of the Brahmins and the language of other communities and castes in the Tamil Nadu. Caldwell travelled extensively in Tirunelveli district examining excavations, studying palm leaf manuscripts, reading the Sangam poems, examining coins and records which resulted in his *A Political and General History of the District of Tinnevelly* in 1881, which was published by the Madras government. In terms of his evangelism, he managed to convert many underprivileged castes but was most known for his work on the language and on the history of Tirunelveli district. He is credited with giving a stimulus to the growing Dravidian movement and the non-Brahmin movement. According to social scientist M. S. S. Pandian, 'His contribution to both Christianity in South India and to the cultural awakening of the region is unmatched in the last two hundred years.' However, there are those who have criticized Bishop Caldwell as being paternalistic and divisive and somewhat flawed in his research of the region although admittedly his sociological insights were important and revealing.

The Catholic church was the first to take root in India. Protestantism, which came later, first appeared in South India with the German Lutheran missionaries. Frederick IV, the king of Denmark, sent two missionaries in 1706, Bartholomaus Ziegenbalg and Henry Pluetschau, to the Tranquebar trading station which was in Danish hands. As soon as Ziegenbalg arrived in the Tamil country, he assiduously began to learn Tamil, and invited a local Tamil pandit to teach him. He would sit by school children as they learned the language and draw letters repeatedly on the beach sand. He mastered Tamil within three months of his arrival and with so much proficiency that he soon translated the New Testament and published it in 1715 in a printing press that he set up in Tranquebar.

Ziegenbalg had requested the Danish court to create Tamil fonts from the drawings of the script and letters that he sent them. He also published Hindu religious texts in German, translated Christian texts into Tamil, and worked on grammars and dictionaries to facilitate cultural understanding. Of course, Ziegenbalg's time in Tranquebar was not without challenges and he was cast into jail for several months at one point for converting locals to Christianity. He also faced a lot of hostility from the Catholics. He died young at the age of thirty-six in Tranquebar having always suffered ill health, leaving behind a remarkable legacy of scholarship and understanding.

Ziegenbalg was followed to India by Johann Fabricius and other missionaries like C. F. Schwartz who came to Tranquebar in 1750. Schwartz, like others before him, was a linguist who very quickly learned Tamil and Telugu as well as Arabic and Persian, which facilitated his engagement with the nawab of Arcot. He became great friends with the Maratha ruler Tulaji in Thanjavur. He came to be known as the Royal Priest of Thanjavur and helped with multiple administrative matters from diplomacy to alleviating food shortage in the kingdom. Schwartz was even trusted by the enemies of Tulaji such as Hyder Ali of Mysore, as he was known for his honesty and integrity. In the middle of all his commitments, he continued with his evangelical work and was held in high esteem in the region.

The notion of honesty and personal integrity was inextricably linked with many of these missionaries. William Carey, whose work was largely in Calcutta and Serampore, was another outstanding missionary who established the Baptist church in India.

With the arrival and establishment of the British East India Company, new rules were framed for missionaries forbidding explicit conversions. The British sensed that this could impact their trade goals and although they brought in 1,600 chaplains on their trade ships, these were primarily for the British seamen on their long voyage to India and for the English community in Madras within the precincts of Fort St. George. The beautiful St. Mary's Church in the Fort is the oldest Anglican church in not just the city of Madras but possibly the first Protestant church built east of the Mediterranean. It was built in 1680 and is a fine example of early colonial architecture. Elihu Yale and Robert Clive were both married there.

The Church of South India, as early as in 1947, brought the plethora of Protestant churches from Lutheran and Methodist to Anglican under one umbrella. Like the Catholic Church, it too has been responsible for setting up schools and colleges of a high standard and great repute across Tamil Nadu. Many of these institutions continue to be supported by the Church yet run by trusts.

Mention must be made of the beautiful church architecture of South India. These reflect the influence of the Portuguese, Dutch, and British as they were built in various periods of European colonization. The style of building could be baroque or Gothic with towering spires and beautiful stained glass windows. Churches like the renowned Velankanni Church in Nagapattinam which draws pilgrims of diverse faith from across India and the world are imposing in their architecture. The church of Our Lady of Snows with the stunning wooden statue of Mary in Tuticorin is another magnificent example of Christian art and architecture in Tamil Nadu.

It is estimated that half the country's Christians live in South India. Around 37 per cent of Christians in India identify as Catholic and the rest belong to other denominations. From mystics to feminists, practising Christians in India have explored multiple ways of worship and for living by their creed.

Chapter 25

From Company to Empire

It was not the British Government that seized India, but a private company run by an unstable sociopath.

William Dalrymple, historian

SEVERAL DUTCH, GERMAN, ENGLISH, AND FRENCH PAINTINGS OF THE eighteenth and nineteenth centuries in the grand houses and palaces of European kings and nobility would usually include a dark-haired boy in the corner of a grouping of people of the household. These were enslaved children, mostly from Africa and many from India, who were taken away in trading ships from their homes to serve in bondage at the great European households. These little figures were dressed in keeping with other figures in the portrait, but the giveaway would be the silver cuffs or collars with padlocks around their necks indicating slavery and servitude. The fact that the acquisition, use, and display of children in wealthy households was more common than assumed is an indication that in pursuit of the wealth of the colonies there were no limits to what the colonizers considered commodities.

Perhaps the most symbolic of these is the portrait of Elihu Yale by an unknown artist, now in the Yale Center for British Art in New Haven, Connecticut. In this eighteenth-century painting, Yale is seen with William Cavendish, Duke of Devonshire, his son James, and a lawyer called Tunstal. There is an enslaved child in the picture, obviously serving them; in an ironical twist, that even the painter was not likely to be aware of, there are young white children playing in the background, their lives no doubt very different from that of the child who was serving inside. Yale, once governor of the East India Company at Fort St. George, acquired a massive fortune while in India mostly from trading in diamonds. As the founder-benefactor of Yale University, he donated what would amount to about £200,000 by today's standards to the institution which was named after him. Recently, Yale University apologized formally for the links of its early donors to the slave trade, especially Elihu Yale, who had until then been seen largely as a philanthropist, until it was discovered that he had also been a slave trader. The historian Joseph Yannielli, who studied at Yale and teaches at Aston University in the UK, examined the archives at Fort St. George and says Elihu Yale had an enormous capacity to make money as 'he was in charge of directing the Indian Ocean slave trade. In the 1680s a devastating famine (in Southern India) led to a labour surplus and Yale and other company officials took advantage of it, buying hundreds of slaves and shipping them to the English colony on Saint Helena'. David Blight, the Yale historian, says, '…on the Indian subcontinent, the trade in human beings along its coasts as well as inland…was very old. (And Yale) oversaw many sales, adjudications, and accountings of enslaved people for the East India Company.' As in the case of Elihu Yale, many company agents and officials of the East India Company profited hugely from the trade in slaves (which began as early as 1684) as well as the trade in commodities—spices, cotton, silk, indigo dye, saltpetre, sugar, spices, tea, and later opium as well. By the mid-1700s and 1800s, the British East India Company accounted for about half the world's trade.

Before we look at the impact of the East India Company and its later transformation, it is relevant to recall that in an earlier chapter, we talked about the foundations of the British empire. These were made during their wins in the Carnatic Wars when the English with much foresight sided with the Wallajah nawabs and defeated Chanda Sahib of the Carnatic sultanate who ruled at the behest of the Mughals. Post the steady decline of the Mughal empire, all their allies and vassals either created their own kingdoms or were conquered by other rulers. The Marathas, for instance, brought much of western India under their influence. There were other rulers like the Hyderabad nizams who also assumed control of their territories. In time, many of these fell into British hands with their rulers either defeated or rendered insignificant.

After some critical battles were fought, such as at Trichy between the British and their allies and the French and their allies between 1751 and 1755, and the Battle of Plassey in 1757 with Robert Clive of the East India Company defeating the nawab of Bengal, the stage was firmly set for British control across much of India and all the way up to Burma. The Mysore Wars brought the British in direct conflict with Hyder Ali and his son, Tipu Sultan, which impacted the Tamil country with terrible devastation in terms of lost lives, lost agricultural land, and lost livelihoods. Similarly, the Thanjavur kingdom was acquired by the British after the ruler Tulaji died without an heir. Over time, through various treaties that involved the payment of large sums of money to the English for the kingdom's defence, the talented young ruler Serfoji was reduced to a ruler in name only.

As Rajayyan points out, during the time of famine in the Thanjavur area, Serfoji did try to assist the ryots, the small farmers or cultivators, who were struggling to survive. However, Serfoji had little real power and was helpless because of his arrangement with the East India Company and was restricted by various factors such as the outbreak of war, by the rules of the Madras Council (run by the Company) and by the very fact that it was a protectorate. During the last decade of the eighteenth century, Serfoji could not do much to help his subjects, the farmers and tillers who were starving, although he tried to temporarily suspend the collection of duties. Ultimately, by both strategy and cunning, the British created a situation by which Serfoji himself became convinced at the futility of holding on to administrative power. A settlement was drawn up, in 1799, curiously titled as 'Treaty for Cementing the Friendship and Alliance between the Company and the Rajah of Tanjore on a permanent foundation'.

In time, the English dominance across Tamil Nadu over the other European powers became clear. The French, who were the last to buckle, were finally defeated after the three Carnatic Wars. Large swathes of Tamilakam soon came under the British East India Company. Coimbatore, Salem, Dharmapuri, and Satyamangalam, known together as Kongu Nadu, were absorbed by the British as they passed hands from the Nayaks of Madurai to the Wodeyars of Mysore and then fell into the hands of Hyder Ali and later his son, Tipu Sultan. Tipu fought the British until his death. He and Hyder Ali courageously fought off the Company's control in Mysore to the best of their ability. Tipu banned the export of sandalwood, pepper, and cardamom from the Malabar coast infuriating the British. Soon after, a detachment of the British led by a Colonel Brown took all of Tipu's forts in Tamil Nadu, in places like Erode and Avarakurichi. Much of Kongu Nadu was held by Mysore because of these wars. Kongu Nadu came under British control. Tipu was killed in battle in Seringapatam in 1799, defending his capital, and the Wodeyars of Mysore were asked to administer the territory as Company subsidiaries. The poignant portrait of Tipu Sultan's sons given as hostages to the British exemplifies the arrogant and triumphalist nature of Company politics in the region. While many places in Tamil Nadu continued to be nominally called trading centres, these places were under British control. Chinglepet, a jagir, was acquired from the nawab of Arcot in return for the services rendered to him for protection from enemies like Chanda Sahib. The nawabs of Arcot too gradually declined and, in 1801, the British stripped the Arcot ruler Nawab Azim-ud-Daula of his powers alleging that his predecessor had secretly aided Tipu, the enemy of the British, during the Anglo-Mysore wars, and that the nawab himself was hostile to the British, regularly violating treaties that had been made between them. The nawab was soon rendered ineffective.

Because of the constant Anglo-French rivalry, an army of local as well as English soldiers was built up in all the presidencies. Their superior weaponry such as guns and cannons as well as training, enabled the British to gain a great deal of control over the land after the defeat of numerous local rulers and sending off the French. After the Battle of Plassey in 1757, the Company's territorial gains as well as wealth accumulation was rapid and astonishing. Robert Clive who was sent from Madras to Bengal won the battle for the Company through treachery and betrayal. Siraj-ud-Daula, the nawab of Bengal, was easily defeated because Mir Jafar, his commander, was bribed by Clive. Bengal was utterly ravaged by the Company and 250 million pounds by current estimate went into the Company's treasury. Clive amassed a huge personal fortune, valued at that time of £234,000, making him 'the richest self-made man' of his day. Clive was given a jagir by the Mughals and a title as well. He obtained exemption from internal duties for the Company as well as for private trade by the Company's members. The corruption unleashed by Clive's example was unprecedented; Company men, particularly those who returned to England from India and who had siphoned off great wealth, began acting like nawabs themselves. They were known as nabobs and lived luxurious lives and like Clive bought political influence and parliamentary seats in Britain, which began to irk those around them, in particular the British parliamentarians who were slowly turning against these Company men. When Clive was summoned before the British Parliament, he famously declared: 'Consider the situation in which the victory at Plassey had placed me!…an opulent city lay at my mercy; its richest bankers bid against each other for my smiles. I walked through vaults which were thrown open to me alone piled on either hand with gold and jewels! Mr. Chairman, at this moment I stand astonished at my moderation'. The British Parliament, however, remained suspicious of Clive. With his reputation lost and his military successes forgotten, Clive committed suicide in 1774.

Meanwhile, in 1765, the young Mughal emperor Shah Alam was forced to surrender the right to collect taxes to Company agents, and the Company became the diwan of Bengal. In an excoriating article in *The Guardian* in 2015, the historian William Dalrymple wrote: 'It was at this moment that the East India Company ceased to be a conventional corporation trading in silk and spices and became something much more unusual. Within a few years,

250 company clerks backed by the military force of 20,000 locally recruited Indian soldiers had become the effective rulers of Bengal. An international corporation was transforming itself into an aggressive colonial power.'

Further distress emanated from Company's policies and taxation measures. The tragic Bengal famine which affected 30 million people (and in which about 10 million people died) occurred after Bengal was taken over by the Company and there were little efforts at mitigation. In fact, despite the obvious distress and deaths, there was no relief from taxation from the Company's administrators. This resulted in large-scale migration from Bengal to other provinces. In Madras, the ryotwari system whereby the cultivator was the taxpayer of the land and its proprietor, which the British initially accepted, was put in place by Thomas Munro in 1820 as governor, but was subsequently destroyed by new taxation rules imposed by the Company and later the Crown. The practice of small landowners being able to sell, lease, or mortgage their lands collapsed as the Company declared that all land had to be taxed whether tilled or not and ruthlessly collected taxes which impoverished the cultivators. A zamindari system with the effort to bring more small cultivators under the umbrella of one landlord was then put in place but that too had its problems and affected small farmers and cultivators. The policy of commercialization of agriculture also begun by the Company and later followed up by the Crown meant that cotton, jute, tea (wherever it could be grown), sugar cane, and tobacco which would have better market value began to be produced instead of food crops that could sustain households and local markets thus strengthening the village economy. But as commercial crops were linked to prices levied by the exporter, many found themselves in further penury. Those who sought help from money lenders also got the rough end of the stick as the British enacted a law allowing money lenders to seize land when there was a payment default. Soon the number of landless labourers grew.

In his analysis of the impact of the Company and British economic policies in the Madras Presidency, K. A. Manikumar, former vice chancellor, Swami Vivekananda University at Sagar in Madhya Pradesh, writes that the money 'looted and carried from India helped to accomplish the Industrial Revolution in England. In India, instead of protecting and encouraging the industries, the East India Company crushed every industry which came into conflict with British industry.' He quotes H. H. Wilson who said, in 1813, that British goods were forced upon India without paying any duty and the manufacturer employed the 'arm of political injustice to keep down and ultimately strangle the competitor with whom he could not have competed in equal terms.'

Artisans and weavers also suffered greatly due to the Company's unfair practices. We are also aware that the imperialist practices of the Company and later the Crown completely brought an end to India's prime position as the world leader in the production of cotton textiles. For instance, the Madras Presidency was forced to export raw material in return for finished goods and the value of these imports rose from ₹11.9 million in 1814 to ₹124 million in 1854–55. The import duty into England of flowered muslins and calicoes, which had to be borne by the producers in India, rose steadily—from 21 per cent in 1800 to 85 per cent in 1813.

On the sustainability of agricultural practices and the critical importance of water resources, Manikumar points out that irrigation tanks were left in great disrepair. In Chinglepet and Tirunelveli, tanks silted up to the point where water could not even flow into them. The collectors, he argues, deliberately refused to spend money on repairing and reviving these age-old water-preserving structures. However, there were exceptions—Arthur Cotton of the Madras Engineering Service in the nineteenth century said it was more important to deal with the problem of irrigation before constructing railways and managed to take concrete steps to construct the upper Kollidam dam despite stiff opposition.

The catalogue of exploitative and repressive actions taken by the East India Company and the complete ruin wrought on India's economy is long and complex. The drain on national wealth, resources, and capabilities greatly affected the lives and livelihood of people across the country. From the nineteenth century onwards, an aggressive policy of expansion of territories was followed by the Company. A new policy of 'paramountcy' was initiated by which the Company's authority was deemed superior to that of any Indian state. What followed was relentless annexation, and extortion of more resources and wealth from the local powers.

The EIC had come under scrutiny by the British Parliament frequently. Its excesses were noted and condemned, including of people like Warren Hastings, the first Governor General of the Bengal Presidency charged initially to bring the Company's corrupt practices under control; ironically, he was called before Parliament for impeachment for corruption himself, although he was later acquitted. Over the early decades of the nineteenth century the British government had had enough from the Company and new charters brought more and more of the Company's jurisdiction and activity under government control. After the Revolt of 1857, the majority sentiment in England was that India was too big a prize to be left in the hands of a private company. An article in the *Illustrated London News* in July 1857 said '...Our house in India is on fire. We are not insured. To lose that house would be to lose power, prestige and character...whether it is desirable that we win India by the sword is no longer a question. Having won it, we must keep it.' The British government took full possession of the territories of the East India Company by the Government of India Act on 2 August 1858. The British Raj had formally begun in India.

BOOK V
The Age of Freedom

Chapter 26

Revolt, Rebellion, and the Road to Freedom

By 1801 the Company had acquired the sovereign rights to all 'little kingdoms'...the vanquished south Indian dynasties and their descendants remained unreconciled and conspired against the Company government.

K. A. Manikumar, historian

THE PALMYRA TREES THAT SURROUNDED THE FORT WERE NOT VERY tall. Tall enough though to hang a man from the fronds. It seemed as if they were chosen with deliberate intent, as a warning, a grotesque ornament of war. From every palm hung bodies, heads slumped forward—men and women and even a couple of children. This was the East India Company's reign of terror inflicted on locals who dared to protest, rebel, and sometimes even attack the British forces and the Company that completely controlled them. The death by hanging of the Marudu brothers, their entire family, and the so called 'rebels' who assisted them, from the palmyra trees surrounding the fort of Thirupputhur was one of the most gruesome mass executions carried out by the East India Company. By the late eighteenth and early years of the nineteenth century, most of Tamil Nadu had come under the sway of the Company, a ruthless corporation which had exploitative politics and profits as its goal. In fact, the use of the word 'rebel' is unjustified as these were people who were fighting for the rights of their communities and for themselves and protesting against an arbitrary authority.

In an earlier chapter, we read the tragic tale of the poligar Veerapandia Kattabomman. Here, we will look at his rebellion and its aftermath in greater detail. Kattabomman was killed because of a refusal to pay unfair taxes, a source of constant friction between him and the British. As the tax arrears to the Company had built up (the nawab of Arcot having surrendered this right to the British), the British took on the rebellious Kattabomman. By the weight of unjust laws and monetary demands many of the local rulers either caved and agreed to the Company's demands or ended up dead. In the case of Kattabomman the Company's directors blatantly decided 'that all subordinate military establishments should be annihilated within the limits now subject to our dominion'. John Bannerman the commander of the East India Company led the British forces against Kattabomman under instructions from Governor General Wellesley. '...the rebellious conduct of Catabomanaig (Kattabomman Nayak), Poligar of Pandalamcourchy (Panchalankurichi) having rendered it necessary to equip a military force for the purpose of suppressing the commotions excited by him, the Right Honourable Governor General has resolved to avail himself of this opportunity, to carry into effect the orders of the Honourable Court of Directors for disarming the whole of the Southern Poligars and for reducing those irregular chieftains to the authority of the Civil Government'. The aim, it was obvious, was to get rid of the poligar system altogether.

Before Bannerman led his forces against Kattabomman, there was ostensibly a move to compromise after the poligar paid some of the arrears. As mentioned earlier, the Collector of Ramnad, Colin Jackson, had treated Kattabomman with appalling arrogance and rudeness during their earlier attempts at talks to resolve the arrears issue. Kattabomman actually wrote to Edward Clive, the governor of Madras, saying, 'I prepared money for the payment of the *kist* and when I intended to set out against my health, Mr. Jackson came to Tirukuttalam which place I reached with the money in full for the payment of the Company's *kist*'.

Soon, however, Kattabomman sensed the swelling mood of rebellion against these outsiders and joined a group called the South India Confederacy, a group of rebels against the British organized by Marudu Pandyan of Sivagangai and another poligar, the son of the poligar of Sivagiri, to take up against the British forces. Meanwhile, Major Bannerman, on orders from Lord Wellesley, took command of an expedition to take on the rebels. Ultimatums given by the British to the rebels were ignored by Kattabomman in Panchalankurichi and they decided to bring him down. Unfortunately, his mud fort had a breach, a crucial point of weakness that the enemy came to know of from Ramalinga Mudaliar who had been sent as a last-minute emissary to Kattabomman. Records indicate that at that point Kattabomman did not actually expect an attack. A heavy cannonade assaulted the vulnerable part of the fort and, despite the storming by the British troops, they were met with courageous and surprising resistance by the poligar's troops led by Kumaraswamy Nayak (also known as Oomathurai), the brother of Kattabomman.

Bannerman records in a letter to the Madras government, 'The attempt was persevered in so long as there was a shadow of success and never was European energy more gallantly displayed than by the officers on this unfortunate occasion.' Bannerman asked for reinforcements and after a pitched battle, the fort was breached, many were killed, and Kattabomman and his brother escaped to join the Marudu brothers' camp while their vakeel Sivasubramania Pillai was taken prisoner along with numerous others. But the raja of Tondaiman's men captured Kattabomman near Sivagangai and handed him over to the British. The raja wrote to Stephen Lushington, the collector, saying, 'on every side in the mountains I had placed my people to find out the hiding place of Kattabomman. He, Oomathurai, his two brothers-in-law and three others were surrounded at Kalapore, on the borders of Sivagangai and caught. When Kattabomman was seized he wished to have slain himself but my people having bound his hands, kept him in confinement.'

Bannerman brought the rebels to a farce of a trial after which Sivasubramania Pillai and several others were executed. To teach the people a lesson, Pillai's body was paraded through the streets of Panchalankurichi, and his severed head exhibited on one of the bastions of the fort. At his trial, Kattabomman proudly accepted all the charges of defiance and rebellion against the government after which he was sentenced to death. Bannerman himself seems to have been quite awestruck by the manner in which Kattabomman met his death. He writes, 'It may not be amiss here to observe that the manner and behaviour of the Poligar during the whole time of his being before those who were assembled yesterday at the examination which took place were undaunted and supercilious. He frequently eyed the Etiapore (Ettayapuram) Poligar, who had been so active in attempting to secure his person, and the Poligar of Sivagiri with an appearance of indignant scorn, and when he went out to be executed, he walked with a firm and daring air and cast looks of sullen contempt on the Poligars to his right and left, as he passed. It was reported to me that [on] his way to the place of execution he expressed some anxiety for his dumb brother (Oomathurai) alone; and said, when he reached the foot of the tree on which he was hanged, that he then regretted having left his fort on the defence of which it would have been better for him to have died.' He was put to death on 17 October 1799.

The tragedy of Kattabomman's rebellion and death consolidated Company rule across the region. Governor Edward Clive established direct Company rule and declared that the poligar system was disbanded, and the English seized everything including forts, arms, and ammunition. More than a hundred years later, an ICS officer, H. R. Pate, found a record of the aftermath of Kattabomman's death in the *Tinnevelly Gazetteer*. Pate says, 'The Panchalankurichi fort was razed to the ground; the site was ploughed over and sown with castor seed and the name of the place was also expunged from all the registers of the district.' Oomathurai was not put to death, although he was captured. He managed to escape and mount a second rebellion, as we will see later.

The Marudu brothers and their families and supporters who were horrifically put to death were even earlier the fulcrum of rebel activity. The idea for the loose confederacy of rebel leaders came from the Marudu Pandyas, brothers Periya Marudu and Chinna Marudu, who were the de facto rulers of the Sivagangai region. Growing up in the last quarter of the eighteenth century, the two brothers had close familial ties to the local king, Muthuvaduganatha Thevar. This ruler was attacked by the forces of the nawab of Arcot who had overlordship of the region under the aegis of the East India Company. With the king killed, one of his wives, Rani Velu Nachiyar, fled with the two young men and many others to neighbouring Virupakshi in Dindigul district which was ruled by Gopal Nayak who gave them sanctuary. In seven years, the brothers learned warfare and military tactics. Periya Marudu, also called Vella Marudu, was an imposing figure, large in stature and strong. He could apparently bend a silver Arcot rupee with his bare hands. Given to hunting and shooting, he was a great sportsman. Chinna Marudu was more the administrator and though naturally good with affairs of state, both brothers were driven to war by the assault from the Company's forces. The Marudu brothers supposedly invented the *valari*, a version of the boomerang which they later used in war to good effect. Ultimately, along with the queen, they returned to Sivagangai and retook the area from the nawab of Arcot. Rani Velu Nachiyar, known locally as Veera Mangai, was perhaps the first Tamil princess to take up arms against the British. Skilled in martial arts, and a proficient horsewoman, she was also a scholar, fluent in Urdu, French, and English. She had great faith in the two brothers and entrusted them with the power to run the region in 1780. After her death in 1796, the brothers became the actual rulers, and they were soon part of a group of rebels against the English and began to spearhead the resistance against them.

Marudu Pandyan's skills were not just militaristic. Historian Rajayyan says that he was one of the greatest political thinkers of that time, and quickly analysed the reasons for the political defeats and ills of the region. He realized that one of the basic issues was the lack of unity among Indians and their frequent treachery and collaboration with the enemy for immediate, short-term political gain. Their often humiliating submission to white authority, without seeing the treachery that was part of British strategy, led Marudu

Pandyan to factor in these aspects as he planned his course. 'He attributed this tragedy in their character to a want of perspective and a vision in grasping the magnitude of the threat that they encountered. Therefore, he served a solemn warning to the people that if these suicidal trends continued, the whole of India would inevitably be reduced to British rule,' says Rajayyan. Marudu Pandyan's words proved prophetic.

At this time, along with the political humiliation and discontent, the economic situation was very grim. Agriculture was in a deplorable state, land rights were ignored, trade practices were corrupt and routinely flouted. Marudu Pandyan declared in Srirangam that it was appalling that people had to seek sustenance from rice water rather than rice itself. The British troops sprawling all over the region demanded a constant supply of grains, vegetables, cattle, and other goods. They seized whatever they fancied from villagers and peasants. Marudu Pandyan complained about this to a British officer, Colonel Agnew. A group of rebels organized by chiefs like Marudu Pandyan, Gopal Nayak, and several others from the Marathas to Dhoondaji Waug of Shimoga all came together and decided as a first step to liberate and capture Coimbatore in April of 1800. Veerapandia Kattabomman had been executed in 1799 but his brother Oomathurai was a part of these forces. Earlier, until his death, the valiant Tipu Sultan frequently sent his forces to assist in the fight against the British. The armies of ordinary people who were suffering under the oppressive and arbitrary rule of the British forces joined these groups of fighting men with whatever arms they had at their disposal. The chiefs had brought sufficient forces with them, but they were not a match for the Company men who had superior artillery, guns, and cannons at their command; at various places, the British forces crushed the rebel groups including those from the Kannada and Maratha regions who joined the Tamil leaders and their troops. The Coimbatore mission was thwarted by the English, but in February 1801, the rebel leaders who were held at the Fort of Palayamkottai were released by their supporters and the Marudu brothers joined these forces in Tirunelveli with 30,000 insurgents from the Marava, Nadar, Parava, and other communities.

The escape was planned and executed with a fine mix of originality and daring. Led by Marudu Pandyan and Gidivetti Nayak, many rebels dressed themselves as pilgrims to Tiruchendur Murugan temple to avoid suspicion as they travelled the roads. Upon reaching the Palayamkottai Fort, many of them disguised themselves as hawkers selling miscellaneous wares. Shevatiah of the Kattabomman clan quietly gained the confidence of the wife of the superintendent of the fort. He pleaded with her that the prisoners be allowed to perform religious ceremonies for their dead; the unsuspecting woman persuaded her husband the superintendent to give permission for conducting the ceremonies. Soon the hawkers turned attackers, snatching arms and ammunition from the sentinels and soldiers guarding the fort. The English commanders dining at that moment in Palayamkottai were taken unawares and by the time they could react, the prisoners who had been released fled into the forests nearby. This triumph for the rebel forces carried out without too much bloodshed captured the public imagination. Collector Lushington reported that the escape was made 'in consequence of a general confederacy and pre-concerted plan'. The execution of the plan, its design, and the suddenness of the attack took everyone by surprise.

In April 1789, at Kollangudi, the British forces were again defeated by Marudu's troops. The British military forces were apparently surprised at the resistance, and Colin Macaulay, the commanding officer of the British forces, issued a public warning to the people of exemplary punishment if they were found to be carrying arms or helping the rebels.

As in several parts of India from the late 1700s onwards, particularly through 1800 and 1801, a spate of incidents of resistance against Company rule occurred continuously in Tamil Nadu under leaders like the Marudu brothers, and several other local rulers and poligars who organized local people against them. Ordinary people from Ramnad, Tirunelveli, Dindigul, Srirangam, Tiruchi, Thanjavur, and other parts of the south marched in large numbers, in disparate armies, to join the rebels. There was an instance where the rebels fighting a fierce battle in Panchalankurichi (Oomathurai's own territory) witnessed many of their brave cohorts being killed. One young soldier whose mother went out to look for him and found him breathing faintly in the midst of the carnage was told by her dying son to save 'swamy' or their leader Oomathurai and not worry about him. The mother, realizing that her son was mortally wounded, at his insistence left him to find a badly wounded Oomathurai nearby. With the help of a few other women, she swiftly attended to him. They soon realized that enemy sepoys were drawing near, and letting out a shriek of lamentation, covered Oomathurai's face with a sheet and told the opposing forces that this was the body of a young man who had just died of smallpox. Panic stricken, the enemy soldiers fled without a backward glance and Oomathurai was saved for the time being.

In 1801, in Srirangam, Marudu Pandyan made an impassioned proclamation that exhorted all Indians to join the struggle. However sketchy the rebels' notions of troubles faced in other regions, it was clear that the firm view that an alien regime cannot control the progress and destiny of the people of this land was increasingly being recognized.

The British administration heard in mid-1801 of the rebel proclamation by Marudu Pandyan which appeared on the fort walls of Tiruchi and in the temple walls of Srirangam. It is an unusual document; Rajayyan calls it 'remarkable' as it displayed a great sense of nationalism and is a call to action against the foreigners. Parts of the proclamation are excerpted below:

> Whosoever sees this paper, Read it with Attention.
>
> To the castes, nations, Brahmins, Kshatriyas, Vysyas, Sudras and Musselmen (sic) that are in the island of Jamboo/in the Peninsula of Jambudweepa /this notice is given.
>
> His Highness the Nawab Mohammed Ali having foolishly given the Europeans place amongst you is become like a widow. The Europeans, violating their faith, have deceitfully made the Kingdom their own and considering the inhabitants as dogs, accordingly, exercise authority over them. There existing no unity amongst you the above castes, who, not being aware of the duplicity of these Europeans have not only inconsiderately calumniated each other, but have absolutely surrendered the Kingdom to them...
>
> ...It is therefore recommended that every man in his place and Palayam fly to arms and unite together in order to make even the name of the low [wretches] cease. Then all the poor and needy will get subsistence. But should thereby any who like dogs, desirous of an easy life, obey the commands of these low wretches, such should be karoo or cut off....Therefore you Brahmins, Kshatriyas, Vysyas, Sudras and Musselmen, all who wear whiskers whether civil of military, serving in field or elsewhere...and all capable of bearing arms, let them in the first place display their bravery...Wherever you find these low wretches destroy them and continue to do so until they are extirpated.. Whoever serves the low wretches will never enjoy eternal bliss after death...
>
> To all living in Srirangam ...Marudu Pandyan prostrates himself at their feet. The sovereigns made and kept forts, mud bastions, churches, and chapels. The great Rajahs and People by the injustices of the low wretches are now reduced to poverty. So great a people as you are, reduced to this state! Grant me your blessings!

An infuriated administration doubled its efforts to subdue the rebels. They also played off one ruler against another and managed to procure some allies from among the local rajas. In 1801, there were fierce battles across much of Tamil Nadu. People in multiple places—Ramnad, Madurai, Dindigul, and Thanjavur—flocked to join the rebels. The English were surprised by the levels of resistance and at times suffered severe defeats with the loss of many lives. The forests of Kalayarkovil soon became a stronghold for the fighters and the British Army led by Agnew found it difficult to tackle the insurgents.

As the year 1801 progressed, more military top brass from the British side were summoned to take charge of the offensives against the rebels. Agnew, Blackburne, and Macaulay were the British officers in command. The insurgents, tired, without food and water for long hours, and mostly moving on foot with their now depleted armaments were finally defeated in October 1801. The Military Despatches to England record the death by hanging of the Marudu brothers, their entire families, and cohorts in a most gruesome manner on 24 October 1801. Marudu Pandyan's head was severed from his body and taken to Kalayarkovil, and his body was buried at Tiruppathur. Oomathurai and Shevatiah were taken to Panchalankurichi and executed in November 1801. Other rebel leaders were banished in perpetuity from Tamil Nadu and sent to Penang by sea, handcuffed and under severe restraint. Many died during the long sea voyage.

Although some historians are of the view that these rebellions were largely localized, they did give significant momentum to a nascent movement of struggle and resistance to an oppressive alien power and led up to the larger movements that soon swept the entire country. Despite the ultimate defeat of the rebel forces, a sense of unity pervaded the struggle. Tamil society by and large was seized of the intrigues—the tragedies and the frequently dramatic situations of a people under attack was reflected in song and dance and poetry mostly of the folk variety, in the form of lullabies, songs of grief and mourning, as well as expressed through folk dances like kummi, all of which had an element of spontaneity. Dheeran Chinnamalai, a Palayakaran from the Kongu region who joined the forces against the British, was valorized by the public. Pulithevan, a leader of the Maravas, who was one of the earliest fighters in this motley group was also much adulated by the local people and his exploits were sung to children as lullabies assuring them that: 'there is nothing to fear while the great Pulithevan who killed a mighty tiger is there with his shining sword to protect him'.

Similarly, the heroism and valour of Kattabomman found its way into popular verse: in a paean of praise, Kattabomman's beauty and the mere glance of his eyes is enough to drive away the evil forces says the poet, calling him 'cousin' and claiming kinship. As Kattabomman's forces prepare for combat, his general Vellaiyan's wife beseeches him to not to go into battle that day as she had a bad dream that foretold his death: 'Pogadhe, pogadhe en kanava / polladha soppanam kandenaiya / pazhum kinaru iddiya kanden / namma maligai thottam azhiyakanden'—the grim foreboding, the end of all that they held dear came to her in a dream which came true. Unable to bear her grief when her husband dies, the legend goes that Vellaiammal committed sati which was quite prevalent until it was abolished by the British later. Another folk ballad some of us knew snatches of, from an old film, spoke of the audacity of the British, who asked a local man to plant cucumbers, thus introducing a vegetable that was unknown locally and to sell it for a price that he set. The verse goes on to berate the man, saying that the coins of the British are no match for our poor local currency and this man desiring that 'white' silver plays up to the white man to gain his favour.

The oral traditions did much to propagate a sense of patriotism but said more about the great valour of the heroic leaders who not only defied the foreigners but were willing to sacrifice their lives in defending their turf and their way of life. Although some of the lore and folk songs and dances were a response to the immediacy of the situation, many songs came into the realm of the popular some years after these events took place so obviously cannot be relied on for historical accuracy. Nevertheless, they served as good tools of communication—much like the war cry or kuravai adopted by the rebels or the betel leaf pierced with a nail called the killah sent from village to village as a silent summons to join the fight.

Although the year 1801 proved to be a disaster in terms of lives and territories lost to the British, the dissidents were never cowed down for long. The Vellore Revolt of 1806 was another key turning point which foreshadowed the Revolt of 1857. It was significant also in that its reverberations were felt across regions and all the way up to Hyderabad.

Vellore Fort served as a base for the military and was often used for specific operations, even from 1791, when Lord Cornwallis first used it for his attack on Bangalore. It has been described as a near perfect 'specimen of native masonry'. Built by the later Nayaks to fortify themselves from attacks by local warring leaders, it had ponds, a temple (later turned into an arsenal by the British), as well as a mosque and a large ditch full of alligators. After the fall of Tipu Sultan, his sons and family, including his wives and servants, were housed in the Vellore Fort. There were large gardens, barracks, and houses all occupied by the British garrison—the troops included not only the commanders but also soldiers and Indian infantrymen.

In 1805, Major Paul Bose decided that the turbans of the sepoys needed to be changed. The new turban designed was supposedly light and cheap and even tried out by a Muslim, a Hindu, and Rajput. It had a leather cockade that was found to be offensive, as animal skin offended the Indian sepoys. Further, a cross affixed to the turban was anathema to Hindu and Muslim sepoys who saw this as being forced on them, and against their religious beliefs. The new regulations also prohibited the use of vibhuti or sacred ash or any other caste marks.

> It is ordered by the regulations that a native soldier shall not mark his face to denote his caste or wear earrings when dressed in uniform; and it is further directed that at all parades and upon all duties, every soldier of the battalion shall be clean shaved on the chin. It is directed also that uniformity shall…be preserved, in regard to the quantity and shape of hair on the upper lip.

Many men stationed at the Vellore Fort in May 1806 refused to wear the new turbans holding that it was against their caste. There was an outbreak of protest from the sepoys who turned up without the new turbans. Those who obeyed the British officers, were jeered at by the rebelling sepoys. As the events cascaded in the ensuing months, it became clear that the turban and dress regulations were only a minor aspect of the rebellion. The main reason, according to historians like Rajayyan, was that the Vellore revolt signified that a far deeper frustration existed, and the endeavour was to revive the insurgency 'under a common banner and to restore the monarchs to their former status of dignity. Collaboration had been so widely concerted as to gain the support from different quarters.' Rajayyan says that apart from the inhabitants of Arcot, during the insurrection, aid came from as far away as the western regions, from as far north as Hyderabad and from parts of the Kannada region although there was no actual uprising in those places. Frustration and disaffection with Company rule that had destroyed much of the countryside saw this sudden spurt of concerted action.

K. A. Manikumar, the historian whose work on the Vellore revolt includes a great deal of material from local accounts as well as from the military records of the British, says that on 9 July 1806, outside guests had been permitted into the fort to attend the wedding celebrations of one of Tipu's daughters, Princess Noor-ul-Nissa, who was confined there. Manikumar says, 'the guests who were invited, thronging the main entrance gate, were full of excitement and bonhomie. This the British officers thought was owing to the prospect of seeing their confined royal relatives once again. Little did they realise that the wedding guests were, in reality, the rebel reinforcements in disguise.' Assistant Surgeon John Dean crossing the parade ground that night later wrote, 'The Mahal was lighted up and the sound of music gave every appearance of mirth and gaiety and I little dreamt that the hand I had so recently shaken, warm with friendship, would in a few short hours be cold as death near the spot where I then stood.' The officers that night did not suspect anything.

In the early morning hours of 10 July at around 2 a.m., a group of sepoys started firing at the European barracks and the officers' quarters. Hastily, the English soldiers were quickly deployed and the officers, shocked and surprised by the onslaught, commanded their men to shoot any sepoy that came out of the fort. Meanwhile, the sepoys and their commanders killed several of the English in their quarters. Colonel John Fancourt who was commandant at the garrison was woken by the sound of firing. His wife, Amelia Fancourt, wrote, '…I looked at my husband. I saw him pale as ashes… "go into your room Amelia" … (he said). I did so as I saw his mind was agitated… I heard him two minutes after, leaving the writing room and go out of the house.' Fancourt was shot just outside his front door and fell dead in his dressing gown. Commanding Officer McKerras was shot while he was exhorting the sepoys on the parade ground and his corpse was kicked and spat upon for haranguing the sepoys about the new turbans. Lieutenant John Eley of the 69th Regiment was killed in the presence of his wife after a chase around a guardroom. Several other British officers were dragged out of their quarters and killed. The British called this 'the Vellore Massacre'—nearly two dozen senior British officers were killed that fateful night. One estimate says that 113 Europeans were killed by the insurgents. Apparently, active communication was kept up between the palace inhabitants and the sepoys outside. Tipu's flag was brought outside and hoisted on the flagstaff in front of a wildly cheering crowd that had assembled in the courtyard. Gold pagodas (the currency of the Company) to the amount of 2,908,733.39 were plundered from the cash chest according to the Military Department Despatches sent to London.

According to accounts, the raging battle in Vellore Fort was ended by Colonel Gillespie in about fifteen minutes. On 13 July, the insurgents were subdued, martial law was declared, and Gillespie along with fellow officers

George Harcourt and Captain Wilson put an end to the siege. The sepoys lost 350 men and more than 500 were caught and imprisoned. Reverberations of this revolt were felt in places like Hyderabad, Wallajahbad, Bangalore, Palayamkottai, and Bellary. Rumours were rife about forced conversions to Christianity and other Company-enforced regulations. Messages went back and forth about how to take down the English soldiers in stealth attacks. Nothing much came of it all, although Vellore demonstrated the success of a coordinated strategy of communication, planning, and military action. The British came down with a heavy hand on the local population after this south Indian rebellion. Nevertheless, it took a decade for them to stifle small uprisings across Tamil Nadu. The disaffection was widespread, and there were also protests from regions like South Arcot against the imposition and collection of taxes from various types of landholdings.

Beyond the struggles of the poor and dispossessed, frequent attacks on officials, especially tax collectors, and an intellectual ferment against Company oppression, were all features of these times. In Madras, bodies like the Madras Native Association, the Madras Hindu Debating Society, and a few others sent petitions to the British Parliament as early as in 1852 as the British government was considering the question of control and renewal of the East India Company's Charter. Repeated petitions and representations made after large public meetings in Madras requested relief from the 'unchecked misrule and oppression' of the Company's administration. They urged a total takeover by the government in London thus protecting India from Company excesses and exploitation and making it 'constitutionally responsible to the people of the country'. However, this happened only the year after the Revolt of 1857, when Britain firmly established total administrative control in India, taking over from the East India Company.

Chapter 27

A Society in Flux

People ate poisonous roots and leaves, dying parents abandoned dying children, many little ones were sold. In some cases, cholera and malaria joined famine and bodies accumulated everywhere....

Rajmohan Gandhi, historian

IT WAS THE WORST OF TIMES; A SEASON OF DARKNESS WHEN THE INDIANS who raised the flag of protest and rebellion in Meerut in 1857 were ruthlessly quelled after large-scale violence that spread across much of North India. The disaffection and the fighting that followed the Meerut uprising extended to other parts of Awadh and later to Delhi and other regions in India including Punjab, Bengal, and as far away as Tripura. The reasons for the revolt were many although the immediate trigger was use of the new Enfield rifle with a cartridge that was coated with lard (from pigs) and tallow enclose with brackets, which was strongly objected to by both Muslim and Hindu sepoys. Spearheaded by a sepoy called Mangal Pandey, this wave of unrest had other causes too. The Doctrine of Lapse, devised by Lord Dalhousie, effectively blocked succession by adoption in the princely states and ensured the annexation of such kingdoms by the British. Rani Laxmibai of Jhansi was one of the principal leaders of the rebellion, having lost her kingdom to the British on account of this policy. The loss of faith in an impartial justice system which clearly favoured the British, the increased burdens of taxation brought about by changes in laws were among other underlying causes. The prejudiced treatment of the sepoys serving in the army added to the discontent.

In the Madras Presidency, although the British were nervous and feared trouble, there was no immediate flowering of rebellion, although a certain restlessness prevailed. To the contrary, groups of citizens from the Madras Presidency actually sent letters of support to the government. It wasn't that they were satisfied with the ruling dispensation but felt that the British Raj was definitely better than Company Raj. The picture changed when it came to the military. Records available at the Tamil Nadu archives suggest that as many as 1,044 sepoys of the Madras army were court-martialled for support to the 1857 uprising. The British Army was already viewed negatively, and the treatment of the sepoys was frequently deplorable both in terms of pay and appointments. S. Muthiah, the historian, in his Madras Musings column says that a messenger from Hyderabad, Syed Aurzurah Husain, was sent to the southern zamindaris of Nagari, Kalahasti, and Venkatagiri, urging them to revolt against the British. He followed this up by instigating rebellion in North Arcot and in Chittoor districts. Reports of disturbances in these regions seeped down further south. In May 1857, Muslims took to the streets in Triplicane, and 'gathered opposite the Prince of Arcot's then residence, Shahdi Mahal on Triplicane High Road, urging him to join the Nizam of Hyderabad in a holy war against the British'. This crowd was soon dispersed by the police. A resident of Triplicane, Syed Hameed Jellah, continued with the crusade. He regularly collected information about the happenings in the north of India and conveyed them not just to civilians but also to the troops who were in the Madras and Chinglepet barracks. He was soon arrested and thrown into prison but stirrings like these were never far from the surface and put fear in the hearts of the administrators. In order to protect the British residents of Madras, the governor Lord Harris created the Corps of Madras Volunteer Guards and 700 infantrymen and 100 cavalrymen were ordered to patrol the streets of Madras during the months following the revolt.

The fact that there were no major reverberations in Madras did not allay the fears of the establishment. A document of the government of Madras's Judicial Department finds reprehensible reports in the press.

> Prominent notice was drawn to the Native Community by the press. The proceedings of Government and its General Administration, as well as in our Military and Political matters, and the supposed discontent caused thereby, especially among our Native Soldiery, were largely descanted (sic) upon....our want of strength was pointed out and most injudicious subjects were discussed. Thus, one newspaper entered into lengthened arguments to prove that greased cartridges of objectionable materials had really been issued...another turned into derision Sir H Lawrence's (Henry Lawrence, Chief Commissioner of Avadh/Oudh) address to the Troops at Lucknow and published a supposed speech in the mouth of a Sepoy in supposed refutation of it. These publications unfortunately do not reach English readers only. They are republished in vernacular newspapers and have a deleterious effect on the Native Community. The policy of annexing Native States on the failure of lineal male heirs may in particular be noticed as having been discussed in very inflammatory language.

The Governor General sent orders to the civil and military authorities in the Madras government on how to deal with seditious material found in public places or with troops and civilians. The offenders were to be caught and exemplary punishment was to be meted out. In February 1858, two activists Ghulam Ghouse and Sheikh Mannu were arrested for displaying placards with 'objectionable' matter on them. In Thanjavur and North Arcot, secret meetings were held among patriots and a great commotion occurred in Salem when rumours swirled that Indian soldiers were soon to take down the British flag in Madras. Several spontaneous instances of struggle and protest against the regime burst across the region with enough momentum to indicate a solidification of the movement against alien rule.

There were, however, as mentioned earlier, many people who backed the government. When Lord Trevelyan, the popular governor, left India, a letter signed by more than 7,500 citizens of Madras expressed their support for a stable and responsible government. In his patronizing reply he said:

> You say that you had hoped to have seen under administration, the introduction of representative Government. My answer is, qualify yourselves for representative institutions and they will be sure to come in good time. You are united under the common protection of the British Crown with a free people who have never grudged to others participation in the political advantages which they themselves enjoy. The real delay is on your part. Cultivate the literature of England which is instinct with the spirit of self-Government…. Above all things strive to attain to a high moral standard. Public morality without which national Government is impossible, is only the aggregate of each man's individual character…

There were little signs of reform although the British government, by an Act of Parliament, took charge. The Government of India Act of 1858 took over from the Company and Queen Victoria became the Queen Empress of India. A statement delivered by Lord Charles Canning in 1858 to the princes and people of India promised reform and non-interference in religious matters. Dalhousie's policy was modified to say that legally adopted heirs would be allowed to succeed as long as they swore allegiance to the Crown. The Towns Improvement Acts of 1865 and 1871 as well as the District Municipalities Act of 1884 and Local Boards Acts of 1871 and 1884 were introduced with the intent to improve local municipalities but nothing much happened, and discontent mounted in the public sphere.

In the Madras Presidency, while public works did not see any remarkable progress, some reforms were attempted by the British in the recasting of the judiciary and in higher education. As far as the judiciary was concerned, the Madras Supreme Court was set up in 1801 and the local courts set up by the East India Company were reconstituted and became the Madras High Court. However, certain religious frameworks were adhered to and rather than attempt to reform these, the British allowed the existence of laws based on Hindu Shastras and the Quran to continue.

There were also some changes made to the education system. The infamous Minute of Thomas Babington Macaulay, politician and historian who came to India and was part of the Governor's Executive Council, needs to be mentioned here. Published in 1835, Macaulay wrote in his Minute 'a single shelf of a good European library was worth the whole native literature of India and Arabia... when we pass from works of imagination to works in which facts are recorded, and general principles investigated, the superiority of the Europeans becomes absolutely immeasurable.' To paraphrase, he hoped that his education plans would create a distinct group of Indians who would be Indian by birth and colour but 'English by tastes, opinions, morals and intellect'. Macaulay advocated the creation of a civil service that would educate and train Indians for administrative work in the best possible English tradition. Earlier, in 1822, Thomas Munro, the governor of Madras, had encouraged the proliferation of schools with the medium of instruction being in Tamil and promoted vernacular learning but Macaulay's ideas shifted the focus to higher education and the spread of English. Essentially elitist in nature and reflecting the superior and racist attitudes of the British administration, it also fuelled inequalities in society, creating deeper divisions among Indians, especially between the educated and the uneducated. His 'downward filtration' theory by which he felt education could seep down to the unlettered over time again stemmed from an arrogance based on a notion of racial superiority. However, English education did take firm root, especially in Tamil Nadu. In time, English spread all across India, and ultimately proved to be a sound base from which the Tamils (and other non-Hindi regions) could connect with the rest of the country, especially during the early days of the nationalist movement and the freedom struggle. The benefits of a Western education and exposure notwithstanding, it was a structure that ensured that only a few could benefit.

One major impact of such initiatives, as pointed out by Japanese historian Miwako Shiga, is that Brahmins (who quickly clambered on to the higher education band wagon), despite being only a small percentage of South India's population, occupied dominant positions in government. In 1896, 53 per cent of deputy collectors were Brahmins, 25 per cent were non-Brahmin Hindus, 6.5 per cent were Muslims, 4 per cent were Indian Christians, and 11.5 per cent were Europeans and Eurasians. In 1912, Brahmins in deputy collector posts were at 55 per cent, non-Brahmins were at 21.5 per cent, Muslims at 10.5 per cent, Indian Christians at 5 per cent, and Europeans and Eurasians at 8 per cent. The statistics were even more skewed when it came to sub judges with 71.4 per cent being Brahmins in 1896 and the figure rising to 83.3 in 1912. Only 21.4 per cent of sub judges were non-Brahmins in 1896, and the figure dips to 16.7 per cent in 1912. There were no Muslim and Indian Christians appointed as sub judges. At the munsif level, too, Brahmins captured most of the posts and this set in place a hierarchy which became deeply entrenched and suited colonial interests. In terms of university education and literacy rates too, there was a preponderance of Brahmins. Shiga says, '…Brahmins were the only community in nineteenth century South India to adjust themselves to the socio-political changes brought about by colonial rule. They acquired Western style education realising that such qualifications were indispensable for gaining power in the new system'. As the imbalance grew, a great deal of resentment set in, creating deep social schisms between Brahmins and non-Brahmins. These structural imbalances would be redefined in later years, especially after the country gained freedom.

The late nineteenth century in Tamil Nadu also saw a great deal of difficulty with colonial measures of taxation and land laws. The ryotwari system set up by Thomas Munro, governor of Madras in 1820, meant that taxes were directly collected from peasant cultivators. While this eliminated middlemen, farmers suffered greatly from harassment and tax demands. The zamindari system, already in place, put the landowners in charge and they in turn collected punitive levels of taxes from the farmers which they paid the colonial administration. The zamindari system was not abolished but continued to exist alongside the ryotwari system which was trying to get farmers in direct contact with the government, cutting out the agents in the middle. Later, this system too became problematic with the government's taxation becoming too heavy.

Another catastrophe that affected the poorest, especially in rural areas, was the Great South Indian Famine which affected Madras, Bombay, Hyderabad, and Mysore in 1876 and 1878 and in 1877 in Madras. This came on the heels of the devastating famines that had already occurred in Bihar and Bengal that wiped out millions. As we now know, it was not just drought that caused these famines but the colonial policy of exporting huge quantities of grain from these regions. Estimates suggest that as much as 320,000 tons of wheat were exported when severe drought was going on. Worse, the relief dispersed to people who flocked to drought relief camps was miserable—1 anna and 450 grams of grain for a man, and slightly less for women and children. This was not simple relief, but wages paid against a day's hard labour. A large number of people, especially weavers and agricultural labourers, signed up as indentured labour for work overseas. William Digby, journalist and humanitarian, and physician W. R. Cornish, Sanitary Commissioner for the Madras Presidency, argued for more relief for each person in addition to paying the starving workers. According to them, the rations doled out by the government were inadequate to support life.

Engravings and prints of the time in the possession of Digby and some illustrations published in London magazines show emaciated women and men and abandoned and dying children. Another illustration depicts the bags of grain lined up for export on Madras Beach with starving men working to load them. An epidemic of malaria also aggravated the situation with many people dying of the disease. Lord Temple, who was in charge of relief at that time, declared that the famine was ended and 'under control' in late 1877, and Digby was said to have remarked, 'a famine can scarcely be said to be adequately controlled which leaves one fourth of the people dead'. More than 8 million people died during this famine in South India. Another outbreak of famine in 1891 in Tamil Nadu in Rasipuram and Pudupalayam also severely affected the local population. A local philanthropist called Kulandaiswami is said to have fed the entire region with porridge and sugar cane—consequently, this outbreak of famine was called kanji thotti panjam.

Two British administrators who were deeply troubled by the callous responses from the officials to the disaster of the famines included William Wedderburn and Allan Octavian Hume who, along with others like Dadabhai Naoroji and Romesh Chunder Dutt, soon established the Indian National Congress in 1885. While many of these people were drawn from a Western, educated elite group in its early years, it did symbolize a political mobilization of sorts. There were other initiatives that fiercely opposed the British Raj and set the country on the course to freeing itself from the colonial yoke. The latter half of the nineteenth century triggered some major shifts all across the country and in Tamil Nadu too the seeds of transformation were sown.

Not the least among the enterprises that were initiated by the citizens of Tamil Nadu at this juncture were newspapers in both Tamil and English. The establishment and development of printing, particularly in the context of the missionaries in Tamil Nadu like Ziegenbalg who imported, adapted, and used printing presses for the translation of the Bible and other Christian texts into Tamil, gave a huge impetus to communication. G. Subramania Iyer, one of the founder members of the newly set up Indian National Congress, and a fierce critic of economic imperialism, along with six other patriotic young men, launched *The Hindu*, a weekly English paper in September 1878. Subramania Iyer partnered with the Triplicane Six as they were known, all young people who were filled with ire at the stiff and racist opposition from British-owned papers to the appointment of an Indian, T. Muthuswamy Iyer, to the Madras Bench. Borrowing a rupee and twelve annas, they set off to a printing press on Mint Street and produced a newspaper. In its first editorial *The Hindu* wrote:

> The principles we propose to be guided by are simply those of fairness and justice, it will always be our aim to promote harmony and union among our fellow countrymen and to interpret correctly the feelings of the natives and to create mutual confidence between the governed and the governors.... In religion we shall observe strictest neutrality; sectarian disputes we shall never allow to appear in our columns...

The tone was moderate, but the intent of objective journalism was clear. In later decades, when the momentum of the national movement built up, the paper adopted a radical stance against the government vis-à-vis the freedom struggle. In 1892, Subramania Iyer also founded a Tamil newspaper, *Swadesamitran*. A fiery journalist, a political activist, and a social reformer, Subramania Iyer, among other things, stood against the orthodoxies of his Brahmin caste to get his young widowed daughter remarried. He also founded, along with others, the Madras Mahajana Sabha to foster national sentiment and reform.

The opposition to the punitive policies of the government grew and newspapers became the instruments that assailed unjust laws and practices. For instance, the levy on salt on Indians was criticized as benefitting the English, the taxes on raw goods exported to England which were again taxed when re-entering India as finished goods also came under fire in the newspapers. There was a growing awareness of impoverishment in various sectors such as among the weaving community and the entire handloom industry was almost wiped out. While papers pressed for more representation in provincial legislative bodies, the All India Congress had its third session in Madras in 1887. It pressed for more reform, passing resolutions which were conveyed to the government to little or no avail until nationalist leaders like V. O. Chidambaram Pillai, who started the India Steam Navigation Company, and the visionary poet and icon of Tamil literature, Subramania Bharati, the reformer Annie Besant, and other stalwarts based in Tamil Nadu plunged into the political fray—soon the impact of the ideas of swadeshi and swaraj started taking root among the masses. But more on this later.

It is important to note that in the late nineteenth century, as all this was going on, the perception of India as a fabled land of learning and mysticism was reinforced by orientalists like William Jones and Max Mueller. A new currency was given to the cultural and spiritual aspects of Hindu culture, which in many ways was an exaltation of Aryan culture. A. Gangatharan, a historian, says, 'Orientalist constructions of Indian antiquity paved the way for prejudicial treatment of the past'. Historian A. R. Venkatachalapathy says that at this juncture something important and transformative happened. William Jones, who was serving as a judge in Calcutta, proposed a family of languages and formulated the idea that Sanskrit, Latin, Greek, and all modern European languages belonged to the Indo-European family of languages, and that Sanskrit was the root of all Indian languages. Venkatachalapathy says that a few decades later in Madras another Englishman, orientalist F. W. Ellis, broadly agreed with this idea of families of languages but said that the south Indian languages were a distinct group, different from the Indo-Aryan language group. He called these the Dravidian languages. He formulated what is called the Dravidian Proof in 1816, and a few decades later Bishop Caldwell expanded this idea in his work, *A Comparative Grammar of the Dravidian or the South Indian Family of Languages*. Gangatharan says that 'Caldwell was one of the first missionary scholars to address the issue of the social conflict with definite categories. He delved deeply into the issue of Brahmin non-Brahmin religious dichotomy and pointed out that it was the Brahmins who injected their Puranic and Vedic superstitions and culture into Tamil life.' With print technology making great advances, Indian texts, both classical and modern, became available in print in both North and South India. In South India, Venkatachalapathy says that Arumuga Navalar, the Tamil Shaivite reformer from Sri Lanka, and following him, C. W. Thamotharanpillai and U. Ve. Swaminatha Aiyar, two Tamil scholars, were among the pioneers who collated literature in Tamil from palm leaf manuscripts from the earliest times, showing a different society, one that was in transition from a tribal society to a state formation, where caste formations were not yet rigid, 'where the entire literature opens up a possibility of a different kind of world'. He points to the pithy four lines from *Purananuru*, 'Yadhum oore yavarum kelir', meaning, 'all towns are our home towns, and all people are my relatives....'

This is the background against which a revival of a strong Tamil identity occurred in the late nineteenth century. The role and presence of south Indians in the national movement is significant and equally so the soon to emerge perceptions of the need to establish and strengthen a distinct non-Brahmin identity as expressed in the Non-Brahmin Manifesto of 1916. The seeds of swadeshi and swaraj were already sown by intellectuals and activists in this period and the transformative social churning and changes of the late nineteenth century set the stage for the fight for freedom.

Chapter 28

Chennai That Was Madras

Life is never dull in Chennai/Madras. There are enough splits in the city to justify perhaps more names and identities.

V. Sriram, writer

FRANCIS DAY WAS IN LOVE. AS HE SAILED DOWN THE COROMANDEL coast from Machilipatnam looking for a place to set up a factory and perhaps a future settlement for the East India Company, Day was clear that among the factors that would impact his decision was the proximity to his secret love, a half-Indian woman with European blood who lived in the port of San Thome where the Portuguese already had a flourishing settlement. Being an impecunious agent of the East India Company, his trajectory to success in love lay in delivering to his superiors a piece of land for which he would be well rewarded and from which they could all obtain profits. He found a small strip of beach by the sea, near the village of Madrasapatnam, positioned at a discreet distance from San Thome, and proceeded with the help of the dubash (an interpreter or translator) Beri Thimmappa to acquire it from the Nayak, Venkatadri Damarla, the local ruler who held it. It was not really the most viable piece of land, it had no natural harbour, but his superior, Andrew Cogan, approved, and in August 1639 the deed was done. The grant was intended to expand trade in the hinterland that offered 'excellent long cloath and better cheape by twenty per cent than anywhere else'. The 'firman' that was granted to Day allowed the construction of a fort and settlement.

Although the beach site on the Bay of Bengal was not the most ideal, the Company was banking on the new settlement with a warehouse and fort becoming the foundation of their success in the future. It would protect and grow their trade in cotton and other goods. Machilipatnam was becoming challenging, and the Dutch at Pulicat were already in competition, and the British needed this spot. Little did they realize that this settlement, and the ancient villages that surrounded it, would become an iconic city, the city of Chennai, once known as Madras, and currently the capital city of Tamil Nadu. There have been diverse theories about the origin of the name Madras, none really satisfactory, but they range from the idea that it was named after the nearby village of Madrasapatnam or after Madrasena, a Portuguese fisherman who had land nearby. Others source it to Madra, a wealthy Portuguese family in the region. Venkatachalapathy, however, says in the early references to the city (even in the eighteenth century) the name Chennapatna, or the town of Chennai, was in use. The British called Fort St. George and the settlement around it Madras, or White Town. This was where they lived and worked. Madrasapatnam and Black Town was where the Indians who supported the colonial enterprise lived. V. Sriram, the historian, says of Chennapatnam that it was 'named after the father of the local chieftain, it was either an existing settlement or one that came up in the area surrounding the place where the British built their enclosure which they grandiosely called Fort St. George.' He adds that old Chennappa was Telugu and so the name that the Tamil Nadu government chose to confer on the city in 1996 'was not Tamil at all'. Pushpa Arabindo, professor of Urban Studies at University College, London, points out,

> the co-existence of colonial and local names indicated the initial dichotomy of the colonial settlement pattern where a foreign enclave existed, segregated from the indigenous population who associated with the foreigners only through trade. In the course of indigenization some of the characteristics of the colonial city were adopted as "modern" … as this grew outwards, it became unclear as to what constituted Madras. So in 1798 an arbitrary line was drawn to define the limits of Madras…including suburban villages and agrarian settlements. Chennai was circumscribed by the larger area of Madras.

The renaming controversy met with some level of resistance, but the name Chennai was locked in and with the passing of time, Madras is more a nostalgic memory and modern Chennai has come to stay.

∽

As we have seen throughout the book, the Tamil region has been settled for millennia and this is also true of the Chennai area. Robert Bruce Foote, the British geologist, unearthed a hand axe dating back over 2.6 million years. Later, Iron Age tools and implements were also found and as historian and archaeologist K. V. Raman has documented, burial urns and a small sarcophagus have been found within the current city's precincts. While there is no documented continuity of human presence after the Palaeolithic Age, a few million years later, Roman coins and painted earthenware were found in areas of the city, indicating a brisk trade with West Asia. Yathees Kumar, the archaeologist, suggests that even though the continuity of human settlement in the area is not recorded, the ongoing excavations across the regions of Tamil Nadu, including in the Chennai area, may throw up more evidence in terms of buried objects and human remains that indicate a kind of continuity of human presence in the region. The numerous neighbouring villages that were woven into the city like the strands of a necklace became an integral part of Chennai but were initially independent villages. The pakkams and oorus, each with their own distinct identity and history, were a repository of Tamil culture and tradition.

Certain areas of the city are older than others. Mylapore was referred to in the writing of Ptolemy the Greek geographer as Mylarphon, even in the second century of the Common Era. St. Thomas, as we know, came to these shores in the early Christian decades and preached the Word of Christ on the beach. The Portuguese settlement of San Thome grew around this sandy terrain and is now a central part of Chennai. Marco Polo, the Venetian merchant and explorer, records that the body of 'Messer Saint Thomas the Apostle lies in this town…having no great population. It is a place where few traders go…. Both Christians and Saracens frequent it in pilgrimage.' When the Portuguese who came to trade in the sixteenth century settled here, it became a small town that dominated the region. Over the next few centuries, San Thome grew and with a population of 5,000 was a White Town like the one in Fort St. George, while adjacent Mylapore served as its Black Town. Even today, the sense of San Thome as a separate town, of an ooru, exists, and some of its streets and buildings still carry a hint of the old Portuguese heritage. Other oorus, the small villages and semi-urban agglomerations, which were pulled into Chennai/Madras include Nungambakkam, Mambalam, Egmore (originally Ezhumbur), Poonamallee, Padi, Manali, Madambakkam, Adambakkam, Tiruvottriyur, etc., and further south, Tiruvanmaiyur, Neelankarai, and other villages. Chithra Madhavan, the historian, says, 'Many of these villages including the interior ones with their ancient temples, which are part of today's Chennai easily date back to the Chola and Pallava times.' Muthiah documented the fact that most Chennai families, even if they have been in the city for many generations, come from other places in Tamil Nadu, migrating to the newly aggregated city from villages near and far. He was also of the view that despite residency in the city, a favourite line of inquiry among Tamilians was the inexplicable desire to know which ooru a person was from. Many families maintain links to their places of origin, especially the Chettiar community, which works hard at preserving a unique and distinct heritage.

Tirumangai Azhwar, one of the Vaishnavite poet-saints of the eighth century, in his poetic compositions speaks of both Mylapore and Tiruvellikeni villages with their ancient temples. The Parthasarathy Swamy temple in Triplicane (anglicized from Tiruvellikeni) is a standout symbol of the Pallava period. Keni means sacred tank, alli refers to the lilies which grew in the midst of the tank, surrounded by groves of tulasi, the holy basil. Another Vaishnavite poet, Pey Azhwar, describes in evocative verse how pearl and coral deposits from the sea that wash ashore on the beach illuminate the entire village of Tiruvellikeni. These temples, in all likelihood, were originally built in the late fifth or sixth centuries CE. Incidentally, Triplicane was the first village to be added to Madras on an annual rent of ₹175 from the sultan of Golconda in 1676. In 1720, after the Golconda dynasty ended, Triplicane was fully annexed into British territory.

Many of the temples were built and rebuilt a few times over the centuries. The Kapalishwar temple in Mylapore has been mentioned in the *Thevaram*. Buddhists and Jains also lived near this temple before the persecution of Jains began around the ninth century. Centuries later, the temple's tank was built on land gifted by the nawab of Arcot. Even now Muslims use the tank on Muharram day. The simple amity between communities symbolized by these spaces and the use of them is a hallmark of Chennai's syncretic culture. The nawabs of Arcot were under the overlordship of the Mughal emperor, many of them tried to keep their territory intact, but were outplayed by the British in the end, either through political manoeuvrings or finally disenfranchised by the infamous Doctrine of Lapse, whereby their areas were ceded to the British. Mention must be made of Nawab Muhammed Ali Wallajah who built the lovely Wallajah Mosque in Triplicane in 1749 and whose generosity again epitomized a high level of inter-faith harmony at the time. Apart from donating land for the Kapalishwar temple tank, he gave elephants to numerous temples and commissioned a painting of *The Last Supper* which he gifted to St. Mary's Church in Fort St. George.

In the Sangam poems, there is a reference to Tondaimandalam, indicating the area around Chennai ruled later by the Pallava kings. The Pallava rulers held sway over the region until about the ninth century, then with the Imperial Cholas dominating Tamilakam, their rule and influence prevailed. After the Chola decline, the Pandyas who surfaced again from Madurai extended their control up to Tondaimandalam. When the Vijayanagar kings controlled this part of Tamilakam, the Nayaks were their regents, and it was from the Nayak of Wandiwash, Damarla Venkatadri, that the land grant was made to Francis

Day. The great poet-philosopher Thiruvalluvar, legends suggest, was born in the region that later became Chennai around the late fourth century. As a much-revered Tamil icon, his ethical and moral values have permeated much of the Tamil psyche.

Subramania Bharati, that most luminous of poets of the twentieth century, who was born in Tirunelveli district in 1882, spent prolonged periods in Chennai, and also died here. More than anyone else in the twentieth century, Bharati stirred the imagination of the Tamil people particularly as the freedom movement was gaining momentum. Patriotism, a love for the beauty of the land, and a freedom beyond mere political freedom, were ideas he expressed lyrically and movingly. Fearlessness, love, and a humanism that embraced all living creatures, were the themes of his poetry. Bharati was also a journalist, activist, and a passionate votary for the emancipation of women, and spoke out against social orthodoxies. Many young Tamil men and women, even those who were not involved in the freedom struggle, were drawn to his poetry.

We must now come to the English who were the founders of the city of Madras. Muthiah (who incidentally was a vociferous voice against the renaming of Madras to Chennai) says that, originally, Fort St. George, named after the patron saint of England, was only a warehouse for the traders with a couple of security guards posted to take care of the goods of trade. However, over the years, this site began to develop. Within the compound, there is the beautiful St. Mary's Church built in 1680, with its gorgeous wooden fretwork and simple balustrades, the oldest Protestant Church in India. Robert Clive and Elihu Yale married here and Job Charnock, the founder of Calcutta, donated the font at the front of the church. Here lie many Company men, both the well known and unknown buried together—these men believed firmly that their mission was to serve and glorify their queen (Queen Victoria) and country. Several buildings were constructed here and are now under the maintenance of the Archaeological Survey of India (ASI) and house the offices of government including the State Legislative Assembly. The original Exchange Building (now the Fort Museum), the King's Barracks, and Admiralty House are among the handsome edifices that still remain. The streets had names like Charles Street, James Street, and Gloucester Street. The Indo-Saracenic style of architecture, with its nod to an Indian aesthetic, is still visible in many buildings in Chennai. As the company that came for trade metamorphosed into the Crown that ruled, Madras metamorphosed too, and not just in terms of architecture.

The local population had no choice but to help to construct the empire regardless of the racism and exploitation embedded in the practice of the new overlords. Local rulers turned a blind eye to the steady and stealthy expansion tactics of the British. Even before the Crown took over, the Company obtained minting rights and, in 1640, coins with images of English royals were minted and in circulation despite the fact that the Mughal emperor's permission was not obtained for this exercise. The list of agents of the Company who made small fortunes through dubious means runs long; Edward Winter, George Foxcroft, and others engaged in corruption and even created small rebellions. Muthiah records an instance when Foxcroft who became governor was asked to dispense justice in the murder of a slave girl called Chequa by her mistress, Mrs Ascentia Dawes. Enquiries were made in England on how to deal with the issue. The English instruction was for Foxcroft to organize a trial by jury—this was the first time ever that British justice was implemented in Madras. Needless to say, the white lady who 'murthered' was declared 'not guilty'.

In 1688, the Madras Corporation was established, the first ever in British India. The Tamil Nadu Archives (called the Madras Records Office then) was established in 1672 in Madras and is the oldest such facility in the world. The third oldest railway station in the country, the first in South India, the Royapuram Railway Station, was established here in 1856, and the Indian Army's oldest regiment is the Madras Regiment which was first set up in 1758. Various other 'firsts' have been ascribed to Madras. The first industrial enterprise, a tannery in San Thome, the first technical institute, now Guindy Engineering College, and the first component manufacturer, India Pistons, all began here. The oldest organized trade union in India was the Madras Trade union founded in 1918.

Many people from around the world and elsewhere in India fetched up in Madras and all of them have left their mark on the city, not just the Tamils. Beginning with the Armenians and the Parsis and Jews who came here to trade but stayed to make the city their home, Chennai has always made space for other communities including Gujaratis, Sindhis, Marwaris, not to mention the Telugu-speaking Komati Chetties, Beri Chetties, and other linguistic groups like Kannada speakers, Malayalam speakers, and Hindi speakers. As people settled in the city some spaces were oriented community wise and profession wise, although much of it was not of deliberate intent; just like other cities people tended to find spaces and build homes wherever was most affordable and most conducive to them, although often there was little choice in the matter. This was particularly true of the early migrants who came to the city.

There is also outward migration—apart from the younger generation moving out to seek greener pastures in terms of jobs and education, Madras has seen communities like the Parsis and the Anglo-Indians dwindling. The Anglo-Indian community in old Madras had settled in areas like Perambur and Royapuram, near the railway lines where many of them had jobs. Their population in these traditional spaces has decreased because many of the younger generation have moved to countries like Australia and those that have remained have also moved out of their traditional homes to newer areas on East Coast Road, and other parts of South Chennai. During the Raj, although the British did not really give them a hand up socially or economically, the Anglo-Indians brought much to the essence of Madras. Behind the quaint, lace curtained windows of their homes, the tinkle of piano keys and lilting Scottish tunes were frequently heard. Their soft chatter was accompanied by cake and Earl Grey tea. They carried on traditions of their mixed heritage with choirs and western classical music, fox trots, and waltzes, but now the metropolis with its ruthless urbanization seems to have swallowed them up.

∽

Chennai's rich cultural and musical traditions have both classical and popular forms. From the Gaana Pattu, which is based on casual real-life situations, set to lilting music (although sometimes dirge-like) and is irreverent in aspect, to the Carnatic sabhas, which are platforms for classical music, Chennai has much to offer when it comes to vibrant artistic expression. Even in the classical domain, there are experiments and caste strongholds in music sabhas—the Brahmin domination in this art form has been constantly challenged, so much so that a democratization is evident just from the sheer proliferation of musical venues that are not the privilege of the exclusive few. There is also a growing interest from young people who adapt Carnatic music to contemporary styles of expression and, given the ease of communication, find themselves reaching a global audience. Many of the great maestros of Carnatic music are from Chennai—from the older generation you have geniuses like M. S. Subbulakshmi, D. K. Pattammal, Semmangudi Srinivasa Iyer, G. N. Balasubramaniam, Ariyakudi Ramanuja Iyengar, T. N. Krishnan, Veena Balachander, Lalgudi Jayaraman, and others. The younger generation is bolder in expression and freer with their creativity, including maestros like T. M. Krishna, who constantly crosses the boundaries of caste and tradition in Carnatic music, the brilliant Bombay Jayashri (yes, she is from Chennai), and the outstandingly gifted Sanjay Subrahmanyan. These musicians scale new imaginative and creative heights.

Chennai is also one of the country's major centres of film-making. Soon after cinema came to India, theatres were built in Madras as early as 1910–12. As it grew as a cultural form in India, it also increasingly reflected contemporary concerns, boldly pushing its boundaries and its audience. Talented actors were spotted by legendary filmmakers like K. Subramanyam and S. S. Vasan. On their watch, the Tamil film industry (referred to as Kollywood—from Kodambakkam, where studios were located) grew and is now the second largest in the country, next only to Bollywood. The Tamil film industry generated ₹3,500 crore in 2023. About 200 films are made in Chennai every year. The heroes and heroines of the Tamil film world include talented actors who have mesmerized audiences in Tamil Nadu and in many parts of the world with their astonishing versatility and prowess. From superstars like Rajinikanth and Kamal Haasan, who have a cult following, to other influential and gifted actors like Sivakumar, Ajith, Surya, Vijay, and the philanthropist actor Vijayakanth, Vijay Sethupathi, Karthi, and Dhanush, these men and women continue to impact vast numbers of moviegoers in Chennai and the rest of Tamil Nadu. Kamal Haasan forayed into politics and currently actor Vijay who is very popular has also entered politics. Rajinikanth famously flirted with politics, and regardless of the path he is on, continues to inspire and delight millions of fans and moviegoers.

Women actors who are popular include a new generation of stars, many of whom have moved into the Kollywood industry from other states. Jyothika, Trisha, Nayantara, Shriya Sharan, Kajal Aggarwal are some stars of the current generation who are very popular. An earlier generation of notable female stars include Jayalalithaa who later became Tamil Nadu's chief minister, Saroja Devi, Sowcar Janaki, Padmini, Savitri, Vyjayanthimala, K. R. Vijaya, Revathi, and others. One of the most iconic and influential actors of Tamil Nadu was Sivaji Ganesan, who left a deep emotional and cultural impact on the Tamils. M. G. Ramachandran (MGR), the actor turned politician, who was chief minister of Tamil Nadu, and his peers like Nagesh, Gemini Ganesan, Muthuraman, Jaishankar, and many other multifaceted screen heroes gave Tamil cinema a heft that was unmatched in other film hubs. In this context, the unusual presence of an American film director Ellis Dungan must be mentioned. Coming to India in the mid-1930s (he lived in Chennai for over fifteen years), he plunged into film direction in the Madras film world directing actors like MGR, and N. S. Krishnan. Even though he never learned Tamil, he brilliantly directed several well-known films such as *Bhaktha Nandanar* (1935), *Sathi Leelavathi* (1936), bringing new techniques into Tamil film-making. Dungan was credited with bringing Subbulakshmi into the film world, directing her to great acclaim in two of her best-known films, *Shakuntalai* (1940) and *Meera* (1945). Some of the most acclaimed directors in Indian cinema—K. Balachander and Mani Ratnam—have been responsible for a radical new vision in cinema. The recent blend of modern, artistically cultural filmmaking has also garnered commercial success—a combination that appeals to a supportive audience. Despite the advent of OTT platforms, going to movie theatres continues to be a great pastime in Chennai. We will look at the current status of the Tamil film industry in more depth in a later chapter.

Chennai today is a modern, cosmopolitan city. With a population of 4.9 million people, it ranks sixth among cities in India. It is a major hub of industry, with the automobile and IT sectors being especially prominent. It also continues to innovate and restore older and less formally structured sectors such as the handloom and cotton textile industry, the revival of which has been welcomed by Chennaites. More on this when we discuss the current status of industry in Tamil Nadu later on.

While communal disharmony does not rear its head much in the city, other deep divides lurk beneath its surface. Caste and class issues still prevail; the yawning gap between the rich and poor is not bridged by aspirations alone, so in places like North Chennai, close to where the British first settled, the squalor has not abated. In a twist of sorts, Pushpa Arabindo points out,

> If Madras was once the colonial name of a growing, modernizing city with Chennai representing the congested indigenous Black Town north of the Cooum River, nearly 200 years later the roles are reversed, with Chennai reimagined as the sprawling postcolonial post modernizing city encapsulating a shrivelled up Madras that now connotes the former colonial areas north of the Cooum river which exhibit rigor mortis.

Poor infrastructure and the lack of steady employment are some of the factors that deepen the deprivation. The unsatisfactory resettlement of people post the tsunami in Chennai in December 2004, and the more recent predicament experienced by the poor post the cyclone and flooding in both 2015 and again in 2023, casts a long shadow on the prospects of economic prosperity for the most vulnerable sections of Chennai.

Chennai in the twenty-first century is firmly focused on development and globalization. One way of tracing the evolution of the city from its origin to the present day is through its architecture. Sriram brilliantly sets this out in his biography of Chennai:

> If at all there is a part of the city that can boast of a lovely skyline incorporating almost all the styles of architecture referred to up until now, it is the beach. Starting from the San Thome end, you cross All India Radio Building, an elegant structure that incorporates several Dravidian motifs in its façade. Next comes the office of the Director General of Police. Known in the service as Chief Office it began life as a Masonic temple in the 1840s before being handed over to the police in the 1860s. Splendidly restored its classical façade is a thing of beauty. Thereafter comes the vast campus of the Queen Mary's College.... ... Copper House, Jeypore House and Pentland Block are beautiful.... After that comes the Lady Willingdon Institute...an art deco structure that has as its neighbour the quaint Ice House now Vivekanandar Illam. The domed and red brick University Examination Hall follows and next to it the vast Presidency College Cricket Ground. Thereafter are three of Chisholm's creations – the Italianate Presidency College Building, the Scottish PWD Building and the Indo Saracenic University Senate House. This is followed by the University buildings all of which complement the Senate House in their skyline and layout.

This is a word picture that can resonate with the Chennaite. Having done long and frequent drives along this vast stretch of road right from early childhood, this beautiful stretch along the beach can trigger evocative memories of Chennai. The statues on the Marina beach side currently include Kannagi poised to hurl the famous anklet, G. U. Pope, Avvaiyar, Tiruvalluvar, and other Tamil heroes. There was a mystery when the Kannagi statue disappeared for a while and suddenly reappeared. The story goes that when Jayalalithaa was chief minister, someone told her that it was bad luck for her on her way to the Secretariat to pass an angry woman who was pointing and cursing the ruler. Apparently the statue was removed and laid face up in a hidden location for a while (no doubt the pointing hand still remained aloft). Later, it found its way back to its location on the beach.

I also recall that from Mowbray's Road where we lived, we would encounter just some yards away another long historic arterial stretch where a motley group of people lived in the garden bungalows and roadside houses of Edward

Elliots' Road now renamed Radhakrishnan Salai. This road began at Gemini Circle (now Anna Flyover), named after Gemini Studios where the movie Moghul S. S. Vasan created fantastical sets and movies for Madras's passionate filmgoers. The stucco of the Gemini twins blowing trumpets on the entrance arch seemed to beckon passersby into a mysterious world of make-believe. The road continued all the way up to Marina Beach. The green lung of the area was the Agri Horticultural Society, and Woodlands Drive In (now Semmozhi Poonga). Right opposite was a favourite place for delicious dosais, filter coffee, and ice creams all to be savoured from within the car—upon the vehicle's window frame an innovative steel tray would be hung with a great clatter to hold the dishes that were brought to the customers in swift succession. Further down was Stella Maris College, the go-to institution for aspiring girl students. Then came the august Music Academy, the repository of Carnatic music built in this location in 1962, although it was first established in George Town in the 1920s. Vasan's Gemini House, a beautiful landmark of the area, was positioned in the corner and has been replaced by a megalith of glass and chrome which houses multinational back offices. A forlorn marble tablet now stands on the kerbside wedged between Maris Hotel and the Chola Hotel. It was once within the compound of Tilak Bhavan which Rajaji had rented from Kasturi Ranga Iyengar of *The Hindu* and where Gandhiji stayed as his guest. It was here that Gandhiji had his early morning idea that transformed a nation—that of satyagraha.

This was a road where eminent lawyers, educationists, and a smattering of film stars lived. Tree-lined and gracious in aspect, there were no tall buildings then and the evening breeze from nearby Marina Beach would offer a cool respite to its residents. A sprawling bungalow, Chandra Vilas, was the residence of C. S. Ayyar, a senior officer in the British Railways. He was the older brother of the Nobel Laureate, distinguished physicist C. V. Raman. Ayyar's son, another Nobel Prize winner, Dr Subrahmanyan Chandrasekhar, grew up in this house with his siblings. Chandra, as he was called, used to bicycle from the house every day down the Marina to Presidency College where he was a physics student. On the same Edward Elliots Road stood the house of a Captain Doraiswamy, a medical officer in the Indian armed services, whose daughter Lalitha was also a student in the same physics honours course as Chandra. Kameshwar Wali, Chandrasekhar's biographer, says Lalitha and Chandra exchanged laboratory records and later at a class party 'Chandra gave Lalitha a sweet smelling rose to pin on her sari'. Wali, recounting this charming anecdote, says that one day, 'seeing Lalitha take her bicycle out to ride back home from college, Chandra followed her all the way on his bicycle'. Chandrasekhar and Lalitha were married six years later in 1936.

The philosopher and former president Sarvepalli Radhakrishnan's house, Girija, still remains on this road, tucked back in quiet solitude amid overgrown trees and an unruly garden that has locked within it a glimpse of a time gone by. The famed Children's Garden School, the first educational institution that welcomes children from all walks of life, castes, and religious affiliations, was located here and the famed Travancore sisters, dancers turned cinema stars Lalitha-Padmini-Ragini, also lived here. Today, the road has a different character. From luggage shops to eateries, a few jewellery stores, and office buildings cut up by a flyover and criss-crossed by smaller roads, this hallowed part of Chennai is being transformed by galloping urbanization. Although now a global city with its crowded malls, branded goods, and coffee shops, Chennai still holds on to its filter coffee and its dosai and idli. These Chennai (or should I say Tamil) essentials have emerged in new avatars. Nevertheless, the city still revels in the fragrance of jasmine, in the soft music of the veena, and the joyous laughter of the modern young Chennaite whether in hijab or in t-shirt and jeans. With its history still playing out, Chennai will continue to fascinate and delight both the visitor and resident by the sheer uniqueness and charm of its character.

Chapter 29
Awakenings and Transformations

The Freedom Struggle and the Dravidian Movement

A prison sentence can be a badge of honour...

Rajmohan Gandhi, historian

FIFTEEN-YEAR-OLD AMBUJAMMAL WAS LOOKING FOR A DISTRACTION. IN the sprawling gardens of her father's home in Luz, lush with mango groves, mini paddy fields, flowering trees and bushes, she tried to find respite in the shade. She needed to escape not just from the heat but from family entanglements that constantly weighed on her. Ambujammal soon heard her father's loud, commanding voice. The visitors had come. When she darted inside and hastily stood next to her timid mother, she was immediately transfixed by the aura of the visitor who had just entered—a skinny man in khadi, who had strode in purposefully with his petite wife beside him; with a single glance he seemed to take in the entire room. Her father seemed to have dropped his stern demeanour for once and her mother all of a sudden dropped her aura of melancholy to welcome the visitors. This was perhaps the most memorable event in young Ambujammal's life. The arrival of Mohandas Karamchand Gandhi in her firmament marked the beginning of a transformative life experience.

The impact of Gandhi on Tamil Nadu was tremendous. He came to the various towns and cities in Tamil Nadu at least twelve times, and seven of his visits were to Chennai. One of his earliest encounters with a Tamil person as a practising lawyer in South Africa was with Balasundaram, an indentured labourer whose employer had beaten him severely. With his front teeth broken, bruised and bleeding, the man stood trembling and crying before him. Gandhiji was shocked at this first instance of severe abuse that he had seen and after protracted negotiations got the man released from his employer. Indentured labourers from Tamil Nadu and other parts of India were no better than slaves in South Africa at that time. The news of Gandhi's efforts reached faraway Madras. Thillayadi Valliammai, a young Tamil girl, joined Gandhi on his march from the Transvaal to Natal while protesting the unjust marriage laws imposed on Indians. Indians could not move between regions without passes and the march itself was labelled illegal and more so the public meetings. She was all of sixteen when addressing meetings and rallies. Arrested and sentenced to rigorous imprisonment for three months, Gandhiji wrote later of his deep sadness and distress at seeing her emaciated and ill in prison. She became dangerously ill but refused the offer of early release. When she came out of prison, she died. 'We mourn the loss of a noble daughter of India, who has set an example of womanly fortitude, pride and virtue that will, we are sure, not be lost upon the Indian community,' wrote Gandhi.

Gandhi's multiple visits to Tamil Nadu were always impactful, drawing huge crowds each time. Of particular significance was his second visit to Madurai in September 1921 when he resolved to abandon a more formal way of dressing and adopt the loincloth that became the image that would define him. Many a time, after the meetings, women would crowd around him and voluntarily give up the gold on their person. Like Ambujammal who met him as a young girl in Chennai, hundreds of women began to follow his lead, resorting to wearing khadi and plunging into political activism. Ambujammal herself, like her father, S. Srinivasa Iyengar, a top Madras lawyer, became an ardent follower of the Mahatma. She courted arrest, led protest marches, exhorted women to join her, and even travelled to the Gandhi Ashram at Wardha. When she returned to Chennai, she plunged into social service, setting up the Srinivasa Gandhi Nilayam in Alwarpet. Like Ambujammal, there were thousands of young people in Madras and in the wider Tamil region who felt the impact of this magnetic personality whose vision and message spurred a nation to action. 'Gandhi's influence cut across region, caste and gender,' says Venkatachalapathy.

Let us go back a bit in time. After World War I everything accelerated in the country as a whole, and also in the Tamil country. Media became more powerful and industry began to flourish—it was then that the British realized it would be difficult to keep a colony under strict control while fighting a World War at the same time. So, industry was allowed to grow in Tamil Nadu as in other parts of India. Women's participation in public life increased. Even as industry and other aspects of the economy grew, so did the media. To the surprise of the British, the Civil Disobedience movement too began to grow in strength.

The late nineteenth century, Venkatachalapathy points out, was a remarkable period. The influence of Christianity, discussed in an earlier chapter, created a much needed ferment especially among many Hindus who realized the need for social reform. Venkatachalapathy says this 'created a vibrancy in the south, whereas there was no real challenge in North India which unlike the south, or Bengal and Maharashtra was still carrying the baggage of the Mughals and concerned with cow protection.' The Protestants' focus on social injustice, particularly in southern Tamil Nadu, through the work of people like Caldwell and Ellis, was quite unlike the earlier approach of the Catholics who preferred to work with the elites. This created a momentum for change. Take, for instance, the breast cloth controversy, referred to earlier, among the Nadar women where through several decades of persistent struggle aided by the missionaries, they won the right to cover their breasts. However, the battles to bridge social injustice and schisms were often eclipsed by the natural struggle for freedom.

The Indian National Congress set up in 1885 in Bombay initially only aspired to the representation of Indians in government; the senior Congress leader Dadabhai Naoroji successfully won a seat in the House of Commons in London. Bal Gangadhar Tilak, another prominent leader in the national movement, was one of the early advocates of swaraj or self-rule and was severely critical of the exclusionist nature of British education, their disdainful views of Indian culture and traditions, and the lack of any space for ordinary Indians to participate in their own government. He felt that swaraj would rescue the Indian economy from the evils of exploitation that it had been subject to and would lead to political independence as well. The other rising leaders in the Congress like Aurobindo Ghose, Muhammad Ali Jinnah, Lala Lajpat Rai, V. O. Chidambaram Pillai, and of course the great poet-visionary Subramania Bharati exhorted ordinary people through their fiery speeches, persuasive arguments, and writings in their home regions to join the national movement.

V. O. Chidambaram Pillai, or VOC as he was called, was one of the early heroes of Tamil resistance to British rule. A government pleader and a man of modest means, he was stirred by the maritime history of the Tamils. Noting the monopoly of the British India Steam Navigation Company, despite the great difficulties and impediments that came his way, he raised funds and investors to set up an Indian navigation company. In his biography of VOC, *Swadeshi Steam,* Venkatachalapathy says he launched the Swadeshi Steam Navigation Company in 1906. 'Shouting Swadeshi from the rooftops and thumping its breast, not only did it challenge an international shipping behemoth, it also did not hesitate to take on the might of the Empire.' Already a passionate freedom fighter, a close friend of Bharati, and a member of the Congress party, he was an ardent votary of swadeshi and labour rights. In 1908, he gave a speech in Tuticorin, along with fellow nationalist Subramania Siva, urging the workers of the Coral Mills to protest against their bad working conditions which included poor wages and a harsh work situation. The protest spread and the British soon took note of VOC. Again, in Tirunelveli in 1908, he was arrested along with Siva for sedition at a meeting where he spoke of swadeshi and the boycott of foreign goods, stressing the importance of the Swadeshi Movement. Venkatachalapathy writes: 'The next day, Tirunelveli and Tuticorin erupted in violence. An eerie silence descended on the Tirunelveli marketplace, with shops being shut. Soon a crowd gathered, and amid shouts of *Vande Mataram*, and "V. O. Chidambaram Pillai", marched on the main road where all the government offices were situated. Large-scale destruction of government offices occurred, and despite bans, public meetings and more protests took place, and more violence ensued. When the authorities charged the crowds, instead of dispersing, they counter-attacked. Four people were killed, and many were imprisoned and sentenced to long-term confinement. This came to be known as the 'Tinnevely Riots'. Venkatachalapathy says, 'The protest violence of 13 March marked the high point of the *Swadeshi* movement in south India.'

In jail, VOC was not treated like a political prisoner, but like someone with a criminal conviction and was subject to great torture. He 'was yoked (in place of bulls) to the oil press like an animal and made to work in the cruel sun' according to an account. His travails in prison were such that his dear friend Subramania Bharati, anguished by his situation, wrote, 'Thanneer vitto valarthom sarvesa, eppaiyrai kanneeral kaathom'—'did we grow this crop with water, Lord? No, we nourished it with our tears.' (The film version of VOC's life *Kappalottiya Tamizhan* (1961), magnificently portrayed by Sivaji Ganesan, left not only the audience but the filmmakers themselves in tears as they were making it.) Given the numerous obstacles it faced, the Swadeshi Steam Company was doomed to fail right from the start—not only did VOC have to contend with his British tormentors, but he also had to deal with Indian collaborators and rivals who wanted to stop him. However, for a while, it managed to stay afloat. Ships were leased and indeed one ship, the SS *Gallia*, was actually purchased by the company. In the early years, the company provided regular service between Tuticorin and Sri Lanka against opposition from the British government. The foreign companies threatened by this even offered free passage to passengers and gave handkerchiefs to the travellers as presents. After his release in 1912, VOC was dismayed to see the end of his brave shipping venture and joined the Congress again, only to leave it several times because he did not always agree with its course of action. His fiery patriotism inspired many young radicals. A young man called Vanchinathan who shot dead the Tirunelveli Collector Robert Ashe in a train, on 17 June 1911, and later shot himself, was supposedly distraught by the treatment meted out to VOC, Subramania Siva, and others. VOC was not allowed to enter Tirunelveli district after his release and spent his later years in Chennai, running a kerosene and provision store. He immersed himself in literary commentary and writing, including a commentary on the *Tirukkural*. Towards the end, VOC returned to Tuticorin and spent his last days there in penury. This kappalottiya Tamizhan, the Tamilian who sailed ships, died in the offices of the Indian National Congress in Tuticorin in 1936.

We have spoken about Bharati in many of these pages but must remember that it was at this time, in the first and second decade of the remarkable activism of the early twentieth century, that Bharati's writing (much of it written when he was exiled in Pondicherry because of his political activism) became extremely popular. In poems like *Panchali Sabatham* his tone is feminist, advocating for the emancipation of women; in other poetry, he expresses his love for children, for nature and for Tamil and his country, and it is boundless. As a journalist, he wrote for many papers including the *Swadesamitran* and *The Hindu*. His politics were radical, and he often shocked moderates with his views. In his personal life he was generous to a fault; there is the famous incident of him donating his entire monthly earnings to a poor rickshaw puller, much to his wife Chellammal's consternation—they barely had enough food in the house. He died in Chennai at the early age of thirty-eight after a temple elephant trampled on his already weakened body. He had quietly left Pondicherry (then French territory) where he had lived in exile to avoid arrest as he was banned from British territory. He came into British territory in Cuddalore but was arrested and confined to house arrest. He was later released after an intervention by Annie Besant, who was part of the national movement. 'Had he been alive for another ten years, he would have published more,' says Venkatachalapathy ruefully 'and would have been able to witness his songs sung in the streets.' Another leading light from Madras in the Independence movement was Chakravarti Rajagopalachari, also known as Rajaji or C. R. He was one of the closest deputies of Mahatma Gandhi in Madras and an ardent nationalist who later was appointed the last Governor General of India before the country became a republic. He also served as the premier of the Madras Presidency and later the chief minister of the state. A brilliant lawyer and interlocutor, Rajaji was a prolific writer as well. The Mahatma called him his 'conscience keeper'. Although later he was involved in unpopular political strategies, his integrity was never in question—to the contrary, his principled approach to life and politics shone with a rare and ineluctable radiance. As a child who had devoured his translations of the Ramayana and the Mahabharata, watching his funeral procession on Christmas day in 1972 from a vantage point, I recall a feeling of deep sadness. Not because of a tenuous connection with him through the people who knew him well, but because his stories were profound, and popular with many, and as a writer his tales were laced with the sorrows and the tragedies of the lives of the poorest communities in Tamil Nadu and were extraordinarily moving. They gave me a glimpse of a world in which crushing poverty, indebtedness, alcoholism, and societal taboos blighted the lives of many, especially women.

Rajaji spearheaded the Vedaranyam Salt March in the south which mirrored Gandhi's Dandi March in 1930 and was imprisoned in Tiruchi jail. He took part in the Vaikom Satyagraha (1924–25) against untouchability. This was the first non-violent satyagraha to protest lower caste people being banned from entering the roads leading to the Vaikom temple by the Travancore royal family. Ezhava leaders like T. K. Madhavan, and Kerala Congress leaders like George Joseph, were involved. Periyar, along with Rajaji and others, drew Mahatma Gandhi's attention to the struggle.

There were many other luminaries who became passionate nationalists and embraced the Gandhian ethos and left their mark on Tamil Nadu. Movements like Home Rule (1916–18), the Khilafat Movement (1919–22), and the Non-cooperation Movement (1920–22) brought masses of people into the struggle for freedom. Annie Besant who came to India from Ireland as a theosophist was the first woman president of the Indian National Congress and was a strong advocate of Home Rule in India. In Madras, where she spent most of her time (and where she later died in 1931), she established the Theosophical Society, given to esoteric philosophical views and adopted young Jiddu Krishnamurti, whom she proclaimed the new messiah. Although he became one of the most influential philosophers of his time, J. K. as he was later known, rejected the Besant umbrella, evolving his own distinct mode of philosophical enquiry. Annie Besant continued her ardent commitment to India's independence as an avowed secularist and champion of women's rights and was admired by both Gandhi and Jawaharlal Nehru.

Another woman who rose to prominence at this time was Muthulakshmi Reddy, the social reformer who worked tirelessly for the abolition of the Devadasi system and for the welfare of women, particularly destitute girls. She was a medical practitioner and the first female student to be admitted to a men's college in Pudukkottai where she was born. She trained as a doctor in the Government Ophthalmic and Maternity Hospital in Chennai. She was appointed to the Madras Legislative Council in 1926 and was the first woman legislator in British India. Drawn into political activism from early adulthood, she also developed a deep interest in social reform, especially in the upliftment of women. Influenced by Annie Besant, and later by Gandhi, Muthulakshmi's contributions in the field of medicine, education, and in championing the cause of women in Tamil Nadu was immense. Her fight against the Devadasi system, where women dancers dedicated to temples often faced severe abuse, especially from the men who 'sponsored' them and were their patrons, was born of her own personal experience as the daughter of Chandrammal, a Devadasi. She found the road to reform and abolition long and difficult, meeting with stiff opposition even from many women dancers of the Devadasi community like Bangalore Nagarathnamma and Duraikannu Ammal. The tragedy of a young Devadasi, Shanpakavalli, who wrote a poignant and distressing letter to P. Varadarajulu Naidu, for his paper, *The Tamil Nadu,* before taking her own life at the age of thirteen triggered Muthulakshmi into action.

Muthulakshmi Reddy wrote an appeal for the abolition of the Devadasi system to *The Hindu* describing the case.

> …the innocent, virgin Dasi girl, Shanpakavalli…could not think of any other alternative, but ending her worthy and noble self, thereby hoping that the nation would be moved to acts of compassion and mercy at the very deplorable lot of her community girls…
>
> …is it not fair or just on our part to try and root out a system that forcibly converts good, healthy, normal children…into miserable and undesirable human beings…

Muthulakshmi goes on to quote from the girl's letter:

> Owing to my evil karma I was born to a Dasi mother who died in my 10th year. Then my grandmother showed me much affection and brought me up. I loved to listen to the stories of the Ramayana, and I

> used to pray daily that I should be blessed like Sita with a husband like Rama. One day my grandmother advised me to undergo the dedication ceremony that I may become a prostitute. I did not listen to her evil advice...Then I attained my age in my 13th year. Again, she pressed me... Even then I impressed upon her that I might even consent to get myself wedded to a dog with all the sacred rites but never lead the life of a Dasi.

The tipping point for Shanpakavalli came when her grandmother allowed a rich older man access to her room, and he actually entered it. Dressed as a man she ran away from the house. Sadly, this did not end well. The girl ends the letter avowing to kill herself because though she saved herself from being sexually abused by the man, the shame of running away was too much for her.

> When readers go through my letter, I would have left this world for the other so I may plead before my Creator for my poor sisters who may be in similar circumstances like myself. I hope my death would teach my grandmother a lesson.

Anguished by this, Muthulakshmi hoped that a nation's conscience would be moved to act. Along with Moovalur Ramamirtham, another social activist, she worked tirelessly to abolish the Devadasi system. It took till 1947 to pass the bill to abolish the system, but Muthulakshmi and Ramamirtham never gave up fighting persistently for the passage of the bill.

Another social reformer who took up the cause of widows, who were often left destitute on the deaths of their husbands, was Sister R. S. Subbalakshmi, herself a child widow. She used the title of 'sister' in order to identify with all the child widows and widows who were in dire straits. The Icehouse in Triplicane, originally kept for refrigeration of goods from abroad, became a Widows Home with the government letting Sister Subbalakshmi use the premises. Her work was important because it underlined the need for the social and economic rehabilitation of many young women who had little wherewithal after they were abandoned by their families. A complete mainstreaming of widows gradually occurred, and such homes no longer needed to exist. Much of this social change is because of the work of Sister Subbalakshmi and her co-workers.

Besides such initiatives, others need to be noted. Many accounts of Tamil participation in the freedom movement do not give adequate space to the contributions of Tamil Muslims. Raja Mohamad says that Muslims 'proved their religious faith as well as true patriotism by enthusiastically participating in the Non-cooperation Movement. Very soon the Hindus and Muslims realized the strength of unity, mutual trust, and co-operation'. The Khilafat Movement originating in Turkey, where that country's territorial integrity was at stake, had caught the Indian public's imagination. As Gandhiji was a firm supporter of the movement, he advocated that Non-cooperation should be combined with the Khilafat Movement both for its own success and to support the sultan of Turkey. When he toured the south with Muslim leaders like Muhammad Ali and Shaukat Ali, great crowds turned out in support—and this included Hindus as well. For instance, Varadarajulu Naidu of Thanjavur was warned by the police for his speech in support of the movement and the sultan of Turkey. A member of the Madras Legislative Council, Yakub Hasan, went to London in 1919 to campaign for the Khilafat cause. It cannot be forgotten that large numbers of ordinary Muslims played a role in the struggle against the British. The writer Khushwant Singh said 'Indian freedom is written in Muslims' blood, their participation in the freedom struggle was much more, in proportion to their small percentage of population.'

Tamils did their bit in the nationwide movements that marked the first decades of the twentieth century—protests against the oppressive Rowlatt Act, the Jallianwala Bagh Massacre, and the growing Civil Disobedience Movement.

It was during this period that an event of great importance for the Tamil people took place. In 1916, with the birth of the non-Brahmin movement, T. M. Nair, and P. Theagaraya Chetti, who were originally in the Congress Party, formed the South India Liberation Federation, later called the Justice Party, and sought to end Brahmin domination in the Indian National Congress where they found the majority of office bearers were Brahmins. Venkatachalapathy says, 'The ground rules of politics changed with Non-Brahmins staking a claim to political power'. Disillusionment with the Congress had set in when these leaders saw intense competition taking place within the movement, with the Brahmins undercutting them at every stage. In 1916, they released the Non-Brahmin Manifesto, a document written in English, which 'was framed within the Enlightenment liberal discourse' says Venkatachalapathy. 'The lived experience plays a very important part in transformations' he adds, 'whether it is Pietermaritzburg, where a Gujarati lawyer is thrown out of a train, or as in the case of Periyar (E. V. Ramasamy) who encountered a situation in the Cheranmadevi Gurukulam. This was where the Congress activist and polyglot V. V. S. Aiyar had started a school with a national curriculum with funds collected from the Congress Party and from the public. The caste fissure comes in. It transpires that Brahmin students and non-Brahmin students are served food separately, and this causes a furore.' We have seen how Brahmins had a disproportionate amount of jobs and influence in government and education for centuries. Now there were serious protests about the privileged position the Brahmins enjoyed in Tamilakam from other castes.

With the Montagu-Chelmsford Reforms of 1918 in place with the Government Act of India 1919, gradual concessions were being made by the British to include Indians in government, as they recognized the need to accommodate growing democratic aspirations in the country. Many of the Brahmin leaders in Congress saw the writing on the wall and quickly roped in people like E. V. Ramasamy and Varadarajulu Naidu into the party. However, the demand for proportional representation, and in jobs, was strongly voiced by the non-Brahmin leadership. These demands found massive support. Leaders like Periyar and Naidu used the discontent to effect lasting change. They had been unsuccessful so far in getting elected to various political offices and were defeated by Brahmin groups, the Mylapore faction led by several lawyers as well as the Vembakkam Iyengars and the Chetpet Iyers. Another group was headed by Rajaji from the Congress party. The Egmore faction was led by *The Hindu*'s editor, Kasturi Ranga Iyengar. The Justice Party was initially one of the factions and all these groups worked to convince the British authorities that they were the appropriate group to take up power in any plan for constitutional devolution. The Non-Brahmin Manifesto of December 1916 had pointed out:

> Not less than 40 million out of 41.5 million, who form the population of this Presidency (composite Madras state), are non-Brahmins... they make little or no use of their influence among the masses for the general political advancement of the country. In these days of organised effort, they maintain no proper organisation for protecting and promoting their common interests and for preventing professional and other politicians, with hardly any corresponding stake in the country, from posing as their accredited spokesmen. Nor have they a press of their own to speak the truth on their behalf. Their political interests, therefore, as compared with those of the Brahmins, who number only about a million and a half, have materially suffered.

The goal of wider representation, which was one of the principles of the Justice Party, pushed it to contest the 1920 elections and they won in the Madras Presidency. They continued to win elections as the major opposing party to the Congress and won the presidency elections until 1937. They participated in a British-led representative government arguing that India was not ready yet for self-rule and opposed Annie Besant's Home Rule movement. The party line was that if self-rule came to be, Brahmin domination would continue. Opponents to this indicated with levels of anger that this was a throwback to the British 'Divide and Rule' policy. Further criticism included the lack of nuance in the document which bracketed all Non-Brahmins together, not recognizing the history of conflict within Non-Brahmin communities including the age old left-hand-right hand disputes. *The Hindu* commented: 'It can serve no good but is bound to create bad blood between persons belonging to the same Great Indian Community.' It further declared: '…we do not wish to open our correspondence column to a discussion on this subject, as it cannot but lead to acrimonious controversy….' In time, *The Hindu* changed its stance and opened its columns for debate and discussion of the subject.

Perhaps the most important member of the Tamil political scene at this time was E. V. Ramaswamy or Periyar. Periyar's contribution to politics at the societal churn that was taking place would later gave birth to the Self-Respect Movement, which in turn influenced politicians in Tamil Nadu for the next 100 years. Periyar was born in Erode into a merchant family. Initially a member of the Erode Town Council and its chairman between 1917 and 1919, he was forced to resign owing to some accusations levelled at him. He joined the Congress Party in 1920 and was imprisoned during the Non-cooperation campaign of 1921. Periyar advocated strongly for reservations even while within the Congress, but his views were either met with indifference or resistance. He had to constantly battle a local political enemy T. Srinivasa Mudaliar and in 1925 left the Congress in disappointment and disgust as he felt he could not make much progress while in the party. Between 1925 and 1929, he set up the Self-Respect Movement, speaking in meetings across the state; one of the movement's principal aims was to remove Brahmins from power, diminish Hinduism and bring about social change through swaya mariyadhai—self-respect.

Even as a young boy, Periyar had questioned caste hierarchies as well as Hindu mythological stories and many aspects of the religion itself which he felt were ridden with caste overlays and superstition. A story goes that while on a pilgrimage to Kasi (Varanasi) he was denied entry, food, and shelter in a choultry (rest house for pilgrims) and told that only Brahmins could enter. Due to severe hunger, he decided to dress as a Brahmin so that he could get some food to eat, but it was soon discovered that he was not a Brahmin, and he was then violently thrown out on the streets. A bitterly disillusioned Periyar turned from religion and became an atheist. He was shocked to later learn that the choultry he had sought to enter was actually owned by a wealthy non-Brahmin. The fact that shastras and rules had their roots in religion, which he felt created divisions within society, made Periyar question the very nature of religion itself.

In later years he campaigned against Brahmins and the Hindu religion itself. He famously said, 'If you see a Brahmin and a snake, kill the Brahmin first.' In a recent article in *Frontline*, Karthick Ram Manoharan says that critics have railed against Periyar's speeches against Brahmins and Hinduism but says that 'movements for social justice that challenge subordination and inequality do not always conform to civil language: offensive speech is often resistance speech'. In *Viduthalai* in 1957, Periyar himself said that 'the rationale behind such speeches was meant to raise indignation among the backward and oppressed castes of their lowered position in society.' He further said that there was no further violent action that followed his words. Periyar's close and deep lifelong friendship with Rajaji was touted as evidence of his opposition only to Brahminism and not Brahmins themselves.

The principle of Self-Respect, according to Periyar, went beyond the political freedom that the Congress party and other nationalist parties sought. He described it as Arivu Viduthalai Iyakkam, a movement to liberate the intellect. Social changes introduced by the movement included marriages conducted without Hindu rituals and Hindu priests. Tamil Nadu became the first state to legalize marriages without a Brahmin priest. Widow remarriage was also encouraged by Periyar. Eugene Irschick, the Dravidian historian, says, 'the goals of the Self Respect Movement reflected the ideas of the Siddhars and the nineteenth and twentieth century Christian missionaries. They were heavily influenced by the writings of Ramalingaswami and Subramania Bharati....' These ideas spoke to a 'golden age' of egalitarianism and prosperity, especially in terms of food availability. Periyar was able to reach a wider group of influential people including those connected to the Congress and Justice Party through his stirring speeches as well as through journalism. He owned and backed several publications such as *Kudi Arasu*. Irschick says what was important about the Self-Respect Movement was that it aided the quota system or representation of the lower strata in various government services become a reality.

Periyar took over the Justice Party and renamed it Dravida Kazhagam in 1944. In the 1930s his movement had melded with the Justice Party. In the decades that followed, the Dravidian movement would become the basis for a new Tamil identity.

Chapter 30

An Unprecedented Freedom

Live in the present, shape the future.
Subramania Bharati, poet and writer

16 AUGUST 1947. LIKE THE REST OF INDIA, THE PEOPLE OF MADRAS STATE woke to a new dawn of freedom. Like their counterparts all across India it was a morning that commenced with the hope that this newly born nation would brim with opportunities for life and livelihood for the citizens of a new democratic republic. Two small girls sitting at the doorstep of their home in Thanjavur clapped their hands in glee as the aroma of cardamom and saffron emanated from the family kitchen, celebrating this unique day. They were glad they did not have to wear their thick khadi pavadais anymore in deference to their Gandhian father's advisory. He had freed them too in a way from the rigours of a Gandhian life and told them that as citizens of a free India, they could be whoever they wanted to be. The farmer in Tirunelveli who worried about drought and rain and a disappointing harvest from his miniscule plot of land, sat with his neighbours who read the newspaper that announced the birth of a free India. He did not know what it could mean for him. All across the state that had once been a stronghold of the British, there was rejoicing and hope that this new nation would deliver; there were rumours of communal strife in parts of India that trickled down to the south, but as a citadel of relative communal and ethnic harmony, at least for that time, the state safeguarded its own—whether Tamil, Telugu, Kannada, Gujarati, Hindu, Muslim, or Christian.

Fast forward to 1967. The farmer in Tirunelveli found that a free India brought no profound change to his situation. In fact, if anything, his situation was worse; frequent drought in recent years diminished harvests of rice and other crops; mortgaged land and a heavy debt burden meant that his future and that of his family was perilous. The girls in Thanjavur had fared better, though. Free India for them was also the freedom to embrace new choices; they moved to study in colleges in Madras, found exciting new professions but held on to the core of the ideology that they grew up with, welcoming the new measures of education and social justice that had opened new doors for them and their counterparts.

In the first twenty years of a free India, the changes that came were varied; faster progress in some states, slower in others. Jawaharlal Nehru, free India's first prime minister, who was passionate that the country should be a secular, strong parliamentary democracy and emerge as a modern nation, promoted science and technology from the 1950s onward. The Government of India set up high-level engineering and technical institutions like the Indian Institutes of Technology, the Regional Engineering Colleges, and research centres like the Indian Institute of Science. Several institutes of management were set up, and a plethora of industries, dams, and hydroelectric projects, satellite and space projects, and defence establishments all functioned under the government's own aegis, setting up pathways to technological progress.

In Madras, a particularly striking event occurred in 1967. The Dravida Munnetra Kazhagam (DMK), the Tamil regional party whose antecedents lay with the Dravida Kazhagam and earlier the Justice Party, swept to power in the state. This was an astonishing electoral result in which the Congress was completely routed. The Congress never again got the opportunity to form a government in the state.

From Independence onwards, the Congress had continued to be very popular across states in India and Tamil Nadu was no exception. But, in time, across India, regional grievances with regard to food shortages, price rise, and other issues would lead to significant losses for the Congress party in state elections. In 1950, the states were reorganized linguistically. The renewed call for a separate Telugu-speaking Andhra state, first made in 1948, created problems for Madras with agitators demanding an immediate agreement on the creation of Andhra. When the issue was first raised, soon after Independence, Potti Sriramulu, a freedom fighter and Gandhian who had fasted many times during the freedom struggle and for Dalit upliftment, was caught up in the cause. Gandhi once said of him, 'If only I have...more supporters like him I will win freedom from British rule in a year.' Potti Sriramulu wanted Madras as the capital of Andhra, and neither Prime Minister Jawaharlal Nehru nor Home Minister Vallabhbhai Patel or Pattabhi Sitaramayya, the Congress president, agreed to this, although they did concede to the demand of a separate Andhra without Madras in it. Potti Sriramulu went on fast to press for his demands; tragically, he died in December 1952 after fifty-six days of fasting. The linguistic reorganization would go on to cost many more lives.

In Madras, the decline of the Congress set in post 1953, with opposition, among other things, to the Congress's education scheme in rural schools led by Rajaji who headed the government at the state. It was called the Modified Scheme of Elementary Education but dubbed 'Kula Kalvi Thittam' or a 'caste based' and family-specific education scheme by its detractors. Its intention was to lessen a child's school hours and impart professional skills from the family's occupation by which he meant that they would get trained in the vocation of their parents. This was seen as being caste oriented as professions tended to be caste based. The scheme was immediately perceived as discriminatory and was highly unpopular. This forced the celebrated elder statesman to resign. D. Veeraraghavan's insightful study, *Half A Day for Caste?* sets out the ideas behind Rajaji's educational scheme, the processes, and the controversy it generated and explains that, among other aspects, the senior statesman refused to see that such a system would further solidify the social and educational inequities that already existed. The book reproduces two cartoons published in *Viduthalai*. The first cartoon from 27 July 1953 shows a Brahmin woman teaching her young son and the other half of the cartoon shows a boy on a bull outside with the caption: 'The New Education Scheme—The Aryan boy is being taught how to read by his mother and the Dravidian boy is riding a buffalo.' The second cartoon on 1 August 1953 with a student standing in front of his teacher is titled: 'The Students Are to Learn A Hereditary Occupation. Teacher: What's your father's occupation? Student: Bootlegging Sir.' The caption further says: 'The elementary teacher, following Rajaji's advice, is looking for a place to impart vocational training.' Under fierce opposition from many constituents, from the legislative bodies to the media and even from within his own party, the scheme was dropped upon Rajaji's resignation. Veeraraghavan says, 'As Chief Minister, Rajaji took many bold decisions which found mass acceptance. The de-control of food, the Tanjore Tenant and Pannayil Protection Bill, the Tanjore Tenancy Regulations, his defence of the history of the handloom weavers—all created mass goodwill. A social conservative, averse to radical socio-economic changes, he was deeply committed to the preservation of traditional rural society.' Unfortunately, this decision did not find favour with people in the state.

Kumaraswami Kamaraj, the capable Congress leader who opposed the educational scheme, and whose experience and skills in party building brought him to the helm of the Congress party nationally and in Madras state as well, took over the reins from Rajaji. Rajaji's grandson, the renowned writer and scholar Rajmohan Gandhi, describes the events of this time in his book *Modern South India*. He writes that much of Tamil country was delighted by the ascension of Kamaraj 'a man of few words who had never gone to university and spoke little English, a bachelor whose sole concern it seemed was the ordinary person's well-being....' As chief minister, he recorded more than modest success in the fields of education and industrialization. He was the pioneer of free mid-day meals for children in schools, a scheme that was built upon later by the politicians that followed. Kamaraj found support from an unexpected quarter. Periyar, delighted at the appointment of Kamaraj, the first non-Brahmin chief minister of the state, openly expressed his approval. This is when the complexion of the Congress altered, and it ceased to be a Brahmin-dominated party in Madras.

The DMK under C. N. Annadurai was building itself up slowly. This once trusted lieutenant of Periyar, a shrewd politician, had broken away from the original Dravida Kazhagam and founded the Dravida Munnetra Kazhagam. According to Venkatachalapathy, 'over the 1950s he built a party that expressed the dissatisfaction of Tamils with the Indian state especially the imposition of Hindi'. They had also given up the idea of a separate Dravida Nadu which they had espoused well into the 1950s, along with their opposition to the imposition of Hindi in Madras, something which had been going on even in the decades before Independence. Giving up the idea of a separate Dravida nation made more people comfortable with their ideology. The DMK profited from the general discontent with Congress rule and the perception that the state was being controlled by the Congress government in power at the centre. With films like *Velaikari* (1949), written by Annadurai, and *Parasakthi* (1952), which was scripted by Annadurai's political heir, M. Karunanidhi, starring the popular actor Sivaji Ganesan, showing an indifferent government and a suffering Tamil people, the tide was slowly turning against the Congress.

The impact of Tamil films on the minds of people soon became a phenomenon in the decades ahead, contributing as it did to powerful image building. Several film personalities found that they could make their way on to the political stage from the platform of film. However, even from the early years of cinema, a unique link was established between cinema and politics in Tamil Nadu. Some of the more prominent figures from the world of cinema who would leave an indelible mark on Tamil politics included Karunanidhi, M. G. Ramachandran, Sivaji Ganesan, N. S. Krishnan, M. R. Radha, Jayalalithaa, and several others. The movies at the time were heavily into Tamil nationalism and social causes which helped these figures move into politics and use their popularity to win elections. Kolkai padal is a kind of leitmotif in many films where a song would convey a political message but set to memorable music. MGR's famous song 'Naan aanai ittal, adhu nandathuvittal ingu ezhaiagal vedhanai padamattal' roughly translates to: If I issue a command and it happens, the poor, as long as they live will not suffer, not fall into an ocean of sorrow.

M. Bhaktavatsalam took over as chief minister in 1963 after Kamaraj voluntarily stepped down under his own scheme, the Kamaraj Plan, which he had structured requiring top officials and administrators to quit office after a particular tenure and devote themselves to party work. Bhaktavatsalam soon faced angry protests at the attempt by the central government to impose Hindi in the state. The Hindi agitations spread like wildfire across Madras. A fervent attachment to a distinct identity and pride in the linguistic and cultural heritage of the Tamils came bubbling up to the surface and unleashed a violent reaction in the state. The fires raged fiercely especially as the Official Languages Act was passed by the central government in 1963 declaring that Hindi was the official language. Nehru had earlier in 1959 given the country, particularly the non-Hindi speaking states, an assurance that Hindi would not be imposed agreed with the associate language status of English as an alternative for government communication, but this did not satisfy the agitators as it did not appear to be a watertight arrangement. In fact, Annadurai had famously declared that if numerical superiority was the logic behind the imposition of Hindi, we would have to settle for the crow as the national bird instead of the peacock as they were obviously more in number. When the bill was introduced in Parliament there were objections from the DMK members who did not like the use of the word *may* instead of *shall* in Section 3 of the bill. The sentence read 'The English language *may*...continue to be used in addition to Hindi'. Nehru assured Parliament that in this case, *may* had the same meaning as *shall* at which point the DMK members wanted to know why *shall* could then not be used. The bill was passed that year without any change in wording.

In an editorial in January 1965, when the switch over to Hindi as the sole official language came into effect, *The Hindu* cautioned, 'Hindi is to be installed formally as the principal official language of the Union from the 26th of this month, but the process can prove painful and confusing, unless the authorities seeking to bring about the change watch their step carefully....' On that day, and on the days that followed, massive rioting broke out in the streets of Madurai, in Madras city, and in many parts of the state. Many thousands of college students joined the protest. There were bloody clashes with Congress workers, particularly in Madurai. In Madras, 3,000 DMK workers were taken into custody including Annadurai. Thousands of single-minded protestors marched across Napier Bridge in Madras to Fort St. George to petition the chief minister. The protests would get worse.

The first act of self-immolation was by twenty-seven-year-old Chinnaswamy of Kizhappazhuvur in Tiruchi district. As an aside, this was one of the stranger and more tragic aspects of the Tamil psyche. It was glorified as a kind of martyrdom, so much so that such deaths would happen time after time. On 27 January, two other young men in Madras set themselves ablaze, pouring petrol over themselves and lighting themselves up. One was T. M. Sivalingam, a twenty-four-year-old DMK party worker, and the other was a married father of three young children, thirty-four-year-old V. Ranganathan of Virugambakkam, a Post and Telegraph employee, and a devoted party worker. *The Hindu* reported that he was heard shouting 'Tamil Vazhga' (Long Live Tamil) and 'Hindi Ozhiga' (Down with Hindi). During this time, as many of our generation remember, school children left their classrooms and ran out of schools in many instances of forced school closures for the next few months. T. S. Subramanian recalls how even as an eleven-year-old in school, he would follow the happenings with great interest and assisted in writing graffiti on neighbourhood walls until his father dragged him away by the scruff of his neck and punished him, his father being a nationalist and also unwilling for his son to get caught up in such activities.

Over seventy people died in the violent two weeks that followed until finally, in February of that year, Prime Minister Lal Bahadur Shastri (who had taken over after the death of Nehru in 1964) assured the people of the state that Nehru's original assurance about the continuation of English in official communication and in important areas like the civil services examinations would continue. The people of Tamil Nadu appeared mollified and in time the agitations slowly ceased. There were, however, more troubles and burdens to bear for the general public. Karunanidhi, Annadurai's protégé, protested the renaming of a village where the Dalmia Cements factory was established saying it was a Hindi name that had no place in the deep south. He lay down on the railway tracks to signal his opposition. In addition, the scarcity of rice in the markets caused by droughts in 1965 and 1966 was greatly affecting people.

The inability of the Congress government to tackle rice scarcity and rising disillusionment and public anger meant that when the state went to polls, the DMK won a stunning majority. Annadurai had campaigned on the slogan of 'oru roopavukku moonru padi arisi latchiyam, illendral, roopavukku oru padi nichiyam, adhuvum illai enral muchandiyil savukkadi engalukku'—our goal or ideal is three seers of rice for one rupee, if not one rupee for a seer is definite and if not, we can be beaten on the streets. This promise mesmerized a large number of voters. The DMK also used the star power of MGR, the film actor turned politician, who was a prominent campaigner for the party, and with a resounding victory established a new politics in Tamil Nadu. The fallout of the promised rice scheme where they ended up offering one rupee for only one seer of rice, irked the Nadar community who were the largest community of traders and retailers of rice and felt that this was detrimental to their business. However, because of Annadurai's personal popularity the administration was successful.

It is important at this point to emphasize a troubling aspect of Tamil society that has influenced the community and continues to influence it—the deep-seated hold that caste identity has on Tamils. This impacted Tamil politics quite strongly in post Independent India. Although Gandhian politics and Dravidian ideals had inspired many Tamils during the freedom movement, and saw diverse caste groups come together, the simmering divisions were never far beneath the surface. The Congress party even under Kamaraj saw instances of caste clashes between Dalits and Thevars. Pasumpon Muthuramalinga Thevar was the main Thevar patriarch of the three divisions of Thevars—the Kallars, the Maravars, and the Ahamudaiyars. There was a violent caste clash between Dalits and Thevars in a place called Kaumudi where a young fiery Dalit leader, Immanuel Sekaran, was murdered by the Maravars of the Thevar community because he seemingly disrespected Muthuramalinga Thevar by supporting the Pallars, a Dalit group. Although Muthuramalinga Thevar, a close friend of Subhas Chandra Bose, was a reformer, a nationalist, a labour unionist, and a fierce supporter of the Temple Entry Movement for Dalits, as the head of the Thevars, he was arrested by Kamaraj and put into jail briefly. An already weakened Congress lost the Thevar vote after this. Muthuramalinga Thevar is today considered a divinity by many in the Thevar community. V. Sasikala, Jayalalithaa's close aide, belongs to the community.

It was this aspect of the Tamil psyche that led to the emergence of parties like the DMK and has marked Tamil politics ever since. Venkatachalapathy says, 'In Anna, the emergent backward castes saw a leader who could take them to political power. He skilfully repackaged Periyar's iconoclastic ideas to make them palatable in the public domain. Periyar's rustic atheism became onre kulam, oruvane devan (One God, One Community) in a skilful appropriation of the venerated mediaeval Tamil saint Tirumular. When Periyar went about breaking the idols of Pillaiyar [Ganesha], Anna famously observed that he would neither break the idol nor the coconut (in worship)'. In a Man In The News column published in *The Hindu* in March 1967, as Annadurai assumed office, the writer says, 'from the humble house in the handloom town of Kancheepuram to the historic Fort St. George is a meteoric rise for the short-statured, soft-spoken politician, but one paved with obstacles and worries and setbacks. Radiant and upcoming Annadurai is now a mature 58 year old whose features bear witness to the long years of effort.'

In July 1967, a few months after becoming chief minister, Annadurai steered a resolution in the state assembly renaming the state Tamil Nadu instead of Madras and this was passed after a consensus since this had been a long-standing demand of the state. He also modified the language policy by opting for a two-language formula (Tamil and English) instead of the three-language formula adopted in neighbouring states, which included Hindi. Annadurai organized the first and second World Tamil Conferences, the first one in Madras in 1968, which clearly established the global status of Tamil language and literature. The icons of Tamil culture were all memorialized on Marina beach in Madras. Not so much the politicians, but those who were scholars and heroes of the Tamil world. Annadurai also legalized the Self-Respect marriages, amending the Hindu Marriage Act, the brainchild of his erstwhile mentor Periyar. In 1969, within two short years of assuming office, Annadurai died of stomach cancer at the age of fifty-nine. M. Karunanidhi succeeded him as chief minister.

Karunanidhi, one of the Dravidian movement's strongest leaders, was inspired by the speeches of Periyar and the ideals of the Justice Party. The DMK ruled Tamil Nadu intermittently for five terms under him. He was the longest serving chief minister of the state. We have already mentioned his early fiery activism in the context of Hindi imposition. Karunanidhi was a natural politician, and gradually became extremely popular, especially among the rank and file of the DMK party despite his lack of formal schooling. In many ways, he was of the Anna school of political sophistication, but keen on establishing his own identity. Karunanidhi set out his own set of symbols, such as the invocation to Tamil Thai at public events, to reinforce the Tamil identity. He also paid attention to his party cadres and began referring to them as 'udan pirappukal' or blood brothers, shoring up their loyalty and support to him.

S. Narayan, former bureaucrat, points out that 'the politicization of administration as well as the change in the class structure of the administration enabled the DMK to push forward the social justice agenda that had been the basic feature of the Periyar movement'. New schemes to help the poor with housing was implemented with newly instituted bodies like the Slum Clearance Board. Other development indicators also improved in the state. Building upon Periyar's initial efforts, reservation for various backward caste groups was brought up to 44 per cent. The Sattanathan Commission appointed by Karunanidhi in 1971 looked into the matter of the 'creamy layer' where many had been exploiting the benefits of reservation and edging out more deserving groups. They recommended an MBC or Most Backward Class quota which was worked into the reservation structure. In time, the legislative process brought the reservation quota for Backward and Scheduled classes up to 69 per cent in the state. Karunanidhi, over his many periods in office, set up many welfare schemes for the people, including increasing health care in the state, looking into the rehabilitation of leprosy patients, adding eggs to the mid-day meal scheme, creating habitations such as the Periyar Ninaivu Samathuvapuram, an important project to enhance community living among different castes across many rural areas. He abolished hand-pulled rickshaws and also added to public expenditure on higher education and gave concessions to small industries and to the health and social welfare sectors.

In 1972, the movie star and politician MGR, who was a prominent member of the DMK, decided to leave the party and form his own. He accused the ruling DMK echelons of increasing corruption and Karunanidhi of promoting his own family members. Karunanidhi was also filled with ire at MGR's popularity. It was estimated that half the DMK party members were members of MGR fan clubs or Rasigar Manrams. MGR established the Anna Dravida Munnetra Kazhagam (ADMK), later called the All India Dravida Munnetra Kazhagam (AIADMK). He focused on mobilizing the party and used the medium of film, like many successful Tamil politicians, to further increase his popularity with the Tamil public. In films like *Netru Indru Naalai* (1974), *Idhayakani* (1975), and *Indru Pol Endrum Vazhga* (1977), MGR would play the underdog, a rickshaw puller, a peasant, and other such roles, always identifying with the vulnerable, thus enhancing his image with ordinary people. MGR after defeating the DMK in 1977 held power for the next decade and more. He exuded a powerful persona and won every election in the state till his death in 1987.

MGR's presence ensured the dominance of the Dravidian parties ever since the rout of the Congress in 1957. D. Suresh Kumar, senior editor at *The Hindu*, and a keen political analyst, says that Biju Patnaik, the Odia politician, once tried to bring MGR and Karunanidhi together and Karunanidhi agreed that he would be the party president while MGR would continue to be chief minister. Suresh Kumar says that MGR went back on the proposal as Panruti Ramachandran, a top DMK member, advised him not to. This was because, as Ramachandran clarified later, the leaders might get together but what of the cadres? The two parties continue to dominate state politics to this day. Throughout his political career, MGR saw the masses as his base and never wooed the middle class. Neither did he care for criticism from the media. He knew that his voters were rural people and women and developed an ideology which placed the needs of the poor at the top. His numerous welfare schemes included the landmark expansion of the mid-day meal scheme, initiated by Kamaraj, which brought undernourished children from impoverished households into schools. The development of technical education including the establishment of polytechnics flourished during his time, offering young people opportunities that colleges offering regular degrees could not. He was deified and adored by the people of the state. When he died in 1987, grief-stricken rioters roamed the city of Madras, damaging property, threatening people, and mourning the departed leader with violence and terror.

It is necessary to note at this point that the welfarist impulse exhibited by both Dravidian parties was woven into a broader social reform impulse and plans to reform politics and economics in keeping with the Dravidian vision of social justice. Welfare policies gained greater momentum given the competitive politics between the DMK and the AIADMK. MGR, coming as he did from a background of deep poverty and deprivation, emphasized the role of nutrition in children. This certainly advanced the human development indicators in the state, its health and nutrition outcomes and, at a broader level, inter-caste harmony as children of all castes had to sit together to eat in schools. There is debate about the disbursement of 'freebies' as they are called—when fiscal expenditure is driven by competitive populism there is a risk of capsizing public finances.

After MGR's death the AIADMK saw an internal tussle between his wife, Janaki, and J. Jayalalithaa and the party split, fighting each other, including over the two leaves symbol of the party. Janaki became the chief minister for a month or so with the rebel faction of Jayalalithaa not supporting the AIADMK in the assembly. There was chaos and confusion in the assembly after which President's rule was established. Fresh elections were called in 1989 and there was a contest between these two split factions, the Congress under veteran leader G. K. Moopanar who sought to revive the party's presence in the state, and the DMK led by Karunanidhi. The DMK won 150 seats and the Jayalalithaa faction just 27. This set the stage for one of the most appalling incidents in the state assembly.

Karunanidhi's resounding victory (he returned to power after thirteen years) 'proved that he could play the waiting game', says Suresh Kumar. It was during the presentation of the budget on 25 March 1989 that the horrific episode took place. Describing the incident to *The Print*, K. N. Arun, senior journalist and now professor at the Asian College of Journalism, who was in the assembly that day said: 'Jayalalithaa was disheartened (by the election results) and had decided to resign from her MLA seat (Bodinaickanur) and drafted a letter which was handed to M. Natarajan, husband of V. K. Sasikala (ousted AIADMK leader and aide of Jayalalithaa).' Arun recalled that at that time, a raid was conducted at Natarajan's residence in Chennai's Abhiramapuram on charges of cheating. 'The very same evening, Jayalalithaa's resignation letter mysteriously found its way to then Tamil Nadu assembly speaker M. Tamilkudimagan. The speaker issued a notification the same day accepting the resignation but had to recall it the following day.' It was in this context that the AIADMK planned the disruption citing breach of privilege of the assembly on 25 March. 'Jayalalithaa shouted that a kutravali (a criminal) should not present the budget,' said Arun. 'Karunanidhi then made a remark that left Jayalalithaa visibly shaken. Immediately, AIADMK MLA K. A. Sengottaiyan and a few others moved forward to snatch the copy of the budget and Sengottaiyan pushed the CM,' Arun said.

Violence broke out on the floor of the assembly, with DMK and AIADMK members hurling budget documents, mics, and slippers at each other, according to those present there. Arun said that the MLA Thirunavukkarasar, who was sitting next to Jayalalithaa, said that he tried to shield her from the front, while K. K. S. S. R. Ramachandran, a current DMK minister who was an AIADMK MLA in 1989, guarded her from the back, and Congress leader G. K. Moopanar covered her from the side. Arun observed all these events. As Jayalalithaa was walking out, in the confusion that prevailed, her sari was pulled, and tore at the point where it was pinned to her blouse. Karunanidhi's and Jayalalithaa's versions of the events were different. What was true was that her sari was pulled and torn.

Suresh Kumar says, 'The year 1990 saw Karunanidhi play a key role in the launch of the National Front headed by V. P. Singh's Janata Dal…and he (VP) went on to become prime minister and implemented the Mandal Commission…. More than three decades later, the DMK, a passionate advocate for the equitable representation of marginalized groups and social justice, remained politically indebted to Singh for his gesture. It installed a statue of the raja of Mandal facing the Marina in November 2023.'

In 1991, Karunanidhi's government fell and as Tamil Nadu readied itself for another poll, in May of that year, a human bomb, Dhanu of the LTTE, assassinated Rajiv Gandhi, the former prime minister, who was campaigning in the state for the upcoming national elections, in Sriperambudur near Madras. This changed the course of electoral politics in the state. Jayalalithaa came to power on a massive sympathy wave as her party was in alliance with the Congress and became Tamil Nadu's youngest chief minister at the age of forty-three.

We must recall some facts about Jayalalithaa here. MGR's political heir, and close confidante, she was in power off and on from 1991 onwards. She first rose to prominence upon the death of MGR and was selected as the general secretary of the AIADMK from 1988 to 2016. Emerging like her mentor and patron MGR from the world of film, she overcame the challenges of a difficult childhood to enter the world of the Tamil cinema where her mother, Sandhya, was a minor actor and pressured the young girl to join the film industry. Academically brilliant, Jayalalithaa studied at the well-known Presentation Convent Church Park in Madras and was highly popular in school. She had begged her mother to allow her to continue to college after school, but Sandhya found that ends were hard to meet, her profligate husband having died leaving her with two young children to care for. Trained in classical music, and proficient in playing the piano, Jayalalithaa gave up her dreams of college and joined the film business instead. Articulate and strong-minded, she was known for her diction and superlative expositions. Indira Gandhi and Khushwant Singh actually came down to listen to her maiden speech in the Rajya Sabha in March 1984 on the 'greatness of women'.

Even in her first term, 1991 to 1996, she enjoyed adulation and deference from her followers and the public. Suresh Kumar says, 'Tamil Nadu was soon introduced to an unprecedented VVIP culture where she remained insulated from the people. Vehicular traffic would be stopped for hours for her convoy to pass. Her close confidante Sasikala Natarajan emerged as an overarching extra constitutional authority. Murderous attacks were orchestrated against critics of Jayalalithaa and her government's policy.' Political opponents including Prime Minister Narasimha Rao were subjected to humiliation.

In 1993, when there were repeated highway robberies in the state, she told the assembly, 'Those who were caught for indulging in these robberies speak Telugu. Prime Minister Narasimha Rao is a Telugu man and you can draw your own conclusions.' The chief minister then went on the offensive and made the sensational charge that the events were part of a conspiracy hatched by New Delhi [the Narasimha Rao government] to dislodge her government. She went on to say that the Congress (I) high command was adept at destabilizing state governments, as it had done in the case of its own Veerendra Patil regime in Karnataka by engineering caste and communal riots.

Early on, after assuming office, Jayalalithaa had declared she would draw a token salary of one rupee. This decision later became her nemesis. The then Janata Party leader Subramanian Swamy launched a legal onslaught against her, accusing her of amassing wealth disproportionate to her known sources of income.

In 1995, Jayalalithaa conducted a lavish wedding for her foster son, V. N. Sudhagaran—the nephew of Sasikala, with the granddaughter of Tamil cinema's legendary actor Sivaji Ganesan. The image of Jayalalithaa and Sasikala leading the wedding procession with the groom and bride all bedecked in gold and diamonds created a sense of revulsion and rage among the public, but Jayalalithaa was apparently unapologetic.

This era is often viewed as a particularly troubling phase in Tamil Nadu's political history, marked by actions that overshadowed Jayalalithaa's significant contributions. Despite her notable efforts to protect the state's interests in the Cauvery water issue, ensure constitutional backing for a high level of communal reservations, and introduce social reforms such as baby care initiatives for girls and dedicated women's police stations, her administration's controversial measures left a darker impression on this period.

There were other factors at play by the time of the 1996 elections. Moopanar broke with the Congress party and formed the Tamil Maanila Congress as Narasimha Rao had announced an alliance with the AIADMK. V. Gopalasamy (Vaiko), a powerful personality in the DMK, broke with Karunanidhi over the increasing prominence given to his son M. K. Stalin within the party. Some of his loyalists also followed suit. During electioneering those who were opposed to Jayalalithaa warned the public against her. Even Rajinikanth famously said 'even God cannot save Tamil Nadu if Jayalalithaa returned to power'. He spoke against the prevailing 'bomb culture' in the state as the film director Mani Ratnam's house was subject to a bomb attack. Because one of Jayalalithaa's ministers, R. M. Veerappan, was present at a meeting where this was said, she sacked him. The Pattali Makkal Katchi founded by Ramadoss in 1989, a caste-based party representing the Vanniyars, entered the political landscape.

Karunanidhi won this election. When asked how he won such a massive victory, he quipped, 'Jayalalithaa is the reason'. Stalin was appointed mayor of Chennai and did some commendable work during his tenure including the construction of flyovers to deal with the city's burgeoning traffic. Among one of the chief minister's early actions was to initiate legal action against Jayalalithaa for amassing wealth; she was released on bail and thereafter vowed never to wear jewellery. She had tied up with the BJP, meanwhile, and when L. K. Advani the then home minister refused to help her dislodge the DMK government, she bided her time and delivered a punch—voted out the national NDA coalition government headed by A. B. Vajpayee, of which the DMK was a member, by refusing to support the government during a no-confidence motion. The Vajpayee government fell short by one vote. At this opportune moment, the DMK too joined hands with the BJP and a couple of DMK members actually found themselves in the central government's cabinet.

Jayalalithaa faced legal hurdles. She was convicted in the Pleasant Stay Hotel case, and she and Sasikala were also convicted in two TANSI land deal cases. The High Court suspended their sentence and the conviction was deemed to be suspended. She could not contest the 2001 election personally but fielded a dummy candidate and filed nominations in three other seats. Although her nominations were rejected, her party won the state.

It was soon clear that the AIADMK had been returned to power but Jayalalithaa as a convicted person could not take office. Nevertheless, Fathima Beevi (the first woman judge of the Supreme Court of India) who was governor of the state hurriedly administered the oath of office to Jayalalithaa and her cabinet. This was struck down by the Supreme Court in September of the same year and a humble nominee of Jayalalithaa, an obscure first term MLA from Theni, O. Panneerselvam, became chief minister.

Soon the cases against Jayalalithaa were quashed and she was actually acquitted in the hotel case. On her birthday in February 2002, Jayalalithaa, who had stood in a by election in Andipatti, won her seat in the assembly back and said that this was the best birthday present she had ever received. She was back in the chief minister's seat. Meanwhile, even before she came back to office, the AIADMK arrested an aging Karunanidhi in a midnight gate crash at his residence, with policeman charging him with corruption. That case was later dropped due to insufficient evidence. It was a dramatic event televised for everyone to see, as the Maran brothers (sons of Karunanidhi's nephew, Murasoli Maran) who owned SUN television dramatically telecast the event. The sight of an ailing, elderly, sobbing man, a former chief minister arrested in his lungi at midnight, being dragged away by the police stunned not only the state but all of the country. Jayalalithaa had thought she would avenge her earlier imprisonment, but this proved to be another costly error for her in the long run. There were dramatic developments following this. Union ministers T. R. Baalu and Murasoli Maran were arrested on charges of obstruction of justice, Governor Fathima Beevi resigned for the role she had played. Stalin, Karunanidhi's son, was arrested as well.

Meanwhile, the Vajpayee government in Delhi sent a delegation, including the veteran political leader George Fernandes, to Chennai. Disturbed by the way the arrests were conducted, the delegation condemned the detention of the union ministers, arguing that the chief minister's actions had paved the way for chaos and warned that if this course was not corrected immediately, the country could face an unprecedented threat to its unity and integrity. Maran went directly to the Chennai Central Prison, met with Karunanidhi, and then told reporters that Karunanidhi's health condition was very bad and 'we wonder whether he will come out alive'. He said the Jayalalithaa government would be responsible if anything happened to him. Karunanidhi refused to apply for bail, which led a surprised Jayalalithaa to order his release on 'humanitarian grounds'. Later, Karunanidhi became emotional at a press conference, recounting the suffering he had endured. Jayalalithaa's by now well documented tensions with the press came to the fore around this period. There were several incidents including the controversial arrest of a Sun TV reporter who had earlier presented an investigative report when Jayalalithaa's convoy brushed against journalists protesting Karunanidhi's arrest in the Secretariat. The next day more than 100 journalists, reporters, and editors went on a rally and were arrested and then released. Later, at another DMK rally, police beat up journalists near the DGP's office on Dr Radhakrishnan Road, when the DMK had a public meeting at Seerani Arangam. Again, in 2003, Jayalalithaa went after *The Hindu*, for certain critical reports and editorials. This was another blatant assault on media freedom. The speaker of the Tamil Nadu assembly held that the newspaper's editors, its senior reporters, and its publisher were in breach of privilege of the house. Arrest warrants were sent out and the police were sent to search their houses. It was a shocking and direct attack on the free press and Kuldip Nayar, the veteran journalist, filed a the privilege motion in the Supreme Court and the Vajpayee government promised to send central forces to protect *The Hindu*. Jayalalithaa made a tactical withdrawal, but she continued to file defamation suits against numerous journalists. The media was as much her enemy as her political foes.

Those were unpredictable years in Tamil Nadu. The chief minister's unpopularity grew. There were transport strikes, she tried to take over Queen Mary's College and only stopped when the students protested. She also introduced some unpopular bills in the assembly including a ban on animal sacrifices in temples and a ban on 'religious' conversions. She would soon roll back these measures. But then she also set up welfare measures like the Amma canteens or 'unavagam' where good food would be sold for low cost; packaged drinking water was also sold at ₹10 per litre at 50 per cent the cost of regular bottled water. While this populism endeared her to the masses, she shunned advice and even interaction with her peers.

The state elections over the next few rounds saw the emergence of the popular film star Vijayakanth who had great mass appeal and was also known for his philanthropy. According to Jayanthi Natarajan, even on film sets he would walk around and enquire if everyone had eaten before sitting down to eat himself. Combining philanthropy and personal generosity with success as a film star was a sure shot to successful politics. Tamil Nadu's fabled success of politicians who have moved from the film world into the political landscape also ensured Vijayakanth's success. He made a firm dent in the vote share between the two major parties but won only a single seat. Even today while Kamal Haasan and Rajinikanth continue to enjoy huge star power (despite the poor performance of the former's party at the polls) their fans (and others) still fervently wish to see these stars at the helm of power. Vijayakanth was in and out of an alliance with Jayalalithaa but his party the Desiya Murpokku Dravida Kazhagam (DMDK) slowly diminished in importance after his death in 2023.

It must be mentioned that the civil war in Sri Lanka continually impacted Tamil Nadu in a general sense with ordinary people being extremely incensed as reports and horror stories from the heart of the war emerged in the media. The public was genuinely anguished by the Sri Lankan Tamil cause, but strangely it was never made an election issue, says veteran journalist Subramaniam who covered Sri Lankan Tamil politics from 1981 till 2010 and knew the LTTE supremo, Prabhakaran (and many other Sri Lankan Tamil leaders) well and had interviewed him several times. The DMK and AIADMK politicians often used the issue as an emotional hook to protect ethnic Tamils, and for political jockeying, but the cause itself never made it to any election manifesto.

Another aspect that needs to be mentioned in the Tamil political landscape was the growing stranglehold of Karunanidhi's family on the party. The party was dubbed the 'Dynasty Munnetra Kazhagam' at one point. Initially, there were political problems for Karunanidhi from his Madurai-based son, M. K. Alagiri, whose followers went on a rampage in Madurai and burnt buses. Later when things quietened down, Stalin, his other son, emerged as the victor not just within the party but as his father's unspoken successor. Karunanidhi's smart, articulate, and sophisticated daughter, Kanimozhi, who is a poet and Tamil scholar and has a deep understanding of politics also began to make her mark politically. She is currently a Member of Parliament in the Lok Sabha from Thoothukudi. The family also bought into various film production companies and almost all films that were made in Tamil Nadu had to be distributed by one of these family-owned houses.

Suresh Kumar succinctly narrates the political timeline of the period. 'The 2014 parliamentary election saw Jayalalithaa emerge as a strong and undisputable leader who would surpass the electoral achievements of her political mentor MGR. This was the time when a Narendra Modi wave was sweeping several parts of the country, and the image of the Congress was at its lowest ebb. The DMK, which pulled out of the United Progressive Alliance government just months before the polls, faced a piquant situation as it was unable to find strong allies. That's when Jayalalithaa declared the AIADMK would go it all alone in the polls. A highlight of the election was when Jayalalithaa reeled out statistics to establish that Tamil Nadu was far ahead of Modi's Gujarat in several sectors and she rhetorically posed: "Who is better, Gujarat's Modi or Tamil Nadu's Lady?" Stalin, who had by then begun to shoulder the burden of the DMK's campaign on account of Karunanidhi's frail health, had sought to butt in saying, "Not Lady or Modi, it is my Daddy".' The AIADMK won that election.

A curious thing happened in 2014. Jayalalithaa's old disproportionate assets case, from eighteen years ago, came back to haunt her. A special court to deliver the verdict was set up in Bengaluru and Jayalalithaa and her companion Sasikala were summoned before the court. She left Chennai as chief minister but went to prison in the neighbouring state capital as a felon. Sasikala took the blame on herself, but the verdict went against Jayalalithaa. She had to do jail time. There was turmoil in Tamil Nadu and O. Panneerselvam, Jayalalithaa's loyal deputy, took the oath of office as chief minister. He and several other ministers took their oaths in tears. After twenty-one days, she was given bail and returned to Chennai and took the oath of office once again. In the 2016 assembly election that followed Jayalalithaa again won and this time, despite failing health, she actually saw through some important schemes such as writing off farmer loans and providing free power to handloom weavers.

During an earlier tenure she managed to get a favourable verdict on water disputes with Kerala in the Mullaiperiyar Dam issue and with Karnataka over the Cauvery imbroglio. These were some of the biggest triumphs of her government. Jayalalithaa died after a prolonged illness in December 2016.

In the events that followed, her close associate Sasikala, who was very unpopular within the party, made several attempts to grab power, setting up a tussle between Panneerselvam and Edappadi Palaniswami. The latter replaced Panneerselvam. Sasikala, after serving a long jail sentence, was quietly eliminated from active political roles as she was also largely unpopular with the public, who saw her as a negative influence on their beloved Amma and the cause of her ruination.

Meanwhile, Karunanidhi, the great DMK patriarch, one of Tamil Nadu's tallest leaders and five-time chief minister, champion of social justice, Dravidian visionary, and a lifelong votary of the Tamil language as a writer and poet, died at the ripe old age of ninety-four in 2018. He had been voted to the assembly thirteen times and never lost a single election. The state mourned the passing of one of its brightest sons.

When Covid struck, Palaniswami as chief minister proved his mettle and ably dealt with the situation. In the 2021 elections, held in the midst of the pandemic, Stalin, who had full command of the DMK, emerged as the victor, forging strategic alliances with Vaiko and several other parties using strategists; Palaniswami also scored well in the polls. With the state still reeling under Covid's second wave and severe oxygen shortage, Stalin deftly handled the crisis. Subsequently, his agenda for the state's development is clear—he has sought greater investment in Tamil Nadu and implemented popular measures like ticketless travel for women, among other things. His cabinet is peopled by savvy ministers who seem to have a clear agenda and know what they need to deliver for the state's progress. He has however come in for criticism for promoting his son, Udhayanidhi Stalin, currently a minister in his cabinet. In the recent Lok Sabha polls in 2024 Stalin pulled off a clean sweep, and though the BJP has been able to make some inroads into Tamil Nadu, they did not win a single seat from the state. The AIADMK appears to be on the decline at this point in time.

Despite the heavy political feuds and bitter rivalries between the two major Dravidian parties, one needs to note that there was no dismantling of one government's social and economic schemes and welfare measures by another and despite the contention of persistent corruption, the schemes targeting the poor were never undone. Stalin seems determined to continue on this path.

Let us go back now to our two girls and the farmer in Tirunelveli whom we encountered at the beginning of this chapter. The farmer from Tirunelveli managed to survive for a few decades, although his debts slowly eroded his health. He did not live long. His children escaped though; they got free meals at school and availed of other state benefits that pulled them out of their difficult circumstances. They abandoned the land, moving to small towns nearby and managed to set their own young children on pathways to progress. As for the girls, they are elders now, women of substance who have been able to take bold decisions in their lives as this is a progressive state. Looking back at the great changes they have witnessed, the transformations they lived through, and all the history played out in front of them, they have reasons to hope as well as reasons to feel cautious. Their families have spread their wings outside of Tamil Nadu, become global citizens. They themselves have tried to adapt to a new digital world, even as they have witnessed the tragedies of a global pandemic, calamitous floods, and other natural disasters. And yet, the women are resolutely anchored here, negotiating the complexities of the evolving social, political, and economic environment in a place they call home.

Chapter 31
A Progressive and Paradoxical State

Issues of quality be it in education or healthcare and consequent disparities in human development can possibly be addressed within the domain of subnational politics and policy implementation.

Kalaiyarasan. A, Vijayabaskar. M, political economists

A SHAFT OF LIGHT BREAKS THROUGH A MONSOON SKY. AS I DRIVE through the interior of the state, the threat of rain is never far, but I learn that this is something that one lives with; it may come with force and destroy the seedlings in the fields or be a gentle patter that will be quickly absorbed by a scorched earth. Ramu who has four daughters but not the son he had hoped for is reconciled to the lack of a male child as well as the unpredictability of rain. He continues to steadfastly farm his 3-acre plot while cycling 6 or 7 kilometres every other day to check the accounts in a small textile factory near Erode, the town closest to his village. Ramu knows the value of education, being something of an accountant himself and is keen to send his daughters to study in Erode once they are a little older. 'I can't send them just yet, they are girls after all,' he tells me. He is quick to say that he values the local primary school in the village—the children are fed a nutritious meal, and his wife can spend time helping him on the farm. And are you happy with the education, I ask him. 'Three of them top their classes, then it must be a good education, right?' pat comes his reply.

The latest Performance Grading Index 2.0 report from the Niti Aayog on school education for the year 2021-2022, which assigns a score for each state based on seventy-three indicators, has placed Tamil Nadu seventh in the country after Chandigarh, Punjab, Delhi, Kerala, Gujarat, and Puducherry. In the same report, Tamil Nadu was ranked third in terms of universal access and preventing dropouts; second among the bigger states in infrastructure and facilities, third in terms of inclusivity and equity in education, and third in teacher education and training. However, although Ramu may not yet be aware of this, despite all the positive indicators of progress in education, the learning outcomes in Tamil Nadu schools are not great. Paradoxically, the state fares well in higher education. The number of colleges, the student-to-teacher ratio, and reasonable infrastructure puts it at the top compared to other states in the country. Eighteen institutions of higher learning from Tamil Nadu are ranked among the 100 best institutions in the country, according to the 2023 rankings. As one travels through rural Tamil Nadu one notes sprawling white buildings with trimmed gardens and white walls set off the highway; it is not unusual to see some of them nestled within swathes of paddy, although the encroachment into farmland possibly impacts local agricultural practice. Nevertheless, if Ramu's daughters make it out of school, there is a good chance that they will flourish in Tamil Nadu's colleges.

The Fault Lines of Caste

There is a darker side to Ramu's life. His younger brother, Bharathan, had fallen in love with a Dalit girl from a neighbouring village. There was a great outcry and fierce opposition from his family; from his aging parents as well as relatives and neighbours of the same community, the Thevar caste. Despite desperate entreaties from Bharathan, the family refused to accept the situation and Ramu too joined the family in opposition to the idea of marriage between the young people. The Dalit family was threatened with violence and as Ramu recounts to me, the local panchayat leaders and the police were firmly on the side of the Thevars, a powerful community that had always harboured a bitter enmity with the Dalits. A group of miscreants (possibly family members, confesses Ramu) were directly involved in an arson attack on some Dalit houses, including that of Bharathan's girlfriend, and next day, in the dead of night, many of the Dalit families left their houses and disappeared from the village. The story does not end there, Ramu said. 'My brother doused himself with kerosene and set fire to himself right outside our house,' he says. 'It's been three years, and my parents are completely destroyed. I deeply regret my part in it. The girl's family fled from here and have never been seen here since and the people from that community are now terrified of us,' he adds. Without any prompting from me, Ramu launches into a bitter and deeply sad diatribe on the folly of caste divides that cost his younger brother's life. In many cases, either the boy or girl have actually been murdered, and while the DMK has promised to end honour killings, nothing has actually been done about it, says journalist Udhav Naig who keenly follows the issue.

Ramu's family, like many millions of others, especially in certain districts of southern Tamil Nadu, belongs to the Thevar or Mukkulathor community as it is called, which in turn comprises other sub-caste groupings within it—these caste groups belong to the Other Backward Caste (OBC) or Most Backward Caste (MBC) depending on the sub-grouping. The enmity between these groups and others, particularly with Dalits, continues to be a festering wound in the social fabric of Tamil life. The history of caste violence in Tamil Nadu has been nothing short of horrific and although the Dravidian vision of social justice and equality are an integral part of every political party's agenda and indeed every government that has ruled Tamil Nadu since Independence, there has been little alleviation of the problem. One of the main ideals of the Dravidian movement was to eradicate caste differences, particularly the domination of Brahmins over non-Brahmins. While this was largely successful in the political sphere, as in the area of reservation for example, the social divides between communities and castes continue to prevail in Tamil Nadu. The Dravidian vision followed by the demand for social reform and social justice has not always been implemented at the ground level. Apart from numerous examples of the perpetuation of terrible caste crimes, one cannot help but remember the harrowing experiences of the gifted writer Perumal Murugan. His book *Madorbagam* (One Part Woman) aroused so much caste ire and bigotry even from within his own community, that he had to go into hiding for a long period to save his and his family's lives. Ironically, in Chennai city and indeed in other cities in Tamil Nadu, while caste names in many public places, particularly road names, have been removed, there has been a mushrooming of small caste organizations with names that clearly indicate affiliations. The normalization of caste organizations compounds the problem and criminal groups within these organizations are the worst offenders. Disgruntled, unemployed youth are often drawn to these organizations and many of them get set up to be hostile to other caste groupings. The Dalits suffer the most in this regard. Puthiya Tamilagam party founder and leader, Dr K. Krishnasamy, said that more than fifty murders were recorded in the southern districts since the DMK came to power in 2021. He accused the various Thevar groupings who had historically perpetrated violence against the Scheduled Castes and the OBCs of continuing in their course. 'To truly abolish caste discrimination and hierarchy we have to identify the extent and type of oppression faced and perpetrated by a community and address it. Dravidian ideologues have comfortably obfuscated who they are oppressing,' he said. Traditional antagonism also exists between the Vanniyars and Thevars.

In December 2022 in Vengaivayal, a remote hamlet in the Pudukkottai district, human faeces was found floating in the water tank of the Dalit village.

The public outcry against this shocking act was widespread but no culprit was brought to justice. In August 2023, in Nanguneri town in Tirunelveli district, three boys from a dominant caste entered the small one-room house of Ambikapathi, a Dalit Anganwadi worker, and assaulted her two young children, a boy and a girl, seventeen and fourteen years old. There was already a history of assault and abuse in this case; the children, especially the young boy, had been taunted for his caste and forced to do menial jobs for the three boys and was beaten when he failed to deliver. The mother sent in a letter of complaint to the school authorities. One fateful night, the three entered Ambikapathi's house and attacked the two children with sickles, injuring them severely. It has been a long and difficult road to recovery. Psychological trauma, grievous physical injuries, and several surgeries and medical treatments later, they are slowly recovering. Meanwhile, two other local murders have taken place, and the message is clear. Caste hierarchies have to be respected, and social traditions of superiority have to maintained. Violence and death are often the consequences.

There are many more stories of hate and caste violence in contemporary Tamil Nadu. Discriminatory practices, whether it is the separate glass system still stealthily maintained in many village tea shops, or isolating Dalit students in village schools, reveal a deep-rooted bias that persists in contemporary Tamil Nadu. Vasugi Bhaskar, the editor of *Neelam* magazine, sponsored by film director Pa. Ranjith, speaks passionately to me about the need to publicly articulate the discrimination and injustice meted out to Dalits. In 2023, when Dalits were not allowed into Draupadi Amman temple by caste Hindus in Melpathi village in Villupuram district, it led to violence perpetrated on Dalits who attempted to challenge the discriminatory practice and enter the temple. Bhaskar made a forty-five-minute documentary, *Melpathi*, on the aftermath of the clashes and the film was acclaimed at a film festival in Germany. Bhaskar's documentary reveals the shocking nexus between the powerful castes and local authority and the need to persist in the struggle.

Bhaskar tells me that the Dravidian narrative had its limitations. While Brahmin hegemony was removed by the movement and political representation was widened, it did not really translate into functional representation of all groups, especially of the SC and ST communities. The Justice Party's main focus was political power, he says, although social and cultural reform was also very central to their platform. But it never became a mass movement, says Bhaskar. SC/ST community members were appointed directly in a representational way even during the colonial period. Erstwhile political leaders like Rettamalai

Srinivasan, M. C. Raja, Veeraiyan, and L. C. Gurusamy were strong Dalit voices, but post-Independence, Dalits have become largely voiceless, he says. Currently Bhaskar is working on collating information and data post-Independence on Dalit leaders in all parties on their roles, goals, and specific achievements and equally important, on the articulation of their vision for the community. He says if at least 70 to 80 per cent of the centrally sanctioned schemes for Dalits were to actually reach them it would make a big difference. Amidst the state and centre's tussle for funds, the only money returned to the central government as unspent are the SC/ST funds, says Bhaskar. He gives an example of the blatant circumventing of schemes; for instance, if cows are donated to poor farmers across the state, those of the OBC and MBC caste would be given cows from the funds allocated for that purpose, whereas poor Dalit framers would be awarded this from the SC/ST funds that could be used for other welfare schemes. There is very little monitoring from local banks with regard to the many loans intended for Dalit farmers, many of which are not disbursed at all, stemming purely from caste prejudice. Another issue is political representation within parties which is abysmal, according to Bhaskar. There are numerous such issues of blatant discrimination and when Dalits attempt to come together to fight injustice, they are labelled as fringe groups or isolated and viewed with suspicion; Dalit consolidation remains a distant dream.

Paradoxically, despite a less than bright social and political situation for Dalits in the state, there is reportedly a growth of SC/ST entrepreneurs. Senior journalist T. Ramakrishnan writes that Tamil Nadu, a front-ranking state in MSMEs, has recorded a growth of SC entrepreneurs although it does not in any way match the population of the community. Ramakrishnan says that the proportion of SC-owned enterprises, in terms of all India figures of SC enterprises, shows 6 per cent SC ownership in micro enterprises, 8.2 per cent in small enterprises, and 6.3 per cent in medium enterprises. K. S. Bhagyalakshmi of the Dalit Indian Chamber of Commerce and Industry, who is herself a beneficiary of a new state government scheme to help SC enterprises, feels that the state does take tangible steps in encouraging Dalit entrepreneurship. Her enterprise is the production of eco-friendly bags in cotton and jute, and she also invests in training young entrepreneurs. Echoing Bhaskar's views, Ramakrishnan says, 'The common complaint among many entrepreneurs is the reluctance of banks to provide loans. Though an official of the State Level Bankers' Committee (SLBC) brushes it aside, the document containing the agenda...of the SLBC meeting...stated that about 10,370 applications (for loans) were pending at the end of September 2021 for 139.25 crore rupees.'

Powering through to Progress

Despite the questionable situation of Dalits in the state being a part of economic progress, a collation of facts and statistics about the diverse economy of Tamil Nadu does indicate that the state is developing into a modern twenty-first-century economy that is part of a global register. Tamil Nadu today stands as a powerhouse of India's manufacturing scene, and the state is the country's second-largest economy. The ambition is to grow into a trillion-dollar economy by 2031. As it stands, Tamil Nadu's economy has grown by approximately 10 per cent per year which is very commendable and such a goal could well be within the state's grasp by 2034. This, of course, would mean that many sectors of industry would have to grow, such as agriculture, manufacturing, construction, utility services, transport, hospitality, financial services, etc. However, the impediments and challenges to achieving this goal are many including corruption at various levels, and this is a stumbling block to economic achievement.

The automobile and IT sectors are among the most dominant industries in the state. Guidance Tamil Nadu, a nodal government agency set up to promote and facilitate investment in the state, says that Tamil Nadu is one of the top ten automobile hubs in the world. It is also number one in tyre manufacturing globally. Chennai has an annual (already installed) capacity to produce 1.7 million vehicles and is home to major original equipment manufacturing (OEM) companies like Hyundai Motors, BMW, Daimler, Renault-Nissan, Ford Motors, Ashok Leyland, TVS Motors, and Yamaha Motors. The state does not lag behind in the electric vehicle sector either and generates employment for more than 26,000 people. The world's largest electric scooter plant, Ola Electric Mobility, is planning to produce 10 million electric two wheelers by 2030.

Looking at the human aspect of the change and growth in Tamil Nadu's industry, a much-touted statistic is that 42 per cent of all women working in Indian factories are from Tamil Nadu. What is an even better picture is that women in the service and manufacturing sectors account for about 64 per cent of the workforce. The present Industries minister, Dr T. R. B. Rajaa, points out that 'this means that women are not just involved in menial jobs but (are) participating in the economic mainstream'. Other areas where women triumph in Tamil Nadu is that 92 per cent have a bank account, 52 per cent of government employees are women compared to 36 per cent nationally, and quite remarkably the dropout rate of girls in secondary schools is only 2.5 per cent while all India data shows 12.3 per cent girl-student dropouts nationally. This takes me back to the story of Ramu and his daughters; he is determined, whatever the challenges, to push his daughters out of poverty. His voice was more vociferous than that of his wife. Kamala, his wife, tells me that she is still afraid of the unspoken social norms of their caste which she fears the girls will not adhere to should they pursue higher education.

So, the growth story of business in Tamil Nadu is an encouraging one. Long time business journalist Sushila Ravindranath, who has detailed the growth in the state in the late 1980s in her book *Surge*, says, 'The state can keep surprising you…the *poppadums* served in UK pubs are made in Tamil Nadu….' Though the Tamil Nadu Industrial Corporation (TIDCO) was set up in 1965, it took a while for it to successfully partner up with private businesses. Foxconn, a Taiwanese company, assembles iPhones in two factories in Tamil Nadu. Other aspects like infrastructure and connectivity all across the state have been enhanced. Special industrial zones have been steadily aiding business, not to mention a highly skilled work force, especially in engineering and technology, that drives success.

On the other hand, family business groups have also done really well, collaborating when opportunities arose with partners abroad. Some of them are the Murugappa Group, the MRF group, and the TVS group. Family businesses have thrived for several generations, and brought innovation, valuation, and enterprise to Tamil Nadu's business culture. Their origins may have been humble, but it took just one or two ideas and a flash of genius to see potential opportunities. Anita Ratnam, dancer, writer, and cultural activist, who belongs to the TVS family, tells me that her great grandfather, T. V. Sundaram Iyengar, first began his business in the small village of Thrissur, now in Kerala (it was the Madras Presidency those days), with a cycle repair shop. It appears that a few years before that, Sundaram Iyengar was the only young person in their ancestral village with a transistor radio and he would sit with other village people in the evenings and listen to various kinds of programmes. During one broadcast an Englishman spoke of how Indian industry would thrive if people started thinking of themselves as bosses and not just as workers. This could have triggered ideas in him, says Anita. He went on to ply buses between Madurai, Tirunelveli, and Thrissur and he was so concerned about maintaining punctuality that he organized a platoon to sweep the roads ahead of the buses plying, for fear of nails and other sharp objects on the country roads that could puncture the tyres. Later, along with his five sons, he began a multi-generational family company and never looked back. There are other stories of founders of family companies who put themselves at risk, faced multiple challenges, and ended up with a legacy that stands the test of time.

Ravindranath points out that many family companies are now run by fifth-generation owners. 'The Murugappa Group seen as an arch conservative Chettiar group once…were the original pioneers…and have evolved with each generation. They are a close knit family where the elder's word is final,' she says. While hierarchy does exist in many family companies, and misogynism prevails, overtly or subtly, there are also heartening examples of women at the helm of family companies. Many family groups also have international collaborations and are recognized globally. A younger generation of well-educated scions, often with management degrees from abroad, carefully steer their way within these family groups, often starting on the shop floor and working their way up the ladder. This is not to say that family businesses have not had their share of problems. Inter-family legal disputes, financial woes, and other challenges have often come in the way of growth.

It is necessary to briefly touch on the IT sector as Tamil Nadu has a very visible national and global profile in this regard. Despite the fabled reputation of Bengaluru as the great software hub, Tamil Nadu's story is an equally riveting one with the sector growing in leaps and bounds in recent years. It is not unusual to see young people, including young women, late at night in corporate buses that ply the IT spaces, willing to work long night shifts to service clients on the other side of the world. Software exports touched a record of ₹2 lakh crore during the years 2022–23. We must not forget that digitization, including in government services and sectors, is another transformative aspect in Tamil Nadu which creates efficiencies of various kinds, from banking to travel for the ordinary Tamilian. Startups in the state find encouragement from government and angel investors, creating an enabling environment for new kinds of businesses ranging from ready to eat food and masalas to digital publishing and a host of other quirky but successful ventures.

Alongside successes in relatively new business sectors, traditional and old businesses of the state, such as the mass production of garments for export from places like Tiruppur, and leather manufacturing from Ambur and Vellore, and motors and pumps from Coimbatore, still have a strong presence in the state. While power looms are producing textiles, particularly saris, that are competitively priced as opposed to the handloom sector, there is a palpable revival of the handloom textile heritage as well. Traditional handloom saris in both silk and cotton are a part of Tamil Nadu's rich artistic and crafts heritage. Tiruvalluvar himself was said to be a weaver; so, it is a proud and historic Tamil profession. Recent archaeological excavations in Sangam and pre-Sangam sites have revealed small bits of textiles among the antiquities as we have seen earlier. The excellence of skilled weavers and craftsmen from a long historical tradition in Tamil Nadu has been well established. We also know about the West's exploitative trade in Indian textiles and handlooms over many centuries. Despite the setbacks it has had to deal with, in recent years, the handloom industry has seen a great revival, with support from government agencies as well as NGOs such as the Crafts Council of India, which was originally set up by Kamaladevi Chattopadhyay, the Gandhian social reformer, who was the first head of the All India Handicrafts Board and founded the Crafts Council of India. Besides reviving the many lost arts of India, Kamaladevi was also deeply concerned about the lives and livelihood of craftspeople, and this is at the forefront of handloom revival in Tamil Nadu. Handloom weaving is the largest informal sector next to agriculture in Tamil Nadu although when it comes to retailing and marketing it falls into the more organized sectors of small- and medium-scale businesses.

Although there are aspects of the handloom industry today that deserve to be commended, and it is a fact that state government support has been steady over the past several decades after the disastrous impact of colonial rule, some current trends are a cause for concern. Recent studies have shown a steady decline in the work force in the handloom industry with a younger generation abandoning the profession and seeking fresh pastures. Technology backwardness is also another problem that the industry faces, and although government schemes are in place for a revival, it is not clear how much of these actually reach weaver families. However, the magic of the Kanchipuram silk sari still prevails. Jamakkalams (carpets/blankets) from Bhavani, Kora saris from Coimbatore, Madurai sungudi saris, Salem venpattu, Arani silk, Tribhuvanam silks, and the vegetable-dyed Kandangi saris from Chettinad all carry the GI tag proudly, indicating their place of origin and edging their way into global recognition.

Sreemathy Mohan, textile specialist and entrepreneur, tells me that the Covid years gave her an opportunity to get involved in the business. Initially a researcher in cultural history and textiles, she found herself directly engaging with Tamil Nadu's rural economy, setting her on a practical track that enabled her to not just understand the handloom business but also the lives of the people behind it. 'The weaver is at the heart of everything,' she says. Working with them directly, eliminating middlemen, and creating a productive and collaborative atmosphere has aided her success. Currently, Sreemathy promotes her textiles via social media and through her website. 'Every day is a learning experience,' she says. Her knowledge of textile history, the use of old designs, and her interest in reviving this with an eye to the client's inclination and interest has helped her business to grow. 'I have come to appreciate the exceptional artistry and intricacy achieved by handlooms which surpasses what machines can produce. This experience has taught me the value of teamwork and has led me to focus on design interventions based on consumer trends, as well as reviving near extinct handicrafts.' She adds, 'My efforts have been directed towards creating a diverse range of products incorporating fusion weaves, ensuring fair wages for weavers and artisans, and providing skill training for job opportunities. This approach enables us to offer premium products and pay higher wages to artisans. Exploring niche applications of handlooms in drapery, upholstery and infant clothing has further expanded our scope of work.' In addition, with her passion for reviving Madurai's famed sungudi or tie dye saris brought into Tamil Nadu by Saurashtrian migrants several centuries ago, she has actively contributed to the Kaikattu Sungudi project where a team of artisans from Nilakottai have showcased their skills in adapting to making hand-knotted sungudi.

Sreemathy, like many entrepreneurs in the current landscape of Tamil Nadu, has learned to leverage social media well. Many use YouTube and Instagram to promote their products. Saving on marketing and advertising costs, young entrepreneurs have come to realize that often all you need to effectively market your products is a mobile phone. From new-fangled innovative home products to selling packaged food, offering catering services, selling a variety of craft goods and numerous other items, an informal economy, like in other parts of India, has blossomed in Tamil Nadu as well.

Writing the World

We have touched upon the arts and culture of the Tamil people in past eras in various chapters. In the early to mid-twentieth century, in Tamil Nadu, the creative outpouring in the region was often fuelled by writers and thinkers who were first and foremost social reformers or politicians, such as Periyar, Rajaji, Annadurai, and Subramania Bharati, whose passionate writing was deeply rooted in the political world. But we must also remember a pivotal point in the early twentieth century that saw the remarkable work and discovery of the old palm leaf manuscripts by people like U. Ve. Swaminatha Iyer, which was transformative in nature and impacted our understanding of Tamil history and literature in a spectacular way. Several decades later, popular writers like Kalki Krishnamurthy brought Tamil history alive to ordinary readers. The popularity of his *Ponniyin Selvan* story remains alive in cinematic expression with Mani Ratnam's successful adaptation of the film in 2022 with music by A. R. Rahman and starring many of the big names in Tamil filmdom. Around the same period as Kalki, Pudhumaipithan, a radical writer with socialist leanings, shocked certain echelons of Tamil society. His fictional heroes were oppressed ordinary people, prostitutes, rickshaw pullers, beggars, and villagers. He dealt head-on with subjects that were not always comfortable, and many critics were hostile to his writing. Another widely respected writer of recent times was Asokamitran, translator and author of over eighty books, whose work is laced with irony and humour. He probes the depths of modern life in his writing. He was awarded the Sahitya Akademi prize for his work *Aalayam* in 1991. One of Tamil Nadu's most well-regarded writers of our times, his wry but diligent scrutiny of life places his work in a class apart. Another much admired writer, Sujatha, appealed to a large Tamil readership. Sujatha (the pen name of S. Rangarajan) was an engineer and worked in civil aviation as a senior technical functionary. He lived in Delhi for more than a decade. His short stories, plays, detective stories, and science fiction, influenced by writers such as Ernest Hemingway and Kurt Vonnegut, were very popular.

The radical voice of Perumal Murugan has shaken both the old and new generation by challenging existing social norms. Taking on the prejudices within his own community, Murugan has dealt with serious threats to his life and yet soldiers on, a powerful voice whose themes touch the raw core of human existence. Earlier, Indira Parthasarathy, Jeyamohan, Jayakanthan, Sundara Ramaswamy, and many others added complex and rich dimensions to a treasure trove of new Tamil writing. Na. Muthuswamy brings new themes and vigour to Tamil theatre. Incisive and sharp, the work of Imayam (the pen name of V. Annamalai), rooted in a Dravidian sensibility explores the social inequities that are present to this day. Women writers of distinction include Chudamani Raghavan whose mastery of the short story threw light on women in the 50s and 60s negotiating specific social structures. I must pause here to say that having witnessed first-hand Chudamani's acute sensitivity and courage despite the physical challenges that kept her at home, I have been inspired by her vision and humanity. Her soft demeanour belied an iron will and a humorous awareness of life's many ironies. During her lifetime, she was not widely recognized, but after her death, her writing and the story of her life have attracted great attention, and a play titled *Chudamani* frames her life and work in a haunting manner.

Bama's *Karukku*, an example in courageous writing that exposed exploitation and abuse, is another standout work of our times. Sivasankari's stories have heartened generations of women trapped in difficult situations. C. S. Lakshmi or Ambai, with her inimitable feminist voice, explores the courage and character of women in her powerful short stories. A modern ensemble of young women writers and poets speak their truths unhesitatingly—from Salma and Sukirtharani to Arundhati Subramaniam and K. Srilata, the voices of these women reflect the contemporary Tamil—engaged, unafraid of controversy, and challenging given perspectives. For example, the poetry of Salma confronts the challenges and the spaces to which women can be confined, and her work and voice break free from a traditional world of Tamil (Muslim) women to fearlessly explore and express the inner lives of women. Of her poetry, Perumal Murugan says, it was pivotal in 'establishing the feminist literary movement as a distinct voice during the 1990s'. The works of many of these writers are available in translation through the efforts of translators like the retired judge of the Madras High Court, Justice Prabha Sridevan, and editor and translator Mini Krishnan whose tireless efforts on this front have taken the Tamil identity to a global platform. Mini Krishnan's contribution to the dissemination of Tamil literature is worth mentioning. As an editor with Macmillan India, and later with Oxford University Press and others, she has produced excellent translations of award-winning books from many south Indian languages.

In a blog post 'Unprofessional Translation' Prabha Sridevan, who came to translation after a distinguished tenure as a judge, has written powerfully about her work with Chudamani's stories. 'I almost felt Chudamani's presence while I wrote. I have written about it in my translator's note to "Seeing in the Dark". It felt like I got into her skin, a kind of transmigration of soul.... Translation is like acting. We have to understand the "other", the character who we are portraying and only then it will work.' Prabha Sridevan has translated fifteen works from Tamil since 2011. Translations have conveyed the intricacies of the Tamil world to an outside audience.

Cultural Conundrums

In music and dance, experimentalism and radicalism melded with tradition in the true Tamil style and range from the original and early grace and genius of Balasaraswati, Bharatanatyam's greatest exponent, who brought the dance form to the world's stage from behind the pillars of temples, to the boldness of Rukmini Devi who brought Sadir into households, and founded the famed dance school Kalakshetra. Following in their footsteps, contemporary dancers like Leela Samson, who led dance schools like Kalakshetra, have created traditions of their own. Other contemporary stars include dancers like Padma Subrahmanyam, Sudharani Raghupathy, Lakshmi Viswanathan, Alarmel Valli, Malavika Sarukkai, Anita Ratnam, and Meenakshi Chittaranjan, to mention a few. The great movement to liberate the devadasi women by social reformers like Muthulakshmi Reddy resulted in an exultant flow of creativity into dance where Tamil women were concerned. As a consequence, Bharatanatyam flowered. Many Bharatanatyam dancers have now transitioned into deeper explorations of the original art form and its music. Internationally acclaimed and nationally recognized for her powerful art, Alarmel Valli's deeply interpretative presentation of traditional work brings a modern idiom to dance expression. She says, 'Dance for me is…a transforming experience, a joyous celebration of life.' This is the aspect that a younger audience identifies with. Valli, like some of her peers, keeps the magic of Bharatanatyam alive for a younger generation.

Dancers had to break social norms and in some cases caste prejudices to claim their creative spaces. Anita Ratnam tells me that for years she has worked on her interpretations of Sita and Andal, the Vaishnavite poet-saint. Her fascination with Andal began at a young age. 'I felt as a Tamil woman if I was going to explore feminist tropes and icons and any kind of female characters in legend, in itihasa, I felt I had to encounter and explore Andal and Sita. Sita had somewhat become an all India descriptor for women and Andal too as a young poet with an overwhelming devotion to her Lord. As we were growing up, we only knew the *Thiruppavai*, the devotional hymns or pasuram that she composed. I heard about *Nachiyar Thirumozhi*, the more radical poetry of Andal, at an Indology seminar in New York in my twenties and was fascinated by what I heard. I could only follow up with this when I was back in India and read the work, much of which was in Manipravalam Tamil which had Sanskrit mixed in it. The passion and eroticism of the work celebrating the body and her physical desire for Ranganatha was very different from the sanctified version that was more common. It was a revelation to me,' she says.

Beyond the formal and classical forms of dance are the more spontaneous folk traditions which still hold good across rural Tamil Nadu. Therukoothu, or street theatre, is still a popular form where myths and stories are enacted—usually during the time of Thiruvizha or temple festivals that add local stories and local heroes to an existing repertoire. In terms of dance forms, kummi, kolattam, silambattam, mayilattam, karagam, and other expressions are ingrained in rural life and often infused with religious fervour, whether it is a dance for Murugan or a fervent prayer to Mariamman. These are more forms of prayer and worship and sometimes simple celebrations that mark village life. None of this has changed much in rural Tamil Nadu.

We have talked about classical music earlier, but it must be emphasized that this has now moved beyond performance to a space for questioning and debate. Beyond Brahmin centrism in certain sabhas, which foreground a traditional approach, there are those who continue to question much of this. The brilliantly gifted T. M. Krishna who has long challenged the sabha culture's narrow vision and practices has been awarded the Sangita Kalanidhi award by the very institution he has long been critical of. But the Music Academy, which bestows the award, rightly stands by it; the nature of the award is essentially a recognition of a sterling musician for a solid body of work, and although this raised much controversy in the music world, even to the point where some earlier awards from the academy were returned in protest, it does mark the fact that an impassioned debate is taking place on what the contours and future of Carnatic music ought to be. Krishna also pushed the boundaries of composition—he sang of poramboke or common land, compositions of the social reformer Narayana Guru, of Periyar, and wrote books like *Sebastian and Sons* where he traces the Dalit Christian history of mridangam makers. He wove music around the poems of Perumal Murugan and at the same time, his mellifluous music and mesmeric voice continues to draw great crowds to his concerts.

Sanjay Subrahmanyan, whose musical genius has been mentioned earlier, is a doyen whose creativity touches the core of the Carnatic spirit while quietly soaring to lofty heights in terms of expression, subject choices, and indeed a repertoire and body of work that has brought him recognition both within the country and internationally. Subrahmanyan's quiet explorations include exciting interpretations of poet reformers like Ramalinga Swami, known as Vallalar, and collaborating with a diverse group of musicians to produce a new album.

Musicians like Sangita Kalanidhi Aruna Sairam have taken Carnatic music to global audiences. Her inspiring music draws from her deep knowledge of Hindustani music, Gregorian chants, and other global musical traditions to extend the boundaries of her performance. Aruna Sairam has performed at the BBC Proms, the first Indian vocalist ever to do so, and at New York's Carnegie Hall, and in Paris and Morocco and in other global arenas, mesmerizing the audience with her extraordinary versatility and depth. There are other younger musicians like Sikkil Gurcharan, and the sisters Ranjini and Gayatri, whose musical talents spring from the deep well of traditional Carnatic music, have boldly and excitingly embraced new frontiers, whether it be explorations of a more modern idiom such as using film music or writing and creating compositions of their own which infuse an old tradition with new energies. The classical music tradition from Tamil Nadu has now catapulted into a global space. Much of this trend can be traced to a breed of young musicians who live in North America and Europe and who have layered traditional tropes with imaginative insights and made it their own.

Tamils at leisure are no different from other Indians. Cricket, tennis, and now chess and football, have seen magnificent growth in Chennai and in the state. K. C. Vijaya Kumar, sports editor at *The Hindu*, tells me that the Tamils support sport in much the way they support movies. 'Politicians too always back sports as they see this as a way to improve local infrastructure for sports,' he says. Cricket and tennis have a long and storied history in the state. One of the stories I have always loved involves a test match between India and Pakistan in 1999. Qamar Ahmed, who reported the match for *The Hindu* wrote that over four days of thrilling play, the game took so many twists and turns that spectators felt for both sides. 'Although Pakistan won this sensational Test by a small margin Indian cricket was not disgraced....' says Ahmed. And then he says, '...the knowledgeable Chennai crowd not only enjoyed every moment of it but heartily cheered both teams. Those who played and those who watched would surely remember this match for the rest of their lives. What was really touching and emotional…was the response from the crowd when Pakistan dared to take a lap of honour to thank them. They greeted and cheered…and gave them a standing ovation.' This was a far cry from the kind of jingoism and fanaticism of these times. Chennai's own Ashwin Ravichandran and earlier Kris Srikkanth and S. Venkatraghavan put their stamp on the game. As to tennis, the city was a training ground for Leander Paes. Of course, the Krishnans, Ramanthan, and Ramesh, and the Amritraj brothers are from Chennai.

Kumar also mentions Chennai's inspiring chess maestro, Viswanathan Anand, whose footsteps are now followed by young R. Praggnanandhaa. 'Indian chess truly has its beating heart within this state fringed by the Bay of Bengal on one side and the Western Ghats on the other.'

There are other sports that energize Tamil Nadu's sports scene such as motor sports in Chennai and Coimbatore. Narain Karthikeyan is 'one of Coimbatore's favourite sons'. Another memorable achievement for Chennai was V. Baskaran leading India to a gold in hockey during the Moscow Olympics in 1980. Baskaran's interest in sports goes beyond hockey to cricket and other sports. Tamil Nadu's women sports stars include the squash duo Dipika Pallikal and Joshna Chinappa who have sparkled in their field. Both Shiny Wilson in athletics and the great P. T. Usha did their time in Tamil Nadu for a period. The boost given by corporate support and sponsorships by companies like MRF, Sanmar, and India Cements go a long way in giving sports and sportspeople a sense of stability while they pursue their sporting careers. Nationalized banks too have accommodated sportspeople, although it must be said their initiatives are mostly only in the larger cities. A brand new development on Tamil Nadu's beautiful extended coastline is the growth of surfing and new icons like Jonty Rhodes have emerged in Kovalam. Fishermen too have taken to this sport in recent times.

∽

Shonali Muthalaly, food critic and senior editor of lifestyle sections of *The Hindu*, says the city still loves its filter coffee with chicory. 'Over the past five years a variety of inventive roasters and brewers have set up cafes in the city, offering cold brews, nitro brews, and espresso tonics in addition to the more conventional cortados, macchiatos and cappuccinos. Inspired by these cafes, customers are geeking out on coffee, and experimenting with a range of brewing equipment, from espresso machines to the Chemex, Hario V60, and Aeropress. Every coffee shop has its own personality: at Beachville, each cup has a distinct geography; Japan-influenced Coffee Trotter serves scones and onigiri rice balls; and now the newly opened Vinyl and Brew, celebrates the romance of old vinyl records along with caffeine,' she says.

With her intimate first-hand knowledge of Chennai's food history, Shonali elaborates on the arrival of international cuisine in Chennai. 'When Dahlia was launched in Nungambakkam twenty-five years ago by a Japanese businessman and his Indian partner, it was designed to cater to Asian expatriates and did not even have an English menu. However, Korean and Japanese food have been getting increasingly popular with the locals and now there are a slew of restaurants including Aeseo, Hokkaido, Nippon, Another Kitchen, and Kuuraku, all serving sushi, hot pots, and ramen. Korean bakeries have also got popular, so popular that the fluffy Korean cheese bun can now be found in most bakeries in the city.'

The city tends to focus more on memorable meals in relaxed spaces with friends and family and Shonali says that this accounts for the popularity of restaurants like Amethyst, Pandan Club, and Pumpkin Tales. Tamil people expect value for money and look for consistency, she adds. 'Hype won't keep a restaurant open here,' says Shonali.

The cuisine of the Tamils may have found global recognition through the simple idli and dosai but many of these foods have assumed new forms. Fine dining too has come to stay in bigger cities like Chennai and Coimbatore. Local foods from the familiar rasam to the ubiquitous curd rice are served at ITC Grand Chola's Avartana, which does a tasting menu firmly rooted in Chennai—French Press rasam and vathakuzhambu are served in test tubes.

The same pride in Tamil culture is seen in nightclubs. Earlier, these were the bastions of pop and rock and techno but now local dancefloors thud to Tamil music with DJs in saris, and clubbers in veshtis, on special 'Tamil nights'. According to Shonali, 'This change of attitude is reflected in the food and cocktails as well: gunpowder idlis, tawa prawns, and beach style bhajis are now on multiple menus. Most bars also acknowledge some of Chennai's favourite flavours in their cocktails. The ITC Grand Chola does The Puli, with tequila and green chilli, served with an appalam and mor milagai. The competitively priced Cycle Gap offers Rootu Thalaive, a drink with vettiver vodka, blood orange, and sea salt air foam. At Pandan Club, The Affair features a splash of refined sea water from Marina Beach along with Pandan Scotch and palm jaggery.'

Inasmuch as tradition and a culture intrinsic to the region is carried in the Tamil DNA today, as we have seen in many instances highlighted in this chapter, there is also a happy embrace of the modern and the global. Some aspects of present-day Tamil Nadu described in this chapter show that while it is a region that remains true to its essence, it can quickly adapt to progress whether it is technological or entrepreneurial. Young boys still play cricket in the streets of cities and small towns and dream of becoming great players. A humble village home can foster a mathematical genius, and a girl who tops her school can become a distinguished scientist. It is a place that nurtures hopes and dreams and at the same time, as we have seen, spectres of discrimination and deprivation dog the footsteps of many. As Tamil Nadu wades deeper into the twenty-first century, and scrambles to keep the promises of equity and social justice that were part of the Dravidian vision, it appears to be a mixed bag—there is much that remains to be done.

Epilogue

The Tamil in Us

A people without history is not redeemed from time,
For history is a pattern of timeless moments...
We shall not cease from exploration
And the end of all our exploring
Will be to arrive where we started...

T. S. Eliot, 'Little Gidding', *The Four Quartets*

In the end is the beginning. We go back now to the starting point about this ancient people, their lives and pasts with questions that can never be fully answered, with explorations that can never be complete, with stories that have no ending. Having trailed through some history, looked at records, lingered at sites where footprints fell thousands of years ago, and heard diverse voices, there is now a clarity about how the passage of time dealt with the people of this part of India. There are, however, many missing beats as records and literature can never present a composite picture. For instance, we have not always been seized of the plight and lives of ordinary people; history's bias can tend to lean towards that which is more visible. But as we tarried at sites and learned from experts, we could see that the anonymous artist, the sculptor, the carpenter, the nomadic trader, the lone writer, and the quiet visionary all left their imprint, and this seeps silently through all the history of the Tamil people. We have been reminded by many scholars that the unheard voices, the travails of ordinary people, and voices of dissent are as important as those which are recorded and obvious.

As this book began with the land and people, we can go back to asking some Tamils what it means to them to be Tamil and if indeed there is a 'Tamil way'. This book began with a gossamer touch on Tamil identity; we find that little or no generalizations can be made, especially as cultural facets of different castes in the region often dominate over larger notions of Tamilness. The notion of identity itself can be dubious as we know, and we are all many things, and our histories too are many. But at the same time, the people of the Tamil region produced literary masterpieces, great works of art, meditative narratives, and indeed had notions of the world and the universe that came from being distinctively anchored in this region. Being Tamil is, therefore, the context from which great beauty, as well as vision, creativity, and strength, have emerged. The much-used 2,000-year-old adage of the poet Kaniyan Poongundranar: 'yaadhum oore, yavarum kelir'—'all towns are mine; all people are my relatives' is a strong vein that runs deep in the Tamil muscle. Beyond the unity of many things for a Tamil, there lies a body of tangible experience—in art, culture, literature, music, cities, and communities, and indeed the language itself. David Shulman, the great linguist, says, 'Tamil is a certain body of knowledge, some of it technical, much of it intrinsic to an ancient culture and sensibility well documented in a continuous literary tradition going back many centuries… In general, I think of *Tamil* as a living being—impetuous, sensitive, passionate, whimsical, in constant movement….'

However, any adherence to a fixed notion of essentialism in Tamil identity may become problematic, as Professor Arjun Appadurai, Emeritus Professor of Media, Culture and Communication at New York University, pointed out in a recent interview with me. He says that such an idea does not consider changeability and fragmentation, and may inadvertently fall into a fixed concept, such as those floated by specific groups, which will be far from the truth. But then what is a Tamil identity, Appadurai asks. What is it that persists over time, is visible and has a signature, and is not just an artefact of a group? Globally, ethnic identities are already on steroids, he suggests, and if one speaks about Tamil exceptionalism, what is the exceptionalism of this exceptionalism that is already claimed by many, like in Maharashtra during Bal Thackeray's time. The continuity of Tamil, without any real break, is perhaps something that is distinct. There is no old Tamil, new Tamil, and if you were to look up a word, it may well give you fifteen meanings going back to the Sangam age. There is a veritable archaeology of the language, says Appadurai, an ethnic Tamilian who grew up in Mumbai and is an expert on the cultural dimensions of globalization.

He points to a very curious aspect of Tamil oratory, which was pointed out earlier by the Tamil Professor Barney Bate, a linguistic anthropologist who taught at Yale, Chicago, and Columbia. His superb book, *Tamil Oratory and Dravidian Aesthetic: Democratic Practice In South India*, made the links between sermonic speeches of the early Protestant missionaries and political speeches of the twentieth century, among other things. Drawing from this, Appadurai says, 'Two things are clear. If you listen to the speeches of the

Dravidian leaders, some of them seem to have mastered centuries of allusions, tropes, metaphors, and poetry and speak like Tamil scholars, whereas the other aspects of their lives are probably less than refined. This is nothing short of amazing. Related to this is the audience reaction to such speeches. They may be auto rickshaw drivers, casual labourers, and less educated citizens, but they applaud, enjoy, and understand this demagoguery. It is understood by all. It is like using Hellenic Greek in modern-day Greece or Elizabethan English in present-day UK,' he quips. 'Surely it is a remarkable thing where the persistence of a literary culture exists over centuries,' he adds.

Perhaps it is this that makes Tamil different, Appadurai suggests; the continuation of a strand of DNA from the Sangam era, an anchoring in that sensibility that puts into place a way of seeing the world. Appadurai also says that there is no fragmentation of the language, as in other parts of the world, so the poetry of the Sangam era remains a surprisingly intact undercurrent in the Tamil context. The cultural independence of Aham, or the inner world and mind, is affixed to the Sangam sensibility, which is also about Puram, the external world—one of gods and kings, war, parting, death—all in fabulous poetry and interwoven with a profound ecological consciousness of the five landscapes that was the Tamil home. Even for those who may not consciously know or draw from the Sangam work today, its fragrance still filters down through Tamil, through the language that they use.

As we discuss the threads that persist even through later religious literature that is heavily strewn with Sanskrit words, we realize that there is the leaping out of a distinctly Tamil sensibility, and this is always obvious. Every Tamilian can quickly turn into a poet; everyone can be a dramatist and an orator. This is an angle, however, that adds heft to more simple notions of identity. The steadiness of a rich literary sensibility feeding consciously or unconsciously into the everyday life of even modern Tamils is a concept that cannot really be dismissed easily.

Beyond the literature and language, what is important to understand, according to the sociologist E. Valentine Daniel, is the special relationship that a Tamil has to his ur or hometown. Daniel explains that the context of the ur could also vary, and it is often just a conversation opener; it could mean also going to the centre of the town from perhaps the outskirts. The word itself can be loaded for the Tamil. For a Tamil abroad, ur can mean India, or even the place from where one's forebears came from. While ur has a fluidity, natu or desam may not, suggests Daniel. The Tamil is also affected by the ur; even his nature can be impacted by the local soil. It is almost as if there is a collective way of being that could be defined by the ur. An extension of this enclose within brackets is the belief among some rural people that some urs will not suit particular castes or jatis. The Tamils also believe that one's gunam or character cannot be altered beyond say twelve years of age, unless a transformative event occurs in their lives. The impact of buddhi or the intellect on gunam whether good or bad is also a Tamil way of perceiving things and gives scope for individual flexibility. I have heard people say 'Avan buddhi enga pocchu?'—'Where did his mind/intellect go?' almost as if there could be a disassociation between the person's gunam and buddhi. Added to this is also the notion of a person's fate or jatakam, which many Tamils believe impacts his or her way of life. There is the added near fatalistic idea of 'talai eruttu' or 'head writing', says Daniel. 'Tamils believe that at the time of birth, Katavul (God) writes a script on every individual's head and that the course that each individual's life takes…is determined by this script. The script or writing of God on one's head, is known as talai eruttu.'

Daniel explores more such peculiarities distinct to the Tamil mind. One important aspect is the values that Tamils place on deference. Daniel says, 'Among Tamils deference behaviour is signified through a variety of culturally calculated manipulations of space; standing when a superior sits, squatting on one's haunches when the respected one sits on a chair, standing to the side (rather than directly in front) of an elder when speaking to him, sitting to the left of an honoured guest at a meal, building a house so that it does not exceed the temple tower in height, looking at the ground when walking through an audience of respected elders, not looking a teacher straight in the eye when he castigates you and so on.' The daily behaviour of the Tamil can be interpreted in multiple ways that can signify an anchoring in family, ur, jati, adding up to gunam that is perceptibly 'being a person the Tamil way'.

What gives the Tamils another base of identity is the land from where it all starts, the land, which is still being excavated, where buried treasures throw new light on an ancient world, according to Thangam Thenarasu, who is Tamil Nadu's Minister for Finance, Human Resources Management, Pensions, Electricity, and Archaeology and holds other portfolios. He is a Tamil scholar whose knowledge of the culture and history of the Tamils is extensive. On the origin of the language which we have touched upon earlier, he speaks with great clarity. 'If you look at the early settlements in Keezhadi or Porunthal, a writing system seems to have emerged even before Ashokan Brahmi… This evidence is in other sites like Kodumanal also. So Tamil Brahmi was either earlier or parallel to Ashokan Brahmi. The development of "Vatteluthu" from Tamil Brahmi occurred possibly even during the period of the Kalabhras,' he says. Pallava Grantha came after, another writing form more common in northern Tamilakam where the Pallavas ruled, and Prakrit was also a language that was spoken in the region with a lot of Sanskritic influence along with Tamil. We know too that the copper plates of kings with royal announcements were often a mix of Sanskrit and Prakrit written in Pallava Grantha with Tamil in between, especially in the prasastis or the invocatory verses of praise at the beginning.

Thangam Thenarasu relates a charming malapropism that reinforces how usage can transform a language. Kudumiyan Malai, as we know, is a Pallava cave temple with magnificent musical notations dedicated to Shiva. Its original name is Tirunalakundram. In Sanskrit 'nala' is 'suha' and 'kundram' is 'giri' so another name for the place is Suhagiri. There is a tale that must be told about how the temple's name underwent a radical change. One day, the local king came to worship at the temple and the priest placed the garland from the deity on his neck. The king found a strand of hair in the garland and was enraged; the terrified priest was then rescued by the deity himself who showed that the hair had come from his own locks. Suhagiri from Tirunalakundram becomes known as 'sikagiri' or 'hair' mountain and this in turn becomes 'kudumiyan' malai or the mountain of the man of the tuft or hair. Another instance that fascinated me as a child was how the original name of a bridge near Marina Beach was Hamilton's bridge and the Tamil pronunciation made it 'Ambatta Varapadhi' which again came to be called Barber's Bridge as 'ambattan' is the Tamil word for barber and transposed back into a totally different name.

Thangam Thenarasu says that this the reality of Tamil—classical and grand but yet able to live with the other. The Tamil people created a civilization of their own, a culture and language right from the neolithic period and it reached great heights because of a distinct way of life. 'It is not just about a sophistication of a people but the fact that they could put their resources to good use. For instance, long before iron was used in many parts of India, we made implements with it and used it to develop our day-to-day standards of living. Towns and settlements prospered because of such thinking. In Keezhadi, one can see complete systems in place for water drainage, for wells, and for public use. This is distinct and we have corroborative evidence from literature and archeology that proves the advances in these ancient settlements.' Coming to the essential nature of the Tamil people, Thangam Thenarasu points to the great tolerance that Tamils exhibit; he believes it is fallacious to assume that there is a fanaticism about our language and culture. Let us not forget, the Tamil people adored MGR who was a Malayali, he points out. Tamil Nadu also easily coexists with other neighbouring states despite issues like the Mullaiperiyar Dam and that of the Cauvery water. There is a free movement of people here from other states. Mutual respect and learnings from others are also a laudable trait, says the minister. There is unity in our diversity, whether it is about religious beliefs or lifestyles, we have the ability to support and even take part in other people's events and festivals. An enlightened politician whose broad vison encapsulates the essence of Dravidian ideology, he represents also a modern pragmatist who is keen to contribute to the state's progress.

'Being Tamil is a conscious emotion for me,' says Jayanthi Natarajan, former cabinet minister in the UPA government. A lawyer and outstanding parliamentarian, Natarajan's moorings are firmly in Chennai. Born into a political family, her grandfather was M. Bhaktavatsalam, former chief minister of Tamil Nadu. Growing up, Natarajan saw many sides of the Tamil identity but was also anchored in a national consciousness which stemmed from a strong line of freedom fighters and followers of Mahatma Gandhi. On the other side was the affiliation to a Dravidian ethos. P. T. Rajan, her great uncle, was chief minister when the Justice Party was heading the Madras Presidency. But the dialogue within the family was always civil and respectful despite being on opposite sides of the political spectrum. Natarajan says that the national movement was a great draw for the family and everyday conversations and meetings with national leaders like Gandhi, Nehru, Patel, and others were commonplace. A sense of the Tamil identity grew upon her as she grew older. And it was one that was fashioned from viewing certain traits such as tolerance, respect for others, and a humaneness that embraced a larger world. She recalls that during the linguistic division of states when Potti Sriramulu was fasting for Andhra, her grandfather's uncle exhorted him from his deathbed saying, 'Don't forget that Tamilakam is from Venkatam in the north to Kanyakumari in the south,' holding a firm belief in a geographically larger Tamilakam which was important to many Tamilians of that time.

The Tamils absorb much from outside the space they exist in, feels Jayanthi. For instance, it is not uncommon to find names like Tagore, Nelson Mandela, Kennedy, Clinton, Lenin, and Stalin bestowed on people, even those living in small towns. That is because there is an awareness and admiration even from an older generation of the heroes and leaders who live elsewhere. 'Tamils have a global awareness,' says Jayanthi, 'a willingness to recognize the good that exists in other shores.' Extending this, 'There is an obvious pride among Tamilians in their composite culture. We would get biryani for Eid, cut cakes at Christmas, and there was absolutely no hesitation in sending us to convent schools,' she adds.

Modernizing the language is another phenomenon that shows the open-mindedness of the Tamils who easily import words from other languages. This is a far cry from the notion that most Tamils are language purists. 'Dar agittenga,' meaning "you have become scared" is one usage; "dar" from the Hindi, meaning fear. The importing of words from other languages was often done to suit the occasion. For instance, the use of the word "ji" is becoming as common as using "sir" and "avunga",' says Jayanthi.

Going on to other perceived traits of the Tamils, Jayanthi speaks with pride about Tamil women. Tamil women are courageous and have a broader vision and know that they need to fight for their place within the house and in society. They fight en bloc against social evils like alcoholism, they vote en bloc too when they perceive support for the causes they hold dear. Most of this would devolve around the upliftment and welfare of their families. We know the apocryphal story of a woman who single-handedly fought a tiger to save her child—this exemplifies the extent that Tamil women go to, to defend their own, she adds.

The popular film star Kamal Haasan also spoke to me about Tamil society. His view was that casteism is the biggest bane of Tamil society. 'The metros smudge the issue, and you think everything is fine until you go into the villages and encounter the reality of the situation. Political action to ameliorate such evils as caste will happen only when politics becomes people-centric and does not remain ideology-centric. Their well-being should become the plan, which is why one cannot be bound by ideology alone without people being at the heart of it.' He rues the impact of caste politics. He feels that films can go beyond entertainment to convey social messages that can positively impact Tamil society.

K. Asokan, editor, *Hindu Tamil Thisai*, a seasoned journalist and litterateur, says, 'Though several movements have laid an emphasis on a pure and separate Tamil, free from the influences of other languages, the basic Tamil tendency to find the best anywhere in the world and assimilate it is important as it adds to the vigour and youthful spirit of the mother language. Reading our iconic poet Bharati's line, "Bring here all artifacts", I take artifacts as new words of artistic value or aesthetically exotic diction. Particularly, Tamil has never hesitated to take in several good words and turns of expression from Sanskrit, one of the ancient languages in India, and from Arabic as well.'

Dr Vedachalam, a discerning scholar and expert, whose enlightening conversations and perspectives shaped much of the flow of this work over multiple journeys within Tamil Nadu, stresses that, 'Tamilians are an ancient civilization who while celebrating the classical nature of their literature accept words from other languages in their lexicon. This is a unique characteristic much in consonance with the hospitality that Tamils show to strangers that turn up on their shores. Anybody can freely speak in their mother tongue and live peacefully in the Tamil country. People professing different religions live in Tamil Nadu, and Tamilians live harmoniously with them. In India's history, another distinctly religious and cultural movement that emerged from Tamilakam first is the Bhakti movement.' He suggests that this movement brought ordinary people closer to their spiritual moorings using moving poetic language. While there was sectarian strife at times, in his view, the Tamils are, by and large, a tolerant people. The advent and practice of Buddhism, Jainism, and later Islam and Christianity took very firm root in the Tamil landscape, he adds, and persisted despite the challenges (even violent ones) that they sometimes confronted.

Vedachalam adds that in India's civilizational history, even from the time of proto-history, Tamilians were literate and had a script. Echoing the ideas expressed by Thangam Thenarasu, he says, 'Excavations in Tamil Nadu have established that Tamilians wrote their names in Tamil-Brahmi script more than 2,000 years ago on the pottery that they used. These Tamilians had forged trade and commerce as well as cultural relationships with other parts of the world. Documents in Tamil are available in several countries, from West Asia to Southeast Asia, and Tamilians have been living for centuries in many countries of the world. The large Tamil diaspora has often contributed substantively to their adopted countries,' he says.

A more challenging perception that ploughs through sanctified notions of Tamilness has also been expressed. For instance, Subramaniam, the excellent guide to many things Tamil, who journeyed with me all through Tamil Nadu examining Tamil history and sites, reminds me of a trenchant poem of Subramania Bharati which speaks of Tamilians as being impervious to their own situations and surroundings 'like buffaloes in the rain'.... Subramaniam loosely translates a caustic poem of the great poet who speaks of a certain fatalism in Tamils; as an analogy, Bharati says, 'even when it rains and the entire surroundings are wet, Tamils will walk where it is wet, eat where it is wet, sleep where it is wet, and will not help themselves in any way. Even if many die in the rain, they will say it is fated after all....' Coupled with this strange sense of fatality is also a pervasive sense of hope for divine support through all of life's tribulations expressed through rituals such as fire walking, sticking sharp instruments into one's face, and multiple other cultural practices that seek to alleviate personal misery. Many Tamils believe that the protection, preservation, and support to family deities is vital for the sustenance of their families and for future generations

An important contextualization of this sense of Tamil identity without sacrificing the actuality of Tamilness comes from Professor Radha Sarma Hegde of New York University, who grew up in Chennai. Her diaspora experience of a more global world feeds into her notions of her own Tamil self and her perceptions. 'Being Tamil…yes, a significant part of my identity relates to growing up in postcolonial Madras (now Chennai) with the language, sounds, tastes, and politics. Being Tamilian was always about asserting a local identity that was distinct from the national or often what was simply constructed as the north. The authentic Tamilian is, no doubt, an illusory construct but one that takes many inflections. All kinds of statements circulate both within India and globally about an essentialized Tamil identity. For instance, Tamils are smarter, more fluent in English, superior with math skills, more cunning etc. Stereotypes about Tamilian accents, traditionalism and success continue globally and serve as fodder for the media. I am not sure if any of these beliefs and images are particular to "Tamilness". However, I do believe that the power of the diverse histories that frame Tamil culture will continue to recharge the imaginary about what being Tamil means in the global world,' she says.

Perhaps it is appropriate at this point to touch on a global journey that could summarize the acme of Tamil diaspora experience. Take the case of Shyamala Gopalan, a young student of life sciences who bravely set out, at the age of nineteen in 1958, to study in America with the sole ambition of finding a cure for cancer. There, she plunged into black movements of protest in California, married a black man, and has two daughters who have been taught to work hard and to always know that they can achieve anything. Coming from a progressive Tamil background, Gopalan's values included diligence, courage, and determination. At the time of writing, her daughter Kamala Harris is in the running for the highest office in America.

The Tamils of the diaspora and the Tamilians who live outside Tamil Nadu like other ethnic communities from India have added much to the catalogue of Tamil achievements but whether their ethnicity is of any relevance is a moot point. The connection to a Tamilness springs more from a claim on them that would often emanate from the home region rather than from the subjects themselves. A discussion of the global Tamil diaspora would require at least a chapter in itself, but it is important to state that there are many like Shyamala Gopalan who left for better opportunities and better lives. From the nameless labourers who suffered and struggled, emigrating to do hard labour whether in the West Indies, Malaysia, or elsewhere, to the newer emigres who moved because of opportunities in higher education and employment. Tamils, like others, have impacted the societies into which they transplanted themselves. They are numerous examples: the Chettiars, the traditional financiers of Tamil Nadu, went to Malaysia and made fortunes early on. There are others like Dr Chandrasekhar who won the Nobel Prize, Sundar Pichai, Indira Nooyi, and several hundreds of other emigrants from Tamil Nadu whose successes may have redefined them in many ways but would likely always hold fast to their Tamil identity.

Another fascinating story is that of a non-Tamil who became an honorary Tamil and has lived in the region for over forty years building his businesses, his connections, and just loving and being many things Tamil. Ranvir Shah is something of a Renaissance man in Chennai. A garment exporter who is working to revive the famous Madras Checks (the brand name is Original Madras), he also restores old temples and houses in the heart of Tamil Nadu, sponsors festivals of art and music, and supports writers, scholars, and artists. Shah tells me that as a Jain who moved to Tamil Nadu and found Vaishnavism (although he was never bound by religiosity), he wonders what is this space that has nurtured so many religious traditions—Buddhism, Jainism, Saivism, and much more? His own discovery of the Somaskanda Murthy, which he has co-opted into his emotional and spiritual lexicon, makes him wonder if there is some unknown magnetic force that has drawn him into the heart of Tamil culture. He set up Prakriti Foundation twenty-five years ago to promote arts, culture, and learning and it was a discovery for him as everything was available for exploration—classical music, classical dance, contemporary dance and music too, and he soon became an enabler who could transmit much of this to a wider public.

Shah looks at a new kind of cultural engagement where one can examine, analyse, and question older traditions, be a disrupter of sorts, promote discussion and turn things on their head without taking away from the core of the tradition. It may open a political arc, but he feels that even a traditionally inclined Tamil person will open themselves up to see the new expression. 'The audience here is ready to engage with the new, to debate and discuss and perhaps absorb,' he says. Not only that, in his business, he has observed that Tamils can embrace the new as well. He hears simple farmers talk about something learned from YouTube, their daughters going away to get educated, and these days, many of them returning to work in the same professions, strengthening and modernizing it.

In another layer of his life, in the non-profit sector where he does a lot of philanthropic work, Ranvir Shah says that he has seen a great sea change. 'This is all a part of modern Tamil Nadu,' he says, where 'there is a progressive support to multiple communities such as transgender people, HIV-affected people, mental health, all emanating from enlightened judges, from clear-headed government officials and policies.' This is what makes this state special, according to him.

As I discovered through travel and conversations, readings and encounters in rural villages as well in small town and cities, the notion of Tamilness varied, depending upon literacy, custom, traditions, and rituals. The consciousness of a particular sense of Tamilness was a broad sweep, and embedded within this were centuries of community customs and traditional practice. This notion of a community within the larger cultural moorings of being a Tamilian emanates from a strong caste identity. As mentioned earlier in this book, caste identity is a constant; intertwined with ideas of pseudo honour which sometimes violently impacts the lives of ordinary Tamils, whether it is anti-Dalit clashes or, at the more personal level of inter-community marriages, where family honour is seen as being affected when young people marry outside their communities. So much so that violence or death is often a tragic outcome of these situations. The recent shocking instances which indicate (at the time of this writing) the rise in heinous caste crimes mentioned in an earlier chapter such as human faeces being thrown into the common overhead tank in a village in Pudukkottai district in 2022, and a machete attack on a young Dalit school boy and his sister by classmates highlight the pervasiveness of caste violence in many areas in the state. According to activists, dominant caste groups tend to gang up to commit atrocities against these most underprivileged of Tamils. Bhaskar, the editor of *Neelam* magazine, tells me that his Tamil identity is of less relevance to him than his Dalit identity, especially when there are constant and concerted attacks on Dalits in Tamil Nadu.

To go back to the strong affinity to the language among Tamils, journalist Kolappan, who is steeped in Tamil culture, history, and present-day politics, emphasizes that while all linguistic groups are moored in their own identities, the Tamils, even from ancient times, projected the language as the base of identity and even existence. For example, he says that Thirumular, the

Shaivite poet, one among the sixty-four Nayanmars, in his magnum opus the *Tirumantiram*, says, 'God created me well so that I could sing his praise well (in Tamil) by the Tirumantiram of Thirumular'. Kolappan points out other such insights. Thirunavukkarasar, the Shaivite saint, also says, 'just as I will not forget water flower and incense, neither will I ever forget Tamil songs set to sweet music'. Another Shaivite poet saint Thirugnanasambandar identifies himself as Tamilgnanasambandar in many places in his work, such is the passion for the language. Tamil is the basic link that brought people together, says Kolappan, and regardless of the divisions of politics and faith, it was language that bound people. Beyond the Tamil language, as we need to remind ourselves, is also the Tamil spirit that it embodies; a modern-day poet like Salma finds her own path cutting through many contemporary social shackles and reflects the same courage as the Avvaiyars, the Andals, and the Karaikal Ammaiyars of the Sangam age. However, it is important to note that most of those I spoke to eschew the notion of retaining a 'purist' Tamil, although in usage, many letters have been aptly Tamilized and an older Sanskritized version of these letters have been changed. However, the use of Telegu, Sanskrit, and even the odd English word that has become a part of the Tamil lexicon is viewed as adding to the beauty and layering of the language.

Gopalkrishna Gandhi speaks of the peculiar geography of the Tamil region, a rather pendulous shape that connects it more with its Sri Lankan neighbour in the south in terms of linguistic affinity although it has been 'cradled' by the religion that came from the north of India. Yet, once its separatist dreams were dissolved, like Kashmir, Tamil Nadu 'nestled sub nationalism in the larger arena of nationalism...and this took the sting out of geography'. The integration with the Indian union became important, he says. The Tamil identity is 'more about wanting to be herself or himself without wanting either self-alienation or alienation from the other...what is essentially wanted was recognition. Now what is needed is cherishing.' Only M. S. Subbalakshmi was cherished thus, he goes on to say, although many exceptional Tamils like Rajaji have been recognized in the north as the calendar of events placed him in the forefront of history. A. R. Rahman is another person from the south whose genius is both recognized and cherished, and an important fact about them is that they held on to their GPS so to speak, and did not move away even to places like Mumbai, unlike many other Tamils who were exceptional individuals in terms of their achievements.

Gandhi quotes a lovely interchange between Rahman and him. When Gandhi asked Rahman about the famous lyrics of 'Khwaja Mere Khwaja' by

Javed Akhtar, Rahman gently corrected him to say that the lyrics are by an unknown Sufi poet in Nagore who gave Rahman the original Urdu lyrics. When Gandhi enquired how long it took Rahman to set it to music, 'Twelve minutes' was the prompt reply. 'One of the Tamil chemistries is the amazing comfort with numbers. Ramanujan was the global example. Rahman saying twelve minutes and Subbalakshmi telling me that at the Moscow festival she was first asked to sing for five minutes and then they said sing for three minutes. "Am I the Blue Mountain Express?" she asked me, but she did it,' he says. This is important, Gandhi feels as it 'deprivileges numbers from caste'. He also agrees with Appadurai's idea of the five tinai being the basis of Tamil social organization, different from other regions of India, firmly anchored to the natural landscape of Tamilakam. This is a unique Tamil way of looking at the world.

The distinct story of the Tamils is, in the end, a story of multiple narratives, of the multitude of poets and kings, artists, builders, writers, resisters, scholars, and ordinary people who with language as their sacred base built their history in temples, mosques, churches, fields, and factories, searching as many people do for answers to the mysteries of the human experience. Their origins, buried in pre-history, brought to light by diligent explorations and archaeological endeavours, traced the continuity of a civilization that goes back nearly 5,000 years. Their progress from the beauty of the early Brahmi inscription carved on the brow of an ancient Jain cave through Sangam poetry, through the poetics and grammar of the *Tolkappiyam*, to the uplifting aphorisms of the *Tirukkural* found on Tamil Nadu's state transport buses, all signal a continuity that is quite uncommon. The philosophies that moulded them range from simple surrender and devotion, as expressed through Bhakti poetry, through the asceticism of Jain and Buddhist thought, through Islam and Christianity which were readily embraced, down to the atheism of Periyar and Dravidian ideology. Their lived experience is diverse yet sometimes similar, marking out the singularity of a Tamil essence, and despite the often deep divide of caste, class, and creed, being a Tamilian is the foundation on which all else is built.

Acknowledgements

This book owes its existence to my dear and long-standing friend, my editor and publisher David Davidar. About five years ago, David suggested that I write a history of the Tamils and there was no question but that it would be a daunting task. Although a native Tamil speaker and one who is rooted in the region, there was much that I was ignorant of, and researching this book gave me enriching and indelible insights into the history, culture, arts, and literature of an ancient and sophisticated people. Covid put a temporary stop to progress, but David was quick to pull me back on track and was determined to extract this book out of me, which he did. Being a part of the Aleph family of writers and working with David, one of India's best editors, has been a privilege. It's been a journey that has been challenging and inspirational for me and my gratitude is immense. It is important to mention that David clarified that there is space for serious but non-academic writing for general readers and this spurred me on to write about this vast and absorbing subject.

I would like to also acknowledge with gratitude the incredible patience and support of Pujitha Krishnan, my editor at Aleph, who I have had the good fortune to work with; she quickly set in place a rhythm of work that enabled me to complete the project, offering solutions and clarifications when I couldn't see a way forward. Her insightful editing sharpened the manuscript greatly. I would also like to thank Aayushi Gupta at Aleph for her painstaking efforts with this book.

There are many others who have helped me gather information and gain perspective; I owe them all so much. I would like to thank:

T. S. Subramanian, my colleague and good friend, was the key person who helped shape the research and content of this book. He was Associate Editor of *Frontline* and earlier in *The Hindu* and has in-depth knowledge of Tamil history and archaeology. A gifted and insightful writer, he has written extensively about India's nuclear power, missile, battle tanks, and oil and natural gas programmes. He tirelessly and meticulously (and with unfailing cheer and enthusiasm) curated journeys and multiple site visits across Tamil Nadu for four years and more, arranged travel and meetings with Tamil experts—scholars, historians, archaeologists, and opened a whole new world of the Tamils for me. He also fact-checked the early drafts of the book. His generosity in terms of sharing knowledge, finding references, and spending time helping with this book knew no bounds.

Dr V. Vedachalam, the renowned scholar, writer, award-winning epigraphist, archaeologist, and author of over twenty-five books on Tamil epigraphy, history, and archaeology greatly contributed to the making of this book. I had the privilege of travelling across Tamil Nadu with him and Subramanian, learning and understanding the history and culture of the Tamils over lengthy conversations. Dr Vedachalam with his broad base of knowledge that extended from the history of Jainism in Tamil Nadu to temple art, architecture, numismatics, epigraphy, was very generous with sharing information and insights offering perspectives that were unique and enriching. G. Moorthy, the talented photographer who travelled with us and procured many official sanctions during our visits, and of course for his outstanding photographs, many of which are in this book.

Dr G. Thirumoorthy, who retired as Assistant Professor, Department of Ancient History and Archaeology, for remarkable insights through conversations and site visits to Mamallapuram and Salavankuppam where he was the principal excavator. He is knowledgeable about south Indian temple art and architecture and in the archaeology of northern Tamil Nadu. Thanks to Dr S. Kannan of Madurai who was Associate Professor of History, Annamalai University, Chidambaram, for helping me with research material and information, particularly on the European presence in Tamil Nadu. My gratitude to Dr P. S. Sriraman who was Superintending Archaeologist in Chennai Circles of the Archaeological Survey of India, for several illuminating conversations and an unforgettable visit to the Brihadeeswara temple.

One of the great doyens of South India's history whose pioneering work on epigraphy and archaeology has added a wealth of new perspectives on the region is the distinguished scholar and author Dr Y. Subbarayalu. He was most gracious and generous in sharing his time and knowledge with me on several occasions for which I am very grateful. I had a memorable interaction with Dr K Rajan, historian, archaeologist, and epigraphist whose work on the Kodumanal site yielded many exciting discoveries. I am also grateful to Kudavayil Balasubramanian, the remarkable historian of the Cholas, who gave me a wealth of information during visits to Thanjavur, regaling me with perspectives and stories that are not always to be found in books. Mr Balasubramanian, former curator and publication manager at the Saraswathi Mahal Library, Thanjavur, is a well-known archaeologist and an expert in numismatics, music, and dance as well. I thank Professor Sampath Kumar who retired from the Asian College of Journalism, Chennai, and was former Editor of the BBC's Tamil Osai radio programme in London, for his profound insights on Tamil society, which he generously shared with me. I thank Professor Kanaka Ajithadoss, an authority on Jainism for illuminating conversations.

Dr Thangam Thenarasu, Minister for Finance and Human Resources Management and other portfolios in the Government of Tamil Nadu, who was very encouraging in his support of this project. Despite a very demanding schedule as a senior cabinet minister, he unhesitatingly gave me time for conversations and illuminating discussions emanating from his own passion for history and archaeology.

Mr Kamal Haasan for his insightful and sensitive input for the book. He generously gave me time in the midst of a full daily schedule and discussed various aspects of Tamil culture, politics, and identity. I am very grateful too for the scholarly and illuminating conversation with Dr A. X. Alexander, former Director General of Tamil Nadu Police, whose distinguished career track included Intelligence. His deep interest in South Asian history with a particular focus on Christian history stems from his earlier experience as a lecturer at St. Joseph's College in Tiruchi and in Loyola College, Chennai, before he joined the Indian Police Service.

Dr J. Raja Mohamad, a scholar in Tamil Islamic history, particularly in the maritime history of Tamil Muslims, is the author of numerous books and papers. He was formerly Director of the Government Museum in Pudukkottai and currently Director Centre for Islamic Tamil Cultural Research Jamal Mohamed College Tiruchirappalli. He has been generous with sharing his specialized knowledge and gave me elevating and inspiring insights into Tamil history.

S. Anwar, historian, writer, and award-winning documentary filmmaker, who is deeply interested in the history and culture of Tamil Nadu, enlightened me on much of Tamil history during our numerous discussions and interactions over the several years of researching and writing this book. His documentary *Yaadhum* on Tamil Muslim identity and history won a Bronze Remi award at the 48th Houston International Film Festival. His sensitive and progressive approach to not just Tamil history, but Indian history brought me much enrichment.

Dr A. R. Venkatachalapathy, one of the finest historians in India today, a prolific and gifted writer and translator, is a Professor at the Madras Institute of Development Studies, Chennai. He has published extensively in English and Tamil; from the writings of Bharati and Pudumaipithan to the biography of V. O. Chidambaram Pillai and produced several other tracts and books on the social, cultural, and intellectual history of Tamil Nadu. A very dear friend, he has been a great source of clarity, inspiration, and illumination and for always showing me the larger context of history during my many discussions with him.

The first of the many journeys of discovery for this book about many things Tamil including important narratives of Tamil history, temple art and architecture began with my dear friend Chithra Madhavan, scholar and historian par excellence. During the early years of working on this book, a memorable trip to Kanchipuram with Chithra got it all going for me, and I thank her deeply for that.

Gopalkrishna Gandhi, historian, writer, the author of several books, former bureaucrat, and a cherished and valued friend for sharing reflective ideas. I thank him for multiple enriching conversations, for shining a light on many things, and for an inspiring breadth of vision and idealism so hard to find these days. And personally, for me, this is a treasured and much valued friendship that I set much store by.

The distinguished Dr Arjun Appadurai, Emeritus Professor in Media, Culture and Communication at New York University, was a marvellous source of information and insights especially on Tamil identity and this work benefitted much from conversations with him over Zoom and in person when I was working on this book. His perspectives threw a whole new light on issues of community, history and identity.

I must acknowledge with gratitude the input of the late Dr R. Nagaswamy, a leading light in Tamil history, iconography, epigraphy, and archaeology, the author of numerous books in English and Tamil in these subjects. He was kind enough to meet me on several occasions and despite his frail health, spent several hours with me each time I visited. His marvellous scholarship and range of knowledge was stunning; his passing has left a void for many students of Tamil history and culture.

It was the constant encouragement, push and motivation from my friend Rita Chaudhuri that got me over the finish line with this work. She showed me how a structured way of working can facilitate progress. Rita is a multi-faceted management leader with years of experience in global multinational companies and works with CEOs and management teams on goal setting and performance delivery. She certainly helped me with that. The many sessions with her discussing the book made a huge difference to the writing exercise.

I would like to thank another very dear friend, Radha Sarma Hegde, who grew up in Chennai, remembers it as Madras and now teaches at New York

University. Her constant friendship, encouraging conversations, and invaluable writing insights gave me the support I needed at all the right times. Like Rita, she also helped greatly to bring in a clarity of thought and her analytical insights improved the content.

A very special word of thanks to some other dear friends Ranvir Shah, Sushila Ravindranath, Jayanthi Natarajan, Anita Ratnam, and Prasanna Ramaswamy, who specifically discussed many book ideas with me and gave me a slew of insights that greatly enriched my understanding of Tamil culture and politics. My very dear friend in Boston, Dr George Verghese, formerly Professor at MIT, read several early chapters of the book, and his comments greatly sharpened the text. I would like to express my sincere gratitude to Mansi Gandhi whose amazing wisdom and understanding of human nature saw me through some challenging days.

Several colleagues in *The Hindu* have gone out of their way and helped me with the work on this book. *The Hindu*'s Editor, Suresh Nambath readily facilitated support from within the organization. I owe a huge debt of gratitude to D. Suresh Kumar, Deputy Resident Editor of *The Hindu*, Tamil Nadu, an expert in state politics who not only gave me perspectives and information over lengthy conversations but also helped with specific rich information for the narrative.

B. Kolappan, Senior Deputy Editor of *The Hindu*, an expert on Tamil history and politics, has shared books, conversations, and perspectives all drawn from his own expertise in the region. My gratitude to him for all his help. K. C. Vijayakumar, Sports Editor of *The Hindu*, gave me comprehensive insights on the state of sports in Tamil Nadu. Shonali Muthalaly, Associate Editor at *The Hindu*, shared her knowledgeable insights into what entertains modern Tamils, on eating out, and on the cuisines of Tamil Nadu. Rosella Stephen, Associate Editor, *The Hindu*, unhesitatingly supported this project with her boundless resourcefulness and marvellous creative energies. I also thank Murali N. Krishnaswamy, Deputy Editor, *The Hindu*, who gave me timely help with the manuscript and invaluable assistance that allowed me to wrap up the work. I thank K. Asokan, Editor of the *Hindu Tamil Thisai* for his illuminating insights for the book. Nahla Nainar, of *The Hindu* in Tiruchirapalli, a prolific and sensitive writer, arranged many meetings for me with assiduous kindness, and what is more, drew me into the warm circle of her distinguished and scholarly family, including letting me catch a glimpse of the brilliance of her grandfather, Syed Mohamed Husain Nainar, Reader and head of the department of Arabic, Persian, and Urdu, who wrote and translated many scholarly papers about Tamil history and antiquity. I will always be grateful to her. A very special word of thanks to R. Vengadesh, News Photographer, *Hindu Tamil Thisai*, who was enormously helpful in video documentation. I also thank Udhav Naig for his timely assistance.

This book could not have been completed without the support and assistance of two people, K. N. Parthasarathy and R. Ramesh of *The Hindu*. Their tireless help right from the very beginning, from organizing travel to tracking down references and innumerable other tasks that kept coming up over the many years of this work, made this book possible.

K. Venkatesan of *The Hindu* in Tiruchi, and S. Narayanan of *The Hindu* in Madurai, whose assistance was invaluable through the years of travel and research—their strenuous efforts during my travels and their support went a long way in the making of this book. A special word of thanks to N. S. Srinivasan of Tiruchi who again accompanied me during my many journeys and ensured smooth passage every time. I thank photographers B. Velankanni Raj, and M. Moorthy of Tiruchi for their contributions. M. Esakiappan, News Editor, *The Hindu Tamil Thisai*, Madurai, helped get the permissions and sanctions for visits to temples in the Tirunelveli region. I am grateful to him. K. R. Naresh Kumar, retired Chief Librarian, Vibha Sudarshan, Chief Librarian, and S. K. Subrramanya, Associate Chief Librarian helped hugely with research and patiently responded to all my requests. Vibha took upon herself a lot of additional reference checks.

The Archaeological Survey of India (ASI), a marvellous repository of invaluable material, has been a great source from which I drew much for this book. More important, many top officials of the ASI, expert historians, and archaeologists have been unfailingly helpful and facilitated site visits and gave permissions that furthered my research and added much to this work. Dr T. Arunraj Director, Pandit Deendayal Upadhyaya Institute of Archaeology, ASI, who was Superintending Archaeologist Tiruchi Circle earlier, Dr A. Anil Kumar, Superintending Archaeologist Tiruchi Circle, ASI, and Dr V. P. Yathees Kumar, Assistant Superintending Archaeologist now posted to New Delhi but earlier in the Tiruchi Circle, with great kindness accompanied us on several site visits and gave me superb insights into many excavated sites. Thanks to Dr V. Muthukumar, Assistant Superintending Archaeologist, Tiruchi Circle, for his support and assistance. He along with Yathees Kumar helped us get special permission to view places not open to the public. I also thank Dr S. Nanthakumar, Archaeology Officer, Karur. There are others in the ASI, Conservation Assistants, who in different locations in Tamil Nadu assisted me. My thanks to D. Seetharaman and S. Sankar in Thanjavur, P. Vignesh, N. Jothi, S. Vijayakumar, Vellinathan also at the Brihadeeswara temple in Thanjavur, V. S. Paramasivam in Sittanavasal, V. S. Balasundaram in Kudumiyanmalai, S. Divakar and B. Senthil Kumar at Darasuram, D. Sridhar at Gangaikondacholapuram, and N. Jothi and V. Deivasigamani also at the Gangaikondacholapuram temple.

My mother, Menaka Parthasarathy, a keen observer of my progress (in life and in this book) spurred me on with frequent queries, offering perspectives, insights, and stories that had a great bearing on how I approached many of the topics in this book. Her deep understanding of the Tamils has had a profound impact on my writing. My husband, Lakshman, as always, generously made time and pored over countless pages of the manuscript, offering blunt but constructive criticism and prodding me to get going whenever I faltered.

I am deeply grateful to the rest of my dear family for constantly cheering me on, for being curious about my progress, and wondering, I am sure, whether I would ever get this done. I am also thankful for my supportive group of friends who are like my extended family (they know who they are) who are probably as relieved as I am that I actually got to the finish line.

I may have inadvertently omitted mentioning some names, and for that I apologize. I am very grateful to everyone who made this book possible.

Image Credits

A near perfect jar with a beautifully crafted lid at Adichanallur. Courtesy Nirmala Lakshman.

Urn burial site at Adichanallur. Courtesy G. Moorthy.

A well laid-out Sangam age site at Keezhadi. Courtesy G. Moorthy.

A multi-tiered terracotta ring well at Keezhadi. Courtesy G. Moorthy.

One of the earliest Tamil Brahmi inscriptions, third century BCE, Mankulam. Courtesy G. Moorthy.

Caves of Jain monks at Arittapatti village. Courtesy G. Moorthy.

The empty sanctum sanctorum at the Salavan Kuppam Murugan temple. Courtesy B. Velankanni Raj.

The five unfinished great stone monolithic rathas at Mamallapuram. Courtesy B. Velankanni Raj.

Sculptures including that of Shiva and Parvati at the Kailasanatha temple. Courtesy B. Velankanni Raj.

A series of pillars portraying the history of the Pallava dynasty at the Vaikunta Perumal temple. Courtesy B. Velankanni Raj.

Bas relief of Jain Tirthankaras on a hillside in Kazhugumalai. Courtesy G. Moorthy.

The yakshi Ambika in Kazhugumalai. Courtesy G. Moorthy.

Standing Brahma at the Pasupathi kovil. Courtesy Nirmala Lakshman

Chola sculptures of Ganesha and his servitors at the Brahmapurisvara temple. Courtesy G. Moorthy.

Painting on the ceiling of the Jain rock-cut shrine at Sittanavasal. Courtesy Nirmala Lakshman

An overview of the Airavatesvara temple. Courtesy G. Moorthy.

Nataraja temple at Chidambaram. Courtesy G. Moorthy.

Brihadeeswara temple at Thanjavur. Courtesy G. Moorthy.

Inscriptions on the northern outer wall of the Brihadeeswara temple. Courtesy G. Moorthy.

The hollow vimana of the Brihadeeswara temple. Courtesy G. Moorthy.

Gangaikondacholapuram temple built by Rajendra Chola I. Courtesy G. Moorthy.

The majestic vimana of the Brihadeeswara temple at Gangaikondacholapuram. Courtesy G. Moorthy.

Vijayanagara paintings at Tirumal Iruncholai temple. Courtesy G. Moorthy.

The Golden Lotus Tank. Courtesy G. Moorthy.

Nataraja bronze from Kulasekara Nallur. Courtesy D. Krishnan.

Early Chola bronzes portraying Krishna with Satyabhama and Rukmani. Courtesy D. Krishnan.

Shiva marrying Parvati at the Meenakshi temple. Courtesy G. Moorthy.

Sculptures of the Nayaka rulers at the Madurai Meenakshi Temple. Courtesy G. Moorthy.

The Chola seal in the Tiruvalangadu copper plates. Courtesy M. Srinath.

The Tiruvalangadu copper plate charter at the Government Museum, Chennai. Courtesy M. Srinath.

The Lakshminarasimha bronze, Tiruchirappalli District. Courtesy M. Srinath.

A painting of Portuguese traders arriving in a ship. Courtesy Nirmala Lakshman

Paintings at Tiruppudaimarudur temple. Courtesy Nirmala Lakshman.

Luz Church in Madras. Courtesy G. Moorthy.

A view of the North Street of Fort St. George. Courtesy ASI, Chennai Circle.

A view of St. Thomas Mount, near Madras. Courtesy ASI, Chennai Circle.

Marina Beach, Chennai. Courtesy K. V. Srinivasan.

Chennai's Central Railway Station. Courtesy R. Ragu.

Notes

INTRODUCTION: THIS JASMINE COUNTRY

x 'devoted the rest of his long life': A. K. Ramanujan (tr.), *Poems of Love and War: From the Eight Anthologies and the Ten Long Poems of Classical Tamil*, New York: Columbia University Press, 1985.

x 'they embody values but do not': Ibid., p. 286.

x Whether these people were the original: K. A. Nilakanta Sastri, *A History of South India: From Prehistoric Times to the Fall of Vijayanagar*, New Delhi: Oxford University Press, 1958; Noboru Karashima (ed.), *A Concise History of South India: Issues and Interpretations*, New Delhi: Oxford University Press, 2014.

xi Rise, brothers, rise, the wakening: Sarojini Naidu, *The Golden Threshold*, London: William Heinemann, 1920, p. 31.

xiv For the Tamil villager ooru is: E. Valentine Daniel, *Fluid Signs: Being a Person the Tamil Way*, Berkeley: University of California Press, 1984, pp. 63–68.

xv 'For her devotees, Tamilttay': Sumathi Ramaswamy, *Passions of the Tongue: Language Devotion in Tamil India, 1891–1970*, India: University of California Press, 1997, p. 19.

xv '…one cannot get along in Tamil': David Shulman, *Tamil: A Biography*, London: Harvard University Press, 2016, p. 14.

xvi 'to be a civilized being': Ibid., p. 2.

xvi 'Tamil means something like knowing': Ibid.

xvi 'Tamil is astonishingly rich in': Ibid., p. 13.

xvi 'tend to be Tamilized': Ibid.

xvi As of May 2024, 89.6 million: 'Tamil speaking countries', WorldData.info, July 2024, available at https://www.worlddata.info/languages/tamil.php.

xvii The ancient Sangam text *Purananuru*: A. K. Ramanujan, 'Ecology', *Second Sight*, New Delhi: Oxford University Press, 1986, p. 59.

xix In places like Singampunari in Sivagangai: Sruthisagar Yamunan, 'As jallikattu supporters grow more insistent, Dalit voices of protest against bull-taming emerge', *Scroll.in*, 19 January 2017.

xx He likened the attempt to reduce Tamil identity: Ramachandra Guha, 'To reduce Tamil identity to Jallikattu is both farcical and tragic', *Hindustan Times*, 21 January 2017.

CHAPTER 1: EMERGENCE

2 'represents a paradigm shift in thinking': R. Prasad, 'Stone tools offer insights into history of human evolution', *The Hindu*, 31 January 2018.

3 Redware urns have been found in these: Yathees Kumar in conversation with the author.

4 Raja Mohamad suggests that these cave paintings: J. Raja Mohamad in conversation with the author, Pudukkottai, May 2018.

5 'In the period between the fourth and third centuries': T. S. Subramanian, 'Unearthing an industrial past', *Frontline*, 10 August 2012.

6 'a complete gemstone industry': *A Note on Kodumanal —Report by Dr. K Rajan*, 2013.

6 'The habitation part of the site': Ibid.

8 Sakthivel also reminds us that about: Sakthivel and Pon Vasanth in conversation with the author, Keezhadi, May 2018.

8 'The most important historical inscriptions': Iravatham Mahadevan, 'An epigraphic

perspective on the antiquity of Tamil', *The Hindu*, 24 June 2010.
9   **Shulman writes about the 'sensational':** Shulman, *Tamil*, p. 22.
9   **'The Jambai inscription marks a donation by':** Ibid., p. 23.
9   **'1) potsherds with Tamil Brahmi inscriptions':** Dr Y. Subbarayalu, *Archaeology and the Cankam Literature with Special Reference to Inscribed Pots and Herostones*, Paper presented at the World Classical Tamil Conference, Ulaga Tamizh Semmozhi Manadu, Coimbatore, June 2010.
9   **'star names such as Asatan, Asalay(a)':** Ibid.
10 **'[L]iteracy was confined to only the elite sections':** Ibid.
10 **'the Prakrit-speaking merchants...(who were)':** Ibid.
10 **'The spread of the knowledge of writing through':** Ibid.
10 **There is more Prakrit in the pottery:** Ibid.

BOOK I: THE AGE OF POETRY

CHAPTER 2: LITERATURE AS HISTORY
13 **The development of a rich classical:** K. A. Nilakanta Sastri, *Writings in the Hindu*, Chennai: THG Publishing Private Limited, 2019, p. 33.
14 **'All of us have a natural propensity':** Ibid., p. 67.
15 **'They say the Tamil land where I am headed':** Shulman, *Tamil*, p. 38.
15 **'The traveller is safe on the highway':** Ramanujan (tr.), *Poems of Love and War*.
16 **'The ancient poets composed in Tamil':** Ibid.
16 **'these poems are *classical*, i.e., early':** Ibid.
16 **'both categories of poetry had, notwithstanding':** K. Kailsapathy, *Tamil Heroic Poetry*, Oxford: Clarendon P., 1968, p. 4.
16 **'Those treating wars, exploits of kings':** Ibid., p. 5.
16 **'We do not know enough of':** Ibid., p. 6.
17 **The *Tolkappiyam* has three books dealing with:** Shulman, *Tamil*, pp. 30, 31, 203, 205, 219, and 305.
17 **'this (context) is sweeping, and includes':** Martha Ann Selby, Indira Viswanathan Peterson (eds.), *Tamil Geographies: Cultural Constructions of Space and Place in South India*, New York: State University of New York Press, 2008, pp. 24–25.
17 **'What She Said':** Ramanujan (tr.), *Poems of Love and War*, p. 244.
18 **'In his country, summer west wind blows':** Ibid., p. 7.
20 **'Rains in season':** Ibid., p. 76.
20 **'O man of the seashore, where old women':** Ibid., p. 31.
21 **In the Chola country watered by the Kaveri:** Sastri, *A History of South India*, p. 125.
22 **What remains at the core of:** Ibid., p. 138.

CHAPTER 3: OF HEROES AND KINGS
23 **'Forbearance of kinsmen's wrongs, a good':** Ramanujan (tr.), *Poems of Love and War*.
24 **Scholars like Kesavan Veluthat of Delhi University:** Kesavan Veluthat, *The Early Medieval in South India*, New Delhi: Oxford University Press, 2009, p. 23.
24 **'it has been more profitably considered':** Ibid.
24 **Sastri says that to begin with, the Tamils firmly:** Sastri, *A History of South India*, p. 107.
24 **As noted, most of the actual information about heroes:** Kailsapathy, *Tamil Heroic Poetry*, p. 16.
25 **'Like the heroes who, wishing to go':** Ramanujan (tr.), *Poems of Love and War*, p. 221.
26 **'Like the tiger's cub of curved stripes':** Sastri, *Writings in the Hindu*, p. 52.
26 **'He could uproot mountains; fill up the sea':** Kailsapathy, *Tamil Heroic Poetry*, p. 38.
27 **Kautilya, or Chanakya, as he was called:** K. A. Nilakanta Sastri, *The Pandyan Kingdom from the Earliest Times to the Sixteenth Century*, London: Luzac, 1929, p. 14.

28   **This was around 300 BCE, when:** Karashima (ed.), *A Concise History of South India*, p. 26.
28   **Pliny the Elder, in the years just before:** Ibid., pp. 70–71.
28   **Many gold medallions which were found were:** Ibid., p. 73.
28   **Pliny the Younger (1st century CE) in a letter:** Ibid.
28   **'shows every sign of being the work of a man who':** G. W. B. Huntingford (ed.) (tr.), *The Periplus of the Erythraean Sea, by an Unknown Author: With Some Extracts from Agatharkhides 'On the Erythraean Sea'*, London: Taylor & Francis, 2017, p. 5.
28   **He speaks of Kalliena (Kalyana in Bombay harbour):** Ibid., pp. 49–50.
28   **'there are two very celebrated marts':** Ibid., p. 49.
29   **He documents journeys to the Travancore coast of the kingdom:** Ibid., p. 50.
29   **The exports from this region are large quantities:** Sastri, *A History of South India*, p. 126.
29   **The cotton from the region was said to be:** Ibid., p. 126.
29   **'Under the guardianship of the gods of enduring glory':** Sastri, *Writings in the Hindu*, p. 77.
30   **He quotes the *Ahananuru* collection of Sangam poetry:** Srinath Perur, 'Lost cities #3 – Muziris: did black pepper cause the demise of India's ancient port?', *The Guardian*, 10 August 2016.
30   **Karashima says that old Chinese records mention:** Karashima (ed.), *A Concise History of South India*, p. 76.

CHAPTER 4: LIFE OF THE TIMES
31   **'The general impression left on the mind by this early':** K. A. Nilakanta Sastri, *The Colas Vol. 1*, Madras University Historical Series No. 9, Madras: University of Madras, 1955, p. 546.
32   **'That which men call food comes from water':** George L. Hart, Hank Heifetz (eds.), *The Four Hundred Songs of War and Wisdom: An Anthology of Poems from Classical Tamil: The Purananuru*, United Kingdom: Columbia University Press, 1999, pp. 15–16.
32   **'Niragam porundiya uragattiru', meaning:** Ibid., p. 169.
34   **'The unlettered hunters…spent the day in hunting':** Sastri, *Writings in the Hindu*, p. 70.
35   **'by eating flesh by day and night the edges':** Ibid., p. 53.
35   **The voices of women are clear, and as Ramanujan:** Ramanujan (tr.), *Poems of Love and War*, p. 268.
35   **Much of the imagery is physical, referring to her eyes:** Ibid., p. 269.

BOOK II: THE AGE OF EMPIRE

CHAPTER 5: LIONS OF THE EARTH
41   **The concept of a sacred lineage of kings starting:** Karashima (ed.), *A Concise History of South India*.
43   **'sits upright and gazes forward':** D. Dennis Hudson (tr.), *The Vaikunta Perumal Temple at Kanchipuram*, India: Prakriti Foundation, 2009, p. 161.
43   **The Pulangurichi inscription written in classical:** Y. Subbarayalu, *South India Under the Cholas*, New Delhi: Oxford University Press, 2012, pp. 27–35; Karashima (ed.), *A Concise History of South India*, p. 60.
44   **A copper inscription of the time states:** Sastri, *A History of South India*, p. 135.
44   **However, several expert scholars such as Sastri:** Ibid., pp. 90–92.
46   **Many inscriptions largely specify grants of villages:** C. Minakshi, 'Administration and Social Life under the Pallavas', *Madras University Historical Series*, University of Madras, No. 13, 1938, pp. 6–13.
46   **The next mention of a Pallava king:** Sastri, *A History of South India*, p. 93.
46   **'The only incident which could have shaken badly':** C. Minakshi, *The Historical Sculptures of the Vaikuntha Perumal Temple*, New Delhi: Archaeological Survey of India, September 1939, p. 10.

51 **Dr Nagaswamy, archaeologist and epigraphist par excellence:** R. Nagaswamy in conversation with the author, Chennai, April 2019.

CHAPTER 6: KANCHIPURAM: A CONFLUENCE OF CULTURES

53 **'as the jasmine among flowers, as Vishnu':** Dr Prema Nandakumar, 'Kanchipuram', Hindupedia.com, available at https://www.hindupedia.com/en/Kanchipuram.

53 **'This used to be a huge lake filled with lotuses':** Chithra Madhavan in conversation with the author, Kanchipuram, July 2018.

54 **'squared realm whose east-west axis':** Selby, Peterson (eds.), *Tamil Geographies*, p. 87.

54 **Hudson sees this construct in the layout:** Ibid., pp. 113–114.

54 **'the Self, the wholeness of the personality':** Carl Jung, *Psychology and Alchemy*, United Kingdom: Taylor & Francis, 2014.

54 **'in the olden days, when living in the world':** Selby, Peterson (eds.), *Tamil Geographies*, pp. 111–112.

55 **A volume compiled by scholars that commemorates:** A. Aiyappan, P. R. Srinivasan, (eds.), *Story of Buddhism with Special Reference to South India*, Chennai: Department of Information and Publicity, Government of Madras, 1960.

55 **There are two temples on the granted land:** G. Thirumoorthy in conversation with the author, Jaina Kanchi, March 2019.

57 **'a beautiful banner among women, as dear to':** Chithra Madhavan in conversation with the author, Kanchipuram, March 2019.

57 **'this Emperor, who has vowed to protect the whole':** Ibid.

58 **'Harasya Hara haasa Roopam Athi maanam':** Ibid.

58 **The temple was also the tallest structure of the times:** Ibid.

58 **This is the only temple in India:** R. Nagaswamy, 'Lecture on Kailasanath Temple', Tamil Heritage Trust, Chennai, June 2017.

59 **According to Hudson, these lions could well:** Hudson (tr.), *The Vaikunta Perumal Temple at Kanchipuram*, p. 15.

59 **'the vimana tower as viewed from outside the':** Ibid., p. xvi.

60 **'The vast Sky forever black / The Lights of Sun and Moon':** Ibid., p. 17.

60 **'In a time long ago / He lay down on a soft':** Ibid., p. 21.

61 **So, an entire series tracing the Pallava royal lineage:** Minakshi, *The Historical Sculptures of the Vaikuntha Perumal Temple*, p. 5.

62 **'However, the Dravida style may not have been':** Ibid., p. xiii.

63 **'the remains of a great city that has been':** William Chambers, 'Some Account of the Sculptures and the Ruins of Mavalipuram, a Place a few Miles North of Sadras, and known to Seamen by the name of the Seven Pagodas', *Asiatick Researches*, Vol. 1, 1788, pp. 145–170.

63 **James Fergusson, called 'the first historian of Indian art':** James Fergusson, *History of Indian and Eastern Architecture*, London: J. Murray, 1876.

63 **And centuries before, Ptolemy referred:** 'Mahabalipuram—Sculpture by the Sea', Archaeological Survey of India, available at https://artsandculture.google.com/story/mahabalipuram-sculpture-by-the-sea-archaeological-survey-of-india/_wXB5vhuL90aJA?hl=en.

65 **To corroborate the theory that all the five Ratha:** G. Thirumoorthy and T. S. Subramaniam in conversation with the author, Mamallapuram, February 2020.

66 **The second person was perhaps a blacksmith who:** Balaji Gopalakrishnan, 'Discovering the Sculptor of Mamallapuram', *Journal of Indian History and Culture*, No. 23, September 2017, pp. 36–37.

66 **'these artisans were patronised by kings as well as by':** Ibid., p. 35.

CHAPTER 7: DIVINE ORIGINS AND EARTHLY ARRANGEMENTS

68 **Visaya is one such name and Rastra:** C. Minakshi, 'Administration and Social Life Under the Pallavas', p. 37.
69 **By the time of the Great Pallavas:** K. K. Pillay, *The Caste System in Tamil Nadu*, Chennai: MJP Publishers, 2007, p. 37.
69 **'polities formed around Brahmin royal':** Shulman, *Tamil*, p. 145.
69 **Minakshi says that there are plenty:** C. Minakshi, 'Administration and Social Life Under the Pallavas', p. 159.
69 **Minakshi suggests that Brahmins:** Pillay, *The Caste System in Tamil Nadu*, p. 39.
69 **This could well be the same as:** Ibid., p. 38–39.
70 **Most of these queens, especially the:** Minakshi, 'Administration and Social Life under the Pallavas', p. 160.
70 **The term mahamatra is also inscribed:** Ibid., pp. 51–52.
70 **'Brahma Sri Raja who was a friend':** Ibid.
71 **'Why, this man has heaps of riches drawn':** Ibid., p. 58.
72 **The present Uyyakondan Vaykkal which takes:** Ibid., pp. 94–110.
72 **'The king of Kanchi had been suffering':** Ibid., p. 113.
72 **Notably Sastri has also mentioned:** Ibid., pp. 119–120.
73 **'A king needed the authority of':** Karashima (ed.), A Concise History of South India, p. 91.
73 **While there is much more information:** Minakshi, 'Administration and Social Life under the Pallavas', pp. 124–127.
73 **An inscription dated in the ninth year:** Ibid., p. 128.
74 **Areca nuts, oil seeds, paddy, medicinal plants:** Ibid., pp. 71–83.

CHAPTER 8: THE CITADELS OF FAITH

77 **'Though the kings of the earlier period followed':** Karashima (ed.), *A Concise History of South India*.
78 **As previously noted, there is very:** Sastri, *A History of South India*, p. 130.
78 **'When the curtain rises again towards':** Ibid., p. 130.
78 **the Dravida Sangha which he established:** R. Champakalakshmi, *Airavata: Felicitation Volume in Honour of Iravatham Mahadevan*, Chennai: Varalaru.com, August 2008.
78 **Further historical evidence of the dominance:** Karashima (ed.), *A Concise History of South India*, p. 85.
79 **The Kalyani inscription clearly says that:** Minakshi, 'Administration and Social Life under the Pallavas', p. 69.
79 **Dennis Hudson says that this monastery may:** Selby, Peterson (eds.), *Tamil Geographies*, pp. 111–112.
81 **The poet-saint then burst into the now:** 'Thirunavukkarasu Nayanar - Part- II Establishing the Truth - The Ocean that Floated on a Sea', Shaivam.org, available at https://www.shaivam.org/devotees/thirunavukkarasu-nayanar-part-2-ocean-that-floated-on-sea/#gsc.tab=0.
81 **'We are slaves to no man / Nor do we':** R. Champakalakshmi, *Religion, Tradition, and Ideology: Pre-colonial South India*, New Delhi: Oxford University Press, 2011, p. 65.
81 **He regrets his association with the Jains:** Ibid., p. 65.
82 **The historian Champakalakshmi points out that:** Ibid., p. 63.
82 **Ramanujan in his *Hymns for the Drowning*:** A. K. Ramanujan (tr.), *Hymns for the Drowning: Poems for Visnu*, New Delhi: Penguin Books, 1993, p. ix.
83 **Their geographical environment is thus:** Champakalakshmi, *Religion, Tradition, and Ideology*, p. 56.
85 **'the tall enclosing prakara wall defines this mandala':** Hudson (tr.), *The Vaikunta Perumal Temple at Kanchipuram*, p. 11.

CHAPTER 9: MADURAI AND THE ACME OF PANDYA CULTURE

87 'He saw the Pantiyan's great city of Maturai': R. Parthasarathy (tr.), *The Cilappatikāram: The Tale of an Anklet*, New Delhi: Penguin India, 1993.
87 'like distant thunder the sound': Ibid., p. 136.
87 'appeared to stop them': Ibid., p. 139.
87 In this epic poem, supposedly composed by the monk-prince Illango: Ibid., p. 143.
88 'The south wind from Maturai blows': Ilango Adigal, Alain Daniélou (trs.), *Shilappadikaram*, New Delhi: Aleph Book Company, 2016.
89 More fully, it was called: Iravatham Mahadevan, Michael Witzel (eds.), *Early Tamil Epigraphy from the Earliest Times to the Sixth Century AD (Oipse)*, Volume 62, United Kingdom: Harvard University Press, 2003, p. 94.
89 A second century BCE inscription in: Ibid.
90 'When I bade him goodbye from my heart': 'Ettuthokai—Kalithokai 1–36 Palai', 'Sangam Poems Translated by Vaidehi', available at https://sangamtranslationsbyvaidehi.com/ettuthokai-kalithokai-palai-1-36/.
90 A translation of some of the *Paripatal* poems: V. N. Muthukumar, Elizabeth Segran (trs.), *The River Speaks: The Vaiyai Poems from the Paripatal*, India: Penguin Random House, 2012, p. 47.
90 In *Madurai Through the Ages*, D. Devakunjari: D. Devakunjari, *Madurai Through the Ages: From the Earliest Times to 1801 A.D.*, India: Society for Archaeological, Historical, and Epigraphical Research, 1979.
91 'In the huge city where drums roar': 'Pathuppattu—Mathuraikanchi', 'Sangam Poems Translated by Vaidehi', available at https://sangamtranslationsbyvaidehi.com/pathuppattu-mathuraikanchi/.
91 'things in the market of Koodal do not': Ibid.
91 'rise up to the sky, with many': Ibid.
91 'older women of fine beauty / with': Ibid.
92 'Did you go to study sweet Tamil verses': Selby and Peterson (eds.), *Tamil Geographies*.
92 The local Tamil people were: V. Vedachalam in conversation with the author, Madurai, September 2021.
93 Because of the long reign of the Pandyas: R. Nagaswamy in conversation with the author, Chennai, April 2019.
93 Epigraphy, as the renowned historian and epigraphist: K. V. Raman, *Some Aspects of Pandyan History in the Light of Recent Discoveries, Sri S, Subramania Ayyar Endowment Lectures 1971-72*, Madras: University of Madras, 1979, pp. 1–4.
95 Tamilakam was conducive for Jain asceticism: Kanaka Ajithadoss in conversation with the author, Chennai, 2022.
95 The town of Pudukkottai itself: Sampath Kumar, '3,000-year-old rock art with symbols found in Pudukkottai', *Times of India*, 2 August 2021.
96 'When overtaken by portentous calamity': T. V. Sivanandan, 'What is Sallekhana?', *Summit of Peace*, India: The Hindu, 2018, p. 58.
96 In other words, there were specific: Ibid.
97 Even though it was a time of Brahmanical: V. Vedachalam and T. S. Subramanian in conversation with the author, Sittanavasal, 2019.
98 'The art of painting in the cave temple at': Karl Khandalavala, Moti Chandra, T. N. Ramachandran (eds.), *Lalit Kala*, No. 9, New Delhi: Lalit Kala Akademi, April 1961, p. 52.
100 The art historian C. Sivaramamurthi: T. S. Subramanian, 'Opulent Sculptures', *Frontline*, 24 October 2008.
100 'From above the temple looks': Ibid.
101 'the concentric arrangement of walls': Benoy K. Behl, 'Sacred Spaces', *Frontline*, 18 July 2008.

102 **To this day, during the temple's Chitra:** T. S. Subramanian in conversation with the author, Madurai.
103 **The temple area sprawls over 17 acres:** V. Vedachalam, G. Sethuraman, *The Sculptural Splendours of Meenakshi Temple*, Chennai: Arulmighu Meenakshi Sundareshwarar Temple, 2019, p. 28.
104 **Raman points out that another inscription:** K. V. Raman, *Temple Art, Icons and Culture of India and South-East Asia*, New Delhi: Sharda Publishing House, 2007, p. 17.
104 **'this Alavayil is the place where Annal':** Porchelvi Jeyaprakash, Magnificent Meenakshi Temple-7, *Facebook*, 5 September 2020; Dr C. Santhalingam's lecture on the history of inscriptions in the Meenakshi Sundareswarar Temple, Madurai at Tamil Virtual University, 27 October 2022.

CHAPTER 10: NO FAINTNESS IN THEIR HEARTS
107 **'They fear evils that other men':** 'This world lives...', *The Rich Vegetarian*, 12 January 2007, available at https://therichvegetarian.com/this-world-lives/.
107 **If we look at the origins and early stories:** Sastri, *The Pandyan Kingdom from the Earliest Times to the Sixteenth Century*, p. 15.
107 **'dark complexion, wearing a bright and long':** C. Sivaramamurti, *Kalugumalai and Early Pandyan Rock-cut Shrines*, India: N. M. Tripathi, 1961, p. 9.
108 **In the same text, the Pandya ruler's might:** Ibid.
108 **The more realistic (and possibly earliest reference):** Sastri, *The Pandyan Kingdom from the Earliest Times to the Sixteenth Century*, p. 15.
108 **Y. Subbarayalu says that the antiquity of the first:** Karashima (ed.), *A Concise History of South India*, p. 47.
108 **The riches of the Pandya kingdom, of which:** Huntingford (ed.) (tr.), *The Periplus of the Erythraean Sea*, pp. 53–54.
108 **Fragments from *Indica*, the work of Megasthenes:** E. A. Schwanbeck, McCrindle, John Watson, S. Sedgefield, *Ancient India as Described by Megasthenês and Arrian*, India: Thacker, Spink, 1877, pp. 113–114.
108 **Some twentieth century scholars like E. A. Schwanbeck:** Ibid., pp. 66–67.
108 **'The Pandean nation is governed by':** Ibid., pp. 158–159.
109 **'the sovereignty (of the land) Herakles':** Ibid., p. 202.
109 **'a number of minor principalities ruled over by':** Sastri, *The Pandyan Kingdom from the Earliest Times to the Sixteenth Century*, p. 18.
109 **'we may assign a length of say, 150 to 200':** Ibid.
109 **He also points out that the kind of references made in:** Ibid.
109 **'Great king':** Ramanujan (tr.), *Poems of Love and War*, p. 115.
110 **As K. V. Raman points out, in spite of:** Raman, *Some Aspects of Pandyan History in the Light of Recent Discoveries*, p. 1.
110 **However, the significant contributions made by:** Ibid., pp. 2–3.
110 **The earliest mention of a Pandya king:** Ibid., p. 4.
110 **'characteristic appellation of the Pandyas':** Ibid.
110 **V. Vedachalam in his book *Parakrama Pandyapuram*:** V. Vedachalam, *Parakrama Pandyapuram*.
110 **'he of many sacrificial spaces':** Sastri, *A History of South India*, pp. 114–115.
111 **'a great conqueror and a liberal patron of':** C. Sivaramamurti, *Amaravati Sculptures in the Madras Government Museum*, Madras: Government Press, 1956, p. 10.
111 **Apart from specific information on:** T. S. Subramanian and V. Vedachalam in conversation with the author, July 2021.
111 **'by the donee and his descendants:** Sastri, *The Pandyan Kingdom from the Earliest Times to the*

112 *Sixteenth Century*, pp. 22–23.
112 The story goes that this Kamakaani generously: Ibid., p. 89.
112 'The early Pandya dynasty, from the days': T. S. Subramanian (tr.), *Pandya Nattu Varlarrumurai Sumuga Nilaviyal*, Thanjabur: Dhanalakshmi Pathipakam, 2019.
113 'a resplendent sun (emerging) from: Sastri, *The Pandyan Kingdom from the Earliest Times to the Sixteenth Century*, p. 41.
113 'bringing about the restoration of his own': Ibid.
113 'is clear that Cendan Kutran and his son': Y. Subbarayalu, *South India Under the Cholas*, pp. 29–32.
113 From his time onwards, Pandya kings: Sastri, *The Pandyan Kingdom from the Earliest Times to the Sixteenth Century*, pp. 37 –55.
114 Nedumaran's rule extended from Madurai: V. Vedachalam, A. Kalavathy, *Pandyan Ninraseer Nedumaram*, Thanjavur: Dhanalakshmi Pathipakam, 2019.
115 **In a highly ornate Tamil portion of the grant:** Sastri, *The Pandyan Kingdom from the Earliest Times to the Sixteenth Century*, pp. 41–44.
115 'worshipped the lotus feet of Pasupati and gave away': Ibid., p. 58.
116 **Of course, there were battles fought and:** Ibid., pp. 39, 40–45, 59, 61, 62.
116 **For instance, even the smaller victories over local:** Ibid., p. 60.
117 **one of the inscriptions names someone:** Ibid., pp. 44–60.
117 **When Madurakavi died around 770 CE:** Ibid., p. 60.
117 **The Madras Museum Plates speak of unnamed enemies:** Ibid., p. 62.
117 'conquest of Malainadu, and his destruction': C. Sivaramamurti, *Kalugumalai and Early Pandyan Rock-cut Shrines*, p. 12.
117 **The son of Nedunjadayan, Srimaran Srivallabha:** Ibid.
117 **The Sinnamanur plates mention his success over:** Ibid.
118 **The Sinnamanur plates, according to Sastri:** Sastri, *The Pandyan Kingdom from the Earliest Times to the Sixteenth Century*, p. 78.
119 **Significantly, and perhaps poignantly:** C. Sivaramamurti, *The Great Chola Temples: Thanjavur, Gangaikondacholapuram, Darasuram*, New Delhi: Archaeological Survey of India, 2007, p. 8.
119 'from this time on till almost the end of the thirteenth century': Sastri, *The Pandyan Kingdom from the Earliest Times to the Sixteenth Century*, p. 139.
120 'raised himself and his country in the': Ibid.
120 'the five brothers who were Sultans': Ibid., p. 180.

CHAPTER 11: ENTERPRISE AND OPULENCE: ASPECTS OF PANDYA CULTURE
121 **Since my eyes rejoiced to see the glory:** Parthasarathy (tr.), *The Cilappatikāram*, p. 111.
121 **In the audience hall rested the handsome Pandya:** A. Q. Husaini, Mankuti Marudanar (trs.), *The History of the Pāndya Country*, Madras: Selvi Pathippakam, 1962, p. 25.
122 **One Puram poem offers cautionary:** Sastri, *The Pandyan Kingdom from the Earliest Times to the Sixteenth Century*, pp. 32–33.
122 **Although a monarch's power may seem:** Husaini, Marudanar (trs.), *The History of the Pāndya Country*, p. 15.
123 **These early Pandya rulers:** Sastri, *The Pandyan Kingdom from the Earliest Times to the Sixteenth Century*, pp. 32–33.
123 **Legend has it that when Rome was attacked:** Husaini, Marudanar (trs.), *The History of the Pāndya Country*, p. 7, pp. 18–20.
124 **Kalamar and ulavar who were cultivators:** Sastri, *A History of South India*.
124 **Rajan Gurukkal points out:** Rajan Gurukkal, 'Non Brahmana Resistance to the Expansion of Brahmadeyas: The Early Pandya Experience', *The India History Congress*, Vol. 45, 1984, pp. 161–163.

126 **Caste and land ownership also:** Raman, *Some Aspects of Pandyan History in the Light of Recent Discoveries*, pp. 42–44; T. S. Subramanian in conversation with the author, September 2020.
126 **It appears that women barely covered their chests:** Husaini, Marudanar (trs.), *The History of the Pāndya Country*, pp. 30–32.
126 **Notions like honour and courage were highly regarded:** Ibid.
126 **By this time, a great many Arab:** Ibid., p. 51.
127 **The province is the finest and noblest in the world:** Ibid., pp. 67–68.
127 **'Here are no horses bred; and thus':** Ibid., pp. 68–69.
127 **'They bind the horses for 40 days in a stable':** Ibid.
127 **Marco Polo also points out:** Ibid., p. 69.

CHAPTER 12: ABNEGATION, DEVOTION, AND FAITH
128 **In theology…philosophy:** Champakalakshmi, *Religion, Tradition, and Ideology*, p. 29.
128 **'to see the splendour of Vishnu praised':** Parthasarathy (tr.), *The Cilappatikāram*, p. 110.
128 **'Since my eyes rejoiced / To see':** Ibid., pp. 112–115.
129 **Another much established fishing:** T. S. Subramanian in conversation with the author, Madurai.
131 **David Shulman has suggested that this may:** Shulman, *Tamil*, p. 94.
131 **'uses the pathways of analysis and contemplation':** Gopalkrishna Gandhi, *The Tirukkural: A New English Version*, New Delhi: Aleph Book Company, 2015, p. xxvii.
131 **'Valluvar's vision':** Ibid., p. xxv.
131 **'…gender equality is not a concept that detains':** Ibid., p. xxxvi.
132 **In *Shilappadikaram*, after the wronged:** Shulman, *Tamil*, p. 99.
132 **'No survey of Jainism':** Mahadevan, Witzel (eds.), *Early Tamil Epigraphy from the Earliest Times to the Sixth Century AD (Oipse)*.
134 **The city of Madurai saw a great:** V. Vedachalam in conversation with the author, Madurai, April 2019.
136 **'within the structural edifice of':** R. Umamaheshwari, *Reading History with the Tamil Jains: A Study on Identity, Memory and Marginalisation*, New Delhi: Springer, 2017, p. 197.
136 **'from whom it is easier to seek':** Ibid., p. 199.
137 **Champakalakshmi suggests that Bhakti:** Champakalakshmi, *Religion, Tradition and Ideology*, p. 616.
137 **'in the Paripatal poems':** Nammalwar, Archana Venkatesan (tr.), *A Hundred Measures of Time—Tiruviruttam*, New Delhi: Penguin Books India, 2014, pp. 6–7.
137 **'a crusader and his denunciation':** Champakalakshmi, *Religion, Tradition, and Ideology*, pp. 65–66.
138 **'the Tamil Jaina communities narratives':** Umamaheshwari, *Reading History with the Tamil Jainas*, pp. 12–13.
138 **'these stories signify the efforts':** Ibid., pp. 209–210.
139 **'as both heir and progenitor':** Nammalwar, Archana Venkatesan (tr.), *A Hundred Measures of Time—Tiruviruttam*, p. 5.
139 **Vishnu is praised as the (source of):** Ibid., p. 64.
139 **The masters of the earth cleave / to:** Ibid., p. 67.
140 **'Maran who wears as a garland':** Ibid., p. 75.
140 **'though the impulse of Bhakti was':** Ibid., p. 9.
142 **'in relating the Sanskrit Vedic tradition':** Champakalakshmi, *Religion, Tradition, and Ideology*.

CHAPTER 13: THE TIGER CREST: THE GREAT CHOLA MONARCHY
145 **Let me speak out to this rich country's:** Sastri, *The Colas Vol. 1*, p. 51.
146 **'remain singing on the state of Tanjai':** Ibid., pp. 132–133.

146 'He (Vijayalaya) of the solar race took': Ibid.
147 'a place of a thousand lingams': Kodavayil Balasubramanian in conversation with the author, Thanjavur, January 2019 and September 2021.
150 The ruthlessness and cunning of Aditya: Sastri, *The Colas*.
150 'throne, a palanquin, drums, a palace': Ibid.
151 'His army having crushed at the head': Ibid.
152 the historic Rajaditya having agitated: Ibid.
152 For example, the Karandai plates: S. R. Balasubrahmanyam, *Early Chola Temples: Parantaka 1 to Rajaraja 1 (A.D. 907-985)*, New Delhi: Orient Longman, 1971, p. 3.
153 She also lived well into the reign: Ibid.
154 'with a view to dispel the blinding': Jayasree Saranathan, 'Rajaraja I taking revenge on the assassins of Aditya Karikala – VIII', Viyayvaani.com, 24 April 2023, available at https://www.vijayvaani.com/ArticleDisplay.aspx?aid=6474.
155 'legitimately claim to have laid': Balasubrahmanyam, *Early Chola Temples*.
155 He next 'destroyed the': Ibid.
156 'excelled Sri Rama by crossing the sea': Sastri, *The Colas*.
157 'Rajaraja's son, the Master of Policy': Ibid.
157 'The fearless Madurantaka crossed': Ibid.
158 'the king of Ceylon out of fear': Ibid.
159 'by introducing a fresh, and': Sastri, *The Colas*.
160 As long as the moon crested deity: Ibid.

CHAPTER 14: THE FACETS AND FUNCTIONS OF CHOLA SOCIETY
161 The Chola kingdom grew...into an extensive: Sastri, *A History of South India*, pp. 163–164.
161 'concept of a highly centralised state': Veluthat, *The Early Medieval in South India*, pp. 4–5.
161 'to the understanding of the history': Ibid.
162 'Most *brahmadeyams* revolved': Ibid.
163 Queens and princes were mentioned: Subbarayalu, *South India Under the Cholas*, p. 212.
163 In the earlier years of Chola: Ibid., p. 224.
163 There were about 100 adhikaris by the time: Ibid., p. 225.
163 Tirumantira-olai or olai was the king's: Ibid., pp. 225–231.
163 Some of these territories had other suffixes: Sastri, *The Colas*.
164 The urar was the corporate body: Subbarayalu, *South India Under the Cholas*.
164 The full length of a measuring rod: T. S. Subramanian in conversation with the author, Chennai, July 2021.
165 In another instance, recorded: Subbarayalu, *South India Under the Cholas*.
165 'a veritable classical written constitution': R. Nagaswamy in conversation with the author, 11 April 2019.
166 King: Parakesarivarman who conquered Madurai: Ibid.
167 Other communities like this were: Ibid.
168 However, the two divisions were not: Karashima (ed.), *A Concise History of South India*.
168 Subbarayalu says the history of the Tamil country: Subbarayalu, *South India Under the Cholas*.
170 '...networks around each of the great temples': Shulman, *Tamil*, p. 163.

CHAPTER 15: REACHING THE SKY: AN IMPERIAL VISION
171 The Hindu temple functions: George Michell, 'The Temple as a Link between the God and Man', *The Hindu Temple: An Introduction to Its Meaning and Forms*, Chicago: University of Chicago Press, 1988, p. 61.
171 'paintings of late and degenerate age': S. K. Govindaswami, 'Thousand Years Old Chola Frescoes Reported Discovery in Tanjore Temple', *The Hindu*, 11 April 1931.

172 **'extended the frontiers of Indian painting':** S. K. Govindaswami, 'A New Link in Indian Art: The Chola Frescies of Tanjore', *The Hindu*, 7 June 1931.
173 **Govindaswami's discovery of the Chola:** P. S. Sriraman in conversation with the author, Brihadeeswara Temple, Thanjavur, January 2023.
174 **'While Rajaraja's memory was inerasably':** P. S. Sriraman, *Chola Murals: Documentation and Study of the Chola Murals of Bṛihadisvara Temple, Thanjavur*, New Delhi: Archaeological Survey of India, 2011, p. 57.
176 **He had to be a person of passion and vision:** Jaykumar Bharadwaj in conversation with the author, Thanjavur, February 2019; Kodavayil Balasubramanian in conversation with the author, January 2019; V. Vedachalam in conversation with the author, October 2019.
176 **'It is a rare feat, considering the limited':** S. R. Balasubrahmanyan, *Middle Chola Temples: Rajaraja I to Kulottunga I*, Faridabad: Thomson Press Limited Publication Division, 1975, p. 36.
177 **'wherein the builder himself has left':** T. S. Subramanian, 'Written in stone—Big Temple's inscriptions reveal a King's passion', *The Hindu*, 24 September 2010.
178 **'In addition to donating wealth, Rajaraja':** Sriraman, *Chola Murals*, p. 8.
179 **The Chola societal sensibility was thus:** Kodavayil Balasubramaniam in conversation with the author, Thanjavur, September 2021.
179 **While not much is known of its early history:** Sastri, *A History of South India*.

CHAPTER 16: PINNACLES OF ARTISTIC VISION
181 **Innumerable endowments helped the temple:** Sriraman, *Chola Murals*, p. 3.
181 **The Shaivite poet-saint Thirugnanasambandar sang:** 'Alandurainathar Temple', TempleFolks.com, available at https://templefolks.com/temple-pedia/alandurainathar-temple.
182 **Though the epithet of Parakesari is not tagged:** V. Vedachalam in conversation with the author, Pullamangai, October 2019.
182 **Details of a village assembly that met at the temple:** Balasubrahmanyam, *Early Chola Temples*, pp. 46–47.
182 **'The noblest artistic expression of Parantaka I's time':** Ibid., p. 276.
186 **'a bee at the lotus feet of Parantaka':** Ibid., p. 3.
187 **'the sanctity attached to the temple of Chidambaram':** R. Nagaswamy, Chidambaram Temple, Tamil Arts Academy, Chennai, 2018.
187 **Thereafter Rajaraja was said to have encouraged:** R. Nagaswamy and V. Vedachalam in conversation with the author, Chennai, 2022 and 2023.
188 **He also built a bathing ghat and water tanks:** T. S. Subramanian (ed.), *Epic Saga of the Cholas: Their Art, Temples and Heritage*, Chennai: The Hindu Group Publishing Private Limited, 2023, pp. 83, 86.
190 **'puzzling however that in the innumerable':** Job Thomas, *Chola Bronzes*, Chennai: Cre-A, 2018, p. 47.
191 **'the pose is familiar, but it has nothing':** John Eskenazi, Daud Ali, Vidya Dehejia, et al., *Chola: Sacred Bronzes of South India*, London: Royal Academy of Arts, 2006, p. 47.
191 **Similarly, the postural minutiae of images:** Thomas, *Chola Bronzes*, 2018, pp. 54–56.
191 **There is a lot more to the process, but:** Ibid., p. 56.
192 **'Oh lord of Ranga / I see the exquisite curves of your calves':** Ibid., p. 33.
192 **'O Lord, O Venkata / Would that I were a step':** Ibid., p. 112.
192 **'The image was cast on the lines of the *dhyanasloka*':** Subramanian (ed.), *Epic Saga of the Cholas*, p. 328.
193 **'it is a classical example and the best known':** Ibid., pp. 328–329.
193 **John Guy, Senior Curator of South and Southeast:** Eskenazi, Ali, Dehejia, et al., *Chola: Sacred Bronzes of South India*, 2006, p. 22.
193 **'A good number of metal images':** Subramanian (ed.), *Epic Saga of the Cholas*, p. 361.

CHAPTER 17: THE SPIRES OF FAITH

194 **South India is studded with gigantic temples:** B. Venkataraman, *Temple Art Under the Chola Queens*, New Delhi: Thomson Press (India), Publication Division, 1976, p. xiii.
195 **Historians such as Champakalakshmi:** Champakalakshmi, *Religion, Tradition, and Ideology*, 2011, p. 19.
196 **He also later lived in Srirangam:** P. R. Ramachander, 'Saint Ramanuja—The Great Social Reformer Born in 1000 years back', *Asian Journal of Professional Ethics and Management*, Vol. 9, No. 1, April–June 2017.
197 **The inscriptions of Shankara are available:** Karashima (ed.), *A Concise History of South India*, p. 149.
197 **This philosophy and other offshoots:** Champakalakshmi, *Religion, Tradition, and Ideology*, p. 450.
200 **'That other religions were actively':** Subramanian (ed.), *Epic Saga of the Cholas*, p. 407.
200 **'They belong to the periods of':** Ibid.
200 **'The simple architecture of the pillars':** Ibid., p. 410.

CHAPTER 18: THE CHERAS: THE EMPORIUM OF INDIA

201 **The fine ships of the Yavanas:** Tayan Kannanar, 'Akananuru', Vaidehi Herbert (tr.), available at https://sangamtranslationsbyvaidehi.com/ettuthokai-akananuru-121-300/.
201 **Directly below this place is:** Wilfred Harvey Schoff, The Periplus of the Erythraean Sea: Travel and Trade in the Indian Ocean by A Merchant of the First Century, London: Longmans, Green, and Co., 1912, available at https://www.forgottenbooks.com/en/readbook/ThePeriplusoftheErythranSea_10051357#0.
202 **Then come Naura (Kannur) and Tyndis:** Ibid.
202 **Besides this there are exported:** Ibid.
203 **west of Koodal city where flags sway:** Kannanar, 'Akananuru', Herbert (tr.), available at https://sangamtranslationsbyvaidehi.com/ettuthokai-akananuru-121-300/.
203 **A further reference to Muziris also:** Perur, 'Lost cities #3 – Muziris: did black pepper cause the demise of India's ancient port?', *The Guardian*.
203 **A fifth-century map of the world:** Ibid.
203 **'Musiri, a city at the height of prosperity':** R. Nagaswamy, 'The Chera Coins - Dr. R. Nagaswamy', Tamil Arts Academy, TamilNation.org, available at https://tamilnation.org/heritage/chera/.
203 **'this was a centre of paramount importance':** Perur, 'Lost cities #3 – Muziris: did black pepper cause the demise of India's ancient port?', *The Guardian*.
204 **In addition, Nagaswamy explains that:** R. Nagaswamy in conversation with the author, Chennai, 6 and 11 April 2019.
204 **Ptolemy has also mentioned Ay:** Karashima (ed.), *A Concise History of South India*, pp. 47–48.
204 **Even though there is obvious confusion:** Sastri, *A History of South India*, p. 107.
205 **After a somewhat turbulent rule:** Ibid., pp. 107–108.
206 **Only a crowned king could take:** V. Vedachalam in conversation with the author, Thanjavur, September 2021; Madurai, March 2022; and Tirunelvu, January 2023.
206 **Two of the coins that were discovered:** Ibid.
206 **This firmly places the kings, the literature:** Ibid.
207 **This legend highlights the sense of honour:** Ibid.
211 **'There were many Cheraman Perumals':** S. Divan in conversation with the author, Palayamkottai, July 2023.
211 **To organize trade to their treasury's advantage:** Sastri, *A History of South India*, p. 107.
212 **Among these are 12 Roman gold:** R. Nagaswamy, 'The Chera Coins—Dr. R. Nagaswamy', Tamil Arts Academy, TamilNation.org.

212 **Around the eighth century they resurfaced:** V. Vedachalam in conversation with the author, Thanjavur, September 2021; Madurai, March 2022; and Tirunelveli, January 2023.

BOOK III: THE AGE OF TRANSITION

CHAPTER 19: TURMOIL AND TUMULT: THE MADURAI SULTANS AND THE VIJAYANAGAR KINGS

215 **The pupil of the eye has never seen:** Barkur Narasimhaiah, *Metropolis Vijayanagar: Significance of Remains of Citadel*, New Delhi: Book India Publishing Company, 1992, p. 1.
215 **According to Sastri, the first forays of the northern:** Sastri, *A History of South India*, p. 207.
216 **Raja Mohamad cites the example:** Raja Mohamad in conversation with the author, Tiruchi, July 2023.
217 **Temple accounts, including a few inscriptions:** V. Vedachalam in conversation with the author, 2019, 2021, and 2023.
217 **According to historian Andre Wink, the mutilation:** André Wink, *Al-Hind: The Making of the Indo-Islamic World*, Germany: Brill, 1990, pp. 301–306.
217 **'The temple was normally looted, redefined':** Richard M. Eaton, 'Temple Desecration and Indo-Muslim States', *Journal of Islamic Studies*, Vol. 11, No. 3, 2000, pp. 282–319.
217 **'The Mohammedan invaders were particular':** Narasimhaiah, *Metropolis Vijayanagar*, p. 2.
218 **'bent before the aggressor (the Delhi Sultan)':** S. Srinivas, 'Hoysala Ballala III, the Leader of Resistance Movement in South India', *Ithihas Kaleidoscope of Indian Civilization*, 7 October 2020, available at https://ithihas.wordpress.com/2020/10/07/hoysala-ballala-iii-the-leader-of-resistance-movement-in-south-india-2/.
219 **According to B. Narasimhaiah, retired:** Narasimhaiah, *Metropolis Vijayanagar*, p. 8.
219 **'The pupil of the eye has never seen a place':** Ibid., p. 1.
220 **He also enlisted Muslims:** Ibid.
221 **'he was gallant and perfect in all things':** Robert Sewell, *A Forgotten Empire (Vijayanagar): A Contribution to the History of India*, London: Swan Sonnenschein & Co. Ltd., 1900, pp. 121–122.
221 **'he (the king) was in no way less':** Sastri, *A History of South India*, p. 258.
222 **T. S. Subramanian highlighted the restoration:** T. S. Subramaniam, 'Lime Washed Sculptures to be Revealed', *The Hindu*, 11 December 2009.
222 **Krishnadevaraya, around 1525 CE, covered:** Ibid.
222 **The inscriptions in the temple, in Telugu:** Ibid.
223 **The older Dravidian temples mostly only:** V. Vedachalam in conversation with the author on several occasions.
223 **the Tamil staples, dosai and idli:** S. Kannan in conversation with the author, Madurai, March 2024.
225 **It was not just the influx of migrants, but the general:** Lennart Bes, *The Heirs of Vijayanagar: Court Politics in Early Modern South India*, Leiden: Leiden University Press, 2022, p. 394.
225 **Apparently, many Islamic appellations were:** Ibid., pp. 394–396.
226 **'Muhammadan activities on the northern frontier':** R. Sathyanatha Aiyar, *History of the Nayaks of Madura*, Oxford: Oxford Unievrsity Press, 1924, p. 7.

CHAPTER 20: THE NAYAKS IN TAMIL COUNTRY

227 **The history of the Nayaks…comprises the history:** Ibid., p. 1.
227 **Karashima notes that the number of Nayaks:** Karashima (ed.), *A Concise History of South India*, p. 195.
228 **Karashima quotes the Portuguese horse merchant:** Ibid., pp. 195–196.
228 **Apparently in the early years of the Nayak:** Ibid., p. 198.
228 **However, the system wasn't always smooth:** Ibid., p. 200.

228 'We, the people belonging to *Idangai*': Ibid., pp. 200–202.
229 'carries the history of South India': Aiyar, *History of the Nayaks of Madura*, p. 2.
229 Nelson apparently relied too heavily on information: Ibid., p. 29.
229 According to Aiyar, William Taylor's: Ibid., p. 34.
229 Aiyar draws from epigraphical information in Sewell's: Ibid., p. 39.
230 The Koyiloluhu records indicate that Viswanatha spent: Ibid., p. 53.
230 'set a thief to catch a thief': K. Rajayyan, *History of Tamil Nadu 1565-1982*, Madurai: Raj Publishers, 1982, p. 56.
230 Rajayyan out that: Ibid., p. 63.
231 One Nayak ruler of Madurai, according to: Ibid., p. 64.
231 His brand of proselytizing involved adapting: Aiyar, *History of the Nayaks of Madura*, p. 94.
231 The Jesuit records say that he had 200 wives: Ibid.
232 The Naique of Madurai sent his ambassador: Ibid., p. 123.
232 'held to imply ipso facto, a change of political': Ibid., pp.123–124.
232 'her vigor and diplomacy gave the Nayak kingdom': Ibid., p. 219.

CHAPTER 21: THE GRAND MARATHAS OF THANJAVUR
234 The condition of the members of this royal house: William Hickey, *The Tanjore Mahratta Principality in Southern India: The Land of the Chola, The Eden of the South*, 2nd Edition, Madras: Foster Press, 1874, p. xxx.
234 'She is like a violet, existing in seclusion': Ibid., p. 2.
234 'the independence of the Tanjore Mahratta dynasty': Ibid., p. 87.
235 'they are a fine pair': Ibid., pp. 78–79.
236 He was also paid one fifth: Ibid., p. 136.
236 'including a love for music and dance': Kombai S. Anwar, 'Thanjavur emerged as a thriving cultural capital under the Marathas', *The Hindu*, 26 April 2018.
236 'The painting of the tawaif or courtesan': Ibid.
239 Serfoji instituted a 'Tanjore band': Karashima (ed.), *A Concise History of South India*, p. 248.

CHAPTER 22: TAMIL BY BIRTH, MUSLIM BY FAITH
240 I feel I have to be the best version of a person: Sucheta Dasgupta, 'I feel I must embody the best version of my faith: Rana Safvi', *Asian Age*, 20 April 2024.
240 Raja Mohamad has set up a research centre: Raja Mohamad in conversation with the author, Tiruchi, July 2023.
241 Gold dirhams are recorded in property transactions: Kombai S. Anwar in conversation with the author, Chennai, July 2023.
241 Apparently, there was a complete synthesis with: Raja Mohamad in conversation with the author, Tiruchi, July 2023.
242 'prince among medieval travellers': Sastri, *A History of South India*, p. 201.
242 'possesses vast treasures and wears upon his': Ibid., pp. 201–202.
243 The traveller Ibn Battuta, who visited Calicut: Hassan J., Manu T., Sukesh Kumaradas, et al., 'Arab Accounts of Malabar History: The Early Episodes', *Heritage: Journal of Multidisciplinary Studies in Archaeology*, Vol. 8, No. 1, December 2020, p. 793.
243 Security and justice are so firmly established: Ibid., pp.793–794.
244 Tipu included them in his army: Kombai S. Anwar, *Yaadhum*, 2013, 51 min; Kombai S. Anwar in conversation with the author, Chennai, July 2023.
244 'When I undertook the journey of tracing': R. Ilangovan, 'Celebrating diversity', *Frontline*, 19 February 2014.
245 The early epigraphists like K. V. Subramaniam and Hultz: J. Raja Mohamad, *Maritime History of the Coromandel Muslims: A Socio-Historical Study on the Tamil Muslims 1750–1900*, Tiruchirappalli: Jamal Mohamed College, 2022, p. 45.

246 **The idea was to build a naval presence:** Muhammed Aslam E. S., 'Political Economy of Zamorin and Religious Conversion to Islam', *Café Dissensus*, 15 February 2016.
247 **Pearl, chank shell, and ruby trading:** Susan Bayly, *Saints, Goddesses and Kings: Muslims and Christians in South Indian Society, 1700–1900*, New Delhi: Cambridge University Press, 1989, pp.79–80.
247 **This is a distinguishing feature of wealthy Marakkayar:** Muhammed Abdulla Shabeerali. M, 'History and Culture of Tamil Muslims, and Muslim settlements in Tamil Nadu', *Academia.edu*, p. 7.
247 **It was mainly Muslim and Malay trading ships:** Mohamad, *Maritime History of the Coromandel Muslims*, pp. 68–69.
247 **'you can say that they were the outer':** Kombai S. Anwar in conversation with the author, 2022 and 2023.
248 **'thrifty, enterprising, and industrious':** Edgar Thurston, K. Rangachari, *Castes and Tribes of Southern India*, Madras: Government Press, 1909, pp. 198–205.
248 **They were also called Guthirai Chettigal:** Shabeerali M., 'History and Culture of Tamil Muslims, and Muslim settlements in Tamil Nadu', p. 8.
248 **There are other smaller Muslim communities:** Ibid., p. 9.
248 **He suggests that as the early Arab:** J. Raja Mohamad, *Islamic Architecture in Tamil Nadu*, Chennai: Government Museum, 2004, p. 21.
248 **There were no minarets or minars:** Ibid., p. 31.
249 **Further the names of the four Khalifas:** Ibid.
249 **The mosque is likely to have been constructed:** Ibid., p. 32.
249 **During the first few centuries of Islam's:** Ibid., pp. 32–33.
250 **The inscription details a maximum amount:** Ibid., pp. 33–34.
250 **Other mosques like the Juma Masjid at Periyapattinam:** Ibid., pp. 34–35.
250 **In the film *Yaadhum*, as Anwar moves forward:** Kombai Anwar (dr.), *Yaadhum*, 2013, 51 min.
251 **Raja Mohamad speaks of an important stage:** Raja Mohamad in conversation with the author, Tiruchi, July 2023.

BOOK IV: THE AGE OF THE EUROPEANS

CHAPTER 23: THE MERCHANTS OF COLONIZATION

255 **The Europeans needed spices, cloves, pepper, indigo:** Rajayyan, *History of Tamil Nadu 1565-1982*, p. 90.
255 **Well before the time of the famed Portuguese:** 'Vasco da Gama', History.com, 18 December 2009, available at https://www.history.com/topics/exploration/vasco-da-gama.
256 **In 1453, Constantinople, the capital of the Byzantine:** Mark Cartwright, '1453: The Fall of Constantinople', World History Encyclopedia, 23 January 2018, available at https://www.worldhistory.org/article/1180/1453-the-fall-of-constantinople/.
256 **Meanwhile Christopher Columbus also set out:** 'Christopher Columbus', Royal Museums Greenwich, available at https://www.rmg.co.uk/stories/topics/christopher-columbus.
256 **The Portuguese explorer Vasco da Gama:** 'Vasco de Gama', History.com.
256 **Da Gama's voyage began in 1497 from:** Shane Winser, 'Vasco de Gama', *BBC History*, 17 February 2011, available at https://www.bbc.co.uk/history/british/tudors/vasco_da_gama_01.shtml.
257 **He finally died in Cochin in 1524:** 'Vasco de Gama', History.com.
257 **One account says how in 1525, the Portuguese:** Maddy, 'Mammali Marakkar–Regent of the seas (Regedor do Mar)', *Historical Alleys*, available at https://historicalleys.blogspot.com/2016/03/mammali-marakkar-regent-of-seas-regedor.html.
257 **By 1510, the Portuguese had acquired Goa:** 'Portuguese Colonial Enterprise',

SelfStudyHistory.com, 26 January 2015, available at https://selfstudyhistory.com/2015/01/26/portuguese-colonial-enterprise/.
257 **They set up trade centres in Punnakayal in Tuticorin:** K. M. Mathew, *History of the Portuguese Navigation in India, 1497-1600*, New Delhi: Mittal Publications, 1988.
258 **Henrique Henriques, a Portuguese merchant:** Karthik Madhavan, 'Tamil saw its first book in 1578', *The Hindu*, 21 June 2010.
259 **The Dutch East India Company was established:** Kim Martins, 'Dutch East India Company', WorldHistory.org, 31 October 2023, available at https://www.worldhistory.org/Dutch_East_India_Company/.
259 **The Dutch came to Tamilakam in 1605:** 'The Dutch Connection', *The Hindu*, 2 July 2013.
259 **They constructed a fort called Geldria in Pulicat:** Ibid.
260 **He also published other books in Tamil:** Simonetta Carr, 'Bartholomäus Ziegenbalg – The First Protestant Missionary to India', PlaceForTruth.org, 12 July 2022, available at https://www.placefortruth.org/blog/bartholomaus-ziegenbalg-the-first-protestant-missionary-to-india.
260 **Finally, in 1824, the Anglo-Dutch Treaty:** Alice B. McGinty, 'Angloe-Dutch Rivalry in India', *Current History*, Vol. 11, No. 63, 1946, pp. 383–388.
260 **The charter also specified that any trader who did business:** 'East India Company', Britannica.com, available at https://www.britannica.com/topic/East-India-Company.
261 **'semi-sovereign privileges to rule territories':** William Dalrymple, *The Anarchy: The East India Company, Corporate Violence, and the Pillage of an Empire*, London: Bloomsbury Publishing, 2019, p. 9.
261 **After many years Hawkins was asked:** Clements R. Markham (ed.), *The Hawkins' Voyages During the Reigns of Henry VIII, Queen Elizabeth, and James I*, Cambridge: Cambridge University Press, 2011.
261 **Roe came to Surat in 1615 and made his way:** Adil Ahmad, 'Finding Sir Thomas Roe', IndiaHeritage.in, available at https://indiaheritage.in/finding-sir-thomas-roe/.
262 **'was well aware of the dignity of his country':** N. S. Ramaswami, *The Founding of Madras*, New Delhi: Orient Longman, 1977, p. 13.
262 **Ptolemy mentions the town of Maisolos from where:** 'Masulipatnam and the story of a special fabric', ThePaperClip.in, available at https://thepaperclip.in/masulipatnam-and-the-story-of-a-special-fabric/.
262 **'Masulipatnam chintz was becoming popular':** N. S. Ramaswami, *The Founding of Madras*, pp. 18–19.
263 **Bombay, for example, was gifted as part of the dowry:** 'Charles II, Catherine of Braganza and Bombay', Royal Collection Trust, available at https://www.rct.uk/collection/exhibitions/eastern-encounters/the-queens-gallery-buckingham-palace/charles-ii-catherine-of-braganza-and-bombay.
263 **In 1632, the sultan of Golconda:** Y. Vittal Rao, 'The East India Company and Andhra', *Indian History Congress*, Vol. 20, 1957, pp. 236–240.
263 **Soon Madras became the headquarters:** '22nd August 1639: Madras (now Chennai) is Founded by the East India Company', MapsofIndia.com, available at https://www.mapsofindia.com/on-this-day/22nd-august-1639-madras-now-chennai-is-founded-by-the-east-india-company.
265 **Although he was captured, tried, and hanged:** 'Katta Bomman's Rebellion, 1792-95', IndianCulture.gov.in, available at https://indianculture.gov.in/node/2838808.
265 **The First Carnatic War was fought between 1740 and 1748:** 'Carnatic Wars', Heritage-History.com, available at http://www.heritage-history.com/index.php?c=resources&s=war-dir&f=wars_carnatic.
266 **Neither side had any decisive victories:** Priscilla Adebomi Adeyemi, 'Treaty of Aix-La-Chapelle', ResearchGate.net, 7 December 2023.

CHAPTER 24: CHRISTENDOM IN TAMILAKAM

267 **Evangelical missions had developed within:** D. Dennis Hudson, *Protestant Origins in India: Tamil Evangelical Christians, 1706-1835*, Michigan: William B. Eerdmans Publishing Company, 2000, p. 186.

268 **He was called the 'white brahmin':** R. Champakalakshmi, Sanjay Subramanyam, 'India: Politics and the economy', Britannica.com, 6 September 2024, available at https://www.britannica.com/place/India/Politics-and-the-economy#ref485983.

268 **Max Mueller has called him:** S. Rajamanickam, *The First Oriental Scholar*, India: De Nobili Research Institute, 1972, p. iv.

268 **'I was not born in the land of the *Parangis* (foreigners)':** Bayly, *Saints, Goddesses and Kings*, p. 390.

269 **'their writings are still an important source':** Ibid., p. 241.

269 **Given that the date of Jesus's crucifixion is 33 CE:** 'Saint Thomas, Saint Thomas Mount, India', *TravelPhotographyGuru.com*, available at https://www.travelphotographyguru.com/travel-blogs/saint-thomas-st-thomas-mount-india.

269 **'the legends of St. Thomas predate the arrival':** Bayly, *Saints, Goddesses and Kings*, p. 244.

269 **Some scholars such as Arthur Coke Burnell, W. R. Phillips:** A. F. J. Klijn (ed.), *The Acts of Thomas*, Leiden: E. J. Brill, 1963, p. 73.

269 **'the body of Messer Saint':** K. V. Raman, *The Early History of the Tamil Region*, Madras: National Art Press, 1957, p. 20.

270 **'the Portuguese had no doubts about St. Thomas having':** V. Sriram, *Chennai: A Biography*, New Delhi: Aleph Book Company, 2021, p. 12.

270 **The king of Portugal in 1546 sent a memo:** Stephen Neill, *A History of Christianity in India: The Beginnings to AD 1707*, Cambridge: Cambridge University Press, 1984, p. 160.

270 **Then the Goan Inquisition in 1561 persecuted:** Anant Kakba Priolkar, *The Goa Inquisition: Being a Quatercentenary Commemoration Study of the Inquisition in India*, Bombay: Bombay University Press, 1961.

271 **'Our pearls even went to the court of Cleopatra':** A. X. Alexander in conversation with the author, Chennai, August 2023.

271 **'the *Maduraikanchi* text of the Sangam period':** Edgar Thurston, K. Rangachari, *Castes and Tribes of Southern India: P to S*, Madras: Government Press, 1909.

272 **Another local community called the Maravas:** A. X. Alexander in conversation with the author, Chennai, August 2023.

272 **When Francis Xavier arrived in Goa in 1542:** Neill, *The Early History of Christianity in India*, p. 134.

273 **'it often happens to me to be hardly able':** Paul Halsall, 'St. Francis Xavier: Letter from India, to the Society of Jesus at Rome, 1543', Fordham University, 1998, available at https://sourcebooks.fordham.edu/mod/1543xavier1.asp.

273 **Susan Bayly says that it was Francis's personality:** Bayly, *Saints, Goddesses and Kings*, p. 329.

273 **Alexander says its annual festival 'transcends religion':** A. X. Alexander in conversation with the author, Chennai, August 2023.

274 **Thol Thirumavalavan, Member of Parliament:** 'Christianity has become flexible to India's caste system', *The Hindu*, 6 January 2024.

275 **'a searing indictment of caste-based oppression':** Bama, *Karukku*, Mini Krishnan (ed.), Lakshmi Holmström (tr.), New Delhi: Oxford University Press, 2014.

276 **'refused to shed their caste identity':** 'Watch | Caste discrimination in Christianity', *The Hindu*, 11 January 2024.

276 **'presided over dramatic mass baptism ceremonies':** Bayly, *Saints, Goddesses and Kings*, p. 390.

277 **'In the heart of this my last sermon lie':** 'Reverend G. U. Pope: "Student of Tamil"', TamilNation.org, available at https://tamilnation.org/literature/pope.

277 **'His contribution to both Christianity in South India'**: Y. Vincent Kumaradoss, *Robert Caldwell, a Scholar-missionary in Colonial South India*, New Delhi: ISPCK, 2007.

279 **Around 37 per cent of Christians in India:** Ariana Monique Salazar, '8 key findings about Christians in India', Pew Research Center, 12 July 2021, available at https://www.pewresearch.org/short-reads/2021/07/12/8-key-findings-about-christians-in-india/.

CHAPTER 25: FROM COMPANY TO EMPIRE

280 **It was not the British Government that:** William Dalrymple, 'The East India Company: The original corporate raiders', *The Guardian*, 4 March 2015.

281 **'he was in charge of directing the Indian Ocean':** Geeta Pandey, 'Elihu Yale: The cruel and greedy Yale benefactor who traded in Indian slaves', *BBC*, 13 March 2024.

282 **However, Serfoji had little real power:** K. Rajayyan, *South Indian Rebellion: The First War of Independence, 1800–1801*, Mysore: Rao and Raghavan, 1971, p. 219.

282 **'Treaty for Cementing the Friendship and Alliance':** Edmund Burke, *The Works of the Right Honourable Edmund Burke*, London: J. C. Nimmo, 1887, available at https://www.gutenberg.org/files/15679/15679-h/15679-h.htm.

282 **Tipu was killed in battle in Seringapatam in 1799:** Richard Cavendish, 'Tipu Sultan killed at Seringapatam', History Today, 5 May 1999, available at https://www.historytoday.com/archive/months-past/tipu-sultan-killed-seringapatam.

282 **The nawabs of Arcot too gradually declined:** K. Rajayyan, 'British Annexation of the Carnatic, 1801', *Indian History Congress*, Vol. 32, 1970, pp. 54–62.

283 **Siraj-ud-Daula, the nawab of Bengal:** 'How Robert Clive's Loot From Bengal Made Him Richest "Self-made Man" in Europe', *News18.com*, 9 September 2021.

283 **Clive amassed a huge personal fortune valued:** Suki Haider, 'Hero and villain: Robert Clive of the East India Company', Open.edu, 9 November 2020, available at https://www.open.edu/openlearn/history-the-arts/history/hero-and-villain-robert-clive-the-east-india-company/#:~:text=When%20Clive%20had%20first%20arrived,100%20million%20in%20today's%20money.

283 **'Consider the situation in which the victory':** Nicholas Hoover Wilson, *Modernity's Corruption: Empire and Morality in the Making of British India*, New York: Columbia University Press, 2023.

283 **With his reputation lost and his military:** 'Lord Clive', Oxford Reference, available at https://www.oxfordreference.com/display/10.1093/oi/authority.20110803095618416.

283 **'It was at this moment that the East India':** Dalrymple, 'The East India Company: The original corporate raiders'.

284 **In Madras, the ryotwari system whereby:** Karashima (ed.), *A Concise History of South India*, pp. 267–268.

284 **'looted and carried from India helped to accomplish':** K. A. Manikumar, 'Lecture om Nationalism Against Economic Imperialism in British India', Manonmaniam Sundaranar University, Tirunelveli, p. 3.

284 **'arm of political injustice to keep down':** K. M. Munshi, *The Ruin that Britain Wrought*, Bombay: Padma Publications Limited, 1946, p. 4.

285 **For instance, the Madras Presidency was forced:** 'Merchants and Markets: 1757-1857', *History of Indian Economy*, New Delhi: IGNOU, 2018, p. 18, available at https://egyankosh.ac.in/bitstream/123456789/44535/1/Unit-26.pdf.

285 **The import duty into England of flowered muslins:** Karuna Dietrich Wielenga, *Weaving Histories: The Transformation of the Handloom Industry in South India, 1800-1960*, Oxford: Oxford University Press, 2020, p. 192.

286 **'Our house in India is on fire. We are not insured':** Mark Cartwright, 'Fall of the East India Company', World History Encyclopedia, 26 October 2022, available at https://www.worldhistory.org/article/2096/fall-of-the-east-india-company/.

286 **The British government took full possession:** 'British colonialism in India', *BBC History*.

BOOK V: THE AGE OF FREEDOM

CHAPTER 26: REVOLT, REBELLION, AND THE ROAD TO FREEDOM

289 **By 1801 the Company had acquired the sovereign rights:** K. A. Manikumar, *Foreshadowing the Great Rebellion: The Vellore Revolt, 1806*, New Delhi: Orient BlackSwan, 2021, p. 20.
289 **'that all subordinate military establishments should be':** Rajayyan, *South Indian Rebellion*, p. 91
290 **'the rebellious conduct of Catabomanaig (Kattabomman Nayak)':** Ibid., p. 92.
290 **'I prepared money for the payment of the *kist*':** Rajayyan, *South Indian Rebellion*, p. 75.
290 **'The attempt was persevered in so long as':** Ibid., p. 81.
291 **'on every side in the mountains I had placed my people':** Ibid., p. 82.
291 **'It may not be amiss here to observe':** Ibid.
291 **'The Panchalankurichi fort was razed to the ground':** H. R. Pate, *Madras District Gazetteers: Tinnevelly Volume I*, Madras: Government Press, 1917, p. 85.
292 **Historian Rajayyan says that he was one:** Rajayyan, *South Indian Rebellion*, p. 47.
293 **'He attributed this tragedy in their character':** Ibid., p. 48.
294 **'in consequence of a general confederacy':** Ibid., p. 199.
295 **It is an unusual document:** Ibid.
295 **Whosoever sees this paper, Read it with Attention:** B. Kolappan, 'Letter alerting British military about Marudu brothers' Srirangam declaration discovered', *The Hindu*, 16 June 2023; B. Kolappan, 'The first declaration of war against the British from Srirangam', *The Hindu*, 16 June 2022.
297 **'specimen of native masonry':** K. A. Manikumar, 'Vellore Fort: Site of India's First Sepoy Mutiny', PeepulTree.World, 17 November 2021, available at https://www.peepultree.world/livehistoryindia/story/monuments/vellore-fort.
298 **'under a common banner and to restore the':** Rajayyan, *South Indian Rebellion*, p. 343.
299 **'the guests who were invited, thronging the main entrance':** Manikumar, *Foreshadowing the Great Rebellion*, p. 31.
299 **'The Mahal was lighted up':** Ibid., pp. 31–32.
299 **'I looked at my husband. I saw him pale':** Sydney C. Grier, 'The Mutiny at Vellore in 1606', *Bengal: Past and Present*, Vol. 28, No. 55–56, 1924, p. 172.

CHAPTER 27: A SOCIETY IN FLUX

301 **People ate poisonous roots and leaves, dying parents:** Rajmohan Gandhi, *Modern South India: A History from the 17th Century to Our Times*, New Delhi: Aleph Book Company, 2018, p. 214.
301 **Records available at the Tamil Nadu archives:** N. Rajendran, 'The Impact Of The 1857 Revolt In Tamilnadu', *People's Democracy*, Vol. 31, No. 15, 15 April 2007, available at https://archives.peoplesdemocracy.in/2007/0415/04152007_1857.html.
302 **'gathered opposite the Prince of Arcot's then':** 'Madras and the 1857 Revolt', *The Hindu*, 29 May 2011.
302 **Prominent notice was drawn to the Native Community:** Rajendran, 'The Impact Of the 1857 Revolt in Tamilnadu'.
303 **'You say that you had hoped to have seen under':** D. Mohan (ed.), *Tamil Nadu's Contribution to the Freedom Struggle*, Chennai: Government of Tamil Nadu, 2023, p. 48.
304 **'a single shelf of a good European library':** Thomas Macaulay, 'Macaulay's Minute' in H. Sharp, Alexander Richey (eds.), *Selections from Educational Records: 1781-1839*, New Delhi: National Archives of India, 1965, p. 109.
304 **One major impact of such initiatives:** Karashima (ed.), *A Concise History of South India*, p. 273.

305 **'Brahmins were the only community in nineteenth century':** Ibid., p. 277.
306 **William Digby, journalist and humanitarian:** 'Plarr's Lives of the Fellows', Royal College of Surgeons of England, 2011.
306 **'a famine can scarcely be said to be adequately':** Mike Davis, 'Late Victorian Holocausts: El Niño Famines and the Making of the Third World', *New York Times*, 2001.
306 **Two British administrators who were deeply:** A. Moin Zaidi (ed.), *The Encyclopaedia of Indian National Congress: 1885-1890, The founding fathers*, New Delhi: S. Chand, 1976, p. 609.
307 **G. Subramania Iyer, one of the founder members:** 'About Us', *The Hindu*, available at https://www.thehindu.com/aboutus/.
307 **The principles we propose to be guided by are simply:** 'Ourselves: Editorial published on September 20, 1878', *The Hindu*, 13 September 2013.
307 **In 1892, Subramania Iyer also founded:** 'Swadesamitran', AmritMahotsav.nic.in, available at https://amritmahotsav.nic.in/district-reopsitory-detail.htm?6811#:~:text= Swadesamitran%20 (friend%20of%20self%2Drule,newspaper%20(an%20English%20daily).
307 **He also founded along with others, the Madras:** 'The Madras Mahajana Sabha (1884)', IndianCulture.gov.in, available at https://indianculture.gov.in/node/2820175#:~:text=The%20 Madras%20Mahajana%20Sabha%2C%20a,Iyer%2C%20and%20P%20Ananda%20Charlu.
308 **'Orientalist constructions of Indian antiquity paved the way':** A. Gangatharan, *Cultural Aspirations: Essays on the Intellectual History of the Colonial Tamil Nadu*, Morrisville: Lulu Press Incorporated, 2017, p. 14.
308 **Historian A. R. Venkatachalapathy says:** A. R. Venkatachalapathy, *Chennai Not Madras: Perspectives on the City: Perspective on the City*, Chennai: The Marg Foundation, 2006.
308 **Venkatachalapathy says that a few decades later in Madras:** A. R. Venkatachalapathy in conversation with the author, Chennai, May 2024.
308 **'Caldwell was one of the first missionary scholars':** Gangatharan, *Cultural Aspirations*.

CHAPTER 28: CHENNAI THAT WAS MADRAS
310 **Life is never dull in Chennai/Madras:** Sriram, *Chennai*, p. xxxvi.
310 **'excellent long cloath and better cheape':** S. Muthiah, *Madras Rediscovered: A Historical Guide to Looking Around, Supplemented with Tales of 'Once Upon a City'*, Madras: EastWest Books, 1999, p. 2.
311 **Others source it to Madra, a wealthy Portuguese:** K. V. Raman, *The Early History of the Madras Region*, Chennai: C. P. Ramaswami Aiyar Foundation, 2nd Edition, 2008, pp. 108–109.
311 **Venkatachalapathy however says in the early:** Venkatachalapathy, *Chennai Not Madras*, p. 1.
311 **'named after the father of the local chieftain':** Sriram, *Chennai*, p. xii.
311 **He adds that old Chennappa was Telugu:** Ibid.
311 **'the co-existence of colonial and local names indicated':** Pushpa Arabindoo, 'Geography of a Lingua Franca, History of Linguistic Fracas' in Venkatachalapathy, *Chennai Not Madras*, pp. 21, 24.
311 **Robert Bruce Foote, the British geologist:** T. S. Subramanian, 'A discovery that changed the antiquity of humankind who lived in Indian subcontinent', *The Hindu*, 27 May 2013.
311 **Later, Iron Age tools and implements:** Raman, *The Early History of the Madras Region*, 1957, p. 3.
312 **'Messer Saint Thomas the Apostle lies in this town':** Ibid., p. 33.
312 **'Many of these villages including the interior ones':** Chithra Madhavan in conversation with the author, August 2018 and March 2019.
312 **Many families maintain links to their places of origin:** Muthiah, *Madras Rediscovered*, p. 260.
313 **Even now Muslims use the tank on Muharram Day:** S. Anwar in conversation with the author.

314 **Muthiah (who incidentally was a vociferous voice:** Nirmala Lakshman, *Degree Coffee by the Yard: A Short Biography of Madras*, New Delhi: Aleph Book Company, 2013, p. 27.
315 **The English instruction was for Foxcroft:** Ibid., p. 40.
317 **The Tamil film industry generated:** 'Kollywood generates 3,500 crore in 2023', *Times of India*, 1 January 2024.
318 **With a population of 4.9 million people, it ranks:** 'Chennai, India Population, 2024', World Population Review, available at https://worldpopulationreview.com/cities/india/chennai.
318 **'if Madras was once the colonial name of a growing':** Venkatachalapathy, *Chennai Not Madras*, p. 31.
319 **'If at all there is a part of the city that can boast of a lovely':** Sriram, *Chennai*, pp. 132–133.
320 **'seeing Lalitha take her bicycle out':** Kameshwar. C Wali, *Chandra: A Biography of S. Chandrasekhar*, Chicago: Chicago University Press, 1991, p. 178.

CHAPTER 29: AWAKENINGS AND TRANSFORMATIONS: THE FREEDOM STRUGGLE AND THE DRAVIDIAN MOVEMENT

322 **A prison sentence can be a badge of honour:** Rajmohan Gandhi, *Modern South India*, p. 266.
323 **'We mourn the loss of a noble daughter of India':** Mahatma Gandhi, *The Collected Works of Mahatma Gandhi*, Vol. 12, 1913–1914, New Delhi: The Publications Division, p. 357.
323 **'Gandhi's influence cut across region, caste and gender':** Venkatachalapathy in conversation with the author, Chennai, May 2024.
324 **'created a vibrancy in the south, whereas there':** Ibid.
324 **'Shouting Swadeshi from the rooftops':** A. R. Venkatachalapathy, *Swadeshi Steam: V.O. Chidambaram Pillai and the Battle against the British Maritime Empire*, Gurugram: Penguin Random House, 2023, p. 8–9.
325 **'The next day, Tirunelveli and Tuticorin':** Ibid., p. 213.
325 **'The protest violence of 13 March marked':** Ibid., pp. 214–215.
325 **'was yoked (in place of bulls) to the oil press':** S. Dorairaj, 'Doyen of Swadeshi shipping', *The Hindu*, 2001.
325 **'did we grow this crop with water, Lord?':** Prema Nandakumar, *Poems of Subramania Bharati*, New Delhi: Sahitya Akademi, p. 55.
325 **In the early years, the company provided:** Venkatachalapathy, *Swadeshi Steam*, pp. 161–162.
325 **The foreign companies threatened:** Ibid., p. 163.
326 **'Had he been alive for another ten years':** A. R. Venkatachalapathy in conversation with the author, Chennai, May 2024.
327 **A brilliant lawyer and interlocutor:** Vasanthi Srinivasan, *Gandhi's Conscience Keeper: C. Rajagopalachari and Indian Politics*, Ranikhet: Permanent Black, 2009.
327 **Annie Besant who came to India from Ireland:** Joanne Stafford Mortimer, 'Annie Besant and India 1913-1917', *Journal of Contemporary History*, Vol. 18, No. 1, 1983, pp. 61–78.
327 **In Madras, where she spent most of her time:** 'Annie Besant (1847 - 1933)', *BBC*, 2014.
328 **the innocent, virgin Dasi girl, Shanpakavalli…could:** 'Mrs. S Muthulakshmi Reddi—Letter to The Hindu—Dedication of Girls to Temple—An Appeal For Its Abolition', *The Hindu*, 22 June 1927.
329 **'When readers go through my letter, I would have left':** Ibid.
329 **The Icehouse in Triplicane:** V. Sriram, 'A century of sisterhood and social reform', *The Hindu*, 3 August 2012.
329 **'proved their religious faith as well as true patriotism':** J. Raja Mohamad, 'Contributions of Muslims in the Freedom Struggle' in D. Mohan (ed.), *Tamil Nadu's Contribution to the Freedom Struggle*, Chennai: Government of Tamil Nadu, 2023, p. 357.
330 **'Indian freedom is written in Muslims' blood':** Rabia Shireen, 'Contribution Of Muslims To India's Freedom Struggle', *The Cognate*, 15 August 2022, available at https://thecognate.com/contribution-of-muslims-to-indias-freedom-struggle/.

330 'the ground rules of politics changed with Non-Brahmins': A. R. Venkatachalapathy in conversation with the author, Chennai, May 2024.
331 The Justice Party was initially one of the factions: Eugene F. Irschick, *Tamil Revivalism in the 1930s*, Chennai: Cre-A, 1986, pp. 30–31.
331 Not less than 40 million out of 41.5 million: 'Dravidian movement', *Frontline*, 18 July 2003.
332 'It can serve no good but is bound': M. S. S. Pandian, *Brahmin & Non-Brahmin: Genealogies of the Tamil Political Present*, New Delhi: Permanent Black, 2003, pp. 1–7.
332 He joined the Congress Party in 1920: Irschick, *Tamil Revivalism in the 1930s*, p. 89.
333 'If you see a Brahmin and a snake': Markandey Katju, 'Justice Katju: Whatever his motives, Periyar helped the British', *The Week*, 18 September 2018.
333 'movements for social justice that challenge': Karthick Ram Manoharan, 'Did Periyar call for a genocide of Brahmins?', *Frontline*, 29 March 2024.
333 'the rationale behind such speeches': Ibid.
333 'the goals of the Self Respect Movement': Irschick, Tamil Revivalism in the 1930s, p. 89.
333 Irschick says what was important: Ibid.

CHAPTER 30: AN UNPRECEDENTED FREEDOM
334 Live in the present, shape the future: N. Nanivarman, 'Ilankai Tamil Sangam', Sangam.org, 7 January 2008, available at https://www.sangam.org/2008/01/Bharathiar.php?uid=2727.
335 'If only I have…more supporters like him': 'Potti Sriramulu', AmritMahotsav.nic.in, available at https://amritmahotsav.nic.in/unsung-heroes-detail.htm?42.
336 It was called the Modified Scheme of Elementary Education: D. Veeraraghavan, *Half a Day for Caste?: Education and Politics in Tamil Nadu, 1952-55*, New Delhi: Leftword, 2020, p. 57.
336 'As Chief Minister, Rajaji took many bold': Ibid., p. 125.
336 'a man of few words who had never gone': Rajmohan Gandhi, *Modern South India*, p. 366.
337 'over the 1950s he built a party that expressed': Venkatachalapathy in conversation with the author, Chennai, May 2024.
338 'Hindi is to be installed formally as the principal official': 'Editorial', *The Hindu*, 19 January 1965.
339 One was T. M. Sivalingam, a twenty-four-year-old DMK: 'Editorial', *The Hindu*, 28 January 1965.
340 'In Anna, the emergent backward castes': 'From the archives: C. N. Annadurai | In letter and spirit', *India Today*, 11 January 2022.
341 'from the humble house in the handloom town': 'Man in the News A Mellowed Annadurai as Helmsman', *The Hindu*, 3 March 1967.
341 'the politicization of administration as well as': S. Narayan, *The Dravidian Years: Politics and Welfare in Tamil Nadu*, New Delhi: Oxford University Press, 2018, p. 40.
342 It was estimated that half the DMK party members were: Ramaswamy Sastri, 'A Chronicle of the DMK Split', *Economic and Political Weekly*, Vol. 9, No. 13, 30 March 1974.
344 'proved that he could play the waiting game': Suresh Kumar in conversation with the author.
344 'Jayalalithaa was disheartened (by the election results) and had': Akshaya Nath, 'The "torn sari" that shaped Amma—what happened to Jayalalithaa in TN assembly on 25 March 1989', *The Print*, 19 August 2023.
344 'The very same evening, Jayalalithaa's resignation letter': Ibid.
344 'Karunanidhi then made a remark that left Jayalalithaa': Ibid.
344 'The year 1990 saw Karunanidhi play a key role': Suresh Kumar in conversation with the author.
345 mother Sandhya was a minor actor: B. Kolappan, 'The reluctant actor and politician', *The Hindu*, 17 November 2021.
345 Even in her first term, 1991 to 1996, she enjoyed: B. Kolappan, 'AIADMK leaders emerge from Jayalalithaa's shadow', *The Hindu*, 27 December 2016.

345 **unprecedented VVIP culture where she:** M. R. Venkatesh, 'Rajni's "revenge" on traffic-stopper Jaya', *The Telegraph*, 11 March 2008.
345 **Her close confidante Sasikala Natarajan:** Anna Issac, 'The rise and fall of VK Sasikala', *News Minute*, 18 June 2024.
345 **Murderous attacks were orchestrated against:** Indulekha Aravind, 'Eulogised in death, Jayalalithaa leaves a checkered legacy', *Economic Times*, 11 December 2016.
345 **Political opponents including Prime Minister Narasimha:** Girish Nikam, 'Jayalalitha announces withdrawal of AIADMK support to Congress(I)', *India Today*, 31 March 1993.
346 **The then Janata Party leader Subramanian Swamy launched:** Suresh Kumar in conversation with the author.
346 **In 1995, Jayalalithaa conducted the lavish wedding:** '1995 lavish wedding and more: All you need to know about Jaya's DA case', *Firstpost*, 30 September 2014.
346 **Despite her notable efforts to protect the state's interests:** Ibid.
346 **'even God cannot save Tamil Nadu':** Anna Isaac, 'Rajinikanth once swung an election with one sentence: Does Thalaivar still have that clout?', *News Minute*, 31 December 2017.
346 **prevailing 'bomb culture':** Anupama Subramanian, 'Bomb threat to Mani Ratnam Entertainment', *Deccan Chronicle*, 3 October 2018.
346 **Because one of Jayalalithaa's ministers:** G. C. Shekhar, 'Jayalalitha drops minister from Cabinet for sharing dais with Rajnikanth', *India Today*, 30 September 1995.
347 **Among one of the chief minister's early:** 'The DA case fact file: All you need to know about the 20-yr-long legal battle', *News Minute*, 14 February 2017.
347 **Jayalalithaa faced legal hurdles:** The Hindu Net Desk, 'Jayalalithaa: a political career with sharp rises and steep falls', *The Hindu*, 6 December 2016.
347 **The High Court suspended their sentence:** T. S. Subramanian, 'Can she or can't she?', *Frontline*, 28 April 2001.
347 **Fathima Beevi (the first woman judge:** N. Chithra, 'Fathima Beevi: SC's 1st Woman Judge Who Swore In A Convicted Jayalalithaa As CM', *Free Press Journal*, 24 November 2023.
347 **the AIADMK arrested an aging Karunanidhi:** T. S. Subramanian, 'Tamil Nadu's Shame', *Frontline*, 7 July 2001.
347 **That case was later dropped:** 'Police drop flyover case against Karunanidhi', Rediff.com, 21 May 2007, available at https://www.rediff.com/news/2007/may/21tn.htm.
347 **who owned SUN television dramatically:** Vaasanthi, 'Looking Back At A Political Shocker: When Jayalalithaa Ordered The Arrest Of DMK Head M. Karunanidhi', *Reader's Digest*, 18 May 2020.
348 **Union ministers T. R. Baalu and Murasoli Maran:** Sujan Dutta, Habib Beary, 'Avenger Amma's Revenge Raj', *The Telegraph*, 30 June 2001.
348 **unprecedented threat to its unity and integrity:** George Fernandes, S. S. Dhindsa, V. K. Malhotra, 'Reign of terror in TN: NDA report', Rediff.com, 2 July 2001, available at https://m.rediff.com/news/2001/jul/03tn13.htm.
348 **Maran went directly to the Chennai Central Prison:** 'Karunanidhi last rites LIVE updates: Final journey of Kalaignar from Rajaji Hall to Marina Beach underway', ABPLive.com, 8 August 2018, available at https://news.abplive.com/news/india/m-karunanidhi-last-rites-live-updates-high-court-starts-hearing-on-case-challenging-burial-at-marina-739021.
348 **Karunanidhi refused to apply for bail:** Vaasanthi, 'Looking Back At A Political Shocker: When Jayalalithaa Ordered The Arrest Of DMK Head M. Karunanidhi', *Reader's Digest*.
348 **Karunanidhi became emotional at a press:** D. Suresh Kumar, 'When emotions overwhelmed Karunanidhi', *The Hindu*, 8 August 2018.
348 **There were several incidents including:** 'Jaya refuses to hear media complaint on reporter's arrest', *Times of India*, 4 July 2001.
348 **The next day more than 100 journalists:** 'Of Lathicharge, assault and intimidation: Reporter's diary from Jayalalithaa's times', *News Minute*, 9 December 2016.

348 **Later, at another DMK rally:** 'DMK MLA's death pushes toll to six', *Times of India*, 13 August 2001.
348 **Jayalalithaa went after *The Hindu*:** Arun Ram, 'The Hindu editors arrested for attacking Jayalalitaa's authoritarian ways', *India Today*, 24 November 2003.
348 **The speaker of the Tamil Nadu assembly:** 'Committee to Protect Journalists', *Attacks on the Press in 2003 - India*, February 2004, available at https://www.refworld.org/reference/annualreport/cpj/2004/en/55963.
348 **Kuldip Nayar, the veteran journalist, filed:** 'Press across nation rallies behind The Hindu', *The Tribune*, 9 November 2003.
348 **Jayalalithaa made a tactical withdrawal:** Aditya Iyer, 'The art of defamation: Jayalalithaa's most useful tool', *Hindustan Times*, 29 July 2016.
349 **There were transport strikes, she tried to:** '"Touch me not": Tamil Nadu government has filed over 70 defamation cases on media', *News Minute*, 17 January 2015; Apurva Vishwanath, Dharani Thangavelu, 'Supreme Court pulls up Jayalalithaa for misusing defamation law', *Mint*, 25 August 2016.
349 **'Dynasty Munnetra Kazhagam':** 'Dynasty Munnetra Kazhagam? Udhayanidhi Stalin Anointed Heir To The Party Throne', *Swarajya*, 4 July 2019.
350 **M. K. Alagiri whose followers went on a rampage:** 'DMK workers continue rampage in TN', Rediff.com, 21 September 2000, available at https://m.rediff.com/news/2000/sep/21tn.htm.
350 **The family also bought into various:** N. Madhavan, 'DMK Inc.', *btMag*, 26 December 2010.
350 **'The 2014 parliamentary election saw Jayalalithaa':** Suresh Kumar in conversation with the author.
350 **'Not Lady or Modi, it is my Daddy':** 'It is my daddy, says Stalin in twist to "Modi vs Lady" argument', *Business Standard*, 22 April 2014.
350 **Jayalalitha's old disproportionate assets case:** 'Jayalalithaa convicted in the disproportionate assets case', *Business Standard*, 27 September 2014.
351 **He has however come in for criticism:** Arun Janardhanan, 'Stalin son Udhayanidhi appointed deputy CM of Tamil Nadu amid cabinet reshuffle', *Indian Express*, 29 September 2024; Saikat Kumar Bose (ed.), '"Not Position, But Responsibility": Udhayanidhi Stalin On Getting Top Post', NDTV.com, 29 September 2024.

CHAPTER 31: A PROGRESSIVE AND PARADOXICAL STATE
353 **Issues of quality be it in education or healthcare:** Kalaiyarasan A., Vijayabaskar M., *The Dravidian Model: Interpreting the Political Economy of Tamil Nadu*, New Delhi: Cambridge University Press, 2021, p. 229.
353 **In the same report, Tamil Nadu was ranked third:** 'Performance Grading Index (PGI) 2.0', New Delhi: Ministry of Education, Government of India, 2021–22.
354 **Eighteen institutions of higher learning from Tamil Nadu:** Ibid.
355 **'To truly abolish caste discrimination and hierarchy':** Udhav Naig, 'Papering over the caste violence in Tamil Nadu', *The Hindu*, 3 December 2023.
356 **Bhaskar tells me that the Dravidian narrative had:** Vasugi Bhaskar in conversation with the author, Chennai, July 2024.
357 **Ramakrishnan says that the proportion:** T. Ramakrishnan, 'A steady growth of SC entrepreneurs', *The Hindu*, 21 January 2022.
357 **'The common complaint among many entrepreneurs':** Ibid.
358 **The ambition is to grow into a trillion-dollar economy:** *Towards one trillion: Accelerating Tamil Nadu's progress to become a trillion-dollar economy*, Chennai: Deloitte and FICCI, April 2023.
358 **As it stands, Tamil Nadu's economy has grown:** Ibid., pp. 4–5.
358 **Guidance Tamil Nadu, a nodal government agency:** Sai Sudha Chandrasekaran, 'Home to

the highest number of factories in India - 39,512 units', InvestIndia.gov.in, available at https://www.investindia.gov.in/state/tamil-nadu.

358 **The world's largest electric scooter plant, Ola Electric Mobility:** Mallika Suri, 'Ola Electric Business Model - GrowthX Deep Dive', GrowthX.Club, 29 August 2024, available at https://growthx.club/blog/olaelectric-business-model.

358 **'this means that women are not just involved':** The Hindu, 'The Hindu - Tamil Nadu Women's summit 2024', 19 mins 40 secs, YouTube.com, 30 July 2024, available at https://www.youtube.com/live/OovFO0OI6Io?si=ZTyrGq39G2wHSQDa.

359 **'The state can keep surprising you...the':** Sushila Ravindranath, *Surge: Tamil Nadu's Growth Story*, New Delhi: Westland Limited, 2016, p. xvii.

360 **Later, along with his five sons, he began:** Anita Ratnam in conversation with the author, Chennai, August 2024.

360 **'The Murugappa Group seen as an arch conservative Chettiar':** Ravindranath, *Surge*, p. xxvii.

360 **Software exports touched a record of ₹2 lakh crore:** Pavithra K. M., 'Data: Software Exports from STPI Units Quadrupled between 2010-11 & 2022-23; Six States Account for 95% of the Exports', Factly.in, 21 June 2024, available at https://factly.in/data-software-exports-from-stpi-units-quadrupled-between-2010-11-six-states-account-for-95-of-the-exports/#:~:text=Between%202021%2D22%20and%202022,)%20Act%201992)%20were%20Rs.

361 **Recent studies have shown a steady decline:** R. Ravi Kumar, Dr S. K. Gopal, 'Overview of Tamil Nadu Handloom Industry: A Study from Government Reports', *International Journal of Research and Analytical Reviews*, Vol. 7, No. 1, February 2020, p. 63.

361 **'The weaver is at the heart of everything':** Sreemathy Mohan in conversation with the author, Chennai, August 2024.

362 **But we must also remember a pivotal point:** Yazhiniyan, 'Tamil Nadu is on a mission to read palms, bit by byte', *Times of India*, 7 February 2023.

364 **'establishing the feminist literary movement as a distinct':** Salma, *i, Salma: Selected Poems*, K. Srilata, Shobana Kumar (trs.), New Delhi: Red River Publications, 2023, p. 110.

364 **'I almost felt Chudamani's presence while I wrote':** Prabha Sridevan, 'Guest Post by Prabha Sridevan', *Unprofessional Translation*, 2 January 2017, available at https://unprofessionaltranslation.blogspot.com/2017/01/guest-post-by-prabha-sridevan.html.

365 **'Dance for me is...a transforming experience':** Alarmel Valli, Alarmelavalli.org, available at https://www.alarmelvalli.org/.

365 **'I felt as a Tamil woman if I was going to explore':** Anita Ratnam in conversation with the author, Chennai, August 2024.

367 **'Politicians too always back sports as they see':** K. C. Vijaya Kumar in conversation with the author, Chennai, August 2024.

367 **'Although Pakistan won this sensational':** Qamar Ahmed, 'A Befitting Climax', *The Hindu*, 1 August 1999.

368 **'one of Coimbatore's favourite sons':** K. C. Vijaya Kumar in conversation with the author, Chennai, August 2024.

368 **A brand new development on Tamil Nadu's beautiful:** Ibid.

368 **'Over the past five years a variety of inventive':** Shonali Muthalaly in conversation with the author, Chennai, August 2024.

EPILOGUE: THE TAMIL IN US

371 **A people without history is not redeemed from time:** T. S. Eliot, 'Four Quartets – Extract', Poetry Archive, available at https://poetryarchive.org/poem/four-quartets-extract/.

372 **'Tamil is a certain body of knowledge, some of it technical':** Shulman, *Tamil*, p. 2.

372 **There is a veritable archaeology of the language:** Arjun Appadurai in conversation with the author.
373 **It is almost as if there:** Daniel, *Fluid Signs*, pp. 64–85.
374 **'Tamils believe that at the time of birth':** Ibid., p. 4.
374 **'Among Tamils deference behaviour is signified through':** Ibid., p. 297.
374 **'If you look at the early settlements in Keezhadi':** Thangam Thenarasu in conversation with the author, Chennai, July 2024.
375 **'It is not just about a sophistication of a people':** Ibid.
376 **'Being Tamil is a conscious emotion for me':** Jayanthi Natarajan in conversation with the author, Chennai, July 2024.
377 **We know the apocryphal story of a woman:** Ibid.
377 **'The metros smudge the issue, and you think everything':** Kamal Haasan in conversation with the author, Chennai, July 2024.
377 **'Though several movements have laid an emphasis':** K. Ashokan in conversation with the author, Chennai, August 2023.
378 **'Tamilians are an ancient civilization who':** V. Vedachalam in conversation with the author, Madurai, July 2023.
379 **'Being Tamil …yes, a significant part of my identity':** Radha Sarma Hegde in conversation with the author, Chennai, August 2023.
380 **'The audience here is ready to engage':** Ranvir Shah in conversation with the author, Chennai, July 2024.
381 **all linguistic groups are moored:** B. Kolappan in conversation with the author.
382 **speaks of the peculiar geography:** Gopalkrishna Gandhi in conversation with the author, Chennai, August 2023.

Bibliography

Aiyangar, M. Srinivasa, *Tamil Studies or Essays on the History of the Tamil People, Language, Religion and Literature*, Madras: The Guardian Press, 1914.

Aiyangar, Sakkottai Krishnaswami, *The Beginnings of South Indian History*, New Delhi: Alpha Editions, 2020.

Aiyappan, A., Srinivasan, P. R. (eds.), *Story of Buddhism with Special Reference to South India*, Chennai: Department of Information and Publicity, Government of Madras, 1960.

Aiyar, R. Sathyanatha, *History of the Nayaks of Madura*, Oxford: Oxford University Press, 1924.

Allen, Charles, *Coromandel: A Personal History of South India*, London: Little, Brown, 2017.

Amrith, Sunil, *Unruly Waters: How Mountain Rivers and Monsoons Have Shaped South Asia's History*, London: Penguin Books Limited, 2018.

Andal, *The Secret Garland: Andal's Tiruppavai and Nacciyar Tirumoli*, Archana Venkatesan (tr.), Gurugram: Harper Collins, 2016.

Archaeological Survey of India, *Glimpse of Iconic Site Adichanallur*, Trichy: Archaeological Survey of India.

Arimugam, Oor Eliya, *Alwargal*, Chennai: Visa Publications, 2016.

Ayyar, P. V. Jagadish, *South Indian Customs*, New Delhi: Asian Educational Services, 2001.

Badhreenath, Sathyabhama, *The Brihadisvara Temple Thanjavur*, New Delhi: Archaeological Survey of India, 2010.

Baker, Christopher John, *The Politics of South India 1920-1937*, Cambridge: Cambridge University Press, 1976.

Balasubrahmanyam, S. R., *Early Chola Temples: Parantaka I to Rajaraja I*, Bombay: Orient Longman, 1971.

———*Middle Chola Temples: Rajaraja I to Kulottunga I*, Faridabad: Thomson Press (India) Limited, 1975.

Bayly, Susan, *Saints, Goddesses and Kings: Muslims and Christians in South Indian Society 1700-1900*, Cambridge: Cambridge University Press, 2003.

Bes, Lennart, *The Heirs of Vijayanagar: Court Politics in Early Modern South India*, Leiden: Leiden University Press, 2022.

Bhandarkar, R. G., *Early History of the Dekkan*, Varanasi: Bharatiya Publishing House, 1975.

Bhosle, Pratap Singh Serfoji Raje, *Contributions of Thanjavur Maratha Kings*, Chennai: Notion Press, 2017.

Champakalakshmi, R., *Religion, Tradition, and Ideology: Pre-colonial South India*, New Delhi: Oxford University Press, 2011.

Chandramurthi, M., Vedachalam, V., *Parakramapandiyapuram*, Chennai: Kalaitthai Pathippagam, 2002.

Dallapiccola, Anna L., Singh, Kuldip, Singh, R. G., *Thanjavur's Gilded Gods: South Indian Paintings in the Kuldip Singh Collection*, Mumbai: The Marg Foundation, 2018.

Dalrymple, William, *The Anarchy: The East India Company, Corporate Violence, and the Pillage of an Empire*, London: Bloomsbury Publishing, 2022.

Daniel, E. Valentine, Fluid Signs: Being a Person the Tamil Way, Berkeley: University of California Press, 1984.

Devakunjari, D., *Madurai through the Ages: From the Earliest Times to 1801 AD*, Madurai: Arulmigu Meenakshi Sundareswarar Thirukkoil, 2018.

Dharmaraj, J., *History of Tamil Nadu (1565-2020)*, Sivakasi: Tensy Publications, 2021.

Duraisamipillai, Avvai, *Cherar Varalaru*, Chidambaram: Meyyappan Pathipagam, 2022.

Emmanuel, Dominic, *Christianity, Hindutva, Conversion: Understanding the Challenge*, Mumbai: St Pauls, 2022.

Eskenazi, John, Ali, Daud, Dehejia, Vidya, et al., *Chola: Sacred Bronzes of South India*, London: Royal Academy of Arts, 2006.

Gandhi, Gopalkrishna, *The Tirukkural: A New English Version*, New Delhi: Aleph Book Company, 2015.

Gandhi, Rajmohan, *Modern South India: A History from the 17th Century to Our Times*, New Delhi: Aleph Book Company, 2018.

Gangatharan, A., *Cultural Aspirations: Essays on the Intellectual History of the Colonial Tamil Nadu*, Morrisville: Lulu Press, Incorporated, 2017.

Gnanadurai, P. M., *The History of Anglicanism in Tamil Nadu*, Chennai: Christian Literature Society, 2012.

Govindacharya, Alkondavilli, *The Divine Wisdom of the Dravida Saints*, Poona: The Oriental Books Supplying Agency, 1902.

Hancock, Mary E., *The Politics of Heritage from Madras to Chennai*, Indiana: Indiana University Press, 2008.

Hardgrave Jr., Robert L., *The Nadars of Tamilnad: The Political Culture of a Community in Change*, New Delhi: Manohar Publishers and Distributors, 2006.

Hart, George L., Heifetz, Hank (eds.), *The Four Hundred Songs of War and Wisdom: An Anthology of Poems from Classical Tamil: The Purananuru*, United Kingdom: Columbia University Press, 1999.

Hickey, William, *The Tanjore Mahratta Principality in Southern India: The Land of the Chola, The Eden of the South*, Madras: Foster Press, 1874.

Hudson, D. Dennis, *Protestant Origins in India: Tamil Evangelical Christians, 1706-1835*, Richmond: Wm B Eerdmans Publishing Co. and Curzon Press Ltd, 2000.

———*Protestant Origins in India: Tamil Evangelical Christians, 1706-1835*, Michigan: William B. Eerdmans Publishing Company, 2000.

———*The Vaikunta Perumal Temple at Kanchipuram*, Chennai: Prakriti Foundation, 2009.

Huntingforf, G. W. B. (ed.) (tr.), *The Periplus of the Erythraean Sea*, London: Routledge, 2016.

Husaini, A. Q., Marudanar, Mankuti (trs.), *The History of the Pāndya Country*, Madras: Selvi Pathippakam, 1962.

Husaini, S. A. Q., *The History of the Pandya Country*, Madras: Selvi Pathippakam, 1962.

Irschick, Eugene F., *Tamil Revivalism in the 1930s*, Madras: Cre-A, 1986.

Jouveau-Dubreuil, G., *The Pallavas*, V. S. Swaminadha Dikshitar (tr.), Pondicherry: V. S. Swaminadha Dikshithar, 1917.

———*Pallava Antiquities*, V. S. Swaminadha Dikshitar (tr.), New Delhi: Asian Educational Services, 1994.

Jung, Carl, *Psychology and Alchemy*, United Kingdom: Taylor & Francis, 2014.

Kailasapathy, K., *Tamil Heroic Poetry*, Oxford: Clarendon P., 1968.

———*Tamil Heroic Poetry*, Chennai: Kumaran Book House, 2002.

Kalaiyarasan, A., Vijayabaskar, M., *The Dravidian Model: Interpreting the Political Economy of Tamil Nadu*, New Delhi: Cambridge University Press, 2021.

Kamath, Suryanath U., *Krishnadevaraya of Vijayanagar and His Times*, Bangalore: IBH Prakashana, 2009.

Kanjamala, Augustine, *The Future of Christian Mission in India: Toward a New Paradigm for the Third Millennium*, Bengaluru: Theological Publications, 2016.

Karashima, Noburu (ed.), *A Concise History of South India: Issues and Interpretations*, New Delhi: Oxford University Press, 2014.

Karashima, Noboru, *Ancient to Medieval: South Indian Society in Transition*, New Delhi: Oxford University Press, 2009.

Kasinathan, Natana, *Cherar Mazhavar Varalaru: Tholliyal Nookil*, Chennai: Manivasagar Pathippagam, 2023.

Kersenboom, Saskia C., *Nityasumangali: Devadasi Tradition in South India*, New Delhi: Motilal Banarsidass Publishing House, 2021.

Kulke, Hermann, Kesaapany, K., Sakhuja, Vijay (eds.), *Nagapattinam to Suvarnadwuipa: Reflections on the Chola Naval Expeditions to Southeast Asia*, New Delhi: Manohar Publishers and Distributors, 2010.

Kunnatholy CMI, Abraham, *St. Thomas' Christians in Madhya Pradesh: A Historical Study on Apostolic Church of St. Thomas*, Bangalore: Asian Trading Corporation, 2007.

Lakshman, Narayan, *New Crossroads: Reinventing Dravidian Politics for the 21st Century*, Singapore: Institute of South Asian Studies, 2022.

Lakshman, Nirmala, *Degree Coffee by the Yard: A Short Biography of Madras*, New Delhi: Aleph Book Company, 2013.

Lawson, Philip, *The East India Company: A History*, London: Taylor & Francis, 2014.

Love, Henry Davison, *Vestiges of Old Madras 1640-1800*, Vol. 2, New Delhi: Mittal Publications, 1995.

———*Vestiges of Old Madras 1640-1800*, Vol. 4: Index Volume, New Delhi: Mittal Publications, 1995.

Madhavan, Chithra, *History and Culture of Tamil Nadu*, Volume 1, New Delhi: D.K. Print World Ltd., 2008.

———*Sanskrit Education and Literature in Ancient and Medieval Tamil Nadu: An Epigraphical Study*, New Delhi: DK Printworld Private Ltd., 2013.

———*Vishnu Temples of South India–Volume Three*, Chennai: Dr. Chithra Madhavan, 2010.

Mahadevan, Iravatham, Witzel, Michael (eds.), *Early Tamil Epigraphy: From the Earliest Times to the Sixth Century AD*, Chennai: Cre-A, 2003.

Manikumar, K. A., *Foreshadowing the Great Rebellion: The Vellore Revolt, 1806*, New Delhi: Orient BlackSwan, 2021.

Michell, George, *The Hindu Temple: An Introduction to Its Meaning and Forms*, Chicago: The University of Chicago Press, 1988.

Minakshi, C., *Administration and Social Life Under the Pallavas*, Madras: University of Madras, 1938.

——*The Historical Sculptures of the Vaikuntha Perumal Temple*, New Delhi: Archaeological Survey of India, September 1939.

——*The Historical Sculptures of the Vaikunthaperumal Temple, Kanchi*, New Delhi: Archaeological Survey of India, 1999.

Mohamad, J. Raja, *Art of Pudukkottai: Art and Architecture*, Pudukkottai: Hitesh Kumar Makwana, 2003.

——*Islamic Architecture in Tamil Nadu*, Chennai: Government Museum, 2004.

——*Maritime History of the Coromandel Muslims: A Socio-Historical Study on the Tamil Muslims 1750-1900*, Tiruchirapalli: Jamal Mohamed College, 2022.

——*Muslims of Tamil Nadu in the Indian Freedom Struggle*, Tiruchirappalli: Jamal Mohamed College, Centre for Islamic Tamil Cultural Research, 2019.

Mohan, D. (ed.), *Tamil Nadu's Contribution to the Freedom Struggle*, Chennai: Tamilarasu, 2023.

Molony, J. Chartres, *A Book of South India*, London: Methuen & Co Ltd., 2004.

Munshi, K. M., *The Ruin that Britain Wrought*, Bombay: Padma Publications Limited, 1946.

Muthukumar, V. N., Segran, Elizabeth Rani (trs.), *The River Speaks: The Vaiyai Poems from the Paripatal*, Gurugram: Penguin Random House, 2012.

Nagaswamy, R. (ed.), *Sangam: Numismatics and Cultural History: Essays in Honour of R. Krishnamurthy*, Chennai: New Era Publication, 2006.

Nagaswamy, R., *Gangaikondacholapuram*, Madras: Government of Tamil Nadu, 1970.

——*The Kailasanatha Temple: A Guide*, Chennai: Department of Archaeology, Government of Tamil Nadu, 1969.

——*Tamil Nadu, The Land of the Vedas*, Chennai: Tamil Arts Academy, 2018.

——*Uttaramerur: The Historic Village in Tamil Nadu*, Chennai: Tamil Arts Academy, 2003.

——*Uttiramerur: Ooparum Varalatru Perur*, Chennai: Tamil Arts Academy, 2003.

——*Visnu Temples of Kancipuram*, New Delhi: DK Printworld Private Ltd., 2011.

Naidu, Sarojini, *The Golden Threshold*, London: William Heinemann, 1920.

Nair, Geetha, Mekkoth, Vineetha (Eds.), *Aquality: Tales from the Depths: Short Stories*, Thiruvananthapuram: Folio, 2024.

Nammalvar, *A Hundred Measures of Time: Tiruviruttam*, Archana Venkatesan (tr.), Gurugram: Penguin Random House, 2014.

——*Hymns for the Drowning: Poems for Visnu*, A.K. Ramanujan (tr.), Gurugram: Penguin Random House, 1993.

Narasimhaiah, Barkur, *Metropolis Vijayanagar: Significance of Remains of Citadel*, New Delhi: Book India Publishing Company, 1992.

Narayan, S., *The Dravidian Years: Politics and Welfare in Tamil Nadu*, New Delhi: Oxford University Press, 2018.

——*The Dravidian Years: Politics and Welfare in Tamil Nadu*, New Delhi: Oxford University Press, 2022.

Natarajan, B., *Tillai and Nataraja*, Madras: Mudgala Trust, 1994.

Neill, Stephen, *A History of Christianity in India: The Beginnings to AD* 1707, Cambridge: Cambridge University Press, 1984

Palaniappan, K., *The Great Temple of Madurai*, K. Thiagarajan (tr.), Madurai: Arulmigu Meenakshi Sundareswarar Thirukkoil, 2004.

Pandian, M.S.S., *Brahmin & Non-Brahmin: Genealogies of the Tamil Political Present*, New Delhi: Permanent Black, 2003.

———*Brahmin and Non-Brahmin: Genealogies of the Tamil Political Present*, Ranikhet: Permanent Black, 2017.

Parthasarathy, R. (tr.), *The Cilappatikaram : The Tale Of An Anklet*, Gurugram: Penguin Random House, 2004.

Pate, H. R., *Madras District Gazetteers: Tinnevelly Volume I*, Madras: Government Press, 1917.

Pillay, K. K., *The Caste System in Tamil Nadu*, Chennai: MJP Publishers, 2007.

———*Historical Heritage of the Tamils*, Chennai: MJP Publishers, 2008.

Polo, Marco, *The Book of Ser Marco Polo: The Venetian Concerning the Kingdoms and Marvels of the East*, Henry Yule (tr.), London: John Murray, 1903.

Ponmudy, K., *The Dravidian Movement and the Black Movement*, Chennai: University of Madras, 2009.

Pritam, Ruchi, *Grandeur of the Cholas*, Chennai: ICT Academy Publications, 2023.

Rajagopal, S. (ed.), *Kaveri: Studies in Epigraphy, Archaeology and History*, Chennai: Panpattu Veliyiittakam, 2001.

Rajan, K., *Churning the Ocean: Maritime Trade of Early Historic Peninsular India*, Thanjavur: Manoo Pathippakam, 2019.

Rajayyan, K., *History of Tamil Nadu 1565-1982*, Madurai: Raj Publishers, 1982.

———*South Indian Rebellion: The First War of Independence, 1800–1801*, Mysore: Rao and Raghavan, 1971.

———*South Indian Rebellion 1800-1801: The First War of Independence*, Vandavasi: Akani Veliyeedu, 2012.

Ramachandra Dikshitar, V. R., *Origin and Spread of the Tamils: A Course of Two Lectures Delivered Under the Sankara Parvati Endowment, University of Madras*, Madras: The Adyar Library, 1947.

Raman, K.V., *Some Aspects of Pandyan History in the Light of Recent Discoveries*, Madras: University of Madras, 1972.

———*Temple Art, Icons and Culture of India and South-East Asia*, New Delhi: Sharda Publishing House, 2007.

Ramanujan, A. K. (tr.), *Poems of Love and War: From the Eight Anthologies and the Ten Long Poems of Classical Tamil*, United Kingdom: Columbia University Press, 2011.

———*The Interior Landscape: Love Poems from a Classical Tamil Anthology*, New Delhi: Oxford University Press, 1994.

Ramaswami, N. S., *The Founding of Madras*, New Delhi: Orient Longman, 1977.

Ramaswamy, Sumathi, *Language Devotion in Tamil India, 1891-1970*, Berkeley: University of California Press, 1997.

———*Passions of the Tongue: Language Devotion in Tamil India, 1891–1970*, India: University of California Press, 1997.

Ravindranath, Sushila, *Surge: Tamil Nadu's Growth Story*, New Delhi: Westland Limited, 2016.

Sastri, K. A. Nilakanata, *A History of South India: From Prehistoric Times to the Fall of Vijayanagar*, New Delhi: Oxford University Press, 1958.

———*Studies in Cola History and Administration*, Madras: University of Madras, 1932.

———*The Colas*, Vol. 1: To the Accession of Kulottunga I, Madras: University of Madras, 1935.

———*The Colas*, Vol. 2, Madras: University of Madras, 1937.

———*The Pandyan Kingdom: From the Earliest Times to the Sixteenth Century*, London: Luzac & Co, 1929.

Schwanbeck, E. A., McCrindle, Watson, John, Sedgefield, S., *Ancient India as Described by Megasthenês and Arrian*, India: Thacker, Spink, 1877.

Selby, Martha Ann, Peterson, Indira Viswanathan (Eds.), *Tamil Geographies: Cultural Constructions of Space and Place in South India*, New York: State University of New York Press, 2008.

Seth, Mesrovb J., *History of the Armenians in India: From the Earliest Times to the Present Day*, London: Luzac & Co., 1897.

Sethuraman, G., Vedachalam, V., *The Sculptural Splendours of Meenakshi Temple*, Madurai: Arulmigu Meenakshi Sundareshwarar Temple, 2019.

Sewell, Robert, *A Forgotten Empire (Vijayanagar): A Contribution to the History of India*, London: Swan Sonnenschein & Co. Ltd., 1900.

Shulman, David, *More than Real: A History of the Imagination in South India*, Cambridge: Harvard University Press, 2012.

———*Tamil: A Biography*, London: Harvard University Press, 2016.

Sivanantham, R., Rajan, K., Sakthivel, K., Paranthaman, S., et. al (eds.), *Mayiladumparai: Beginning of Agrarian Society: 4200 Years Old Iron Age Culture in Tamil Nadu*, Chennai: Department of Archaeology, Government of Tamil Nadu, 2022.

Sivanantham, R., Seran, M. (eds.), *Keeladi: An Urban Settlement of Sangam Age on the Banks of River Vaigai*, Chennai: Government of Tamil Nadu, 2019.

Sivanantham, R., Baskar, J., Prabhakaran, M., Thangadurai, T. (eds.), *Porunai: River Civilization*, Chennai: Department of Archaeology, Government of Tamil Nadu, 2022.

Sivaramamurti, C., *Amaravati Sculptures in the Madras Government Museum*, Madras: Government Press, 1956.

———*Kalugumalai and the Early Pandyan Rock-Cut Shrines*, Bombay: NM Tripathi Private Limited, 1961.

———*Mahabalipuram*, New Delhi: Archaeological Survey of India, 2006.

———*Mahabalipuram*, New Delhi: Archaeological Survey of India, 2004.

———*Vijayanagar Paintings*, New Delhi: Government of India, 1985.

Srinivasa, P. T., *History of the Indian People. Life in Ancient India in the Age of the Mantras*, Burbank: Creative Media Partners, LLC, 2016.

Srinivasan, Vasanthi, *Gandhi's Conscience Keeper: C. Rajagopalachari and Indian Politics*, Ranikhet: Permanent Black, 2009.

Sriram, V., Chennai: A Biography. New Delhi: Aleph Book Company, 2021.

Sriraman, P. S., *Chola Murals: Documentation and Study of the Chola Murals of Brihadisvara Temple, Thanjavur*, New Delhi: Archaeological Survey of India, 2011.

Stein, Burton (ed.), *Essays on South India*, New Delhi: Munshiram Manoharlal Publishers Pvt. Ltd., 1997.

Stein, Burton, *The New Cambridge History of India*, Cambridge: Cambridge University Press, 2005.

Stephen, S. Jeyaseela, *Goodbye to Tamil Motherland: The Rise of Labour Migration Overseas and the Society, 1729-1890*, New Delhi: GenNext Publication, 2019.

Subbarayalu, Y., *South India Under the Cholas*, New Delhi: Oxford University Press, 2012.

———*Studies in Cola History*, Chennai: Surabhi Pathippakam, 2001.

Subramanian, T. S. (ed.), *Epic Saga of the Cholas: Their Art, Temples and Heritage*, Chennai: The Hindu Group Publishing Private Limited, 2023.

———*Pandya Nattu Varlarrumurai Sumuga Nilaviyal*, Thanjavur: Dhanalakshmi Pathipakam, 2019.

Sudhakar, G. (ed.), *Popular Uprisings in India: With Special Reference to Tamil Nadu 1750-1857*, Chennai: CPR Institute of Indological Research, 2015.

Swaminathan, S., *The Early Cholas: History, Art and Culture*, New Delhi: Sharada Publishing House, 1998.

Tee, Sangeetha Shinde, The Book of Anglo-Indian Tales, Chennai: Anglo-ink, 2019.

Thomas, I. Job, *Paintings in Tamil Nadu: A History*, Chennai: Oxygen Books, 2010.

———*Chola Bronzes*, Chennai: Cre-A, 2018.

Thangappa, M. L. (tr.), Venkatachalapathy, A. R. (ed.), *Love Stands Alone: Selections from Tamil Sangam Poetry*, New Delhi: Penguin Random House, 2013.

Thurston, Edgar, Rangachari, K., *Castes and Tribes of South India*, Vol. 1-A and B, Madras: Government Press, 1909.

Trautmann, Thomas R., *The Madras School of Orientalism: Producing Knowledge in Colonial South India*, New Delhi: Oxford University Press, 2009.

Umamaheshwari, R., *Reading History with the Tamil Jainas: A Study of Identity, Memory and Marginalisation*, New Delhi: Springer, 2017.

Vedachalam, V., *Kazhugumalai Samanapalli*, Thanjavur: Dhanalakshmi Pathipagam, 2021.

———*Pandiyanattu Oorgalin Varalaru*, Thanjavur: Dhanalakshmi Pathipagam, 2019.

———*Pandya Nattil Vanigam, Vanikar, Vanika Nagarangal*, Thanjavur: Dhanalakshmi Pathipakkam, 2024.

———*Varalatril Jeshthadevi: Moodhevi Vazhipadu*, Thanjavur: Dhanalakshmi Pathipagam, 2024.

Veeraraghavan, D., *Half a Day for Caste: Education and Politics in Tamil Nadu 1952-55*, A. R. Venkatachalapathy (ed.), New Delhi: LeftWord Books, 2019.

Veluthat, Kesavan, *The Early Medieval in South India*, New Delhi: Oxford University Press, 2010.

———*The Political Structure of Early Medieval South India*, Hyderabad: Orient BlackSwan, 2012.

Venkatachalapathy, A. R. (ed.), *Chennai not Madras: Perspectives on the City*, Mumbai: Marg Publications, 2006.

———*Subramania Bharati: Writings in The Hindu*, Chennai: THG Publishing Private Limited, 2022.

Venkatachalapathy, A.R., *Swadeshi Steam: V.O. Chidambaram Pillai and the Battle Against the British Maritime Empire*, Gurugram: Penguin Random House, 2023.

Venkataraman, B., *Temple Art under the Chola Queens*, Faridabad: Thomson Press (India) Limited, 1976.

Walpole, Beth, *Venture of Faith: A Brief Historical Background of the Church of South India*, P. C. Dass Babu (ed.), Chennai: The Christian Literature Society, 2014.

Wilson, Nicholas Hoover, *Modernity's Corruption: Empire and Morality in the Making of British India*, New York: Columbia University Press, 2023.

Wink, André, *Al-Hind: The Making of the Indo-Islamic World*, Germany: Brill, 1990.

Zaidi, A. Moin (ed.), *The Encyclopaedia of Indian National Congress: 1885-1890, The founding fathers*, New Delhi: S. Chand, 1976.

Index

Accutavikanta (Kalabhras king), 78
Acheulian tools, discovery of, 2
Achyuthadevaraya, King (ruler of Vijayanagara), 222–3, 225, 227–8
Act of Parliament, 303
Adan, Udiyan Cheral (Chera king), 208
Adhiyaman, story of, 23
Adichanallur, xiii, 1–2
Adigan of the Bright Lance, 117
Adi Varaha cave temple, 63
Advaita Vedanta, philosophy of, 196–7
Advani, L. K., 347
Adyar, Battle of (1746), 265
Agastya, sage, 14–15, 90
Agattiyam (Tamil grammar compiled by Agastya), 14
agricultural practices, sustainability of, 285
Agri Horticultural Society, 320
Aham, 16, 22
Ahananuru (Sangam poem), 203
Ahmed, Qamar, 367
Airavatesvara temple, Darasuram, 189, 197
Aiyar, Sathyanatha, 229
Aiyar, U. Ve. Swaminatha, x, 13, 308
Aiyar, V. V. S., 330
Ajanta cave paintings, 97
Ajithadoss, Kanaka, 95
Ajivika, philosophy of, 194
Akhilesh, Kumar, 1
Akhtar, Javed, 383
Alagiri, M. K., 350
Alam, Shah (Mughal emperor), 283
Alexander, A. X., 270
Alexander the Great, 108
Ali, Hyder, 278, 281. *see also* Tipu Sultan
All India Dravida Munnetra Kazhagam (AIADMK), 342–3, 347
All India Handicrafts Board, 361
Amaravati River, 206
Ambalavana Swamy temple, in Manur, 125
Ambikapathi, 356
Ambujammal, 322–3
Ambur, Battle of (1749), 266
Ammal, Duraikannu, 328

Amuktamalyada (poem), 221
Anandar, Arul, 276
Anand, Viswanathan, 368
Ananthapadmanabhaswamy temple, in Thiruvananthapuram, 221
Anci, Netuman, 26
Anglo-Dutch Treaty (1824), 260
Anglo-French rivalry, 263, 283
Anglo-Mysore wars, 283
Anna Dravida Munnetra Kazhagam (ADMK), 342
Annadurai, C. N., 337–9, 341
Anwar, Kombai S., 27, 29, 236
Aparajita (Pallava ruler), 50, 52, 74, 118, 150
Appadurai, Arjun, 372–3
Arabic Tamil, development of, 246
Arabindo, Pushpa, 311, 318
Arab merchants, 29, 241, 246, 248, 255
Archaeological Survey of India (ASI), 4, 314
ardha mandapam, 103, 188, 223
Arikesari, Maravarman (Pandya king), 114
Arittapatti rock-cut caves, 89
Arivu Viduthalai Iyakkam movement, 333
Arjuna Ratha, 64
Arokia Matha Church, 275
Arrian (Greek writer), 108
Ashe, Robert, 326
Ashoka, Emperor, 24, 28, 79, 93, 204
Ashokan Brahmi inscriptions, 374
ashtanga vimana (a vimana with eight aspects), 185
Ashvamedha, Vedic sacrificial rituals of, 46
Ashwatthama (son of Drona), 45
Asokan, K., 377
Athan, Chelva Kadungo Azhi (Chera king), 209
Athan, Perum Chorru Udiyan Cheral (Chera king), 204
Atirachandeswara temple, 66
Atyanta Kama Pallava, 50
Augustus (Roman emperor), 28, 271
Avanisimha (Lion of the Earth), title of, 44
Avantisundari Katha, 72
'Avvai' festival, 23

Avvaiyar (Tamil woman poet), 34
  Ahananuru, 16, 21
  Athichudi, 23
  Kondraivendan, 32
  Purananuru collection, 23, 25
Ayyanar, 130
Ayyar, C. S., 320
Azhwar, Budhat, 83
Azhwar, Kulasekhara, 186
Azhwar, Pey, 83, 313
Azhwar, Poygai, 83
Azhwar, Tirumangai (Vaishnava saint), 59–60, 62, 146, 313
Azim-ud-Daula, Nawab, 282

Baalu, T. R., 348
Bahmani sultanate, 220
Balachander, K., 318
Balasaraswati, 365
Balasubrahmanyam, S. R., 155, 176
Balasubramaniam, Kudavayil, 147, 178–9
Balasubramaniam, V., 8
Ballala III (Hoysala king), 218
Bannerman, John, 290–1
Barbosa, Duarte, 220
Baskaran, V., 368
Bate, Barney, 372
Battuta, Ibn, 218, 243
Bayly, Susan, 268–9, 274, 276
Beevi, Fathima, 347, 348
Behl, Benoy K., 101
Bengal famine, 284
Besant, Annie, 308, 326–28, 332
Beschi, Constanzo, 131, 276
Bes, Lennart, 225
Bhadrabahu (Jaina seer), 95
Bhagavata (worshipper of Vishnu), 97
Bhagavata kings, 42
Bhagiratha, sage, 63
Bhagyalakshmi, K. S., 357
Bhaktavatsalam, M., 338, 376
Bhaktha Nandanar (1935), 318
Bhakti movement / ideology, 48–9, 77, 79, 81, 82, 85, 97, 98, 104, 126, 135, 142–3,193
Bharatanatyam, 36, 177, 365
Bharati, Subramania, xvi, 308, 314, 324–5, 333
Bhartiya Janata Party (BJP), 347
Bhaskar, Vasugi, 356
Bhimavarman, King, 41, 51

Bhonsle, Mallojee, 234, 235
Bijapur, sultans of, 235
black pepper, trade of, 29–30, 240
'blue water' policy, 257
Bodhidharma, 55
Bombay Presidency, 263
Bose, Paul, 298
Bose, Subhas Chandra, 340
Brahmadeya, 73–4, 162
Brahmakshatriyas, 69
Brahma, Lord, 37, 48, 57, 67, 69
Brahmanical religion, 78, 97, 129, 137, 197
Brahmapurisvarar temple, Pullamangai, 182
Brahmin non-Brahmin religious dichotomy, 308
breast cloth controversy, 275, 324
Brihadeeswara (the Immense God) temple, at Tanjore, xii, 98, 147, 171, 187, 192, 197, 198, 236
British East India Company, 247, 280, 281, 285, 289–90, 292
  ascendency in the Carnatic region, 263
  attack on the French fleet at Masulipatnam, 266
  Carnatic wars, 263
  establishment of, 278
  factory in Surat, 261, 264
  Plassey, Battle of (1757), 263, 281, 283
  policy of annexing Native States, 302
  Seringapatam, Battle of (1799), 282
British India Steam Navigation Company, 324
British Parliament, 283, 285, 300
British Raj, 148, 286, 301, 306
bronzes, of the Chola period, 153, 190–3
Buddhavarman (Pallava ruler), 47
Buddhism, 37, 77, 79, 378
Buddhist monasteries, 71, 159, 200
Buddhist viharas, 71, 195
burial urns, discovery of, 2
Burnell, Arthur Coke, 269

Cabral, Pedro, 257
Calcutta Presidency, 263–4
Caldwell, Robert, 277
Canning, Lord Charles, 303
Cape of Good Hope, 256, 260
Carey, William, 278
Carnatic music, 36, 239, 316, 366, 367
Carnatic Sabhas, 316
Carnatic Treaty of 1792, 265

Carnatic Wars, 263–6, 281, 282
cartazes (Portuguese licensing system), 247
caste, xviii, 33, 274, 354–7, 365
caste structures / system, 21, 167, 354–7
caste violence and divide, in Tamil Nadu, 355
Catholic Church, 258, 268, 278–9
Cauvery water issue, 351, 376
Cavendish, William, 280
cave paintings, 4, 93, 96–7, 117, 173
Chakravarthi, Sibi, 149
Chalukya dynasty, 44, 51, 74, 78, 156
Chambers, William, 63
Chandiramurthy, M., 110
Charles II, King, 263
Charnock, Job, 314
Chattopadhyay, Kamaladevi, 361
Chaturvedimangalam, Rajaraja, 185
Chenguttuvan, Kadal Pirakkotiya, 207, 209
Chera dynasty, 18, 24–8, 203, 208, 212
  history of, 204
  Karur (Vanchi) capital city of, 205
  Roman 'factory', 211
  Three Crowned Kings, 204
Cheral Irumporai dynasty, 9
Cheral, Kalangaikanni Narmudi (Chera king), 207
Cheral, Uthiyan, 25
Chettiar community, xiii, 312
Chetti, P. Theagaraya, 330
Chidambaram temple, 177
Chidambara Rahasya, 199
Children's Garden School, 321
Chinappa, Joshna, 368
Chinese Pagoda, 79
Chinglepet, jagir of, 282
Chinnamalai, Dheeran, 297
Chithirai festival, 105
Chokkanatha, Vijayaranga, 232
Chola, Aditya (Chola king), 74, 118, 149–51, 180
Chola, Arinjaya (Chola king), 153
Chola empire, 18, 24–5, 32, 112, 215
  administrative system of, 162
  art of temple building, 188
  belief systems, 200
  Bhakti movement, 194
  conflicts with Pandyas, 147
  end of, 215
  gold coins, 155
  Imperial Cholas, 146, 186, 196

Karikal, king, 18
  in Sangam age, 145
  Thanjavur as capital of, 145, 234
Thirupurambiyam, battle of, 150
Chola I, Rajendra (Chola king), 146
  military successes of, 158
Chola III, Rajendra (Chola king), 215
Chola, Kulottunga, 119, 168
Chola, Manimudi, 115
Chola, Parantaka (Chola king), 112, 119, 151–2
Chola, Rajendra (Chola king), 149, 185, 217, 245
Chola, Sundara (Chola king), 154
Chola, Uttama (Madurantaka Uttama Chola), 154–6
Chola, Vijayalaya (Chola king), 118, 145–6, 180, 183
  capturing of Thanjavur from Muttarayar chief, 146, 149
  Thiruvalangadu copper plate of, 146
Chola, Vikrama (Chola king), 188
Choliswaram (Rajeswaram/Brihadeeswara) temple, Gangaikondacholapuram, 188
Chonaka Mappila community, 241
Choolamani, Maravarman Avani, 113
Christian communities, in Tamil Nadu, 274
Christian doctrine, teaching of, 268–76
Christianity, ix–x, xviii, 257–8, 269–72, 277
  development in Tamilakam, 267
  in the Malabar region, 258
Christian Nadar community, 275
Church of England, 277
Church of Our Lady of Snows, 273
Church of South India, 279
Civakacintamani, 132
Civil Disobedience Movement, 322, 330
civil services examinations, 339
Clive, Edward, 290–1
Clive, Robert, 265–6, 279, 281, 283, 314
Coelobothros, 203
Coimbatore, 9, 19, 29, 117, 205, 231, 282, 293, 360, 361, 368–9
colonial administration, 305
Columbus, Christopher, 256
Constantinople (capital of the Byzantine empire), 256
Coote, Eyre, 266
copper plate inscriptions, 45
Cornish, W. R., 306

Cornwallis, Lord, 297
Coromandel Moplahs, 248
Corps of Madras Volunteer Guards, 302
Cotton, Arthur, 285
Crafts Council of India, 361
cultural conundrums, 365–70
Cutler, Norman, 92

Dabhra Sabha, 186
Da Cruz, John, 271–2
da Gama, Vasco, 255–6
Dakhinabades (Dakshinapada), 28–9
Dakhni language, 248
Dakshina Meru (the Meru of the south), 198
Dakshinamurthy, carving of, 99
Dakshinapada (the Southern Way), 92
Dalavaipuram copper plates, 118, 124
Dalhousie, Lord, 234, 301, 30
Dalit community, powering through to progress, 358–62
Dalit entrepreneurship, 357
Dalit Indian Chamber of Commerce and Industry, 357
Dalit upliftment, 335
Dalmia Cements factory, 339
Dalrymple, William, 261, 283
Daniel, E. Valentine, xiv, 373
Danish Lutheran Mission, 259
Dantivarman (Pallava king), 51, 70
Danvers, F. C., 231
Darasuram temple, 188
Darsana Sara (Jain religious work), 78
Dawes, Ascentia, 315
Day, Francis, xii, 263, 310
de Albuquerque, Afonso, 257
de Almeida, Francisco, 257
Dean, John, 299
de Britto, John, 276
Dehejia, Vidya, 192
de Lally, Comte, 266
Delhi sultanate, 218
de Nobili, Roberto, 231, 258, 267, 268, 276
De Romanis, Federico, 203
Desiya Murpokku Dravida Kazhagam (DMDK), 349
devadasis, 237, 328–9
Devanagari script, 59
Devaraya (Vijayanagara king), 220
Devaraya, Narasimha (Saluva king), 220
Devi, Rukmini, 365

Dhammapala, 55
Dhanu (human bomb of the LTTE), 345
Dhanvantri Mahal, 238
Dharanikondakoshan, 42
Dharmaraja Ratha, 64
Dharmasena, 71, 80
Dhyana Marga, 55
Diaz, Bartholomew, 256
Digby, William, 306
Dikshitar, Muthuswami, 239
District Municipalities Act of 1884, 303
'Divide and Rule' policy, 332
Divya Desam, 82
Divya Prabandam, 84, 146
Doctrine of Lapse, 234, 301, 313
Drake, Francis, 255
Draupadi Amman temple, 356
Dravida Kazhagam, 333, 335, 337
Dravida Munnetra Kazhagam (DMK), 335, 337, 341, 343, 347
Dravida Sangha (community of monks), 78
Dravidian architecture, in Muslim mosques in Tamil Nadu, 244
Dravidian cultural self, xiii
Dravidian culture, xv
Dravidian languages, xv, 308
Dravidian movement, xix, 277, 333, 355
Dravidian Proof, 308
drought relief camps, 306
Dupleix, Joseph François, 264
 capture of Madras and Fort St. George in 1746, 265
Durga, Goddess, 59
 as Mahishasuramardini, 184
Durvasa, sage, 89
Dutch East India Company, 259, 260, 278
Dutt, Romesh Chunder, 306

Eastern Chalukyas, 156
Eaton, Richard, 217
Ekambareshwar temple, Kanchipuram, 222
Eley, John, 299
Elizabeth I, Queen, 260
Elliot, Walter, 155
Ellis, F. W., 308
Erode Town Council, 332
Erythraean Sea (Red Sea), 28
Ettuthokai, 16, 36

Fabricius, Johann, 278

Fa Hien, 71
Fancourt, Amelia, 299
Fancourt, John, 299
Fergusson, James, 63
Fernandes, George, 348
First War of Indian Independence (1857), 285
fishing community, 21
Five Chariots (Pancha Rathas), 47, 63–4
Five Great Assemblies, 123
Foote, Robert Bruce, 1, 311
Fort St.George (Madras), 263, 280–1, 311, 314, 339, 341
Fort William (Calcutta), 263
Foxconn (Taiwanese company), 359
Foxcroft, George, 315
Frederick IV (king of Denmark), 259, 278
French East India Company, 263, 264

Gandhi Ashram, Wardha, 323
Gandhi, Gopalakrishna, 131
Gandhi, Indira, 64
Gandhi, Mohandas (Mahatma), 277, 376
    Dandi March (1930), 327
    impact on Tamil Nadu, 322, 333
    Vaikom Satyagraha (1924–25) against untouchability, 327
Gandhi, Rajiv, 345
Gandhi, Rajmohan, 336
Ganesan, Sivaji, 264, 325, 337, 346
Gangaikondacholapuram, city of, 147, 158–9, 188
Gangatharan, A., 308
Gautamanenum, Ilan, 1197
Gauthamanar, Palai, 207
ghatikas, 71, 79
Ghose, Aurobindo, 324
Ghouse, Ghulam, 303
Gillespie, Colonel, 299
Goan Inquisition (1561), 270
gold dirhams, 240, 241
'golden age' of egalitarianism and prosperity, 333
Golden Hind (ship), 255
Golkonda sultanate, 235
Goloubew, Victor, 191
Gopalan, Shyamala, 379
Gopalasamy, V., 346
Government Act of India of 1919, 331
Government of India Act of 1858, 303
Government Ophthalmic and Maternity

Hospital, Chennai, 328
Governor's Executive Council, 304
Govindaswami, S. K., 171
Grantha script, 48, 111
Great Indian Community, 332
Great Revolt of 1857, 297, 300
    protest and rebellion in Meerut, 301
    use of the Enfield rifle, 301
Great South Indian Famine, 281, 305–6
Guha, Ramachandra, xx
Guindy Engineering College, 315
Gunapadeya copper plate, 46
Gupta, Parameshwara Lal, 211
Gurukkal, Rajan, 124
Gurukulam, Cheranmadevi, 330
Guru, Narayana, 366
Guthirai Chettigal, 248
Guy, John, 193

Haasan, Kamal, 377
Hakluyt Society, 28
handloom industry, 307, 361
Harcourt, George, 300
Harisena, 46
Harris, Lord, 302
Hasan, Yakub, 330
Hawkins, William (English Khan), 255, 261, 262
Hegde, Radha Sarma, 379
Hema Sabha, 186
Hemingway, Ernest, 363
Henry, Prince (Navigator from Portugal), 255
Herakles, story of, 108–9
Herbert, Vaidehi, 91
Hickey, William, 235
higher learning, institution of, 71, 353
Hindi, as official language of India, 338
Hinduism, 194–5, 332–3
Hindu Marriage Act, 341
Hindu religious practice, 217
Hindu, The, 14, 172, 307, 326, 328, 331–2, 338, 341, 348, 367
Hirahadagalli copper plates, 46, 68, 74
Hiranyavarman, King, 41–2
Hiuen Tsang, 49, 51, 54, 71, 79
Home Rule movement (1916–18), 327, 332
Hooghly, Battle of (1759), 260
Hough, James, 269
House of Commons, 324
Hudson, Dennis, 43, 79

Index   431

Hume, Allan Octavian, 306
Huntingford, G. W. B., 28
Husain, Syed Aurzurah, 302
hydroelectric projects, 335

Ibn Abdullah, Mohamed Ibn Hameed, 249
Ignatius, Francis, 272
Ilanjetchenni, 25
Ilantiriyan (Chola king), 44
iluvaipaddikol, 164
Imayavaramban (Chera king), 205, 208
Indian Institute of Science, 335
Indian Institutes of Technology, 335
Indian National Congress, 306–7, 324, 326
  alliance with AIADMK, 346
  Brahmin domination in, 330
  education scheme in rural schools, 335
  non-Brahmin leadership, 331
Indo-European family of languages, 308
Indra, Lord, 19, 21, 36, 65, 87, 89, 118, 136
Indus Valley civilization, xv
inter-faith harmony, 313
irai ili nilam (tax free land), 66
Iravatham, 8, 89, 110, 132
Iron Age, 3–4
Irschick, Eugene, 333
Irukkuvelir, Bhuti Vikramakesari, 183
Irumporai, Perum Cheral, 209
Irumporai, Yanaikatchey Mandaran Cheral, 25
Isabella, Queen, 273
Islam, 378
  in the Tamil country, 29
Islamic architecture in Tamil Nadu,
  development of, 251
ITC Grand Chola, 369
IT sector, in Tamil Nadu, 360
Iyengar, Kasturi Ranga, 331
Iyengar, S. Srinivasa, 323
Iyer, G. Subramania, 307
Iyer, T. Muthuswamy, 307
Iyer, U. V. Swaminatha, 207, 363

Jackson, Colin, 265, 290
Jafar, Mir, 283
Jahangir, Emperor, 261–2
Jainism, 37, 77, 80, 98
  ascendency of, 78
  decline of, 77, 138
  marginalization of, 79
Jainism-Brahmanical conflict, 80

Jallianwala Bagh Massacre, 330
jallikattu (bull baiting) sport, xix–xx
Jamal Mohamed College, Trichy, 240
James I, King, 261
Janata Dal, 344
Jayalalithaa, J., 337, 340, 343–4, 346, 350
Jellah, Syed Hameed, 302
Jesuit missionaries, 269
Jeyaprakash, Porchelvi, 104
Jinnah, Muhammad Ali, 324
Jones, William, 308
Joseph, George, 327
Jouveau-Dubreuil, Gabriel, 61
Jung, Carl, 54
Jung, Muzaffar, 266
Jung, Nazir (Nizam of Hyderabad), 266

Kadungon (Pandya king), 48
Kadungon, Ilan, 206
Kafur, Malik, 120, 148, 215–18, 251
Kailasanatha temple, Kanchipuram, 50, 55–6, 59–60, 70, 98, 172
Kailasapathy, K., 16
Kakatiyas of Warangal, 218
Kalabhra period, 42
Kalabhras (Kalappalar), 43–4, 78, 145
kalamkari, 225, 262
Kalavazhi Naarpadhu, 207
Kalidasa, 53
Kalithokai (Sangam work), 35, 36, 90
Kalliena (Kalyana in Bombay harbour), 28
kalyana mandapa, 222–3
Kalyani inscription, in Burma, 79
Kamaraj, Kumaraswami, 336
Kamaraj Plan, 338
Kamba Ramayanam, 7
Kampana, Kumara, 219, 228
Kanakavalli Tataka, 72
Kanchipuram, 42, 45, 48, 53–67, 154
  Buddhist vihara in, 79
  as cradles of Jain, Buddhist, Shaivite, and Vaishnavite, 77
  Ekambareshwar temple, 222
  Kailasanatha temple, 172
  Pallava temples in, 61
  Varadaraja Perumal temple, 164, 222
  World Heritage site, 62
Kannan, S., 223, 257
Kannaradevan, Adittan, 151
Kanyakumari, xi, 31, 114, 148, 150, 152, 231,

245, 259, 272, 376
Kapalishwar temple, in Mylapore, 313
karanams, 238
Karikala II, Aditya, 154
Karikal, King, 18, 20, 25–7
Karthikeyan, Narain, 368
Karunanidhi, M., 337, 341–2, 344–5, 347
Karuppudaiyar Palli, 249
Kasakudi copper plates, 45, 48, 70
Kattabomman, Veerapandia, 264, 289–91, 293, 296–7
Kaveripattinam (Puhar) port, 19
Kazimar Periya Pallivasal (Big Mosque), 93
Keralan Nambudiri Brahman caste group, 269
Khan, Jalaluddin Ahsan, 218
Khan, Khusrau, 217
Khatikabhumi, 98
Khilafat Movement (1919–22), 327, 330
Khilji, Allaudin, 120, 215, 251
Khusru, Amir, 120
Kilkanakku (Eighteen Minor Works), 80, 131
Killivalavan (Chola prince), 45
King, William, 1
Kio-chen-ru, 30
Kocchadayan (Pandya king), 115
Kochadai Ayyanar temple, 129
Kodandarameswara (Adityarameswara) temple, 151
Kodimarathu Siru Nainar Palli (Dravidian style mosque), 249–50
Kolappan, B., xviii
Kollywood, 317–8
Koneriswarar temple, Ponnamaravathy, 168
Kongu Cheras, 206
Kongu Nadu, 282
Koodal Azhagar temple, 58, 93
Koranaganatha temple, in Tiruchi district, 182, 184
Kotravai (mother goddess), 17
Krishnadevaraya, King (ruler of Vijayanagara), 220–2, 225, 227, 229–30
Krishna III (Rashtrakuta king), 152
Krishnamurthy, Kalki, 49, 155, 363
Krishnamurti, Jiddu, 327
Krishnan, Mini, 364
Krishnan, N. S., 337
Krishna, T. M., 316, 366
Krita Yuga, 50
Kulandaiswami, 306
Kulasekhara, Maravarman, 120

Kulasekhara, Ravivarman, 217
Kulottunga I (Chola king), 159, 187, 193, 196
Kulottunga II (Chola king), 159
Kulottunga III (Chola king), 160
Kumaravishnu I (Pallava ruler), 47
Kumar, D. Suresh, 274, 342, 344, 345, 350
Kumar, K. C. Vijaya, 367
Kumar, Yathees, 3, 311
Kundavai Chaturvedimangalam, 164
kuravar people, 17
Kurram plates of Mahendravarman, 69
Kurran, Chendan, 43
Kuruntokai, 16, 35, 36
Kutran, Cendan, 113
Kuttuvan, Palyanai Selkelu (Chera king), 207

Labbai (Hindu converts to Islam), 247
Ladan temple, 94, 117
Lakshmi, C. S., 364
land grants, 313
Lawrence, Henry, 302
Laxmibai, Rani, 301
Levant company, 260
Local Boards Acts of 1871 and 1884, 303
London Missionary society, 277
Louis XIV, King, 263
Lushington, Stephen, 291, 294

Macaulay, Colin, 294
Madhavan, Chithra, 53
Madhavan, T. K., 327
Madrasapatnam, 310–11
Madras Civil Service, 229
Madras Corporation, 315
Madras Council, 282
Madras Hindu Debating Society, 300
Madras Legislative Council, 328, 330
Madras Mahajana Sabha, 307
Madras Native Association, 300
Madras Presidency, 263, 266, 286, 301, 304, 327, 331
Madras Regiment (Indian Army), 315
Madurai, 19, 80, 87, 88, 90
    Azhagar temple in, 221, 224
    development of Islamic architecture in, 251
Maduraikanchi, 91, 109, 123
Madurai Mission, 131, 276
Madurai Sultanate, 105, 120, 218
    establishment of, 217
Madurakavi, 117

Magellan, 255
Mahabalipuram, 47, 63
    Buddhist vihara in, 79
Mahabharata, 15, 45, 47, 204
Mahadevan, Iravatham, 8, 89, 110, 132
Mahadevi, Sembian, 153
Mahadevi, Sri Vanavan, 118
maha mandapam, 223
Maharaja, Varaguna, 116
Mahavamsa, 151
Mahendravarman I (Pallava ruler), 47–8, 71, 80
    battles with the Chalukya king Pulakesi II, 48
    conflict with the Pandya dynasty, 114
    as follower of Jainism, 48
    Mattavilasa Prahasana (play), 48, 71, 79
    reconversion to Saivism, 48
    temples built by, 48
Mahendravarman II (Pallava king), 49
Maheshwaras, 42
Maheshwari, Uma, 138
Malai, Kudumiyan, 375
malaria, epidemic of, 306
Malay trading ships, 247
Malligai Maanagar (city of jasmines), 89
Mandagapattu inscription, 48
mandala, concept of, 54
Mandal Commission, 344
mandapa vihara, 63
Mandela, Nelson, 376
Mangammal, Rani, 232–3
maniams, 238
Manikumar, K. A., 284, 298
Manimekalai (Sattanar), 22, 35, 45, 132
Mannu, Sheikh, 303
Manoharan, Karthick Ram, 333
Manuel I (Portuguese king), 256
Mappila community, 241–42
Marakkayar community, 247–48
Maran, Murasoli, 347–48
Maratha dynasty, 237
Marathas of Thanjavur, 234–39
Marudu brothers, 289
    hanging of, 289, 296
    invention of valari, 292
    victory against British forces, 294
Marulnikki, 80
Maruthanar, Mangudi, 91
Masulipatnam (later known as Machilipatnam), 262, 264
Maurya, Chandragupta, 22, 27–28, 108
Mauryan empire, xii, 90
Mayon (god of mullai), 36
McCrindle, J. W., 108
Meenakshi Sundareswarar temple, 89, 102
Meenakshi temple, 93, 223, 227
    Golden Lotus tank, 223
    Vijayanagar-Nayak additions to, 224
Meen Pudi Thiruvizha festival, 129
megalithic burial sites, 4
Megasthenes (Greek historian), xii, 27, 204
    as ambassador to Chandragupta's court, 28
    Indica, 28, 108
Meru, idea of, 198
Michell, George, 59
Military Department Despatches, 299
Minakshi, C., 44, 46, 68
Ming dynasty (China), 219
Minute of Thomas Babington Macaulay, 304
Modified Scheme of Elementary Education, 336
Modi, Narendra, 350
Mohamad, J. Raja, 4–5, 214, 240–1, 244–8, 250
Montagu-Chelmsford Reforms of 1918, 331
Moopanar, G. K., 343
Moors Mopulars, 241
Moplahs, 241
Most Backward Class (MBC) quota, 342, 355
MRF group, 359
Mrikandu, Rishi, 83
Mudali, Ariyanatha, 103
Mudaliar, Ramalinga, 290
Mudaliar, T. Srinivasa, 332
Mudal Tiruvanthadhi, 83
Mudukudumi, Palyagasalai, 111
Mueller, Max, 268, 308
Mughals, 264
Muhammad, Prophet, 211
Mukkulathor community, 354
Mullaiperiyar Dam issue, 351, 376
Munro, Thomas, 284, 304
Murattu Kaalai (1980), xix
Murthy, Somaskanda, 380
Muruga, Lord, 23, 36
Murugan, Perumal, 355
Murugappa Group, 359
Musical Trinity, 239

Muslim Arab traders, 240
Muthalaly, Shonali, 368
Muthiah, S., 302
Muziris port, 29–30
Mysore Wars, 281

Naccinarkkiniyar, 45
Nachiyar, Rani Velu (Veera Mangai), 292
Nachiyar Thirumozhi, 365
Nachiyar, Thuluka, 101
Nadar community, 340
Nagapattinam, 79
Nagarathnamma, Bangalore, 328
Nagaswamy, R., 65, 92, 177
Naidu, P. Varadarajulu, 328
Naidu, Varadarajulu, 330, 331
Nair, T. M., 330
Nakula-Sahadeva Ratha, 64
Nalanda University, 55
nalavai (daily durbars), 34
Nalayira Divya Prabandham, 74, 101, 195, 210
Nambi, Nambi Andar, 195
Nandivarman (Pallava ruler), 42–3
Nandivarman II (Pallava king), 51, 165
Nandivarman III (Pallava king), 52
Naoroji, Dadabhai, 306, 324
Narasimhaiah, B., 217, 219
Narasimhapotavarman, King, 72
Narasimhavarman I (Pallava king), 62
  consolidation of the Pallava empire, 49
  disputes with Nedumaran, 114
  naval expedition to Sri Lanka, 49
  passion for art and for building temples, 48
  victory against Chalukya king Pulakesi II, 49
Narasimhavarman II (Pallava king), 49, 56, 79
Narasimha, Vira, 220
Narasinga Asthram, 95
Narasinga Perumal cave temple (Yoga Narasimha temple), 94
Narayan, S., 341
Narendra, Rajaraja (Eastern Chalukya ruler), 159
Narkottran, Korkai Kizhan, 111–2
Natarajan, Jayanthi, 349, 376
Nataraja sculpture, 64
Nataraja temple, at Chidambaram, 186
Nathamuni (Vaishnavite theologian), 82, 195
National Democratic Alliance (NDA), 347
Nattrinai, 36
Natya Shastra, 51

Nayagam, Tirumandira Olai, 245
Nayaka, Muppidi, 217
Nayaka, Narasa, 220
Nayaka, Tuluva Narasa, 220
Nayak, Gidivetti, 293
Nayak, Gopal, 291–2
Nayak, Lingama, 226
Nayak, Muttu Virappa, 231
Nayak, Nagama, 229
Nayak of Wandiwash Damarla Venkatadri, 313
Nayaks of Madurai, 229, 282
Nayak, Tirumalai, 129, 223, 227, 231, 232
Nayak, Viswanatha, 231
Nayanar, Sundaramurti, 172
Nedumaran, Ninraseer (Chola king), 197
Nedunchezhiyan, Parantaka (Pandya king), 18, 25, 95, 100
neeradum mandapa, 223
Nehru, Jawaharlal, 328, 335
Nelliappar temple, in Tirunelveli district, 102
Nelson, J. H., 229
New Testament, 278
Neytal lands, 21
nidu bhukti, 111
Niharili Chola Chaturvedimangalam, 185
Nikator, Selecus, 108
Nisumbasudani temple, 183
Niti Aayog, on school education, 353
Nizami culture of Hyderabad, 216
Non-Brahmin Manifesto of 1916, 330
non-Brahmin movement, 277, 330
Non-cooperation Movement (1920–22), 327
Noor-ul-Nissa, Princess (Tipu's daughter), 299
nritta mandapam, 223
Nunes, Fernão, 225, 228

Official Languages Act, 338
Ola Electric Mobility, 358
ooru, notion of, xiv
original equipment manufacturing (OEM), 358
Other Backward Caste (OBC), 355
Ottomans, 256

Paari Vallal, story of, xvi
Paes, Domingo, 220
Paes, Leander, 367
Palaeolithic Age, xiii, 1
palayakaran, 230
Palayamkottai, fort of, 293

Pallankoyil copper inscription, 55
Pallava cave temple, 375
Pallava Grantha, 70, 375
Pallava kingdom
    conflict with the Pandya dynasty, 114
    end of, 52
    establishment of, 77
    Great Pallavas, 47, 69
    interactions with the Gupta kings, 48–9
    Sripurambiyam, battle of, 52
    Tamil origin of, 45
Pallavamalla, Nandivarman, 70, 73, 84
Pallavamalla, story of, 41–2, 47
Pallava temples, 61
Palli, Irrataikulam, 249
Pallikal, Dipika, 368
Palli, Thurukka Nainar, 250
Panchalankurichi fort, 291
Pancha Marabu and Kootha Nool (dance forms), 36

Pandey, Mangal, 301
Pandian, M. S. S., 277
Pandya, Arikesari Parakrama, 250
Pandya dynasty, 17, 24, 33, 74
    cave temples of, 94
    conflicts with the Chola dynasty, 97, 114, 120–1
    conflict with the Pallava dynasty, 114
    decline of, 118
    impact on Tamil culture, 88
    Jain monuments, 95
    temple construction, 100
Pandya I, Mara Varman Sundara (Pandya king), 147
Pandya inscription, 103
Pandya, Jatavarman Kulasekhara, 249
Pandya, Jatavarman Sundara, 120
Pandya, Jatavarman Vira, 120
Pandya, Kulasekhara, 91
Pandya, Maravarman Kulasekhara, 120, 127
Pandya, Maravarman Sundara (Pandya king), 119
Pandyan, Jatavarman Kulasekhara, 119
Pandyan, Jatavarman Sundara, 120
Pandyan, Jatavarman Vira, 120
Pandyan, Maravarman Kulasekhara (Pandya ruler), 215
Pandyan, Marudu, 290, 292, 293, 296
Pandyan, Sundara, 217

Pandyan, Vira, 217
Pandyas of the Second Empire, 119
Pandya Vaadyamaaryar, 104
Pandya, Varaguna (Pandya ruler), 74
Panneerselvam, O., 350
Pappu, Shanti, 1
Paramasivan, S., 98
Parameswaravarman I (Pallava king), 49
Parameswaravarman II, 42
paramountcy, policy of, 285
Paranjothi (poet-saint), 89
Parantaka I (Chola king), 169, 182, 186
Parantaka, Jatila, 122
Parantaka, Sri (Viranarayana Sadayan), 118
Paravar community, 258
Paripatal poems, 36, 90, 91
Parivirajakar, Vatta Somayaji, 94
parliamentary democracy, 335
Parsvanatha (Jain Tirthankara), 200
Parthasarathy Swamy temple, 313
Parvati (Hindu goddess), 183, 274
Pataliputra, 204
Pate, H. R., 291
Patel, Vallabhbhai, 335
Patil, Veerendra, 346
Patnaik, Biju, 342
Pattali Makkal Katchi, 346
Patthitrupattu (Sangam age anthology), 5, 25, 204
Pattinapalai, 26, 29
Pattupattu, 14
Paul III, Pope, 272
Peddana, Allasani, 221
Pepys, Samuel, 262
Performance Grading Index 2.0 report, 353
Periplus of the Erythraean Sea, The, 25, 28, 108
Periya Kovil (Big Temple), 171
Periyapuranam (Sekkizhar), 69, 195, 199
Periyar Ninaivu Samathuvapuram project, 342
Periya Tirumozhi (Tirumangai), 84
Perumal, Cheraman (Chera king), 199, 210
Perur, Srinath, 30
Peruvazhudi, Palyagasalai Mudukudumi, 110
Peter Padukam, 102
Peter, Rous, 102
Phillips, W. R., 269
Pidari Ratha, 64
pilgrimage, notion of, 85
Pillai, T. V. Umamaheswaran, 171
Pillai, V. O. Chidambaram (VOC), 310, 324–5

Pillay, K. K., 69
Pillivalai (Naga princess), 45
pit burials, 3
Plassey, Battle of (1757), 263, 281, 283
Pleasant Stay Hotel case, 347
Pliny the Elder, 28, 110
Pliny the Younger, 28
Plutschau, Heinrich, 259
Poligar of Pandalamcourchy (Panchalankurichi), 290
poligar system, 232–3, 291
political consciousness, xv
Polo, Marco, 127, 242, 312
Pondicherry, xiii, 264
Pondicherry, Treaty of (1754), 266
Pongal festival, xvii
Ponniyin Selvan story, 363
Poongundranar, Kaniyan, 372
Pope, G. U., 131, 277
Portugal, 256, 258–9, 260, 270, 272
Portuguese missionaries, 260
Prabandam, 86
Praggnanandha, R., 370
Prakriti Foundation, 382
Prakrit language, 9–10, 47
Prithvipati I (Ganga king), 150
Protestant missionaries, 372
Puhar, port of, 29
Pujyapada (monk), 78
Pulakesi II (Chalukya king)
  battles with Pallava king
  Mahendravarman, 48
  Narasimhavarman I, 48–9
Pulalur, battle of, 49
Pulankurichi inscription, 43, 78, 113
Pundarikaksha temple, 75
Puram, 16, 22
Purananuru (ancient Sangam text), xvii, 16, 18, 204, 309
Puravi Eduppu festival, 132

Quilon Syrian copper plate, 241

Radhakrishnan, Sarvepalli, 321
Radha, M. R., 337
Raghavan, Chudamani, 363
Raghuvamsa (Kalidasa), 107
Rahman, A. R., 363, 382
Raigad Fort, 235
Rai, Lala Lajpat, 324

Rajagambhira Tirumandapam, 189
Rajagopalachari, Chakravarti, 326
Rajan, K., 5
Rajan, P. T., 376
Rajaraja I (Chola king), 162, 195, 200
  arts of war and administration, 155
  conquests of, 156
  religious tolerance, 156
  victories against Pandyas, 156
Rajaraja II (Chola king), 197
Rajarajesvaram temple, 158
Rajasambavanai, custom of, 74
Rajasimha II (Pandya king), 118, 151
Rajasimha, Maravarman (Pandya king), 115
Rajasimhanar, Cheramannar, 185
Rajayyan, K., 230
Rajendra II (Chola king), 189
Rajendra Kala Vidyadharan, title of, 245
Rakkayi Amman temple, 222
Ramachandran, M. G. (MGR), 317, 337, 339, 342–3, 345, 350, 376
Ramachandran, T. N., 97
Ramakrishna, K. Amarnath, 6
Ramakrishnan, T., 357
Ramamirtham, Moovalur, 329
Raman, K. V., 64, 93, 104, 110, 269, 311
Ramanuja, 197
Ramanujan, A. K., x
Ramaswami, N. S., 261
Ramaswami, Periyar E. V., 131–2, 331
Ramaswamy, E. V., 332
Ramaswamy, Sumathi, xv
Ramayana, xvii, 15, 182, 219, 224
Ranganathaswamy temple, in Srirangam, 101
Ranganatha temple, Srirangam, 231
Rao, Jadow, 234–5
Rao, Narasimha, 345–6
Rashtrakuta dynasty, 51, 74, 149
Rasigar Manrams, 342
Ratnakarandaka Shravakachara, 96
Ratnam, Anita, 359, 365
Ratnam, Mani, 155, 318, 363
Ravichandran, Ashwin, 367
Ravindranath, Sushila, 359
Razzaq, Abdur, 219–20, 243
Rea, Alexander, 3, 61
Reddy, Muthulakshmi, 328, 365
redware urns, discovery of, 3
Reformation in Europe, 256
Regional Engineering Colleges, 335

Index 437

Renaissance in Europe, 256
Rhodes, Jonty, 368
Richelieu, Cardinal, 264
rock-cut temples, 47–8, 93, 117
Rockfort Temple (Tiruchirappalli), 55
rock paintings, 4, 36
Rodin, Auguste, 190
Roe, Thomas, 261
Roman Catholic Church, 258
Roman Catholicism, 270
Roman coins, 9, 28, 123, 206
    punch-marked coins, 213
Rowlatt Act, 330
royal patronage, 48, 55, 71, 74, 78–9, 98, 125, 143, 174, 198, 200, 223, 258, 270
Royapuram Railway Station, 315
ryotwari system, 284, 305

Sadayan, Parantaka Viranarayana, 118
Sahib, Chanda, 266, 281
saidu ittavi, 223
Sairam, Aruna, 367
Sairam, Sangita Kalanidhi Aruna, 367
Shaiva Nayanmars, 78
Shaiva Siddhanta, philosophy of, 197
Saluva dynasty, 220
Samantha Kulam, 147
Samanthanarayana Chaturvedi Mangalam, 147
Samantha Narayana Vinnagaram temple, 147
Samudragupta (Gupta king)
    Allahabad pillar of, 45–7
    southern campaign of, 46
Samur, Sonegan, 245
Sangam Age, xvii, 77, 88, 194
    First Sangam, 14
    Third Sangam, 14
Sangam literature, 27, 29, 240
Sangam poetry, 19–20, 27, 30
sangharamas, 54
Santhalingam, C., 104
San Thome, 258, 312
Sasikala, V., 340, 350–1
Sastri, Nilakanta, 13, 107, 161, 172
Sastri, Syama, 241
Satavahanas, 46
Sathyamurthy, T., 4, 173, 222
sati, practice of, 35, 297
Sattanathan Commission, 342
Saurashtrian communities, 105
Scheduled Castes, 355

Schwanbeck, E. A., 108
Schwartz, C. F., 278
Schwartz, Friedrich, 237
SC/ST funds, 357
Sekaran, Immanuel, 340
Self-Respect Movement, 332
Selkezhukuttuvan, Palyanai (Chera king), 208
Sendalai inscriptions, 146
Sengayvan, Moodha Amanan Athur, 206
Sengottaiyan, A., 344
Senguttavan, King, 18
Serfoji I (Maratha ruler), 239
Serfoji II (Maratha ruler), 236
Seringapatam, Battle of (1799), 282
Sethupathi, Kilavan, 231
Seven Years' War (1756–1763), 266
Sewell, Robert, 220
Shah, Ranvir, 380
Shankaracharya, Adi, 196
Shastri, Lal Bahadur, 339
Shiga, Miwako, 304
Shilappadikaram (*The Tale of the Anklet Bracelet*), 23, 29, 89–90, 93, 94, 110, 123, 130, 134
Shilpa Sastras (rules of sculpture), 191
Shiva ganas, 22
Shiva, Lord, 89, 199
    Ananda Tandava, 192
    as Brahmapurishvarar, 181
    as Dakshinamurthy, 184
    sculptures of, 65
Shiva Chudamani (the crest jewel of Shiva), 50
Shiva Nataraja bronze, 190
Shore Temple, 47, 63
Shulman, David, 7, 14, 69, 131, 170, 372
silver coins, of Chera kings, 9
Simhavarman, King, 43, 44–5
Simhavishnu (Pallava king), 41, 42, 44, 55, 113
Singh, V. P., 344
Siraj-ud-Daula, Nawab, 283
Sittanavasal cave paintings, in Pudukkottai, 95, 96, 117
Sivalingam, T. M., 339
Sivaramamurti, C., 100, 107, 111, 117, 119, 193, 200
Sivaskandavarman, Yuva Maharaja, 46
Siva, Subramania, 325
Skanda Purana, 189

slave trade, 259, 281
Slum Clearance Board, 342
Smythe, Thomas, 260
Soame, Stephen, 260
social injustice, 324
social justice, 334
    Dravidian vision of, 343, 355
Society of Jesus (the Jesuits), 272
Somaskanda, sculptures of, 67
South India Confederacy, 290
South India Liberation Federation, 330
spice trade, 242, 247, 260, 262
sportspeople, from Tamil Nadu, 367–9
Srikkanth, Kris, 367
Sringeri Sharada Peetam, 219
Srinivasan, K. R., 67
Srinivasan, Rettamalai, 356
Sripurambiyam, battle of (880 CE), 52
Sriramulu, Potti, 335, 376
Srivallabha, Srimaran (Pandya king), 97–8, 117, 118, 217
srivimana, 176
SS *Gallia*, 325
Stalin, M. K., 346
Stalin, Udhayanidhi, 351
State Legislative Assembly, 314
State Level Bankers' Committee (SLBC), 357
Stein, Burton, 161
Stella Maris College, 320
St. Joseph of Nazareth, 276
St. Mary's Cathedral, 93
Strabo (Roman historian), 28, 108
Straits of Magellan, 260
Subbalakshmi, M. S., 382
Subbarayalu, Y., 5, 108
Subrahmanyan, Sanjay, 317, 366
Subramaniam, K. V., 245
Subramanian, T. S., 5, 62, 75, 100, 222, 339
Subramanyam, K., 317
Sudhagaran, V. N., 346
Suenas of Devagiri, 218
Sufism, 245
Sundarar (Bhakti poet-saint), 199
Sundareswarar, Kalyana, 103
Sunni Muslims, 247
Suvargal (Father Mark Stephen), 275
Swadesamitran (Tamil newspaper), 307, 326
Swadeshi Movement, 325
    in south India, 325
Swadeshi Steam, 324

Swami, Ramalinga, 366
Swamy, Subramanian, 346
Swamy, Vandi Marriccha, 251
swayambhu (self-manifested) lingam, 89
Syrian Christians, 269

Tabula Peutingeriana, 203
Taittiriya Upanishad, 85
Takkolam, battle of, 152, 156
talamana, 191
talasampohita karana, 97
Talikota, Battle of (1565), 229
Tamilakam, 53
    boundaries in the Sangam age, 33
    development of Christianity in, 267
    early history of, 4
    functioning of, 31
    Kalabhra rule in, 111
    links with European society, 256
    mosques of, 248
    politics and power relations, 68
    religious beliefs, 36
    Saiva Siddhanta, philosophy of, 197
    three crowned kings of, 204
    topography of, ix, 1
Tamil Brahmi inscriptions, 9, 13, 26, 30, 31, 37, 89, 132
Tamil Christian literature and philosophy, 268
Tamil culture, xv, xix, 13
    Aryanization of, 15
    Palaeolithic phase of, 2
    strengths of, xiv
Tamil diaspora, 378–80
Tamil films, xix
    impact of, 337
Tamil foods, 223
Tamil Hindu families, xiv
Tamil identity, 376
    Dravidian movement, 333
    notion of essentialism in, 372
    sense of, xvi, xvii–xx, 371, 379
Tamil language, xv
    relation with Sanskrit language, xvi
Tamil lexicography, 131
Tamil literary works, 80
Tamil Maanila Congress, 346
Tamil Muslims, 240–1, 244
    social divisions among, 246
Tamil Nadu, x
    caste violence and divide in, 355

cities and towns of, xii
economy of, 358
English dominance across, 282
growth story of business in, 359
impact of Gandhi on, 322
language and culture of, xiv–xvii
rural economy, 361
women's participation in public life in, 323
Tamil Nadu Archives, 315
Tamil Nadu Industrial Corporation (TIDCO), 359
Tamil Nadu State Department of Archaeology, 7
Tamilness, notion of, 381
Tamil people
  agitations against Hindi language, 339
  caste identity, 340
  identity of, xiv
  linguistic and cultural heritage of, 338
  as original inhabitants of India, x
Tamil revivalism, in the nineteenth century, xv
Tamil Sangam, ix–x
Tamizh Thai (anthropomorphic mother goddess), xv
Tanjaik-kon (Tanjai narpukalalan, lord of Tanjai), 146
Tanjaimamanikovil Vishnu temple, 146
Tanjore / Thanjavur, xii, 334
  Brihadeeswara temple, 198
  British annexation of, 234
  Chola capital of, 145, 234
  Marathas of, 234–9
  Nayaks of, 231, 235
  paintings, xxi, 98
  Rajarajesvaram temple, 181
  as rice bowl of Tamil Nadu, 145
  Tenancy Regulations, 336
  Tenant and Pannayil Protection Bill, 336
  Thanjavur Palace, 239
  Thanjavur Quartet, 237
TANSI land deal cases, 347
Tarisapalli, 241
tax-free land, 73
Temple Entry Movement for Dalits, 340
temple worship, 191
Terminalia arjuna, 185
Thamirabarani, rivers of, 33
Thamotharampillai, C. W., 13, 308
Thapar, Romila, 139

Thenarasu, Thangam, 374, 375
Theosophical Society, 327
Thevaram, 74, 81, 197
Thevar community, 340
Thevar, Muthuramalinga, 340
Thevar, Muthuvaduganatha, 292
Thirugnanasambandar (Saiva poet saint), 103–4, 114, 179
Thirukkovaiyar (poem), 92
Thirukkurungudi temple, 242
Thirumoorthy, G., 62
Thirupputhur, fort of, 289
Thirupurambiyam, battle of, 118, 150
Thiruvalluvar, 314
Thiruvidaimarudur, 165
Thiruvilayadal Puranam, 95
Thomas Christians, 269–70
Thomas, Job, 190
Thomas, St., 270, 273
Three Crowned Kings, 24, 204–5
Thurston, Edgar, 271
Tiger Cave, 63, 67
Tilak, Bal Gangadhar, 324
Tinnevelly Gazetteer, 291
Tinnevely Riots, 325
Tipu Sultan, 244, 281
  fall of, 298
  fight against the British, 282, 293
  Seringapatam, Battle of (1799), 282
Tirthankaras, 98
Tiru Alandurai, 182
Tirukailai Padigam, 176
Tirukkural (Tiruvalluvar), xiv, 37, 80
Tirukoshtiyur temple, 197
Tirumantiram, 187
Tirumayam Fort, 36
Tirumurai, 141
Tirunavukkarasar (Appar), 80
  Thevaram poems of, 81
Tirunavukkarasar (Shaivite saint), 48, 179
Tiruparittikunram Jain temple, 55
Tirupavai, 139
Tirupullamangai, 181
Tirupurambiyam, battle of (880 CE), 74
tiru ulagalandhakol, 164
Tiruvacakam, Pope's translation of, 277
Tiruvalluvar, 32, 80, 361
Tolkappiyam (Tamil grammar text), xviii, 14, 16, 17, 21, 36, 37, 204, 383
Tondaiman dynasty, 27

Tondaiman, Samantha Narayanan (Pandya general), 147
Towns Improvement Acts of 1865 and 1871, 303
Treaty of Aix la Chapelle (1748), 265
Trevelyan, Lord, 303
Tripurantaka, sculptures of, 198
Tughlaq, Muhammad Bin, 216, 218
Tuticorin, 93, 130, 257–9, 270, 273, 277, 279, 325–7
TVS group, 359

Udayachandra (Pallava general), 51
Udayagiri cave temple, near Sanchi, 94
Udhaya Marthanda Perum Palli, 250
Udiyanjeral, King, 18
Umamaheshwara temple, Konerirajapuram, 152–3
UNESCO protected group of monuments, 62
UNESCO World Heritage site Mahabalipuram/Mamallapuram, 47
unfair trade practices, 264
United Progressive Alliance (UPA), 350
untouchability
  concept of, xviii
  Vaikom Satyagraha (1924–25) against, 327
upliftment of women, 328
Usha, P. T., 368
Uttiramerur inscription, 165
Uyyakondan Channel, 233
Uyyakondan Vaykkal, 72

Vaazhiyathan, Selva Kadungo, 207
Vaigai River 8, 90–1
Vaikunta Perumal temple, in Kanchipuram, 42–3, 46, 51, 56, 59, 61, 69–70, 84–85, 165
Vaishnava saints, 62, 82, 146, 195
Vaishnavism, 48, 54, 82, 84, 140, 221, 380
  concept of, 196
Vaishnavite Azhwars, 78, 117, 143
Vajapeya, Vedic sacrificial rituals of, 46
Vajpayee, A. B., 347
Vajranandi (monk), 78
valangai/idangai rebellion, against the Nayaks, 228
Valliammai, Thillayadi, 322–3
Vanavarayar, Sembiyan Mahabali, 182
Vanniyars, 346
Vanpukazh Muvar (Three Celestially Famed Kings), 204

Van Sirappu, 32
Varadaraja Perumal temple, Kanchipuram, 222
Varadaraja Swamy temple, Kanchipuram, 164
Varaguna, Maran Sadaiyan (Pandya king), 52, 125, 150
Varagunavarman II (Pandya king), 118
Varman II, Nandi (Pallava king), 147
Varuna, Lord, 21, 23, 39
Vasan, S. S., 317
vasanta mandapa, 223
Vatteluthu, 55, 375
Vedachalam, V., 92
Vedaranyam Salt March, 327
Vedic gods, worship of, 21
Vedic sacrifices, 43, 110
  rituals of Ashvamedha, 46
Vedic yagnas, 37
velan-kudi (peasants), 33
Velanvagai (non-Brahmin villages), 162–3
veli of land, 21
Vellore Revolt of 1806, 297–9keshu
Veluthat, Keshavan, 24, 139, 161
Velvikkudi copper plates, 113
Velvikkudi village, 111
Venkatachalapathy, A. R., 308
Venkataraya III (Vijayanagar king of Chandragiri-Vellore), 263
Venkatesan, Archana, 137
Venkatraghavan, S., 367
Venni, Battle of (130 CE), 25
vetar people, 17
Vettuvankovil temple, 99
vibhuti (sacred ash), prohibition on the use of, 298
Victoria, Queen, 275, 303, 314
Vijayalaya Choliswaram temple, 183
Vijayanagar empire, 219
  administration of, 228
  building of Vishnu and Shiva temples in, 223
  decline of, 226, 227, 229
  Nayak stewardship, 228
  rule over the Tamil regions, 219
  Talikota, Battle of (1565), 229
village assemblies, 66, 72, 125, 165, 182
village communities, 195
Vira, Naraloka (Chola king), 188
Viranarayana, Parantaka (Pandya king), 118, 150
Virappa, Ranga Krishna Muttu, 232

Vishnugopa of Kanchi, 45–7
Vishnu, Lord, 42–3, 77, 83, 118, 185
Viswanathaswamy temple, in Vedaranyam, 23
Vonnegut, Kurt, 363

Wallajah Mosque, in Triplicane, 313
Wallajah, Muhammad Ali Khan, 266, 313
Wandiwash, Battle of (1760), 266
War of Austrian Succession, 265
Waug, Dhoondaji, 293
weaving community, 307
Wedderburn, William, 306
Wellesley, Governor General, 290
Western Chalukyas, 156
Whitman, Walt, xx
widow remarriage, 333
Wilson, Captain, 300
Wilson, H. H., 284
Wilson, Shiny, 368
Wink, Andre, 217
Wodeyars of Mysore, 282
women's position in society, 35

Woodlands Drive In (now Semmozhi Poonga), 320
World Tamil Conferences, 341

Xavier, Francis, St., 270, 273, 276

Yaadhum (film, 2013), 29, 243–4, 250, 386
yaga kundam (ritual fire pit), 246
yagnas, 112
Yale Center for British Art, in New Haven Connecticut, 280
Yale, Elihu, 280–81, 314
Yale University, 280
Yannielli, Joseph, 281
Yavanas, 20, 21, 29–30, 124, 201, 203, 208–9
Yoga Narasimha temple, at Yanaimalai, 95, 116–7

zamindari system, 286, 307
Zamorin of Calicut, 271
Ziegenbaulg, Bartholomeus, 259–60
Zvelebil, Kamil, 137